Nature and the Human Spirit
Toward an Expanded Land Management Ethic

Edited By

B. L. Driver
Daniel Dustin
Tony Baltic
Gary Elsner
George Peterson

Nature and the Human Spirit
Toward an Expanded Land Management Ethic

EDITED BY:

B. L. Driver
Daniel Dustin
Tony Baltic
Gary Elsner
George Peterson

VENTURE PUBLISHING, INC. • 1999 CATO AVENUE • STATE COLLEGE, PA 16801-3238

Production Manager: Richard Yocum
Graphic design, layout: Naomi Q. Gallagher
Editors: Naomi Q. Gallagher, Diane K. Bierly, and Katherine Young
Cover © 1987 Estate of High Cloud, Robert Wayne Means
Cover Design: Sandra Sikorski, Sikorski Design
Printing and Binding: Jostens Printing and Publishing

Library of Congress Catalogue Card Number 96-60358
ISBN 0-910251-82-7

Then in the Arctic half-light of the canyon,

all existence fades to a being with my soul

and memories and the sounds of the Big

Blackfoot River . . .

Eventually, all things merge into one,

and a river runs through it . . .

I am haunted by waters.

Norman Maclean (1976)

A River Runs Through It

Acknowledgments

We would like to thank several individuals and organizations for helping make this text a reality. First and foremost, we thank the 50 contributors, many of whom traveled long distances to participate in two workshops associated with the text's development in addition to the long hours spent writing their chapters. Their dedication to the project is reflected in the text's content. Second, production of the text would not have been possible without the financial assistance of the Rocky Mountain Forest and Range Experiment Station of the United States Department of Agriculture Forest Service in cooperation with San Diego State University's Foundation and Venture Publishing. Finally, we extend a special thank you to the Nebraska faithful: Joyce Hart for her typing skills and for managing the voluminous correspondence associated with the project, and Gene Lamke for his administrative assistance.

DESCRIPTION OF COVER PAINTING:

Artist: High Cloud Robert Wayne Means (1942-1990)
The End of the World (1987)
Size: 24 inches x 36 inches

The painting featured on the cover is the artist's interpretation of the Lakota legend of the end of the world (described in the Preface) and depicts an old woman designing quillwork on a buffalo robe at the edge of the Bad Lands in South Dakota.

High Cloud Robert Wayne Means
(1942-1990) Native American
(Lakota Sioux).

(photograph courtesy of Rhoda Mills)

About the Artist

High Cloud Robert Wayne Means (1942-1990) was born to Bruce and Della Mae Means in Pine Ridge, South Dakota. His family included six brothers and two sisters, all of whom showed artistic merit, so it was no surprise when he developed an interest in art at a young age. High Cloud attended the Holy Rosary Mission School at Pine Ridge and later joined the Navy. Upon his return, he studied Art at Creighton University in Omaha, Nebraska.

Although High Cloud traveled to many places and for a time lived in Texas and California, his Lakota Sioux heritage and traditions endured and influenced his artwork. He not only pursued painting, but also worked with such media as wood, leather and textiles. In the photograph on the facing page, High Cloud is pictured in a traditional Lakota costume with a ceremonial white buffalo robe, all of which he created.

According to his sister, Rhoda Mills, of Pine Ridge:

I'll always remember Robert Wayne . . . and what a kind person he was. When I was little and he came to see me, he always brought me a bag of cookies. That was him—always giving to people no matter who they were.

Many thanks...

In part, it was High Cloud's painting "The End of the World" that inspired this work. Dan Dustin purchased the painting from a gallery in 1988 when he was taken with the art and the legend it portrayed. After many months of searching for High Cloud to request permission to reproduce "The End of the World" for the text cover, Dustin believed he would be unable to use it since High Cloud could not be found.

When I saw a photograph of "The End of the World," I could not allow the search to be abandoned. Many thanks to the following people who helped me find the path that led to High Cloud and, hence, permission to reproduce his painting on the cover of *Nature and the Human Spirit*:

Dan Dustin for the initial information and history of "The End of the World;"

John R. Kostura of the Native American Artist's Home Page for his insight into Native American Arts and Crafts and for posting a notice on the Internet which led to High Cloud's family;

Jim Greene for responding to the posting and pointing me to Brother Simon of Red Cloud Schools;

Brother Simon, Arlene and Dennis Means, and Irene Means who were kind enough to help me find Rhoda Mills of Pine Ridge, South Dakota, and the rest of the Means family; and

a special thanks to the Means family and Rhoda Mills, sister of High Cloud Robert Wayne Means, for her kindness, patience, insight, and generous help so that "The End of the World" could take its rightful place as this book's cover and for supplying a rare photograph of High Cloud to enhance his biographical sketch.

We regret that we never had the chance to meet High Cloud ourselves.

Michele L. Barbin, Production Assistant
Venture Publishing, Inc.

Table of Contents

SECTION III: DESCRIBING DIVERSE PERSPECTIVES

Chapter Eight: Against Uniformity: Prehistoric Language Lessons for Modern Land Managers 119

Philip Kopper

PART A: ETHNIC AND CULTURAL PERSPECTIVES

Chapter Nine: Diverse Native American Perspectives on the Use of Sacred Areas on Public Lands 127

Louis Redmond

Chapter Ten: African American Naturifocal Values 135

Rachel Bagby

Chapter Eleven: Hispanic Perspectives and Values 145

Maria Teresa Garcia

Chapter Twelve: Feminist Perspectives, Female Ways of Being, and Nature 153

Karla Henderson

SECTION V: RESEARCH DIRECTIONS

SECTION VI: SUMMARY: WHERE DO WE GO FROM HERE?

Preface

According to Lakota legend, at the edge of the Bad Lands in South Dakota an old woman sits by a fire designing quillwork on a buffalo robe. Each time the woman gets up to gather more wood for the fire, her wolf dog unravels the work she has done. When the woman returns she must always start over. The legend tells us that if the old woman ever finishes her quillwork it will be the end of the world.

In our efforts to advance social science knowledge and apply that knowledge to public land management, we are not unlike the old woman in the Lakota legend. As we carefully weave new threads of learning into the fabric of policy and practice, one dog or another waits in the shadows watching for an opportunity to unravel our work. And though we see the individual threads of learning as we weave them, the larger pattern of understanding often escapes us. We hesitate to step back from our work for a broader perspective lest the dogs creep in, but we must for the pattern is not complete. So as we weave, we cast our eyes about, searching for the larger meaning of the things we do. And as we search, we see empty places in the pattern, and these empty places draw us to them, so that, by our weaving, we may make the pattern whole. In this way, it is possible to imagine that if we ever finish our quillwork, we, too, will have discovered the purpose and end of the world.

Nature and the Human Spirit has been written with the Lakota legend well in mind. Its subject matter consists of the hard-to-define and hard-to-measure values and benefits that enrich the meaning of human-kind's relationship with the natural world. These values and benefits are the empty places in the pattern of our understanding. They are the object of the quillwork we have carefully woven into the pages that follow. Our task has been a humbling one, and while we are pleased with the final product, we understand it is only a beginning and there will always be more work to do. Although wolf dogs may unravel some of what we have done, we, and others, will keep returning to weave again. Ours has been but a first step in what promises to be a most rewarding intellectual, emotional, and spiritual journey toward a deeper understanding of our relationship with the Earth that sustains us.

Foreword

Jack Ward Thomas, Chief
USDA Forest Service
Washington, DC

One of the first things I did as Chief of the Forest Service was to put a picture of Aldo Leopold beside one of Gifford Pinchot in the headquarters office in Washington, DC. This was appropriate because Leopold pioneered arguments for managing lands from an ecological perspective in order to sustain those lands over time to meet societal needs. In fact, Leopold's ideas are key to the managerial philosophy of sustainable ecosystems management which the Forest Service (Thomas, 1994), other federal and state land management agencies, and many large private forest industries have adopted in recent years.

This text builds directly on Leopold's philosophy. Its title and practically all of its chapters call for an expanded land management ethic that promotes ecosystems sustainability. This is pure Leopold. He stated in his foreword to *A Sand County Almanac*, "that land is a community is the basic concept of ecology, but that land is to be loved and respected is an extension of ethics" (Leopold, 1949: xix). Leopold (1933) had elaborated his concept of a "conservation ethic" even earlier, so when the editors and authors of this text advocate an expanded land management ethic oriented toward ecosystems sustainability, they are in excellent company.

Leopold, a hunter and angler, never advocated that the land should not be used, but rather that it should not be used up. As a manager and administrator of public lands during his early career, and later as a college professor, he taught that the land must be respected and viewed ". . . as a community to which we belong. . . ." However, Leopold was not overly optimistic that his world-view, which he called an "ecological conscience," would be widely accepted. He was aware of opposing forces preventing humans from modifying their thinking and behaviors in ways necessary to reflect such an ethic. Since these forces continue to exist today, this text should help facilitate the concept of sustainable ecosystems management by promoting the expanded land management ethic envisioned by Leopold over six decades ago.

While the text is oriented to land managers, it will also be useful in the policy arena to help elected officials and policymakers better understand what Leopold meant by an "ecological conscience." It also should help those of us who establish policies for the public lands better appreciate the nature-based values and experiences that serve to renew and fulfill the human spirit. I know of no other reference directed to land managers that looks at these values of nature so comprehensively. Further, other works on this topic do not demonstrate as clearly the connection of these values with material well-being. Given its in-depth coverage of this broad spectrum of deep nature-based values and experiences and its offering of many diverse perspectives about these values, the text will contribute significantly to policymakers' understanding of why these values must be considered more carefully in resource allocation decisions than they have been in the past.

The text maintains a carefully balanced perspective on its very difficult topic. The editors have succeeded in their attempt to include authors who represent a diversity of views on ways in which humans value and use the public lands. In this way, the text emphasizes that public lands can be managed to better accommodate the psychologically deep nature-based human values within a multiple-use managerial framework. It shows that opportunities can be provided to renew the human spirit at the same time and place that traditional uses take place. Indeed, the text demonstrates ways in which all land-related values and uses are interrelated and mutually sustaining.

Because the text focuses on the broad role of nature in sustaining the human spirit, some of the authors expand Leopold's concept of an "ecological conscience" to include a "spiritual" orientation toward the Earth. Both concepts recognize the fact that we humans must use the land to meet our needs, and both propose wise use, with respect and concern for future generations. Rolston, Chapter One, makes an intriguing case for a spiritual orientation to the Earth by referring to the classical definition of "spiritual" as "that to which humans are bound" and then considering some ways in which we humans are bound to our "spaceship earth." Within this context, remember that astronauts who viewed the Earth from outer space returned with new respect for its finiteness and for how closely we humans are bound to it and to each other. Several of those astronauts have written that this was truly a spiritual experience for them. I wonder how such a view of the Earth by all humans might influence our ideas about the need for an expanded land management ethic?

Perhaps the real difference between Leopold's "ecological conscience" and a "spiritual" orientation toward the land is that the latter points out our subjective response to the extreme complexity of managing the public lands both to meet societal needs and to sustain ecosystems. As emphasized by the editors in their introductory chapter, this complexity makes us humble and stimulates a sense of awe about natural systems—responses commonly recalled when people attempt to put into words what a nature-based spiritual experience means to them. I have stated elsewhere that ecosystems are not only more complex than we think—they are more complex than we humans *can* think. If these systems are indeed more complex than we can think, then by definition we are operating in the realm of risk and uncertainty. This means that resource management decisions will have both subjective and objective components.

The introductory chapter cautions readers against assigning a narrow sectarian, religious, or mystical meaning to the words "spirit" and "spiritual" because the words are used in a much broader sense throughout the text. Much care is taken not to imply actions or ideas that would violate the doctrine of separation of church and state. Friesen addresses this concern in Chapter Twenty-Two. She proposes that purposeful management of the public lands, in part to renew the human spirit as that concept is developed in the text, has nothing to do with the clauses of the First Amendment to the Constitution of the United States pertaining to the "establishment, promotion or prevention" of a religion. Friesen's position is that nature-based spiritual benefits are generic to all users, whether holders or nonholders of sectarian religious beliefs.

Friesen's position is supported strongly in the Describing Diverse Perspectives section of the text, which is written by authors from different countries and by authors who represent different users of the public lands in the United States, including users from different subcultures and those with commodity interests. This section clearly shows that the types of nature-based spirit-renewing benefits defined by the editors in their introductory chapter are common across all types of users, whether a timber cutter, a hunter, a member of an environmental organization, a hiker, or a Native American. Indeed, the purpose of this text is to articulate clearly these commonly held values and to explore how they can be integrated into the practice of multiple-use sustainable ecosystems management. This is in line with the policy of the USDA Forest Service that ". . . ecosystem management must include consideration of the physical, emotional, mental, spiritual, social, and economic well-being of people and communities" (USDA Forest Service, 1995).

Wondolleck, in Chapter Twenty-Three, makes the excellent point that there is never just one technically defined "right" public land management decision. There is a set of possible decisions that defines the range of alternative feasible allocations that can meet to varying degrees the competing biophysical and social objectives that must be considered when making allocation decisions. Each reflects a different set of "value mixes," including value judgments about what is fair for future generations. Thus, these decisions are in the realm of ethics whether we recognize it or not. We, therefore, need better and more widely accepted philosophical guidelines for land policy and managerial decisions. We need the expanded land management ethic called for in this text.

This text is timely because it is clear that a growing number of people recognize and deliberately seek the spiritual benefits the public lands can provide. The text shows that these benefits have grown in importance as more people—now about 85 percent in the United States—live in essentially urban areas and as rapid social changes of many types have accelerated the pace and complexity of life. Because of these changes, increasing numbers of people use the public lands to cope with modern life and as a foil for negative aspects of urban living, to generate and restore adaptive energies, to renew their spirit away from the city, and to learn about natural processes. This text should help elected officials and administrators and managers of public natural areas better understand the complex intangible benefits those areas provide and how they enrich the lives of all Americans. With that improved understanding we can all do a better job of managing those areas for all of their uses and benefits whether they be city parks or state or federally administered lands.

Literature Cited

Leopold, A. (1949). *A sand county almanac and sketches here and there.* New York, NY: Oxford University Press.

Leopold, A. (1933). The conservation ethic. *Journal of Forestry, 31:* 634-643.

Maclean, N. (1976). *A river runs through it.* Chicago, IL: The University of Chicago Press.

Thomas, J. (1994). The forest service ethics and course to the future. USDA Forest Service, Washington, DC, 12 pp.

USDA Forest Service. (1995). Human dimensions in ecosystems management: A concept paper. Washington, DC.

Section

I

Introduction and
Need for Text

*Clearly, we are moving toward a new era in the
stewardship of public lands. This new era is one in
which we must blend environmental values with the
needs of people in such a way that the [public lands]
represent diverse, healthy, productive, and sustainable
ecosystems.*

President William J. Clinton (1993)

NATURE AND THE HUMAN SPIRIT: OVERVIEW

B. L. DRIVER
Rocky Mountain Forest
and Range Experiment Station
USDA Forest Service
Fort Collins, Colorado

DANIEL DUSTIN
La Mesa, California

TONY BALTIC
Rocky Mountain Forest
and Range Experiment Station
USDA Forest Service
Fort Collins, Colorado

GARY ELSNER
Recreation, Heritage
and Wilderness Resources Staff
USDA Forest Service
Washington, DC

GEORGE PETERSON
Rocky Mountain Forest
and Range Experiment Station
USDA Forest Service
Fort Collins, Colorado

Introduction

In the spring of 1992, the editors met to consider the "spiritual" meanings that nature holds for human beings and to consider if and how a more thorough understanding of these meanings could improve management of the public lands. Spiritual meanings, as the editors conceive them, refer to the broad range of hard-to-define and hard-to-measure values and benefits that relate to the deep psychological or higher order human needs that characterize what is called in this text the "human spirit" and that is derived in part from humankind's relationship with the natural world.

To help guide thinking on this topic, the editors organized a focus group which met in Santa Fe, New Mexico, in June 1992. That focus group included representatives from a wide range of backgrounds, interests, disciplines, and occupations so it could reflect the broadest possible spectrum of views about how the public lands help maintain and renew the human spirit. One of the questions asked of the focus group was whether a text was needed to increase understanding of the topic, "Nature and the Human Spirit." The response was affirmative and this text represents the results of the subsequent efforts.

Introduction

The Problem

At one time, approximately two-thirds of the United States was public domain held in federal ownership. Many of its national parks, national forests, fish and wildlife reserves, and areas administered by the Bureau of Land Management and other federal agencies have since been carved out of that original public domain. Today these lands constitute over one-third of the United States and they are managed to meet the specified needs and values of the American people, needs and values that the democratic political process has decided could not be met if the lands were privately owned. These needs and values have evolved over time and in turn have precipitated legislative changes governing public land management.

The USDA Forest Service (USFS) is a case in point. As one of the world's largest and most effective land managing agencies, the USFS plays a central role in the stewardship of natural resources in the United States. To guide that stewardship effort, Gifford Pinchot, the first Chief of the USFS, issued his "Wise Use" book nearly a century ago. Pinchot felt that the national forests should be managed for all of their multiple uses, but in the early years management focused primarily on watershed protection, timber production, mining, and grazing. Although these uses remain as important as ever, the USFS has broadened its managerial focus considerably—especially since passage of the Multiple Use and Sustained Yield Act of 1968—to include noncommodity uses commonly referred to as amenity services. This expanded focus in the USFS and other public land management agencies was brought about by a variety of changes in society.

In the 1950s, '60s, and early '70s, social changes such as increased mobility, free time, income, and knowledge about available opportunities accelerated demands for outdoor recreation on the public lands in the United States. This burgeoning demand prompted an inventory of the nation's supply of outdoor recreation resources by the Outdoor Recreation Resources Review Commission (1962) and an expansion of areas and facilities to accommodate the heightened demand.

While increasing demands for outdoor recreation opportunities certainly changed the policies of public land managing agencies, that growing demand does not adequately explain the increased valuing and use of natural areas for maintaining and renewing

the human spirit. Instead, three major trends have contributed to this emphasis on spiritual values. The first trend involves the major demographic and cultural changes taking place in America, changes that have caused the 1980s and 1990s to be called the "Age of Anxiety." These changes include the faster pace of life, stresses caused by concentrating people in urban areas, the growing number of single-parent families, the maturing of the "baby boomers," many of whom have become pessimistic about their career opportunities and those of their children, and other causes of perceived lack of predictability and control. The second trend is widespread concern about "lifestyle management" oriented toward increased physical activity, proper nutrition, avoidance of substance abuse, the creation and nurturance of more satisfying personal and family relationships, stress management, and growing interest in mental dispositions and orientations that contribute to a perceived sense of fitness and to mental or inner peace. The third trend has been increased concern for the biophysical integrity and health of the natural environment, and contributions of the physical environment to the quality of one's life.

These and other changes in society have caused a large and growing number of people to explore both old and new orientations to life including taking less stressful jobs, moving to the country, or just testing new modes of thinking and behaving. Not only has this testing resulted in a diversity of personal reflections on the meaning of life, but it has also enhanced awareness and increased use of the public lands in ways that go beyond outdoor recreation and that contribute uniquely to the psychological essence of life. The purposeful use of these lands to maintain and renew the human spirit is the topic of this text.

While public land managers are sensitive to the psychologically deep, nature-based values, they are experiencing difficulty in fully understanding them and in designing and implementing actions to accommodate them. Herein lies the problem—while these values are extremely hard to define, legislation such as the 1976 National Forest Management Act mandates that all relevant values be explicitly incorporated into management planning. Carrying out this and similar mandates is made all the more difficult because these hard-to-define, spirit-renewing values and uses can conflict not only with the values underlying more traditional uses of the public lands but also with one another. Working with citizens to sort out these competing values and to turn this conflict into a learning process that creates positive results is a difficult and largely uncharted management task. Nonetheless, if the public lands are to be managed in the best interests of all, all values attendant to those lands and their existence must be considered.

In sum, if public land managers are to be responsive to the changing needs and values of an increasingly multicultural citizenry in management planning, they must work toward a fuller understanding of those needs and values. This text responds to that challenge by reasoning that public land management policies and practices can be expanded to integrate better these values with the values related to commodity production and the more conventional notions of amenity resource management.

The Values of Focus

The focus group that met in Santa Fe, New Mexico, in June 1992, helped identify key dimensions of the hard-to-define nature-based values that help maintain and renew the human spirit. But before the editors could outline the general content of the text and assign authors to write chapters that comprehensively covered the topic, they needed a more in-depth understanding of how natural areas help maintain and renew the human spirit. To gain that understanding, the editors reviewed the relevant literature and asked a large number of people what these hard-to-define nature-based spiritual experiences meant to them. As a result of these efforts, the editors recognized that they were, indeed, dealing with an abstract topic—one that reflects the moral and ethical aspects of land usage and the ascendancy of higher emotions and refinements of thought and feeling toward the land, nature, and cultural resources. At this level of abstraction, the editors and authors are dealing with feelings, thoughts and values that are ethereal and intangible and, therefore, hard to define and measure.

While these abstractions were useful for structuring thought, they provided little guidance for making recommendations about how managers of the public lands could do a better job of providing opportunities for spiritual renewal. Given this need

to be more discrete, the editors focused on the following ways that natural areas help maintain and renew the human spirit:

- Nature-based spiritual experiences. As elaborated on shortly, these experiences cover but include much more than sectarian, evangelical religious experiences. The editors know these nature-based, spiritual experiences cannot be defined adequately to the satisfaction of everyone but they include: introspection and reflection on deep personal values; the elements of human devotion, reverence, respect, wonder, awe, mystery or lack of total understanding; inspiration; interaction with and relationship to something other and greater than oneself; sense of humility; and sense of timelessness, integration, continuity, connectedness, and community.

- Sense of place, special place, and attachment to place. Included here is appreciation of "Early American Landscapes" (EALs) and places such as the Old West and colonial New England.

- Use of natural areas for mental well-being and associated effects on physical well-being.

- Cognitive appreciation of heritage/historic sites and areas for a sense of cultural continuity, appreciation of cultural roots and meanings, and the understanding of a society's credos, fiber, and temperaments that these historic resources inspire and teach.

- Deep reflective recreational values of natural areas best reflected by Aristotle's notion that leisure should achieve excellence of the soul and mind which is much deeper than escape, social interaction, skill testing, and other values sought during leisure.

- Nature-based archetypes of human existence and experience as defined by Jung (1964) and elaborated by Campbell (1988).

- Nature-based, multisensory, aesthetic experiences which include but go beyond the visual/scenic experience.

- Representations and expressions of artistic interpretations of nature.

Each of these dimensions is described in one or more chapters in the text.

The editors recognize that complex and deep psychological human experiences can also be associated with other stimuli (e.g., listening to the second movement of Mozart's Clarinet Concerto or Beethoven's Fifth Piano Concerto). However, some of these experiences do depend on natural environments, and many people deliberately seek out nature for such experiences.

While each of the above dimensions of the hard-to-define nature-based values discussed in the text can be viewed as a separate category of experience, the editors believe that each contributes to a holistic maintenance and/or renewal of the human spirit. The editors also believe that Leopold's (1949) concept of an "ecological conscience" implied the need for what can be called a "spiritual orientation" to the land. Such an orientation calls for wise use that accommodates the hard-to-define values and concerns about future generations. An expanded land management ethic would reflect such a spiritual orientation to the land. Indeed, the title of the text explicitly refers to the "human spirit" as central to such an expanded ethic.

Research has shown that seeking desired experiences such as spiritual growth, introspection, and value clarification are important reasons for engaging in many outdoor recreation activities. While these and related motivations certainly denote elements of the use of natural environments for spiritual fulfillment and renewal, they are not addressed explicitly because of the following: considerable qualitative and quantitative research already has been done on the motivations of outdoor recreationists (cf. Driver, Tinsley, and Manfredo, 1991); managerial technologies such as the Recreation Opportunity Spectrum (Driver, Brown, Gregoire, and Stankey, 1987) and agency visual or scenic resource management systems are on-line that help managers accommodate the experience preferences identified by past motivational research; and the editors do not want the text to leave the impression it focuses on outdoor recreation per se.

In closing this section, the editors caution the reader not to assign a narrow sectarian religious interpretation to the word "spiritual" because that is not how the editors and the other authors use the word. The editors respect the sectarian religious uses of nature, but they do not recommend or imply ideas or actions that violate the doctrine of separation of church and state as expressed in the clauses of the First Amendment to the Constitution of the United States pertaining to the "establishment, promotion or prevention" of a religion. This volume focuses on the much broader, nature-based, spiritual values that are generic to all users of the public lands no matter what their secular or religious beliefs might be.

Managerial Orientation

As stated previously, the fundamental problem addressed by the following chapters is that public land management agencies must explicitly consider the hard-to-define nature-based values even though these values and associated uses make managing the public lands more complex. The text attempts to reduce this managerial complexity by:

1. identifying the essential dimensions of nature-based, spiritual renewal;

2. describing each of these dimensions in nontechnical language;

3. showing the commonalities in these dimensions of nature-based spirituality across different types of users of the public lands;

4. recommending specific managerial orientations and practices related to these hard-to-define values; and

5. identifying additional research that can aid managers in accommodating these values.

Over the past several decades, different laws have established a large number of goals for public land management agencies. Those laws require that agencies promote national economic development in efficient ways, create flows of revenue to the U.S. Treasury, be fair, maintain the sustainability of basic ecosystems, be responsive to the public, and be good stewards of the land for future generations. These goals frequently conflict and must be addressed within constrained fiscal appropriations and with limited objective information about alternative management actions that various citizens would like to see implemented, the good and bad and short- and long-term consequences of each alternative action, and the costs, benefits, and values of each. Just as the traditional goals of public land management agencies can conflict, the deep psychological and higher order human spirit-renewing values and uses also can be conflicting.

These values are deep psychologically because for many people they represent what psychologists call "core values" which reflect basic beliefs and orientations to life—and even to the land. As such, these values have high emotional content which can exacerbate conflicts between the holders of these values and other stakeholders who have equally strong but different values regarding the public lands. This potential for conflict represents the greatest challenge facing managers of the public lands. For that reason, many chapters in the text strongly advocate a participative style of management of the public lands under which collaborative partnerships are established that involve all people who have a stake in those lands. The authors also recommend a philosophy of management that recognizes there is seldom, if ever, just one technically defined "right" allocation but instead a range of alternative feasible allocations that will meet the values and interests of different stakeholders to varying degrees.

Before agencies can manage for the hard-to-define values, they must not only conceptualize a working definition of them, but they must also understand the implications of these values for management of the public lands. For example, managers certainly need to understand how one type of use impacts other actual and potential types of use. They must also understand how cultural diversity affects different uses and values. The agencies must also better understand their responsibilities and opportunities as nurturers of possibilities for discovery and learning. This is particularly important in view of the fact that the latest census (1993) of the United States population shows that about 85 percent of the people live in urban areas and that there is a negative correlation between the size of one's community and the amount of knowledge one is likely to have about natural ecological processes. It has only been recently that public land management agencies have started to realize the significance of these environmental education opportunities and responsibilities.

For managers a central value of this text is that it can aid them in dealing with actual and potential conflict among stakeholders with different values in a way that produces positive results for all people who value, use, and derive benefits from the public lands—and that is all Americans. This aid is not so much defined by the specific options and activities recommended in the text as it is by the process it presents. It is a process that requires mutual respect, honesty, openness, understanding, give-and-take, and continuing learning among policymakers, managers, stakeholders, and the public at large.

Organization and Content of Text

The text is organized into six sections including:

Section I: An introduction which details policy and management needs;

Section II: A weaving of the context within which ideas about nature and the human spirit are subsequently discussed;

Section III: An exploration of those ideas from a variety of ethnic, cultural, personal, professional, and international perspectives;

Section IV: A detailing of related public land management issues and concerns with recommendations for action;

Section V: An examination of research approaches for studying nature and the human spirit including an extensive list of research questions and a potential program of research; and

Section VI: Summary.

The text represents not so much the end of something as it does a beginning, a much longer journey that aims at a better understanding of what social science can and cannot offer in the quest for insight about the nature of humankind's spiritual relationship with the Earth. Thus, while the editors think there is much to commend in the text, we do not suppose that the story it tells is complete. There is more. What the editors offer you is a modest beginning. May it serve you well in your own way.

Literature Cited

Campbell, J. (with Moyers, B.). (1988). *The power of myth*. New York, NY: Doubleday & Co., Inc.

Clinton, W. J. (1993, October 16). A proclamation (released in conjunction with the National Forest Products Week). Washington, DC: Office of the Press Secretary.

Driver, B., Brown, P., Gregoire, T., and Stankey, G. (1987). The ROS planning system: Evolution, basic concepts, and research needed. *Leisure Sciences, 9* (3):203-214.

Driver, B., Tinsley, H., and Manfredo, M. (1991). The paragraphs about leisure and recreation experience preference scales: Results from two inventories designed to access the breadth of the perceived psychological benefits of leisure. In B. Driver, P. Brown, and G. Peterson (Eds.). *Benefits of leisure* (pp. 263-286). State College, PA: Venture Publishing, Inc.

Jung, C. (1964). Approaching the unconscious. In C. Jung (Ed.), *Man and his symbols* (pp. 1-94). New York, NY: Dell Publishing Company, Inc.

Leopold, A. (1949). *A sand county almanac and sketches here and there*. New York, NY: Oxford University Press.

Outdoor Recreation Resources Review Commission. (1962). *Summary report* (and 27 other reports). Washington, DC: Government Printing Office.

United States Census Bureau. (1993). 1990 census of population and housing. Washington, DC: U.S. Department of Commerce Bureau of the Census, Data User Services Division.

The Role of Public Lands in Maintaining and Rejuvenating the Human Spirit

GARY ELSNER
Recreation, Heritage and Wilderness Resources Staff
USDA Forest Service
Washington, DC

FRANK SNELL
Division of Recreation and Wilderness
USDI Bureau of Land Management
Washington, DC

DARRELL LEWIS
Natural Resources Management Branch
US Army Corps of Engineers
Washington, DC

WILLIAM SPITZER
Recreation Resource Assistance
USDI National Park Service
Washington, DC

Introduction

People can shape the landscape, and the landscape can shape people. A beautiful landscape, like the canyon country of the American Southwest, can bring peace of mind, a new level of creativity, an increased appreciation of the arts, and a heightened respect for nature. It can result in a new, or renewed, you.

Now more than ever before, public land managers need to understand the full range of benefits derived from human interactions with the natural world. They need to understand the human dimension of ecosystem management. Successfully incorporating the concerns of humans into ecosystem management means giving equal consideration to social as well as physical and biological concerns.

Recognition of the human dimension is, of course, the first step. This dimension is complex and includes the spiritual, ethical, cultural, historic, aesthetic, economic, and social. Planning for the human dimension requires sound information about a broader spectrum of benefits than public land managers have concerned themselves with in the past. This, in turn, requires cooperative input from land managers, researchers, and the various populaces in whose trust the public lands are overseen.

Humans are but one part of the natural world—one of many species. The greatest and most powerful forces on Earth are forces of nature, and we need to connect with nature to better understand our place in it. It is becoming clearer to public land managers that people visit forests, parks, and other natural areas to be close to nature, to be re-created, and to renew their spirit. It is appropriate, then, that the land managers' business is called "recreation." Providing opportunities for the American people to recreate and renew their spirit through interactions with the natural world is the job of the public land manager.

Over the last three decades researchers have helped public land managers identify and understand the importance of many nature-based benefits (see Driver, Brown, and Peterson, 1991). While these understandings have been valuable, they have also been incomplete. While profiting from research on economic benefits, environmental benefits, psychological benefits, and social benefits, researchers have yet to study the more elusive benefits of nature-based recreation that may stem from a possible relationship between nature and the human spirit. By "study" researchers mean an organized knowledge-gathering approach that strives to understand this relationship in terms of both our past and present associations with nature; an approach that involves land managers, multicultural members of society, and other interested parties.

Recreation land management has evolved rapidly in the United States, especially since the 1960s. Much of the planning emphasis has been on the quantitative aspects of outdoor recreation (e.g., the number of visitors, the number of sites needing maintenance). Many past studies focused on what people were "doing" in nature. Now a study of what people are "feeling" in nature is needed. In recent years the quantitative aspects have been augmented by qualitative considerations. Thus an augmentation of insights—not a substitution of the qualitative for the quantitative—is required. And it is in this qualitative realm that researchers can best begin to examine the hard-to-define benefits.

This challenge of seeking the best balance between the quantitative and the qualitative is comparable to the search for balance between preservation and development of the natural world. Land managers must balance saving the wilderness with protecting the rural landscape and small towns and the authenticity of our nation's past that they represent (see Bruns and Stokowski, Chapter Twenty-Nine, in this volume). The bottom line is a healthy sustainable ecological base.

It is difficult, if not impossible, to predict the future—especially as it relates to the needs and values discussed in this text. The one thing we can predict is that values and needs will change with regard to public lands. Douglas County, Oregon, for example, was at one time the timber capital of the world. The single most important public land value was commodity production commensurate with long-term productivity. Today, a relatively short time later, public land values have changed dramatically. Much of the public now values preservation of biodiversity on the same lands that previously were valued for commodity production.

How can public land managers respond to these changing values? Land managers need to keep in mind that the capacity of the land to satisfy spiritual and other intangible needs depends on the fundamental, holistic health of the land, just like commodity production. So, if the health of soil, water, air, vegetation, and animal populations is maximized, the capacity of the land to satisfy a wide range of public needs—from preservation to commodity production—will be maximized. In today's terminology, this is called good ecosystem management.

In his book *Earth in the Balance: Ecology and the Human Spirit*, Vice President Al Gore (1992) concludes that:

> When considering a problem as large as the degradation of the global environment, it is easy to feel overwhelmed, utterly helpless to effect any change whatsoever. But we must resist that response, because this crisis will be resolved only if individuals take some responsibility for it. . . . Perhaps most important, we each need to assess our own relationship to the natural world and renew, at the deepest level of personal integrity, a connection to it. And that can only happen if we renew what is authentic and true in every aspect of our lives. The twentieth century has not been kind to the constant human striving for a sense of purpose in life. . . . We retreat into the seductive tools and technologies of industrial civilization, but that only creates new problems as we become increasingly isolated from one another and disconnected from our roots. . . . More people than ever before are asking, "Who are we? What is our purpose?" . . .
>
> Perhaps because I have ended up searching simultaneously for a better understanding of my own life and of what can be done to rescue the global environment, I have come to believe in the value of a kind of inner ecology that relies on the same principles of balance and holism that characterize a healthy environment. . . . The key is indeed balance—balance between contemplation and action, individual concerns and commitment to the community, love for the natural world and love for our wondrous civilization. This is the balance I seek in my own life . . .
>
> For civilization as a whole, the faith that is so essential to restore the balance now missing in our relationship to the earth is the faith that we do have a future. We can believe in that future and work to achieve it and preserve it, or we can whirl blindly on, behaving as if one day there will be no children to inherit our legacy. The choice is ours; the earth is in the balance (pp. 366-368).

Why Study the Spirit/Nature Relationship?

Why is it necessary to study the spirit/nature relationship, and what will be gained from it? For years public land managers have understood that people often visit forests and parks in order to get close to nature or to be renewed. But what does this mean, and how can the land and recreation opportunities be managed so these benefits may be realized?

The knowledge gained from pursuing the first part of this question will result in an improvement in researchers' ability to articulate the meaning of the spirit/nature relationship. If that's the first goal, what kinds of talents and skills are needed to attain this goal? A variety of people can help achieve this goal, and they are people that are not often associated with natural resource management. They include philosophers, poets, artists, theologians and social scientists. They also include other groups that researchers know well but may not have taken the time to talk to about spirit/nature relationships. They include Native Americans, Hispanic Americans, African Americans, women, representatives from various forest industries, and others (see Section III, Describing Diverse Perspectives, in this volume).

Once spirit/nature relationships are understood, how can the land be managed so that the associated benefits can be realized? Land managers need to understand much more precisely what they can do as land managers to assist in the spiritual renewal of people who visit these natural areas. Managers need to understand what different environmental characteristics tend to contribute toward a renewal of spirit for each culture.

How Important Is Renewal of the Human Spirit?

How important is this renewal? Isn't it just one more benefit that can be obtained by visiting natural areas? Of course it is, but it is one of the most important benefits, one that would be hard to replicate in human-built environments. The authors believe that renewal of the human spirit is important for the individual to enjoy a full life and to be a productive member of society, for the members of a family to regain their vigor, motivation and interests in the family unit, and for members of the community and the nation to maintain a long-term productive role as economic agents and as socially responsible citizens.

Throughout the twentieth century more and more people have lived in urban and suburban areas and fewer and fewer in rural areas. Many people feel that this physical detachment from the land results in a loss of touch with nature and in many cases even the knowledge of how to enjoy nature. If

nature is inherently important to humans, how should land and information be managed so that people do not lose the benefits that can be derived from nature? In this regard, a better understanding of spirit/nature relationships should help managers reconnect the American people with the natural world.

Public land managers and educators may be perpetrating the perception that nature is something that happens "out there." A democratization of environmental education is thus in order. Educators and land managers must link people to nature where they live if they are to see and understand themselves as part of nature and value it. Certainly some of these important nature-based benefits could be realized closer to home. Certainly the benefits for children at risk could be significantly realized. Findings from ecobiology seem to indicate that a person's need for contact with nature is genetically formed. This need likely transcends many of our cultural differences. People may be separated from the land as much by urban living and modernity as by race or income.

Some might assume that managing resources in order to facilitate the renewal of the human spirit applies only to wilderness and other pristine environments. At this point in time, however, with the cultural evolution that has taken place in the United States, many urban/suburban people receive a renewal of their spirit from nature-based areas that have significant developments such as trails, interpretive signing, and other recreation facilities. So, managers are concerned with the entire spectrum of settings from the urban to the rural to the most primitive and remote.

Managers frequently hear visitors to the public lands speak of their "special place." It is an intriguing term that has a wide range of meanings (see Roberts, Chapter Four, in this volume). It can refer to a certain campground that has been visited by several generations of the same family, or a historic homestead. In all cases "special places" are part of the public estate that elicit strong personal and nostalgic feelings. "Special places" can refer to a broad area of a state or region, but in most cases they refer to a specific and rather small piece of public land. Visitors often request that these "special places" receive special management attention. For managers, the benefits to an individual from a solo trip into a wilderness area, the benefits to friends spending a week together on a wild river, or the benefits to a family discovering their roots in a National Historic Park, are obvious. Managers need to continue emphasizing the use of these designations. As Darrell Lewis (1994) testifies:

> *In southwestern Washington State, Spirit Lake, nested at the foot of Mt. St. Helens, was my "special place." I can still remember the quiet deep waters of the lake reflecting the beauty of Mt. St. Helens. It was my personal definitive memory of natural grandeur. The volcanic explosion that ripped away the top of the mountain and all but obliterated my "special place" had an emotional impact on me. I still feel like something valuable has been taken from me.*

Special areas can often be managed within the usual management guidelines; however, if they need special protection which is not provided under the national system, it is possible for agencies to provide a special administrative designation. For example, the Bureau of Land Management uses the designation Areas of Critical Environmental Concern to bring special management attention to selected natural areas. This designation, and others like it, could also be used to safeguard hard-to-define values.

Managers have a number of tools that should prove useful in managing public lands for hard-to-define values. They include concepts from ecosystem management, overall ecosystem health, the human dimension of ecosystem management, and methodologies such as Visual Resource Management and the Recreation Opportunity Spectrum (Driver, Brown, Stankey, and Gregoire, 1987) which can assure the maintenance of the beauty of the landscape as well as the complete range of recreation opportunities.

Another important reason to pursue this work is that our public lands contain "chapters" of American history. You can still visit landscapes where our nation's history unfolded. Whether they tell the story of the Civil War, farming methods of the 1800s, the cultural characteristics of the Anasazi, the history of colonial New England, or the cowboy era of the Old West, it's all out there on the public lands. Visiting these areas and in some sense reliving the experience is important to many Americans.

Conclusion

What, one may finally ask, should be the federal government's position on the spirit/nature relationship? Most people would probably say it's not appropriate for the government to have a position on whether this relationship exists or not, because the fact is that there is a relationship between people and nature. The manager's concern should be, does one manage in a way that alienates many people concerning this relationship or does one manage in a way that identifies these communities of interest and responds to their needs? The authors suggest that managers take the initiative and use this overall effort to better understand the increasingly multicultural users of the public lands, and to reevaluate management practices to see if managers can make improvements in how the public is served.

To provide responsive and responsible public land management for our increasingly multicultural citizenry, managers must better understand their valuing of nature. Public land managers are committed to providing opportunities for realizing the hard-to-define values discussed in this text, and they look forward to meeting that challenge.

Literature Cited

Driver, B., Brown, P., and Peterson, G. (Eds.). (1991). *Benefits of leisure.* State College, PA: Venture Publishing, Inc.

Driver, B., Brown, P, Stankey, G., and Gregoire, G. (1987). The ROS planning system: Evolution, basic concepts, and research needed. *Leisure Sciences, 9(3),* 203-214

Gore, A. (1992). *Earth in the balance: Ecology and the human spirit.* Boston, MA: Houghton Mifflin Company.

Lewis, D. (1994). Personal communication.

Section II

Weaving the Context

When despair for the world grows in me

and I wake in the night at the least sound

in fear of what my life and my children's lives may be,

I go and lie down where the wood drake

rests in his beauty on the water, and the great heron feeds.

I come into the peace of wild things

who do not tax their lives with forethought

of grief. I come into the presence of still water.

And I feel above me the day-blind stars

waiting with their light. For a time

I rest in the grace of the world, and am free.

Wendell Berry (1968)

NATURE, SPIRIT, AND LANDSCAPE MANAGEMENT

CHAPTER 1

HOLMES ROLSTON, III
Department of Philosophy
Colorado State University
Fort Collins, Colorado

Nature, Science, and Spirit

Both the words "nature" and "spirit" are complex with tapestries of meaning. Etymologically, "nature" goes back to a Greek and Latin root, *gene (g)nasci, natus,* to give birth, to generate. The word "spirit," from the Latin, *spiritus,* contains the root idea of "breath," with parallels in both the Greek and Hebrew languages, naming the unseen air that inspired life. In their origins nature and spirit are surprisingly similar, nature being the creative, generative powers on Earth, spirit being the animating principle that raised life from the ground. Thus, in the Hebrew scriptures, the Spirit is the giver of life, animating the dust and generating the Earth and its swarms of creatures. Early peoples, understandably, found this creativity sacred; if anything at all is to be sacred, surely this fundamental vitality at the ground of our being must be sacred.

Modern Western peoples with a science-based world-view have been inclined to contrast nature and spirit. Since the Enlightenment, aided by a Cartesian dualism of mind and matter, and endorsed by the successes of physics, astronomy, chemistry, geology, meteorology and such physical sciences, the concept of nature has been dominantly mechanistic; that is, spiritless. Nature works like a clock, a machine. Nature is matter in motion, energetic matter, a realm of objective causal networks, value free in itself. Humans, by contrast, are inward with psychologically felt experience, self-conscious awareness, value-driven preferences, with what philosophers call *Existenz*; what theologians call spirit. Humans have minds that operate on matter; humans have souls separate from their bodies.

Biology, as well as physics, is a science, and it too has depopulated the world of spirits. We do not live in an enchanted world; the phenomena are not the work of fairies, angels, and demons. (That disenchanting of the world was already begun by the Western monotheist traditions for whom the natural world was sacred creation but not full of particular spirits.) There is no entelechy, no spooky life force in organisms; they are made of ordinary elements, ordinary chemicals, organized in biochemical processes. Biology is a causal science; hence the successes of molecular and evolutionary biology—the secret of life is in the DNA, in genetic variations on which natural selection operates, producing the myriad species over the millennia. Forests are not haunted; they are causal systems determined by natural processes which humans can, if they wish, learn about and manage as natural resources. Such biology can banish spirit from nature allowing it only, if at all, in human life.

But there is another mood in biology, never too comfortable with the phenomenon of life viewed reductively as so much clockwork—as nothing but matter in motion. Perhaps nature in the heavens has been reduced to celestial mechanics, but nature on Earth is a different story. Earth is the only planet with life, so far as we know, and the story of matter here has been animated, often spectacular. Biology is a historical science; DNA codes this earthbound vitality that emerges and develops over the millennia— the generation of the swarms of creatures, resulting at length in humans with their remarkable minds, hands, and spirits. So biologists are not always comfortable with the merely physical explanations; life seems more than physics and chemistry, though it requires that. There is a vitality, animation, spiritedness in living beings that makes life more than its precursors in the nonlife sciences.

Biology, too, is a natural science, and the explanations in biology, though they advance beyond those in physics, remain natural. But to a person pondering this spirited behavior of matter such explanations can seem right as far as they go, but not all that needs to be said. The story is of the steady evolution of more out of less, of the persistence of life in the midst of its perpetual perishing, and, in the end, of the evolution of spirit, of our spirits, which, today, we have to reckon with. The assembly is of materials, complexity out of simplicity, but there comes with it autonomous life out of dead matter, biofunction out of nonfunctional antecedents, and, with sufficient neural organization subjectivity or felt experience arises out of objectivity or mere things. Once there was a world with only matter and energy, but later there appeared within it information centers, and later still, incarnate subjects. Molecules, trillions of them, spin around in complicated ways and generate the unified, centrally focused experience of mind.

Science is the most recent and sophisticated discipline for studying the secular, empirical world. And it is often thought that science—whether physics, astronomy, geology, chemistry, or biology—chases out the sacred, but this is proving to be a superficial impression. Ernst Mayr, one of the most eminent living

biologists, says, "Virtually all biologists are religious, in the deeper sense of this word, even though it may be a religion without revelation. . . . The unknown and maybe unknowable instills in us a sense of humility and awe" (Mayr, 1982, p. 81). In that sense, what impressed the ancients is still impressive after biological science—the rising of life from dust, its inspiration. Man and woman arising from all the intermediate steps (trilobites, dinosaurs, primates) from the maternal Earth is not less impressive, rather more so, than Aphrodite rising from the seas. We moderns find ourselves asking again whether the phenomena of natural history are a response to the brooding winds of the Spirit moving over the face of these earthly waters. The phenomena could be revealing the noumena, something deep and ultimate in, with, and under the passing appearances.

Biologists are "religious in the deeper sense of the word," claims Mayr (1982), and that prompts a closer look at the word "religion," a word with an impressive, if checkered, history. The Latin root, *religio*, contains two elements *re-* and *ligare,* with the idea of binding, seen in the English word "ligament," or in "obligation." The *re-* intensifies the binding; religion is that to which we are most deeply committed. "Religion is ultimate concern," insisted the famous theologian Paul Tillich, in a widely accepted definition; "it is the state of being grasped by something unconditional, holy, absolute" (Tillich, 1957, p. 59). Religion, concluded Rudolf Otto in a classic study, is "the sense of the holy" (Otto, [1923] 1958). "One's religion," according to Frederick Ferré, in a memorable address to the American Academy of Religion, "is one's way of valuing most intensively and comprehensively" (Ferré, 1970). The naturalist philosopher John Dewey, found that "whatever introduces genuine perspective is religious" (Dewey, 1934, p. 24).[1] One's religion is one's governing world-view when this reaches the dimension of depth, when it encounters the sacred, what is sometimes called the numi-

---

[1]Religion is complex, and there are also many pejorative definitions of religion, loaded with the users' dislikes. The Jewish theologian Martin Buber said, "I must confess that I don't like religion very much, and I am very glad that in the Bible the word is not to be found" (quoted in Smith, 1967, p. 33). The Protestant theologian Karl Barth added that religion is the action of those "who have fallen out of their relationship with God." For this reason, he claimed, "Religion must die. . . . In God we are rid of it" (Barth, 1933, pp. 246, 248). The protest is often against the institutional, dogmatic, intolerant dimensions of religion. James Leuba collected 47 classic definitions of religion (Leuba, 1912).

nous. The conviction arises that the phenomena require deeper explanation in the noumena; the explanations of who humans are and where they are, and of the meaning in life do not lie on the surface of things, but have to be penetrated to discover a presence, a power, in, with, and under everyday, empirical experiences.

Religious persons have often referred to this sense of something beyond the secular, or everyday order, as the "supernatural," and so religion, some think, has conveyed commitment to the supernatural, to, in polytheist traditions, gods, or, in the monotheist traditions, God, or to other ultimates such as Brahma or nirvana. With the rise of science, the contrast between the natural and the supernatural becomes more intense, with science appealing to a causal order, typically mechanistically conceived, and said to be natural, and religion appealing to a divine presence, said to be supernatural. Since there is no "spirit" in mechanism, "spirit"—often called "soul"—was typically thought to be supernatural, both the human "spirit" and the cosmic, divine "Spirit." That, too, produces a contrast between nature and spirit and now it may be said that religion differs from science, in that science takes all things to be natural, but religion believes in the supernatural, something unseen and transcendent that perfuses, or permeates, the empirical, natural order. Mayr (1982), however, while not believing in the supernatural, finds nature itself to be mysterious; he encounters the genesis of something out of nothing, of life out of matter and energy with awe and humility. He finds in nature that he sees as a biologist something before which he is reverent.

Mayr's (1982) religion in the deeper sense is also meant to leave institutional religion and denominationalism behind. Religions, as convictions about what is ultimately valuable, have needed to be passed from generation to generation; they are convictions about which people have wished to act in concert in their communities. Hence religions have become social forces, carriers of culture and institutions. Religions, as social forces, have promulgated creeds, sought converts, preached, and taught. Religions, as carriers of culture, have built churches, temples, ordained priests and clergy, organized communities with their scriptures, and have authorities and financial budgets. Religions as institutions, have conducted persecutions, endorsed wars, sent out missionaries, and the like. But in the confrontation of persons with nature, this aspect of religion is not in central focus.

One needs to notice that persons never confront nature except as they do so with cultural eyeglasses. People see nature through world-views that are supplied to them by these social institutions which include religion, philosophy, science, politics, economics, and art. Still, people confront nature, to some extent at least, as a world other than culture, as primordial nature; and what are people to make of it? A fundamental answer is that nature generates religious experiences in this deeper sense. If land managers wish to bypass the word "religion," owing to its institutional, denominational, and cultural dimensions, nature nevertheless generates "spiritual" experiences. One may find oneself, as a spirit, wondering about this inspirited inventiveness of nature. One may find oneself in a mood of reverence.

Of late, astronomers and the physicists themselves have been impressed by how the universe is well-organized (despite its increasing disorganization over time). The world, according to the recently prominent anthropic principle, is a fine-tuned universe, and was destined to produce life right from the start twenty billion years ago. So cosmological nature, even if one still thinks of nature as energetic matter in motion, can seem to have spirit among its possibilities (Barrow and Tipler, 1986; Davies, 1983; Leslie, 1989). Many, perhaps even most, physicists today think that cosmology is compatible with some kind of monotheism. Victor Weisskopf (1983) is explicit:

> *The origin of the universe can be talked about not only in scientific terms, but also in poetic and spiritual language, an approach that is complementary to the scientific one. Indeed, the Judeo-Christian tradition describes the beginning of the world in a way that is surprisingly similar to the scientific model.* (p. 480)

Whatever one makes of astronomical nature, in biological nature on Earth there arises the life that, experienced and reflected on over the centuries, has so persistently seemed sacred, something mysterious, an animation otherwise as yet unknown in the universe. In organisms, there is organization based on a principle radically different from anything found in merely geophysical or geochemical nature:

accumulating information storage localized in the species lines, transmitted over the millennia, spreading around the globe, increasing in diversity and complexity. Superimposed on the background physical organization of the universe, superimposed on the background increase of entropy, there appears more organization than ever before by many hundreds of orders of magnitude. The secret of it all, the biologists say, is these coding molecules, the DNA that "knows how" to organize matter in these spectacular ways. The result is the difference between the Earth and the moon.

Molecular biologists are providing a naturalistic account of all this synthesis of life in increasing detail. There remains yet much to be known. But what then? After the scientific descriptions are done, is that all there is to be said? Photosynthesis and the trophic pyramids in ecosystems have been explained; has life been explained away? Once, in ancient Israel, Moses thought that the burning bush, not consumed, was a miracle. Modern people hardly believe any more in that sort of supernatural miracle; science has made such stories incredible. But what has it left instead? A self-organizing nature that, over the millennia, organizes itself into photosynthesis that drives a synthesis of higher life forms, supporting trophic pyramids in ecosystems with millions of species, continuing for millennia—life as a strange fire that outlasts the sticks that feed it. This is hardly a phenomenon less marvelous even if, after bioscience, one no longer wants to say that it is "supernaturally" miraculous.

Indeed, in the original sense of "miracle"—a wondrous event, without regard to the question whether it is natural or supernatural—photosynthesis and the life it supports is the secular equivalent of the burning bush. The bush that Moses watched in the wilderness was an individual in a species line that had perpetuated itself for millennia, coping by the coding in its DNA, fueled by the sun, using photosynthesis, and surviving without being consumed. To go back to the miracle that Moses saw, a bush that burned briefly without being consumed would be to return to something several orders of magnitude less spectacular. The bigger miracle, even though one knows some of the steps by which this genesis operates, requires more, not less reverence.

After a survey of evolutionary natural history Loren Eiseley (1957) concluded:

I would say, that if 'dead' matter has reared up this curious landscape of fiddling crickets, song sparrows, and wondering men, it must be plain even to the most devoted materialist that the matter of which he speaks contains amazing, if not dreadful powers, and may not impossibly be . . . but one mask of many worn by the Great Face behind. (p. 210)

A landscape that has reared up such a spectacle, which can seem to veil Spirit in, with, under, and behind it, is quite a challenge for landscape management. It makes landscape management a matter of ethics as well as of science.

In nature there is no religion; the fauna and flora are incapable of ultimate concern with things holy or sacred. Only humans have, in that sense, a spiritual life. Only humans can be reverent about anything. But there is no religion without a concept of nature (see Kaza, Chapter Three, in this volume); there is no experiencing of nature without, sooner or later, moving to values at religious levels—if one remembers what religion means in the deeper sense. Nature stimulates spiritual experience; that was true once upon a time in the paleontological past when humans with spirits emerged out of nature; that is true again today, when one confronts nature as both the source of and a foil for spirit. Religions have shaped all cultures which have also been shaped by science and which grew up in a Judeo-Christian ambience. Part of such shaping of culture is to provide a concept of nature. Without that understanding, humans will never know who they are because they do not know where they are. Humans will know neither their ultimate origins nor their ultimate duties. As will be next seen, landscape management, in the end, is connected to metaphysics.

Landscape Policy and Spiritual Values

In the twentieth century, there has been a trend toward privatizing religion; religion—especially in its institutional forms—is difficult to deal with in a pluralistic government which believes in separation of church and state. The state must be neutral toward religion which is a matter of personal choice. Religion is a matter of one's spiritual life; that is not the province of government, and hence not the concern of public landscape managers. And yet, when one is dealing with natural history, with landscapes, with the generative, creative nature that has just been discussed, one faces collective choices about something fundamental. Some ethical choices are made by individuals, but in other cases citizens must choose together. Unless landscapes, with their natural histories, on both public and private lands, are protected by national, state, and local policy, they will be inadequately protected.

If one of the values of landscapes is provided by spiritual responses to nature, religions are then forced to become public and to join in shaping the public ethic. For many persons today, especially in an increasingly urban society, the principal opportunities to experience natural history—wildlands and wildlife, scenic vistas, primeval nature—take place on public lands, as these have been designated for conservation and preservation. Most remaining natural areas are public lands—national forests, parks, wilderness areas, seashores, grasslands, wildlife refuges, lands under the Bureau of Land Management, state or county parks and forests.

One of the constitutional freedoms in the United States is religious freedom, but one cannot be free to practice his or her religion if one of the sources of its inspiration is unavailable, if there is no longer any natural history to experience spiritually. The spiritual values that one may wish to defend on landscapes are often the softer, more diffuse ones, but that does not mean they are unessential or unreal, but that they are deeper and more philosophical. There is nothing denominational about this, since persons are free to experience nature spiritually in diverse ways. Indeed, that is one interesting feature of nature-based spiritual experience: it need not be structured institutionally in orthodox ways but is open-ended. Another important feature is that here, more than elsewhere, the multiple denominations, indeed the plural faiths, are likely to find common ground. Since all faiths, each in its own way, find nature sacred, they together endorse the conservation of nature for its power to generate spiritual experience.

A pristine natural system is a spiritual resource, as well as a scientific, recreational, aesthetic, or economic one. Indeed, although landscape managers commonly think of nature as "natural resources," they can, from the sacred point of view, profane experience and nature alike if they see nature as merely resource. This is something like seeing God, or parents, or the sacraments as a resource. A forest, a mountain, a prairie is more than resource, instrumental to civilization, more than even a religious resource. It is a primeval, wild, creative source. Here religious persons can bring a perspective of depth on wildland conservation. If landscape managers do not find that such perspective of depth fits their usual categories of landscape management, their perspectives need to be deepened or they will miss important values on landscapes.

Managers need to see forests, for example, as a characteristic expression of the creative process. In a forest, as on a desert or the tundra, the realities of nature cannot be ignored. The forest is both presence and symbol of forces in natural systems that transcend human powers and human utility. Like the sea or the sky, the forest is a kind of archetype of the foundations of the world. The central "goods" of the biosphere—forests and sky, sunshine and rain, rivers and earth, the everlasting hills, the cycling seasons, wildflowers and wildlife, hydrologic cycles, photosynthesis, soil fertility, food chains, genetic codes, speciation and reproduction, succession and its resetting, life and death and life renewed—were in place long before humans arrived, though they have lately become human economic and social resources. The dynamics and structures organizing the forest do not come out of the human mind; a wild forest is something wholly other than civilization. It is presence and symbol of the timeless natural givens that support everything else.

A pristine forest is prime natural history, a relic of the way the world was for almost forever. The forest as a tangible preserve in the midst of a culture contributes to the human sense of duration, antiquity, continuity, and identity. A visit there regenerates the sense of human late-coming and sensitizes us to our novelty. In the primeval forest humans know the most authentic of wilderness emotions, the sense of the sublime. We get transported by forces "awe-full" and overpowering by the signature of time and eternity.

"The groves were God's first temples" (Bryant, 1992). "The trees of the Lord are watered abundantly; the cedars of Lebanon which he planted" (Holy Bible, Psalms 104.16). John Muir (1901) exclaimed, "The forests of America, however slighted by man, must have been a great delight to God; for they were the best he ever planted" (p. 331). Such forests are a church as surely as a commodity. The forest is where the "roots" are, where life rises from the ground. Trees pierce the sky, like cathedral spires. Light filters down, as through stained glass. The forest canopy is lofty; much of it is over our heads. In common with churches, forests invite transcending the human world and experiencing a comprehensive, embracing realm. Forests can serve as a more provocative, perennial sign of this than many of the traditional, often outworn, symbols devised by the churches. "I find that I get goose pimples much more often in a wilderness than I do inside a church."

Being among the archetypes, a forest is about as near to ultimacy as one can come in the natural world—a vast scene of sprouting, budding, flowering, fruiting, passing away, passing life on. Mountaintop experiences, the wind in the pines, solitude in a sequoia grove, autumn leaves, the forest vista that begins at one's feet and disappears over the horizon—these generate experiences of "a motion and spirit that impels . . . and rolls through all things" (Wordsworth, 1992). One feels life's transient beauty sustained over chaos. A forest wilderness is a sacred space. There many will recognize God's creation, and others may find the ultimate reality or a nature sacred in itself. A forest wilderness elicits cosmic questions. One of the obligations of landscape managers is to preserve nature as a sanctuary for these spiritual experiences.

Land, Earth, and the Ground of Being

Landscape managers may not need to be cosmologists; that might be expecting too much of them. But they do need a global perspective; they need to rise from the earth beneath their feet to the planet Earth on which they live and move and have their being. They may not need to think about the whole universe, but they do need to think about the whole land that they inhabit. They may not need to think about heaven, or the heavens, but they do need to think about Earth, and they need to think deeply about foundations and fundamentals, about the spirited vitality that characterizes our home planet.

Land is not where one *makes* a living; it is where one *lives*, and this can be seen if one enlarges the scope from earth to Earth. Landscape management is part of managers' responsibility to Earth. Landscape management can seem specific enough; managers know what the assignments are on the forty acres, or four thousand acres, or forty thousand acres under their charge. Managers know who has grazing allotments where, or who wants to purchase the timber. Managers have surveyed recreationists who use the region they manage, they know who the constituents are in their district. A responsibility to Earth, by contrast, might be thought the most remote of managerial responsibilities. An Earth ethic seems so grandiose and vague beside one's concrete responsibilities to one's children, or to next door neighbors, or to fellow citizens.

But not so: one's responsibility to Earth is the most fundamental, the most comprehensive of responsibilities. Landscape managers increasingly have to figure their responsibilities into this larger picture. Though foreshadowed in the past by the sense of belonging that many peoples have had on their landscapes, loyalty to the planet is the newest demand in ethics, a new possibility that could also prove the highest level of duty. Responsibility at this level is always religious—in the deeper sense. Perhaps one will first say that this is a matter of appropriate respect for Earth, but later one will begin also to see that this is a matter of appropriate reverence for life, and for the planet that generates life. The UN Secretary General, Boutros Boutros-Ghali, closed the 1992 Earth Summit with an imperative: "The Spirit of Rio must create a new mode of civic conduct. It is not enough for man to love his neighbor; he must also learn to love his world" (Boutros-Ghali in UNCED, 1992a, p. 1). "We must now conclude an ethical and political contract with nature, with this Earth to which we owe our very existence and which gives us life" (Boutros-Ghali in UNCED, 1992b, pp. 66-69).

The twentieth century has been the century of seeing Earth ecosystemically, as a whole, the home planet. Viewing Earthrise from the moon, the astronaut Edgar Mitchell (1971) was entranced:

Suddenly from behind the rim of the moon, in long, slow motion moments of immense majesty, there emerges a sparkling blue and white jewel, a light, delicate sky blue sphere laced with slowly swirling veils of white, rising gradually like a small pearl in a thick sea of black mystery. It takes more than a moment to fully realize this is Earth . . . home. My view of our planet was a glimpse of divinity.

Mitchell, quoted in Kelley,
at photographs 42-45

Mitchell has an overview of the terrestrial Earth, a total landscape and a seascape view, and his response is that he is seeing God.

A first response here may be that the astronaut has gone to extremes. Earth is not divinity, nor is dirt to be loved like God and neighbor. The astronaut has quite confused nature and spirit. Landscape managers, who ought to be good hard-nosed scientists, must stick to the facts and not get carried away in mystical interpretation. Earth is, after all, just earth. Earth is, in a way, a big rock pile like the moon, only one on which the rocks are watered and illuminated in such way that they support life. No doubt Earth is valuable, but that is because humans are able to value it. We use its natural resources and put landscape managers in charge of either sustaining or exploiting these resources. But it is really human life that is valued and not the Earth, except as instrumental to life. We do not have duties to rocks, air, ocean, dirt, or Earth; we have duties to people, or living things.

And yet is it so amiss to see this home biosphere as the sphere of divinity? Consider all the complexity and diversity, integrity, richness, natural history and cultural history—the whole storied natural and cultural history of our planet. Say, if you like, that Earth is only a big rock pile, mere matter, but, as Eiseley (1957) insisted, when one considers the story these rocks spin, it must indeed be plain to the materialist that matter contains dreadful powers. Really, the story on these landscapes and seascapes is little short of a series of "miracles," wondrous, fortuitous events, unfolding potential; and when Earth's most complex product, *Homo sapiens*, becomes intelligent enough to reflect over this cosmic wonderland, everyone is left stuttering about the mixtures of accident and necessity out of which humans have evolved. But nobody doubts that this is a precious place, a pearl in a sea of black mystery. Earth could be the ultimate object of duty, short of God. And if one cannot get clear about God, there is ample and urgent call to reverence Earth.

Earth is dirt, but here one finds revealed what dirt can do when it is self-organizing under suitable conditions with water and solar illumination. One can, if one insists on being anthropocentric landscape managers, say that it is all valueless except as a human resource, though valuable in that respect. But one will not be valuing Earth objectively until one appreciates this marvelous natural history. Maybe the planet is not supernatural, but it is surely super in being natural. This really is a superb planet. The astronaut Michael Collins (1980) recalled being awed:

> *The more we see of other planets, the better this one looks. When I traveled to the Moon, it wasn't my proximity to that battered rock pile I remember so vividly, but rather what I saw when I looked back at my fragile home—a glistening, inviting beacon, delicate blue and white, a tiny outpost suspended in the black infinity. Earth is to be treasured and nurtured, something precious that* must *endure.* (p. 6)

There is the real assignment in landscape management. Managers do not know who they are and where they are until they realize that they are managing a little bit of a precious pearl in a sea of black mystery. That may be metaphor but it is just as true a claim as any bit of hard-nosed science. Those experiences, which, as Mayr (1982) testifies, are widespread in virtually all biologists, are spiritual in this deeper sense. And here landscape managers will find it increasingly required to join with those who are religious in admiration and respect for this marvelous planet that we inhabit. For the appropriate admiration and respect sooner or later passes over to a reverence.

No other species can be either responsible for or religious toward this planet, but *Homo sapiens* carries a responsibility that assumes these spiritual dimensions. In a planetary, environmental age, spirituality requires combining nature and grace at new levels of insight and intensity. Nature is grace, whatever more grace may also be. The geophysical and biological laws, the evolutionary and ecological history, the creativity within the natural system we inherit, and the values these generate, are the ground of our being, not just the ground under our feet. Ultimately, there is a kind of creativity in nature demanding either that one spells nature with a capital N, or pass beyond nature to nature's God. If anything at all on Earth is sacred, it must be this enthralling creativity that characterizes our home planet. If anywhere, here is the brooding Spirit of God. If there is Spirit anywhere, this is a spirited place. If there is any holy ground, any land of promise, this promising Earth is it. That is why, in the end, landscape management is a spiritual duty.

Literature Cited

Barrow, J. and Tipler, F. (1986). *The anthropic cosmological principle*. New York, NY: Oxford University Press.

Barth, K. (1933). *The epistle to the Romans*. New York, NY: Oxford University Press.

Berry, W. (1968). The peace of wild things. In *Openings*. New York, NY: Harcourt, Brace & World, Inc.

Bryant, W. (1992). A forest hymn. In J. Kaplen (Ed.), *Bartlett's Familiar quotations* . Boston, MA: Little, Brown & Company, Inc. (Canada) Limited.

Collins, M. (1980). Foreword. In R. Gallant. *Our universe*. Washington, DC: National Geographic Society.

Davies, P. (1983). *God and the new physics*. New York, NY: Simon and Schuster, Inc.

Dewey, J. (1934). *A common faith*. New Haven, CT: Yale University Press.

Eiseley, L. (1957). *The immense journey*. New York, NY: Vintage Books.

Ferré, F. (1970). The definition of religion. *Journal of the American Academy of Religion, 38*, 3-16.

Holy Bible, King James Version. Psalms:104:16.

Kelley, K. (Ed.). (1988). *The home planet*. Reading, MA: Addison-Wesley Publishing Company, Inc.

Leslie, J. (1989). *Universes*. New York, NY: Routledge, Chapman, and Hill, Inc.

Leuba, J. (1912). *A psychological study of religion*. New York, NY: Macmillan Publishing Company, Inc.

Mayr, E. (1982). *The growth of biological thought*. Cambridge, MA: Belnap Press.

Muir, J. (1901). *Our national parks*. Boston, MA: Houghton Mifflin Company.

Otto, R. [1923] (1958). *The idea of the holy*. New York, NY: Oxford University Press.

Smith, R. (1967). *Martin Buber*. Richmond, VA: John Knox Press.

Tillich, P. (1957). *The Protestant era*. Chicago, IL: University of Chicago Press.

United Nations Conference on Environment and Development (UNCED), (1992a). *Final meeting and round-up of conference* (UN Document ENV/DEV/RIO/ 29, 14 June).

United Nations Conference on Environment and Development (UNCED), (1992b). Text of closing UNCED statements. In *Report of the United Nations conference on environment and development. Vol. IV* (UN Document A/CONF.151.26).

Weisskopf, V. (1983). The origin of the universe. *American Scientist, 71*, 473-480.

Wordsworth, W. (1992). Lines composed a few miles above Tintern Abbey. In J. Kaplan (Ed.), *Bartlett's Familiar quotations* (16th ed.) (p. 373). Boston, MA: Little, Brown and Company.

FOUR CORNERS OF HUMAN ECOLOGY: DIFFERENT PARADIGMS OF HUMAN RELATIONSHIPS WITH THE EARTH

GEORGE PETERSON
Rocky Mountain Forest and Range Experiment Station
USDA Forest Service
Fort Collins, Colorado

CHAPTER 2)

Introduction

This text focuses on the psychologically deep nature-based values and experiences that add essence to life by touching the human spirit. While the topic of nature and the human spirit is elusive, the purpose of the text is application. It is to help public policymakers and managers of the public lands define and implement a set of land management ethics that not only explicitly recognize hard-to-define nature-based human values but also set the moral standards necessary for achieving and maintaining sustainable human and biophysical ecosystems. Thus, the text considers the human value framework needed to achieve ecosystems management—the managerial scheme adopted in recent years by all the federal land management agencies and many of the large land management corporations.

The purpose of this chapter is to better understand the diverse human values that challenge natural resource managers as they struggle to adopt the land management ethics which are necessary to implement the philosophy of ecosystems management. Accordingly, this chapter examines the "human ecology" of ecosystems management,

with human ecology defined as the study of relations between humans and their environment. These relations are determined by how people value their environment.

While there are laws and professional principles and tools that help establish policies and practices to guide management of the public lands, such policymaking and management remain, nevertheless, a highly political endeavor. Jack Ward Thomas, Chief of the USDA Forest Service, recognized this when he said in testimony before a committee of the U.S. House of Representatives that ". . . all managerial decisions are moral, not technical" (1994). They are moral because they require accommodating some people's values and not accommodating others. This challenge is not a new one. As an ancient philosopher once stated:

As every knowledge and moral purpose aspires to some good, what is in our view the good at which the political science aims, and what is the highest of all practical goods? As to its name there is, I may say, a general agreement. The masses and the cultured classes agree in calling it happiness, and conceive that 'to live well' or 'to do well' is the same thing as 'to be happy.' But as to the nature of happiness they do not agree. . . .

Aristotle, 1985

It is thus incumbent on public policymakers and managers of the public lands to try to understand the many views of "happiness" that lead to different human orientations to the Earth.

Preference-Based Human Values

Understanding humans' Earth-related values requires clarification of the word "value" because the values people hold are responsible for the ethical, cognitive, and behavioral paradigms they adopt. In turn, these paradigms express the diverse values that challenge the land manager.

In this chapter I accept as a premise that "value" is a property *attributed* to things by human preference (Peterson, Driver, and Brown, 1990). Spinoza states, "We do not desire a thing because it is good, rather it is good because we desire it" (Santayana, 1896). Other premises (e.g., that there are intrinsic values in nature, Rolston, 1982) are perhaps more appealing to some readers, but this chapter leaves alternative premises to other authors. While these other perspectives might favor a more absolute concept of value as something to be discovered rather than created by human preference, the U.S. Constitution derives the just powers of government from the consent of the governed and requires Spinoza's definition. Political sovereignty resides with the individual. While it is true that human preference may depend on objective properties inherent in things, the politically meaningful values are those which are articulated by individuals as preferences; there is no way for intrinsic values to be articulated with political validity other than as human preferences. These preferences may be self-directed or other-directed, according to the choice of the individual. One might choose to seek personal advantage and competitive gain, strive for communal equality or equity, or sacrifice self for the good of another.

Held values are deeply rooted beliefs about what is good, true, and beautiful (Brown, 1984). They are the foundations of religion, ethics, and so-

cial propriety. Assigned values are the products of personal and collective choices. Collective or social choices become institutionalized through legislation and litigation. They protect one from the tragedy of the commons (Hardin, 1968), protect the weak against the strong, and enable the fulfillment of needs that cannot be served through individual effort. Within and upon the institutional context thus created, we assign personal values by making individual choices.

Preference-based values can exist at three levels: operative, conceived, and object (Morris, 1956). One assigns operative values by the choices one makes. Operative values include economic values, further operationalized as exchange ratios among things, or between a thing and a sum of money, where money serves as a parameter of exchange and represents other things it might purchase. Conceived value is the value assigned by the choices one believes one ought to make. Conceived and operative value ought to agree, but don't necessarily. Object value is the value assigned by the choices the perfectly rational and fully informed person would make. It is the domain of the preferable, as opposed to the preferred. Statesmen, educators, philosophers, and evangelists normatively advocate conceived values and strive to understand object value. Politicians and economists, however, work with operative values. Santayana (1896) further differentiates between "aesthetic" and "moral" value. An aesthetic value is an expression of preference for a thing that is an end in itself. Moral value is a preference to avoid pain and suffering, that is, preference for a thing that is a means to a greater good. Moral value ultimately derives from an aesthetic end.

Just as people have different preferences and, hence, different values, species have different preferences, also. One can say, for example, that clean, naturally flowing streams in Alaska are of "functional" value to salmon, and that salmon in such streams are of functional value to bears. Whether nonhuman species are sentient and capable of conscious preference is debatable. It is possible, however, for humans to conceive and altruistically to prefer functional value on behalf of nonhuman species. One may also value such species themselves, thereby assigning human preference-based "derived" value to the things that are of functional value to other species.

There may be many derived values of which one is unaware and that may be thought of as latent and awaiting "discovery" because the natural and social processes by which the things preferred (and thus valued) are not fully understood and depend on other things. These things would be preferred if their role in the satisfaction of needs and wants were understood, but knowledge and experience are inadequate.

Value created by human preference is not a static phenomenon. Interaction with the environment through life is a continual learning experience about oneself, about the environment, and about the relationships between the environment and the quality and meaning of human life. This experiential learning process constructs and modifies the values that generate the preferences one expresses through personal and social choice. Thus, the land manager not only faces the values and preferences then extant but must also anticipate future different values.

Four Corners of Human Ecology

In the preceding section I defined value as a property attributed to things by human preferences. The definition is the cornerstone on which this chapter rests. Having established that definition, this section will now consider four extreme paradigms of human ecology that span the range of values by which humans define and evaluate their relationship to the Earth. It is a journey through four "corners" of ethical geography. These corners are dominion, stewardship, participation, and abdication. The values people hold drive their environmental choices, and those values and choices express various positions relative to these four paradigms.

Dominion

Dominion implies rule by a monarch, so the dominion paradigm places *Homo sapiens* in the role of governor or king of the Earth. As such, humans can adopt the role of "bad king" and try to conquer and exploit the domain for short-term personal gain without concern for long-term effects on others. Or, they can adopt the role of "good king" and try to protect the domain and serve the well-being of all.

Obviously, the "bad king" role will not allow humankind to persist over time as it fouls the Earth on which it depends. In either case, humankind places itself in a role of superiority and priority over the rest of nature and sees itself as nature's highest purpose. The "good king" role, however, leads to the stewardship paradigm.

Stewardship

The stewardship paradigm places *Homo sapiens* in the position of statesman—caretaker of the Earth, managing the Earth in trust as an agent for some employer or client. That client might be the human race, now and in the future; it might be all living things; it might be the Earth itself; or it might be a symbiotic relationship between *Homo sapiens* and other species. Different clients may imply different strategies.

Participation

The participation paradigm places humans in a role of symbiosis and/or equality of rights with other species.[1] In the symbiotic sense of this paradigm, the purpose of human existence is to serve the symbiosis by constructing cooperative and complementary relationships through which all species are better off.

The equal rights form of the participatory paradigm replaces the statement, "All humans are created equal," with "All species are created equal." Human beings are seen as one of many equal participants in the Earth's ecosystem, without special rights or privileges not held by other species. There is no right to cause harm to the rights of other species.[2] Participatory equality may mean either equality of process rights or equality of substantive rights. Equality of process rights means equal protection under the law and equal opportunity to *pursue* (not possess) life, liberty, and happiness. Darwin would recognize this form of the participatory paradigm as "survival of the fittest."

Equality of substantive rights, on the other hand, means equality in *possession* of life, liberty, and happiness. At this extreme, the distribution of well-being must be divided equally (communally) among all species (including *Homo sapiens*), not distributed more heavily to the more successful competitors. Under both symbiosis and equality of substantive rights the more powerful competitors (e.g., *Homo sapiens*) must impose limitations upon themselves in order to maintain harmony and/or equality (or equity) because other species have neither the voice nor the choice to impose those limitations.[3]

Abdication

In the abdication paradigm *Homo sapiens* renounces all claim to the right to prosper when that right conflicts with the functional values of other species. *Homo sapiens* is both in competition with other species (e.g., the spotted owl) and prey to predator and parasite species (e.g., the smallpox virus, polio and HIV viruses, tapeworms, liver flukes, and criminals). In deference to the functional values of these competitive and predator species, the abdication paradigm requires us to lay down our arms and serve their needs, even if it means extinction of the human race or reduced quantity and quality of human life. It is difficult to believe, however, that even the most devoted "abdicator" will not try to avoid the mosquito that carries malaria or yellow fever or the criminal who carries a gun, so there may be more involved than meets the eye.[4]

The purpose of this discussion of four corners of human ecology has been to demonstrate the diversity of ways human values toward the Earth might express themselves and to urge the reader to think about what constitutes an acceptable environmental ethic. It will become apparent that I believe the stewardship model is the one that is necessary to create and maintain a land management ethic that will accommodate the deep psychological human experiences discussed in this text. Some readers might prefer the participation model for these purposes, but I think the model is infeasible politically, economically and socially. The stewardship model I recommend is one that makes *Homo sapiens* the custodian that manages the Earth for all species but does not grant equality between human and infrahuman species.

Scientific Perspectives on the Human Dimensions of Human Ecology

Use of a General Systems Approach to Guide Science

Thus far I have adopted a human preference definition of value to serve as the conceptual framework for analyzing and understanding human relationships with the Earth and other species. Using that framework of human ecology, I described four extreme ethical paradigms that reflect different sets of values and preferences that determine how humans will relate to their physical environment. I now turn to the question of how to analyze and evaluate scientifically the role of value in human ecology and how value-based human preferences direct personal and social choices.

For the purposes of this chapter, I recommend a general systems approach to guide scientific inquiry about the role of value in the relationships among humans, other species, and the Earth (Ashby, 1958; Berrien, 1968; Von Bertalanffy, 1950). I accept the scientific method as the correct method of inquiry, but I require it to be guided by general systems theory to assure that not only the parts of human ecology, but also the interactive relationships among these parts are examined. Science may decompose human ecology, but it must not discard the residue of that decomposition. Simply put, knowledge of the parts is necessary and useful, but not sufficient; a scientific holistic approach is needed. But this word "holistic" can be problematic.[5]

Too many scholars now use the word "holism" as the intellectually proper way to think about human ecology without defining what they mean by the word. Thus, "holism" means different things to different people and causes much confusion. The following discussion describes briefly five different uses of the word holism. The purpose of the discussion is to elevate the concept out of its mysterious quagmire into the scientific domain of general systems theory.

1. General systems theorists accept the scientific method as a useful and powerful tool for obtaining, organizing, and applying

knowledge. However, they see much that science does and has done as narrow, overly specialized, and incomplete, especially with regard to human ecology. They see human ecology as a complex maze of mutually causal processes. The whole is greater than the sum of its parts and cannot be understood by understanding the parts individually or separately. Effective understanding of the whole as well as the parts requires study of the parts in the context of the whole, including the organization (interaction) among parts and the properties and behaviors of these parts within the context of a mutually causal whole. Challenges to "wholeness" are simply matters of scale (i.e., how one draws the boundary of the whole system in question). General systems theorists do not reject science. They want it to be more complete and in proper context. To them, the "residue" of decomposition of the whole into parts is the interaction and organization among parts that cause the whole to be greater than the sum of the parts.[6]

2. Gestaltists believe it is possible to understand human ecology only as a gestalt (i.e., as a whole picture that conveys meaning only as a whole picture, such as the face of a friend). One can recognize, appreciate, and perhaps even describe to some extent the gestalt, but one cannot meaningfully decompose or analyze it, even in general systems terms. We see and experience only the whole gestalt, and that whole gestalt is all that is possible to see and experience. Decomposition by scientific reduction or general systems analysis destroys the meaning of the whole and contributes no useful knowledge about it.

3. Scientific nihilists are angry and/or existential. They view science with suspicion and distrust, sometimes (but not necessarily) from a position of scientific illiteracy. Like Dostoyevsky (1983) in *Notes from the Underground*, they stick their tongues out at any Crystal Palace that promises to improve things through scientific knowledge and technology. They deny the existence of a rational or scientific basis for knowledge and may even advocate rejection of scientific institutions, methods, and constructs. They are adversaries of the scientific method as a way to obtain, organize, and apply knowledge about the human relationship with the Earth.

4. Mystics see holism as a spiritual or religious relationship with the Earth. Mother Earth is the source of life, and one must relate to her with respect and reverence. For mystics, holism is a religious sect that has beliefs, deities, rites, rituals, duties, and codes of conduct, including prescriptions regarding the human relationship to the Earth, that do not necessarily have any relationship to science. Holism is a symbol or religious icon, not a body of scientific knowledge. The path to knowledge and proper behavior is through "holistic" inner peace and/or mystical revelation of truth unknowable by other means.

5. Holistic groupies don't have the slightest idea what "holism" means. For diverse reasons they espouse the cause and tag along with the holistic crowd. They eagerly learn and speak the language without knowing the meaning of the words. They confuse familiarity with understanding. The words have no connection with meaning based in experience, though the groupies smile, nod in approval, and wave the flags of holism when they hear the words.

In summary, in this section I proposed that the scientific method, as applied in terms of the general systems approach, is the appropriate way to inquire holistically into the role of value in the relationships among humans, other species, and the Earth. I accept the scientific method as the correct method of inquiry, but require that method to examine not only the parts of human ecology, but also the interactive relationships among these parts. Science may decompose human ecology, but it must not discard the residue of that decomposition. Simply put, knowledge of the parts is necessary and useful, but not sufficient.

Illustrative Contributions of Several Disciplines

Several scientific disciplines study the values, beliefs, and behaviors that drive human ecology. These disciplines offer different perspectives on the origins and effects of values as they affect personal, social, and institutional behavior toward the Earth. To illustrate some of the results of research that has been guided by these different perspectives, I now look briefly at the results of some studies of human ecology that have been done within the disciplines of environmental psychology, social psychology and anthropology, and economics. Space does not allow an extensive review, and the objective of this discussion is to present only a few illustrations. Much remains to be done in search of integration and application of these and other perspectives. Paraphrasing Boulding and Lundstedt (1988), the academic disciplines are continents of the mind, separated by broad oceans with high tariff barriers, no safe harbors, and apparently no realization that specialization without trade is worthless.

ENVIRONMENTAL PSYCHOLOGY

Twenty-five years ago the environmental psychologist Kenneth Craik (1970) coined the phrase "environmental disposition" and suggested that human beings have deeply rooted definable and measurable psychological dispositions toward the physical environment—dispositions that help to drive environmental attitudes, preferences, and behaviors. Craik and McKechnie developed a personality test called the "Environmental Response Inventory" (ERI) that was accredited by the American Psychological Association and published commercially (McKechnie, 1970, 1971).

The ERI describes individual personality in terms of several independent dimensions of environmentally relevant held values. These held values are deeply rooted and are difficult to change. They vary significantly among individuals and various segments of the population, and they tend to motivate environmental behaviors and choices. Managers need to understand the diversity and political implications of such held values. They are at least partially responsible for one's choice of which one of the previously described ethical paradigms of human ecology to champion, and they are behind much

of the conflict that managers encounter. Further, environmental decision makers may hold environmental dispositions that differ from those of their publics without understanding these differences thereby adding fuel to the fire (Craik, 1970). Additional development and application of this kind of research will contribute greatly to an ability to manage public wildlands effectively. Needed also is more psychological research into the processes and experiences that mold environmental disposition and the held values it represents, especially values that lead to social dysfunction (e.g., see Csikszentmihalyi, 1993; Kellert and Wilson, 1993). Especially needed from psychologists is research that defines and better measures the importance of the deep psychological nature-based human experiences on which this text focuses.

SOCIAL PSYCHOLOGY AND ANTHROPOLOGY

Failure to understand and effectively respond to the rich diversity of environmental values held by people, and especially cross-cultural differences, leads to ineffective and even destructive environmental management. Interpersonal and intercultural differences in such values lead to important differences in personal behavior and social organization and in the way people use and depend on various characteristics of the natural and built environment.

A study done in Los Angeles many years ago asked people from various geographic, social, and income groups in the Los Angeles area to draw "cognitive maps" of what they considered to be their "neighborhood" (Orleans, 1972). People from the San Fernando Valley (professional and middle- to upper middle-class) drew maps lacking in local detail but showing major features of the entire metropolitan region with surprising accuracy which indicated a regional but locally superficial concept of neighborhood. Their identity tended to be tied to social and transactional space, rather than to local geographic space. People from low-income, ethnic neighborhoods tended to draw very detailed maps of a few square blocks surrounding their homes. These people seemed to have their identity tied to a local geographic space. They were, so to speak, "urban villagers" (Gans, 1962). Land management policies that are insensitive to such differences can have devastating effects on the affected populations.

An example comes from a now forgotten but once famous, then infamous public housing project in St. Louis. In the early 1960s, this high-rise housing project was hailed as one of the outstanding architectural achievements of the year. It took underprivileged people out of the ghettos and placed them in a reasonably comfortable physical setting intended to be a solution to their physical and social problems. Within a few short years, the project became a social war zone and shortly thereafter was torn down.

What went wrong? Middle-class, white environmental values imposed themselves on low-income, ethnic values with what appeared through the eyes of the white middle-class to be the solution to a perceived problem. The physical solution destroyed the social organization and environmental identity of the people from the disrupted neighborhoods. If the planners and architects had understood the relationship between the stabilizing social organization of the community and the physical neighborhoods, they might have avoided much pain and expense. Is there, perhaps, a parallel between the devastating effects of disturbed social organization on the one hand and disturbed ecological organization on the other?

The Territorial Imperative (Ardrey, 1966) describes *Homo sapiens* as a creature that identifies with and defends personal, tribal, cultural, and social space. Different cultures relate to social and physical space in different ways. In personal conversations with Edward T. Hall, I learned about proxemics and differences across cultures.[7] For example, Northern Europeans have difficulty conversing with Southern Europeans and Arabs because of differences in the "spatial bubble" they carry around as the personal territory they defend against strangers. The southerner wants to be close, while the Scandinavian needs an arm's length.

Another idea gleaned from these conversations concerns "privacy." In some cultures, "privacy" means physical exclusion of others from one's personal space—"You can't touch me," or "you can't see me." In other cultures where physical privacy has tended to be an unachievable luxury, privacy means "I can't hear you," or "I am not speaking to you." The authors of *Community and Privacy* (Chermayeff and Alexander, 1963), describe people as having conflicting desires for social interaction, on the one hand, and for physical and social privacy on the other.

What, if any, are the effects of adaptation on environmental values? A study of the recreational preferences and experiences of teenagers (Peterson, 1977) found at one extreme that white males preferred exotic activities, such as hang gliding, skiing, sailing, and white water canoeing. They had very little experience with such activities, however, perhaps implying incongruity between preference and opportunity. At the other extreme, black females tended to prefer things that were easy to do in the local neighborhood, and there was a strong correlation between preference and experience. Do such findings suggest adaptation to environmental opportunity, or do they reflect deeply rooted held values that differ across cultures? Should public policy respond to manifest demand as driven by such forces, or should there be an effort to expand the opportunities and change the preferences of groups that have adapted to limited opportunity sets?

A study of crowded beaches in the Chicago area (Peterson and Neumann, 1969) found that a majority of visitors preferred scenic natural experiences. Those seeking the urban social experiences offered at the settings in question were a minority. Why had the majority accepted an inferior substitute for the experience it preferred? Perhaps it had to accept what was available within its constraints of time and money.

Van Arsdol, Sabagh, and Alexander (1964) studied the perception and reality of environmental hazards in Southern California. Among other things they found that people who were most exposed to air pollution and noise (low income nonwhites) tended to be least aware and concerned about these things, while people who were least exposed (suburban whites) tended to be most aware and concerned. The authors concluded, "It may be that, while nonwhites are concentrated in smog areas, the intrusion of social hazards in such areas and the preoccupation of such populations with other social problems may have obscured their perception of environmental hazards." Perhaps adaptation and numbing also have a role. Perhaps the environmental values people hold may not be the best indicators of what is good for them in some cases or how they may behave in the future. Shortly after this study was done, Watts burned. Is this local phenomenon a prototype of the larger destiny of *Homo sapiens* as we slowly adapt, like boiled frogs, to a gradual worsening of our environmental habitat?

A rich literature in environmental psychology, anthropology, social psychology, and other social sciences describes an incredible diversity of human values at work in our environmental relationships. Past and ongoing research also seeks to understand the processes by which values form and influence the behaviors they drive. I have only scratched the surface here with a few illustrations. I now turn the discussion to the neoclassical microeconomic model of our human relationship with the Earth. While the other social sciences (as illustrated previously) search for understanding through empirical observation, the economic model is axiomatic deductive, deriving its propositions about human value and value-driven behavior from assumptions and rules of logic.

ECONOMICS

The neoclassical economic model of our human relationship with the Earth is both narrow and complex. The Earth and all its components are input factors in processes by which people and firms produce things they can sell (or barter) for a profit or consume for direct utility. Those aspects of the economic model most relevant to the larger question of human ecology are:

1. the economic definition of value,
2. the question of whether money can substitute for all environmental values,
3. values that do and do not involve legal property rights,
4. external diseconomy, and
5. distributional equity, including intergenerational sustainability. (It should be noted that this economic model is not universally accepted, especially in the realm of human ecology.)

According to the economic definition, the justification of value that underlies neoclassical microeconomic consumer theory is consumer sovereignty. This justification is consistent with and derives from the democratic principle that sovereignty resides in the individual. It is assumed that individual preferences operate within a framework established by social choice, usually a framework of laws and institutions that bound or create the choice sets available to individuals and/or impose penalties and incentives for different choices. This institutional framework also defines and protects rights. In general, econom-

ics does not attribute rights and consumer sovereignty to nonhuman species except as social choice may define nonhuman sovereignty and nonhuman rights as, for example, with the Endangered Species Act (1973), or as individuals attribute such rights and sovereignty by their personal choices.

Economic goods and services are viewed as instruments for humans to achieve their personal objectives, and the economic values of these instruments are therefore derived from the values of the objectives they serve (Hicks, 1956). However, it is essential to understand that economic values do not necessarily reflect the value of the objectives or functions served. It is the relative scarcity of the goods and services that determines the magnitude of economic value. Ornamental diamonds are more "valuable" (in economic terms) than water, but water serves a much more valuable function. Rock stars and football quarterbacks are much more "valuable" than school teachers, but school teachers perform a much more valuable service.

One of the most fundamental economic questions facing land managers is whether effective substitutes exist to meet all the environmental preferences of public land stakeholders. The absence of substitutes means that nothing the manager can do will ameliorate a loss that accompanies a management action (or failure to act). As stated by an angry young woman in a discussion of compensation for the Exxon Valdez oil spill, "You mean to tell me I've been raped, and you think there is some amount of money that will make me feel like it didn't happen?" Public and private actions often impose costs and benefits for which just compensation is difficult or impossible.

What about values that are not rights? When justified by social merit, the government may take a right, such as a property right, by the principle of eminent domain. Such a taking requires just compensation. It is sometimes necessary, however, to invade values that the law does not define as rights. The resulting losses are real, but because no legally protected rights are involved, there may be no obligation to compensate. Land managers must understand and cope with stakeholder values that are and are not legal rights, that can and cannot be compensated, and for which there may or may not be a feasible and peaceful resolution.

There are also many values that focus on things that markets cannot serve effectively because private enterprise has no incentive to produce (or refrain from producing) the things that affect these values (e.g., public goods). Such uncompensated and unproduced costs and benefits cause wasteful allocation of resources in the form of external diseconomies. Some of these externalities involve legal rights, while others do not, and this raises two basic dilemmas:

1. all values are real, but not all stem from legal rights; and

2. some rights are efficiently enforceable and others are not.

Economists call the result "market failure" (Randall, 1983).

Land management also often gives benefits to some stakeholders while imposing losses on others. Some of these effects are direct and others are indirect. The question thus created is one of distribution and equity. Distribution of costs and benefits is a technical economic question that can, in economic theory, be exposed by technical means. On the other hand, equity is a political problem that cannot be decided by economic technical means unless or until the political process defines a technical (legal) resolution.

Distribution and equity come to a head in intergenerational allocation. In order to describe intergenerational distribution of costs and benefits, it is necessary to predict the future. And, in order to select the action that is fair, it is necessary to represent future generations in the political and economic negotiations. Both problems appear to be insurmountable. Economists generally take the approach that intergenerational values must be represented by the preferences of the present generation. Standard practice is to represent the future by means of a discount rate. Any discount rate greater than zero means costs and benefits at some future time do not affect the present decision. People at that time and beyond have no rights at all.

Sustainable use and development of natural resources into future generations requires new ways of responding to hard-to-define values, the hardest of which are the unknown values land managers and land users will hold and assign in the future. Tonn (1991) proposes a judicial body at the Supreme Court level to examine and adjudicate intergenerational conflicts.

From this brief discussion, one can see that information about values that economics can provide is important and useful to some, but not all, of the questions the land manager confronts. The same is true for the other disciplines discussed in this section.

I have recommended that general systems theory is the holistic approach that should be used to guide scientific approaches to understanding the human ecology component of ecosystems management. The discussion in this section shows that the theories and methods of different disciplines can help us better understand the different types of values and preferences that direct human orientations and behaviors toward the Earth. Ethics and religion also affect those orientations and behaviors.

Ethics and Religion

Ethics and religion focus on beliefs about what is right and wrong. The various forms of these beliefs are both the causes and outcomes of our environmental values, beliefs, and behaviors. They are things at the heart of what one holds to be the purpose of life. The values flowing therefrom are strong and deeply rooted. The behaviors driven by these values are important, essential, and not easily changed. Because different religious values, doctrines, and dogmas lead to different systems of environmental ethics, they share responsibility for the shape of human ecology (as evidenced by Kaza, Chapter Three, in this volume).

Some ethical philosophers argue that the environment has intrinsic value apart from any human preference or appreciation. One such argument attributes primary rights to nonhuman creatures (e.g., Stone, 1974), and from that argument flows an ethical framework of secondary rights defining human duties toward nonhuman things and requiring the performance of those duties. Another argument holds that biological information has been "learned" genetically over eons of time and cannot be replaced if lost. This argument attributes great "intrinsic" value to this information and leads to the conclusion that *Homo sapiens* has a responsibility to protect other species and do nothing that would lead to their extinction (Rolston, 1982).

Still another argument is that nature is unbalanced, that the human race has acquired the power to destroy itself, the Earth, and other living things thereon. Because of this position of power, the argument states, humans have an ethical responsibility to nurture and protect. And there is also the position that a person who lives now has a responsibility toward other people who live now and toward future generations, that one must not act upon the environment in ways that cause harm to others. This concept of avoiding harm through the environmental relationship draws some support from the common law principle that there is no right to cause harm which is the basis of the police power by which government regulates private behavior.

These ethical positions express hypothetical preferences that people and their laws may or may not hold. Some such positions have been codified, in part, in common and statutory law and therefore define real values by virtue of sovereignty (e.g., the Endangered Species Act, 1973; the National Environmental Policy Act, 1969). Unless the laws, the courts, or individual humans hold such positions as preferences, however, they are not values that managers need be concerned about in an operative sense. They are to be advocated by teachers, philosophers, preachers, and evangelists, but unless they own sovereignty, they must not drive policy that is supposed to be an expression of the will of the people under a government that derives its just powers from the consent of the governed.

In addition to their role in philosophy, law, and social custom, ethical values find expression through religious institutions. Religion takes many forms and has been the driving force behind both the best that humanity has become, and much human conflict, human suffering and human abuse of the Earth and its nonhuman inhabitants.

To discuss all ramifications of the role of religion in the relationship between humans and the Earth is an overwhelming task. Instead, I focus briefly on the resolution of an apparent conflict among dominion, stewardship, and participation in the Judeo-Christian framework. The Judeo-Christian line of religious thought sometimes receives the criticism that it advocates exploitation of the Earth for the sake of human comfort and convenience. The accused principle is apparently an interpretation of statements like the following in the Old Testament (Holy Bible a):

And God said, Let us make man in our own image, after our likeness: and let them have dominion over the fish of the sea, and over the fowl of the air, and over the cattle, and over all the earth, and over every creeping thing that creepeth upon the earth. So God created man in his own image, in the image of God created he them. And God blessed them, and God said unto them, Be fruitful, and multiply, and replenish the earth, and subdue it: and have dominion over the fish of the sea, and over the fowl of the air, and over every living thing that moveth upon the earth. (Genesis 1:26-28)

The exact meaning of the Hebrew word for "dominion" in the original text is not clear, and neither is the intention of the scholars who translated the word into English. It is interesting, however, to embark on a logical expedition that leads to some interesting implications. Assume the words "dominion over" mean sovereign authority to govern. At least two opposite concepts of the intent of government are possible. At one extreme the Sovereign uses power over "the fish . . . sea . . . fowl of the air, and . . . every living thing . . . upon the earth" to exploit them for self-serving purposes. At the other extreme the Sovereign uses power to protect and maintain both humans and all things " . . . that moveth upon the earth." The two extremes represent a good sovereign and a bad sovereign, both of whom have "dominion over." Thus, application of this Old Testament Hebrew concept of "dominion over" the Earth boils down to how one chooses to interpret it.

The New Testament (Holy Bible b) also offers choices of interpretation when it quotes Jesus as stating that the greatest commandments are:

Thou shalt love the Lord thy God with all thy heart, and with all thy soul, and with all thy mind. This is the first and great commandment. And the second is like unto it, Thou shalt love thy neighbor as thyself. (Holy Bible [b], Matthew 22:37-39).

The first commandment requires that one understand and obey the preferences of "God" (or "nature," as you may choose) and have a "good will" that is in harmony with the laws that govern the universe (Kant, 1955). Given this framework of law (natural and/or divine, as you may choose), the second commandment requires each person to value the welfare of neighbors as much as the welfare of self. The Apostle Paul (Holy Bible c) amplifies this concept by stating, "Let no man seek his own, but every man another's wealth" (Corinthians 10:24). This statement by Paul advocates a society wherein all become enriched by working for the good of each other.

We may choose, if we like, to generalize the definition of "neighbor" to include all nonhuman living things as well as all other people and thereby encounter the stewardship or participatory paradigms. Confining the definition of "neighbor" to include only human beings leads to the same conclusion if one recognizes that individual actions affect others now and in the future through environmental as well as interpersonal relationships.[8]

These arguments lead to alternative ethical maxims for interpersonal relationship:

1. serve the good of others without regard to self;

2. serve the good of all in order to obtain benefits to all;

3. serve the good of others in order to obtain benefits to self; and

4. serve self without regard to effects on others.

Defining "self" as *Homo sapiens* and "other" as the nonhuman rest of the Earth, these maxims become:

1. serve the good of the Earth without regard to the good of *Homo sapiens*;

2. serve the good of *Homo sapiens* and the Earth holistically in order to serve the good of the whole;

3. serve the good of the Earth in order to obtain benefits to *Homo sapiens* through our relationship with the Earth; and

4. serve the good of *Homo sapiens* without regard to the good of the Earth.

None of these maxims is tenable without knowledge of and respect for "what goes around comes around." That is, service to any goal, including blind service to self, without understanding the ultimate effects of the reactions of others and of the Earth on that goal will ultimately be destructive.[9] Combining the interpersonal and environmental frameworks leads to an enlightening and self-evident (but too often ignored) truth about the dependence of love of neighbor and love of self on the environmental relationship. We humans are inseparably linked to each other through the Earth on which we live. We cannot ignore the ecological and intergenerational externalities of our personal and social choices and still claim to "love our neighbors as ourselves," even if we only include other humans beings in the definition of "neighbors."

Ecosystem Management

The four ethical paradigms of human ecology discussed earlier seem coincident with various concepts of "ecosystem management" being championed by academic groups and public agencies. At one extreme, ecosystem management seems to mean managing ecosystems in a way that places protective barriers and shields between nature and human influences. It sees humankind as something outside nature, as an enemy and disrupter of the balance, harmony, and sustainability that nature allegedly strives toward. This type of ecosystem management apparently fails to see nature as also including volcanos, earthquakes, ice ages, meteorites, hurricanes, tornadoes, supernovas, and the second law of thermodynamics.

An alternative interpretation is that because of uncertainty about the relationship between long-term human welfare and the condition of the nonhuman components of ecosystems, we must maintain the status quo in ecosystems and even strive to move toward conditions that would prevail in the absence of human influences. Under this interpretation, protection of threatened and endangered species, for example, is not an end in itself. These species are seen as indicators of uncomfortable change toward an uncertain future. The purpose is to achieve and maintain the present and future conditions that most favor human welfare, with fear and ignorance being the parents of conservatism. A pending decision to eradicate the smallpox virus, for example, demonstrates that preservation of species is not the end, but a means to an end. Apparently, the smallpox virus serves no useful purpose, and its extinction will cause no harm.

A middle road is to characterize human beings in two roles:

1. as one of many participatory components in the greater ecosystem, a component that has become a dominant and potentially destructive agent; and

2. as a being capable of reasoned choice and control of self and of the whole, either for the good of all components, or for sustainable improvement in human welfare.

Some see these purposes as inseparable (i.e., that sustainable improvement in human welfare can be achieved only by managing self and the greater ecosystem for the good of all). In any case, humans cannot achieve effective management of self within the ecosystem and management of the greater ecosystem including self without an understanding of how the whole thing works.

These paradigms, perceptions, value systems, and applications of human ecology are complex and poorly understood. Managers of the public lands face diverse and too often conflicting values, all clamoring for attention, including values that are hard to define and even more difficult to serve. Difficult though the task may be, managers need to understand these things in order to better serve the will of the people, to avoid unnecessary conflict, and to cope with those conflicts they cannot avoid.

Summary

Four paradigms form ethical corners of "human ecology," or the complex relationship between people and the Earth:

1. dominion,
2. stewardship,
3. participation, and
4. abdication.

These paradigms stem from preference-based human values that have their roots in environmental personality, social psychology, culture, and religion.

The theory or doctrine of "holism" seems to have become the intellectually correct way to think about human ecology. Properly understood, "holism" is concerned with how to obtain and organize knowledge about human ecology and advocates study of the whole as being greater than the sum of its parts, either as a system of mutually causal interactions or as a gestalt or cognitive organism that decomposition destroys.

General systems theory, environmental personality, social psychology and culture, economics, other disciplines, and ethics and religion offer partial explanations of the environmental values, beliefs, and behaviors that challenge land managers, and each raises questions that natural resource managers must understand and address.

Ecosystem management is a modern rediscovery of all these ideas and an attempt to integrate them into a scientifically and ethically holistic approach to natural resource management. Hopefully

the diverse perspectives clamoring for attention under the ecosystem management banner will eventually coalesce into a useful tool.

Whether one views the proper relationship between *Homo sapiens* and the Earth as exploitive dominion, benevolent service and stewardship, passive participation, or abdication is a matter of personal choice and, perhaps, religious or ethical belief. Objective logic seems to dictate, however, that one cannot be comfortable in a house that is not maintained in good condition. In this respect, several roads lead to Rome. Though the reasons may differ, the conclusion is the same: happiness is something one gets by giving it away, and if the Earth is not happy, neither are we.

Endnotes

[1] A less extreme version of the participation paradigm would replace "equality" with "equity." Equity is a political concept, however, which requires the assignment of "fairness" weights to the different participants. One is then left hanging by the question, "Who defines what is fair?" The key point of the participation paradigm as a corner in the model is the attribution of rights to all living things. As the dominant species capable of reasoned action, *Homo sapiens* then inherits by default the responsibility to protect the rights of all living things and to perform the duties implied by those rights, either in a relationship of equality, or in a relationship of equity, if equity can be defined. Effective assignment of rights to other species is, however, a matter of law in the public domain and of personal or corporate choice in the private domain.

[2] Under common law there is no right for one person to cause harm to another. This common law principle is the justification for the police power under which governments regulate private activity, such as through zoning ordinances, licensing powers, and building codes. Attribution of rights to nonhuman species expands the common law principle to include relationships between humans and nonhumans.

[3] In the long run, however, involuntary limitation may be the unavoidable outcome of failure of voluntary limitation. It is interesting to speculate that "survival of the fittest" ultimately will require reasoned self-restraint by *Homo sapiens*, given the

dominant influence of human activity, in order to avoid a natural backlash of involuntary restraint (Wynne-Edwards, 1965).

[4]The Threatened and Endangered Species (TES) Act appears to border on the abdication paradigm because in effect it assigns infinite value to a designated species. Extinction of the species is not acceptable, and all human activity that leads to extinction must step aside no matter what the cost. The TES Act is not necessarily an abdication position, however. It can be interpreted as a conservative response to uncertainty about the relationship between long-term human welfare and the health of the ecosystem in which we participate (a derived value relationship) with threatened and endangered species serving as indicators of negative departure from the status quo.

[5]Webster Third New International Dictionary (1965) defines "holism" as (1) "the philosophic theory first formulated by Jan C. Smuts that the determining factors in nature are wholes (as organisms) which are irreducible to the sum of their parts and that the evolution of the universe is the record of the activity and making of these wholes," and (2) "a theory or doctrine according to which a whole cannot be analyzed without residue into the sum of its parts or reduced to discrete elements."

[6]Wilson (1965) gives a simple example of a physical system whose performance transcends the performance of its components. One simple change in the organization among identical components causes opposite behavior of the system. It is this organization among components that remains as the "residue" when decomposition analyzes only the behavior of individual components. The individual parts are not capable of producing the system behavior, yet knowledge of their individual behaviors is necessary to understand how they will behave as a system when organized into some interactive relationship.

[7]Edward T. Hall was a Professor of Anthropology at Northwestern University, where the author was also a member of the faculty. Professor Hall authored such books as *The Hidden Dimension* (1966) and *The Silent Language* (1959).

[8]Unfortunately, it is probably not possible for nonhuman creatures to choose voluntarily to seek the "wealth" of *Homo sapiens* in the same way it might be possible for *Homo sapiens* to seek the "wealth" of nonhuman creatures.

[9]Although nonhuman species that lack the capability for reasoned action appear, on face value, to act blindly, exclusively, and instinctively in their own self-interest, their behavior is constrained by natural checks and balances, such as equilibrium with other species, Wynne-Edwards' (1965) self-regulating mechanisms, and genetically learned holistic behaviors that enhance survival. Our greatest strength, reasoned action, seems to have given *Homo sapiens* some degree of "freedom" from this "balance of nature." Our ultimate destiny, however, will depend on whether we are able to conceive and perform holistic reasoned actions that enable sustained improvement in the human condition. The preferences of "nature" are neither easily nor long ignorable.

Literature Cited

Ardrey, R. (1966). *The territorial imperative*. New York, NY: Atheneum Publishers.

Aristotle. (1985). *Nicomachean ethics*. Indianapolis, IN: Hackett Publishing Company, Inc.

Ashby, W. (1958). General systems theory as a new discipline. *General Systems Yearbook, 3*, 1-6.

Berrien, F. (1968). *General and social systems*. New Brunswick, NJ: Rutgers University Press.

Boulding, K. and Lundstedt, S. (1988). Value concepts and justifications. In G. Peterson, B. Driver, and R. Gregory (Eds.). *Amenity resource valuation: Integrating economics with other disciplines* (pp. 13-22). State College, PA: Venture Publishing, Inc.

Brown, T. C. (1984). The concept of value in resource allocation. *Land Economics, 60*(3):231-246

Chermayeff, S. and Alexander, C. (1963). *Community and privacy*. Garden City, NJ: Doubleday & Company, Inc.

Craik, K. (1970). The environmental dispositions of environmental decision-makers. *The Annals of the American Academy of Political and Social Science, 389* (May), 87-94.

Csikszentmihalyi, M. (1993). *The evolving self: A psychology for the third millennium*. New York, NY: HarperCollins Publishers.

Dostoyevsky, F. (1983). *Notes from the underground*. New York, NY: Bantam Books.

Gans, H. (1962). *The urban villagers*. New York, NY: The Free Press.

Hall, E. (1959). *The silent language*. Garden City, NJ: Doubleday & Company, Inc.

Hall, E. (1966). *The hidden dimension*. Garden City, NJ: Doubleday & Company, Inc.

Hardin, G. (1968). The tragedy of the commons. *Science, 62*, 1243-1248.

Hicks, J. (1956). *A revision of demand theory*. London: Oxford University Press.

Holy Bible (a), King James Version. Genesis 1:26-28.

Holy Bible (b), King James Version. Matthew 22:37-39.

Holy Bible (c), King James Version. Corinthians 10:24.

Kant, I. (1955). The metaphysics of morals. In D. Bronstein, Y. Krikorian, and P. Wiener (Eds.). *Basic problems of philosophy* (pp. 100-108). Englewood Cliffs, NJ: Prentice-Hall.

Kellert, S. and Wilson, E. (Eds.). (1993). *The biophilia hypothesis*. Washington, DC: Island Press.

McKechnie, G. (1970). Measuring environmental dispositions with the environmental response inventory. In J. Archaea and C. Eastman (Eds.). *Edra Two: Proceedings of the 2nd annual environmental design research association conference*. Pittsburgh, PA: Carnegie-Mellon University, Office Service Department.

McKechnie, G. (1971). *Environmental response inventory*. Palo Alto, CA: Consulting Psychologists Press.

Morris, C. (1956). *Varieties of human value*. Chicago, IL: University of Chicago Press.

Orleans, P. (1972). Differential cognition of urban residents: Effects of social scale on mapping. In R. Downs and D. Stea (Eds.), *Cognitive mapping: Images of spatial environments*. Chicago, IL: Aldine Publishing Company.

Peterson, G. (1977). Recreational preferences of urban teenagers: The influence of cultural and environmental attributes. In *Children, Nature, and the Urban Environment: Proceedings of a Symposium-Fair* (pp. 113-122). USDA Forest Service General Technical Report NE-30. Upper Darby, PA: Northeastern Forest Experiment Station.

Peterson, G., Driver, B., and Brown, P. (1990). The benefits and costs of recreation: Dollars and sense. In R. Johnson and G. Johnson (Eds.), *Economic valuation of natural resources*. Boulder, CO: Westview Press.

Peterson, G. and Neumann, S. (1969). Modeling and predicting human response to the visual recreation environment. *Journal of Leisure Research, 1* (3), 219-237.

Randall, A. (1983). The problem of market failure. *Natural Resources Journal, 23*, 131-148.

Rolston, H. (1982). Are values in nature subjective or objective? *Environmental Ethics, 4* (2), 131.

Santayana, G. (1896). *The sense of beauty*. New York, NY: Charles Scribner's Sons.

Stone, C. (1974). *Should trees have standing?* Los Altos, CA: William Kaufmann, Inc.

Thomas, J. W. (1994, February 3). Testimony of the Chief of the USDA Forest Service before the Subcommittee on Oversight and Investigations Committee on Natural Resources, United States House of Representatives, concerning "new directions for the forest service."

Tonn, B. (1991). The court of generations: A proposed amendment to the U.S. Constitution. *Futures,* June, 482-498.

Van Arsdol, M., Jr., Sabagh, G., and Alexander, F. (1964). Reality and the perception of environmental hazards. *Journal of Health and Human Behavior, 5*, (Winter), 144-153.

Von Bertalanffy, L. (1950). An outline of general systems theory. *British Journal of Philosophical Science, 1*, 134-165.

Webster's Third New International Dictionary (Unabridged). (1966). Springfield, MA: G. & C. Merriam.

Wilson, W. (1965). *Concepts of engineering system design.*
New York, NY: McGraw-Hill.

Wynne-Edwards, V. (1965). Self-regulating systems in
populations of animals. *Science, 147,* 1543-1548.

COMPARATIVE PERSPECTIVES OF WORLD RELIGIONS: VIEWS OF NATURE AND IMPLICATIONS FOR LAND MANAGEMENT

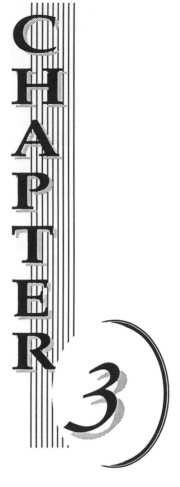

STEPHANIE KAZA
Environmental Program
University of Vermont
Burlington, Vermont

All religions have evolved in specific places, often with specific relationships to the surrounding lands. Every religion both shapes and is shaped by the culture in which it flourishes. Religious doctrines, practices, and moral philosophies have played a significant role in determining cultural attitudes and behaviors towards the natural world. Most land management practices reflect the values of the associated dominant religious traditions, either directly or indirectly. The purpose of this chapter is to explore eight major world religions and their views of nature, highlighting doctrines and teachings as they pertain to land management. It is my hope that this material can serve as a stimulus for discussion, raising awareness of cultural values in current management policies and inspiring dialogue on appropriate environmental ethics for public lands.

The eight major world religious traditions I treat include three from the west (Judaism, Christianity, and Islam) and five from the east (Hinduism, Jainism, Taoism, Confucianism, and Buddhism). For each, I explore principles related to land management, examining four areas:

1. the spiritual significance of nature,

2. ethical guidelines applicable to the environment,

3. land management practices recommended in the religious teachings, and

4. current activism on behalf of the environment.

These religions have been chosen for their significant contributions to world cultures—both in philosophical content and in sheer numbers of practitioners. They also are the traditions most involved in international ecoreligious dialogue or most referred to by scholars in environmental ethics. Here I sketch the broadest picture of commonly accepted beliefs, understandings, or practices held by most members of a tradition.

This overview is limited in several dimensions. First, it would not be possible to treat all world religions and all variations of any single tradition in such a study. Subgroups within traditions vary tremendously in codes of behavior, rituals, religious interpretation of texts, and institutional lines of authority. Certainly there are many differences and disagreements among sects as to text interpretation, daily life practices, religious governance, and degree of religious authority for the individual or the community. The pursuit of this level of study must be left to the interested reader.

Second, because religions evolve in geographical, historical, political-economic contexts, it may or may not be useful to apply their philosophical frameworks outside the source culture. Some religions have spread easily and been well-received on new shores as a welcome contrast to local religious practice. Others have stayed more or less in their region of origin, establishing cultural ties over thousands of years. In either case, the relationships between culture, religion, and, sometimes, the legal system are so entwined that guidelines for land management may not transfer from one culture to another. However, across the globe there is a long history of syncretism, or the influence of one religious tradition on another to create new forms and philosophies. Even now in the United States, land managers are being influenced and challenged by Native-American experiences of the land as sacred.

Third, all religions can be criticized for falling short of their own professed ideals. There have been and are continuing to be serious failures among religious practitioners who don't "walk their talk," either interpersonally or interinstitutionally. Religions in the past have frequently imposed their doctrines and ways of life on other cultures with serious impact on local and indigenous cultures. Intolerance of religious difference has escalated to militarism, war, and genocide time and time again, taking thousands of lives and destroying whole cultures. In some cases, religious zeal has been addressed directly against the land, causing major changes in habitat structure and function. Is there a religion which has not been a party to some significant loss of human, plant, or animal life on the earth? The scope of this chapter, however, precludes an in-depth review of the history of religious assault on people and ecosystems.

Finally, my sources are limited by their own points of view; they do not represent official positions of established denominations. I have looked specifically for recent revisionist articles by religious scholars and writers concerned about religious relationship with the environment. My aim is to suggest ways in which religious tradition and ethical principles are relevant to land management issues of today. Ecotheologians and those concerned with environmental revisioning of their faiths are still a very small voice in the institutional religious conversation. Here I bring them forward as creative visionaries, helping to bridge the gap between traditional moral guidelines and modern ecological crisis. The chapter is offered to provide a stepping stone for further discussion among field staff, policymakers, and all those charged with the responsibility of serving the public in caring for the land.

Western Religious Traditions

Judaism

Judaism is the oldest of the recognized world religions after Hinduism, dating back 4000 years to the ancient Hebrews, a pastoral, nomadic, and later agricultural people. Christianity, and later Islam, share some common roots in the Jewish tradition, history, and teachings. Judaism developed in the lands of Israel as a covenant relationship between one supreme God and God's recognized people. Because this area is strategically located at the junction of Africa, Asia, and Europe, it has been invaded by many major political powers over the centuries. With each successive wave of displacement, Jews migrated to more stable countries, spreading their influence and people all around the world. In Germany during World War II almost a third of the Jewish population was deliberately exterminated in the Holocaust. Jews, though numbering less than 13 million, (just under six million in North America), still see themselves as part of a continuous lineage connected to the original homeland of Israel, now the official Jewish nation state.

Jewish tradition is a way of life as well as a religion, with strong emphasis on family/lay life and the study of religious texts. In modern Judaism, there are no monastic orders or priests; Jewish rabbis or spiritual leaders serve as members of the community and are active in education, social service, and worship. Jewish dietary laws and other social customs date back to early agricultural practices which reflect the relationship of the people to the land.

SPIRITUAL SIGNIFICANCE OF NATURE

The Jews consider themselves the chosen people, cared for and watched over by one supreme God, Yahweh, who created the universe. Jewish appreciation for the environment is grounded in a respect for life as God's creation in all its manifestations. The goodness and abundance of the biophysical world is seen as a testimony to God's greatness. Nature is not an abstract concept but the physical realm where humans encounter God. Plants and animals hold intrinsic value because they are part of God's creation.

The Hebrew Bible creation story in which God gives dominion over all creatures to humans as God's servants has been discussed extensively by Hebrew and Christian scholars (Katz, 1994). In the Jewish tradition, the nature of this responsibility has been interpreted consistently as benevolent stewardship (Solomon, 1992). Since Jews believe the world belongs to God stewardship means caretaking, not ownership. Thus all instructions on behalf of the land are expressed from a theocentric world-view, reinforcing the covenant relationship between Jews and God. Judaism emphasizes neither extreme of domination or preservation, but rather supports conservation and wise developmental use (Katz, 1994).

Diversity of species is enumerated and appreciated in the Hebrew Bible, especially in the story of Noah's ark, and in the *Pereq shira*, the Chapter of Song (Solomon, 1992). The Jewish scriptural world includes many references to trees, animals, birds, and the land, reflecting the people's indigenous relationship with their homeland. A person's primary relationship is with God, but relative to other organisms, humans are perceived to be at the top of a hierarchy of value and intelligence above animals, with animals above plants, and plants above inanimate elements.

ETHICAL PRINCIPLES

In addition to the Bible itself, there are three sources of ethical guidelines for Jewish people:

1. *halakhah*:—rules and statutes in the Mishnah and Talmud along with their commentaries;

2. *aggadah*:—nonjuristic literature of exegesis, homilies, parables, and proverbs; and

3. *tefillah*:—prayers and liturgy (Helfland, 1986).

Fundamental to Jewish community practice is a culture of self-restraint where freedom is a blessing to be harnessed for beneficial good, both for the human community and for the natural world. The fundamental laws of self-restraint are the Ten Commandments which were given through Moses (Schorsch, 1992).

Ethical relations with nature begin with blessing (*berakhah*). A traditional *Kiddush* or ceremonial blessing, is recited over bread and wine on Sabbaths and holy days; other blessings for trees, animals, the new moon are part of Jewish culture (Rose, 1992). The desire for peaceful relations with the world is expressed in the traditional greeting, *shalom aleichem*, peace be unto you. Jews are encouraged to develop virtue through *mitzvahs* or commandments to do good deeds, including protection of trees and compassionate actions towards animals.

Jewish dietary laws (*kashruth*) spell out strict codes for acceptable and unacceptable foods and methods of food preparation. These reflect a general emphasis on caring for one's own body as God's creation, maintaining good health as one aspect of religious practice. Orthodox Jews eat only *kosher*, or allowed, foods which have been prepared in a ritual way and meats slaughtered in a humane ritual fashion.

LAND MANAGEMENT

Jews believe their prosperity as a people depends on their obedience to God's covenant which includes a caring, loving attitude toward the land with effective regulation of human use. A number of land management practices support sustainable use of marginal lands. The Hebrew Bible commands that lands be given a sabbath year rest every seventh year, paralleling the weekly sabbath rest from human activity. This means crop rotation and letting fields lie fallow to recover soil fertility.

In the Hebrew Bible, Jews are commanded not to destroy fruit trees in times of war. The phrase *bal tashchit*, no wanton destruction or despoliation, is now interpreted by some as applying broadly to trees, animals, rivers, and personal property as well. *Bal tashchit* is a moral law meant to maintain respect for God's creation (Katz, 1994). It forbids destruction of property that could be of social use to the community.

Specific regulations within the *Mishnah* place limits on grazing rights (*yishuv ha-aretz*), monitor water use, define areas for waste disposal, regulate sewage disposal, and provide open space around cities (*migrash*). Excess production of foul smells or loud noises are also prohibited to maintain environmental quality. Based as it is in a desert climate where water is scarce and trees provide precious shade, water and trees hold a special place in Jewish culture. Many prayers call for the blessed rain, the living water (*mayim chayim*). Tree planting and protection for green belt space are central to town planning.

The yearly agricultural cycle is celebrated in the Jewish holidays which are determined by the full moons. The high holy days, Rosh Hashannah and Yom Kippur, are held in the harvest months of fall. On *Tu Bi Shevat*, the New Year for Trees, children and families plant trees in their communities. Other holidays are pilgrimage festivals which reflect the history and tradition of journeying to sacred land sites to reconsecrate human relationships with them as holy (Pick, 1992).

ACTIVISM

In 1902 the Zionist Movement established the Jewish National Fund to renew and redeem the land. Since Israel attained independence in 1948, the Fund has sponsored the planting of 180 million trees, with 11 million in the 9000 acres around Jerusalem. Unfortunately the Palestinian *intifada* has burned over a million of these in recent uprisings. Five percent of Israel is protected in national forests and parks managed under the Ministry of the Environment as of 1989. The Nature Reserves Authority, founded in 1964, manages 385 reserves on 450,000 acres. Since 1990 a number of Noah's sanctuaries have been established as animal shelters (Rose, 1992).

In the United States, a Jewish environmental group, Shomrei Adamah, encourages synagogues to highlight the ecological aspects of the Jewish holidays, especially *Tu Bi Shevat*. They have developed a high school environmental curriculum and a resource manual for congregations and are providing outreach and coordination around Jewish environmental activism.

In Philadelphia, a Jewish Eco-Kosher Project focuses on expanding traditional dietary guidelines to include ecological practices. They suggest ecologically acceptable foods are those which do not ruin the earth (*bal tashchit*), show respect for animals (*za'ar ba'alei chayim*), protect one's own body from harm (*sh'mirat haguf*), do not oppress workers and exploit customers (*oshek*), and share food, money, work, and time with the poor (*tzedzkah*).

Jewish rabbis have been active in international environmental discussions at the Rio Summit, the Assisi meeting, the Parliament of the World's Religions, and other global gatherings.

Christianity

Christianity was founded by followers of Jesus Christ almost 2000 years ago as an outgrowth of Judaism. The religion spread quickly through the Mediterranean countries and on to northern Europe. Missionaries and emigrants took it further to North America, South America, Asia, and Africa, establishing churches and monastic orders across five continents. The three largest groups today are the Catholic Church (900 million), Eastern Orthodox (125 million), and Protestants and Pentecostals (622 million). Ethnic, cultural, and theological differences mark hundreds of different branch groups, from Christian Scientists to Baptists, Episcopalians to Mormons, Coptic Christians to Mennonites.

The primary source of scriptural wisdom is the Bible which includes the Old Testament or Hebrew Bible, and the New Testament teachings of Jesus and his followers. This single text is interpreted by various traditions as the literal revealed word of God, wisdom stories for moral life, or historical records of theological interpretation. Christian thought is closely associated with the philosophical tradition of western Europe as it evolved through the Middle Ages, Renaissance, Enlightenment, and Age of Industrialism. Christian religious organizations, especially the Catholic Church, have played a powerful political and historical role in determining the fate of the European landscape.

SPIRITUAL SIGNIFICANCE OF NATURE

Like Jews, Christians believe in one supreme transcendent God who rules over all the earth. God is the creator, the ultimate provider, the sole governor, and the final judge of human behavior. Teachings from the Old Testament emphasize a covenant relationship between people and God and a command to keep God's laws in caring for plants and animals. Teachings in the New Testament focus more on human relations and the rewards of living in fellowship with the body of Christ, the larger Christian community. This reflects the urban orientation of early Christians as compared to the agriculturally based Jews (Baker, 1990).

Christian attitudes toward nature show two opposite themes: transcendence and communion. The transcendent theme, well-developed in the Protestant tradition, is marked by two key ideas:

that personal salvation rests on one's own unmediated relationship with God (not the rest of creation), and that God blesses his chosen ones with material well-being (Palmer, 1992). The physical world is seen as a place of travail and turmoil, to be transcended through salvation. The experience of redemption is a release from nature and the difficulties of the ephemeral body. During the settling of North America the natural world was often seen as threatening and dangerous, feared for its wildness. Christian missionaries felt a moral call to save the souls of heathen savages (the Native Americans) and to bring civilization to wild areas through taming and settling the land. From a Christian perspective, the primary value of the natural world lay in the usefulness of its forests and rich soils.

The communion or sacramental view is represented by St. Francis, the Catholic monastic who lived close to the earth in relation with trees and birds, sun and moon. Modern Christian ecotheologians have picked up this theme, interpreting the creation as an expression of God's faithful loving kindness (Nash, 1991). All members of the creation are seen as products of God's love and recipients of ongoing love. This view endows nature with intrinsic moral significance, a contrast to other views which place moral importance solely on human beings. Christian readings of the book of Genesis, the creation story, generally interpret "dominion" as ecologically beneficial, a command against abuse of God's creation. Humans are to act in the image of God as his responsible representatives, for which they have been given particular rational, moral, and creative capacities. This role is often described as steward, caretaker, or manager—a role associated with conservation and a wise use orientation to natural systems.

Modern Christian writers such as McFague (1992), Berry (1988), and McDaniel (1990) suggest an ecological revisioning of Christian attitudes towards nature. They offer an inclusive evolutionary creation story (Swimme and Berry, 1992), an emphasis on interrelatedness and interdependence, and a role for humans as cocreators with God (McFague, 1992). Nash (1991) expands the Christian idea of sacrament to include the whole universe, with nature as locus for spiritual experience, a medium for revelation.

ETHICAL GUIDELINES

Though there are many interpretations of the Bible, Christians generally agree that Jesus' teachings and personal example are key to Christian ethics. Perhaps the two most important principles are love and justice. Love is the ground of all being; God is love—the process of creation is an act of love. Love is taught as service, respect, giving to self and others, mercy, compassion, and kindness; it is an expression of relationality. Dimensions of love applied to an ecological context include:

1. beneficence: loving service to the environment;

2. other-esteem: valuing and respecting the integrity of the other as a gift of God;

3. receptivity: recognizing love's dependency on relationship, both between humans as they directly and indirectly affect the land, and between humans and nonhumans;

4. humility: expressed as simplicity, frugality, and restraint from overuse of the environment; and

5. communion: the bonding power of solidarity and friendship with others (Nash, 1991).

Grace is the experience of God's love in a personal context; "green grace" is the experience of the healing power of God's love through a connection with the natural world (McDaniel, 1993).

Christian sin or wrongdoing has generally described immoral acts between people—lying, stealing, adultery, and so forth—which break the bonds of love. From an ecological perspective, sin would result in an alienation between people and God (and God's creation), a disrespect for the interdependent relations between all creatures, and a human self-centeredness out of proportion to reality (McFague, 1992). In this sense, the Fall from paradise is perennial, manifesting in ongoing ecological transgressions (Nash, 1991). Sins persist not only in individual relations but also in cultural relations and institutions, perpetuating patterns of nonharmonious relations with the environment.

Justice is a necessary condition for love; injustice is social sin. Justice, from a Christian perspective, is the definition, negotiation, and application of moral rights. Responsibilities to others are defined by socially agreed upon rights. Nash (1991) suggests a list of environmental rights to prevent ecocide, or thoughtless destruction of the earth. Among these are sustainable productivity, protection from pollution, and preservation of biodiversity. The Judeo-Christian rights perspective has been the basis of public law in western Europe and the United States, shaping much of the debate on endangered species, wilderness use, and animal welfare.

LAND MANAGEMENT

Most of the Christian guidelines for land management practices are suggested in the Old Testament or the Hebrew Bible (described under Judaism). The New Testament covers a much shorter time frame, represents fewer authors, and does not generally contain laws pertaining to secular matters. Christianity was initially conceived as a religion of individual faith for specially chosen people. It gained ground during a time of political upheaval; converts were urged to invest in their own personal salvation rather than a long-term view of sustainable ecological relations.

As institutional Christianity spread from the Mediterranean, it officially denounced local gods and goddesses associated with forests, streams, and mountains. The natural world was dedivinized to make clear the omnipotence of the one God above all others (Page, 1992). This process undermined indigenous land management practices based on respect for local deities. In many places heresy to the new ways was met with death; many atrocities were justified in the name of one God. Some modern ecotheologians suggest the need for official church reexamination of and repentance for its legacy with regard to indigenous peoples and environmental degradation (Rajotte and Breuilly, 1992).

ACTIVISM

Representatives of Christian denominations have been very active in global dialogue on ecology and religion (Granberg-Michaelson, 1992). The World Council of Churches (WCC) at its 1990 convocation in Seoul, Korea, pledged its efforts towards "Peace, Justice, and the Integrity of Creation." A further report to the WCC laid out principles for advancing this program based on a liberation theology praxis (Birch, Eakin, and McDaniel, 1990). In the United States, this work is being carried out by the North American Conference on Religion and Ecology (NACRE), the National Religious Partnership for Life (NRPL), and the Center of Respect for Life and Environment (a subgroup of the Humane Society). Individual churches have projects of ecojustice, environmental awareness and celebration, recycling, and interfaith environmental leadership (Morton, 1993).

Christian groups have been encouraged to observe the new United Nations Environmental Sabbath Day on June 5th. At least two other sects have established additional church celebration days for the earth (June 21st is Nature Day for Swedish Lutherans, and September 1st is Conservation Feast Day for Greek Orthodox). In former East Germany and the Philippines, church leaders have taken strong initiatives to oppose local environmental despoliation, risking denominational sanctions for their strong statements.

Islam

The word Islam comes from the root Arabic letters s. l. m.—Sin, Lam, and Mim—which means to be in peace, to be integral whole. Islam is a revealed religion, established through the experience of the Prophet Muhammad (570-632 CE). As a human messenger—prophet for Allah, the Alone God—the Prophet Muhammad delivered the *Qur'an* as the speech of God. According to Islamic belief and practice, one who consciously submits to the will, law, and guidance of Allah finds peace within, with all creatures, and with the Creator (Aasi, 1993).

Islam is historically and theologically related to Judaism and Christianity which share a similar emphasis on one supreme God. It was founded in the city of Madinah in the sixth century and quickly spread to Mecca and the rest of the Arabian peninsula. Within less than a hundred years, Islam had moved into China, India, Europe, and Africa. Long before the European Renaissance, the Islamic movement made significant contributions to world culture, art, and architecture. Despite many geopolitical challenges, conquests, and displacements, Islam has continued to spread throughout the world. Muslims now number over a billion, with the largest contingent in North America being African Americans (Aasi, 1993).

SPIRITUAL SIGNIFICANCE OF NATURE

Muslims believe that the one God, Allah, created everything, commands everything, and holds an ongoing creative role in the dynamic unfolding of the universe. Allah is sovereign over heaven and earth, with power over all beings. The natural and human world is seen by Muslims as the Creation of God, full of signs of his power and goodness. Though the gifts of creation are given for human use they are primarily meant to evoke devotion, praise, and gratitude for the good works of Allah. As such, Muslims are expected to treat nature with care and respect (Timm, 1994).

The human role with respect to the creation is as designated vice-regent (*khalifah*) for Allah who gives this authority to people as a test of their obedience and loyalty to God (Timm, 1994). According to Muslim belief, people have been given the role of God's servant (*abd Allah*), to receive the grace flowing through him. In this relationship between Creator and human, God is clearly absolute.

Nature, in the Qur'an, is a "theophany which both veils and reveals God" (Nasr, 1992). Humans are seen as immersed in the Divine, yet unaware of it because of their own forgetfulness and negligence (*ghaflah*); this can be overcome by remembrance (*dhikr*). The Muslim sense of pattern reflects the perceived music of proportionality in plants, animals, crystals, and planetary motion. In these forms, order and harmony, interrelationship of parts, and complementarity of functions and roles are revealed (Nasr, 1993).

For Muslims, the protection of nature is a spiritual duty. To protect the environment is to preserve its value as a sign of the Creator and to respect the laws of nature made by the Creator. The Prophet Muhammad considered that humankind was not the only community of beings and that all living creatures were worthy of protection (*hurmah*) and kind treatment (Izzi Dien, 1990). The environment is God's gift to all ages and the context for all human relationships as they are established in justice (*'adl*) and equity (*jhsan*).

ETHICAL PRINCIPLES

Islam is understood as a way of life, *manhaj hayat*, encompassing a person's entire orientation to the world. Ethics or values are thought to reside in the soul as a state, *hay'a*, that is conditioned by upbringing and one's perception of virtue. Good ethics, *khuluq hasan*, reflect a good Muslim upbringing and strongly internalized Muslim values. The fundamental Muslim expectation is to practice good (*al-ma'ruf*) and prohibit evil (*munkar*). The community call to this imperative is handled by volunteers (*muhtasib mutatawi*) or appointed persons (*al-mutatawi*). Care

for the environment falls legally under the jurisdiction of the official *muhtasib*, as well as matters of public health, food and water practices, and proper slaughter. In practice today, however, the office is mostly concerned with making sure the daily prayers are called on time (Izzi Dien).

The five pillars of Islamic practice are *shahadah* (statement of faith), *salat* (five daily prayers), *sawm* (fasting during Ramadan period), *zakat* (sharing of wealth to purify it), and *hajj* (pilgrimage to holy sites). The *Shari'ah*, which literally means the "source of water," is the source of both legal rules and ethical principles for Muslim behavior. Types of actions fall under five categories:

1. obligatory (*wajib*) or what one is obliged to do as a Muslim;

2. devotional and ethical actions (*mandub*) or what one is encouraged to do to be a virtuous person;

3. permissible actions (*mubah*) or what one may do;

4. abominable actions (*makruh*) or those which are morally but not legally wrong; and

5. prohibited actions (*haram*) which are strictly forbidden.

Muslim sources for ethical guidelines are drawn directly from the Qur'an and its commentaries in the Hadith, derived Islamic law, and interpretation of the law. All environmental practices for Muslim cultures are thus based in religious law.

LAND MANAGEMENT

According to Islamic law, there are three types of land: developed (*amir*), undeveloped (*mawat*), and protective zones (*harim*) (Dutton, 1992). Developed lands refer to any land with human settlement or agricultural activity, whether in a large city or rural area. The root of the word *amir* means alive. Undeveloped lands (*mawat*) are those which are neither settled nor cultivated. Islamic law states that if someone brings this (dead) land to life (i.e., develops it), they own it. Development in this sense means putting a hedge or wall around the land, irrigating the land, clearing the area of trees and rocks, plowing the land, planting crops or trees, or putting up a building. This kind of development may have serious consequences in the form of ecological fragmentation of the land (Dutton, 1992).

Around all developed lands are protected zones, *harim*. These zones belong to the owner of the developed land with which the harim is associated. This may be an area for gathering firewood or pasturing livestock, or the area around a community well. Whereas undeveloped land is not owned by anyone (until brought to life), harim zones are always owned by individuals or communities. A *hima* is an area of undeveloped land set aside to remain unused, wild, or to protect pasture. In the past, large areas have been set aside by Muslim rulers to support war animals. Now most himas are smaller, with an estimated 3000 existing in Saudi Arabia in the mid 1960s (Dutton, 1992). Use restrictions include prohibitions on grazing, grass cutting, or tree cutting. The local village headman is responsible for "managing" these areas, adjusting the restrictions from year to year, to meet village needs. Himas would seem to hold the greatest potential for land conservation and biodiversity preservation.

Owners of developed land pay a regular tax or *zakat*. Zakat is not a tax on income or products but rather a socioreligious obligation for those with more to help those with less. The tax is collected by the community and redistributed to the poor, sick, and needy in the local area (Vadillo and Khalid, 1992).

ACTIVISM

The challenge for Muslims concerned about the environment is to highlight aspects of Islamic law and faith traditions that support an ecological perspective. Foreign laws may be legally binding, but Muslims believe that only Islamic law is morally binding. This creates some barriers for international cooperation on environmental issues, since non-Islamic law carries less weight with Muslims. However, under the continual pressures of western colonial domination many Muslim countries have discarded much of the divine law in favor of secular laws (Nasr, 1993). Some of those most concerned about this loss are actively engaged in resisting western domination in order to maintain Islamic culture. To the extent that environmental activism, even through religious organizations, is perceived as "western," it may also be resisted by Muslims as one more aspect of colonization (Nasr, 1993). Several Muslim groups have formed to increase awareness about animals and the environment. Muslims also have been present at a number of global interfaith environmental conferences.

Eastern Religious Traditions

Hinduism

Hinduism is the oldest of the recognized world religions, originating in India as far back as 3000 BCE (Before Common Era) with no one single identifiable founder. More than a religion, it is regarded as a way of life reflecting the development of Indian culture over centuries. The actual name for the religion in the scriptures is the Vedic religion, or religion of the *Vedas* (scriptures); also *Sangtama Dharma*, the perennial wisdom and righteousness, the "Eternal Religion" (Venkateswaran, 1993). The four *Vedas—Rig*, *Yajur*, *Sama*, and *Atharva Vedas* —are the primary source for religious knowledge. These revealed texts are supplemented by the equally important *Upanishads* and other interpretive writings and works of Hindu law.

Hindus believe in one Supreme Being, but the divinity arises in many forms including many gods and goddesses. Three of these form the Hindu trinity: Brahma, the creator; Vishnu, the sustainer and preserver; and Shiva, the destroyer of evils and dissolver of the universe. Of the four living subtraditions, three are dedicated to worship of each of the forms of the trinity; the fourth group worships Shakti, the Divine Mother. For Hindus, the universe goes through endless cycles of creation, preservation, and destruction. The unifying theme in all Hindu creation stories is that this cyclical process depends on the supreme will of God; God and nature (*Prakriti*) are one and the same (Venkateswaran, 1993).

SPIRITUAL SIGNIFICANCE OF NATURE

A strong sense of place is pervasive throughout Hindu tradition, representing an unbroken lineage of knowledge of holy sites for thousands of years. Hindus regard their mountains, rivers, and forests as sacred and filled with universal consciousness (*brahman*) (Chapple, 1994). The rivers Ganga (Ganges), Yumna, Sarasvata, and Sindhu and the earth (Prthivi) are seen as female deities; the fire (Agni) and wind (Maruts) as male deities. Hindus regularly make pilgrimages (*parikrama*) to the sacred rivers and mountains, reconsecrating them by ritual circumambulation (Prime, 1992).

Sanctity of life is central to Hindu religion; protection of cows even in crowded city streets reflects the belief that God may take many different life forms. Humans do not act as special servants or stewards for God, nor are different species assigned degrees of value (Dwivedi, 1990). The practice of *ahimsa*, or nonharming, is based in an understanding of reincarnation. All souls are thought to move through different forms from lifetime to lifetime, reflecting the quality of one's deeds. Animals may have been one's parent in an earlier lifetime or may become one's future child; thus it is important to treat them kindly (Dwivedi, 1990).

Plants, likewise, are regarded as having divine powers. Hindus believe that each tree has a *Vriksa-devata*, tree deity, which lives inside it. This deity is worshipped with prayers and offerings of water, flowers, and sweets; cutting of trees is considered a sinful act. Hindus see tree planting and protection as religious duty. Herbal plants have long played an important role in Indian medicinal practice. Ayurvedic medicine, one of the world's great herbal healing systems (along with Chinese medicine and the western European herbal tradition), draws on the special properties of plants to improve harmful spiritual and physical conditions (see Montes, Chapter Seven, in this volume). Ancient Hindu yoga practices also contribute to a strong respect for a healthy body which lives in spiritual harmony with the world (see for example Iyengar, 1979).

ETHICAL GUIDELINES

The Hindu religion has developed an elaborate caste system which marks individuals as members of four main castes and hundreds of subcastes. Guidelines for behavior are determined by caste. The system has degenerated over time into a hierarchical and oppressive social structure, raising human rights issues especially for the lowest caste, untouchables. In some areas, cows are regarded as more holy than untouchables. It has been suggested that the ecological effect of resource partitioning according to caste has been very efficient in reducing economic competition (Dwivedi, 1990). However, under British industrial demands and job opportunities the system has broken down.

Hindu tradition encourages three principles of moral practice: *yajna* (sacrifice), *dhana* (giving), and *tapas* (penance). Interpreted ecologically, these provide means of replenishing the earth, society, and the soul. *Yajna* means thinking of others that will follow and providing for replacement of what

one uses. *Dhana* means giving labor, time, money, or material goods to replenish social relations out of gratitude for what has been given already. *Tapas* means exercising self-restraint by fasting, meditating, or abstaining from sexual activity to replenish one's internal spiritual environment (Prime, 1992).

There are four aims of life in Hindu tradition:

1. joy in the sensual, sexual, artistic, and aesthetic forms of expression;

2. economic and social fulfillment;

3. morality as in duties to people, animals, and plants; and

4. salvation or liberation—union with God.

According to Hindu belief, one can attain liberation from the endless cycle of birth and death by one of four spiritual paths—the ways of knowledge, love and devotion, selfless action, and meditation (Venkateswaran, 1993).

LAND MANAGEMENT

Early Vedic teachers gave great weight to the importance of trees. Gurus gave spiritual instruction under trees; trees were symbols of patience and tolerance. Hindu literature is filled with references to forests and trees; the bond between Indian people and trees is strong. Forests are seen as critical to self-identity formation for Hindus. Unfortunately in modern times, forests and sacred ancient trees are suffering the impacts of increasing population pressure (Prime, 1992).

There are three types of forest in Hindu tradition: *shrivan* (source of prosperity), *tapovan* (the contemplative forest), and *mahavana* (the great natural forest where all species find shelter). A *shrivan* includes groves of fruit trees (*vanakhandi*) and dense woodland (*ghana*) for fuel collection maintained by a village committee of elders. Each village ideally has five great trees representing the five primary elements of earth, water, fire, air, and ether—the totality of the universe. The *tapovan*, home of sages, was to be left natural and untended, a place apart from worldly activity for the quiet life of spiritual centers or *ashrams*. In the past it was thought that the presence of spiritual teachers protected the forest and all who dwelled within it. Now modern sanctuaries must be protected by legal regulation and guards (Prime, 1992).

Followers of Gandhian economics promote cottage industry as compatible with sustainable land conservation measures. Gandhi advocated village self-sufficiency and local rule and responsibility. He promoted genuine self-government and economic independence based on local resource availability. The root of his social teachings is based in the spiritual wisdom tradition of *ahimsa*, nonharming. His guidelines for development included maintaining the health of local forests as contexts of stability for village life (Chapple, 1994).

ACTIVISM

An offshoot of Hinduism founded by Guru Maharj Jambaji in the late fifteenth century thrives today as the Bishnois community in the Marwar area. In his youth, Jambaji witnessed the impacts of a severe drought and reasoned that if trees were protected, the community would survive. Among his religious injunctions was a ban on cutting any green tree. About 300 years later, a nearby king sent his soldiers to harvest the abundant trees to build a new palace. The villagers protested on religious grounds, protecting the trees with their bodies. Soldiers massacred 363 people; eventually the king withdrew the operation and gave the Bishnois state protection for their beliefs (Dwivedi, 1990). Today the community continues to protect trees with fierce devotion, and has served to inspire the internationally famous Chipko movement.

The *Chipko Andolan* (movement to hug the trees) takes its name from similar actions in 1973 and since, when villagers in the town of Gopeshwar formed a human chain to prevent the local forest from being cleared for a sports equipment factory. Women, in particular, showed strong leadership in protecting trees, recognizing the presence of tree deities. Ten years later a similar movement happened in Karnataka and spread to adjoining districts. Gandhi's term *satyagraha*, or persistence in search of truth, has been adapted to these forest movements. Forest *satyagraha* means persistence in search of truth pertaining to the lives of trees (Dwivedi, 1990).

An impressive tree planting program in India was started by Balbir Mathur in the 1960s. It was his idea to distribute trees free as *prasadam* or spiritual blessing, blessed by holy sages. By 1989, Trees for Life had a large office in Delhi with a network of volunteers all over India. In one year they planted over 700,000 trees. Perhaps the greatest blessing ritual took place at Sarnath in 1990 when His Holiness the Dalai Lama blessed over three million walnuts, apricot, papaya, and guava seeds to be given to 300,000 pilgrims during his Kalachakra teachings (Prime, 1992).

Jainism

The Jains religion originated in India over 5000 years ago and currently has over seven million followers, primarily in India, with about 100,000 in North America, Britain, Europe, Africa, and Australia. Jains practice the teachings of Mahavira XXIV and last prophet of the Jain time cycle, born in 599 BCE and alive during the time of the Buddha. He is credited with consolidating the teachings of a long lineage of prophets who consistently held to principles of peace, harmony, and renunciation. The word Jain means follower of the Jainism, those human teachers who have attained omniscience through spiritual practice of asceticism and nonviolence toward all living creatures (Jain, 1993).

SPIRITUAL SIGNIFICANCE OF NATURE

In Jain cosmology, the universe has no beginning or end, nor a single creator. That which has no consciousness, *ajiva*, has five substances:

1. motion (*dharma*),
2. rest (*adharma*),
3. space (*akasha*),
4. matter (*pudgala*), and
5. time (*kala*).

That which has consciousness, the soul or *jiva*, takes form in a body which accumulates subtle material particles or karmic "dust" (*asravas*). All beings are thought to have *jiva*, including animals, trees, and stones. Jains consider plants to be a lower form of physical body with only the sense of touch; microorganisms and small animals have two, three, or four senses. Next highest are animals with five senses; humans and advanced animals possessing rationality and intuition (*manas*) are regarded as the highest form of soul. As a highly evolved form of life, humans hold ethical responsibility for environmental protection and harmony (Singhri, 1993).

The central Jain teachings are contained in two statements: *Ahimsa parmo dharmah* (nonviolence is the supreme religion); and *Parasparopagraho jivanam* (all life is bound together by mutual support and interdependence). All aspects of the natural world are seen as existing in physical and metaphysical relationship with each other. The principle of nonviolence applies not only to physical acts but also to thoughts; violence is defined by the intention to harm—the absence of compassion for the other. Jain scriptures are very clear on prohibition of injury, abuse, oppression, torture, or killing of any creature or living being.

Three other important teachings help define the Jain view toward the environment. *Anekantavada*, the doctrine of manifold aspects, describes reality as multifaceted and ever changing; this doctrine recognizes the existence of an infinite number of viewpoints reflecting the time, place, and state of mind of the viewer and the view. *Samyaktva*, equanimity, promotes a live and let live attitude, avoiding dogmatic, intolerant, aggressive, harmful, and unilateral attitudes towards the natural and human world. *Jiva-daya* (compassion, empathy, and charity) means caring, tending, and protecting all living beings. Jains pray for universal friendliness, forgiveness, and fearlessness towards all living beings (Singhri, 1993).

ETHICAL PRINCIPLES

The Jain code of conduct is based in the five *vratas* or vows:

1. *ahimsa* (nonviolence—no killing);
2. *satya* (truthfulness—no lying);
3. *asteya* (no stealing);
4. *brahmacharya* (chastity); and
5. *aparigraha* (nonmaterialism).

Consistent with the vow of *ahimsa*, Jains practice strict vegetarianism, eating only vegetables and dairy products. Cruelty to animals is forbidden, including keeping animals in captivity, depriving them of food and drink, or overburdening them (Singhri, 1993).

Central to the Jain way of life is the ethic of moderation and self-restraint. Waste and pollution are seen as acts of violence, preventable by reducing one's needs and wants. Desires for excessive use of natural resources should be curbed to keep consumption levels reasonable. Those that accumulate wealth are advised to distribute the surplus to reduce material attachment. Giving time and chari-

table donations are considered part of a Jain's social obligations. Thus the Jains have founded and maintained many schools, colleges, hospitals, clinics, orphanages, and relief camps (Singhri, 1993).

LAND MANAGEMENT/ACTIVISM

Jain environmental concerns have focused primarily on animals. They have traditionally maintained hospitals and homes for sick and old animals. A group of Jains is actively promoting a wildlife sanctuary on the outskirts of London. Two groups of Jain ascetic monks have special practices for avoiding killing of small animals. Shvetambara and Digambara monks carry a whisk broom to sweep in front of them as they walk to prevent stepping on insects. Terapanthis monks also wear a cloth over their mouths to prevent swallowing insects (Chapple, 1994).

Some of the Jain development projects in rural communities include work in tree planting and solar energy. Recently, the Jains declared March 28th as "Ahimsa Day" to be celebrated as a new religious holiday related to environmental concerns. Mahatma Ghandi's spiritual leadership based on nonviolence was strongly influenced by Jain philosophy (Chapple, 1994).

Taoism

The philosophy of Taoism was developed and popularized in the sixth century BCE by Lao Tzu and Chuang Tzu, contemporaries of Confucius. The name derives from the primary text by Lao Tzu, the *Tao Te Ching*, a small book of verse describing the way of harmony with nature. This time in China during the Chou dynasty was a period of great intellectual creativity, sometimes called the age of the one hundred philosophers (Tucker, 1994). Today Taoism is known more as a philosophy than an organized religion, though there are some temples in the west as well as the east. A wide range of people, including naturalists, environmentalists, vegetarians, alternative health practitioners, and new paradigm physicists are influenced by it.

SPIRITUAL SIGNIFICANCE OF NATURE

Taoists believe the Tao to be the self-existent source of all things. It is the cosmic, the mysterious, the nameless, the all-pervasive, the eternal, the ultimate reality of nature (Ip, 1986). It is neither a god nor personified creator. The Tao is called "the way" by Lao Tzu, referring to the path of return to the original principle. The *Tao Te Ching* emphasizes unmediated intimacy with the natural world, particularly through the flowing and yielding qualities of water. Other important metaphors for the Tao are the valley, womb, vessel—all images of receptivity and productivity (Tucker, 1994).

Nature is described as dynamic and ever changing, reflecting the interplay of two primary forces, *yin* and *yang*. These represent all opposites, for example: male/female, increase/decrease, light/dark, initiating/yielding. In the Chinese system, these opposites are not exclusionary but rather complementary. In any given situation, yin and yang forces govern the sense of energy and direction shaping the outcome. These can be studied by observing the natural world closely for weather and seasonal patterns, river meanders, bird flight, earth movement, and other indicators of energy dynamics. According to Taoist beliefs, the environment is a primary determining condition for one's own actualization or enlightenment. The actions of humans are not separate from those of nature; the enlightened sage is one who acts in accordance with the movements of the Tao (Chung, 1993b).

ETHICAL GUIDELINES

Te, the broad category of virtue in the Taoist tradition, is defined as moral power reflecting the fundamental truth in nature (Ames, 1989). It is the potency, the vitality and power sustaining and transforming all beings. *Te* appears in humans through *wu-wei*, nonegocentric action, or action which harmonizes with the flow of the Tao. *Yu-wei*, in contrast, is willful, intentional, or unnatural activity which goes against the flow of nature.

Taoists value simplicity and spontaneity which allow one to respond to the subtle and dynamic changes in any interaction. Peaceful coexistence with nature is fundamental to Taoist activity. Lao Tzu sees little need for human superstructure (institutions, governments), believing this creates artificial separation between people and the natural world. He urges a return to the most basic intimacy, basing one's lived truth in the experience of the Tao (Ip, 1986).

LAND MANAGEMENT/ACTIVISM

The way of the Taoist sage provides a model for minimal impact on the environment. Invisible, enfolded, unobtrusive yet fully aware, the sage moves easily through the natural world, disrupting nothing in the landscape. He or she practices Lao Tzu's three methods of life enhancement: to keep to the original "oneness," maintain one's vital energy, and persist in the practices for longevity (Chung, 1993b).

The sage uses methods of transformation to help situations move from conflicting mode, the destructive or waning cycle of the Five Elements, to creative mode, the nourishing or increasing cycle. In the destructive mode, metal harms wood (axes, chain saws), wood harms earth (through buildings stuck in the ground), earth harms water (dams), water harms fire (squelching of spirit and beauty of life), and fire harms metal (industrial pollution). In the creative mode, the cycle is turned at any point where it is harmful. Then metal nourishes water (purification of aquifers), water nourishes wood (growth of forests), wood nourishes fire (creating stability of spirit), fire nourishes earth (creating ashes to feed the earth), and earth nourishes metal (slowly forming in the undisturbed depths). The path of return to the Tao is based in the process of transformation; the sage cultivates methods for meeting conflict and turning it to creativity (Chung, 1993b).

Confucianism

Confucianism as a philosophy, religion, and way of life is an important element in Chinese, Korean, and Japanese traditions. It is named after Confucius (551-479 BCE), the philosopher, educator, statesman, and visionary whose thoughts have influenced Asian culture and political relations for two millennia. Important texts include the *Analects of Confucius*, *Mencius*, the *Great Learning*, and the *Doctrine of the Mean*. The Confucian system offers a model of human conduct that promotes the ideal harmonious society based in cosmological relations (Tucker, 1994).

SPIRITUAL SIGNIFICANCE OF NATURE

Central to the Chinese world-view is the sense of the universe as constantly changing, unfolding, filled with *ch'i* or vital force or power. This view is neither cyclic nor spiral but rather transformational, with emphasis on the continuity of being (Wei-ming,

1989). There is no single creation story or personification of good and evil. Creativity is seen not as the creation of something out of nothing, but as a transformation of what already exists into another form. All life forms are part of the continuous flow of *ch'i*; human life is thus organically connected to stones, trees, animals. The movement of *ch'i* is influenced by the dynamic tension between *yin* and *yang* forces which are complementary and interdependent.

Confucians describe human beings as filial sons and daughters of the universe. The ideal just society is one that functions in harmony with nature with human activity adapted to the rhythms of the natural world (Tucker, 1994). A moral ruler will respect the laws of nature in the creation of a benevolent government. Confucians use the image of concentric circles to describe their relationship with the cosmos: at the center is the individual self, encircled by family, teachers, friends, government, and finally the universe. Harmonious relations at each level are thought to promote harmonious relations throughout the ordered universe.

ETHICAL GUIDELINES

In the Confucian world order people are seen as basically good. This inherent goodness is brought out through education and taking personal responsibility for one's life. Confucianism emphasizes relational ethics based in a view of nature as an interdependent network of wholes and parts. In choosing to act, one considers the balance of yin and yang forces, timing, the mean position or the Golden Path (the most strategic position from which to deal with change), and the status (role, position, duties) of the people in the situation (Chung, 1993a).

One's humanity is achieved only with and through others in society. Concern for social harmony tends to hold priority over concern for environmental harmony. Through self-discipline and self-improvement, the individual becomes a better member of his or her family and of society (Chung, 1993a).

LAND MANAGEMENT/ACTIVISM

Chinese and other north Asian landscapes have been actively managed for thousands of years with agriculture as the primary use. Sustainable agricultural practices have been essential for maintaining high human population levels. Most of this is highly regulated through the state to achieve pragmatically an adequate distribution of food. Under Chairman Mao, millions of trees were planted, although some of these projects were ultimately unsuccessful. While Confucian philosophy encourages harmonious relations between people and the natural world, in practice these have been stretched by the pressure on the landscape of increasing population. In many places China's landscape is scarred and deforested, reflecting years of intensive use. As China heads toward a period of rising materialism, it seems likely that Confucian influence will protect the interests of the state more than the environment.

Buddhism

The word Buddha means the "awakened one"; the practice of Buddhism is based in waking up to or becoming enlightened by the interdependent nature of reality. Sakyamuni Buddha taught in the Ganges River basin of northeastern India around 500 BCE. Buddhism flourished in India until the thirteenth century when it disappeared from there as a result of several waves of foreign invasion under Islam rule. By then, however, it had spread to southeastern Asia (Burma, Cambodia, Laos, Siam, Sri Lanka, and Viet Nam), to central and east Asia (China, Japan, Korea, Mongolia, and Tibet), and the Himalayas (Bhutan, Ladak, Nepal, and Sikkim). Today there are over 250 million Buddhists, with approximately five million in the United States. Most of these are of Asian descent, but the number of Euro-American Buddhists is increasing as Buddhism becomes established in the latest wave of adoption in North America (Sopa and Jones, 1993).

Central to the Buddha's teaching is the path of the Middle Way. This means avoiding the sensory extremes of asceticism and hedonism and the philosophical extremes of eternalism and nihilism (Sopa and Jones, 1993). The Buddha explained causation through multiple causes, asserting that nothing arises independently but rather depends on specific conditions. Buddhists do not believe in a creator god or an ultimate cause. All existence is seen as impermanent and empty of an independent self. The Buddha exhorted his students to investigate the teachings for themselves and find their own liberation from suffering through personal insight and compassion. According to the Mahayana path, one cultivates *Bodhicitta* mind and aspires to enlightenment in order to serve others (Sopa and Jones, 1993).

SPIRITUAL SIGNIFICANCE OF NATURE

The central teaching of interdependence (*pratitya samutpada*) has been symbolized in the Hua-Yen school of Buddhism by the metaphor of the Jewel Net of Indra (Cook, 1989). This net stretches in all directions to infinity; at each eye or knot of the net lies a jewel of an infinite number of facets. Each jewel reflects all the other jewels in the net, representing both mutual causality and mutual identity. According to Buddhist understanding, one who wakes up to this ungraspable complexity gains a perspective of the self as completely dependent on other beings for its existence. This insight is congruent with the modern ecological view of natural systems. In this view, nature is both context or matrix for all relationships and a significant influence on human consciousness.

According to Tenzin Gyatsu His Holiness the Dalai Lama (1992), the sanctity of nature inspires the practitioner to understand the Buddhist teachings. Direct study and experience of the natural world is of high value in Buddhist practice, especially Zen. One goal of meditation is to reduce distractions and false conceptions in order to become more intimate with the processes of nature (Shaner, 1989). Buddhist rituals are aimed at regenerating the vitality of the earth. The Buddhist law of *karma,* or cause and effect, states that today's thoughts, words, and deeds shape the experiences of the future; likewise, the environmental crisis of today has been shaped by thoughts, words, and deeds of the past.

In Japanese Buddhism, nature aesthetics have played an influential role in cultural activities such as tea ceremony, flower arranging, and poetry. Five spiritual qualities of nature are particularly valued:

1. *aware* (a poignant appreciation of the passing nature of beauty);

2. *yugen* (the mysterious depths of complexity in nature);

3. *wabi* (the beauty of simplicity and poverty);

4. *sabi* (the beauty of solitude and tranquillity in nature); and

5. *yojo* (sensitivity to the relational and dynamic quality of nature) (Odin, 1991).

ETHICAL GUIDELINES

The early Buddhist texts tell many stories admonishing disrespectful behavior toward the environment. Some of the precepts or rules for monks prohibit cutting down trees, polluting or wasting water, eating meat, and harming animals (Kabilsingh, 1990). These are all reflections of the first precept, no killing. Each of the five precepts (no killing, no stealing, no lying, no use or offering of intoxicants, and no misuse of sex) has important environmental ramifications for patterns of consumption and land use (Nhat Hanh, 1993).

Buddhist ethics are based in three practices: sila (morality), dhyana (meditation), and prajña (wisdom) (Macy, 1990). These support an ethic of self-restraint in which the practitioner resists the temptations of the three poisons—greed, anger, and delusion. Excess greed causes overuse of ecosystems, expansionism for profit making, and possessiveness of privately owned property. Excess anger causes a destructive attitude towards the natural world. Excess delusion causes inappropriate use or despoliation of ecosystems through ignorance of consequences (De Silva, 1990).

Buddhists take refuge in the Triple Gem—the *Buddha, dharma,* and *Sangha.* One vows to develop oneself to become enlightened (*Buddha*), to understand the teachings or truth (*dharma*) of interdependent nature, and to seek and help build a Buddhist ideal society (*Sangha*) (Sivaraksa, 1990). In the Mahayana tradition, one aspires to the *Bodhisattva* ideal, one who has attained enlightenment but returns to serve others. The Bodhisattva practices two kinds of love: *karuna* or compassion for all beings and their suffering, and *metta* or loving kindness, prayers for the health and equanimity of all beings (Kaza, 1993). Buddhists understand all beings to include not only humans, but also plants, animals, rivers, and mountains.

LAND MANAGEMENT

Because Buddhism developed in a tropical forest setting, trees have always been highly regarded. The Buddha was born under a tree and gained enlightenment at the foot of the bodhi tree (*Ficus religiosa*). Big trees are thought to be inhabited by spirits and should therefore be protected. Over the centuries, it has been debated whether plants have Buddha nature or not; the Tendai school in China supported the full awakening of plants (LaFleur, 1990). More procivilization interpretations make plants the exception to the no killing precept for practical agricultural reasons (Schmithausen, 1991). Killing plants directly as in tree cutting is seen as more harmful than indirect harm caused by pesticide use. According to Buddhist thought, the intention to harm causes almost greater injury than the act of harming itself.

Buddhist principles as they apply to land development, especially in southern countries, would include spiritual development at the foundation. In contrast to the usual sense of development as increasing desire for and production of material goods, a Buddhist approach would reduce needs and desires and increase spiritual satisfaction (Sivaraksa, 1993). Increased spiritual awareness is seen as a critical factor in restructuring the collective consciousness of society towards the environment. This could include greater emphasis on local sense of place as part of the *Sangha* or religious community (Devall, 1990).

ACTIVISM

There are two opposing views in Buddhism towards activism: one regards it as a distraction from achieving inner awareness and enlightenment, the other sees engaged social work as a path to enlightenment. Those who see activism as a distraction are unlikely to be supportive of religious response to environmental crisis unless it directly affects monastic retreat centers. The Sarvodaya movement in Sri Lanka, in contrast, demonstrates socially engaged Buddhism on behalf of community development and ecological sustainability. Villagers join in *shramadana* projects (shared labor), giving of their time and effort to create a well, a school, or an orchard for the community. Over 400 villages have participated in self-organized trainings to bring a Buddhist focus to local development activities (Macy, 1983, 1990).

In Thailand, forest monks are taking leadership in protecting village forests from clear-cutting for state contracts. Wearing orange robes of ordination as protectors of the forest these monks perform religious ceremonies with large trees. Similar ceremonies have been carried out in the United States in connection with Earth Day and Arbor Day celebrations at Zen temples (Batchelor and Brown, 1992). Eco-Tibet, a support group in the United States, has drawn attention to environmental devastation since the Chinese invasion in the 1950s. Forests have

been denuded, lakes dammed, and uranium waste dumped as China has displaced and destroyed the Tibetan population. His Holiness the Dali Lama has proposed that Tibet be declared a zone of *ahimsa*, the entire country an ecological and human rights preserve (Batchelor and Brown, 1992).

Implications for Public Land Management

Each of the world's major religions has something to offer in the discussion of emerging ethics and principles for caretaking of public lands. Certainly none of these religions will be adopted as official guides for policymaking on U.S. lands (see Friesen, Chapter Twenty-Two, in this volume). It is also true that pieces of religions cannot be lifted out of cultural context and adopted in piecemeal fashion elsewhere. While U.S. land managing agencies are prohibited from adopting a religious orientation in setting policy, they can consider the merits of world religious metaphysical views as they might inform agency choices. This may help illuminate the Judeo-Christian philosophical relationship with U.S. regulatory law and suggest alternative interpretations more in keeping with current religious ecological revisioning (Engel, 1990).

Examination of the ethical basis of land management policies can only benefit from broad ranging dialogue on many important religious concepts. Ideas from other traditions may be reframed in a different context and incorporated where appropriate. It may be that careful consideration of different religious values will help in resolving land management conflicts, especially those arising out of cultural difference. The land manager who develops a sensitivity and vocabulary around values issues will be able to be more articulate and helpful in mediating conflicts that threaten deeply rooted religious practices.

In the spirit of interfaith dialogue and investigation, I offer some possible starting points for consideration. From each of the eight traditions, I highlight one central concept or practice, looking briefly at the implications for management practices on public lands. I suggest that such experimental dialogue encourages flexible and creative thinking that may be helpful in the context of emerging ecocentric values.

Western Traditions of Land Management

From the *Jewish* tradition, one might bring attention to the concept of the *Sabbath,* letting the land rest. Though this originally applied to a desert agricultural environment where soils were poor, it easily translates to lands under pressure from over-harvesting, excess recreation use, trail erosion, and diversion of waters. Policies that allow the land and waters to rest would limit tourist traffic, closing areas off for recovery every five to ten years as needed. Forest product harvesting such as food collecting would be monitored and periods of rest included following poor years. Clear-cutting would be regulated with the overall health of the landscape in mind to reduce stress of runoff, soil loss, and loss of wildlife habitat in impacted areas.

From the *Christian* tradition, one might consider the ramifications of *love.* Land management employees who love the lands they care for will make more responsible decisions than those who are detached or removed from the area. To deeply love a place provides a powerful motivation for on-the-ground knowledge of one's region. Love promotes intimacy of observation, and this makes good natural history. Good natural history promotes ecological understanding which can support management strategies based directly on what the land can sustain. To love and respect the land as sacred is to protect the opportunity for people to experience the land as source of spiritual inspiration.

From the *Islamic* tradition, I suggest an ecological application of the practice of *remembrance.* Calls to wake up and remember the powerful presence of the land and all the plants and animals who depend on it can increase attention and awareness of the divine spirit. The public servant caring for federal or state lands can take on the role of one who calls for remembrance. This might be through education, representation at public hearings, conflict negotiation, or user group training sessions. To call for remembrance is to call for strong attention to what is at hand, to remember the human place in the divine cosmos. The public employee responsible for land stewardship can use this call to evoke high standards of public behavior.

Eastern Traditions of Land Management

From the *Hindu* tradition, one might reflect on *karma,* the law of cause and effect. Analysis of environmental problems from the perspective of multiple causes helps expose points of view, historical patterns, power relations, and political/economic forces at play. Acknowledging these, one can see the choices and policies which have determined the present condition of the landscape. One can also consider the implications of present actions in creating the future. The decision-maker observing the law of karma would take into serious account the impacts of public lands policies on future generations. Likewise, managers in North America would consider impacts of U.S. land agency policies on international negotiations for resource use.

From the *Jains,* I highlight the practice of *ahimsa,* nonharming. This means restraint from both the thought of harming and the act of harming. Public land managers could serve as examples to visitors and user groups, encouraging an attitude of minimum disturbance to life and maximum promotion of the well-being of species. This might be a broadened application of the minimum impact philosophy suggested for backpacking in wilderness areas. By setting standards for users, land managers educate and increase awareness of the value of life in public lands.

From the teachings of *Taoism,* one could consider the possibilities for *wu-wei,* nonegocentric action or action that is in harmony with nature. This might provide guidance for ecological restoration of creek channels, estuaries, and forests. Native plant regeneration from a local seed source would harmonize with watershed genetics. Leaving downed wood or snags for woodpecker homes and grubs would replenish the soil fertility. Keeping the flow of creeks, rivers, and estuaries free and active would allow aquatic ecosystems to flourish. The Taoist approach would do less instead of more where a small action was enough to turn an ecosystem from degeneration towards health.

From *Confucianism,* I suggest the concept of *ch'i,* or energy flow. Land managers might try to understand forest regions in terms of vital energy flow through the watersheds, the food chain, or the decomposition cycle. This fits well with ecological modeling, and it also includes the ch'i that moves through the people working with the land to sustain healthy movement of energy. Students of ch'i would learn to recognize it in diverse forms from slow and stable (bristlecone pines) to swift and ephemeral (hatch of mayflies). Likewise, ch'i flows in different ways through long-established indigenous populations versus new settlers to an area.

From *Buddhism*, one might consider the ecological concept of *interdependence*, the interconnected, interrelational nature of existence. This concept lends itself easily to a systems perspective, with a management focus on bioregion, watershed, or landscape. With this understanding, a manager might seek ways to protect wildlife corridors, reconnect stream channels, remove road barriers, or connect trail systems. One might also engage in public hearings that encourage community participation in decision making and shared responsibility.

Conclusion

Perhaps this chapter can serve as a starting point in stimulating conversation about the concepts behind public service commitments on behalf of parks and protected areas. In most public land management agencies, religion is a de facto forbidden topic. This is due not only to legal requirements of separation of church and state in policy making, but also to collegial respect for personal beliefs. However, religious traditions have much to offer the discussion on land management values. In the act of reviewing the meaning of different ethical codes, one becomes more aware of the implicit codes underlying all decisions affecting the land. Everyone carries a set of values assumptions shaped by personal experience, upbringing, education, and cultural conditioning. A land manager is no exception to this. Discussions about religious values can help clarify one's own personal values and how they affect one's management choices at every institutional level.

I offer this work in the spirit of tolerance for diverse perspectives and willingness to learn about the many attitudes and cultural ties with the natural world. The world's religious traditions represent thousands of years of careful thinking, consideration, testing, and winnowing to essentials. What has lasted over the centuries is what holds meaning. As more and more people turn to public lands for spiritual experience, land managers will need to recognize the role of religious values and be willing to include them in policy considerations. It is my hope that this material can help raise awareness of cultural values in current management policies while inspiring dialogue reflecting on our rich and vital relationships with the public lands.

Literature Cited

Aasi, G. (1993). A portrait of Islam. In J. Beversluis (Ed.), *A sourcebook for the community of religions* (pp. 67-72). Chicago, IL: Council for a Parliament of the World's Religions.

Ames, R. (1989). Putting the *Te* back into Taoism. In J. Callicott and R. Ames (Eds.), *Nature in Asian traditions of thought* (pp. 113-144). Albany, NY: State University of New York Press.

Baker, J. (1990). Biblical views of nature. In C. Birch, W. Eakin, and J. McDaniel (Eds.), *Liberating life: Contemporary approaches to ecological theology* (pp. 9-26). Maryknoll, NY: Orbis Books.

Batchelor, M. and Brown, K. (Eds.). (1992). *Buddhism and ecology*. London, UK: Cassell Publications.

Berry, T. (1988). *The dream of the earth*. San Francisco, CA: Sierra Club Books.

Birch, C., Eakin, W., and McDaniel, J. (Eds.). (1990). *Liberating life: Contemporary approaches to ecological theology*. Maryknoll, NY: Orbis Books.

Chapple, C. (1994). Hindu environmentalism: traditional and contemporary resources. In M. Tucker and J. Grim (Eds.), *World-views and ecology* (pp. 113-123). Lewisburg, PA: Bucknell University Press.

Chung, D. (1993a). A portrait of Confucianism. In J. Beversluis (Ed.), *A sourcebook for the community of religions* (pp. 58-61). Chicago, IL: Council for a Parliament of the World's Religions.

Chung, D. (1993b). A portrait of Taoism. In J. Beversluis (Ed.), *A sourcebook for the community of religions* (pp. 86-87). Chicago, IL: Council for a Parliament of the World's Religions.

Cook, F. (1989). The jewel net of Indra. In J. Callicott and R. Ames (Eds.), *Nature in Asian traditions of thought* (pp. 213-230). Albany, NY: State University of New York Press.

De Silva, P. (1990). Buddhist environmental ethics. In A. Hunt-Badiner (Ed.), *Dharma Gaia: Harvest of essays in Buddhism and ecology* (pp. 14-19). Berkeley, CA: Parallax Press.

Devall, W. (1990). Ecocentric Sangha. In A. Hunt-Badiner (Ed.), *Dharma Gaia: Harvest of essays in Buddhism and ecology* (pp. 155-164). Berkeley, CA: Parallax Press.

Dutton, Y. (1992). Natural Resources in Islam. In F. Khalid and J. O'Brien (Eds.), *Islam and ecology* (pp. 51-68). London, UK: Cassell Publications.

Dwivedi, O. (1990). Satyagraha for conservation: Awakening the spirit of Hinduism. In J. Engel and J. G. Engel (Eds.), *Ethics of environment and development* (pp. 201-212). Tucson, AZ: University of Arizona Press.

Engel, J. (1990). The ethics of sustainable development. In J. Engel and J. G. Engel (Eds.), *Ethics of environment and development* (pp. 1-23). Tucson, AZ: University of Arizona Press.

Granberg-Michaelson, W. (1992). *Redeeming the creation*. Geneva, Switzerland: World Council of Churches Publications.

Gyatso, T. (1992). A Tibetan Buddhist perspective on spirit and nature. In S. Rockefeller and J. Elder (Eds.), *Spirit and nature: Why the environment is a religious issue* (pp. 109-123). Boston, MA: Beacon Press.

Ip, P. (1986). Taoism and the foundations of environmental ethics. In E. Hargrove (Ed.), *Religion and environmental crisis* (pp. 94-106). Athens, GA: University of Georgia Press.

Iyengar, B. (1979). *Light on yoga*. New York, NY: Schocken Books.

Izzi Dien, M. (1990). Islamic environmental ethics: law and society. In J. Engel and J. G. Engel (Eds.), *Ethics of environment and development* (pp. 189-198). Tucson, AZ: University of Arizona Press.

Izzi Dien, M. (1992). Islamic ethics and the environment. In F. Khalid and J. O'Brien (Eds.), *Islam and ecology* (pp. 25-36). London, UK: Cassell Publications.

Jain, N. (1993). A portrait of Jainism. In J. Beversluis (Ed.), *A source book for the community of religion* (pp. 76-79). Chicago, IL: Council for a Parliament of the World's Religions.

Kabilsingh, C. (1990). Early Buddhist views on nature. In A. Hunt-Badiner (Ed.), *Dharma Gaia: Harvest of essays in Buddhism and ecology* (pp. 8-13). Berkeley, CA: Parallax Press.

Katz, E. (1994). Judaism and the ecological crisis. In M. Tucker J. and Grim (Eds.), *World-views and ecology* (pp. 55-90). Lewisburg, PA: Bucknell University Press.

Kaza, S. (1993). Planting seeds of joy. In F. Hull (Ed.), *Earth and spirit: The spiritual dimension of the environmental crisis* (pp. 137-148). New York, NY: Continuum.

LaFleur, W. (1990). Sattva—Enlightenment for plants and trees. In A. Hunt-Badiner (Ed.), *Dharma Gaia: Harvest of essays in Buddhism and ecology* (pp. 136-144). Berkeley, CA: Parallax Press.

Macy, J. (1983). *Dharma and development*. West Hartford, CT: Kumarian.

Macy, J. (1990). The greening of the self. In A. Hunt-Badiner (Ed.). *Dharma Gaia: Harvest of essays in Buddhism and ecology* (pp. 136-144). Berkeley, CA: Parallax Press.

McDaniel, J. (1990). *Earth, sky, gods, and mortal: Developing an ecological spirituality*. Mystic, CT: Twenty-Third Publications.

McDaniel, J. (1993). Ecological Christianity: Dialogue with Buddhist and Native-American traditions. *Ecojustice Quarterly, 13* (4),12-15.

McFague, S. (1992). A square in the quilt: One theologian's contribution to the planetary agenda. In S. Rockefeller and J. Elder (Eds.), *Spirit and nature: Why the environment is a religious issue* (pp. 39-58). Boston, MA: Beacon Press.

Morton, J. (1993). Environment and religion: The evolution of a new vision. In F. Hull (Ed.), *Earth and spirit: The spiritual dimension of the environmental crisis* (pp. 119-132). New York, NY: Continuum.

Nash, J. (1991). *Loving nature: Ecological integrity and Christian responsibility.* Nashville, TN: Abingdon Press.

Nasr, S. (1992). Islam and the environmental crisis. In S. Rockefeller and J. Elder (Eds.), *Spirit and nature: Why the environment is a religious issue* (pp. 83-108). Boston, MA: Beacon Press.

Nasr, S. (1993). *The need for a sacred science.* Albany, NY: State University of New York Press.

Nhat Hanh, T. (1993). *For a future to be possible.* Berkeley, CA: Parallax Press.

Odin, S. (1991). The Japanese concept of nature in relation to the environmental ethics and conservation aesthetics of Aldo Leopold. *Environmental Ethics, 13*(4), 345-360.

Page, R. (1992). The Bible and the natural world. In E. Breuilly and M. Palmer (Eds.), *Christianity and ecology* (pp. 20-34). London, UK: Cassell Publications.

Palmer, M. (1992). The Protestant tradition. In E. Breuilly and M. Palmer (Eds.), *Christianity and ecology* (pp. 86-96). London: Cassell Publications.

Pick, P. (1992). Tu Bi Shavat: A happy new year to all trees. In A. Rose (Ed.), *Judaism and ecology.* London, UK: Cassell Publications.

Prime, R. (1992). *Hinduism and ecology: Seeds of truth.* London, UK: Cassell Publications.

Rajotte, F. and Breuilly, E. (1992). Treatment for the earth's sickness—the church's role. In E. Breuilly and M. Palmer (Eds.), *Christianity and ecology* (pp. 98-108). London, UK: Cassell Publications.

Rockefeller, S. and Elder, J. (Eds.). (1992). *Spirit and nature: Why the environment is a religious issue.* Boston, MA: Beacon Press.

Rose, A. (Ed.). (1992). *Judaism and ecology.* London, UK: Cassell Publications.

Schmithausen, L. (1991). The problem of the sentience of plants in earliest Buddhism. *Studia Philologica Buddhica Monograph Series VI.* Tokyo: International Institute for Buddhist Studies.

Schorsch, I. (1992). Learning to live with less: a Jewish perspective. In S. Rockefeller and J. Elder (Eds.), *Spirit and nature: Why the environment is a religious issue* (pp. 25-38). Boston, MA: Beacon Press.

Shaner, D. (1989). The Japanese experience of nature. In J. Callicott and R. Ames (Eds.), *Nature in Asian traditions of thought* (pp. 163-182). Albany, NY: State University of New York Press.

Singhri, L. M. (1993). *The Jain declaration on nature.* Cincinnati, OH: Federation of Jain Associations in North America.

Sivaraksa, S. (1990). A Buddhist perception of a desirable society. In J. Engel and J. G. Engel (Eds.), *Ethics of environment and development* (pp. 213-221). Tucson, AZ: University of Arizona Press.

Sivaraksa, S. (1993). *Seeds of peace.* Berkeley, CA: Parallax Press.

Solomon, N. (1992). Judaism and the environment. In A. Rose (Ed.), *Judaism and ecology* (pp. 19-53). London, UK: Cassell Publications.

Sopa, G. and Jones, E. (1993). A portrait of Buddhism. In J. Beversluis (Ed.), *A sourcebook for the community of religions* (pp. 45-47). Chicago, IL: Council for a Parliament of the World's Religions.

Swimme, B. and Berry, T. (1992). *The universe story.* San Francisco, CA: Harper.

Timm, R. (1994). The ecological fallout of Islamic creation theology. In M. Tucker and J. Grim (Eds.), *World-views and ecology* (pp. 83-95). Lewisburg, PA: Bucknell University Press.

Tucker, M. (1994). Ecological themes in Taoism and Confucianism. In M. Tucker, and J. Grim (Eds.), *World-views and ecology* (pp. 150-162). Lewisburg, PA: Bucknell University Press.

Vadillo, U. and Khalid, F. (1992). Trade and commerce in Islam. In F. Khalid and J. O'Brien (Eds.), *Islam and ecology.* London, UK: Cassell Publications.

Venkateswaran, T. (1993). A Portrait of Hinduism. In J. Beversluis (Ed.), *A sourcebook for the community of religions* (pp. 62-66). Chicago, IL: Council for a Parliament of the World's Religions.

Wei-ming, T. (1989). The continuity of being: Chinese visions of nature. In J. Callicott and R. Ames (Eds.), *Nature in Asian traditions of thought* (pp. 67-78). Albany, NY: State University of New York Press.

Additional Reading

Beversluis, J. (Ed.). (1993). *A sourcebook for the community of religions.* Chicago, IL: Council for a Parliament of the World's Religions.

Breuilly, E. and Palmer, M. (Eds.). (1992). *Christianity and ecology.* London: Cassell Publications.

Engel, J. and Engel, J. G. (Eds.). (1990). *Ethics of environment and development.* Tucson, AZ: University of Arizona Press.

Helfand, J. (1986). The earth is the Lord's: Judaism and environmental ethics. In E. Hargrove (Ed.), *Religion and environmental crisis* (pp. 38-52). Athens, GA: University of Georgia Press.

Hull, F. (Ed.). (1993). *Earth and spirit: The spiritual dimension of the environmental crisis*. New York, NY: Continuum Publishing Corp.

Hunt-Badiner, A. (Ed.). (1990). *Dharma Gaia: Harvest of essays in Buddhism and ecology*. Berkeley, CA: Parallax Press.

Khalid, F. and O'Brien, J. (Eds.). (1992). *Islam and ecology*. London: Cassell Publications.

LaFleur, W. (1989). Saigyo and the Buddhist value of nature. In J. Callicott and R. Ames (Eds.), *Nature in Asian traditions of thought* (pp. 183-209). Albany, NY: State University of New York Press.

McDaniel, J. (1994). The garden of Eden, the fall, and life in Christ: A Christian approach to ecology. In M. Tucker and J. Grim (Eds.), *World-views and ecology* (pp. 113-123). Lewisburg, PA: Bucknell University Press.

PLACE AND SPIRIT IN PUBLIC LAND MANAGEMENT

ELIZABETH ROBERTS
The Naropa Institute
Boulder, Colorado

CHAPTER 4

Introduction

Viewed as a life-support system, the Earth is an environment. Viewed as one's home, the Earth is a collection of places. In common parlance, the word "place" is used with little explanation. One may say that events and activities "take place," that something is "out of place," or that someone has a good "sense of place," but rarely does one go on to consider the full import of place in one's life. In this chapter, I explore in depth the human nature interaction called "place." I document its essential role in fostering our identity, our attitude towards the land and quality of inner life, and its relevance to public land management.

A place is a spatial part of the environment that one is related to through one's experiences, imagination, or feelings. It is through place that a mobile organism makes sense of its habitat. Experiences of place allow one to orient and identify with the environment and make the world of space meaningful to oneself.

The built environment of houses, towns, cities and rural communities represents a multitude of places in which people weave the meaning of their lives. However, the places of the human-made world cannot, by themselves, satisfy the human spirit. People are inevitably part of a larger world, a natural world people did not make and do not control. In this chapter it is this world of undeveloped natural places that I am concerned with—specifically the 30 percent of U.S. lands managed by federal agencies in the public interest.

The policies and actions of the USDA Forest Service, the National Park Service, the Bureau of Land Management, the Fish and Wildlife Service, and the Bureau of Reclamation traditionally have been influenced by the Newtonian/Cartesian world-view which treats nature as something separate from us, as simply the backdrop for the human drama. This "backdrop" of commercial and recreational resources has been managed by the agencies for maximum human use and consumption. In this context the task of the land manager has been to referee among the competing uses put forth by a growing number of pressure groups and special interests, while attempting to assure both politicians and the general public that this endeavor is sustainable—an increasingly difficult if not impossible task.

The research reviewed in this chapter will clearly demonstrate that in order to fully understand the human need for place, land managing agencies need to reconsider the human/nature relationship. Research from both the physical and social sciences suggests that humans are not separate from nature. Indeed, the very meaning of place derives from our experience of connection or coherence with a territory.

It is through our relatedness with the natural world that we gain our most basic orientation to life. Through sensual, cognitive and intuitive interactive processes with their surroundings people create the experience of place. The places people experience, in turn, enable them to locate themselves externally and internally. Externally, they orient by telling one *where* one is. Internally, they become part of one's psychological and cultural identity, telling one *how* one is to be here. This reciprocity at the heart of connection with place is multidimensional. It extends from the most elementary level of physical grounding to the psychological and cultural realms of intellect, symbol, and emotion. And it opens one to the spiritual domain of ultimate belonging and meaning.

This emerging ecological world-view is taking hold throughout all culture. It is evident not only among environmentalists but also in the growing field of holistic health, the new emphasis on ecopsychology practices within the therapeutic community, the rise in educational and religious programs designed to help people bridge "the spirit–nature gap," and the quantum growth in ecology programs, wilderness schools, outdoor classes, and the wilderness recreation industry.

For the public land manager, place offers an alternative value around which the growing pressures for a new land ethic can be integrated. It suggests an expanded definition of the public interest, a fresh rationale for the importance of public lands, and a means for uniting social and environmental goals.

An Age of Placelessness: The Sociological Context

At the end of the twentieth century humankind finds itself struggling to come to grips with a world dramatically different from anything the species has ever inhabited. According to estimates by the 1980 census, more than 80 percent of U.S. citizens now live within sprawling urban and suburban constellations (Hough, 1990). Before this explosive growth of the city, the visual edge between town and country was clear and well-defined. The town or city drew its character from its regional setting. From the outside looking in or the inside looking out, one had no question about one's place in the larger natural world.

Now as the century comes to its close, suburban expansion continues to engulf the rural environment. The surrounding lands are the raw materials for housing, subdivisions, industrial parks, malls, mobile homes and used car dumps. What is left of the natural landscape within metropolitan environments is fragmented in remnant ravines and river valleys, ponds and pockets of farmland. The identity of the contemporary city now is largely dependent on the character of its built form, and in most large cities the built form has lost its character (Hough, 1990).

The loss of a sense of natural place in urban life has many faces:

1. the ecological diversity of regional landscapes is replaced by horticulture;

2. the parks, gardens and formal open spaces of most cities have been subjugated to universal design standards which further diminish regional identity;

3. climate control has seduced us indoors; and

4. cars have not only destroyed the pedestrian niche in cities, but also they have turned the natural surroundings into the "drive by" and our public lands into "windshield experiences."

As landscape architect Michael Hough (*1990*) notes:

> *North American cities appear to be places of unlimited and one-way energy systems. Living in this context gives people free rein to attitudes that accept high consumption, pollution, and complete freedom of choice as a normal way of life.* (p. 92)

The loss of regional identity was accepted as the necessary by-product of increasing human efficiency, comfort, and consumption. The bioregional influences which at one time gave uniqueness and meaning to human dwelling—the response of the built form to climate, local building materials and craftsmanship—are today overlooked as building materials are universally available and as climate is controlled by artificially modifying the interior environment of buildings.

The design of office buildings, apartment blocks and suburban housing tracts is often repetitive and bland; chain retail outlets and strip developments along arterial roads are seldom aesthetically pleasing. Streets without sidewalks, walled residential enclaves, and houses that lack front porches give more emphasis to security and commuting than to a feeling of neighborhood. As crime rates rise in North American cities, these precautions may seem prudent, but as Relph (1976) warned, these landscapes and cityscapes tend to "create an environment without significant places" (p. 143).

Humanity has been living a massive experiment. Now, after some years of this grand experiment, the shift away from what is distinctive to what is identical, from daily interaction with natural places to an indoor life, and from an Earth alive with meaning to one that is essentially real estate has begun to show its dark side. In an attempt to overcome what was thought of as the "limits" of nature, humans have eliminated the very connections that give meaning to their lives.

A growing number of contemporary researchers and analysts have begun to question the trade-offs people unwittingly made in order to live inside an artificially heated, cooled, and lighted world. They point out, for example, that for the first time in human history, exposure to sunlight has become erratic in duration and timing. And they suspect that the fact that most people are no longer wakened by the dawn, drawn outdoors for much of the day by their way of life, or lulled to sleep by darkness, may help to explain why almost a third of U.S. citizens suffer from sleep or mood problems (Wehr, 1989).

Some psychotherapists and clinical psychologists point out that modern people are experiencing a spiritual famine in their lives, and that alcohol, food, and drug addictions are futile attempts to fill the spiritual emptiness left by our loss of contact with nature (Jaffe, 1990; Johnson, 1987; Schroeder, 1990).

Still others point to the high costs in quality of family and community life. The daily rhythm of life has become a series of isolated events—separate nodes of activity between home life, shopping, recreation and work made accessible only by a paved environment of highways. Recreation is sought in mega-commercial entertainment centers—a world that has no connections with either the ecological or the cultural realities of the place. The make-believe world of marketing, consumerism and the multimedia have become so compelling and persuasive that many people now live within these illusions (Sack, 1988). Unsustainable stress, dissatisfaction, loneliness, materialism, loss of community, and political disengagement are some of the suspected results.

Most people quickly adopted this indoor way of life, but a number of physical and social scientists tell us that evolutionarily humans are still creatures of natural place. Like all other living beings, the human species evolved over millions of years to respond to the cycles of the Earth and sun with predictable biochemical and behavioral changes. According to the Biophilia hypothesis, this has imbued *Homo sapiens* with a deep, genetically based, emotional need to affiliate on a regular basis with the rest of the living world. Meeting this need, according to scientists such as Kellert and Wilson, may be as important to the health of the human spirit as forming close personal relationships (Kellert and Wilson, 1993).

As psychologist Stephen Kaplan notes:

if you just look at the statistics of spouse, child and drug abuse, it's plain there are a lot of pressures out there today that people have trouble absorbing. Nature could play a terribly important, although as yet almost unrecognized, role in reducing some of their stress.

Kaplan and Kaplan, 1989

This last statement is supported by comparing the overall themes of two bodies of research. Much of the research in environmental psychology, for example, has focused on city life and the built environment. Its concern is usually the negative impact of environmental stressors such as the noise, crowding, traffic and pollution endemic to urban areas (see Evans and Cohen, 1987).

In contrast, a good part of the research on natural environments has looked at the positive psychological benefits people draw from their experience in natural places ranging from parks to wilderness areas (Hartig and Evans, 1993H). Not surprisingly, the desire to escape urban stressors is seen as an important motivation for seeking natural places in which to restore body, mind and spirit (Schreyer and Knopf, 1984).

Adding to this psychological and sociological data, a few political scientists now speculate that the evidence of a dwindling engaged citizenry in the U.S. may also be a result of the loss of a sense of belonging to natural place.

> *Public life, as we all too often experience it now, is very much like a Big Mac—it can be replicated in exactly the same form anywhere. And just as our acceptance of placeless food consumed under placeless yellow landmarks weakens both our sense of food and of place, so too does the general placelessness of our political thought weaken both our sense of politics and of place . . . to put it more positively, public life can only be reclaimed by understanding and then practicing its connection to real identifiable natural places.*

Kemmis, 1990, p. 6

Perhaps the greatest problem is that what people ignore, people can also forget. While the experience of natural place is demonstrably important to the human psyche and spirit, the recognition of this need becomes obscure in urban and suburban settings. Like any other genetically based trait, whether it is fully expressed depends on learned responses to actual places (Wilson, 1984). Without such connections, the resulting indifference to nature can easily encourage the further degradation of the natural world.

The Science of Place: A History of the Research

Geography is the academic field first identified with the study of place. Since World War I, empirical studies have been the norm of American geography. Applying this mode to regional analyses, Hartshorne (1939) explicitly focused on "things" in his positivist treatment of area differentiation. This was accomplished through attention to the location of objects in geometric space, with geographers delineating spatial patterns and the overall distribution of such objects. He considered studying the connecting links among phenomena, but he concluded that it was more important to focus on "a particular circle of facts" than to search for relationships (Hartshorne, 1939, p. 120).

In contrast, cultural geographers working in the middle part of this century were interested in showing links, particularly among native peoples, between the physical environment and people's ways of life, noting feedback mechanisms between ecosystems and the human world. Culture was seen in constant interaction with nature, with people making choices in shaping both landscape and behavior to maximize their standard of living, while preserving the integrity of their physical place to enable future use. The psychological and spiritual dimensions of such relationships were not a major cause of study; instead, it was the functional realm that predominated, with studies still being oriented to "things" in a place (i.e., descriptions of their material form, spatial extent and utility as natural resources [see Clarke, 1971]).

Behavioral geographers employed positivistic methods to study people's functional relationship with place, at times looking into people's feelings for place using quantitative methods (e.g., Eyles, 1985; Taylor and Townsend, 1976). Some humanistic geographers researched the importance of the emotional realm in human relationships with place using a more reflective approach, concentrating on such topics as aesthetics and interpretations of artistic representations of place (see Hay, 1988). Affective ties or "bonds" were examined on occasion, and they were found to develop gradually through long residence in a defined place (Tuan, 1974). Tuan (1980) later separated rootedness from sense of place, believing that an appreciation of place in the latter is a self-conscious condition; he did not refer to the residential mobility (i.e., rootlessness) of modern people in his development of this conceptual division.

The material functions of place had now been combined with the emotional realm by a few geographers, but something was still missing. Phenomenological research tried to fill the gap. Phenomenologists believe people constitute their life worlds by holding objects unreflectively in their consciousness and forming a relationship with them. Phenomena are defined as the "objects of experience," which only have meaning when one's intentions and/or actions also are taken into account (Pickles, 1988). For example, a landscape business with row after row of cedar and pine trees, evenly spaced, does not invite us to sit or to bring a picnic and spend the day. On the other hand, similar trees growing irregularly in a natural forest with dappled light and mulch underfoot calls us to linger, to be silent, to listen. It is one's intention and the qualities of the setting that interact to cocreate one's experience of place.

Motivated by concern for environmental problems and an interest in the attitudes that helped create them, a number of geographers in the past decade have broadened their investigations to include indigenous peoples (e.g., Bonnemaison, 1984; Hay, 1988; Murton, 1987). Empirical studies using sensitive research methodologies were launched to focus on these people's relationships with place. These studies demonstrate that the world of nature and the dwelling places of Homo sapiens need not be so dichotomous. For traditional people, nature and human habitat were one big, if not always happy, family where the twoleggeds were just folks along with coyote, raven, deer and water bug. Rituals reaffirmed ties to place in conscious ways, and storytelling further solidified beliefs, connecting indigenous people with place through the wisdom of elders. This resulted in a minimal degree of conscious separation between people and their place. They joined together to form a whole (see Hay, 1988).

In the past two decades another door to understanding the place experience has been opened through the framework of systems theory (Bateson, 1979). Through the groundbreaking research of two Chileans, Humberto Maturana and Francisco Varela, researchers are given a fresh understanding of how the human—through perceptual and cognitive functions—cocreates an experience of place out of the complexities of nature. This new work in cognitive science has begun to bridge the traditional fields of geography, epistemology, psychology, and biology.

The work of Maturana and Varela, known as the Santiago theory, is based on a systems view of life which maintains that both humans and places are best understood as living organisms; organisms that undergo constant structural changes while at the same time preserving their pattern of organization (Maturana and Varela, 1987). According to this research, humans interact with their environment through a process called "structural coupling" (i.e., through recurrent interactions, each of which triggers structural changes in each system). However, both living systems are autonomous. The environment only triggers the structural changes; it does not direct them. Humans not only self-organize their structural changes, but also they specify which patterns in the environment trigger them. By specifying which patterns in the environment

trigger the changes, we "bring forth our world," as Maturana and Varela put it.

This theory of cognition is compatible with the theory of perception developed by James Gibson (Gibson, 1979). The traditional post-Cartesian account of perception describes it as an internal process whereby an initially meaningless mass of sensory data is built up into an internal representation of the external world. Gibson overcomes this long held dichotomy between perceiver and perceived by showing that perception is a relationship between the organism and its environment taken together. To explain this he coined the word "affordances." The various surfaces of the environment afford one perception as one moves through them and they move by one. The senses are not passive mechanisms receiving data. They are active, exploratory systems attuned to dynamic meanings or patterns already present in the environment. This insight that one's true nature arises from one's relationships with others does not apply only to relations with other humans or human systems, but to all other living beings as well as to patterns of inanimate matter (i.e., to the physical setting).

Environmental educator Dolores LaChapelle gives an example of how this process occurs in her rock-climbing classes:

> *All along we have been developing the concept that it is not the human who does it. At first it's the boulder which 'affords' the foot a hold on it. Later on the mountain when it gets scary, we . . . help people to see that the mountain 'affords' their passage . . . that happens on good climbing rock. On bad climbing rock . . . a mountain may not afford climbing at all.*
> LaChapelle, 1988

These new theories overcome the Cartesian division of mind and matter and have far-reaching implications for the management of public lands and the study of place. From this perspective, developing an authentic sense of place is implicitly moral as well as physical and psychological. It calls for a kind of praxis in which one sees oneself in proportion, in harmony, a part of a larger whole. It asks one to relate to all others that live and all systems that support life fittingly, for they are the context and cause of one's own life.

While science offers important clues to the understanding of natural place, the reductionist focus of traditional scientific methodology can never adequately reveal what makes a place. Under the reductionist model, researchers try to understand the everyday things of their world by eliminating their context. As a matter of principle this traditional approach abstracts from the given to arrive at neutral, "objective" knowledge. It necessarily severs the process of one's relatedness. Place, however, has no meaning as an abstraction. Only in the particular does it possess the power to inform, locate, and safeguard people, to shape her or his character and culture, to cocreate with people the meaning of her or his life. To treat place as an abstract piece of the environment is to disconnect people from the world.

The Role of Place in Orientation: Knowing *Where* One Is

There is a continual need for a mobile organism to be oriented in space and time. From humanity's earliest collective history, people have needed to know where they are and how to be in the terrain they encounter. Territoriality is linked with this sense of place.

> *What is common to all human societies is their need for a sense of place—a feeling of living in an environment which has boundaries and identity.*

Marsh, 1988, p. 27

From the human perspective it is possible to identify with quite large geographic regions. Among geographers, a region is defined as a part of the Earth that is distinctive from other areas and which extends as far as that distinction extends. It is characterized by internal similarities of land forms, climate, and human settlement (Seamon and Mugerauer, 1985). People may identify themselves as being from New England, the Southwest, or the Pacific Coast. These identifications mean something more than political boundaries. They imply certain similarities of speech, personality, and way of life. While a regional sense of place in this largest context can be rather superficial, it does precede any academic or political attempt to clarify boundaries.

The importance of regional identity is being reemphasized today by the growing bioregional movement. The word "bioregionalism" is from the Greek *bios* (life) and the French *region* (itself from the Latin *regia* [territory], and earlier *regere* [to rule or govern]). Etymologically, bioregionalism means "life territory, place of life" (Andrus, Plant, Plant, and Wright, 1990).

For the contemporary bioregionalist, each natural region has its own inherent character, which is distinguishable from one place to the next. It is this overall character of a bioregion, its geomorphology, water regime, soils, plants, animals and birds that express the regional personality or *genius loci* of the place. The *genius loci*—literally the spirit of place—is an old Roman concept denoting the general atmosphere or character which is the most comprehensible property of any place. The *genius loci* is determined by how things are here. It helps us to identify ourselves and our place within the larger whole (Norberg-Schulz, 1980, p. 14).

For bioregionalists, a healthy regional identity requires a heightened awareness of natural place. They see the geographical region as the basis for culture, politics, and economics as well as the body of metaphors from which our spirits draw their sustenance (Dodge, 1981). Every regional place is, of course, comprised of many local places. The nearby grove one goes to for solitude, the river or lake where the family spends its holidays, the state park or historical landmark that the children visit for a history lesson, all work together to orient one's life in space. They tell one where one is in the round of things.

Landscape is still another concept used to orient people in space. It is perhaps the most common demarcation of regional space used today by public land managers, planners, and architects concerned with the management of "noncommodity" resources. It has come to hold primarily an aesthetic meaning and is often used as a technical term for the analysis of visual environments. As a result, landscapes are more often seen as scenery for interpretation than as places of human experience (Hough, 1990).

Although the experience of nature as a place is strongly related to landscape, its experiential dimensions of place are qualitatively greater. Landscape is part of any immediate encounter with the natural world, and so, as long as people can see, people cannot help but see it no matter what their purpose. This is not so with a sense of place for it is constructed in one's experiences, memories, and affections through repeated encounters and complex associations. From this perspective, the landscape itself is not necessarily a place. For all its visual and sensed immediacy, it is often experienced as a backdrop. According to Webster's, landscape is "a portion of land which the eye can comprehend in a single view, especially its pictorial aspect" (Webster's, 1971). Unlike concepts such as landscape or environment, place is not simply a condition of the surrounding territory. It is rather "a situation of connectedness" (Seamon and Mugerauer, 1985, p. 4) in the relationship between people and their world.

The Role of the Human Body

As discussed in the previous sections, people find themselves not "in front of" the world, confronting it as if it were a picture, but "in the midst of" things, experiencing them from a particular place. Reflection on the ordinary words used to describe one's gestures of orientation yields the obvious fact that orientation flows most directly from one's upright posture. People elaborate the meaning of distance, and say "far away," "very close," "near to hand," or "over there." People structure places through distance and this immediately introduces them to nearness which, in turn, forces upon their body all the modalities of intimacy as well as estrangement. Orientation, then, is the bodily experience of place derived from the physical stance of one's being. In the most literal sense, this knowledge is the ground on which one stands (Grange, 1985; Tuan, 1977).

This experience of orientation can be spiritual as well as physical. Also contributing to the experience of orientation are one's perceptual "place-making" or "structural coupling" capacities and senses. Through them one encounters the hundreds of natural cues that each place provides—the colors, sounds, smells, the changing quality and duration of light, the magnetic shifts, a panorama scaled to the human nervous system—these and a hundred other sights and sounds insure survival and give one an existential foothold on the Earth.

The human body is built to resonate with its situation. Surroundings can be felt as gloomy, bright, light, threatening, overwhelming or enticing. It is a sign of the remarkable delicacy of the human somatic capacities that an almost limitless range of values can be detected. The meaning arising from this bodily evaluation of place suggests that the human body is in constant resonance with the surrounding territory.

The Role of the Physical Setting

If the "where" of knowledge is rooted in one's flesh, it is also embedded in the territory in which one stands. Three historically distinct literatures find their nexus in the empirical investigation of the role of the physical setting of place: landscape assessment, spatial cognition, and human spatial behavior. Although I will not provide a comprehensive review of these extensive literatures, I will outline qualities that I believe are likely to increase the probability of some landscapes becoming important places for individuals and cultures.

First, place associations seem more likely to be formed around unusual features than mundane ones. These are landscape features that facilitate memory and cognitive mapping. They help answer the question "how do I find my way back to this desirable place?" or "how do I avoid a place I have learned is dangerous?" The cognitive mapping and wayfinding literatures have already examined the characteristics of memorable features. Those features of a setting that contribute to its memorability have long been grouped under the term "legibility" (Lynch, 1960). The more one is familiar with a particular region, the smaller and more detailed these memory referents may be. While a first-time tourist in the desert southwest may only notice the large arches and mesas, the person who lives nearby or is a frequent traveler to the region may find legibility in the positioning of a few creosote bushes.

Garling, Lindberg, Carreiras, and Book (1986) provide a somewhat more detailed analysis suggesting three characteristics of easily remembered environments:

1. differentiation,
2. degree of visual access, and
3. the complexity of the spatial layout.

Differentiation is the degree to which parts of the environment are unusual or distinctive, visual access the degree to which the environment is easily seen, and the complexity of the spatial layout is the amount of information that must be comprehended to move through a particular environment. In a natural trail environment other research suggests the related dimension of discontinuity (Gusteke and Hodgson, 1980), noting that people seem to pay particular attention to those locations where a trail moves from one landscape type into another. This last finding is echoed in studies of the built environment that report the importance of edges and thresholds in defining a positive sense of place (Alexander, 1977).

In addition to visual memorability, the perceived functional utility of a setting can help to foster a sense of place. For some, the principal utility of a place is simple biological survival. One needs to understand the dangers and opportunities provided by an environment. Does it offer food or shelter? Does its topography endanger one's life? These characteristics or "affordances" are those perceived elements of a place that make it hospitable to humans. Kaplan and Kaplan (1989) have developed a similar thesis into a theory of landscape preference which proposes that settings likely to be preferred by humans are those that support their evolved desire "to seek and make sense of information."

Other theories focus on landscape aesthetics with emphasis on the physical characteristics of vegetation or rock forms (Daniel and Schroeder, 1979; Zube, Sell, and Taylor, 1982). In a comprehensive phenomenological analysis of the meaning of place in human orientation and identification, Norberg-Schulz (1980) identifies three types of landscape:

1. the "cosmic" landscape of the desert;
2. the "classical" landscape of valleys, hills and basins; and
3. the "romantic" landscape of forest and mountain.

Each landscape is analyzed for its typology and physical features, its impact on regional identity and the localized sense of place experienced within it. This type of interpretive study and subjective analysis offers excellent insight into the meaning of a place's *genius loci* as well as the meaning of ecological and cultural "fitting."

If one gains one's existential foothold in space by being able to orient oneself, knowing where one is, one also has to be able to identify oneself with the environment; that is, one has to know how one is in a certain place.

The Role of Place in Personal Identity and Character: Knowing *How* One Is

For the adult human being, feelings, expectations, and ideas about natural places grow out of a life's unique and shared experiences. This identification process occurs as one grows up. The child grows up in green, brown or gray spaces, she or he walks or plays on concrete, earth or moss under a cloudy or serene sky, she or he grasps and touches hard or soft things, she or he experiences heat and cold. Thus, the child interacts with the environment and develops perceptual patterns or structures which determine her or his future experiences.

This knowledge of place can be direct and intimate or it can be indirect and mediated by symbols. One may know a state park intimately after repeated family holidays there, while one only knows about the Grand Canyon through stories or movies. While most research suggests that direct experience of natural places is most influential in developing a psychological bond with nature, it is characteristic of human symbol-making species that one can become passionately attached to, influenced by, and identified with places of which one has only limited sensory experiences.

As other chapters in this volume testify, the patterns or affordances people register and the meanings they make of them as they grow are strongly influenced by their cultural upbringing. Anthropological research demonstrates that culture can influence personal perception to such a degree that different people will have significantly different experiences of the same place. For example, in the same natural region, the semiarid plateaus and mesas of northwestern New Mexico, five groups of people live quite close to each other (Hopi, Navaho, Hispanic, Old Settler, and New Age newcomer), but each maintains its distinctive world-view and particular life ways.

By keeping the encounters and the stories fresh, a culture keeps the places themselves alive in the collective imagination. Throughout history, the communal life is filled with stories about places known for their good views, their good fishing, their dangerous spots. There are the places people go for solitude, and the areas sports enthusiasts gather.

There are places young people are taken for certain teaching, and places where the dead are buried. In all cultures some places are recognized as numinous, loaded with meaning and power. These particular locales come to be recognized as important or sacred because of the repeated stories that are told about them. It is the remembered place that excites and directs the mythic imagination of a people (Snyder, 1990).

All people share the search for meaning and rootedness in a place. Like trees, people spring from somewhere and the human search for connectedness with the Earth and each other is universal. One's search for a sense of place links one on a horizontal level. Surrounding the experience of how one relates to a particular place is that of how this place relates to its larger context, the space around it. This longing to feel integrated is coded in one's DNA—it is the desire for what Jung (1960) calls a "kinship with all things." To identify with a place is to belong to it, and to belong is to feel human.

Within the global environmental movement, new forms of activism and ecophilosophy such as deep ecology and ecofeminism emphasize the need for individuals to expand their sense of self to include all life forms, as well as ecosystems and the planet Earth itself. By developing this "ecological" self, deep ecologists argue that environmentally responsible behaviors will follow more spontaneously, as a function of self-interest (Bragg, 1994). This ecological construct of the self involves a belief in the fundamental connectedness of human beings with the rest of the natural world. Experiencing ecological self involves seeing oneself as part of an encompassing biophysical/psychological/spiritual relationship and one's behavior as contingent on the state of being of others in this relationship (e.g., plants, animals, humans, the atmosphere, landscapes). What is focal in the ecological construct of self is not the ego self, but the relationships of the person to the natural environment (including other human beings).

Another body of sociological and psychological research suggests specific ways in which people's encounter with natural places, particularly places that feel wild or undomesticated, can contribute to such an ecological self. Two interrelated conditions from which many people living in the modern world suffer—anomie and alienation—are pointed to as examples. An anomic person finds himself or her-self faced with myriad choices in life, bombarded by stimuli, moving rapidly through a set of unrelated experiences in a condition of separation. As Richard Mitchell notes, such a person feels "unsupported by significant others, free to choose from meaningless alternatives, without direction or purpose, bound by no constraint, guided by no path, comforted by no faith" (Mitchell, 1983, p. 173). The anomic person feels adrift, pushed about, and plagued by an uncertainty that renders even routine and normal tasks very difficult.

Alienation, on the other hand, occurs when someone finds her or his world too predictable. Again, Mitchell (1983) summarizes the contributing factors. When a person:

> *. . . perceives his world as constrained by social forces, bound over by rule and regulation at every turn to the extent that personal creativity and spontaneity are stifled; when she knows what she will and must do in a given situation regardless of her own interests, she experiences alienation.* (p. 179)

The effect of these conditions on someone is that she or he comes to feel powerless and indifferent, lethargic, uninvolved and lost. Researchers can reasonably say that these two conditions are harmful to human well-being. Mitchell (1983) argues that certain activities provide opportunities for people to break out of their anomie and alienation. Such experiences enable people to encounter a freedom and creativity that breaks their emotional treadmill and opens new possibilities for them. One may add to Mitchell's (1983) contention that certain activities bring these outcomes the argument that the place in which these activities occur contributes equally to the healing outcomes.

For example, for ten years the Kaplans monitored the responses of teenagers and adults who experienced nine to fourteen days in a wilderness area of 17,000 acres in rural Michigan (Kaplan and Kaplan, 1989). Most of the people had little previous experience in wild lands. The program was based on immersion in nature, and learning skills such as tracking, compass reading, and outdoor cooking. In addition, each participant spent 48 hours completely alone in a vigil called a "solo."

The most striking results of this study and others like it is the consistency of the findings. Participants universally experience inner discovery, enthusiasm for the experience, and the desire to make "nature" a part of their future lives. Of course, long before there were such programs, tribal peoples sent their young males into the wilderness for self-affirming and spiritually awakening experiences known as vision quests. These cultures understood that in a natural place in which one can confront her or his fears, prove mastery, and quiet one's life, one also becomes capable of shaking off the learned helplessness that hinders inner change. It becomes easier for one to figure out what matters and what doesn't. Life becomes deeper, more meaningful, and more vital.

The number of outdoor programs and schools that now use public lands as a teaching place confirm that the unfamiliar and relatively wild nature of the place experienced contributes to the achievement of their goal of personal transformation. Gerald Golins researched how such programs impel a psychological shift in many people and how the natural environment contributes to this process. One way is through its evocative quality. Wild places are unfamiliar and captivating. They engage the person's senses and increase her or his receptivity to the surrounding stimuli, thus increasing the likelihood of developing a deep sense of connection to the place and expanded sense of self (Golins, 1978).

Historian Roderick Nash reminds us that etymologically the root of the word "wild" was "will" with a descriptive meaning of self-willed, willful, or uncontrollable. Wilderness is self-willed land or self-willed place (Nash, 1988). The opposite of wild is domesticated. Domesticated places are tame, cultivated, controlled, and predictable. While there is a clear need for domesticated natural settings, (places which reassure us with their familiarity and utility), the research in this area points to the fact that a great many of the psychological and spiritual benefits derived from place experiences are predicated upon an encounter with that which is unfamiliar, unknown and uncontrolled—the wild.

Stephen Bacon has analyzed the Outward Bound process and his thinking reveals yet another way in which the outdoors contributes to the inner healing of the people who go there. He speaks of the importance of sacred place. Implicit in the experience of sacred place is the concept of transformation and change. When one experiences a natural place, especially in the context of programs like the wilderness solo or vision quest, one accepts the

possibility that some kind of transformation may occur. This acceptance may not be conscious but it is there, and it makes change, growth, and healing possible (Bacon, 1983).

Kaplan and Talbot (1983) similarly argue that wild places offer a larger framework to life and rich possibilities not considered before. The visitor is in another world and the world is a coherent place. "Coherence" is the sense of continuity, a perceived interrelatedness of all the perceived elements of the situation (Kaplan and Talbot, 1983). This coherence is not dependent on the scale of the place or the aesthetics of the setting, but is rather a consistency between what one sees and what one knows about the world as a whole:

> *It is coherent not because it matches one's ways in the everyday world (which, of course, it does not do) but because it feels 'real,' because it matches some sort of intention of the way things ought to be, of the ways things really are, beneath the surface layers of culture and civilization.*
>
> Kaplan and Talbot, 1983, p. 191

When people perceive this coherence between self and place the world seems to fit together. Their experience of place in the natural world suggests the possibility of returning to the day-to-day world from this special "other" world and finding coherence there as well.

Finally, traveling through a wild area or spending extended time alone in one place requires a step-by-step attitude toward one's tasks—a kind of pacing—that can lead to a meditative or contemplative state. This is an advanced state of awareness and of being totally one with what is happening, while remaining fully attentive and aware. This finding is supported by Kaplan and Talbot (1983) who concur that after a person experiences an increase in self-confidence and a feeling of tranquility, there comes an inclination toward contemplation. They posit that this is made possible by the high degree of compatibility between environmental patterns, the inclinations of the individual, and the actions required by the place.

This compatibility and contemplative experience can be very liberating. It can lead to a new intensity of contact with nature, a fascination with it, and a desire to become related to the natural world in a meaningful way. In the end it may be a spiritual experience. They "feel a sense of union with something that is lasting, that is of enormous importance and that they perceive as larger than they are" (Kaplan and Talbot, 1983, p. 195).

Role of Place in the Spiritual Life: Knowing *Who* One Is

While the importance of public lands in cultivating the cultural and psychological sense of place in human life is increasingly being researched and recognized, the role of public lands in orienting and influencing the spiritual life is rarely discussed. The first amendment of the U.S. Constitution frequently is cited as the reason to avoid all such discussion. This wholesale dismissal of the topic not only neglects an important role of public lands, but also serves to obscure the difference between organized religion and one's personal inner journey. It also negates the essential connection between some religions, specifically Native-American religions, and sacred lands (see Friesen, Chapter Twenty-Two, in this volume).

In this chapter, I use the term "spiritual" to refer to the experience of "being related to or in touch with an 'other' that transcends one's individual sense of self and gives meaning to one's life at a deeper than intellectual level" (Schroeder, 1990). In the spiritual experience, therefore, one encounters something greater than oneself. One need not conceptualize the "other" that one encounters in any traditional religious terms.

In classical Western theology, there has been the tendency to "dis-place" the spiritual phenomena experienced. Many contemporary theological texts define spirit solely in abstract terms. Unfortunately, this has lent the study of spirituality a certain rarefied unsubstantial quality. Similarly, the tendency to focus on extraordinary mystical experiences serves to remove spirituality still further from the natural world. As a result, a certain anemic unreality is often connected with the word "spirituality" today.

Both the word and the subject deserve better than this. Spirituality can be understood in such a way as not to exclude the palpable context of one's lived experience of the great mystery of life. Theology may choose to explore ideas more abstractly— within the context of eternity—but for many people the spiritual life is, for the most part, tied to the particular. Listen to Thoreau as he describes the effect of a particular place on him:

> *I see, smell, taste, hear, feel that everlasting Something to which we are allied, at once our maker, our abode, our destiny, our very Selves . . . the actual glory of the universe.*
> Thoreau, 1983

While a distinction between the spiritual and the physical is valid, the spiritual and the material are not necessarily isolated realms. A place will be both material or spiritual depending on how we approach it (Roberts and Amidon, 1991). What then does it mean to experience spirit within the context of a natural place? Several themes emerge in the literature.

First, the need to remove oneself from the familiar, the predictable, the human, in order to hear the voice of spirit is perhaps the most well-documented use of nature for spiritual encounter. The emphasis here is usually on the role of wilderness. The domesticated world is typically felt to be too predictable to approach what Rudolf Otto ([1923] 1958) describes as the "mysterium tremendum," the disturbing, life-changing, encounter of the holy.

Historically this encounter occurs in the wild beyond the boundaries of city and town. The Buddha reached enlightenment under the bo tree on the floodplain of the Ganges. Moses was instructed to take off his shoes so as to respect the sacred ground on which he stood before the burning bush on Mount Horeb. Jesus went into the desert to seek his vision. Mohammed first heard the voice of the angel Gabriel in the lonely cave on Mount Hira outside of Mecca. The Native Americans of the Pacific Northwest still refer to Mount Rainer as Tahoma, "The Mount That Was God" (Lane, 1988).

Mountains and deserts, in part because they were historically difficult for human settlement, have always absorbed the spiritual imagination in one way or another. As Dante describes in the *Divine Comedy*, "midway on the journey in my life," I found myself "within a forest dark," on the way toward a distant "seven story mountain." These are the wild places of undiscovered self that Carl Jung (1960) described and Mircea Eliade found as a pattern in mythologies around the world. Such places have been absorbed within the unconscious mind, the remembrance and reverence for that which is so much more than us (Eliade, 1959).

A second theme found among those who write of their spiritual encounters in the natural world is the experience of being part of a larger whole (Rockefeller and Elder, 1992). Walking slowly through a vast valley as rose begins to tint the sky behind Colorado's Sangre de Cristo range, it may strike one that she or he is only an infinitesimal flicker in the great scheme of things, a feeling altogether different from feeling like just another gnat during rush hour. This perception of being a very small fish in a very big pond, called the "diminutive effect" by some environmental psychologists (Gallagher, 1993), enables one to see oneself in proportion and in a fitting manner relating to all other beings that live and support life. It is the sense that everything is valuable in and for itself and that the whole forms a unity in which each being, including oneself, has a place. It is the beginning of natural piety.

This expanded sense of identification with nature, what deep ecologist Joanna Macy (1993) calls "the greening of the self," is finding scientific support among epistemologists, psychologists, and ecologists. The conventional Western notion of the self, what Alan Watts called "the skin-encapsulated ego" and Gregory Bateson (1979) referred to as "the epistemological error of Occidental civilization," is being replaced by wider constructs of identity, what I called earlier the "ecological self."

The awakening to this larger self is the awakening to the whole. It is a spiritual experience, a response to, wonder at, and appreciation for, the unbelievably vast, old, rich, diverse and surprising cosmos of which one's self is an infinitesimal but conscious part, the part able to sing its praises.

I thank You God for most this amazing day:
for the leaping greenly spirits of trees and a
blue true dream of sky; and for everything
which is natural which is infinite which is yes

e e cummings, 1959

A third theme demonstrating the connection between spirit and nature is the belief that nature is a kind of mask for the holy. Sam Gill points out that the Hopi child discovers early in life that things are much more than they appear. The child is put into a position to learn what is perhaps the most important lesson in his or her religious life: that a spiritual reality is conjoined with, and stands behind, the physical reality (Gill, 1982). In this view, the physical world is understood to simultaneously hide and reveal certain aspects of the divine. Natural places and events are experienced as offering some measure of correspondence to the alternative world of spirit. The experience of "sacrament" within the Roman Catholic church echoes this understanding.

This universality revealed in particularities is at the heart of the spiritual journey as told in countless myths. A tree is a tree, but it also is the "Axis" of the world; a mountain is a mountain, but it also is the Mountain at the center of all worlds; a ridge is only a ridge, but it also is the serpentine power of the Earth spirit made physical before us. This is not an act of infantile fantasy, but rather a conviction that the natural world, in the eyes of human imagination and faith, functions as icon. It incorporates in its evocative powers the utterly transcendent reality to which it points. The landscape through which we make our pilgrimage and the spiritual reality it symbolizes are one and the same (Versluis, 1992). "Split the stick and there is Jesus," "lift the stone and one finds the Lord," said the ancient Gospel of Thomas, knowing the ordinary to be filled with wonder (Lane, 1988).

Still another theme found among spiritual traditions is that of sacred place. The growing number of volumes on bookstore shelves addressing this theme makes clear the developing public interest in this topic. Joseph Campbell (1974) asserts that:

> *. . . the idea of a sacred place where the walls and laws of the temporal world may dissolve to reveal a wonder is apparently as old as the human race.*

For most cultures there is a place—a grove, a mountain, a curve of the land, a spring—where the wondrous power of the divine can be seen breaking into the world's alleged ordinariness. Belden Lane (1988), in his seminal work on sacred place, suggests four rules or axioms which can guide us in seeking to understand the character of sacred place:

1. The first axiom is that sacred place is not chosen; it chooses. We cannot force the encounter. Sacred place is an experience of the imagination that affirms the independence of the holy.

2. A second axiom asserts that sacred place can be ordinary place, ritually revealed as extraordinary. The *loca sacra* is frequently

found to be surprisingly unremarkable. It is recognized by certain acts or ceremonies that are performed there, setting it apart as unique. For example, the most unremarkable forest clearing or lonely stretch of desert can be experienced as sacred by the ritual act of silence which we assume there.

3. A third axiom makes it clear that sacred place "can be tread upon without being entered." Simply being there is not enough. The experience of sacred place is intimately related to our state of consciousness. To the nonseeker there is nothing to be found.

4. A final axiom asserts that the impulse of sacred place is both local and universal. The Great Mystery can be found in a particular place of divine encounter. At the same time, the encounter reminds one that Spirit is never confined to a single locale. (Lane, 1989, p. 15)

These axioms remind us that natural places are not comprised of inanimate matter separate from the realms of spirit and consciousness. The entire surrounding landscape is infused with meaning, creativity, and its own evolutionary story. One's spiritual identity, like one's psychological and cultural identity, is woven into the unfolding of this sacred story through one's deepest experiences of natural place.

Of course, places which are held sacred vary immensely in their nature. The following is a brief topography of some of the more generally recognized reasons for places being valued as sacred.

Physically unique places, with unusually powerful natural patterns, may draw one apart from one's everyday life and into awareness of primal forces. Sacred mountains, high alpine lakes, ancient redwood groves, Glacier, Canyonlands or Yosemite National Parks rarely fail to make a powerful impact on people. Such places stand out. They exemplify an intensity of pattern or unique topography, geology, hydrology, plant or animal life. In the presence of these natural forces one may experience the glory and diversity of creation.

Places where human actions don't dominate, such as extensive backcountry or wilderness areas, allow people the opportunity to shed the self-absorption and self-importance engendered by modern society and the humanized environments of our daily life. In such wildness one can become aware of the greater context within which one is embedded.

Places of important cultural history or context, such as the Lincoln Memorial in Washington, DC, or Chaco Canyon in New Mexico hold before one events, actions, lives and places which stand witness to one's highest values. Abraham Lincoln's memorable address at Gettysburg or the events at Wounded Knee acknowledge unforgettably how the sacrifice of many lives indelibly hallowed the ground there.

Places with special energy conditions such as Hawaiian birth centers, Southwestern vision quest sites or the Hopewell Serpent Mound in Ohio give documentary evidence of the ability of places with unusual electromagnetic field conditions to favorably influence human experience either materially or through one's belief systems. Some have a level of radioactivity which may affect one's mental processes. Others have a pronounced fluctuating magnetic field induced in the earth by action of the sun's energy emissions on the Earth's magnetic field.

Healing places such as vapor caves, mud baths and hot springs are often used for meditation and spiritual practices as well as for physical restoration. Such places may be used as ceremonial sites for performing healings and rites of purification.

Inaccessible places, simply by putting limits on one's desires and actions, remind one in unequivocal terms of the limits of human power. By saying "no" to human access or activity these places convey the significance of restraint—of not letting anything or anyone become all powerful. Likewise, prohibitions on killing or interfering with the natural processes of a place are a powerful statement of honoring the inherent rights of other life.

Through these means, certain natural places have gained the power to move people's hearts and spirits and influence their lives. The sacred places can help one marshall one's inner resources for personal change. They bind one to her or his spiritual or cultural beliefs and strengthen one's sense of belonging to the world. In one's act of "holding sacred," one restores to nature what technology takes out—a sense of mystery, power and inherent value. One acknowledges its ability to forge and strengthen the bonds between oneself and the greater whole to which one belongs.

In the end, each of these traditions reminds the land manager that for a great many people, the natural world is the home of Spirit. Encounters with natural places inspire the capacities of one's imaginative powers and structure our understanding of life's basic goodness. If one lived on the moon, one's experiences of the divine would resemble a lunar landscape. But people don't live on the moon, and it is this Earth in all its natural diversity that is the ground of our experience of all that is spiritual.

Of course one must slow down to experience public lands as a meaningful place. It takes time for most people to come into a more contemplative relation with a place. And it takes longer still to conceive of one's spiritual life in terms inclusive of natural place, so that environmental protection becomes an unquestioned matter of self-defense and care for a region is a form of spiritual practice. But all of the above are demonstrable by-products of the development of a greater sense of belonging to natural place.

Guidelines for Land Management

America's public lands cannot be a panacea for all the problems of modern life. However, as "free" nature becomes more rare it can be expected that the public's value of such lands will shift. Once people lived in an age in which their greatest needs may have been for cheap beef, paper products and minerals. But that age is disappearing along with the health of the land.

Today federally held public lands are being used to provide people with an opportunity to:

1. reawaken their senses;

2. renew their connection with the natural world;

3. engage in activities which help overcome the learned helplessness implicit in a consumer society;

4. stimulate citizenship through the development of regional identity and a sense of belonging to place; and

5. broaden and deepen their spiritual experience.

A central thesis of this chapter is that those who manage our public lands have the responsibility to ensure that their management policies do not obstruct or degrade the public's deep-seated need

for psychological and spiritual connection to (as well as physical contact with) the land. Put more positively, I recommend that public land managers give high priority to the following principles and practices to foster a renewed sense of natural place for all Americans.

i. Protect and Restore Biodiversity

This overarching principle is crucial for all place-centered values. Without healthy and diverse ecosystems capable of sustaining the full spectrum of native biodiversity in North America, the complexity and richness of the person–place experience is permanently undermined. The new emphasis on ecosystem management within public land agencies is an important step in this direction, but only if interpreted through the lens of a rigorous new land ethic as advocated by Aldo Leopold.

At present, 59 percent of all species listed under the Endangered Species Act (1973) are either extinct, declining in population, or their status is unknown. Worldwide, three-quarters of all bird species are declining in population or are threatened with extinction while the entire class of amphibians is losing ground. Conservation biologists estimate that the following groups of animals may "all but disappear" within the next century: primates, larger carnivores, and most of the hoofed animals. In light of these projections, recommendations for more National Parks, the cessation of old-growth logging and the elimination of livestock from western public lands is not sufficient for ensuring long-term biodiversity (Noss and Cooperrider, 1994).

I recommend public land agencies work together to design regional and continental biodiversity reserves, including core areas and corridors, buffer areas, restoration areas and mixed use areas (Noss and Cooperrider, 1994). Such networks must be large enough to provide habitat protection for viable populations of all native species as well as encompass natural disturbance regimes (i.e., fire, floods). Such reserves will require the involvement of Congress in the development of biodiversity protection partnerships between state and private lands. In addition, the management time line for these activities needs to allow for the continuing evolution of species and ecosystems. Although the creation of such a system will be difficult, it is hard to justify anything less if ecosystem sustainability is to be attained.

ii. Integrate Human Culture Within Ecosystem Management Policies

Biological diversity will not be sustained if new ways of managing nature do not also transform how one experiences *her or his* place in nature and how one manages oneself. While there must be limits on how much habitat humans can appropriate to the detriment of other living beings, current population pressures make it unrealistic (and place-centered values make it undesirable) to perpetuate the old, tired and tiring use-versus-preservation debate.

Conservation biologist Ed Grumbine (1994) urges land managers to move beyond preserving *wilderness* to a concern with protecting *wildness* in our country. He reminds us that despite all the lofty pronouncements of preservationists, wilderness is still viewed as a resource for humans. Wildness, on the other hand, as the process and essence of nature, is the *source* of resources and of human existence. Wildness is the generative framework within which all beings inhabit Earth (Grumbine, 1994).

The purpose for protecting wildness within public lands is not to preserve a nostalgic image of nature. Nor is it to try to improve upon it. It is rather for humans to learn a sense of limits from it and to see human habitat, cultures and economies within it. The traditional Euro-American belief in a necessary dichotomy between human development and wild nature has, in large part, led to many of the problems described in this chapter. It is time to conceive of a sustainable cultural partnership with wild nature. The various bioregional and deep ecology movements around the country already are attempting this process. While there are still more questions than answers about the form such regional cultures and economies will take, public land agency personnel have a critical role to play in the developing dialogue.

iii. Increase Designated Wilderness Areas

For the present, the first step in the strategy suggested in recommendations i and ii is to continue to focus on increasing the size and number of designated wilderness areas. These lands are the last remaining remnants of wild diversity. Over 95 percent of the contiguous U. S. has been altered from its original wild state, while only 2 percent is now legally protected through officially designated wilderness areas. To consider allowing any further degradation of this tiny remnant of protected wilderness is a travesty, not to mention a violation of the letter and spirit of the 1964 Wilderness Act (Costanza, Norton, and Haskell, 1992; Grumbine, 1992; Maser, 1992).

At the same time, additional wilderness areas must be set aside immediately to protect them from imminent development. In the determination of areas for protection, biological diversity should be emphasized over the preservation of scenic lands and recreational opportunities. As this chapter demonstrates, it is the essential wildness of a place, rather than the scenery per se, that stimulates most of the psychological and spiritual benefits that are gained from encounters with natural place.

Finally, land management policies must be put in place to prevent wilderness areas from being loved to death in the coming decades. The 1994 management plan for Utah's Canyonlands National Park offered a number of recommendations such as limits on the size of backcountry groups, horsepacking trips and off-road vehicles, which are a good start to the type of regulations that will be necessary if wildness is to survive in the United States.

iv. Reduce Roads

One of the more tangible means of managing public lands for greater biodiversity and wildness is one of the simplest—close roads. By reducing road access into desert and forest areas or wilderness backcountry, land managers can vastly increase the size, integrity and biodiversity of these areas. The passage into the wild place is as important a part of the experience as the arrival at a destination. It is not in the interest of place values to provide easy auto access to dramatic places or view points. This only promotes a postcard scenic view of nature—

nature looked at rather than experienced from within. Moreover, with most of the United States already containing extensive roads, the opportunities for vehicular exploration far outstrip the availability of genuine wilderness experience. While closing roads or converting them into trails may mean a reduction in the number of visitors overall, managers do a larger disservice by allowing overly easy access to wild country; they further the illusion that one can bond with place by racing in and out.

v. Assess Psychological Impacts of Amenity Infrastructure

Future recreational development and amenity infrastructure on public lands should be sensitive not only to their environmental impacts but to their psychological impacts as well. As public agencies respond to the growing demand for more opportunities to engage with nature, a key danger is the over-development of amenity resources, recreational areas, and interpretive programs. At first blush, a ski resort may seem to be a significant improvement over timbering as a use of public lands. However, the rapid development of recreational infrastructure throughout our public lands threatens to undermine many of the benefits of the person–place experience discussed in this chapter.

Too often these well-intentioned amenities fragment natural places into recreational bits. They make it difficult for the visitor to experience a place as a total environment—a whole, a willful place—which is, after all, a very different kind of territory from a "recreational resource."

A corollary to this recommendation is the need for great care with interpretive methods (see Magary, Chapter Twenty-Six, in this volume). Like recreational development in general, interpretative materials and signage need to be sensitive to the importance of solitude, self-discovery and personal investment in the wildlands experience. Interpretive methods should be cautious of taking control of people's experience or doing more than is necessary. Undoubtedly, many hikers and campers on public land (including this author) have at times wished for more trail signs or better facilities. After all, people have become conditioned to expect such conveniences in their lives. However, it is precisely the absence of such amenities and interpretation that encourages one to pay more attention to the land, to learn more about its terrain next time, to make that extra effort which makes all the difference in deepening the human–place encounter.

vi. Design for Regional Authenticity

To foster greater regional identity, I recommend that land managers and landscape architects move beyond the current focus on stunning scenery and tourist values. Scenery alone rarely commands deeply felt emotion or long-term commitment (Tuan, 1980). Landscape design should place greater emphasis on revealing and regenerating the natural process of the region. Appreciation of a region increases the more one delves into its natural history. Further, such practices automatically include the representative landscape as well as the places with unusual scenery. It is often the less visible reference points, boundaries and other symbols of the region, which are the very things that give a place its character and authenticity. In terms of belonging to place, representative landscape is the central expression of regional context for most people.

Another limitation of current landscape design practices is the widespread belief that it can be some kind of panacea applied to beautify or mask the scars created by destructive use of natural resources on public lands. The messages about natural place that are given to residents or visitors when they drive past one of the cosmetic "beauty strips" are inauthentic and deceptive. The public, hoodwinked by a public relations device, is led to believe that all is well in the forest and that it is being safeguarded for future generations. Such environmental deception can have a profoundly negative effect on the human spirit (not to mention on one's faith in government). Honest communication is the foundation of social life because effective interaction requires integrity between the surface and the depth of experience. When one feels that one cannot rely upon surface appearances, one becomes uncertain, distrustful or alienated.

Webster's dictionary (1971) definition of authentic, "reliable, genuine, trustworthy or of undisputed origin," offers clear guidelines for landscape design and land management decisions. First, "genuine" implies that there should be a connection between the surface and the depth of the natural world. After all, there is an essential difference between a "real" experience and a "media" experience. A genuine forest is not merely the facade or appearance of a forest. Behind the surface experience is a healthy forest ecosystem. Second, "undisputed origin" similarly implies a connection between the form of the phenomenon and the processes that produce it. And third, the "reliable and trustworthy" component of land management implies a connection between present and future and between perception and action. Since people must act in everyday life on the basis of the perceptual surface of the lived world, authenticity of place renders the world both reliable and trustworthy.

An essential part of this recommendation is the reevaluation of the whole process of landscape research and evaluation methods. Present methods are almost always biased towards appearance. And they tend to leave out the unmeasurable things that are largely responsible for the aesthetic experience in the first place. As Michael Hough (1990) notes, such aesthetic measurement systems can even leave out total regions such as prairie landscapes that may be perceived as having little or no aesthetic value and which, therefore, get crossed off the list of significant places.

All of the place benefits to humans discussed in this chapter—including orientation, character, coherence, healing, regional identity or spiritual meaning—are undermined by this emphasis on aesthetics over natural processes in landscape design.

vii. Develop Public Lands Restoration Projects

For land management agencies, restoration, rather than recreation, should be the new priority for amenities management. Place benefits are well-served by bringing more people into the restoration process, sensitizing them to the natural processes of the land, and making them aware of the values of participation, while at the same time affecting their willingness to support agency goals and policies.

Public lands restoration projects could be integrated into corporate public awareness campaigns (similar to the Save-a-Highway program) as well as into wilderness programs to help disturbed youth, community development efforts, or the many programs designed for personal growth. Seeking to simultaneously engage people with place while restoring natural areas will encourage more such projects near population centers thus further enhancing regional identity and a nonconsumptive relation with the land. Public lands restoration programs should be structured so that problems are defined with the help of inhabitants of the bioregion with much of the work performed by local people, especially young people.

Restoration work with its themes of scientific understanding, worthy physical labor and local collaboration serves agency goals regarding ecosystem management well. It offers promise, moreover, of returning us to what we so persistently admire in indigenous cultures—a full physical, spiritual and intellectual involvement with the land and the primacy of authentic relationship over management or control.

viii. Support Native-American Religious Freedom

While it is a thesis of this chapter that any natural place can open us to the mystery of spirit, there are specific sacred places that require special and immediate attention (see Redmond, Chapter Nine, in this volume). In 1993 and 1994, testimony before congressional subcommittees identified 44 Native-American sacred places that are currently the subject of disputes concerning land management or development. Because the location of sacred places is often kept secret in traditional Native-American practices, these places reflect only a portion of the total number of places nationwide which are of significance to the spiritual needs and practices of the first people of this land. These 44 sites seem like an appropriate place to begin to honor formally the ongoing spiritual legacy of the Native American to this land. Further, how can land managers fruitfully explore the needs of other sacred places until the native people of this land are given religious freedom legislation which has legally enforceable teeth? Public land agencies should take every available opportunity to support this effort.

Conclusion

In the coming decades, managing public lands with regard to the effect of natural place on the human spirit will require that land managers learn to consider the psychological and spiritual implications—along with the environmental and economic impacts—of their decisions. As the diverse body of research cited in this chapter shows, the places where we spend our time affect the people we are and can become. We appear to be "hard-wired" for our need of a world of natural places. As the landscape becomes more developed and cities become more crowded and stressful, the role of public lands in nourishing this need will only increase.

Consequently, federal land managing agencies are at a profoundly important turning point in their history. The combined pressures of industrial use, preservation, formal and informal recreation are simply not sustainable. A new vision is needed: one that will guide our nation's public lands policy through the coming century. To realize such a vision, land managers will find it necessary to shift their point of reference from resource and recreation management to stewardship of wildness. Nothing less will insure that our children and their children will have the range of natural places that give regional identity to city and settlement, function as home to diverse native species, provide wild and sacred experiences for humans, and in which the entire biotic community is recognized as the teacher of an enduring land ethic to guide human cultures and economies.

Literature Cited

Alexander, C. (1977). *A pattern language*. New York, NY: Oxford University Press.

Andrus, V., Plant, C., Plant, J., and Wright, E. (Eds.). (1990). *Home! A bioregional reader*. Santa Cruz, CA: New Society Publishers.

Bacon, S. (1983). *The conscious use of metaphor in outward bound*. Denver, CO: Colorado Outward Bound School.

Bateson, G. (1979). *Mind and nature*. New York, NY: Dutton.

Bonnemaison, J. (1984). The tree and the canoe: Roots and mobility in Vanuatu societies. *Pacific Viewpoint, 25* (2), 117-151.

Bragg, E. (1994). *Towards an ecological self: Deep ecology meets constructionist self theory*. Australian Psychological Society.

Campbell, J. (1974). *The mythic image*. Princeton, NJ: Princeton University Press.

Clarke, W. (1971). *Place and people: An ecology of a New Guinean community*. Canberra, Aust: Australian National University Press.

Costanza, R., Norton, B., and Haskell, B. (Eds.). (1992). *Ecosystem health, new goals for environmental management*. Washington, DC: Island Press.

cummings, e e (1959). *One hundred selected poems of e e cummings*, (6th ed.). New York, NY: Grove Press.

Daniel, T. and Schroeder, H. (1979). Scenic beauty estimation model: Predicting scenic beauty of forest landscapes. In G. Elsner and R. Smardon (Technical Coordinators), *Our national landscape* (pp. 524-531). (General Technical Report No. PSW-35). Berkekley, CA: U.S. Department of Agriculture, Pacific Southwest Forest and Range Experiment Station.

Dodge, J. (1981). Living by life: Some bioregional theory and practice. In Vandruss et al. (1990), *Home! A bioregional reader*. Philadelphia, PA: New Society Publishers.

Eliade, M. (1959). *The sacred and the profane: The nature of religion*. New York, NY: Harcourt Brace Jovanovich, Inc.

Evans, G. and Cohen, S. (1987). Environmental stress. In D. Stokols and I. Altman (Eds.), *Handbook of environmental psychology* (pp. 571-610). New York, NY: John Wiley & Sons, Inc.

Eyles, J. (1985). *Senses of place*. Warrington, UK: Silverbrook Press.

Gallagher, W. (1993). *The power of place*. New York, NY: Poseidon Press.

Garling, T., Lindberg, E., Carreiras, M., and Book, A. (1986). Reference systems in cognitive maps. *Journal of Environmental Psychology, 6*, 1-18.

Gibson, J. (979). *An ecological approach to visual perception*. Boston, MA: Houghton Mifflin Co.

Gill, S. (1982). *Native-American religions: An introduction*. Belmont, CA: Wadsworth Publishing Co.

Golins, G. (1978). How delinquents succeed through adventure-based education. *Journal of Experimental Education, 1* (2), 26.

Grange, J. (1985). Place, body and situation. In D. Seamon and R. Mugerauer (Eds.). *Dwelling, place and environment* (pp. 71-84). New York, NY: Columbia University Press.

Grumbine, E. (1992). *Ghost bears: Exploring the biodiversity crisis*. Washington, DC: Island Press.

Grumbine, E. (1994). Wildness, wise use, and sustainable development. *Environmental Ethics, 16* (3), 227-249.

Gusteke, L. and Hodgson, R. (1980). Rate of travel along an interpretive trail: The effect of environmental discontinuity. *Environment and Behavior, 12*, 53-63.

Hartig, T. and Evans, G. (1993). Psychological foundations of nature experience. In T. Garling and R. Golledge (Eds.), *Behavior and environment: Psychological and geographical approaches* (pp. 427-457). New York, NY: Elsevier Science Publishers.

Hartshorne, R. (1939). *The nature of geography: A critical survey of current thought in light of the past*. Westport, CT: Greenwood Publishing Group, Inc.

Hay, R. (1988). Toward a theory of sense of place. *The Trumpeter, 5*, 159-164.

Hough, M. (1990). *Out of place*. New Haven, CT: Yale University Press.

Jaffe, L. (1990). *Liberating the heart: Spirituality and Jungian psychology*. Toronto, Canada: Inner City Books.

Johnson, R. (1987). *Ecstasy: Understanding the psychology of joy*. San Francisco, CA: Harper & Row Publishers, Inc.

Jung, C. (1960). On the nature of the psyche. In H. Read, M. Fordham, and G. Adler (Eds.), *The collected works of C. G. Jung* (vol. 8) (pp. 159-234). New York, NY: Pantheon Books, Inc.

Kaplan, R. and Kaplan, S. (1989). *The experience of nature: A psychological perspective*. Cambridge, England: Cambridge University Press.

Kaplan, S. and Talbot, J. (1983). Psychological benefits of wilderness experience. In I. Altman and J. Wohlwill (Eds.), *Behavior and the natural environment*. New York, NY: Plenum Press.

Kellert, S. and Wilson, E. (1993). *The biophilla hypothhesis*. Washington, DC: Island Press.

Kemmis, D. (1990). *Community and the politics of place*. Norman, OK: University of Oklahoma Press.

LaChapelle, D. (1988). [personal conversation].

Lane, B. (1988). *Landscapes of the sacred*. Mahwah, NJ: Paulist Press.

Lynch, K. (1960). *The image of the city*. Cambridge, MA: The MIT Press.

Macy, J. (1993). *World as lover, world as self*. Berkeley, CA: Parallax Press.

Marsh, P. (1988). *Tribes*. Salt Lake City, UT: Peregrine Smith Books.

Maser, C. (1992). *Global imperative, harmonizing culture and nature*. Walpole, NH: Stillpoint Publishing International, Inc.

Maturana, H. and Varela, F. (1987). *The tree of knowledge: The biological roots of human understanding*. Boston, MA: Shambala Publications, Inc.

Mitchell, R., Jr. (1983). *Mountain experience: The psychology and sociology of adventure*. Chicago, IL: The University of Chicago Press.

Murton, B. (1987). Maori territory. In P. Holland and W. Johnston (Eds.), *Southern approaches: Geography in New Zealand* (pp. 91-116). Christchurch, New Zealand: New Zealand Geographical Society.

Nash, R. (1988). Why wilderness? In V. Martin (Ed.), *For the conservation of the earth* (pp. 194-201). Golden, CO: Fulcrum Publishing Co.

Norberg-Schulz, C. (1980). *The concept of dwelling*. New York, NY: Rizzoli International Publications.

Norberg-Schulz, C. (1985). *Genius loci*. New York, NY: Rizzoli International Publications.

Noss, R. and Cooperrider, A. (1994). *Saving nature's legacy: Protecting and restoring biodiversity*. Washington, DC: Island Press.

Otto, R. [1923] (1958). *The idea of the holy*. New York, NY: Oxford University Press.

Pickles, J. (1988). The phenomenological method and social science research. In J. Eyles and D. Smith (Eds.), *Qualitative methods in human geography* (pp. 233-254). Cambridge, England: Polity Press.

Relph, E. (1976). *Place and placelessness*. London: Pion Ltd.

Roberts, E. and Amidon, E. (Eds.). (1991). *Earth prayers*. San Francisco, CA: Harper.

Rockefeller, S. and Elder, J. (Eds.). (1992). *Spirit and nature: Why the environment is a religious issue*. Boston, MA: Beacon Press.

Sack, R. (1988). The consumer's world: Place as context. *Annals of the Association of American Geographers, 78*, 642-664.

Schreyer, R. and Knopf, R. (1984). The dynamics of change in outdoor recreation environments—some equity issues. *Journal of Park and Recreation Administration, 2*, 9-19.

Schroeder, H. (1990). The spiritual aspect of nature: A perspective from depth psychology. In G. Vander Stoep (Ed.), *Proceedings of the 1991 Northeastern Recreation Research Symposium* (pp. 25-30) (General Technical Report NE-145). USDA Forest Service, Northeastern Forest Experiment Station.

Seamon, D. and Mugerauer, R. (Eds.). (1985). *Dwelling, place and environment.* New York, NY: Columbia University Press.

Snyder, G. (1990). *The practice of the wild.* San Francisco, CA: North Point Press.

Swan, J. (1990). *Sacred places: How the living earth seeks our friendship.* Santa Fe, NM: Bear & Company.

Taylor, C. and Townsend, A. (1976). The local sense of place as evidenced in northeast England. *Urban Studies, 13,* 133-146.

Thoreau, H. (1983). Walden. New York, NY: Penguin Books

Tuan, Y. (1974). *Topophilia: A study of environmental perception, attitudes and values.* Englewood Cliffs, NJ: Prentice-Hall, Inc.

Tuan, Y. (1977). *Space and place: The perspective of experience.* Minneapolis, MN: University of Minnesota Press.

Tuan, Y. (1980). Rootedness and sense of place. *Landscape, 24* (1), 3-8.

Versluis, A. (1992). *Sacred earth, the spiritual landscape of native America.* Rochester, VT: Inner Traditions International, Ltd.

Webster's Third World International Dictionary of the English Language—unabridged. (1971). Chicago, IL: Encyclopedia Britannica.

Wilson, E. (1984). *Biophilia: The human bond with other species.* Cambridge, MA: Harvard University Press

Zube, E., Sell, J., and Taylor, J. (1982). Landscape perception: Research, application, and theory. *Landscape Planning, 9,* 1-33.

Additional Reading

Altman, I. (1975). *The environment and social behavior.* Belmont, CA: Wadsworth Publishing Company, Inc.

Bell, P., Fisher, J., Baum, A., and Greene, T. (1990). *Environmental psychology* (3rd ed.). Ft. Worth, TX: Holt, Rinehart, and Winston College Division.

Csikszentmihalyi, M. *Flow: Studies in enjoyment.* (PHS Grant Report N. R01HM 22883-02).

Dovey, K. (1985). The quest for authenticity and the replication of environmental meaning. In D. Seamon and Mugerauer, R. (Eds.), *Dwelling, place and environment* (pp. 33-49). New York, NY: Columbia University Press.

Elkin, B. (1982). The individual and environment. *Journal of experiential education, 5,* 1 Spring, p. 31.

Fishwick, L. and Vining, J. (1992). Toward a phenomenology of recreation place. *Journal of Environmental Psychology, 12,* 57-63.

Gibson, P. (1979). Therapeutic aspects of wilderness programs: A comprehensive literature review. *Therapeutic Recreation Journal, 13* (2), 21-33.

Hart, J. (1984). *The spirit of the earth.* Ramsey, NJ: Paulist Press.

Hiss, T. (1991). *The experience of place.* New York, NY: Vintage Books.

Kaplan, S. (1987). Aesthetics, affect, and cognition. *Environment and Behavior, 19,* 3-32.

Low, S. and Altman, I. (1992). Place attachment: A conceptual inquiry. In I. Altman and S. Low (Eds.), *Place attachment* (pp. 1-12). New York, NY: Plenum.

McAndrew, F. (1993). *Environmental psychology.* Pacific Grove, CA: Brooks/Cole Publishing, Co.

Meyrowitz, J. (1985). *No sense of place.* Oxford, England: Oxford University Press.

Mitchell, M., Force, J., Carroll, M., and McLaughlin, W. (1991). Forest places of the heart: Incorporating special places into public management. *Journal of Forestry, 4,* 32-37.

Relph, E. (1981). *Rational landscapes and humanistic geography.* London, UK: Croom Helm.

Sauer, P. (Ed.). (1992). *Finding home.* Boston, MA: Beacon Press.

Stitch, T. (1983). Experiential therapy. *Journal of Experiential Education, 5* (3), 24.

Stone, C. (1987). *Earth and other ethics.* New York, NY: Harper & Row Publishers, Inc.

Taylor, D. (1990). Nature as a reflection of self and society. *The Trumpeter, 7,* 174-176.

Willers, W. (Ed.). (1991). *Learning to listen to the land.* Washington, DC: Island Press.

Williams, D. and Roggenbuck, J. (1989). *Measuring place attachment: Some preliminary results.* Paper presented at the session on outdoor planning and management. National Recreation and Parks Association Symposium on Leisure Research, San Antonio, TX.

Psyche, Nature, and Mystery: Some Psychological Perspectives on the Values of Natural Environments

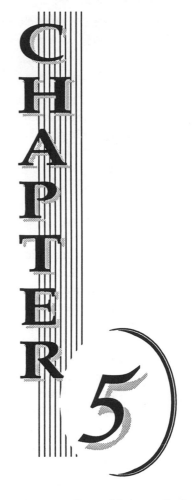

Herbert Schroeder
North Central Forest Experiment Station
USDA Forest Service
Evanston, Illinois

Psychology is a broad and diverse field of study, including many different perspectives and approaches. In a single chapter it is not possible to give a detailed account of how each area within psychology would view the topic of this text. Instead, I first give a general, historical overview of some approaches to psychology and discuss their implications for nature and the human spirit. Then I explore some specific psychological perspectives that may be helpful in understanding the kinds of values and experiences to which this text is devoted.

Historical Overview of Psychological Perspectives

The root of the word *psychology* is the Greek word *psyche*, which can signify soul, spirit, mind, or life. The Latin word *psychologia* (which later entered the English language as "psychology") was first used in the 16th century to refer to the branch of philosophy dealing with doctrines of the human soul. In the late 1800s, however, psychology broke away from philosophy to establish itself as an empirical, scientific discipline. At that time, most psychologists abandoned the concept of soul as irrel-

evant to a scientific understanding of human beings. Rather than speculating on philosophical concepts such as soul and spirit, the first experimental psychologists sought to study the human mind using the empirical methods of the natural sciences.

In 1879 the German psychologist Wilhelm Wundt established the first psychological laboratory. His goal was to analyze the structure of human consciousness in terms of basic elements of sensation and feeling. To do this, Wundt and his students spent long hours carefully observing their own subjective experiences under highly controlled conditions. At about the same time, the American psychologist William James was seeking to understand various mental phenomena in terms of how they function to enhance human survival. While there were fundamental differences between the approaches of Wundt and James, they both shared the basic assumption that valid knowledge of the mind can be gained through careful observation of subjective mental states.

By the early 1900s, however, many psychologists were becoming doubtful about this assumption. The direct observation of mental states did not seem to be leading to the kinds of decisive advances that had been achieved in physics, chemistry, and biology. As an object of scientific study, the human mind began to appear nearly as troublesome as the human soul. This led some psychologists to reject the concept of mind entirely, and to refuse to theorize about mental processes that could not be objectively observed. The psychologist John B. Watson proposed that the purpose of psychology should be to identify stimulus-response laws that directly describe observable behavior. This approach, called behaviorism, was the dominant influence in American psychology from the 1920s through the 1960s.

In the 1960s, mental processes again emerged as a respectable topic for academic research. The new field of cognitive psychology proposed that the human nervous system functions by processing information, much like a computer. Even though internal mental processes may not be objectively observable, cognitive psychologists found that they could make inferences about human information processing by observing how the output of the system (behavior) changes as the input (information) is varied systematically in experiments.

Behaviorism and cognitive psychology are the two most important influences that have shaped the current mainstream of American academic psychology. Dictionaries and textbooks typically acknowledge both of these influences, defining psychology as the scientific study of behavior and mental processes.

To establish psychology as a rigorous science, mainstream psychologists have generally pursued a deterministic approach to understanding their subject matter. Determinism views behavior and mental processes as products of causal factors such as physical and social stimuli, personality traits, attitudes, motivations, and cognitive mechanisms. By understanding the causes that underlie psychological phenomena, a deterministic approach seeks to explain, predict, and (at least to some extent) control mental processes and behavior. The popularity of behaviorism in the field of experimental psychology was largely due to the promise it held for establishing psychology as a rigorous, deterministic science. At the same time, a different form of psychological determinism based on Sigmund Freud's theory of unconscious sexual motivations dominated the clinical field of psychiatry for many years.

Not all psychologists have been committed to a deterministic approach, however. William James, the founder of American psychology, rejected determinism as a philosophy and wrote at length about

will as a faculty of the human mind. Decades later, in the 1960s, Abraham Maslow (1968) identified an emerging group of approaches or theories that lay outside the deterministic camps of behaviorist psychology and Freudian psychiatry. He named this group humanistic or "Third Force" psychology. The humanistic viewpoint holds that people's perceptions, thoughts, and behavior are not simply mechanical effects of environmental and genetic causes. While behavior may be influenced to some extent by environment and heredity, humanistic psychologists believe that behavior also reflects free, creative choices made by individuals.

Some humanistic psychologists believe there is within human nature an innate, creative potential, toward which people will grow, unless they are blocked by social and environmental factors. Maslow (1968) used the term "self-actualization" to refer to this process of growth. Maslow believed that self-actualizing people develop a capacity for "peak experiences" in which the individual sense of self is transcended or extended to include a feeling of identification with a larger reality. Similar notions of transpersonal experience are also found in other Third Force psychologies. Transpersonal experiences include the mystical and spiritual states reported in many religions, as well as similar experiences that occur outside of a religious context. Maslow (1974) believed that such transcendent or sacred experiences could be understood in naturalistic terms and would fall within the domain of a "suitably enlarged science."

Psychology and the Environment

Throughout most of psychology's history psychologists have had little to say about the relationship of people to natural environments. In order to isolate cause–effect relations in human behavior, behavioral and cognitive psychologists have typically placed people in controlled laboratory situations where a few carefully selected variables can be manipulated while everything else is kept constant. In this way, rigor and precision are gained and specific causal hypotheses can be tested. The results of such research, however, do not provide much insight into how people interact with complex real world environments—including natural environments.

Humanistic psychologists have worked in therapeutic settings more than in laboratories, and have been more directly concerned with the issues and experiences that people encounter in real life. The humanistic focus, however, has been primarily on how individuals relate to other people and to society rather than to the nonhuman environment.

In response to this neglect of human/environment issues in psychology, environmental psychology emerged as a distinct subdiscipline in the 1970s (Ittelson, Proshansky, Rivlin, and Winkel, 1974). Environmental psychologists emphasized the need to conduct research outside the laboratory to learn how people interact with real environments in their daily lives. Over the last 20 years, environmental psychologists have studied artificial environments such as cities and buildings, as well as more natural settings such as parks and forests. The motivation for much of this research has been to improve the design and management of the environments in which people live, work, and recreate.

With respect to natural environments, a major goal of environmental psychology research has been to identify, measure, and enhance the benefits that people obtain from interacting with nature. One such benefit of natural settings is their beauty or aesthetic quality. Using psychological scaling techniques, some researchers have measured people's perceptions of landscape aesthetic quality (Daniel and Boster, 1976) and have derived statistical models for predicting aesthetic preferences for natural landscapes (Brown and Daniel, 1984). Others, following in the tradition of William James, have developed theories to explain the origins of landscape preferences in terms of their contribution to human survival and evolution (Appleton, 1975; Balling and Falk, 1982; Kaplan and Kaplan, 1989).

In addition to aesthetics, many individuals report that the experience of serenity or peacefulness is an important benefit of natural environments for them (e.g., Schroeder, 1991). Consistent with this, physiological measurements of heart rate, blood pressure, and brain waves have shown that relaxation and stress reduction occur when people are viewing natural landscapes (Ulrich, 1981). Hull (1992a) has shown that even short visits to city parks contribute to improved moods. To account for these mood and stress-related benefits, Kaplan (1993) has theorized that natural environments provide restorative experiences in which people

are relieved of the need to maintain focused mental attention.

Another benefit of natural environments is the opportunity for people to experience settings that are dramatically different from the artificial environments in which they usually live and work. In some cases, people report that natural areas give them a sense of refuge and an escape from the pressures of urban environments and daily routines (e.g., Schroeder, 1991). In other cases, novelty seems to be an important benefit. For example, in a study of the psychological outcomes of leisure, activities that typically occur in natural areas (hiking, camping, canoeing and lake fishing) were rated highest for satisfying "the person's needs to experience something new, fresh, or unusual; . . . needs not satisfied by their job or daily routine" (Driver, Tinsley, and Manfredo, 1991; Tinsley and Tinsley, 1988).

Qualitative research on people's experiences of natural environments shows that strong emotional ties can exist between people and elements of natural settings such as trees and forests (Dwyer, Schroeder, and Gobster, 1991). Natural features help to create a sense of place; that is, a feeling of identification and belonging that is important to people in cities (Hull, 1992b) as well as in forest recreation environments (Mitchell, Force, Carroll, and McLaughlin, 1993). The deepest and strongest attachments between people and natural environments may give rise to spiritual experiences in which people feel a sense of connection with a larger reality that helps give meaning to their lives (Schroeder, 1990b).

Some environmental psychologists who study benefits of natural environments argue for using a deterministic approach, in which benefits are measured and modeled as a direct product of objective environmental attributes. One advantage of adopting a deterministic approach to benefits of natural environments is that it makes the results of research easier for managers to use. If cause–effect links can be established between environmental attributes and psychological outcomes, it is relatively easy to draw conclusions about how environmental attributes should be managed to enhance benefits for people. This approach to research, with its emphasis on quantitative measurement and predictive modeling, has made important steps toward understanding how the benefits of nature can be enhanced by management.

A deterministic approach to environmental psychology, however, may encounter problems in addressing how natural settings contribute to what Driver, Dustin, Baltic, Elsner, and Peterson in the introduction to this volume call the "deeper psychological essence of human life." Determinism, especially in its more mechanistic forms, leaves little room for anything that can be described as "the human spirit." For example, there may be an inherent contradiction in using a deterministic approach for measuring spiritual values and managing sacred places. Seeking to manipulate and control a natural environment to produce a predictable, measurable stream of benefits may be inconsistent with the experience of awe and humility that characterizes a spiritual view of nature.

In one of the first environmental psychology textbooks, Ittelson, Proshanky, Rivlin, and Winkel (1974) argued against defining the human–nature relationship in terms of simple, stimulus–response determinism. In their view, human beings are not passive products of the environment, but goal directed beings who act on their environment and are, in turn, influenced by it. With respect to the natural environment, they described the problem facing environmental psychology in the following terms:

> If man is to live in harmony and inspire, as part of the natural order of things, his deeper self, a better balance must be found between the integrity of this environment and its destructive exploitation. . . . The centuries-old equilibrium of the human and the natural environment—the physical and psychological accommodation between man and his outer world which allowed him to swim freely in the universe—is dissolving under the impact of a stepped-up technology.
>
> Ittelson, Proshanky, Rivlin, and Winkel, 1974, p. 3

Recently, some psychologists who are concerned about the state of the human–nature relationship have reechoed this sentiment. Calling themselves "ecopsychologists," they assert that the isolation of people from the natural world in western technological cultures has created both an ecological and a psychological crisis. Their solution to the crisis is to bring human culture back into an "integrated relationship" with ecological systems (Segal, 1993). This is more than just a matter of making adjustments in economic, social, and legal institutions. It calls for a radical change in how individual people experience themselves in relationship to the natural world.

While a deterministic approach to environmental psychology seeks to manipulate environments for the benefit of people, ecopsychology addresses a deeper concern: healing the split between the human spirit and the natural world. One way in which ecopsychologists have approached this is by taking the practice of psychotherapy out of the consulting room and into nature. Therapeutic activities are being conducted in the context of wilderness experience programs, and practices such as dream interpretation, long used in psychotherapy to enhance self-understanding and awareness, are now being discussed as a means for transforming the human–nature relationship (Bulkeley, 1991; Schroeder, in press).

Transpersonal psychology could provide a model for understanding and speaking about the deeper psychological connections between humans and natural environments. Maslow (1968) seems to have regarded the highest form of transpersonal experience to be a feeling of identification with all of humanity. Deep ecologist Warwick Fox (1990) has proposed extending Maslow's (1968) transpersonal psychology to include the natural as well as the human world, thus providing a psychological foundation for environmentalism. Maslow himself hinted at this possibility in the preface to the second edition of his book *Toward a Psychology of Being*:

> I should say also that I consider Humanistic, Third Force Psychology to be transitional, a preparation for a still 'higher' Fourth Psychology, transpersonal, transhuman, centered in the cosmos rather than in human needs and interest.
>
> Maslow, 1968, pp. iii-iv

Understanding Hard-to-Define Values

In the introductory chapter of this text it is pointed out that the phrase "nature and the human spirit" includes values that are hard-to-define, poorly understood, elusive, ethereal, and intangible. At the same time, many people regard these values as contributing to the deeper psychological essence of human life. In my view, the hard-to-define character of these values does not result from inadequacies in our current data and theories regarding them. Rather, it is a reflection of the inherent nature of the values themselves.

The hard-to-define character of these values is not a problem per se; it is in fact part of their essence and their strength. A problem does arise, however, when researchers attempt to formulate these values in terms of conventional scientific concepts and methods. Because these "deeper" values originate in a preconceptual, nonverbal domain of human experience, there may be no fixed set of conceptual dimensions, categories, or logical relationships that can completely define or describe them. Thus the scientific process with its requirement for clear, precise definitions and logically rigorous analyses may run counter to the very qualities that enable these values to function as they do in human experience.

More than a century ago, William James ([1892] 1961) pointed out that human consciousness does not consist entirely of clear and distinct mental objects. Surrounding our awareness of any image or idea there is always a "fringe"—a vague, indefinite halo of inarticulate meanings and relations. "The significance, the value of the image is all in this halo or penumbra that surrounds and escorts it" (James, [1892] 1961, p. 33). Stressing the importance of this fringe for human consciousness, James [1892] 1961 called for "the reinstatement of the vague and inarticulate to its proper place in our mental life" (p. 32). I think this call is worth heeding today in our attempts to deal with the deeper, hard-to-define values of natural environments. It simply may not be possible to completely understand and respond to these values in terms of precise, abstract definitions and theories. A more open-ended, experiential approach may be required in which the intellect, the feelings, and the imagination are all engaged.

In the remainder of this chapter I discuss three specific areas of psychology that may help in approaching the hard-to-define values of nature. The three areas—Jungian psychology, phenomenological psychology, and experiential psychology—all fall within the grouping that Maslow (1968) calls "Third Force Psychology." I present some ideas from each of these areas, identify some common themes that run through all of them, and point out some of their implications for understanding the values of natural environments. I then suggest some steps toward a land management ethic that respects the importance of this kind of value in the human–nature relationship.

Finally, I close with some thoughts regarding a particular hard-to-define value that is often associated with nature: the experience of mystery.

Jungian Psychology

Carl Jung was a Swiss psychologist who began his career as a student and close associate of Sigmund Freud. Like Freud, Jung was interested in the relationship between the unconscious psyche and the conscious ego. Freud believed that the unconscious consists entirely of old memories, wishes, and feelings that have been repressed or pushed out of awareness because they are too painful to deal with consciously. Jung differed from Freud in believing that the unconscious mind can also give rise to new thoughts and images that have never been conscious before (Jung, 1964).

Jung (1964) viewed the conscious mind, with its capacity for focused and rational thought, as a recent development in the evolution of the human species. The unconscious mind comprises the older layers of the psyche and is the substrate or matrix from which consciousness has arisen. Unconscious mental processes, by their very nature, lack rationality and clarity of definition. They are therefore often ignored or rejected by the conscious intellect. Nevertheless, the unconscious is a dimension that permeates all of human life. Even apparently well-defined, rational concepts have unconscious, emotional undertones that can give rise to confusion and miscommunication between individuals (Jung, 1964).

Unconscious thoughts and ideas make their way into conscious awareness in the form of symbols. Jung (1964) defined a symbol as a word, image, or action that points beyond itself towards something that cannot be completely grasped by the conscious intellect. Symbolism allows a concrete object such as an animal or a tree to stand for an idea or experience that is intangible, indefinite, or only vaguely understood. For Jung (1964) the key to understanding the unconscious psyche lay in the interpretation of symbols. Dreaming is the most obvious and accessible source of symbols from the unconscious, but such symbolism occurs in virtually all areas of waking life as well.

Jung (1964) believed that certain symbols in dreams and mythology arise from deep, inherited structures in the human psyche. He called these structures "archetypes." Jung (1964) developed the notion of archetypes to account for the fact that similar themes and images have arisen in the mythologies of cultures widely separated in space and time, and that the same images also appeared in the dreams of his patients who were unfamiliar with such mythologies. Archetypes are underlying, instinctive patterns of motives and meanings that are characteristic of humanity as a whole. They constitute a collective unconscious that is shared by all people, analogous to the way in which the basic physical form of the human body is shared.

Because they are associated with deep, instinctual motivations, archetypal symbols and images are highly charged with emotion. In earlier cultures, the archetypal level of the unconscious appeared in the form of numinous nature spirits, evoking awe and giving rise to a sense of "mystical participation" in the natural world. Elements of nature such as trees, mountains, and animals have functioned in this way as archetypal symbols in the myths and rituals of virtually all cultures.

Jung (1964) argued that the modern ego, with its emphasis on rationality and logic, has become detached from the archetypal, instinctive energy of the unconscious. This split in the modern psyche leads the unconscious to express itself in destructive symptoms of neurosis, addiction, and fanaticism. It also contributes to environmental problems and abuses by diminishing our ability to feel the psychological value of the natural world. Jung (1964) illustrated this by noting how we understand the word "matter." The origin of this word is the Indo-European root "mater," which means "mother." Our modern understanding of matter, however, is given in inanimate, physical terms.

> *The word 'matter' remains a dry, inhuman, and purely intellectual concept, without any psychic significance for us. How different was the former image of matter—the Great Mother—that could encompass and express the profound emotional meaning of Mother Earth. . . . As scientific understanding has grown, so our world has become dehumanized. Man feels himself isolated in the cosmos, because he is no longer involved in nature and has lost his emotional 'unconscious identity' with natural phenomena. These have slowly lost their symbolic implications. . . . No voices now speak to man from stones, plants, and animals, nor does he speak to them believing they can hear. His contact with nature has gone, and with it has gone*

> *the profound emotional energy that this symbolic connection supplied.*
>
> Jung, 1964, p. 85

Jung felt that a healthy relationship between the conscious and unconscious minds could be regained through the process of interpreting and integrating into consciousness the symbols that are spontaneously produced by the unconscious. He did not view interpretation of these symbols as a strictly intellectual process, but stressed the importance of experiencing the emotional charge or numinosity of archetypal symbols. He also emphasized that there is no mechanical formula for interpreting these symbols, and that there is no final, complete, or "correct" interpretation of a symbol. A symbol always implies more than what can be grasped consciously; it always remains open for further interpretation. Thus, the interpretation of symbols is a highly individual and creative process.

Jung (1933) also developed a system of personality types which may be of some help in understanding the different ways in which people approach nature—based values. In this system, individuals are identified as either introverted or extroverted. *Introverts* are oriented towards the inner world of concepts and ideas, while *extroverts* are oriented toward the outer world of people and objects. Within each of these two categories, people are further categorized according to which of four basic psychological functions they prefer to use. The *thinking* function is concerned with impersonal, logical reasoning. *Sensation* deals with observable facts and sensory data. The *feeling* function makes judgments according to personal and social values. *Intuition* involves "hunches" and insights into meanings, relationships, and future possibilities. Everybody uses all four functions, but each individual tends to rely on one function more than the others. By combining the introversion—extroversion distinction with the four functions of thinking, sensation, feeling, and intuition, Jung arrived at eight basic personality types. Personality tests based on these types (e.g., Myers and McCaully, 1985) have been used for career guidance and to improve cooperation and understanding among people having different personality types (Hirsh and Kummerow, 1989).

Jung's theory of personality may help explain differences in how people value natural environments. For example, introverted people often feel a strong need for periods of solitude, and might therefore value secluded natural places where they can get away from people. Extroverts are more oriented toward social activity, and might therefore value developed recreation areas where there are opportunities to interact with people. Thinking and sensing types would most likely value nature in terms of its tangible, material, and scientific aspects, while intuitive and feeling types may be more attuned to the social and spiritual values of nature.

Phenomenological Psychology

Seamon and Boschetti (1990) describe phenomenology as the:

> . . . *exploration and description of the essential nature of phenomena—i.e, things and experiences as human beings experience those things and experiences. . . . The aim is clear sightings and interpretation of the phenomenon that the phenomenon would be proud of if it could speak.*

In contrast to the natural sciences and mainstream psychology, phenomenology employs a descriptive and interpretive rather than a theoretical and predictive approach to understanding human experience. Its purpose is not to establish causal relations between events but to understand the meanings of events for people in their everyday lives. This requires approaching phenomena on their own terms as they actually appear in lived experience without imposing a priori theoretical categories on them.

Environmental phenomenology employs a variety of sources and methods, including qualitative descriptions from participants in surveys and interviews, interpretation of works of art and imaginative literature, and the investigator's reflections on his or her own experiences. From individual, idiosyncratic descriptions of particular experiences, phenomenological analysis seeks to identify more general patterns and essential characteristics of a phenomenon (Seamon, 1982).

Like the natural sciences, phenomenological psychology has developed systematic and carefully defined procedures, and strives for accuracy and clarity in its conclusions. At the same time, however, phenomenology recognizes that "existence is ambiguous, filled with light and shadow" and that descriptions of psychological phenomena can perhaps only be "imprecisely precise" (Seamon, 1982).

Phenomenology does not seek a totally objective, value-free perspective from which to view reality. It recognizes and values the presence of the investigator's unique viewpoint and his or her active involvement in the phenomenon. A description of a phenomenon is therefore not judged in terms of external standards of objectivity but in terms of how well the description harmonizes with the way in which the investigator and others experience the phenomenon (Seamon, 1982; Shapiro, 1986).

> *Through understanding, the student realizes more about his own life or is better able to empathize with the worlds of others. . . . The crux of phenomenological work is a genuine wish to look and see, and there are no external props like statistics or legitimacy requirements to guarantee the accuracy of the process. Such a style of study requires care, dedication and trust.*
>
> Seamon, 1982, p. 122

Phenomenologists have noted that people experience events within a context or backdrop of meanings, memories, and anticipations, some of which may not be fully conscious. Keen (1975) calls this backdrop of implicit meanings a "horizon." By means of various styles of phenomenological reflection and interpretation, the meanings within the horizons of events can be "explicated," that is, unfolded or made explicit. By bringing the implicit horizons of experienced events into conscious, reflective awareness, the phenomenologist comes "to see more deeply and more respectfully the essential nature of human existence and the world in which it unfolds" (Seamon, 1982, p. 123).

The phenomenological concept of horizons is, at least in some sense, similar to both William James' ([1892] 1961) concept of the "fringe" and Jung's concept of the unconscious. All three of these notions indicate that there are aspects of human experience that are not immediately apparent to everyday conscious awareness. Jung (1954) himself claimed to have used a phenomenological approach to arrive at his understanding of the unconscious. Phenomenologists have generally not accepted this claim, however, and have criticized Jung for his frequent reliance on theoretical concepts and language borrowed from the natural sciences. In a sympathetic review of Jung's psychology, Brooke (1991) has argued that Jung's underlying vision was indeed that of a phenomenologist, although he lacked a conceptual framework that would allow him to express his phenomenological vision in a philosophically consistent way. Brooke (1991) tries to reconcile Jungian and phenomenological psychology by reframing Jung's psychological insights in more rigorous phenomenological terms.

Brooke (1991) uses Jung's (1989) account of his experience of the African landscape to illustrate a central theme of phenomenology: "intentionality"— the inseparability of consciousness and the lived world. Since Descartes, Western culture has viewed the human psyche as being detached or separate from objective reality. Phenomenology challenges this subject–object dichotomy by observing that, in actuality, experience never occurs separately from the experienced world. That is, consciousness is always directed toward something other than consciousness itself.

Based on this principle (and contrary to the conventional view of modern science), phenomenologists such as Brooke (1991) and Romanyshin (1982) argue that human experience takes place not inside people's heads, but in the world itself. As Jung was watching the herds grazing on the plains of Africa, he had a vivid experience of this essential unity of psyche and world. He saw that "the longing for consciousness is a longing of the world itself" and that "the world itself comes into being in that human light called consciousness" (Brooke, 1991, p. 55). This realization was profoundly liberating for Jung.

> *No longer did his psychic life need to be contained within his European head as an embalmed inner world. . . . Jung's psychological life returned to its original place in the world. Thus he experienced a 'divine peace' and a sense of kinship and harmony with all things.*
>
> Brooke, 1991, p. 55

Another emphasis in phenomenology has been on the role of the body and the emotions in human–environment interactions. This is in contrast to mainstream psychology which has focused primarily on cognition as a mode by which humans interact with the world (Seamon, 1982). Within the body, phenomenologists have discerned a preconscious intelligence or capacity that is revealed in outward bodily motions and that enables people to perform everyday, routine tasks without the need for conscious awareness and thought (Seamon, 1982).

In addition to outward movement, the body also responds inwardly to people, things, places, and events. One aspect of this inward response is emotion. Seamon (1984) uses Wordsworth's poetry as a vehicle for exploring the emotional experience of nature. Wordsworth's poetry describes a strong felt connection between people and nature. Nature is a window opening into a deeper, universal experience with spiritual significance. Beyond the material connections that exist between parts of nature, Wordsworth points to a higher, less readily touched connection, which is felt at sudden, unpredictable moments, and cannot be conveyed in words.

> *Wordsworth suggests that if one desires to see and understand more thoroughly and sensitively, one must realize that such awareness will come through emotional rather than intellectual contact with the world.*
>
> Seamon, 1984, p. 768

Experiential Psychology

Experiential psychology, as formulated by Eugene Gendlin (1962), elaborates on phenomenology's interest in the body as a mode of human experience. In addition to emotion, Gendlin (1962, 1990) describes other, more subtle aspects of inwardly felt, bodily experience. He uses the word "experiencing" to refer to the "partly unformed stream of feeling that one has every moment." Experiencing is a broad, diffuse "inward sensitivity of the body" that plays an important function in our thinking, perception, and behavior.

Experiencing itself does not function according to any fixed, logical order or schema. It is a prelogical and preconceptual dimension, which nevertheless plays an essential role in the meaning of concepts.

> *We cannot even know what a concept 'means' or use it meaningfully without the 'feel' of its meaning. . . . If we do not have the felt meaning of the concept, we haven't got the concept at all—only a verbal noise.* (p. 5)

In the creation of meaning, the flow of experiencing interacts with symbols in a dynamic and open-ended way. (Gendlin, 1962, uses the word "symbol" more broadly than Jung, to include anything that functions as a carrier of conceptual meaning.) From one's initial, vague sense of the meaning of a concept or a situation, one can formulate symbols (words, images, etc.) that specify that meaning more and more precisely. As with Jung's symbols, however, there is no final, correct way of specifying a felt meaning.

Any aspect of it, no matter how finely specified, can be symbolized and interpreted further and further, so that it can guide us to many, many more symbolizations. . . . We can synthesize endless numbers of meanings in it. (p. 16)

The meanings within experiencing are implicit and unformed, but they are not arbitrary. Certain symbols may resonate with a particular aspect of experiencing while others clearly will not. In the process of symbolizing, some of the many possible meanings within the experiential dimension are made explicit by symbols. The flow of experiencing itself may then shift and change in response to the particular symbols that have been used to specify it.

Gendlin (1962) sees the ever-present dimension of experiencing as the basis or motivation of everything we do:

Within experiencing lie the mysteries of all that we are. For the sake of our experiential sense of what we observe, we react as we do. From out of it we create what we create. And, because of its puzzles, and for the desperation of some of its puzzles, we overthrow good sense, obviousness, and reality, if need be. (p. 15)

Modern society, however, does not often support or allow pause for an awareness of this experiential dimension. Instead, one is encouraged to pretend that the meanings of one's words consist entirely of logical and objective references. This can lead to a state of psychological distress:

If our direct touch with our own personally important experiencing becomes too clouded, narrowed, or lost, we go to any length to regain it. . . . For nothing is as debilitating as a confused or distant functioning of experiencing.
Gendlin, 1962, p. 15

Gendlin (1981) formulates a method to enhance one's awareness of the experiential dimension and to enable it to function effectively in psychotherapy. He defines a felt sense as:

. . . a bodily awareness of a situation or person or event. An internal aura that encompasses everything you feel and know about the given subject at a given time—encompasses it and communicates it to you all at once rather than detail by detail. (p. 32)

A felt sense forms when one pays attention to a particular aspect of the ongoing flow of experiencing, making it an object of conscious awareness. Through a series of steps, called "focusing," an individual can attend to the felt sense of a situation or problem, find words or images that resonate with it, and bring about shifts in the felt sense that further the progress of therapy.

Gendlin's (1981) descriptions of felt senses are reminiscent of James' ([1892] 1961) earlier descriptions of the "fringe." Gendlin's (1981) ideas also bear similarities to the phenomenological idea of "horizons" and to some aspects of Jung's notion of the unconscious. One unique aspect of Gendlin's (1981) work is his strong emphasis on the body, specifically the "inward sensitivity of the body," as the mode through which this dimension of human experience takes place.

Gendlin (1981) formulated his focusing method in a clinical context. It has also been applied in the creative arts, but so far its relevance to environmental psychology has not been much discussed. It is easy to discover, however, that felt senses can play a powerful role in the experience of environments. In an earlier paper (Schroeder, 1990a), I described how focusing on the felt sense of a particular natural environment led me to a more articulate understanding and a more vivid experience of the value that such environments have for me.

A Synthesis of Themes: The Implicit Dimension

In this section I attempt to distill some common themes that run through Jungian, phenomenological, and experiential psychology. I present these themes as a series of statements regarding what (for lack of a better term) I call the "implicit dimension" of human experience.

1. There is a dimension of human experience that has been described by various psychologists as implicit, prelogical, preconceptual, subliminal, deep, felt, vague, or unconscious. This dimension has profound consequences for human experience and behavior, even though we usually are not aware of it in an explicitly conscious way.

2. The implicit dimension is rooted in the body. It is not identical to emotion, although it seems to be allied with emotional and instinctive processes. It is a continually present backdrop for conceptual thought and understanding.

3. The implicit dimension cannot be explained, reduced to, or completely grasped in terms of any final or fixed logical schema. It is creative and open-ended, always lending itself to further elaboration and interpretation.

4. It is through the implicit dimension that we sense our relationship to the world. Motivations, meanings, and the felt values of things, events, people, and places come to us through this dimension.

5. The conscious, rational intellect may lose touch with and operate at cross-purposes with the implicit dimension. This can be a source of psychological distress and behavioral problems.

6. On the other hand, the conscious intellect can engage in a creative interaction with the implicit dimension by means of symbols, images, and concepts. This interaction can lead to greater awareness, more articulate understanding, and a more integrated personality.

7. To be effective, this process of interaction must involve not only intellectual concepts, but also emotion, feeling, imagination, and intuition.

8. The process proceeds differently for different individuals. There is no mechanical formula that can be followed in every case. Nevertheless, some generalizations about the process can be made, and methods for fostering it can be developed.

The tendency of the modern, rational intellect to lose touch with the implicit dimension parallels the separation of modern culture from the natural world. When the intellect becomes detached from the implicit dimension, it can only recognize values that are defined in precise rational and material terms. The human relationship with the natural world is then deprived of its psychological and experiential depth. Thus, efforts to heal the split between the cognitive intellect and the implicit dimension within the modern psyche go hand in hand with ecopsychology's efforts to heal the split in the human–nature relationship. This is increasingly recognized by people working in the field of ecosystem restoration:

We will also be exploring the idea of [ecosystem] restoration as . . . a kind of alchemy, through which the initiate struggles to change dross into gold and in the process brings about deep-seated transformations in himself or herself. . . . In this way we hope not only to increase public awareness of restoration, but to strike at what we believe to be the root of our 'environmental' problems, which we believe is located somewhere back there in the human heart and the human mind.

Jordan, 1990, p. 70

A Metaphorical Understanding of Values

The values implied by the phrase "nature and the human spirit" are hard to define because they are rooted in the implicit dimension of experience. As Gendlin (1962) makes clear, this dimension cannot be adequately conceptualized in terms of logical and deterministic concepts like those employed in the physical sciences. This does not mean, however, that these values cannot be conceptualized at all. Conceptualization of hard-to-define values can take place using metaphorical (as opposed to objective and literal) concepts.

The linguist George Lakoff (Lakoff and Johnson, 1980) argues that human understanding is structured to a large extent in terms of metaphors. Metaphors enable one to grasp an area of one's experience in terms of its similarities to another area. In particular, areas of experience that do not have an inherent, clearly delineated structure tend to be metaphorized in terms of areas that are more sharply delineated. For example, one often thinks about one's emotions in terms of metaphors drawn from one's experience of physical spaces, objects, and forces. One may say that one feels "up" or "down," that one is "close" to someone one knows, or that one is "attracted" to a person, place, or thing (Lakoff and Johnson, 1980).

Metaphors are more than just figures of speech. They are a fundamental means by which humans understand the world. Large areas of social and cultural reality are created and defined in terms of metaphorical concepts. One thinks, speaks, and acts on one's metaphorical understandings, yet one is often not directly aware of these metaphors and of how one is using them. Part of the difficulty in communicating across cultures is that different cultures define their worlds in terms of very different metaphors (Lakoff and Johnson, 1980).

Because the deeper values of nature are rooted in an experiential dimension for which there is no clearly delineated, objective structure, a conceptual understanding of these values is most naturally formed in terms of metaphors. It is worth noting that a metaphorical understanding of "value" itself is already implicit in the origins of the words that researchers use to talk about value and related concepts. The word *value* comes from the Indo-European root *wal*, which means "to be strong." The words *emotion* and *motivation* both can be traced to the root *mew*, which means "to push away" or "to move." Metaphorically, then, to say that something has value is to say that it has the strength to move people emotionally and to motivate or push them into action.

The concept of physical motion provides a further metaphorical link between the concept of value and the concept of spirit. In many languages the word for spirit is derived from words meaning wind or breath. Thus, moving air is a common metaphor for spirit. Air is invisible and intangible, yet when it is moving it can be felt and has the power to set visible objects into motion. Based on this metaphor, "spirit" may be understood as an experience in which one is touched or moved by something that can be felt but that cannot be seen or grasped in tangible, concrete terms. I would argue that this kind of metaphorical description gives a more accurate account of the spiritual values of natural environments than do the numerical concepts of value or utility that are employed in economic and cognitive decision theories.

Utility-based models of value and choice are mechanistic, in that they treat value as a quantitative component of a deterministic process. These mechanistic models are useful for dealing with values in a variety of practical decision-making tasks. It is important to recognize, however, that mechanistic models are themselves a form of metaphor (Abram, 1991). As is the case with any metaphor, viewing human values and behavior in mechanistic terms highlights some aspects of reality while concealing other aspects (Lakoff and Johnson, 1980). The growing interest in nature and the human spirit indicates a need to embrace a wider range of metaphors which can represent aspects of our experi-

ence that are missed by a mechanistic understanding.

Implications for an Expanded Land Management Ethic

In moving toward an expanded land management ethic, researchers need to recognize the diversity of world-views held by people who are concerned about natural environments. Different world-views conceptualize the natural world and its values in terms of fundamentally different metaphors. Researchers need to respect the validity of metaphors that differ from their own and search for a common ground of understanding between groups holding different world-views. As part of this process, researchers may need to explore new metaphors for understanding their role with respect to nature. For those researchers steeped in the mechanistic Western world-view, this might mean imagining themselves in roles other than as controllers of a mindless, mechanical world.

In an expanded land management ethic, researchers could conceptualize "values" not only as quantities to be measured and maximized, but as felt experiences that move and motivate people. Reflecting on value experiences could give rise to new understandings and more fitting metaphors for humanity's relationship with the natural world. Recognizing the importance of emotion and imagination in the unfolding of these experiences, land managers might explore ways of integrating art, music, philosophy, and poetry along with science in the practice of restoring and sustaining ecosystems.

An expanded land management ethic must include a recognition that there is no such thing as absolutely objective truth in most areas of human knowledge. In recognizing this, managers allow for the return of an attitude of humility and an experience of mystery in their dealings with the natural world. Mystery is an excellent example of a hard-to-define value because it necessarily implies the presence of something unknown or unknowable. In the next section I offer some thoughts on mystery as an aspect of one's experience of nature.

Toward a Psychology of Mystery in the Experience of Nature

Perhaps the best known writing about mystery in the field of environmental psychology has been in the area of visual landscape preference. Kaplan and Kaplan (1989) have defined "mystery" as a cognitive, informational variable. A landscape is said to have mystery if it is partially hidden or obscured in such a way that one could gain more information by walking further into it. Studies by the Kaplans (1989) and their associates have shown that mystery defined and measured in this way is a strong predictor of landscape preference.

The Kaplans' (1989) research shows that a deterministic approach to mystery is both feasible and useful for the purpose of predicting preferences for landscapes. But the experience of mystery in natural environments involves more than visual preference. Consider the following quote from a qualitative survey about landscape experiences at the Morton Arboretum near Chicago (Schroeder, 1991):

> *Awesome, breathtaking, beautiful areas to wander through, experiencing the sight, the terrain, nature controlling the environment. . . . You can never stop admiring the wonder of it all and dwell on the mysteries of nature that can create such a primitive, almost threatening environment. It's beautiful, and scary. Makes one feel totally insignificant—and alone.*

For this person, the "mysteries of nature" evoke a powerful and moving experience, including feelings of admiration, awe, and fear.

The experience of mystery is the feeling that there is something deeper hidden behind, beneath, or within what is immediately visible. What is hidden may simply be part of the physical landscape, but it may also be something more ethereal—a sense of some numinous presence that cannot be defined in objective terms. Some environments are better able to evoke this intuitive sense than others. Forests may be among the best environments for evoking the experience of mystery because of the way they hide what lies within. Perhaps this is why European folk tales and fairy stories often begin with the hero or heroine entering a forest.

Mystery includes the possibility that what is hidden may be at least partially glimpsed or revealed; but there may also be a sense that what is hidden either cannot or should not be completely exposed. Perhaps one reason that both forest fires and clear-cutting are upsetting to many people is that they strip the land of its mystery in a particularly abrupt and harsh way.

Mystery gives rise to fascination and awe and is an essential element in many religions. The word *mystery* itself is derived from a Greek word referring to certain religions in which secret rites were revealed only to initiates. The original meaning of the word was "to close the lips," that is, to keep silent. The best known of the Greek mystery cults was held in honor of the Goddess Demeter who was linked with the earth, vegetation, and the cycle of the seasons.

The Jungian, phenomenological, and experiential perspectives that I outlined earlier in this chapter provide avenues for exploring the psychology of mystery in the experience of nature. They each imply that mystery is an essential aspect of the psyche itself—that there is an unconscious, implicit dimension of human experience that can never be completely known in conscious, rational terms. This dimension of depth and mystery within the human psyche resonates with the mystery of the natural world:

> *I have occasionally encountered places that call forth a particularly strong felt sense. These places have a special magic or enchantment, as if I had momentarily stepped out of my ordinary reality into a very different kind of world. I don't know exactly what it is about these places that gives them this quality. . . . On a recent visit to the Arboretum I tried focusing on this special felt sense in one place where it occurred. For a few moments I seemed to sense a deep, mysterious silence lying behind and beneath the sights, sounds, and movements of nature. The meaning in this felt sense of silence is still unclear to me, but it seems to be the source of the peace and serenity that I often experience in forests.*
>
> Schroeder, 1990a

The ideas and methods of Jungian, phenomenological, and experiential psychology may help us in understanding the significance of this kind of experience, how it is related to particular kinds of places, and why it is so deeply valued by certain people.

This does not mean that deterministic methods and models should be discarded by psychologists who are studying the human–nature relationship. Deterministic methods are powerful and valuable tools for answering certain kinds of questions. When the goal is to make valid statements about causal connections between objectively defined phenomena, rigorous and replicable scientific procedures are indispensable. But such procedures may be less well-suited for understanding an experience such as mystery. At times they may even be antithetical to this kind of experience. When deterministic science seeks to expose all that is unknown and reduce it to literal, materialistic explanations, it is working to remove mystery from our experience of the world. The purpose in doing this is to gain understanding and control of natural processes. When carried to extremes, however, this kind of understanding may be gained at a high price. In the words of Carl Jung (1964):

> *Modern man does not understand how much his 'rationalism' (which has destroyed his capacity to respond to numinous symbols and ideas) has put him at the mercy of the psychic 'underworld.'. . . We have stripped all things of their mystery and numinosity; nothing is holy any longer.* (p. 84)

Of course, many scientists do have a genuine appreciation for the experience of mystery. Loren Eiseley (1978) believed that the greatest advances in biology were not made by strict reductionists but by scientists who still had "a controlled sense of wonder before the universal mystery" (Eiseley, 1978, p. 190). These scientists had "just a touch of the numinous in their eye, a sense of marvel, a glimpse of what was happening behind the visible" (Eiseley, p. 193). The feeling of awe and mystery that inspired the cave paintings of early humans, Eiseley says, also motivated the work of biologists like Darwin. "Thus the *mysterium* arose not by primitive campfires alone. Skins may still prickle in a modern classroom" (Eiseley, pp. 189-190).

Clough (1992) describes just such a skin-prickling experience that he had after a classroom lecture on molecular orbital theory. Leaving the lecture hall, he felt himself "engulfed by the vision behind the mechanics."

> *All around me I saw and felt electrons in motion. . . . They surrounded, entered, and left me. I was a small puddle of molecules in an ocean of molecules, a pool with energy—events flowing in and out. I felt cared for by a Generosity as intimate as my very breath, as close as the oxygen in my blood, as available as the air.*

> Clough, 1992, p. 21

Clough (1992) interprets his experience in light of a quote he attributes to Albert Einstein:

> *Einstein wrote: 'The most beautiful and profound sensation we can experience is the sensation of the mystical. It is the source of all true art and science. He to whom this emotion is a stranger, who can no longer stand wrapped in awe is as good as dead. It is that deeply moving experience of a power revealed in the incomprehensible universe that forms my idea of God.'* (p. 22)

This view might be compared to that of the Lakota Indians who tell of an unseen source of power that gives movement to the material world. They call this power *Wakan Tanka*, or the Great Mystery (more often but less accurately translated as "Great Spirit"). Similarly, an Osage tradition tells of a time when certain men gathered to discuss the movements of heavenly bodies.

> *In their meetings they formulated the theory that a silent creative power fills the sky and the earth and keeps the stars, the moon and the sun moving in perfect order. They called it Wakonda (mysterious power) or Eawawonaka (causer of our being).*

> Bierhorst, 1985, p. 229

In his exploration of the psyche, Carl Jung seems to have encountered a similar realization of the irreducible *mysterium* of existence. He wrote, "the collective unconscious, it's not for you, or me, it's the invisible world, it's the great spirit. It makes little difference what I call it: God, Tao, the Great Voice, the Great Spirit" (Jung, 1980, p. 375). Thus a numinous mystery confronts us in the inner world of the psyche as well as in the outer world of nature. The outer and the inner worlds are in fact not separate. They are simply two perspectives on the same world, and it is the same mystery—"that fundamental hiddenness out of which everything comes into being" (Brooke, 1991, p. 131)—that we encounter in both.

The effort to understand nature and the human spirit leads toward an encounter with this mystery in the world and in oneself. This is a matter of first-hand experience that cannot be reduced to logical formulas, precise definitions, and predictive models. Through the encounter with mystery one might regain one's sense of awe at the world and one's place in it. Scientific knowledge, whether gained by psychology or physics, can be a vital part of this encounter, but only if one is willing to accept that science cannot reveal and define everything. In Jung's (1976) words:

> Science is the art of creating suitable illusions which the fool believes or argues against, but the wise man enjoys their beauty and their ingenuity, without being blind to the fact that they are human veils and curtains concealing the abysmal darkness of the Unknowable. (p. 57)

Literature Cited

Abram, D. (1991). The mechanical and the organic: On the impact of metaphor in science. In S. Schneider and P. Boston (Eds.), *Scientists on Gaia* (pp. 66-74). Cambridge, MA: MIT Press.

Appleton, J. (1975). *The experience of landscape*. London, UK: John Wiley & Sons.

Balling, J. and Falk, J. (1982). Development of visual preference for natural environments. *Environment and Behavior, 14*, 5-38.

Bierhorst, J. (1985). *The mythology of North America*. New York, NY: Quill.

Brooke, R. (1991). *Jung and phenomenology*. New York, NY: Routledge Chapman & Hall.

Brown, T. and Daniel, T. (1984). "Modeling forest scenic beauty: Concepts and application to ponderosa pine" (Research Paper RM-256). Fort Collins, CO: USDA Forest Service, Rocky Mountain Forest and Range Experiment Station.

Bulkeley, K. (1991). The quest for transformational experience. *Environmental Ethics, 13*, 151-163.

Clough, W. (1992). The common spring. In D. Martin (Ed.), *Science and Christian faith: Beyond dualism* (pp. 21-26). Louisville, KY: Presbyterian Publishing House.

Daniel, T. and Boster, R. (1976). "Measuring landscape esthetics: The scenic beauty estimation method" (Research Paper RM-167). Fort Collins, CO: USDA Forest Service, Rocky Mountain Forest and Range Experiment Station.

Driver, B., Tinsley, H., and Manfredo, M. (1991). The paragraphs about leisure and recreation experience preference scales: Results from two inventories designed to assess the breadth of the perceived psychological benefits of leisure. In B. Driver, P. Brown, and G. Peterson (Eds.), *Benefits of leisure* (pp. 263-286). State College, PA: Venture Publishing, Inc.

Dwyer, J., Schroeder, H., and Gobster, P. (1991). The significance of urban trees and forests: Toward a deeper understanding of values. *Journal of Arboriculture, 17*, 276-284.

Eiseley, L. (1978). *The star thrower*. New York, NY: Harcourt Brace Jovanovich.

Fox, W. (1990). *Toward a transpersonal ecology: Developing new foundations for environmentalism*. Boston, MA: Shambhala Publications, Inc.

Gendlin, E. (1962). *Experiencing and the creation of meaning*. Glencoe, IL: Free Press of Glencoe.

Gendlin, E. (1981). *Focusing*. New York, NY: Bantam Books.

Gendlin, E. (1990). On emotion in therapy (1990 revision). *The Focusing Folio, 9*, 1-49.

Hirsh, S. and Kummerow, J. (1989). *LIFETypes*. New York, NY: Warner Books, Inc.

Hull, R., IV. (1992a). Brief encounters with urban forests produce moods that matter. *Journal of Arboriculture, 18*, 322-324.

Hull, R., IV. (1992b). How the public values urban forests. *Journal of Arboriculture, 18*, 98-101.

Ittelson, W., Proshansky, H., Rivlin, L., and Winkel, G. (1974). *An introduction to environmental psychology*. New York, NY: Holt, Rinehart and Winston, Inc.

James, W. [1892] (1961). *Psychology: The briefer course*. New York, NY: Harper & Row, Publishers, Inc.

Jordan, W. III. (1990). Earthkeeping: A realization. *Restoration and Management Notes, 8*, 70.

Jung, C. (1933). *Modern man in search of a soul*. New York, NY: Harcourt Brace Jovanovich.

Jung, C. (1954). The phenomenology of the spirit in fairy tales. In J. Campbell (Ed.), *Spirit and nature* (pp. 3-48). Princeton, NJ: Princeton University Press.

Jung, C. (1964). Approaching the unconscious. In C. Jung (Ed.), *Man and his symbols* (pp. 1-94). New York, NY: Dell.

Jung, C. (1976). *Letters* (vol. 2). London, UK: Routledge and Kegan Paul.

Jung, C. (1980). *C. Jung speaking*. London, UK: Pan Books.

Jung, C. (1989). *Memories, dreams, reflections*. New York, NY: Vintage Books.

Kaplan, R. and Kaplan, S. (1989). *The experience of nature: A psychological perspective*. New York, NY: Cambridge.

Kaplan, S. (1993). The role of natural environment aesthetics in the restorative experience. In P. Gobster (Ed.), *Managing urban and high-use recreation settings* (pp. 46-49) (General Technical Report NC-163). Chicago, IL: USDA Forest Service, North Central Forest Experiment Station.

Keen, E. (1975). *A primer in phenomenological psychology*. New York, NY: Holt, Rinehart, and Winston, Inc.

Lakoff, G. and Johnson, M. (1980). *Metaphors we live by*. Chicago, IL: University of Chicago Press.

Maslow, A. (1968). *Toward a psychology of being*. New York, NY: Van Nostrand Reinhold.

Maslow, A. (1974). *Religions, values, and peak experiences*. New York, NY: Viking Press.

Mitchell, M., Force, J., Carroll, M., and McLaughlin, W. (1993). Forest places of the heart: Incorporating special spaces into public management. *Journal of Forestry, 91*, 32-37.

Myers, I. and McCaulley, M. (1985). *Manual: A guide to the development and use of the Myers-Briggs Type Indicator*. Palo Alto, CA: Consulting Psychologists Press.

Romanyshyn, R. (1982). *Psychological life: From science to metaphor*. Austin, TX: University of Texas Press.

Schroeder, H. (1990a). The felt sense of natural environments. In R. Selby, K. Anthony, J. Choi, and B. Orland (Eds.), *Coming of age: Proceedings of the twenty-first annual conference of the Environmental Design Research Association* (pp. 192-195). Oklahoma City, OK: EDRA.

Schroeder, H. (1990b). The spiritual aspect of nature: A perspective from depth psychology. In T. More, M. Donnelly, A. Graefe, and J. Vaske (Eds.), *Proceedings of the 1990 Northeastern Recreation Research Symposium* (pp. 25-30) (General Technical Report NE-145). Radnor, PA: USDA Forest Service, Northeastern Forest Experiment Station.

Schroeder, H. (1991). Preference and meaning of arboretum landscapes: Combining quantitative and qualitative data. *Journal of Environmental Psychology, 11*, 231-248.

Schroeder, H. (in press). Seeking the balance: Do dreams have a role in natural resource management? In K. Bulkeley (Ed.), *Dreams of social transformation*. New York, NY: State University of New York Press.

Seamon, D. (1982). The phenomenological contribution to environmental psychology. *Journal of Environmental Psychology, 2*, 119-140.

Seamon, D. (1984). Emotional experience of the environment. *American Behavioral Scientist, 27*, 757-770.

Seamon, D. and Boschetti, M. (1990). (Untitled). *Environmental and Architectural Phenomenology Newsletter, 1*, 1.

Segal, F. (1993, March/April). Ecopsychology: Toward an integration of nature and culture. *Creation Spirituality*, 8-11.

Shapiro, K. (1986). Verification: Validity or understanding. *Journal of Phenomenological Psychology, 17*, 167-179.

Tinsley, H. and Tinsley, D. (1988). An expanded context for the study of career decision-making, development and maturity. In W. Walsh and S. Osipow (Eds.), *Career decision-making* (pp. 213-264). Hillsdale, NJ: Lawrence Erlbaum Associates.

Ulrich, R. (1981). Natural versus urban scenes: Some psychophysiological effects. *Environment and Behavior, 13*, 523-556.

HARD-TO-DEFINE VALUES AS DIMENSIONS OF LEISURE

CHAPTER 6

THOMAS GOODALE
Department of Health, Sport and Leisure Studies
George Mason University
Fairfax, Virginia

GEOFFREY GODBEY
School of Hotel, Restaurant and Recreation Management
The Pennsylvania State University
State College, Pennsylvania

The focus of this text is nature-based experiences and values that lend deep and enduring psychological essence to human life. That strikes us as an excellent way to begin a definition of leisure. It also strikes us as an excellent way to begin a definition of work which is meaningful, pleasurable, and absorbing.

The prefactory language includes moral and ethical aspects of resources, higher aspects of mind, ascendancy of higher emotions, refinement of thought and feeling, sense of place, cognitive and emotional responses, appreciation of life forms, recognition of intrinsic values, introspection, devotion, reverence, respect, wonder, awe, mystery and inspiration. All of this language appears in discussions of leisure since leisure is an ideal, existential, transcendent, and rooted in philosophy and religion. In the family of leisure concepts, too, there is no clear distinction between religion and fly fishing.

Difficulties operationalizing these dimensions of leisure, these hard-to-define values, have meant that leisure researchers usually avoided them in favor of those more readily accessible with available tools. Researchers focus on what is easy to measure. Consequently, they find severe limits to what they can con-

clude about the reduction of leisure, except that it is often complex, ethereal, and ephemeral.

Time is a central dimension of leisure not because leisure is equated with free time, a presumably objective quantity, nor equated even with a subjective, internal, qualitative sense of time, but because leisure transcends time, as in "flow" (Csikszentmihalyi, 1990). In a very real sense, when leisure enters our experience, time leaves: one might even say time is dismissed. However, time is a central element in the realization of meaning and purpose, in the deep and enduring psychological essence of life. Even before Stonehenge, humans were searching for their place in time, place having a temporal as well as spatial dimension. To feel in place is to belong, to have meaning and purpose. Time connects us to hard-to-define values in many ways, and it ties leisure to fly fishing and religion as well. Emerson ([1870] 1929) was not alone in thinking the measure of time should be spiritual. God is in the details and in the moments.

In ancient Athenian philosophy, leisure is an ideal arising from ethics, politics, and conversing with the Gods. *Schole*, or leisure, is the opportunity and ability to develop excellence of the soul. It is also, therefore, the opportunity to achieve happiness since happiness depends on virtuous acts, and virtuous acts display the soul's excellence. Although all freely chosen acts are not virtuous, only freely chosen acts can be. Like Aristotle centuries before, America's founders wrote of life, liberty, and the pursuit of happiness. Later still, Wittgenstein, himself referring to Dostoevsky, agreed that the person who is happy is fulfilling the purpose of existence (in Singer, 1992).

Also in our own century, Josef Pieper (1963) made the most compelling argument linking leisure to philosophy, religion and culture. Whereas Aristotle held contemplation to be the highest and best expression of leisure, Pieper made contemplation the very essence of leisure. Pieper equated leisure with "The Philosophic Act," which is also the title of the companion essay to *Leisure the Basis of Culture.*

> *The philosophic act . . . is an attitude which presupposes silence; a contemplative attention to things in which man begins to see how worthy of veneration they really are.* (p. 18)

Elsewhere Pieper (1963) wrote:

> *Leisure is a form of silence . . . the prerequisite of the apprehension of reality. Silence . . . means . . . that the soul's 'power' to answer to the reality of the world is left undisturbed. For leisure is a receptive attitude of mind, a contemplative attitude, and it is not only the occasion but also the capacity for steeping oneself in the whole of creation. . . . (p. 41)*

In leisure, Pieper (1963) argued, people celebrate the creation and affirm that it is good. And the highest form of celebration is the festival, the union of tranquility, contemplation, and intensity of life. To hold a celebration means to affirm the basic meaningfulness of the universe and a sense of oneness with it, of inclusion within it (p. 43). The point and justification of leisure, Pieper (1963) argued, is that people must be more than mere functionaries, and must:

> *retain the faculty of grasping the world as a whole and realize (their) full potentialities as . . . entitie(s) meant to reach Wholeness. . . . Because Wholeness is what (people) strive for, the power to achieve leisure is one of the fundamental powers of the human soul.* (p. 44)

Leisure and other hard-to-define values of philosophy and religion, of Aristotle and Pieper, have been largely lost in the revolutions brought about by science, technology, capitalism and bureaucracy. Manifestations of those losses include leisure being defined as time left over after work is done and other obligations completed, and time being commodified and shorn of anything spiritual or transcendent. Free time came to be legitimized by function or, perhaps more accurately, exploitation. Once free time was legitimized by social institutions supporting opportunities to rest as a means of increasing production. More recently, free time has become legitimized for providing opportunities to shop, spend and purchase the increased production. But if progress means—as it does to many—ever increasing production and consumption, then failure is inevitable. Leisure as free time valued only for its role in consuming or preparing to produce must, then, also fail.

This led to the next stage of attempting to define leisure. Shorn of commercial and industrial ties and still shorn of its roots in religion and philosophy, leisure was now to be understood scientifically, or at least understood from the perspective of social psychology. From that perspective, leisure is intrinsically motivated activity engaged in when people perceive themselves free to do so. Whatever other shortcomings this definition may have, there appear to be three principal ones. First, little is known about motivations to act and outcomes of acting. Second, individuals who perceive themselves to be free may be fatally wrong and instead of finding leisure find the undertaker. There is a reality, and being ignorant of it or ignoring it does not make a person free. In addition, if Ornstein and Ehrlich (1989) are correct, most people fail to comprehend much of the modern world; in fact, they only perceive about one-trillionth of the events in it. Third, social psychological conceptualizations of leisure provide no framework of values; no moral or ethical context by which to judge motives, perceptions or actions. Rather than find meaning, one finds a void.

In the modern world, leisure has become even more subjective than in the world which existed before industrialization. Leisure is now more individualistic. The choices to be made during time away from work or life in general are more varied, complex and uncertain. The influence of mores and folkways is less absolute. The impact of both primary and secondary social groups on decisions concerning leisure has diminished. Church, family, and neighborhood shape decisions concerning leisure less and less. Multinational corporations stormed into that void seeking to provide ways to occupy people for which they are willing to spend money. Such efforts, part of the massive influence of the combined effects of science, technology, bureaucracy and capitalism, have produced an ordering of life in more absolute ways than humans thought possible. This produced a revolt manifest in existential quests to discover one's essence, one's core being, amidst a sea of meaninglessness. It has led also to a profound alienation which has produced nihilism and fraud in the arts and in the sciences, tribalism among (no longer) social groups, violence as a primary form of entertainment for spectators and, increasingly, participants.

While science, technology, bureaucracy and capitalism brought about miracles of production and have reshaped the material standard of living for most in ways unimaginable to previous generations, they have also led to a preordering of life which is alienating.

> *Human institutions—the state, the government, the civil service, the party, the factory— have become impersonal and anonymous powers of enormous strength which the individual tries in vain to master. Thence arises the growing sense of frustration, anxiety and despair which pervades the Western hemisphere. At the back of it all is man's estrangement from nature.*

Heinemann, 1958, p. 168

Existentialism seeks to counter such impersonal power:

> *The essence of the existential protest is that rationalism can pervade a whole civilization, to the point where the individuals in the civilization do less and less thinking, and perhaps wind up doing none at all. It can bring this about by dictating the fundamental ways and routines by which life itself moves. Technology is one material incarnation of rationalism, since it derives from science; bureaucracy is another, since it aims at the rational control and ordering of social life, and the two—technology and bureaucracy—have come more and more to rule our lives.*

Barrett, 1958, p. 269

In a world in which technology, bureaucracy, and increasing affluence provided more opportunities for leisure but increasingly defined in advance the ways in which those opportunities would unfold, the existential search for the authentic was a natural consequence. The line between work and leisure became artificial for those who viewed the world in existential terms. If there is no "human nature," if one must define or seek to define oneself through authenticating acts, if one must literally bring oneself into being on an individual basis without the comfort and guidelines of religion, the line between work and leisure is meaningless. All activity, whether "work" or "leisure," can potentially contribute to a fundamental task: the task of defining one's self.

While the rational side of humans is viewed as being capable of infinite development by the logical positivistic view of the world often found in science and technology, existentialism sees it as only one facet of our being. In a world in which God has little role to play, the notion of "self" is abstract and in need of further definition. The individual must meet such a need through his or her own actions. As the philosopher Kierkegaard wrote in the middle of the nineteenth century, "When I behold my possibilities I experience the dread which is 'the dizziness of freedom' and my choice is made in fear and trembling" (Kaufmann, 1956, p. 17). Freedom, without the comfort of theological and ethical systems, can produce terror and absurdity. There are no compasses for conduct: there are not even directions.

It is small wonder, then, that many people reject freedom, and thus leisure, in their own lives. In an abstract world our lives are highly programmed. Many people suffer alienation, and such alienation may lead to leisure being used simply as an arena for consumption of the products and services which have been planned for them. Indeed that course of action appears to have taken place within highly industrialized societies. In the absence of leisure, free time is used for watching television, for shopping, for mass-produced tourism "packages," and mass-produced films, magazines and newspapers. The forms of most leisure activities are increasingly shaped by the products and services produced by huge organizations.

This mass consumption of both material goods and experiences is not part of a sustainable culture for several reasons. First, the volume of goods produced has had fundamentally negative effects upon the human habitat. For example, the ozone layer surrounding the Earth, on which our lives depend, is depleting at the rate of 2 to 4 percent per year (Weiner, 1990). Second, the population of the world is doubling and our highly consumptive society does not provide a useful model for such a world (Kennedy, 1992). Third, the United States suffers from a profound loss of sense of community and of spirituality which harm one's sense of well-being and one's contentment. Fourth, levels of formal education are increasing at a great rate, and society is at the forefront of developing models of lifelong learning for the majority. Such a situation means that leisure must increasingly serve as an arena for both acquiring substantive knowledge and exercising it. More typically, however, it has brought about an acquiescence in consumption, a quest for a day at the right beach wearing the right brands of everything. That is frightening not only because the environment cannot sustain it but also because the imagination atrophies if lying on a beach becomes the highest and best use of life imaginable.

Unalienated leisure today is more a question of what is meaningful and what is real than what is pleasurable. Meaning and reality lead to pleasure. As the culture producing qualities of work have been gradually removed in the name of efficiency, leisure has become the realm in which culture must be created and meaning identified and documented. While a privileged minority, who often control the culture which determines what is real, find their meaning in work, for the majority, work is too often unreal and devoid of meaning and significance. In particular, the young have inherited unskilled jobs which are wildly out of synch with their higher levels of education. While their educational attainment may not have increased, their educational sensibilities and awareness have. Leisure is now the arena in which such sensibilities and awareness have the potential to be expressed—or subverted.

Leisure and the values which may emanate from it have become harder to measure because researchers are further away than ever from understanding what leisure means or could mean in their culture. They are further than ever from having commonweal, common language, common cause, common assumptions about what to do about the problems of the world and common ideas about what is needed. If leisure is an individual matter,

invented as part of the invention of self, measuring that invention will surely be profoundly difficult. Attempts at such measurement will harm our understanding of leisure.

It is perhaps understandable, then, that attempts to understand the values associated with leisure have become reductionist. Indeed, our notion of science, which one thinks of more as objective technique than as one philosophy among many, has been used in ways that produce answers which are not only reductionist but reduced *ad absurdum*. Thus, researchers ask people if they are happy, when psychologists increasingly believe people may be simultaneously happy and sad (Csikszentmihalyi, 1990). Researchers also use fixed categories of descriptors for emotions when poets such as Robert Bly (1969), who know different things about emotions from scientists, observe that each emotion is unique, never to be replicated. These difficulties are mirrored in the attempts of recreation and park managers to measure and hence understand what it is they do. As the ideological components of such services have diminished, there have been few attempts to measure the values of such services; the values of such services were, presumably, obvious. Measuring mere participation, therefore, was thought to be sufficient. People are free to choose, it is assumed, and if they attend parks or participate in recreation activities they must be doing so, a priori, because it is worthwhile. Never mind that television viewing, the dominant consumer of free time in our society, is an activity of which participants almost never say they want more. Further, it is an activity which produces mood deterioration—the longer people watch television, the more their moods tend to become negative (Kubey and Csikszentmihalyi, 1990).

Public leisure service providers have used other simple measures to evaluate their services, measures assumed to be "objective," but which are, in fact, highly subjective and difficult to understand. Thus, researchers find in regard to leisure that the greatest constraint on what people do during their leisure is "lack of time." If even a few more questions are asked, however, this answer shifts and usually disappears. A mother categorized as being engaged in "camping" may be revealed as simply housekeeping under inferior conditions upon subsequent observation. People are defined as "boating" when they are really drinking beer and talking, albeit on the water.

If revenue generated by a leisure service agency is measured, it is thought of as an absolute good even though we have no idea what is done with the money. Suppose it is used to hire incompetent political appointees who diminish the quality of communal life with their ineptitude? If "attendance" is measured, suppose most of those who attend are dissatisfied or do things which injure their health or contribute to their obesity?

There is no standard measure of the success of recreation and park services which makes much intellectual sense. Nor has there been much concerted effort to come up with any measures which do. Now these services are locked in a battle of declining budgets in which the major variable is whether they are "essential" or "nonessential." Such a battle is filled with ideological baggage which is inherently hard to measure. Police, one assumes, are "essential," even though they have little to do with criminal justice. Only about 20 percent of reported crime leads to an arrest (and probably most petty crime is not even reported). Only about one-half of those arrested come to trial. Only about one-half of those trials lead to conviction. Only about one-half of those convictions lead to incarceration. Over one-half of those who are incarcerated are rearrested after they are released (Bennett, 1987). In spite of that, the United States has the highest proportion of its population in prison among modern nations and still has among the highest rates of crime. Nevertheless, Americans think more police is the answer. Similarly, America has third-rate fire departments, principally because we measure what is easy to measure—success at putting out fires in burning buildings. In other countries, fire departments are better at enforcing fire codes and providing people with information about how to minimize the risk of fire (Osborne and Gabler, 1993).

What these observations have in common is that the notion of "prevention" is largely ignored. Prevention is difficult to measure. It requires the leap of faith which Americans are no longer willing to make. It is like the decision to "prime the pump" for the next person who will use the well. One does not know who that person may be. Measuring what is not easy to measure, to a great extent, implies distrust. It means, in the absence of proof, anything done in common through government is suspect. Its equivalent in the market sector is quarterly profit. Concern with short-term profit similarly reveals a lack of trust, and trust is necessary if more intangible values are to be measured in any sector. Americans have no faith in the long run, the abstract and intangible, and the collective or common.

It is axiomatic that the most important values are the most difficult to measure. Happiness, wellness, beauty, peace, all are resistant to simple measurement. Those who want easy answers, who want "proof" that is absolute and indisputable show their ignorance of postmodern reality. They also exhibit a fear of living with doubt. In the postmodern world, one lives not so much with competing truths as with competition between those who believe truths can exist a priori and be communicated, and those who believe all truth is manufactured and, once communicated, can be decomposed. Sometimes, then, there seems little except doubt. Living with doubt, of course, requires the development of some sort of faith for life to be meaningful.

In the postmodern world, trust, at least in the realm of human relations, is far from absolute or overarching. No truth is free from stinging criticism. Science is one way, but only one, of finding truth. While postmodernism announces the postscientific era, science continues to be the sine qua non of the university and the corporation. Nonetheless, one lives in a world in which one's very notion of self is in a constant state of change. It is also saturated with communication. As psychologist Kenneth Gergen (1991) observed, new technologies have made it possible to sustain relationships—either directly or indirectly—with an ever-expanding range of other persons. This has led to a state of "social saturation" in which the very ways in which one perceives and characterizes oneself are changed.

Emerging technologies saturate us with the voices of humankind—both harmonious and alien. As we absorb their varied rhythms and reasons, they become part of us and we of them. Social saturation furnishes us with a multiplicity of incoherent and unrelated languages of the self. For everything we 'know to be true' about ourselves, other voices within respond with doubt and even derision. The fragmentation of self-conception corresponds to a multiplicity of incoherent and disconnected relationships. These relationships pull us in myriad directions, inviting us to play such a variety of roles that the very concept of an 'authentic self' with knowable characteristics recedes from view. The fully saturated self becomes no self at all.

Gergen, 1991, p. 7

The fax machine, call waiting, E-mail, improved air travel and other technological changes not only complicate our lives but also put our very identity at risk. In such a situation, as others are incorporated into our self-concept, their desires become ours. " . . . There is an expansion of goals—of 'musts,' 'wants,' and 'needs.' " While one's use of time may not be changed by this condition, one's sense of the necessary is, with the attendant result of making time psychologically more scarce.

All these factors, in combination, make it unlikely that decision makers will fool around with attempts to measure values which cannot be measured easily, and instead will continue producing "factoids" useful in making quick decisions. In the process of doing so, any opportunity to understand the benefits of leisure is largely lost. The meaning of life, Csikszentmihalyi (1990) observed, is "meaning," the making of meaning. The greatest benefit of leisure in postmodern culture is the establishment of meaning through personal acts. To attempt to measure the value of establishing such meaning is a long climb on a slippery slope, a climb on which one needs more than science.

It should come as no surprise, then, that there is a resurgence of interest in philosophy and religion. While some manifestations of that interest are remarkably dysfunctional, so much else is demonstrably good. There are both spiritual and scientific dimensions to biodiversity and ecosystem maintenance, to recycling and vegetarianism, to debt reduction, and to environmental and intergenerational equity. Poets write of bioregions, physicists write of the *Tao of Physics* (Capra, 1984), anthropologists write of *The Dance of Life* (Hall, 1983), physicians explore the parallel course of physics and art (Schlain, 1991). There is a renewal of interest in natural law and rights rooted in something beyond the sovereign state. Americans remain reverential to "being endowed by their creator with certain inalienable rights," and have added a World Charter for Nature and a Universal Declaration of Human Rights. All are tied to achieving some sense of wholeness, coherence, meaning, purpose, and, withal, happiness. To all of that leisure and the natural environment are critical resources.

However hard-to-define might be the values of experiencing the natural world or the dimensions of leisure, we have clear and compelling measures of the ability of the environment and of leisure to sustain life (Ornstein and Sobel, 1989). Those measures demonstrate what is good and right, as Leopold argued, and they demonstrate what one knows from one's own experience. One seeks in leisure no utility. That, as Aristotle argued, is its principal virtue. "To look for utility everywhere ill behooves free and exalted souls" (Stocks, 1936). Modern psychologists agree. One cannot flow by trying to flow. Modern and ancient theologians suggest that to find oneself one must lose oneself. One cannot seek the hard-to-define values of leisure—meaning, wholeness, happiness and peace—because they do not hide. They will find one when one is ready.

They will come on the heels of defining moments of appreciation, exhilaration and enchantment; defining moments of consuming beauty and harmony; defining moments when one shines in an endless drama with its own pace, order, reality and life.

Call the benefits of leisure serendipitous. Call the need for realizing those benefits urgent. Demonstrating those values is not only politically necessary but also affirms the better and higher aspects of moral and ethical, thinking and feeling beings. Leisure provides a basis for faith: valuing leisure is an act of faith. Science may help us define the hard-to-define values of leisure. Might it also one day help define the values of faith? Now that would be serendipitous.

Literature Cited

Barrett, W. (1958). *Irrational man: A study in existential philosophy*. New York, NY: Doubleday & Company, Inc.

Bennett, G. (1987). *Crimewarps, the future of crime in America* (1st ed.). New York, NY: Norton & Co., Inc.

Bly, R. (Ed.). (1969). *The sixties*. Madison, MN: The Sixties Press.

Capra, F. (1984). *The tao of physics* (2nd ed.). New York, NY: Bantam Books.

Csikszentmihalyi, M. (1990). *Flow: The psychology of optimal experience*. New York, NY: Harper & Row Publishers, Inc.

Emerson, R. (1870) (1929). Works and days. *The complete writings of Ralph Waldo Emerson* (pp. 668-678) (Vol. 1). New York, NY: William Wise and Company.

Gergen, K. (1991). *The saturated self: Dilemmas of identity in contemporary life*. New York, NY: Basic Books, Inc.

Hall, E. (1983). *The dance of life*. New York, NY: Anchor/Doubleday.

Heinemann, F. (1958). *Existentialism and the modern predicament*. New York, NY: Harper & Row Publishers, Inc.

Kaufmann, W. (1956). *Existentialism from Dostoevsky to Sartre*. New York, NY: Meridian Books.

Kennedy, P. (1992). *Preparing for the 21st Century*. New York, NY: Random House, Inc.

Kubey, R. and Csikszentmihalyi, M. (1990). *Television and the quality of life*. Hillsdale, NJ: L. Earlbaum Associates.

Ornstein, R. and Ehrlich, P. (1989). *New world new mind*. New York, NY: Simon Schuster–Touchtone.

Ornstein, R. and Sobel, D. (1989). *Healthy pleasures*. Reading, MA: Addison-Wesley Publishing Co., Inc.

Osborne, D. and Gaebler, T. (1993). *Reinventing government—How the entrepreneurial spirit is transforming the public sector*. New York, NY: Plume Books.

Pieper, J. (1963). *Leisure the basis of culture*. New York, NY: New American Library.

Schlain, L. (1991). *Art and physics—Parallel visions in space, time and light*. New York, NY: William Morrow.

Singer, I. (1992). *Meaning in life: The creation of value*. New York, NY: The Free Press.

Stocks, J. (1936). Leisure. *Classical Quarterly, XXX*, 3, 4, (January), 175-185.

Weiner, J. (1990). *The next one hundred years—Shaping the fate of our living planet*. New York, NY: Bantam Books.

Uses of Natural Settings to Promote, Maintain and Restore Human Health

CHAPTER 7

Sharon Montes
Department of Family Medicine
Colorado School of Medicine
Denver, Colorado

Introduction

Long before Hippocrates offered his creed for physicians, humans tried to answer the question: What is health? Many volumes have addressed that question and debate continues today. Within the medical professions, the most commonly accepted definition is that of the World Health Organization:

health is the state of complete physical, mental, and social well-being and not merely the absence of disease or infirmity.

Although the concept of well-being is an abstraction with intuitive appeal, it has never been defined in such a way that explicit criteria can be established to differentiate well-being from the absence thereof. Thus, if one accepts the idea that a definition should clearly differentiate that which is being defined from other related concepts or terms, it is apparent that the word "health" has not yet met that criterion.

The complexity of the concept of health gives me some license as a physician to venture into some realms of health not commonly referred to by the American Medical Association—but which probably should be. With confidence, I discuss the contributions of nature to human health that are widely ac-

cepted within the United States' dominant medical paradigm (nature-derived pharmaceuticals, aerobic exercise done out-of-doors, etc.). I also speculate about the intuitive health-related benefits of nature that have yet to be documented scientifically. These include such things as the health-related spiritual uses of natural areas, of being uplifted psychologically while paying to participate in a cattle drive, or of restoring one's adaptive energies by passively enjoying a sunset, or sitting in a backyard listening to songbirds.

The central themes of this chapter are twofold:

1. more attention needs to be given to health promotion and disease prevention in the United States; and

2. many factors—good nutrition, avoidance of substance abuse, physical exercise, stress management, good social support systems—have considerable scientific documentation as being important dimensions of preventive medicine; but other factors, not having as reliable scientific documentation—recreational, educational, spiritual and other

amenity-related uses of natural environments—probably also contribute greatly to human health.

For many individuals and subcultures those contributions to health seem substantial, and their role in preventive health needs to be understood better. Within many healing traditions, it is impossible to separate the spiritual, mental, or physical aspects of health.

Rising Costs of Healthcare

All literate citizens of the United States are quite aware of continued increases in the costs of healthcare. Senior citizens have seen their life's savings extinguished by the costs of health problems or by the need for long-term care. Costs of emergency room treatment and of other health services have increased much faster than the rate of inflation. Improvements continue to be made in "high tech" medicine that can diagnose or correct health problems and thereby promote longer or better life, but these technologies are expensive. Finally, concerns about malpractice suits increase healthcare costs because physicians must recommend tests and consultations they would not have recommended previously. For these reasons, and many others, the healthcare system in the United States is placing a growing economic burden on individuals, companies, agencies, and society in general—currently representing 13 percent of gross domestic product (Letsch, 1993).

Despite the large amount of money allocated to healthcare costs in the United States, this country does not lead the world in many healthcare indicators such as infant mortality and life expectancy. The United States outspends Australia, Canada, Japan, France and the United Kingdom on per capita healthcare expenditures, yet has a higher infant mortality rate and lower life expectancy rate than each of those countries (U.S. Bureau of Census, 1991).

It is clear to most people both inside and outside the healthcare professions, that the continuing pattern of increasing healthcare costs with less than optimal healthcare outcomes is one of the most pressing problems in the United States. This concern is reflected by the attention now being given these costs within the political arena. More atten-

tion must be given to preventive medicine as one way of solving the healthcare cost problem. Such programs must explore all facets of preventive medicine including those not considered previously, or little considered within the dominant allopathic tradition of medical practice in the United States.

Comparative Medical Traditions

Allopathy, the Dominant Paradigm

While generalizations can exclude important exceptions, it is safe to say that the dominant medical paradigm in the Western world has been derived from the work of Louis Pasteur. It is called the "germ theory of disease." This tradition has become known as the allopathic approach, which is primarily concerned with the diagnosis and treatment of the physical body. Disease—and thus impaired health—is thought to result from physical factors such as infection (e.g., bacteria, fungi, virus) or deficiency (e.g., nutritional, pancreatic deficiency resulting in diabetes). One of the strengths of this tradition is the use of antibiotics to fight infections. This way of looking at physical health is somewhat linear. One event leads to another with traceable and measurable results so diagnoses are possible. Treatment relies on physical cures such as pills, physical therapy, injections, and medical devices such as braces.

While the allopathic tradition—along with better sanitation (which was stimulated largely by that tradition), better nutrition, better housing, and other factors—has contributed, and still contributes greatly to health promotion and maintenance, it has its limitations. Until the last 20 years the allopathic tradition said little about mental or emotional health and their relation to physical health. In addition, the most common causes of death in the Western world today (cardiovascular disease, cancer, accidents) are not clearly attributable to "germs." In recognition of these limitations, other approaches to healthcare exist that are practiced in combination with, or separate from, allopathy.

An increasing percentage of people in the United States are pursuing healthcare either totally or partially using approaches that differ from allopathy.

One estimate is that in 1990 the number of visits to providers of unconventional therapy (425 million) exceeded the number of visits to all U.S. primary care physicians (388 million). Expenditures for these visits were estimated to be approximately $13.7 billion (Eisenberg, Kessler, Foster, Norlock, Calkins, and Delbanco, 1993). Alternative approaches include massage, polarity balancing, use of fewer prescription drugs, kinesiology, reflexology, hypnosis, traditional methods employed by Native American and other cultures (e.g., Ayurvedic and Chinese), megavitamin therapy, and prayer. (Although a higher percentage of respondents to Eisenberg et al.'s [1993] interviews used prayer than any other individual modality except exercise, this area was not explored or discussed in the study.)

So although patients may not be discussing the fact with their physicians, a high percentage of the patients in Eisenberg et al.'s (1993) study were pursuing alternative therapy. The next section describes a few of these alternative traditions with an emphasis on how they relate to nature.

Other Traditions

Homeopathy

This approach to medicine was developed by Samuel Hahemann in the late 1700s and early 1800s and is based on treating disease with compounds that cause symptoms similar to those of the disease being treated. The drugs, which are frequently herbal based, are subjected to a series of dilutions in the same way that Edward Jenner developed the vaccine for smallpox in 1798. In homeopathic theory the more diluted the compound the more potent it is thought to be. After many dilutions all that remains of a therapeutic compound is its energy imprint which in turn works on the "energy" of the patient rather than the physical body. The theory continues to evolve, and today the practice of homeopathy treats the body, emotions, mind, and spirit as a holistic unit. Homeopathy is commonly practiced within the medical establishments of India and countries in Europe and South America.

Ayurvedic Medicine

Although Ayurvedic medicine had its origins in India over 5,000 years ago, it did not become well-known in the United States until the 1980s. This system of preventive medicine and healthcare is based on the belief that an intangible energy body controls physical health. Deepak Chopra, MD, one of the most articulate authors in English on this subject, calls this energy body the "quantum mechanical human body." Through a program of meditation, "living in tune with nature," and regular contact with nature a person can achieve and maintain health (Chopra, 1991). Chopra proposes that living in tune with nature involves harmony with both "internal" and "external" environments. His argument is that individuals are born with an "internal" body type that has a predisposition towards certain imbalances or disease conditions. Externally, weather and environment affect individual types with the potential to exacerbate imbalance and lead to disease. Regular contact with nature can be as simple as leaving a building to feel the sun on one's skin or lying down on a patch of ground in a city park (Chopra, 1991). Thus, a person maintains harmony, balance, and health through careful attention to thoughts, feelings, exercise, proper food selection and preparation as well as meditation and use of selected herbal preparations.

Traditional Chinese Medicine

Beyond homeopathy and Ayurvedic medicine, many of the alternatives to allopathic medical practices in the United States have their bases in the Eastern medical traditions, especially traditional Chinese medicine (TCM).

According to TCM, energy—or chi—flows through the body in channels. Different organs have their own chi channel with each channel influencing, and being influenced by, other channels. The organs are grouped into five pairs which correspond to the five elements of wood, water, metal, earth, and fire. (Note that these are the natural elements.) Each pair is acted upon by two other pairs, stimulated by one and repressed by another. This law of five elements is further refined by a series of other laws which describe even more intricate relationships between the organ systems. In TCM, one system cannot become out of balance without affecting all others. This requires a holistic view of the patient by the physician.

Given the focus of TCM on maintenance of balance and harmony, it by necessity emphasizes preventive medicine. Particularly relevant to the purposes of this chapter and to the larger text, many examples of balance within TCM make reference to balances in nature. Also, many of the remedies used to cure disease within TCM are derived directly from nature with little to no refinement, and many of the preventive medicine, health-maintenance activities (e.g., daily physical and mental exercises such as Tai Chi Chuan and Chi Gong) recommended by TCM are practiced out-of-doors. "You've got to be out in nature every day, physically moving and meditating, or you won't be as healthy as you can be" (Moyers, 1993, p. 285). Furthermore, TCM espouses a philosophy of human life and relationship to other forms of life that can best be described as a spiritual orientation to life. Interestingly, such a spiritual orientation to life—and health—is central to the traditional forms of medicine long practiced by Native Americans.

Respect for and living in harmony with nature is as, or more, prominent in the many Native-American subcultures as it is in TCM. An increasing number of members of other subcultures in the United States are integrating many of the preventive medicine practices of Native Americans into the more traditional approach reflected by allopathy. In summary, it can be said that the traditional allopathic approach to medicine in the United States is being supplemented by alternative approaches, especially those that are more holistic and those that advocate more clearly and strongly the need for individual responsibility for health as well as preventive medicine.

Health and Nature

This section plays on the theme of this chapter that every available means must be pursued for achieving widespread practice of preventive medicine, especially those means that provide positive reinforcement and are cost-effective. One such practice of preventive medicine is the continued and perhaps greater use of natural environments to promote and maintain mental and physical health. The section examines past, current, and possible future relationships between human health and nature.

Plants, Animals, and Minerals

Throughout the world, plants or plant derivatives are used as adjuncts to healing. Plants contribute to healing in three ways: by providing active therapeutic agents (e.g., reserpine, digoxin); by providing basic materials for further drug synthesis (i.e., 95 percent of starting-point materials for steroid production comes from natural sources); and by providing auxiliary agents which act as binders or stabilizers (e.g., algim). In addition to providing active medical agents or building blocks for construction of active agents, plants also provide blueprints for construction of drugs (e.g., aspirin is produced by replicating a chemical formula derived from willow tree bark). Unfortunately, human laboratories are not as efficient as nature; "of 76 pharmaceutical compounds obtained from plants, only seven can be commercially produced at competitive prices through synthesis" (Myers, 1983, p. 92).

Because of strict federal regulations, a relatively small number of plants and plant products with medicinal values have been approved for commercial or experimental use in the U.S. In contrast, approximately one-half of all prescription items in the former West Germany are derived from plants, while Africans depend on plants for 95 percent of their drug needs.

While subject to some skepticism by allopathic physicians, there is also widespread and growing use of herbal remedies. This is evidenced by increased paid subscriptions to health magazines that promote such usages and advocacy of the health benefits of herbs by subcultures (e.g., New Age) that are growing in membership. In fact, the Federal Drug Administration has recently become concerned about undocumented and possibly exaggerated claims of the medicinal values of some herbs and formulations made from plants.

In addition to the above uses of plant products for restoring health, some plants and plant products are used in spiritual ceremonies for health purposes. This group includes plants containing hallucinogenic compounds (e.g., cacti, mushrooms). While these plants and plant products are also used for recreation and relaxation, they are revered within certain cultures and contexts as a means for recreating a relationship between the sacred and the everyday profane aspects of life—an adjunct in maintaining individual and aggregative community well-being.

The natural world offers more than medicinal plants to benefit the health of humankind. The animal world offers benefits that range from obvious commercial uses (e.g., food, clothing) to medical research on animals to better understand ourselves. By understanding why mollusks and bison are immune to developing cancer, maybe we will develop improved technology to prevent or treat cancer in humans. Research on the cardiovascular functioning of hibernating bears might provide insights that will help prevent heart disease in humans. Other health-related uses of animals include derivation of medicines (e.g., antimicrobial, antiviral agents from marine life). Also, some healing traditions draw upon certain animals for the practitioners to avail or align themselves with certain "energies" that particular animals are perceived to have. These animal energies purportedly can be tapped through visions or by contact with the animal or parts of the animal (i.e., feathers, bones, claws, teeth).

In addition to the health-related spiritual uses of plants and animals, some people ascribe health maintenance and healing values to certain minerals. One example is the folk remedy of using copper jewelry to assist in the treatment of arthritis. Almost any alternative bookstore will carry a selection of crystal jewelry. Those crystals are worn, placed on patients, or allowed to sit in water to create elixirs. Each type of crystal or stone is believed to have specific properties to maintain or restore the health of the physical, emotional, mental, and/or spiritual body.

Restorative Properties of Nature

While pharmaceuticals derived from plant and animal products provide health benefits, even greater health benefits probably accrue from the use of natural environments to recover from the stresses and strains of everyday living experienced both at home and at work. Research has shown that pursuit of these restorative, or re-creative, benefits is a primary motivator for many people to select natural environments as places for their leisure. This comes as no surprise to people who know this intuitively, and such judgments were a major force behind the parks and recreation movements in many countries including the United States. These restorative benefits of nature were espoused frequently in the writings of Frederick Law Olmsted,

perhaps the best known park designer (including Central Park in New York city) in the United States. Although the pursuit of psychophysiological recovery can be one of several motivations that simultaneously prompt recreational activity, I focus only on the restorative benefits here and leave the other benefits of recreating in natural settings (e.g., skill development, learning, social cohesion) for discussion elsewhere.

Some scientists have argued that natural environments are preferred by many people over indoor or highly urbanized settings for many recreational pursuits oriented toward psychophysiological recovery because those settings offer therapeutic advantages. Driver and Greene suggest that since humans evolved in natural settings, our sensory mechanisms have been historically tuned over hundreds of thousands of years to find such stimuli attractive so long as we understand them and do not find them threatening (Driver and Greene, 1977). To be sure, some natural stimuli are not relaxing—extreme cold, biting mosquitos, dangerous animals, and nearby lightning strikes—but most elicit responses that do not provoke anxiety.

Roger Ulrich and his colleagues have conducted empirical studies that lend strong support to the hypothesis that for many, if not most, people natural settings and stimuli are much more effective in promoting psychophysiological recovery from stress than urban settings. In addition, Ulrich's well-known hospital study that showed improved recovery benefits to gallbladder surgery patients whose hospital room had a window view of nature over a control group of patients who had a view of a brown brick wall, has led to changes in hospital designs that optimize views of nature (Ulrich, 1984). Also, many hospitals and other medical institutions are now offering patients opportunities to view or care for plants or gardens as a part of their recovery. Over 20 years ago Kansas State University started training horticultural therapists. Originally students were trained in mental health, and graduates mainly worked in psychiatric hospitals. As the profession has developed and wider benefits have been defined (e.g., socialization, fine/gross motor skill development, work and frustration tolerance), further applications and specializations have been created. Current specializations in addition to mental health include gerontology, corrections, community-based programs, developmental disabilities and special education (Mattson, 1992; McAvoy and Lais, Chapter Thirty-One, in this volume).

During the past 15 to 20 years, many other researchers have contributed to a growing body of scientific evidence which suggests that natural stimuli and settings offer not only restorative but health maintenance and promotion benefits. As one example, Stephen and Rachael Kaplan (1989) have expanded and clearly articulated the suggestion by William James ([1892] 1961) (a well-known psychologist of the early 1900s) that natural settings elicit an involuntary cognitive and perceptual process in humans whereby the mind tends to scan with not as much need to attend consciously or voluntarily. The voluntary process demands more energy and concentration and, therefore, can be more tiring mentally (e.g., attending to a work performance or child rearing task). Recent research suggests that the therapeutic benefits of nature can be realized in or near the home. There is a growing body of evidence that indicates that gardening, caring for potted plants, watching fish in an aquarium, or having a pet dog or cat can help reduce hypertension and offer other mental and physical health benefits.

My purpose in this section is not to urge urban residents to return to the country. Nor is it to offer an unrealistic "sanitized" view of nature that ignores the many economic, social, cultural/artistic, and other benefits of the city. Further, I am aware of the psychophysiological benefits afforded by many forms of indoor recreation that are not oriented to nature (e.g., listening to Mozart's piano concertos). I do believe, however, that natural stimuli and settings do provide opportunities for many people to restore adaptive energies to face everyday life. It is not yet totally clear whether this is a consequence of personal preferences of those people or some combination of personal preference and unique therapeutic advantage of natural settings. If it is a consequence of personal preference, options should be preserved, and perhaps expanded, for those health-related restorative benefits to be realized as one part of preventive medicine, assuming that the recipients of these benefits are willing to pay (taxes, use fees, or both) to help cover the costs of providing those opportunities. If there are unique advantages of natural settings over urban settings that are relatively devoid of natural stimuli in eliciting preservation benefits—as there is grow-

ing scientific evidence to support—a serious program of preventive medicine would promote ready accessibility to natural stimuli for the approximately 80 percent of people in the United States who reside in urban areas. While the public lands managed by federal and state agencies would continue to offer opportunities to realize these restorative benefits, the greatest need seems to be to make our cities more livable in many ways, especially by better integration of nature and by designs that promote spontaneous human interaction and reduce aversive visual, auditory, olfactory and other stimuli. This has been done in large and small cities in many other countries.

Other Health Benefits of Uses of Natural Areas

In addition to the stress-mediation benefits of natural areas and their contributions to the development of pharmaceuticals, the recreational use of natural areas provides many other health benefits. Perhaps the best documented are the psychological and physiological benefits of persistent exercise—whether practiced indoors or outdoors. Other probable benefits of outdoor recreation that are documented scientifically include benefits associated with development and nurturance of systems of social support and companionship; mental engagement in activities such as nature study; improved efficiency of one's self-concept from development and application of skills; value clarification through introspection; creative engagement and expression, and spiritual renewal (Driver, Brown, and Peterson, 1991). I return to some of these later in the section "Toward a Positive Program of Preventive Medicine."

Preventive Medicine

Reasons for Little Past Attention

Preventive medicine involves disease prevention as well as health promotion. As briefly mentioned earlier in this chapter, historically this area has received little attention from many U.S. physicians. Contact with nature can be an important part of a plan to promote health and prevent disease.

In ancient China, a physician was paid to keep a patient well. This is in contrast with the traditional allopathic approach in the United States.

Here physicians are paid for what they do *to* the patient, and with the exception of psychiatric and psychological counseling, they are not generally paid for time and effort expended to educate and train patients about what patients should be doing *themselves* to maintain and promote good health. Fundamentally, it is a problem of economics on a national and individual level. Nationally, in the past, a high percentage of research money has been dedicated to diagnosis and treatment of disease rather than disease prevention. In addition, in the United States, most healthcare services are provided by physicians who are paid to do something about a diseased or injured body or part of the body. Until recently, there were few financial incentives for these physicians to practice preventive medicine—although many physicians, due to a commitment to patient well-being, advocate that their patients avoid substance abuse, stop smoking, get enough exercise, be careful about cholesterol, manage their stresses and so on. The fact remains that there have not been strong financial incentives for wide advocacy or implementation of preventive medicine. In addition to little financial reward to physicians for health counseling and education, many health insurance companies have not been willing to pay for the costs of preventive health screening programs or tests such as formal smoking cessation classes or mammograms.

Beyond lack of economic incentives, preventive medicine has some inherent flaws that make it difficult to practice given the U.S. cultural fixation on short-term pleasures and benefits. Investing time, money, and energy in an area today which might contribute towards benefits many years later is to ask physicians, insurance companies, and patients to make a leap of faith that these investments will pay off. Not only are the outcomes not totally predictable over time, but the patients are being asked to change rather ingrained behaviors, many of which give pleasure (e.g., eating unhealthy foods, smoking, not exercising, consuming alcohol). Also, some of the recommended alternative behaviors are viewed as not being pleasurable. For example, large percentages of people who start and then soon drop out of aerobic exercise programs report they stop because "it is not any fun," even though they knew it was good for them.

Despite the problems described above, the need for a national policy, and physician endorsement, of preventive medicine in the U.S. is apparent. Such national programs of preventive medicine have been adopted to some degree by many countries.

Changing Directions

From 1984 to 1989, a twenty-panel committee reviewed all published studies done in the area of preventive medicine. Then in 1989, in the *United States Preventive Services Task Force Guide,* they made recommendations regarding 60 healthcare interventions. There were two conclusions of considerable interest to the theme of this chapter. First, there is a lack of scientific evidence to prove conclusively the efficiency of many interventions (e.g., stool guaiac testing or certain serological and radiological screening tests). This finding reinforced the need to fund more preventive medicine research at a national level. Second, the committee found the most effective interventions are those that encourage a change in patient behavior. These include avoidance of substance abuse, and pursuing a healthy diet and exercise.

Although many physicians in private practice and a few federal and state government agencies have developed and advocated programs of preventive medicine that included adequate incentives and follow-up monitoring and evaluations, recent trends indicate considerable growth in interest in such programs. Some examples follow:

- Since about 1985 many citizens of the U.S. have become more committed to the quality of their lives. Essential dimensions of such "life-style management" where considerable changes in individual behaviors have been evidenced are reduced abuse of drugs and alcohol, reduced use of tobacco, better diets, increased stress management, more involvement in aerobic and persistent exercise programs, and development of good social support systems.

- Considerable growth in organizational wellness programs by private industries and governmental agencies. Many of these reimburse employees the costs of joining and using health clubs.

• Increased attention by the federal government to the problem of healthcare costs, with recommendations for preventive medicine getting more support and attention.

• Increased promotion of preventive medicine by the health/hospitalization insurance companies. For example, in July 1993 Mutual of Omaha agreed to pay clients the costs of their participating in a program based on principles of preventive medicine. This program, developed by cardiologist Dean Ornish, combines diet, exercise, meditation and support groups to reverse coronary atherosclerosis. This announcement was followed by three major medical centers opening "reversal centers."

• Increased promotion of preventive medicine by professional organizations such as the National Recreation and Park Association.

• More books and publications that promote preventive medicine. For example, in the book *Healthy People 2000: National Health Promotion and Disease Prevention Objectives* (U.S. Department of Health and Human Services, 1992) the first three health-improvement areas focused on were exercise, nutrition and tobacco. Particularly relevant to the purposes of this chapter, within the area of exercise, specific "risk reduction" objectives were: reduce to no more than 15 percent the proportion of people aged six and older who engage in no leisure-time physical activity, and increase community availability and accessibility of physical activity and fitness facilities in three categories (hiking, biking and fitness trails; public swimming pools; and areas of park and recreation open space).

Toward a Positive Program of Preventive Medicine

Probably all of the medical traditions in the United States accept the need for greater attention to preventive medicine or "preventive health," and I am sure we will hear much more about that need in the near future.

The Big 6

There is wide consensus within the healthcare community that the following behaviors promote and maintain good health:

1. regular exercise that is somewhat demanding but which is not done to excess;

2. proper nutrition;

3. maintenance of a personally meaningful system of social support, that includes caring friends;

4. stress management, which does not mean total avoidance of stress, but does require some psychological stability;

5. avoidance of substance abuse, moderation in consumption of alcohol, and avoidance of tobacco; and

6. reasonable economic security that affords at least minimal levels of housing, clothing, food, and medical services such as health screening, dental and prenatal care, and vaccinations.

These well-known "Big 6" components of a preventive medicine program have received much attention. Therefore, little comment seems necessary on them except to point out that regular exercise, nurturance and maintenance of friendships, and stress management each take place during the recreational use of natural environments for many people. They thus help define the role of natural environments in preventive medicine.

There are other components whose effectiveness as interventions in promoting health have not been as well-established scientifically as the Big 6. Nevertheless, they are receiving increasing attention within the medical traditions in the United States with less attention within the allopathic tradition. They follow:

• A balance between work and play.

• Engagement in activities that require use and development of skills, including mental skills, that promote the efficacy of one's self-concept(s).

• A system of inner/core values that go beyond gratification of ego that give inner meaning and direction to one's life.

Work and Play

The reader might be surprised that I did not include this component in the first list. Certainly, the medical traditions recognize the needs of a healthy person for recreation. But little can be found in the medical journals and more popular preventive health magazines that promote "serious leisure" beyond criticism of "couch potatoes." Instead, the proponents of leisure for health are the professionals who work within the various subspecialties of that field, especially therapeutic recreation. Furthermore, there is no national policy for leisure in the United States as there is in many other countries (several of which provide subsidies to workers who take vacations). This can, in part, be explained by the dominance of the work ethic in the United States, nurtured by our Puritan ethic.

As a physician, I believe these relationships between health and leisure need to be documented better and given more prominence in preventive medicine programs. Since most Americans spend at least part of their leisure time in natural environments, such recommended efforts will give greater identity and credence to those hard-to-define values of nature.

Meaningful Activities

With the exception of mental healthcare professionals (psychiatrists, clinical psychologists, etc.), most healthcare providers have given little attention—especially in the literature—to the health-related benefits of active engagement in meaningful activities (at work, at play, or elsewhere) and the possession of a healthy self-concept. Such engagement helps prevent depression, assures retention of skills (including cognitive skills under the metaphor of "use them or lose them") that give satisfaction, and helps maintain and improve one's self-concept. Campbell, in his book *The Sense of Well-Being in America*, reports that his long-term program of research on Americans' perceived quality of their lives disclosed that a "healthy self-concept" was one of the five best predictors of high satisfaction with life (Campbell, 1981). While you will find little reference to self-concept in the traditional physiologically oriented medical journals, I know of no physician who would argue with the generalization that patients with healthy self-concepts have an easier recovery from most health problems.

While skill testing and skill development can take place during time not devoted to recreation, leisure offers good—and sometimes the only—opportunities for people to so engage. And many of these opportunities are found in natural settings. Included are opportunities to learn about nature, to relive the Old West, or to better understand Colonial New England or the history and culture of a region or the nation by visiting Gettysburg or an Anasazi ruin. Or one might gain pride from perfecting skills as a fly fisherman or a technical mountain climber. These relationships between nature, self-concept, and health should be documented better as another set of hard-to-define nature-dependent components of preventive medicine.

Inner Values

Many of the increasingly popular alternatives to the allopathic medical tradition either center on, or strongly promote, a sense of inner peace. In most instances this can be termed a spiritual orientation to life. This includes conventional religious beliefs related to a deity and a formal system of institutionalized norms for behavior, but it also can be much broader and might not include religious aspects.

Despite the centrality of spirituality to the nontraditional schools of medicine, I have personally had contact with only two physicians who used the word "spirit" during my seven years of medical training. The first was through my reading of Dr. Bernie Siegel's book, *Love, Medicine, and Miracles* (1986). The second was a staff physician at the hospital where I did my residency. Both advocated greater attention by physicians to the spirituality of their patients. While I personally am favorably inclined toward the views expressed by these two, my perception is that those views caused more criticism than respect among their peers. This probably helps explain the fairly rapid growth in numbers of people who are embracing alternative medical traditions.

More has been written about the link between health and spirituality in the sociology literature than in the medical literature. One very well-designed retrospective study by Dwyer, Clarke, and Miller (1990) has shown the significant impact of religion (again not equating religion with spirituality) on decreasing the mortality rates for all malignancies combined, and for digestive and respiratory cancer, when controls for demographic, environmental, and regional factors known to affect cancer mortality were implemented.

In general, however, relatively little scientific research relates spiritually to health, leaving room for speculation about those relationships. First, it makes intuitive sense to me that a person who has a set of core values that go beyond ego gratification and whose life is directed largely by those values will also by definition have a mentally and physically healthy lifestyle as connoted by words that are key to these systems of belief such as inner peace, balance, respect for all forms of life, and living in harmony. One study has partially confirmed this assessment. A scale called the Index of Core Spiritual Experience assesses personal conviction in existence of some type of higher power (defined by the individual), and the perception of an internalized relationship between this higher power and the individual. People who possess these beliefs showed a decreased frequency of medical symptoms as well as increased life purpose and satisfaction (Kass, Friedman, Lesserman, Zuttermeister, and Benson, 1991).

Second, it is interesting to note that the spiritual orientation to life espoused by the nontraditional approaches to medicine all explicitly include spiritual orientation to the natural world. This is particularly true of TCM and of the medical practices of Native Americans.

Third, while logic would suggest that natural areas are not needed to gain and retain a spiritual orientation to life, it appears that such environments are preferred by many people for such purposes. It seems clear that many people use natural environments for something called "spiritual renewal," which might or might not be related to the spiritual orientation being discussed. In any event, my judgment is that there are sizable preventive health benefits from the spiritual uses of natural areas. It is also my opinion that while these health-related benefits of nature are probably the greatest of any of the benefits considered in this chapter, they will be the hardest to define and measure. But we should try to define and measure them because of their probable magnitude and significance.

Endnote

Over the last few years I have noticed a steady increase in the number of publications about mind, body, and/or spiritual connections to health. They have been written from many perspectives (e.g., Medical Doctor, patient, self-professed healers, witches, shamans). Many of these books convey similar messages. One recurrent theme is that individuals should be increasingly responsible for their own health. The task is to provide information to individuals about how they can best accept that responsibility and what the health outcomes will be. That information should discuss all of the components of preventive medicine, including the spiritual and other health-related uses of natural areas.

Literature Cited

Campbell, A. (1981). *The sense of well-being in America: Recent patterns and trends*. New York, NY: McGraw Hill.

Chopra, D. (1991). *Perfect health: The complete mind/body guide*. New York, NY: Crown Publishers.

Driver, B., Brown, P., and Peterson, G. (Eds.). (1991). *Benefits of leisure*. State College, PA: Venture Publishing, Inc.

Driver, B. and Greene P. (1977). Man's nature: Innate determinants of response to natural environment. In *Proceedings of a symposium fair: Children, nature, and the urban environment* (pp. 63-70). USDA Forest Service, General Technical Report, NE-30, Northeastern Forest Experiment Station, Broomall, Pennsylvania.

Dwyer, J., Clarke, L., and Miller, M. (1990). The effect of religious concentration and affiliation on county cancer mortality rates. *Journal of Health and Social Behavior, 31,*185-202.

Eisenberg, D., Kessler, R., Foster, C., Norlock F., Calkins, D., and Delbanco, T. (1993). Unconventional medicine in the United States: Prevalence, costs, and patterns of use. *The New England Journal of Medicine, 328* (4), 246-252.

James, W. [1982] (1961). *Psychology: The briefer course*. New York, NY: Harper & Row Publishers, Inc.

Kaplan, S. and Kaplan, R. (1989). *The experience of nature*. New York, NY: Praeger.

Kass, J., Friedman, R., Lesserman, J., Zuttermeister, P., and Benson, H. (1991). Health outcomes and a new index of spiritual experience. *Journal for the Scientific Study of Religion, 30* (2), 203-211.

Letsch, S. (1993). DataWatch: National healthcare spending in 1991. *Health Affairs, 12* (1), 94-110.

Mattson, R. (1992). Prescribing health benefits through horticultural activities. In D. Relf (Ed.), *The role of horticulture in human well-being and social development: A national symposium* (pp. 161-168). Portland, OR: Timber Press.

Moyers, W. (1993). *Healing and the mind*. New York, NY: Bantam Doubleday Dell Publishing Group.

Myers, N. (1983). *A wealth of wild species: Storehouse for human welfare*. Boulder, CO: Westview Press.

Siegel, B. (1986). *Love, medicine and miracles*. New York, NY: Harper & Row Publishers, Inc.

Ulrich, R. (1984). View through a window may influence recovery from surgery. *Science, 224,* 420-421.

U.S. Bureau of the Census. (1991). *Statistical abstract of the United States: 1991* (111th. ed.). Washington, DC: U.S. Government Printing Office.

U.S. Department of Health and Human Services. (1992). *Healthy people 2000: National health promotion and disease prevention objectives*. Boston, MA: Jones and Bartlett.

U.S. Preventive Services Task Force. (1989). Guide to clinical preventive services: An assessment of the effectiveness of 169 interventions. *Report of the U.S. Preventive Services Task Force*. Baltimore, MD: William and Wilkins.

Section III

Describing Diverse Perspectives

The range of the human mind, the scale and depth of the metaphors the mind is capable of manufacturing as it grapples with the universe, stand in stunning contrast to the belief that there is only one reality, which is man's, or worse, that only one culture among the many on earth possesses the truth.

To allow mystery, which is to say to yourself, "There could be more, there could be things we don't understand," is not to damn knowledge. It is to take a wider view. It is to permit yourself an extraordinary freedom: someone else does not have to be wrong in order that you may be right.

Barry Lopez (1978)

AGAINST UNIFORMITY: PREHISTORIC LANGUAGE LESSONS FOR MODERN LAND MANAGERS

PHILIP KOPPER
Posterity Press, Incorporated[1]
Chevy Chase, Maryland

CHAPTER 8

Introduction

When rovers from the Old World stumbled upon the New, this continent was already home to many nations. Linguists estimate that the peoples of North America spoke some 700 languages at the time of contact which indicates there were many more de facto cultures. This is a crucial, neglected fact of pre-Columbian life. In terms of human settlement and social organization, North America was remarkably complex before the arrival of Europeans.

Thus the lamentable corollary: one result of European immigration was the eclipse, sometimes partial, often total, of uncounted indigenous cultures. It happened by chance, as through the spread of exotic diseases that decimated native populations, and it happened by intent as through the conquer and convert policies of conquistadors in the Southwest and the lethal xenophobia of the British in the Northeast. What seems most tragic about these facts is a lesson usually invoked in biological and ecological contexts—extinction is forever.

The fact remains that when many human cultures died out, whether because of malice, ignorance or accident, posterity became the poorer for it. Yet a second fact prevails as well today. *We* need not be ruled by those ugly attributes, thanks variously to advances in science, the maturation of democratic practices, and the mixed blessing of the most sophisticated communications systems the world has ever seen. Consequently, I argue that lessons drawn from prehistory may positively affect the governance of public lands, and indeed improve "an advanced land management ethic," the motivating purpose for this volume. My argument runs like this: prehistoric America was magnificently varied in terms of its peoples' cultural identities and achievements; cultural diversity remains a valuable and available asset today; and public policy and modern communications methods can jointly strengthen and enrich America's variegated fabric.

The Wonders of Babel

By one recent count, 22 native languages have managed to survive today in California, which was the single most linguistically varied region on the continent circa 1492. This is less than half the 50-odd languages believed to have been spoken at the time of the first European contact in what became that single state. Probably more languages were spoken there than in all Western Europe. This suggests a cultural complexity of continental magnitude in a single region. By extrapolation, while a region like the Arctic displays a kind of cultural uniformity, prehistoric North America in its entirety must have been a patchwork of remarkable dynamics and variety. Today's cliché, "culturally diverse," can only be used as an understatement.

In terms of linguistics, prehistoric North America was a sprawling, continental Babel. At the time of contact there may have been as many as six dozen language families alive and well on this continent (a family being analogous to the Romance group of the Western Mediterranean). Within each family, of course, there were distinct languages, and within languages there were dialects that were mutually unintelligible. Here is a summary:

- Eskimo-Aleut languages occurred along the northern coast and stretched from west of the Bering Sea to the North Atlantic.

- Macro-Algonquin languages dominated the Canadian Shield and the region that became New England down into the Middle Atlantic states, Wisconsin, the Ohio and Tennessee River Valleys and the central South.

- Aztec-Tanoan languages occurred in the western half of Mexico, in the Southwest Plateau, and central Texas.

- Penutian tongues appeared in the central valley of California and again in Oregon.

- Na-Dene languages were spoken through the thinly populated region of western Canada and central Alaska.

Not a linguist, I was astonished by nuggets of linguistics I encountered when researching my archaeological portrait of the continent before the coming of the Europeans, *The Smithsonian Book of North American Indians*. For example:

- Unlike the Romance languages, some Native-American tongues are not preoccupied with tenses and the placement of actions (and thus events) in past, present or future time. Rather, they highlight such things as an action's duration or its repetitive nature.

- In Kwakiutl, a speaker must say whether an object is seen—both by the speaker and whoever is spoken about.

- In Navajo, a person, beast, or thing cannot be described as narrowly or as simply as by those English words. The very structure of the language compels a Navajo noun to convey a much more fully descriptive range of information. In Navajo, a subject must be revealed as definite or vague; a verb cannot avoid indicating that the subject is round, long, animate, or whether an action is in progress, habitual or brief.

These examples suggest a critical element of Native-American consciousness: that in the Navajo world, for example, humans are not superior to other beings; characteristics of all other things are as worthy of note as any human's traits; and people must order themselves in relation to their surroundings. Compare that notion to the ancient Judeo-Christian tenet that "God said 'Let us make man in our image . . . and let them [humans] have dominion over the fish of the sea, and over the fowl of the air, and over the cattle, and over all the earth.'"

If prehistoric North America was complex in the distribution of languages, its peoples also made a remarkable mosaic of achievements in palpable forms of art and architecture that survive from one side of the continent to the other and from top to bottom. To study this continent's early people through archaeology is to encounter extraordinary work in such realms as practical astronomy, applied engineering, and plain survival, the first goal of any culture.

In prehistoric times, Native Americans thrived in places where most of us moderns might last a week, or at best a couple of seasons. Consider:

- Without wheeled vehicles, the Anasazi of the Southwest transported 200,000 logs across scores of miles in the high desert to Chaco Canyon. There they built huge pueblos and ceremonial kivas of clay-mortared masonry that remain standing three-fourths of a millennium later.

- Without pack animals or iron tools, those we call the Mound Builders moved millions of cubic yards of soil to raise the great earthworks of Moundville, Alabama; Monks Mound and others at Cahokia, Illinois; and Ohio's Serpent Mound.

- With built structures such as "medicine wheels" laid out in circles of stones on bare earth, inhabitants of the trans-Mississippi West calculated and predicted the passage of seasons. The high cultures of Mexico contrived a more accurate calendar than Europe possessed after the vaunted Renaissance.

- Without hard metal, the Woodland people of the Midwest made what we call "banner–stones," now-mysterious objects (possibly atlatl weights) that are as simply beautiful as any nonrepresentational object in the canon of modern art.

Prehistoric Americans created many things whose purposes we have not fathomed. They invested remarkable amounts of time, energy, and inventive skill in creations as diverse as those fist-sized bannerstones, and effigies of humans drawn in gravel outlines hundreds of feet long, and the giant concentric semicircles at the ceremonial center called Poverty Point, Louisiana.

Many cultures that preceded us on this continent thrived in situ for hundreds of generations, and followed an essentially constant life way whether in desert, tundra or forest. By comparison, people of European descent have occupied the Americas for 500 years and have had to experience a few social revolutions in the process. If stability is meritorious, light-skinned descendants of Johnny-come-lately Europeans should bow to the original conservatives, the ancestors of modern Native Americans.

America's ancient cultures created objects and art we cannot fathom because those people saw the world in their unique ways. It is self-evident that these viewpoints have value and deserve the respect of persons holding other views. To suggest the contrary is ridiculous. If I am tempted to impose my imported ethic on all others, I have only to think about trying to survive a winter in ultima Thule. I lack both the practical skills and the mental disci-

pline to get along without accustomed diversions. There is no room for a library in an igloo, nor for an entertainment center save in the repertory of itinerant storytellers. (In the past century anthropologists noted that a story, especially a joke, would make its way from Siberia to Greenland in the relative twinkling of two or three years. The circumpolar Eskimo peoples so treasured oral lore that they made storytelling a kind of profession perhaps because they had so many dark hours to fill in the land of the noonday night. Evidently they had more active senses of humor than anthropologists.)

The many viewpoints glimpsed through the foreshortening lens of history and prehistory offer positive proof of the vulgar adage, "different strokes for different folks." Or "each to his own taste." The need to struggle with the implications of this tenet underlie this volume (see Louis Redmond, Chapter Nine, in this volume). Wisely, I think, we are not as content as our forebears to admire uniformity per se or to accept the "melting pot" metaphor as an ideal.

Putting diversity aside, in scanning America's pre-Columbian past one encounters many notable manifestations of cohesion and cooperation. There had to have been extensive trading, probably along established lines, possibly over very long periods. For example, the bones of tropical birds (perhaps prized for feathered regalia) have been unearthed 300 miles inland from the Gulf of Mexico at Poverty Point. Hundreds of marine shells, richly carved with figures and symbols, have been found in landlocked Oklahoma. A fabulous hunk of obsidian whose geochemical signature proves its origin in the Tetons of Wyoming turned up in the Ohio River Valley where it must have been transported when men traveled only by foot and canoe—before the use of wheeled vehicles or beasts of burden.

Whatever their dramatic differences, the myriad peoples of pre-Columbian America often had enough in common to make common cause when it suited them, at least for many instances or traditions of trade. Those people could cooperate when they had reason to, as twentieth-century Americans must also do however numerous our purposes, beliefs and arguments. (A remark at the signing of the Declaration of Independence comes to mind: "We must hang together or most assuredly we will all hang separately." Hopefully that will be our watchword as we enter the most crowded century in the history of our prolific and prodigal species.)

In local terms, prehistoric Americans recognized equity by birthright between tribes/nations that could not have been equal in terms of might. Anthropological evidence shows that nations in the vicinity of places like modern Glenwood Springs, Colorado, and Yellowstone National Park all had free access to the hallowed resources of hot springs and mineral baths. This seems to have been a widespread convention. Such treasures of the earth were deemed too precious and too special, perhaps too powerful, to be the province of any one people. They must be shared. Similarly, as territories were claimed and altered by tribes along the Columbia River, a tradition arose that guaranteed everyone access to the river for salmon fishing during the spawning run. Territorial boundaries changed from time to time as some people abandoned or fled riverside lands and others claimed them, but whoever had the ancestral right to fish the great river retained the prerogative. Thus they shared what amounted to a public resource—the bounty of the river.

In passing, I must at least note the animosities that Indians visited on each other in both historic and prehistoric times. They waged war brutally. They enslaved each other (and Europeans). They are known to have practiced cannibalism—at least ritualistically in New England and perhaps for dietary reasons in Mexico. They annihilated each other, to judge by the sudden disappearance of some cultures. The archaeological record has many examples of one culture vanishing and another replacing it. Often the cause was plain genocide.

Intertribal conflict was often as bloody, fierce and lethal as any that Europe knew. More important for our purposes, I think, is the fact that all this notwithstanding, prehistoric Americans of rival cultures also found ways to share assets of special value. Now, today, our nation of nations must do no less than cherish and secure such assets for the future. Among them are our public lands, common property for all and resources for our modern and future diversity. The problem is how to forge public policies that assure or enable that. The good news is that at least we have a common language in which to negotiate; we need not talk in signs.

The range of cultures in pre-Columbian America was arguably as broad as it is today if not broader. There were "high" cultures ruled by priestly oligarchies. There was the Iroquois Confederacy of Na-

tions of the Five Tribes that Benjamin Franklin considered a model for an American republic. There were tribes in the Western U.S., located in the Great Basin, whose material culture was virtually bereft of excess or ornament, which led Europeans to think them uncivilized, though they survived for many generations in an inhospitable desert which must be counted as an extraordinary human accomplishment. Let us not make the silly error of assuming a people to be inferior because they lack excess material goods. One common attribute of possession-poor nomadic peoples in Africa, Australia and the Americas is an astonishingly rich oral tradition. Why? One reason is that storytelling preserves knowledge in collective memory: the locations of reliable water sources, edible plants, and so forth. In this manner, these people pass on specific and detailed information from generation to generation with enviable reliability.

Practical Implications

A major lesson evident in the broad sweep of prehistory is the simple premise that diversity has value—diversity in culture and viewpoint as well as diversity in flora and fauna. Consequently, I take exception to the general proposition put forth in the introductory chapter to this volume that managers must be particularly *objective* when responding to users of the public lands. Having lived in the nation's capital for more than 30 years and having watched, sometimes joined, the machinations of government, I believe that the road to accommodation does not lie in objectivity—in honesty, perhaps; in fairness, for sure; in consensus and compromise, certainly. I am certain that devotion to objectivity is at best a well-intentioned canard. At worst it is a mischievous tool designed to let people of special rank or responsibility (e.g., civil servants) feign superiority over other folk.

It seems to me that objectivity can no more be achieved by government organizations than by any other institution outside the most rarefied realms of quantitative science. In government particularly, pleadings of objectivity are too often excuses for obfuscation or for evading difficult decisions. We bureaucrats wrap ourselves in swaddlings of rules that seem to remove the vagaries of making discretionary decisions.

So, in the governance of separate tracts of public land, I would scrap the hope for safe objectivity and the comforting camouflage of uniformity. Instead, I would urge land managers to try to be fair, responsible and willing to make decisions case-by-case on the merits of each situation. We must strive for honesty and evenhandedness over the long haul and across broad horizons.

Obviously, a given acre of land cannot be grazed by one cattleman's stock, cleared for one New Age quester's medicine wheel, and held inviolate as one native tribe's ancestral sacred ground. In the instance of each specific piece of ground, decisions must be made. Those decisions must be made by individuals who base them on specific circumstances in the good-faith belief that across the board there will be grazing land, and retreats for the expression of alternative world-views, and sacred sanctuaries. Then it is the duty of the federal decision maker to help convince the public of the objective fact that the government, as steward, is doing the best it can while respecting all interested parties and serving their overall interests. By and large I think that most groups of the American people will negotiate and compromise if they see that their interests are being seriously considered and sometimes accommodated.

It behooves civil servants to make the best decisions we can without favor or fear. It behooves managers of public lands to tell the public what they are doing, honestly and openly. I think that if we do that, and at the same time let people know about it, the vast majority of our bosses, the American people, will cheer us on and give us the popular support necessary to maintain administrative agencies in a democracy.

As a civil servant, I think every employee of every public agency should believe in what her or his agency is doing, and each agency should inform the public of those doings as completely as it can. By the same token, every manager worth her or his salt—in order to stay worth it—should do things that she or he believes in, lest the salt lose its savor. Our duty lies in honesty and commitment to fairness. Our duty does not lie in weighing alternatives hoping that objectivity will prove one to be better than the other and thus force a choice for us. Our duty also lies in admitting our mistakes when we make them and in spreading the word far and wide about our successes.

The best hope for the preservation of America's special resources and unique assets lies in the adoption of sound general policies that must be constantly custom-fitted to particular circumstances by fair, responsible people who take their work seriously. The intention to act effectively behooves them to abandon the safety of uniform policy in the face of diverse circumstances. The people of the prehistoric Dorset culture did not survive by building round houses out of saplings and bark no more than the Woodland people lived in igloos. Americans of the nation's third century will thrive only if we husband resources such as distinct tracts of public land according to the specific circumstances of each tract, and if we balance the conflicting interests of involved parties in the broadest context.

It is easiest for civil servants to walk in lock step and worship the palest gods, Uniformity and Objectivity. Rules and the very notion of National Policy favor the uniform, the known, the strictly defined. On the other hand, the better public servant recognizes that the public is a variegated body, one that deserves service in diverse ways. If the future is to be rich in potential and if today's management principles are to assure our heirs a portion of what we have inherited, our generation must nurture a fraction of the diversity that this continent has seen. After all, we are to posterity what prehistory was to us—the guarantors of choice.

Endnote

[1]The author was Director of Publications at the National Endowment for the Arts at the time of this writing.

Literature Cited

Kopper, P. (1986). *The Smithsonian book of North American Indians*. Washington, DC: Smithsonian Books.

Lopez, B. (1978). *Of wolves and men*. New York, NY: Charles Scribner's Sons.

Section III

Part A

ETHNIC AND CULTURAL
PERSPECTIVES

Diverse Native American Perspectives on the Use of Sacred Areas on Public Lands

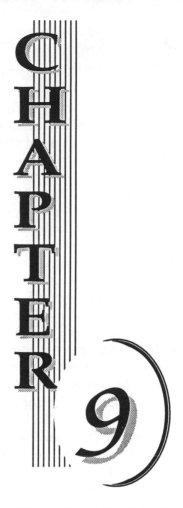

Louis Redmond
Nebraska National Forest
USDA Forest Service
Chadron, Nebraska

One of the problems encountered in misunderstandings between Native Americans and non-Native Americans is the assumption that in some way the world-views of both groups are basically the same. World-view, as defined here, means those basic cultural ideas and underlying undefinable inner stirrings or "voices" of a human being upon which everything else that individual does is based (Bock, 1969; Geertz, 1965). The traditional Native-American world-view, in general, embraces only a few basic premises. The first is that all Nature is sacred. Nature means everything dwelling on planet Earth—rocks, trees, humans, animals, birds, land, water—everything. Second, even the so-called harmful creature has a place in the Circle of Life and, as such, can teach us many things. Third, everything has a right to live, and everything is alive. If, for some reason, the life of a creature must be taken, it is usually only taken after asking forgiveness (cf. Halifax, 1979; Kehoe, 1981; Underhill, 1965).

In general, the world-view of non-Native Americans in the United States is that humans are superior creatures that alone have a God-given "right to life." All other forms of life can be utilized for the benefit of humans without thought or ceremony. What is called "sacred" by Native Americans is viewed as wilderness, barren, or dead by non-Native Americans, and therefore is exploitable.

A second problematic area is the perception by non-Native-American people that there is little diversity among Native-American groups in the application of their world-views (Deloria, 1973). In many ways, this homogeneous perception of the application of one's world-view is a two-way street. Many Native Americans and Native-American groups, for example, deal with non-Native Americans on preconceived notions formed when dealing with other non-Native-American groups or individuals. In truth, both sides exhibit spectrums of behavioral or dogmatic diversity not perceived by, or acknowledged by, the other side. Many times I've heard someone in authority say, "This concept works for the [Iroquois, Sioux, Apache, etc.] that I have dealt with in the past. Why can't these people get the hang of it?" Or from the other side, "Why do all 'whites' think that way?"

Although there is currently an extensive pan-tribal interaction related to traditional activities, there is also a resurgence of intratribal reorientation to individual tribal traditions (Moses and Wilson, 1985). For example, at a recent Sun Dance ceremony, there were Lakota, Mohawk, Blackfoot, Pueblo and Cheyenne participants. However, the medicine man that officiated was an Ogallala Lakota; therefore, the proceedings followed that medicine man's traditional ways, not those of the individual participants. Although the participants were all there in a form of fraternity, each individual as part of a group followed the lead of the medicine man. Continuing with this Sun Dance ceremony, some of the traditions represented believe that a Dancer should be pierced with a leather thong on the last day of the ceremony, while some traditions merely allow for the piercing, while others do not believe in piercing at all. Still others have all but lost any tradition of Sun Dancing due to prohibitions imposed by early missionaries. However, the general perception of the non-Native-American populace is that piercing is mandatory; after all, didn't Richard Harris have to get pierced in *A Man Called Horse* to prove his manliness?

This notion is further solidified by novels and films of the Old West and even in monographs written by anthropologists. That is not to say that all movies, novels, or monographs have reported a homogeneous application of piercing or other customs as pantribal tradition. However, the general public, including land managers, have accepted the view of being able to know about all Native Americans by studying a specific tribal group. This would be the same as a Native-American ethnologist studying the Catholics (or Masons or Trade Unionists or the people of Boise, Idaho) for a few years and saying that she or he could now understand all non-Native Americans. The enormity of this misconception is staggering. Even within the Catholic faith (or the Masons or whatever group) there is great diversity in the ritual and daily practices of its members. So it is within Native-American tribal groups. Within this context, each of the Sun Dance participants noted above was allowed to follow his or her own specific tribal beliefs even though the rest of the ceremony was specifically directed by those of the medicine man.

Both inter- and intratribal diversity is at least as extensive as within the different Christian faiths.

Added to this would be the same fundamental differences existing between Christians, Jews, and Moslems. Moving to another level on the scale would add in New Age activists, Eastern teachings, and confirmed or confused nonbelievers. All aspects of these analogues also exist within the Native-American community. There is little common ground in the belief systems of the Northwestern Nootka, the Southeastern Seminole, the Plains Cheyenne, the Northeastern Mohawk, or the Southwestern Pueblos apart from their same generalized world-view. Even within each of these communities there are believers, nonbelievers, traditionalists, lip service Native Americans, and those who merely go along because it is expected. Some of the people are altruistic, some are greedy. Some demand privacy for ceremonies while others would have a carnival atmosphere and charge fees.

Add to this the problem of defining who is a Native American (Canby, 1981; Price, 1973). Due to a myriad of regulations and tribal statutes, this is an extremely complex issue. In some tribes there are movements currently to enroll or recognize only those tribal members who are a minimum of one-half Native American from that specific tribe. In other tribal groups anyone who can provide definite blood lineage to anyone on the tribal roles from the early 1800s can become an enrolled member. The Bureau of Indian Affairs currently recognizes only those persons who are enrolled members of federally recognized tribes or recognized within the Native-American community as Native Americans. Today there are over 100 tribes that have been terminated (i.e., lost federal recognition) and for which there is no recourse under law as Native Americans (e.g., the Miamis of Indiana). These people were once recognized as Native-American people, but due to bureaucratic manipulation they no longer are. Added to this are an unknown number of tribes that for one reason or another have never had federal status (e.g., the Pomonkeys of Maryland).

Turning to the subject at hand, is it any wonder that federal agencies are stymied in attempting to develop rules and regulations to define the conduct of Tribal Agencies and Native-American groups, especially when dealing with ceremonial or spiritual use of public lands? Whether the Lakota go to the Black Hills in South Dakota to collect lodge poles for ceremonies, or the Ojibwa collect wild rice, or the Zuni culminate certain ceremonies near Zuni Salt Lake by "making salt" for their relatives, or the Northwest Coast Native Americans go fishing, these are all sacred activities. As such, the tribes or individuals request specific things from land managers like privacy. Added to this is usually a list of other, less demanding requests necessary for the proper conduct of the ceremony. Sometimes these are simple requests dealing with the use of rocks for sweat lodges, or at other times access to specific gathering areas. Sometimes there are no requests other than to be left in peace to conduct the ceremonies.

In 1992 at a meeting between a certain Plains tribe and representatives of a government agency, the Native Americans tried to impress on agency personnel, especially land managers, that they needed to collect live trees for upcoming ceremonies. They felt that their treaty rights were being violated once again because they were being forced to get and pay for a permit like the general public, in order to collect the trees necessary for tipi lodge poles. These live poles were necessary for the successful culmination of the ceremonies. The land manager replied that the Native Americans could go into previously burned areas and collect as many lodge poles as they liked from the burnt areas without paying for the permit. Nothing could be said by the Native Americans that seemed to get across to this official that the poles needed *must* come from live trees. Although several attempts were made to describe the ceremonial difference between the use of live and dead trees, the manager could not be dissuaded. The manager's attitude continued to be that a lodge pole was a lodge pole after all.

This misunderstanding was based almost solely on a difference in world-views. For the non-Native-American manager, there was no valid or sensible difference between live or dead lodge poles, especially if the poles were to be used merely as structural supports. In fact, the manager saw benefits in utilizing the dead trees instead of the live trees (less sap to get on oneself). For the Native-American participants, however, the tipi is a living being whose presence is necessary for the proper conduct of this ceremony. Also, there was never any attempt by the land managing agency personnel to explain that the permit needed was so the agency could manage its resources, not to keep track of or dictate to the people. Several points that were viewed as minor for the land manager and her staff were actually taken as major insults by many of the Native-American participants. These points could generally be ascribed to mistrust and prior unshakable agendas couched in differing world-views, not the least being the difference between using live and dead trees.

This particular agency is not the only agency or group that has been hampered by the influence of differing world-views in dealing with Native Americans. Several years ago there were controversies in many parts of the country over Native-American fishing rights. In one of these areas, Native-American fishermen had caught a huge supply of fish to be smoked and dried for their families for the coming winter. Several days after the catch, local townspeople discovered that one of the Native-American groups had "thrown out" a large number of fish. For the townspeople this was wanton disregard for non-Native-American fishermen, both recreational and commercial, who could very well have caught all the "wasted" fish. What the Native Americans had done, of course, was simply remain faithful to their world-view. The fishermen from each family or clan had merely given back a fish, or in some cases several, to the "Grandfather Spirits" that had guaranteed such a successful harvest. Had anyone looked, they would have found that in the mouth of most of the fish was a small bit of tobacco. These fish were offerings of thanksgiving.

This is not to say that all dealings between Native Americans and non-Native Americans end in this manner. The Sun Dance noted above occurs annually on national park lands on a specific date sacred to this Plains Indian group. Both parties sat down almost a decade ago and worked out the methodology whereby the Sun Dance grounds would be restricted to participants, supporters and their families. The national park in question is the traditional site of the Sun Dance for this particular group of a particular Plains tribe. The Sun Dance is a difficult time for the dancers and dance supporters (Spencer, Jennings, et al., 1977; Underhill, 1965). At this Sun Dance, the dancers themselves, and sometimes their supporters, endure four days of fasting without food or water. For many of these participants, stringent rules and taboos are followed for several days, weeks or months prior to arriving at the Sun Dance grounds. The ceremony for most of the dancers is the most sacred and enduring ceremony they will be involved in during their entire life. Privacy is a specific necessity, especially at this Sun Dance. These dancers perform a ritualistic renewal ceremony for the common good, not just to prove their manhood (Halifax, 1979; Underhill, 1965). A carnival atmosphere or even one of open invitation would distract the dancers from praying while they danced during these four days. As human beings, they would begin to wonder if they looked good or were doing everything exactly right, rather than trying to keep a spiritual attitude of what they were attempting to do for their people.

Eight years ago representatives of both sides sat down and talked face-to-face. There were no letters written to heads of departments or tribal councils; no internal meetings to define current policy; just two diverse groups sitting down to discuss the possibilities of assuring the rights and dignity of each side. A permit was issued, a no-fee permit for the records. There were restrictions on the behavior of the participants and their families imposed by national park regulations and the Native Americans themselves. Both sides defined the behavior expected of park users. The behavior designated by the Native-American group for its own participants was far stricter than that required of non-Native-American users of the park. (In such matters, Native-American groups generally do not want any type of special treatment. What they are looking for is what is guaranteed to them in their treaties, and as citizens of the United States under the Bill of Rights. All they are asking for is the right to practice their religious beliefs in the same unrestricted, unmolested manner as other Americans, of whatever faith. Supposedly, the Constitution allows each group the right to this unmolested practice of its inherent religious beliefs. In the past, this has not been allowed to Native-American groups, for whatever reason or bias).

Another private ceremony, sometimes sought on public lands, is the vision quest (Halifax, 1979). Versions of the vision quest are pantribal under different names, but are common in purpose. This purpose, in general, is to fast and pray for usually three to eight days "crying for a vision." During this time, the participant is generally alone with his or her own prayers and introspection. Usually participants seek through praying, fasting and sleep deprivation, to attain a vision that will aid their people in some way or make themselves more useful in some way to their individual people (Halifax, 1979). Dis-

tractions of any sort can prevent these visions. Again, privacy is of the utmost importance. However, this particular ceremony is much more difficult for non-Native Americans to grasp because, although it generally involves only one or at most several individuals, a very large unoccupied area is requested and necessary. In general, these participants seek out areas that have absolutely no development within a five- to ten-mile radius. (Yes, there are vision seekers who do fast and pray within a short distance of highly developed areas, but most prefer completely isolated areas.) Again, this is a very difficult time. The seeker is, as stated, generally alone with his or her own prayers, with no food or water, for the length of time that has been chosen. Typically, it takes the first several days to clear one's mind of the modern world and focus on the needs of the people or the problem one has gone there to divine. Interruptions of even the slightest nature can destroy what has been slowly built up over these several days. These ceremonies are difficult and demanding and can easily be interrupted sometimes causing grave consequences for the individual(s) involved.

An analog of this in the non-Native-American culture is the person who for years has gone to a specific secluded creek to fish. Each year he or she goes and spends a week at the creek totally secluded from anyone. During each trip he or she arrives fully agitated by the "rat race." At the end of the week, he or she is completely at peace with him- or herself and the world, whether or not any fish has been caught. The last year that this person went to the special creek, more fish were caught than any other two years combined. However, on the last two days a family of five camped across the creek. The family's noise and general disruption of the secluded scene sent the person back to the world as agitated as when he or she arrived. Was this person's release each prior year self-induced or a spiritual experience? Why not both?

Another problem, perhaps more obvious, in misunderstandings between Native-Americans and non-Native-American groups is that of language. Although in today's American society, where English is generally the acceptable language of use, many tribal people have been raised with their own language as a primary or at least coequal language. The tribal language itself imparts a different behavior or understanding implicitly when translated into

English. For example, the words "brother" or "sister" can be used within the tribal sense for any living creature with the same effect for the user as the English term defines the word to mean one's family. In other words, whether a Native-American uses the word "brother" or "sister" for another human or uses it to address another species, it still has the implicit relatedness defined in English. This, in general, is a relatively simple psychological attitude for a non-Native American to grasp, but when the terms are used for extended family members, confusion generally begins (e.g., a maternal cousin is a "brother" or "sister" while a paternal cousin may just be "some kind of relative"; an uncle may be recognized as a "father," an aunt as a "mother," etc.). Added to the confusion of actual blood relatives is the case of the friend who is viewed as a "brother" or "sister," "son" or "daughter," and, therefore, has the same relative position within a family that this natural person of blood would occupy in the non-Native-American world.

This, then, is where the trouble of language enters into conceptual discussion. In general, non-Native Americans can grasp the initial uses of terms by Native-American people, but when the terms are used in broader senses, they become lost. At the same time, many Native-American words or phrases imply far more than what is translated. For example, in Iroquois, the greeting phrase in common practice is *Shekon* which translates directly as "still" or "yet." This word is taken from the phrase, *Shekon skennen kowa* which means literally "still peace is great," which is a direct reference to the Great Peace acquired in the forming of the Iroquois Confederacy centuries ago. Among the Iroquois, this implies a time depth of friendship and commitment to peace and each other within the tribes, predating contact by Europeans.

This discussion centers on the relatively complicated definitions of what exactly Native Americans mean by sacredness when addressing public lands. To put this in rather simplistic terms, the Native-American concept moves through a series of concentric, spherical perceptions, each built upon and related to the one before and after, above and below (cf., Storm, 1972). Initially, Native-American people see the Earth as the sacred embodiment of Mother Earth and as such representative of the universe. In the second sphere are notions of world and tribal origin centered in oral traditions. The next sphere

involves generalized geographic places (some of which are origin places also) like the Black Hills in the Dakotas that are considered naturally sacred and related to several levels of belief. Next are specific, individual places like Devil's Tower, Wyoming, (*Mahto Tipishila*), Niagara Falls or Zuni Salt Lake which are specifically sacred (see also Deloria, 1973). The next sphere is specific sites of ceremonies, such as Sun Dances, that are held to be sacred. Then come the sites of ceremonies used for practices such as purification ceremonies that are held as sacred. Last are those places where sacred objects such as prayer pipes are generally stored. All of these are sacred and equal each in its own right, as well as everything that walks, crawls, swims, flies or resides on Earth, in the air, or in the waters. All of these are implicit in the "Religion of the Red Man" and as such cannot be ranked in reality. The place where a sacred pipe is kept is as sacred to the individual pipe carrier and his or her family as is Mother Earth to them and to their people. Devil's Tower is as sacred to a Lakota as is the plot of land where his or her children play. Each of these concentric, spherical perceptions is only complete within the completion of each other concentric, spherical perception.

This, then, is another level of misunderstanding between Native Americans and non-Natives. That many of these ideas can be intuited by non-Native Americans sometimes causes even greater misunderstandings. This is due in part to the misinterpretation that because one or several levels of these spherical comprehensions are reached, that is all there is to understand. Far from it! The really sad part is that many Native-American peoples only understand the depth and complexity of these spherical realms intuitively and from the oral traditions taught from early childhood. For this reason, it is often extremely difficult for a Native-American person to explain fully the meaning of something. It generally ends with an exasperated "But why can't you understand? I've just explained it!" In reality, the Native American may have explained it as fully as possible, but only for another Native American because both are using the shorthand of understanding. They are dealing with the same worldview that begins their own understanding. It is exactly the same when a non-Native American attempts to explain something to a Native American. Many times the initial feeling on both sides is that an understanding has been reached only to find in the future that next to nothing was actually understood.

The lives of Native-American people are also tied to the land upon which their tribe exists or existed prehistorically (cf. Deloria, 1973). The "story of the people" is based upon features across the landscape. The Native-American people can only exist as a full and complete people within the landscape of their oral traditions. Whether it is the Iroquois of the Northeast, the Plains tribes of the Midwest, or the Pueblos of the Southwest, each group relates to both the specific and generalized landscape within each country as children upon Mother Earth. Tradition and religious ritual is intimately tied to locations within each Native-American Nation's home country. Specificality of landscape is not easily understood by the non-Native American who possesses a mobile religion that can be practiced anywhere on Earth. However, there are some specific sacred areas—Jerusalem, Mecca—that are analogous to the landscape relatedness of Native-American religious belief.

This, then, is the reason that tribal groups request unmolested access to specific locations that are currently described as "public" land. Prehistorically these lands "belonged" to, or, more accurately, were lived on by the tribes that request the access. In some cases, as with Niagara Falls for northeastern tribes, non-Native American use, development and whole or partial destruction of a sacred site currently precludes use of the area for ceremony. There is no way that the people that once held these areas as sacred could go there with privacy to perform ceremonial rituals in peace. Other ceremonies such as the Sun Dance at Devil's Tower described earlier can still be performed only with cooperation of others.

The question then becomes why is it necessary for Native-American people to have special access to specific properties within the public domain? The requirements placed on land managers by the separate Native-American Nations or groups would generally not be entertained if they were requested by non-Native-American groups. Do the Native-American people have special rights not available to the general public or specific special interest groups? The answer is emphatically "Yes!" The emphasis is placed by two modes of law: first, the treaties made by each Nation; and second, by the Bill of Rights of the United States Constitution. Although each Native-American Nation is not recognized as having the same rights across the board, treaties with each of the treaty nations do grant special rights, including land use, to individual tribes or nations. Nothing can be said about these in any coherent general sense, and each tribal group must be taken on separately, case-by-case. There is no easy answer to this problem, and each case should and must be taken through the legal system individually.

Most of the original treaties that granted unmolested use of aboriginal lands to the tribes were abrogated by later treaties. Before anything can be said about the later treaties, these original treaties should at least be perused. These treaties, both the original and all subsequent treaties, are legal documents signed between sovereign nations and as such are recognized by international courts (although oftentimes they are ignored by the United States Government). These documents, in truth, are more binding today than they have been in the past and therefore should be checked whenever there are dealings between Native-American nations and managers of the "public" lands.

As for the Bill of Rights and the Constitution, these are used and have been used to specify a strict delineation between church and state without regard to protection of Native-American religious rights. Every single citizen in this country is guaranteed the unmolested right to freedom of religion. No other people in this nation need have specific laws passed in order to practice their inherent religious rights. In the last several decades, however, several such laws have been passed by Congress and another is currently pending. In reality, there can be no such delineation between "church and state" for Native-American people (Canby, 1981; Deloria, 1973; Halifax, 1979; Price, 1973; Underhill, 1965). As stated earlier, all aspects of humanity are enmeshed within all other aspects for most Native-American peoples. The experiment of attempting to delineate these parts into separate areas has been mostly a disaster for Native-American peoples, and many are returning to traditional values because of it. This inherent part of Native-American life was acknowledged in the passage of the Indian Civil Rights Act of 1968 (Canby, 1981).

The right to the unmolested practice of one's inherent religion also takes on special meaning when applied to Native Americans. This is the only group of American citizens whose definitive, historic religion identifies specific landscapes within the boundaries of the United States. Many of these landscapes have been annexed by the subsequent treaties mentioned above and are now "public" lands. For Native Americans to have a full resolution of the right to religious freedom guaranteed by the Constitution, they must be allowed special access to specific areas within publicly owned lands.

Once again, the legalities of these treaties must be realized by both parties. Then the next step is face-to-face consultations. Here I use the word *consultation* because it is implicitly appropriate with representatives of treaty signatories. Although it may seem unnecessary to state or restate, Native-American Nations and their subordinate representatives are special cases. These entities truly do have rights of access to public lands and special use of those lands and resources in many cases that are not reserved to any other group. One thing not generally grasped by land managers is that the treaty rights of these nations transcend the concerns of the Constitution concerning a separation of church and state. The first amendment specifies that no group can be given preferential treatment under the Constitution for the practice of its religion. However, since the time of George Washington, the U.S. Government, and by extension, its agents, has been responsible for representing Native-American people "in all your just rights" (Price, 1973, pp. 384-386). These just rights do implicate special access to public lands not otherwise allowed to any other group of American citizens. However, in reality, Native-American people as a whole are asking for nothing more than what is guaranteed to all other American citizens, the right to speak to their God without harassment or intimidation.

Acknowledgments

I would like to thank Thomas Cook, Loretta Afraid-of-Bear Cook, Ben Rhodd, Peter Swift Bird Jr., Raymond Samudio, Delores White Head, Charlotte Black Elk, Gerald Clifford, Kathleen Russell, Elizabeth Amos and all the many others who have reviewed this work and graciously commented on it. The content, however, is my own and I am fully responsible for it.

Literature Cited

Bock, P. (1969). *Modern cultural anthropology*. New York, NY: Alfred A. Knopf, Inc.

Canby, W., Jr. (1981). *American Indian law in a nutshell*. St. Paul, MN: West Publishing Co.

Deloria, V., Jr. (1973). *God is red*. New York, NY: Dell Publishing.

Geertz, C. (1965). Religion as a cultural system. In W. Lessa and E. Vogt (Eds.), *Reader in Comparative Religion* (pp. 204-216). New York, NY: Harper & Row, Publishing, Inc.

Halifax, J. (1979). *Shamanic voices*. New York, NY: E. P. Dutton.

Kehoe, A. (1981). *North American Indians: A comprehensive account*. Englewood Cliffs, NJ: Prentice Hall.

Moses, L. and Wilson, R. (Eds.). (1985). *Indian lives: Essays on nineteenth- and twentieth-century Native-American leaders*. Albuquerque, NM: University of New Mexico Press.

Price, M. (1973). *Law and the American Indian*. New York, NY: The Bobbs-Merrill Company.

Spencer, R., Jennings, J., et al. (1977). *The Native Americans: Ethnology and backgrounds of North American Indians* (2nd ed.). New York, NY: Harper & Row Publishing, Inc.

Storm, H. (1972). *Seven arrows*. New York, NY: Ballantine Books, Inc.

Underhill, R. (1965). *Red man's religion*. Chicago, IL: University of Chicago Press.

AFRICAN AMERICAN NATURIFOCAL VALUES

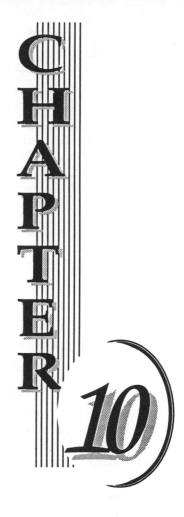

CHAPTER 10

RACHEL BAGBY
Friends of the Ganges
Vallecitos Mountain Refuge
Taos, New Mexico

the earth is a living thing
*is a black shambling bear
ruffling its wild back and tossing
mountains into the sea*

*is a black hawk circling
the burying ground circling the bones
picked clean and discarded*

*is a fish black blind in the belly of water
is a diamond blind in the black belly of coal
is a black and living thing
is a favorite child
of the universe
feel her rolling her hand
in its kinky hair
feel her brushing it clean*

Lucille Clifton, 1993[1]

"Naturifocal," nature + focal, is a word coined by the author to mean nature reverence as a focusing principle of attention and activity. Naturifocal values and related belief systems of African immigrants to the Americas—whether they arrived as free explorers, indentured servants or as slaves, before or after Columbus—were as

diverse as the continent from which they came is vast (Mbiti, 1969; van Sertima, 1976).

According to John Holloway, editor of *Africanisms in American Culture*, the majority of African slaves' cultural heritages reflected civilizations of the clearings and the cities. Slave traders preyed on peoples from these areas because their skills were demanded by colonists.

The people of the clearings were familiar with the cultivation practices for rice, indigo, cotton, yams, maize, sorghum, okra, and sesame. The urban dwellers based their civilization on trade and commerce, and they had strong centralized political authorities. They were also excellent cattlemen and agriculturalists, familiar with the cultivation of yams, maize, corn, okra, palm oil, and sorghum. The Ashanti and Dahomeans in particular perfected art works in stone, bronze, and iron.

The African slaves' cultural heritage was based on numerous West and Central African cultures brought together collectively from Senegambia (Wolof, Mandingo, Malinke, Bambara, Fulani, Papel, Limba, Bola, and Balante), the Sierra Leone coast (Temne and Mende), the Liberian coast (Vai, De, Gola, Kisi, Bassa, and Grebo),

[1]"the earth is a living thing" from *The Book of Light*. Reprinted by permission of the Copper Canyon Press, PO Box 271, Port Townsend, WA 98368

and the Slave Coast (Yoruba, Nupe, Benin, Dahomean [Fon], Ewe, Ga, Popo, Edo-Bini, and Fante). From the Central African coast came Bakongo, Malimbo, Bambo, Ndungo, Balimbe, Badongo, Luba, Loanga, Luango, and Ovimbundu.

Holloway, 1991, p. 11

An oversimplified yet contextually useful summary of common naturifocal world-views underlying primal beliefs and related practices of the areas in which these cultures thrived is as follows:

1. interrelatedness;

2. natural forces communicate through naturally occurring phenomena;

3. emphasis on action and relationship; and

4. notions of mutual obligation.

According to African naturifocal world-views, all within the cycle of Life and death is interrelated. Various natural forces, including human nature, interact/communicate through naturally occurring phenomena (e.g., bodies of water, weather, storms, droughts, and seasons). There is an emphasis on action: relationships with natural forces are actively cultivated through group and individual ritual. Humans *embody* larger-than-human forms of these forces through the expressive use of drums/rhythms/song/musicality of oral delivery and dance. African naturifocal notions of mutual obligation hold that the various worlds in which natural forces operate and are perceived (e.g., the worlds of spirits, humans, and the wild), are actively and mutually responsible for each other (Mbiti, 1969; Mitchell, 1977; and Murphy, 1994).

These principles are the ground in which this chapter is seeded. The proverbs, poems, novel excerpts, and cultural practices discussed herein illuminate resonant relationships between African naturifocal values and those of African Americans. Doing so is essential to this chapter's integrity. Doing so also ensures that the naturifocality I ascribe to African Americans is more than a chocolate-covered polyglot of naturifocal values and practices born of this continent and the mix of peoples with whom African Americans have cocreated this country.

What can racially-based attributes of naturifocal values contribute to an evolving ethic of public lands stewardship? Racially-based inquiries are often suspect in the United States because race is still one of the most destructive ways Americans habitually classify someone as an outsider—"the other," or as "not one of us." But the present search for racially-based naturifocal values has the goal of articulating our collective wisdom about, and actions toward, restorative stewardship. This learning goal transforms what has historically been a destructive dynamic into a potentially creative one.

In the process of learning how to empathize with the "others" ways of "others," respectfully relating to other-than-human nature, one expands one's possibilities for developing different ways of listening to and learning from Life directly. Gathering, respecting, and seeking to understand interracial/intercultural, naturifocal wisdom broadens the experiential foundation upon which to base an evolving restorative land management ethic. This chapter proceeds in the spirit of contributing Native-American wisdom to discussions and decisions affecting our common Life.

What follows is divided into five sections:

1. Claiming Ground,

2. Kneeling Ground,

3. Choosing Ground,

4. Healing Ground, and

5. Fertile Ground.

Each section is introduced, adorned, and sometimes centered around resonant poetry, proverbs, song lyrics and stories that echo the African naturifocal principles outlined above.

"Claiming Ground" maps out conceptual parameters of our exploration—fleshing out the reasons for relying on story, poetry, proverbs, music, and folk practices for *interrelated* evidence of Native-American naturifocal values. "Kneeling Ground" offers examples of revering natural forces as ancestors; examples encoded in Native-American *actions*: cultural arts and social practices. "Choosing Ground" details experiences of *interacting/communicating* with the wild as cathedral, sanctuary, place and partner of freedom and spiritual maturing. "Healing Ground" focuses on how *mutually beneficial relationships* between humans and other forms of nature cocreate revitalizing environmental and social change. "Fertile Ground" draws on each of the four preceding groundings to suggest implications for a restorative land management ethic.

One tree cannot make a forest

Igi Kan Ki s'igbo
Nigerian Proverb

A few words about method and sources. Repetition, unconventional capitalizations, unusual word conjugations and poetic sentence structure are three ways language is placed at the service of this chapter's substance, rather than bending the latter into more familiar forms. Sources which record oral expressions of naturifocal values (e.g., songs and proverbs) are highlighted in deference to the historical place oral tradition holds as a system of communication and knowledge throughout Africa and the African diaspora. "Choosing Ground" ends with a composite text based on testimonies from several Native-American activists, each of whom independently requested anonymity because of the nature of the material. Thus, this chapter is organized to reflect the wild's interdependent diversity in its known and unknown, seen and unseen, identifiable and mysterious expressions.

Receive each section's offerings as initiating glimpses into the living continuum of African Americans' naturifocal values.

Claiming Ground

The Negro Speaks of Rivers

I've known rivers:

I've known rivers ancient as the world and older than the flow of human blood in human veins.

My soul has grown deep like the rivers.

I bathed in the Euphrates when dawns were young.
I built my hut near the Congo and it lulled me to sleep.
I looked upon the Nile and raised the pyramids above it.
I heard the singing of the Mississippi when Abe Lincoln went down to New Orleans, and I've seen its muddy bosom turn all golden in the sunset.

I've known rivers:
Ancient, dusky rivers.

My soul has grown deep like the rivers.

Langston Hughes, 1973[2]

Many questions are confronted at the onset of a quest for contemporary, generalizable African

American expressions of naturifocal values. Scholars debate the ability of Africanisms—naturifocal, spiritual or otherwise—to survive North American slavery's soul-snatching practices. There are those scholars who agree with E. Franklin Frazier in arguing that such practices mitigated against transmitting significant, culturally cohesive legacies from generation to generation of slaves and their post-emancipation offspring (Frazier, 1964). These practices included the dispersal of various language and cultural/kinship groups on arrival in North America while brutally enforcing spirit and culture-breaking practices such as separating children from parents, forbidding the speaking of African languages, silencing drums, and forcing conversions to Christianity.

In contrast to Frazier (1964) and his followers, Herskovits and contemporary scholars argue that abundant evidence of Africanisms are to be found throughout the United States. These scholars support their position by citing striking resonances between contemporary Native-American language, proverbs, music, folk art/tales, literary/fine art, religious/social practices, and that of slaves and their African ancestors (Herskovits, 1958; Holloway, 1991; Thompson, 1983, 1993).

As is true with seemingly conflicting forces in nature, truths in the Frazier-Herskovits (1958) perspectives coexist. For example, the version of Christianity slave masters offered slaves encouraged them to believe their subservience was inevitable and ordained by God. Salvation and freedom were something to expect after death, up there somewhere in Heaven, but definitely not here where all that grows in and depends on earth's dirt for survival. Such beliefs are the antithesis of those that encourage a present, cocreative relationship with Life. Despite this indoctrination effort and shattering of traditions, Native-American Christianity evolved a rhythmic and musical quality in its preaching and ritual styles evocative of that found in Africa and absent from practices of "typical" non-Black Christians.

Another legacy connecting first Negro, then Black, and now Native-American Churches to the African tradition of recognizing the *interrelatedness* of spiritual and social life is the tradition of institutional *actions* toward freedom from social injustice. This tradition finds a naturifocal expression in the environmental justice movement, the national organizing efforts of which were spearheaded by the

---

[2]from *Selected Poems by Langston Hughes.* Copyright 1926 by Alfred A Knopf, Inc. and renewed 1954 by Langston Hughes. Reprinted by permission of the publisher.

United Church of Christ (UCC) Commission for Racial Justice under the leadership of an Native-American minister (Bullard, 1992).

In October 1991, UCC sponsored "The First National People of Color and the Environment Summit" in Washington, DC. Conference delegates adopted seventeen principles of environmental justice (see below). "Mother Earth" focused principles were in large part contributed by Native American delegates; a reflection of their living relationship with the Earth.

In mainstream Native-American culture, however, the reclamation of naturifocal values as a living principle is still in its infancy. This is a predictable legacy of a people forced to migrate from their known land to work another for the benefit of those who viewed and treated them as slaves, less than human, who abused them as other animals are often

Principles of Environmental Justice
Preamble

We The People Of Color, gathered together at this multinational People of Color Environmental Leadership Summit, to begin to build a national and international movement of all peoples of color to fight the destruction and taking of our lands and communities, do hereby reestablish our spiritual interdependence to the sacredness of our Mother Earth; to respect and celebrate each of our cultures, languages and beliefs about the natural world and our roles in healing ourselves; to insure environmental justice; to promote economic alternatives which would contribute to the development of environmentally safe livelihoods; and, to secure our political, economic and cultural liberation that has been denied for over 500 years of colonization and oppression, resulting in the poisoning of our communities and land and the genocide of our peoples, do affirm and adopt these Principles of Environmental Justice:

1. *Environmental justice* affirms the sacredness of Mother Earth, ecological unity and the interdependence of all species, and the right to be free from ecological destruction.

2. *Environmental justice* demands that public policy be based on mutual respect and justice for all peoples, free from any form of discrimination or bias.

3. *Environmental justice* mandates the right to ethical, balanced and responsible uses of land and renewable resources in the interest of a sustainable planet for humans and other living beings.

4. *Environmental justice* calls for universal protection from nuclear testing, extraction, production and disposal of toxic/hazardous wastes and poisons that threaten the fundamental right to clean air, land, water, and food.

5. *Environmental justice* affirms the fundamental right to political, economic, cultural and environmental self-determination of all peoples.

6. *Environmental justice* demands the cessation of the production of all toxins, hazardous wastes, and radioactive materials, and that all past and current producers be held strictly accountable to the people for detoxification and the containment at the point of production.

7. *Environmental justice* demands the right to participate as equal partners at every level of decision making including needs assessment, planning, implementation, enforcement and evaluation.

8. *Environmental justice* affirms the right of all workers to a safe and healthy work environment, without being forced to choose between an unsafe livelihood and unemployment. It also affirms the right of those who work at home to be free from environmental hazards.

9. *Environmental justice* protects the right of victims of environmental injustice to receive full compensation and reparations for damages as well as quality healthcare.

10. *Environmental justice* considers governmental acts of environmental injustice a violation of international law, the Universal Declaration on Human Rights, and the United Nations Convention on Genocide.

11. *Environmental justice* must recognize a special legal and natural relationship of Native Peoples to the U.S. government through treaties, agreements, compacts, and covenants affirming sovereignty and self-determination.

12. *Environmental justice* affirms the need for urban and rural ecological policies to clean up and rebuild our cities and rural areas in balance with nature, honoring the cultural integrity of all our communities, and providing fair access for all to the full range of resources.

13. *Environmental justice* calls for the strict enforcement of principles of informed consent, and a halt to the testing of experimental reproductive and medical procedures and vaccinations on people of color.

14. *Environmental justice* opposes the destructive operations of multinational corporations.

15. *Environmental justice* opposes military occupation, repression and exploitation of lands, peoples and cultures, and other life forms.

16. *Environmental justice* calls for the education of present and future generations which emphasizes social and environmental issues, based on our experience and an appreciation of our diverse culture perspectives.

17. *Environmental justice* requires that we, as individuals, make personal and consumer choices to consume as little of Mother Earth's resources and to produce as little waste as possible; and make the conscious decision to challenge and reprioritize our lifestyles to insure the health of the natural world for present and future generations.

Adopted October 27, 1991 in Washington, DC.

abused. A people surviving such experiences would understandably see the flight away from dirt and animals, flight from naturifocal identities and skills, as a flight toward freedom. Native-American mass migrations to urban areas to find jobs and escape violently enforced Jim Crow laws (pervasive codes of racial discrimination initiated in the Southern United States) were, in part, an expression of this flight pattern. The continuity of Native-American naturifocality suffered in the process.

Where, then, is one most likely to be successful in finding contemporary clues to the values one hopes to understand better? My search for Native-American naturifocal values logically begins in places and populations devoted to preserving traditional wisdom in the face of alienating forces. Helpful clues exist in parallel and usually visually or orally transmitted understandings of Life; encoded languages embedded in cultural expressions of what slaves and their descedants made of conflicts between:

1. the versions of reality inherited from their ancestors;

2. those told them by their masters; and

3. what they were learning about cocreative freedom from Native Americans and from the new land, its rivers, trees, rocks, creatures, winged and many legged ones; the sensually evident forms of Life they came to know in their new home.

Thus, I began my search in folk-based, Native-American, expressive arts and works of contemporary artists who articulate the depth to which their works are informed by that of the folks. Folk arts and their derivatives sprout from the ground of experience that their practitioners devote their lives to preserving.

In her books, Toni Morrison, Nobel Prize winning author, exemplifies Native-American literary traditions based on folk forms. Morrison's works are true to written and oral traditions, both of which are equally potent and vital in contemporary Native-American culture (Taylor-Guthrie, 1994). And the oral tradition depends on lusciously arresting language, rhythm, repetition, and vivid—often nature-based—imagery to transmit knowledge in ways designed to enhance the listeners' retention. Indeed, these arts can expect to be bearers of the naturifocal values that have managed to survive as they have proven to be the signifiers of a myriad of other cul-

tural beliefs, values, practices, and survivalisms (Lovell, 1972; Murphy, 1994; Thompson, 1993).

Kneeling Ground

Generosity, as the highest form of morality in Yoruba traditional terms, is suggested . . . by symbolized offering of something by a person to a higher force through the act of kneeling.

Thompson, 1983, p. 13

Reverence of natural forces as ancestors and voices of the spirits is a widely held practice throughout the African diaspora (Mitchell, 1977; Murphy, 1994). Ysaye Barnwell, a composer and member of the Native-American women's a cappella group Sweet Honey in the Rock, paid homage to this value when she put "Breaths," a poem by Senegalese poet Birago Diop, to music. The song's lyrical melody and cadence lulls us into listening:

. . . more closely / to things than to beings / listen more closely / to things than to beings / 'tis the ancestor's breath / when the fire's voice is heard / 'tis the ancestors breath / in the voice of the water.

Sweet Honey in the Rock, 1988

The song "Breaths" in both its message and cocreation by an African man and Native-American woman embodies the naturifocal belief of interrelatedness. As Barnwell articulates it:

[i]n the African world-view, the invisible world of spirit, humans, and the visible world of nature exist on a continuum and form an organic reality. In Diop's poem 'Breaths' we are reminded of this continuum. In writing the music I tried to create a continuous melody line, rhythms that represent the relationship *[emphasis added] between human rhythmic functions and the laws of nature, and breath sounds representing the breath of life and the presence of spirit in air around us.*

Reagon and Sweet Honey in the Rock, 1993, pp. 264-265

The action called for in "Breaths" is that of listening, paying respect (attending) to natural forces with our ears. Through this action one maintains ancestral connection and receives ancestral guidance. Thus, listening to natural phenomena is a way in which to fulfill one's obligations to ancestral forces.

"Breaths" is requested again and again by Sweet Honey in the Rock audiences of diverse racial, ethnic and socioeconomic backgrounds throughout the United States. One interpretation of the song's popularity is that it evidences contemporary American resonance with African naturifocal values.

My Grandfather Walks in the Woods

Somewhere
in the light above the womb,
black trees
and white trees
populate a world.

It is a March landscape,
the only birds around are small
and black.
What do they eat,
sitting in the birches
like warnings?

The branches of the trees
are black and white.
Their race is winter.
They thrive in cold.

There is my grandfather
walking among the trees.
He does not notice
his fingers are cold.
His black felt hat
covers his eyes.

He is knocking on each tree,
listening to their voices
as they answer slowly
deep, deep from their roots.
I am John, he says,
are you my father?

They answer
with voices like wind
blowing away from him.

Marilyn Nelson Waniek, 1978
from *For the Body*[3]

A related practice of acknowledging and cultivating relationships between human and ancestral natures centers around traditions in both Kongo and southern Native-American communities of planting trees directly on graves to symbolize the idea of immortality.

---

[3]Reprinted by permission of Louisiana State University Press from *For the Body*, by Marilyn Nelson Waniek. Copyright 1978 by Marilyn Nelson Waniek.

There is, in fact, a whole collection of trees in Kongo, each with its special symbolic nuance that comes forward dramatically in the mortuary context. Mbota trees, famous for their extremely hard wood, suggest the hardiness of the elders' spirit and resistance to the force of time. This suggestion may have reinforced the similar use of cedar in black America as a preferred wood for stakes and headboards . . . To this day, the more spectacularly traditional graves in black Georgia and South Carolina often are sited by and, in a few cases, even hidden within woods or clumps of forest.

Thompson, 1991, p. 172

The tradition continues. Thanks to an Native-American environmentalist association—The Center for Environment, Commerce and Energy—Martin Luther King, Jr.'s grave site is now graced with a tree (*The Native-American Environmentalist*, 1990).

Choosing Ground

sitting

on a poem

the mountain writes me

Rachel Bagby, forthcoming
from *Fertile Ground*

Rich is the ongoing tradition of Native-American meetings with spirit, both communal and individual, in the natural cathedrals we call forests. This relation is in part another gift of restrictions on slave's religious freedom. Clandestine praise or prayer meetings and night sings often took place under the protective darkness and distance offered by the deep woods (Simpson, 1978).

During the time of slavery, freepersons of African descent also expressed their spiritual impulses in forests, being unwelcome in white churches, having not yet created their own buildings of worship, or being called to revive their souls in the wild. The following excerpt from Toni Morrison's *Beloved* offers a vivid, fictionalized account of the content of such services.

When warm weather came, Baby Suggs, holy, followed by every black man, woman, and child who could make it through, took her great heart to the Clearing—a wide-open place cut deep in the woods nobody knew for what at the end of a path known only to deer and whoever cleared the land in the first place. In the heat of every

Saturday afternoon, she sat in the clearing while the people waited among the trees.

After situating herself on a huge flat-sided rock, Baby Suggs bowed her head and prayed silently. The company watched her from the trees. They knew she was ready when she put her stick down. Then she shouted, 'Let the children come!' and they ran from the trees toward her.

'Let your mothers hear you laugh,' she told them, and the woods rang. The adults looked on and could not help smiling.

Then 'Let the grown men come,' she shouted. They stepped out one by one from among the ringing trees.

'Let your wives and your children see you dance,' she told them, and groundlife shuddered under their feet.

Finally she called the women to her. 'Cry,' she told them. 'For the living and the dead. Just cry.' And without covering their eyes the women let loose.

It started that way: laughing children, dancing men, crying women and then it got mixed up. Women stopped crying and danced; men sat down and cried; children danced, women laughed, children cried until, exhausted and riven, all and each lay about the Clearing damp and gasping for breath. In the silence that followed, Baby Suggs, holy, offered up to them her great big heart.

She did not tell them to clean up their lives or to go and sin no more. She did not tell them they were the blessed of the earth, its inheriting meek or its glorybound pure.

She told them that the only grace they could have was the grace they could imagine. That if they could not see it, they would not have it.

Morrison, 1987, pp. 87-88

The Native-American tradition of experiencing spiritual deepening in forests finds contemporary expression in Southern Baptist churches still located in the woods near waters which become ongoing baptismal pools. Before the act of baptism, however, comes the reckoning. Witness the testimony of Bernice Regon Johnson Reagon (Reagon and Sweet Honey in the Rock 1993), MacArthur genius grant-winner, daughter of a Baptist minister and founder of Sweet Honey in the Rock:

A sinner was supposed to go through a seeking period. I knew of older cousins and my oldest

sister who began praying to be saved. They did not eat; they also went into the woods to their own praying ground [emphasis added].... In late August 1953, I went to my praying ground. I got up in the middle of the night and went into 'the bottom.' This was a wooded area near our house that I never went to alone during the day. I positioned myself under a tree and began to pray that my sins be forgiven. I was struck with a great fear, and I prayed that as a sign of forgiveness, my fears be removed. I don't know how long I stayed there shaking in fear and praying, but then I felt a great change. I was swept throughout with a quiet and deep calm. I felt quiet inside, the fear was gone, the shakes were gone, and all the sounds of the woods were gone, there was no sound anywhere. Within me was a peace I had never felt before. I got up from my praying place and don't remember the walk back to the house. When I got inside, I woke up my mother and told her what had happened to me and that I felt I had it (p. 138).

The consummate integrity and equitableness of the wild makes it the sanctuary of choice for many Native-American activists. Their composite, anonymous testimony—excerpted in the following two paragraphs—eloquently articulates why they choose the wild as their healing ground. (The statements are unattributed at the activists' request.)

Nowhere else feels as much like home to me as does the wild. If a snake comes out and bites me, well then, I know deep inside of me that snake bite came not because I am Black or a woman or my parent's son, or because that snake was threatened by ignorance of my race, or afraid I would shed some of my dirt on it. If a tree falls down on me and kills me, if lightening strikes, it's not personal, not some consequence of a socialized ism or two or three.

And trees are simply themselves. They're not out to prove anything, nor to make me be like them. Their gifts are offered without discrimination. I don't feel compelled to guard against slipping into my mother's tongue lest I be considered uneducated rather than in love with and proud of the music she squeezes all up into her language. In the woods silence, wordlessness rather, is our shared language. I can feel myself and feel what the wind tells me, hear what the birds say. To be in the wild is much needed relief from so-called civilization.

Healing Ground

Earth is the queen of all beds
Nigerian Proverb

Catherine Sneed, a Native-American woman and former welfare mother, diagnosed with a terminal kidney disease, lay in a hospital bed, reading Steinbeck's *The Grapes of Wrath* (1939). Inspired, she dreamed of transforming fallow land at her job site, the San Francisco jail, into a garden. In the 1930s that same land had been a 145-acre farm. When Michael Hennessey, the sheriff, her boss, and friend, came to visit what he thought was her death-bed, she excitedly told him about the possibility of putting inmates to work cleaning the place up and planting growing things. He said she could as soon as she was out of the hospital. Catherine Sneed left her hospital bed the next day.

She and a group of male and female inmates began clearing the land with their hands because they didn't have tools. One year later, Sneed was healed of her illness and regained the ability to walk by herself; a recovery she attributes to getting her hands in the dirt and helping other people. Thirteen years later, in 1994, the jail garden has evolved to include offshoots—the Garden Project and the Tree Corps—in which released prisoners make healthy contributions to their communities through a series of reentry programs.

> *We use growing stuff, cleaning up garbage dumps and food as a way of saying there is a future for you, for us. There is work that you can do that matters.*
>
> Sneed, 1993

Over 200 inmates and former inmates in the San Francisco Bay area are employed by the associated projects. They grow organic food on prison land as well as on land owned by a diverse community of public and private concerns (e.g., a bakery, Southern Pacific Railroad, and the San Francisco Unified School District). Though jail culture remains racially segregated, Sneed's gardening classes are integrated and bilingual (Spanish and English).

When racial tensions emerge, Sneed reminds her students:

> *We are an organic garden. One of the basic ideas of organic gardening is this idea of diversity. In nature there is diversity, that's what makes health. And in this class, the fact that*

> *you all look different, that's going to make this the best experience that will help you feel better about yourself, that you can do something with your life.*
>
> Sneed, 1993

The life-sustaining "something" Sneed's students do with their lives, in the form of offering organic produce to others, is substantial. Inmates of the San Francisco County Jail grow over 50,000 pounds of produce yearly using the biodynamic French intensive method. The fruits and vegetables of the participants' labors fill bellies of people from diverse races, genders, sexual and spiritual practices, and social classes.

Weekly, produce from the jail's program is delivered to homeless people, senior citizens and AIDS victims. Upscale restaurants like Berkeley's Chez Panisse serve the Garden Project's produce to its well-heeled clientele. Former inmates also share harvests of food and cocreative activity with their families and friends. A portion of the Garden Project's harvest goes to senior citizens who also get bread from the bakery behind which the Project's vegetables grow.

> *A lot of people in our program have preyed on seniors. [The Garden Project offers them a] whole new way of looking at old people. The act of being able to give to people with nothing touches prisoners. Most of them were homeless at the time of arrest. They stood in food lines. They need to know they can do something good.*
>
> Sneed, 1993

Members of the Tree Corps get eight dollars an hour to plant trees in low-income neighborhoods of San Francisco. With 2,000 trees planted during 1993-94, the Tree Corps has a waiting list of people who want to participate. Sneed, a California Department of Forestry appointee to the Urban Forestry Advisory Board, embodies her conviction that our ability to sustain human culture depends upon combining the importance of trees and people (Sneed, 1994).

> *The thing [capitalistic values] that destroys our rainforests is the same thing that has my son wondering whether or not he will end up in state prison. Putting people to work to transform an environment is ecology.*
>
> Sneed, 1994

Fertile Ground

A little rain each day will fill the rivers to overflowing.

Liberian Proverb

Catherine Sneed's gardening and tree planting projects exemplify several transformational consequences of managing land according to African American naturifocal principles. She returned, *claimed*, a portion of San Francisco Jail land to its ancestral use. The work Sneed and her students do requires them to *kneel* and use their hands (the root of the word manage). Inmates and former inmates in the program *choose* to work in the dirt. By doing so they simultaneously revitalize cocreative relationships with their communities and their sense of self-worth. There is a waiting list of people who want the privilege of planting trees, and, through program participants' collective efforts, inner-city communities and ecosystems of San Francisco, are *healing*.

How might land management ethics be transformed in interrelated ways? A sampling of guiding questions and suggested actions toward their answers circles back to the underlying primal values with which we began. These few examples are meant to stimulate continuing asking and answering along similar lines.

How might *reverence* and a sense of *mutual obligation* for the animal and plant elders/ancestors of North America inform a restorative land management ethic? One suggested action is to establish and protect wilderness corridors. By recognizing and cultivating *relationships* between these corridors and urban greenbelt projects such as Sneed's Tree Corps the *interrelatedness of all of life* is served. This means paying attention to both human and other than human dynamics and populations habitually ignored in land management decisions.

What kind of land ethic facilitates *communication with and through naturally occurring phenomena*? One which is informed by people who live close to the ground. Herbalist, granny midwives, and naturifocal tribal elders devote their lives to Life. They safeguard a tradition of mutually beneficial relations with other than human nature and know intimately the impacts on those relations of various land management policies. Including these folk

naturalists on decision-making bodies will expand the depth with which management ethics reflect the wisdom communicated by naturally occurring phenomena.

A land management ethic evolved and implemented by a work force which reflects the diversity of healthy ecosystems is the fertile ground in which restorative naturifocal values can flourish. The partnership model of recruiting students of color into the Forestry Service via Commencement 2000, initiated in California, is one step toward creating such a work force (Hicks, 1990). May similar steps be implemented systemwide to claim, kneel on (respect), choose and heal, our common ground.

Literature Cited

The Native-American Environmentalist. (1990). Volume 1, Number 2.

Bagby, R. (forthcoming). *Fertile ground: Poems*.

Bullard, R. (1992). *People of color environmental groups directory*. Riverside, CA: University of California, Riverside.

Clifton, L. (1993). *The book of light*. Port Townsend, WA: Copper Canyon Press.

Frazier, E. (1964). *The Negro church in America*. New York, NY: Schocken Books, Inc.

Herskovits, M. (1958). *The myth of the Negro past*. Boston, MA: Beacon Press.

Hicks, A. (1990). *Commencement 2000: Pacific southwest region and research station*. San Francisco, CA: USDA Forest Service.

Holloway, J. (Ed.). (1991). *Africanisms in American culture*. Bloomington, IN: Indiana University Press.

Hughes, L. (1973). *Selected poems of Langston Hughes*. New York, NY: Alfred A. Knopf, Inc.

Lovell, J. (1972). *Black song: The forge and the flame*. New York, NY: Paragon House Publishers.

Mbiti, J. (1969). *African religions and philosophies*. New York, NY: Praeger Publishers, Inc.

Mitchell, R. (1977). *African primal religions*. Niles, IL: Argus Communications.

Morrison, T. (1987). *Beloved*. New York, NY: Alfred A. Knopf, Inc.

Murphy, J. (1994). *Working the spirit*. Boston, MA: Beacon Press.

Reagon, B. and Sweet Honey in the Rock. (1993). *We who believe in freedom*. New York, NY: Doubleday & Co., Inc.

Simpson, G. (1978). *Black religions in the New World*. New York, NY: Columbia University Press.

Sneed, C. (1993). Talk given at Applied Deep Ecology Institute. Boulder, CO: Sounds True Recordings.

Sneed, C. (1994). These green things. *Orion, 13*, 3.

Sweet Honey in the Rock. (1988). *Breaths*. Chicago, IL: Flying Fish.

Taylor-Guthrie, D. (Ed.). (1994). *Conversations with Toni Morrison*. Jackson, MS: University Press of Mississippi.

Thompson, R. (1983). *Flash of the spirit*. New York, NY: Random House, Inc.

Thompson, R. (1991). Kongo influences on Native-American artistic culture. In J. Holloway (Ed.), *Africanisms in American culture* (pp. 148-184). Bloomington, IN: Indiana University Press.

Thompson, R. (1993). *Face of the gods*. New York, NY: The Museum for African Art.

van Sertima, I. (1976). *They came before Columbus*. New York, NY: Random House, Inc.

Waniek, M. (1978). *For the body*. Baton Rouge, LA: Louisiana State University Press.

HISPANIC PERSPECTIVES AND VALUES

MARIA TERESA GARCIA

Carson National Forest
USDA Forest Service
Taos, New Mexico

CHAPTER 11

Introduction

The term "Hispanic" generally is defined as relating to or derived from the people, speech, or culture of Spain, or more broadly, the Iberian peninsula (i.e., Spain and Portugal) and the Basque region of the Pyrenees. For federal census statistics and other reporting purposes, the United States Government uses the term Hispanic to categorize certain ethnic groups and applies the following definition: "A person of Mexican, Puerto Rican, Cuban, Central or South American, or other Spanish culture or origin, regardless of race."

While other terms such as Latino, La Raza, Spanish, Spanish-speaker, Mexican American, and so forth, are sometimes applicable, Hispanic is an inclusive noun that refers to the largest group of minorities in this country who comprise "not one nationality, one culture, but many" (Shorris, 1992). According to Shorris in 1990, U.S. Hispanics numbered 22.4 million or 9 percent of the population. By the year 2000, Hispanics are expected to number 30.6 million or 11.1 percent of the population.

Despite the apparent differences between a third-generation Mexican American born and raised in south Texas and a recent immigrant from Central America living in southern California, both share an identifiable cultural legacy. This legacy can be characterized by common traits including descent from European immigrants whose arrival in the New World dates to the 1500s, development of an economic system based on subsistence use of natural resources obtained from communal lands, use of the Spanish language, adherence to the Catholic faith, settlement patterns based on communities consisting of clusters of extended families, strong family ties, and use of fictional kinship organizations such as the *compadrazgo* (godparent system), and religious societies to reinforce familial solidarity and promote social integration.

Of these traits, the most significant is family solidarity. Traditionally, Hispanics were socialized to accept the idea that the responsibility of the individual was to contribute to the group rather than to aspire to personal success (Shorris, 1992). The familial role and its attendant obligations were the focal point of the Hispanic way of life. Retention of these particular traits among contemporary Hispanics, especially those in urban settings, is variable due to acculturation, assimilation, and education.

Yet, as I demonstrate in this chapter, specific examples of how Hispanics use public land or think public land should be managed can be shown to derive from this cultural heritage that emphasizes the family as the most valued social institution.

Historical Background

Great expanses of the United States now constituting all or portions of the states of California, Nevada, Arizona, Utah, Wyoming, Colorado, New Mexico, Texas, Louisiana and Florida, were once integral components of New Spain (i.e., colonial Mexico from 1540 to 1821) and then the Republic of Mexico (1821-1846). For many Spaniards who journeyed to the New World in the sixteenth century, the possibility of a better life in a new land was a primary motivation. Once here, and over subsequent generations, they developed a symbiotic relationship with the land. As a result of this historical association, Hispanics achieved a strong sense of place and personal identity. The land, as such, was much more than a storehouse of natural resources; it was the home of one's immediate family and ancestors. In a sense, "land and family" became synonymous terms, if not a single concept, that embodied certain spiritual qualities.

Rights to the land were acquired from the Spanish sovereign. Much of the land the United States government took possession of during what might be termed the Expansion and Acquisition Era of 1776 to 1867 was populated by people, such as Native Americans and Hispanics, whose rights and claims under previous sovereigns were to be upheld by the new government. It is apparent from the historical record and extant court cases that this extension of rights often did not occur (Carlson, 1990; DeBuys, 1985; Ebright, 1994). The differential manner in which matters were attended to and resolved, which at times appeared to be subject to the whim or necessities of local officials, became a point of contention whose repercussions are still evident in Hispanic and land management agency relationships today.

Some of the disagreements that occur between Hispanics and land managers are rooted in what can be described as fundamentally different approaches to valuing the land. The traditional Hispanic land tenure system has been described as "in many respects the reverse of the Anglo-American system" (Van Ness and Van Ness, 1980). This traditional system is based on a direct relationship to land through one's physical presence and use. This contrasts with the Anglo-American view of land as a speculative commodity.

The historical precedent for the Hispanic view is the original land tenure system brought to the New World by the Spanish in the sixteenth century. Individual and community land grants (*mercedes*) were the principal components of their settlement system. The basic principles of this system derived from Old World concepts, such as *poblacion*, which achieved the sovereign's goal of establishing a presence in sparsely populated lands by enticing settlers with offers of private title to land particularly well-suited for personal needs, such as agriculture and usufruct, a legal term for the guarantee of communal access to and use of woodlands for firewood and other commodities as well as pasturage.

Carlson (1990) discusses the specifics of the system. Land holdings were delineated by natural features on the landscape, such as hills and drainages, or by the boundaries of adjacent land owners. It was an ecological rather than political or administrative approach to land use. To fully appreciate the holistic nature of this concept, it should be contrasted with the section-township-range method which applies an artificial, one dimensional construct (i.e., the grid system) to a naturally contoured surface. The contrast is an apt example of how a culture's world-view or cognitive perception of surroundings can differ radically from another group's.

Often tracts of land were designated by family name, and land and resource values were assessed in relation to personal subsistence use rather than potential commercial gain. Speculation was not allowed, nor was absentee ownership. This system encouraged an intensive reliance on natural resources and an experiential knowledge of the land. Consequently, it engendered strong feelings of attachment and sense of place among landowners. Perceptions regarding quality of life were directly tied to one's relationship with the land.

By the time Mexico obtained its independence from Spain in 1821, the land grant system was firmly established throughout its territories. The Mexican government had pledged to uphold previously acquired grants and continued the practice begun by the Spanish. In 1846 General Stephen W.

Kearney took Santa Fe commencing the Mexican War which made the Southwest part of the United States. Two years later in 1848 the United States and Mexican governments signed the Treaty of Guadalupe Hidalgo. One provision of the Treaty was that property rights obtained during the Spanish and Mexican periods would be upheld if the original grants could be confirmed. By 1890 millions of acres of land were tied up in litigation (Carlson, 1990). This situation set the stage for controversy over land ownership and use that carries over into modern times.

Current Considerations

Today, 90 percent of Hispanics in the United States live in urban areas. They use federal lands, as do thousands of other people each year, primarily for recreation and leisure activities. Data compiled by the USDA Forest Service Pacific Southwest Research Station in Riverside, California, is an important source of information on urban Hispanics' expectations and needs from federal land management. A discussion of these findings is preceded by one based on a rural perspective from northern New Mexico where much of the land base is public domain, and a traditional lifestyle based on subsistence use of forest products is maintained through a strong reliance on federal lands.

A Rural Perspective

The Spanish who settled in New Mexico in 1598 came from what has been described as a world of "patron-client social relations, material wealth, iron tools, food markets, domesticated animals, Aristotelian logic and divine right" (Ford, 1987). But in this part of the New World, the legacy of the sixteenth and seventeenth century domineering conquistador gave way in the eighteenth century to an essentially pastoral way of life (DeBuys, 1985). Like neighboring Pueblo Indians, Spanish settlers in New Mexico developed an economy based on what they could produce on individual agricultural lands coupled with what they could obtain from the surrounding environment. Because communal use of large tracts of unsettled land had been sanctioned and handed down under Spanish law, they came to be thought of as ancestral lands. Further, their relationship with the land assumed an intrinsic,

spiritual value that also passed to succeeding generations.

Woodlands and forest were viewed as pasturage for herds and flocks and as a storehouse of resources including trees, shrubs, herbs, grasses, roots, tubers, berries, and large and small game. These resources were used for food, fuel, building materials, tools, clothing, and medicine. The resultant lifestyle was based on social and economic patterns that were established, respected, and, most important, passed on through prescribed behavioral practices. Isolated by geography and colonial Spanish policies, northern New Mexicans developed and adhered to a provincial way of life.

With Mexico's independence from Spain in 1821 and subsequent changes in commercial restrictions, traders of French and Anglo descent appeared on the scene in New Mexico. They were drawn by a multitude of untapped resources, initially those that could be obtained by a single individual with little or no investment, such as beaver pelts. These activities initiated an era of commodity exploitation that would peak at the turn of the century with large scale mining, timber, and grazing operations. The designation of forest reserves within the public domain began in 1891 with the passage of the Creative Act.

An influx of new citizens representing the federal government and Eastern commercial interests began. Within a relatively short time, the local subsistence-based economy was profoundly affected by and made subordinate to a mercantile capitalist orientation. With the disruption of their own economic system steeped in subsistence use of the land and barter, Hispanics were obliged to participate in a new economic order based primarily on wage labor associated with natural resource extraction industries, most of which took place on federal land.

With wage labor came a market economy, transportation systems, credit, money lending, land speculation, legal experts, entrepreneurs, and rapid changes for people who had been pursuing a simple lifestyle during the previous centuries. Competition for natural resources increased, and many lands which in the past had been used communally now were subject to commercial exploitation and permitting processes. Among the most apparent results of these social and technological developments was a serious deterioration in the environment due to large-scale resource extraction, and financial profit primarily accruing to outside investors. Conflict between local and national needs were evident from the beginning.

The end result of this situation was a transition of most Hispanic settlements from essentially self-sufficient communities to economically depressed villages. Resentment and suspicion of outsiders resulted from the government's inability to integrate traditional lifestyles with contemporary demands for natural resources. Conditions continued to deteriorate after the decline of the timber industry in the mid- to late-1920s. To participate in the cash economy on which they were now dependent, many Hispanics, particularly men, were forced to leave their villages and families to pursue employment in population centers such as Albuquerque, Denver, and Los Angeles. This shift to urban living was a difficult adjustment for many and further disrupted traditional lifestyles.

Faced with a severe economic situation in northern New Mexico, the federal government attempted to ameliorate local conditions to some extent by the establishment of the Vallecitos Federal Sustained Yield Unit in 1948 under the authority of the Sustained Yield Forest Management Act of 1944. The intent was:

> . . . *to promote the stability of forest industries, of employment, of communities, and of taxable forest wealth, through continuous supplies of timber; in order to provide for a continuous and ample supply of forest products. . . .* USDA Forest Service, 1993.

Once again, while the Congressional intent may have been admirable, a narrow interpretation of the mandate by the Forest Service resulted in local residents becoming heavily dependent on a single resource—timber—and an industry which was dominated by outside financial control.

In the 1960s, while the entire country was experiencing political and social upheaval, New Mexico was facing its own crises. Young people, known as hippies, who were rejecting conventional society and seeking alternative lifestyles, flooded into the traditional Hispanic communities. Because their mores and values were so different from the provincial villages, it was inevitable that conflict would occur. Further, caught up in the consciousness raising movement of the time, politically active Hispanics organized into groups such as La Raza Unida and the Alianza Federal de Los Mercedes which promoted a renewed interest in land grant issues and pride in Hispanic heritage.

As described by Gomez-Quiniones (1990), the Alianza was primarily a movement of land grant claimants. Led by Reies Lopez Tijerina, the group consisted of people of all ages, including older persons, and "the motivating force was the desire for the land." The Alianza was a militant critic of government in general and the Forest Service in particular. Throughout the late 1960s the group engaged in high-profile, controversial activity to draw attention to its cause.

In June of 1967 members of the group stormed the courthouse in Tierra Amarilla, New Mexico, with plans to make a citizen's arrest of the District Attorney. The raid resulted in violence, numerous arrests, and eventually investigations into Forest Service activities in the area. These investigations, in turn, led to preparation of the Hassell Report, an internal examination of Forest Service policies which recommended a more flexible and sensitive philosophy of managing federal lands in northern New Mexico. It promoted the concept that as the primary landowner in the region, the Forest Service had an obligation to help maintain economic stability among traditional people (DeBuys, 1985). This was followed in 1984 by *A White Paper Concerning the Management of the Juan Jose Lobato Grant*, another attempt on the part of the Forest Service to address the unique situation it faces in northern New Mexico where personal use of forest commodities is still tied to a cash poor economy.

Within the last ten years there has been some diversification of the northern New Mexican economy with the growth of the tourist industry. However, the majority of new jobs tend to be low paying, seasonal activities with few options for advancement. By the same token, there has been some increase in worker-owned cooperatives and small, community-based businesses centered on traditional arts and crafts, recreation opportunities, and natural and cultural attractions. Enterprises such as these are models for sustainable economic development which Lust, Rivera, Sargent, and Varela (1991) define as one that maintains mutually beneficial and equitable relationships both within the community as well as with society in general. Benefits are maximized and social costs are minimized because local residents are active in both planning and implementation of change.

Even with these changes in economic orientation, however, many people are still dependent on federal resources. In northern New Mexico, relationships between Hispanics and federal agencies, such as the Forest Service, the National Park Service, the Bureau of Land Management and the Army Corps of Engineers, are still fraught with conflict and uncertainty as different segments of the public with diverse demands, needs and interests vie for access to limited resources. Conflicting legislation and divergent missions complicate the land management agencies' roles. Any attempts at conflict resolution must take into account the rural Hispanic community's notion of its historical presence within the Southwest.

An Urban Perspective

Research on the cultural diversity of users of federal lands has increased dramatically in the last few years. Managers, particularly those overseeing wilderness and other designated recreation areas near urban centers, have faced new challenges due to the "diversity of customers, the many uses that they make of the areas, and the diverse experiences that they desire" (Dwyer, 1989).

The Wildland Recreation and the Urban Culture research project at the USDA Forest Service Pacific Southwest Research Station in Riverside, California, was begun as a result of this challenge. Its mission is to develop effective visitor management strategies for wildland recreation areas with an emphasis on different cultural and user groups. The project's publication, *Recreation Research Update* (1990a, 1990b, 1991a, 1991b, 1992a, 1992b, 1993a, 1993b) is an important source of information on studies specifically citing Hispanic patterns of recreational land use. A series of such research findings demonstrate the following:

1. The data indicate that the term "Hispanic" is too broad to identify respondents properly. Minimally, Hispanics can be categorized (and readily identify themselves) as U.S.-born Hispanic, Mexican-born Hispanic, and Central/South American-born Hispanic. Differences in opinions, attitudes and responses are associated with these distinctions. This also suggests that among many Hispanics, Spanish may be their first language.

2. A second conclusion is that Hispanics generally show stronger motivation for social interaction in recreational activity than do non-Hispanic respondents. Among Hispanics there is a definite family orientation and an expressed preference for group activities that include children.

3. Another trend is that visits by Hispanics to recreation areas are shorter, but more intense, and commonly take place on major holidays. Repeat visits to preferred locations are common, and information on desirable places often is obtained from family and friends.

What can be said of these trends relative to what is known about Hispanic culture in general? These findings suggest that many of what might be described as personal values among Hispanics carry over to recreation behavior. The extended family continues to be the primary focus and predominant social unit. Activities are structured to include all age groups, including children, and to coincide with holidays to accommodate and incorporate the maximum number of people. Hispanics appear to rely on personal experience as a source of information. Further, once a desirable location is identified as a recreation spot, Hispanics tend to become attached to specific sites and establish a regular visitation pattern. It appears that the intrinsic values of familial relationships are closely linked to and heighten the value of experiences in the natural world. Any attempt to understand the relationship between urban Hispanics and the land should take this information into consideration.

The Management Challenge

"People can debate issues and seek to reconcile conflicts about the use of specific parcels of land; they cannot be expected to compromise their deeply held values" (USDA Forest Service, 1990). The challenge to land management agencies is to adopt an inclusive and collaborative approach to problem solving and decision making when planning and implementing public land policies (see Henderson, Chapter Twelve, in this volume). As promoted by such community-based groups as the Intercultural Community Leadership Project at Santa Fe Community College in Santa Fe, New Mexico (Blanco,

Chene, Rael de Garcia, and Zee, n.d.), the collaborative approach has its roots in traditional cultures where emphasis is on community needs and interests rather than those of the individual. The collaborative approach recognizes and utilizes cultural diversity and attempts to integrate a variety of perspectives when considering issues and options. Collaboration implies shared responsibility, promotes gender balance, and, unlike hierarchy, encourages peer relationships. The collaborative approach fosters empowerment and self-determination rather than dependence while striving for consensus as a means of resolving conflict. It relies on close effective relations with the publics it strives to serve.

Philosophically, collaboration affords land managers opportunities to interact with and respond to public land users in a more equitable manner than in the past. Collaboration effectively incorporates the idea that humans, too, are part of a healthy, sustainable ecosystem. It accepts the fundamental principle that culture, like nature, is diverse and complex. It accepts the differences in the beliefs and values of the many groups of federal land users and attempts to incorporate alternative perspectives when identifying current and future wants and needs.

In practical terms and in response to concerns of Hispanic communities, land managers can improve relations by such measures as increased hiring of Hispanics (and other Spanish speakers) in all disciplines and particularly in such areas as recreation, law enforcement, public affairs, and information services. In parts of the country where Spanish speakers are known to represent a significant portion of land users, written materials (e.g., permits, signs, brochures, exhibits, press releases) should routinely be available in Spanish. Managers should solicit, interpret, and use opinions from the Hispanic community in the decision-making process. Managers should attempt to find ways to balance regional and national needs with those of local communities and to deal effectively with multicultural perspectives.

Resource management is more difficult than we care to admit. For years, land managers felt that science and technology would provide the necessary tools for the job. Recent experience indicates that true stewardship must take into account social, emotional, political and spiritual considerations as well.

Literature Cited

Blanco, M., Chene, R., Rael de Garcia, C., and Zee, R. (no date). *The Intercultural Community Leadership Project 1991-1993 Program Statement*. Santa Fe, NM: Santa Fe Community College.

Carlson, A. (1990). *The Spanish-American homeland*. Baltimore, MD: The Johns Hopkins University Press.

DeBuys, W. (1985). *Enchantment and exploitation*. Albuquerque, NM: University of New Mexico Press.

Dwyer, J. (1989). "Wildlife management near large urban centers: The need for diversity." Paper presented at Managing America's Enduring Wilderness Resource: A Conference. Minneapolis, MN.

Ebright, M. (1994). *Land grants and lawsuits in northern New Mexico*. Albuquerque, NM: University of New Mexico Press.

Ford, R. (1987). "The new pueblo economy." In *When cultures meet*: *Remembering San Gabriel del Yunge Oweenge* (pp. 73-91). Papers from the October 20, 1984, Conference Held at San Juan Pueblo, NM. Santa Fe, NM: The Sunstone Press.

Gomez-Quiniones, J. (1990). *Chicano politics reality and promise, 1940-1990*. Albuquerque, NM: University of New Mexico Press.

Lust, P., Rivera, J, Sargent, F., and Varela, M. (1991). *Rural environmental planning for sustainable communities*. Washington, DC: Island Press.

Shorris, E. (1992). *Latinos: A biography of the people*. New York, NY: W. W. Norton and Company.

USDA Forest Service. (1990). *Synthesis of the critique of land management planning* (vol. 1) (FS-452). Washington, DC: USDA Forest Service.

USDA Forest Service. (1993). *The principle laws relating to Forest Service activities*. Washington, DC: USDA Forest Service.

USDA Forest Service Pacific Southwest Research Station. (1990a). *Recreation Research Update, 2*(2). Riverside, CA: USDA Forest Service.

USDA Forest Service Pacific Southwest Research Station. (1990b). *Recreation Research Update, 3*(1). Riverside, CA: USDA Forest Service.

USDA Forest Service Pacific Southwest Research Station. (1991a). *Recreation Research Update, 3*(2). Riverside, CA: USDA Forest Service.

USDA Forest Service Pacific Southwest Research Station. (1991b). *Recreation Research Update, 4*(2). Riverside, CA: USDA Forest Service.

USDA Forest Service Pacific Southwest Research Station. (1992a). *Recreation Research Update, 5*(1). Riverside, CA: USDA Forest Service.

USDA Forest Service Pacific Southwest Research Station. (1992b). *Recreation Research Update*, *6*(1). Riverside, CA: USDA Forest Service.

USDA Forest Service Pacific Southwest Research Station. (1993a). *Recreation Research Update, March*. Riverside, CA: USDA Forest Service.

USDA Forest Service Pacific Southwest Research Station. (1993b). *Recreation Research Update, October*. Riverside, CA: USDA Forest Service.

Van Ness, J. and Van Ness, C. (1980). Introduction. In J. Van Ness and C. Van Ness (Eds.), *Spanish and Mexican land grants in New Mexico and Colorado* (pp. 3-11). Manhattan, KS: A. C. Press.

FEMINIST PERSPECTIVES, FEMALE WAYS OF BEING, AND NATURE

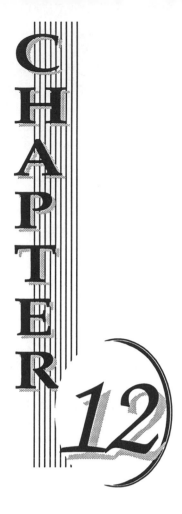

KARLA HENDERSON
Curriculum in Leisure Studies and Recreation Administration
University of North Carolina
Chapel Hill, North Carolina

> *For some women, this vitalizing 'taste of the wild'
> . . . comes through the vision; through sights of
> great beauty. I have felt her when I see what we
> call in the woodlands a Jesus-God sunset. I have
> felt her move in me from seeing the fishermen
> come up from the lake at dusk with lanterns lit,
> and also from seeing my newborn baby's toes all
> lined up like a row of sweet corn. We see her
> where we see her, which is everywhere.*
>
> Estes, 1992, p. 7

This quote from the best seller *Women Who Run with the Wolves*, illustrates a currently popular view about the relationship and connection between nature and women. It represents only one way, an essentialist view, of examining female "ways of being" or values in relation to nature. It is, however, a place to begin in exploring feminist values about nature. These nature-based, feminist values refer primarily to intangible benefits derived from personal experiences that vary greatly from individual to individual. Commonly expressed values or ways of being include a sense of purpose in life, a belief in a connectedness of nature to humans, and a belief in something greater than oneself.

In this chapter, I examine the historical and cultural relationship of women to nature-based, human values and recommend directions for a new land management ethic based on these perspectives. I try to present a range of thinking about feminist perspectives, female ways of being, and nature. My intent is not to focus on a critique of male (i.e., dominant) views about nature. My major goal is to suggest additional perspectives about nature-based, human values which often differ from dominant white, middle-class, heterosexist, able-bodied male views. I do not suggest that female ways of being or the perspectives and values of women/girls are more valid than those of men/boys, but that they are worthy of consideration. Neither males nor females have a monopoly on values, but the voices of women have not always been heard (Gray, 1988).

Analyses of the relationships of feminist perspectives, female values, and nature are warranted to rectify the philosophical biases and the invisibility of women in the past. As Merchant (1980) suggested, values and social structures based on a full expression of male and female talent and focused on maintaining environmental integrity are needed. The costs of excluding the diversity and complexity of female ways of being are high because without these views, the full range of the magnitude, complexity, and interdependence of systems of oppression (both of nature and of females) are not addressed (Fox, 1992; Held, 1990).

An analysis of nature-based, human values in relation to women/girls may be grounded in two world-views: female ways of being and feminist perspectives. To view nature from a female view is to see the relationship between typical feminine and masculine ways of being and what females contribute to balancing the way that any entity, such as nature, is viewed. This essentialist view applauds the characteristics of females and what they can contribute to an understanding of the world. As Estes (1992) suggests in the opening quote, many women see the world through eyes that focus on different aspects of the environment than do most men. From a possible female world-view, typical female values become the yin in relation to the yang stereotypic male views. Both are necessary to create a whole. Thus, females may ascribe certain interpretations to nature-based experiences that may be overlooked if females are not included in the analysis or development of management ethics. Within female ways of being arise particular interpretations of literature, religion, and even recreational experiences, as related to nature (e.g., Anderson, 1991).

Feminist views acknowledge the world as a complementary but different paradigm. Part of the problem with current views of the environment is that differences such as male/female, nature/culture, body/spirit, and intellect/emotions have been placed in false dichotomies that tend to polarize the relationship between people and the Earth. The feminist paradigm has no singular definition but is based on a critique, correction, and transformation of heretofore minimally challenged positions within the dominant culture (Eichler, 1980). Feminism is a philosophy and practice that embodies equality, empowerment, and social change for women and men and that seeks to eliminate the invisibility of women (Henderson, Bialeschki, Shaw, and Freysinger, 1989). Within feminism many viewpoints exist. Viewpoints taken within feminism (e.g., liberal, socialist, cultural, or radical) have a great influence on the way in which projects are undertaken. Thus, when using feminist perspectives as the focus of discussing nature-based, human values, a plurality of views must be kept in mind.

Ecofeminism, or ecological feminism, is an emerging aspect of feminism that addresses the parallel patterns of domination of women and nature. Ecofeminists, who also acknowledge overlapping viewpoints based upon the perspectives taken (e.g., liberal, cultural, radical), describe how understandings of human liberation (feminism) and a concern for interdependence and relationships between humans and nonhumans (ecology) can provide a personal philosophy for both males and females (Henderson and Bialeschki, 1990-91). Ecofeminism is not a monolithic, homogeneous ideology but seeks to reweave new stories that acknowledge and value the biological and cultural diversity that sanctions all life (Diamond and Orenstein, 1990). All ecofeminist views share a common commitment to making visible the ways in which women and nonhuman nature are dominated under patriarchy.

Feminist Perspectives and Female Ways of Being

It is necessary to consider feminist perspectives and female ways of being in addressing nature's values. Values are not necessarily biological, but are created culturally. Further, as already indicated, a singular women's view of nature does not exist. Feminist perspectives and female ways of being are not the domain of women only, but they may be shared by men (e.g., Dustin, 1992) and certainly may not reflect the views of all girls and women. Other researchers and feminists have suggested similarly that the ways many females have expressed their lives can provide new perspectives within the dominant culture (e.g., Gilligan, 1982, in describing moral development; Schaef, 1981, with the Female

System juxtaposed to the White Male System; Belenky, Clinchy, Goldberger, and Tarule, 1986, with women's ways of knowing; and Anderson, 1991, in examining women's writings about nature). These values have been empowering for both women and men despite the neglect and denigration of women in general by dominant societal ethos. For example, a number of women have described essential female ways as respecting life by caring not controlling, harmony not mastery, humility not arrogance, and appreciation not acquisitiveness (e.g., Anderson, 1991; Merchant, 1980).

Another way to illustrate this discussion is to examine the dominance of patriarchy and what it has done to the Earth. A patriarchal view can be contrasted to feminist perspectives and female ways of being that challenge the value hierarchies and the logic of domination. Further, as some feminists have suggested, if the concept of "human" was based on women rather than men, it would be a different concept (Card, 1991).

Feminist and female ways of being related to nature are not necessarily biological, but are likely due to socialization and the positions that women and other nondominant groups have held in the patriarchal society. Almost all Western women have been socialized toward the view that "man" has dominion over nature; some women have resisted this socialization by developing environmental activism and a spirituality based on intuitive values and a relationship with nature. Female ways of being, however, are not solely biological since dualistic thinking, as in male/female, is antithetical to the way nature is (Kaza, 1989). To suggest that men cannot experience nature through feminist values is alienating and is not the experience of some men. One of the major foci of feminist perspectives and female ways of being is to avoid excluding anyone's view, especially if that individual, regardless of biological sex, supports the integrity of all life. In describing feminist perspectives and applying female ways of being to nature-based human values, the diversity of interpretations is obvious. The differences in interpretation offer opportunities for growth.

The diverse historical and cultural associations concerning nature-based, human values are addressed in five areas:

1. perceptions of women and nature,
2. women's spirituality and Earth religions,
3. the exclusion of women's voices,
4. ecofeminism and the parallels between the treatment of women and the treatment of nature, and
5. women as environmental activists.

Perceptions of Women and Nature

The essentialist view suggests that women are closer to nature than men. The biological aspects of women's lives with monthly cycles and the ability to reproduce are cited as reasons for this affinity. If women are closer to nature, they are also assumed to be its caregivers. Women may be closer to nature, however, simply because they have been socialized that way (Ortner, 1974). In describing women as having an embodied knowing or a "lived experience" with nature (Salleh, 1984), we also must acknowledge that lived experience results from a cultural interpretation of experience.

Some researchers suggest that female ways of being may result in different experiences in the outdoors for males and females. Because women's ways of being have been associated with relationships and connections rather than justice and rights, women more often than men are perceived to be more attuned to voices of nature and moments of mystical union in the outdoors. An essentialist female view suggests women are attuned to thousands of simple pleasures in nature (e.g., sensory, aesthetic, spiritual). Simpson (1991), for example, described the journey, and not the quest, that epitomizes the outdoors for a majority of women. Many women have also found the value of shedding socially assigned roles and finding self in experiences with nature (Yerkes and Miranda, 1985). The experience of moral development suggesting that relationships are more important for many women than rights (Gilligan, 1982), has major implications for female values and nature. A concern for others in the outdoors associated with group centered values is a common description of female ways of being in the outdoors (Mitten, 1992). The creation of connections for women may result in a sense of caregiving as the supportive role that holds human culture and natural environments together.

The perceptions associated with the meanings of difference and dichotomous thinking are worth considering in relation to women's perceptions of nature. The tendency of the dominant society has been to dualize or dichotomize life. Thus, we have male/female and culture/nature. The notion also exists that men express creativity through culture and the mind, while women express themselves through nature and their bodies. The problem with this notion is that it suggests that one view must be juxtaposed to another view or may be superior, when in reality many views may be necessary. The dualistic thinking of "either/or" rather than "both/and" has resulted in placing women in a lower status due to the dualism between males and females (Merchant, 1980).

These culturally created differences between women and nature have often been politically and theoretically regressive because they reinforce existing prejudices. On the other hand, to flip-flop the value system as advocated by essentialists, and to place traditionally associated "women's values" in place of the dominant culture may not be altogether useful either. If it is true, as King (1991) suggested, that by virtue of their close relationship to nature, women are more likely than men to care about nature and are better prepared to do something about it, women then become responsible for accomplishing the activist work that needs to be done. The responsibility for environmental activism must be placed upon both males and females if we are to use all of the resources available to solve problems.

Mother Earth, or *Gaia* as the concept of the ancient Mother Earth, is another perception of women's relationship to the Earth that may be misleading. Murphy (1988), however, raises the questions of whether the idea of the planet as a female nurturer (i.e., Gaia) opposes the patriarchal ideology that destroys the environment that sustains life, or whether it reinforces elements of the ideology and limits its effectiveness. He asks whether Gaia imagery subverts patriarchy when it continues the tendency to sex type the planet as female.

A danger in believing that women are inherently closer to nature suggests that biology is the link and that changes cannot occur in either male or female behavior. It must be kept in mind that the meaning of women and nature has been culturally constructed. Neither one has unchanging essential characteristics although we sometimes make that assumption (Merchant, 1980). If it were impossible to change the reality of women or men and nature,

the editors probably would not include a chapter about female values in this text. It is possible to change female and male behavior; therefore we must be cautious about the context dependency of the statements made about female/male values about nature.

Several other contradictions about females and nature are worthy of mentioning. For example, while women are attuned to nature, they are also conditioned to fear it. "Goldilocks and the Three Bears" and "Little Red Riding Hood" are children's stories that socialize a message about girls and nature. The fears generated in women due to the socialization from these stories as well as the rising violence in society also mitigate the possible positive values that might be associated with the outdoors. In addition, although the perception exists of the Earth as mother, the woman as wild and untamable also comes forward. Perhaps what many men fear most is their inability to tame and control nature as well as women. All these contradictions must be acknowledged in understanding women's perspectives in relation to nature.

Women's Spirituality

Women's values about nature have also resulted in the emergence of spirituality and religions associated with female ways of being and the Earth. Religion may be closely associated with spirituality depending on how it is defined. Religious beliefs can also intersect with spirituality and environmental ethics as is true with Goddess religions and other forms of women's spirituality. Gray (1988) suggested that the sacred circle of women addresses the whole planet and a concern for the welfare of the planet.

The rebirth of Earth religions, which are not solely the property of females but are attractive to many women who can no longer relate to traditional religions, "is a part of a broad movement that challenges domination—that seeks to connect with the root, the heart, the sources of life by changing our present relationships" (Starhawk, 1982, p. xiii). These religions often have evolved because of some women's desires to name their experiences in a way different from the past and to reconnect with the ancient past before patriarchy dominated.

The Mother Goddess, as one image of women's spirituality, is fundamentally an immanent deity and the work of creation. Goddess religions stress female symbolism and immanence (i.e., operating within, living, present through the universe). To honor the Goddess, or Goddesses, is to honor traditional female attributes. These religions make the role of women important and stress community, interdependence, and mutual aid. Goddess feminists believe that divine foundations of reality do not force women to deny their bodies and material existence. They accept the naturalness and goodness of things—to see all humans and animals, plants, stars, and rocks as brothers and sisters (Ruether, 1983). In Goddess religions as well as other forms of women's spirituality, communitarian and ecological values are expressed throughout the ideology.

One example of a religion emanating from former Goddess worship is called Witchcraft, Wicca, or the Craft. The myths and symbols are drawn from women-valuing, matristic, Goddess-centered cultures that underlay the beginnings of civilizations. This religion connects with the Goddess who is immanent in nature and is akin to aspects of Native-American and African religions. The focus is to bring human community into harmony with nature. The idea is to rectify personal style along with the struggle against "pollution of patriarchy" (Ruether, 1983). No harm is done to others, but spells may be used to transform one's own consciousness and to purge anger and hatred. These religions are frequently female dominant, but many include men.

The history of patriarchy has been a cumulative effort to break the bond, to drive a wedge between spirit and flesh, culture and nature, and men and women (Starhawk, 1982). The problem with alternative religions in our culture is that they are outside the "dominant" Judeo-Christian views. They also can set women apart from men, suggesting that women possess a different nature which, as has been argued previously, is not necessarily so. Women's spirituality as reflected in these alternative religions, however, has connected female values with nature as an emphasis that is not commonplace in most mainstream religions.

Exclusion of Women's Voices

From feminist perspectives, one must question why women have not been more visible in the theory and practice surrounding values and nature. Both women's as well as men's views are needed for level-

ing value hierarchies. Just hearing the views, however, is not enough unless the ideas are incorporated into the dominant power structure. Many females have trouble speaking about nature-based, human values surrounding their attitudes and experiences in the outdoors because they have not had a chance to speak and write about their experiences. Naming experiences is a power that shapes reality into a form that serves the interests and goals of the one doing the naming (Gray, 1988). Until women have an opportunity to name and talk about their experiences, they will have little power to challenge the patriarchal hierarchies. One of the reasons why *Women Who Run with the Wolves* has sold so well may be that these stories represent for many women what they have been unable to articulate in the past because of the invisibility of their voices.

Because the stories and experiences of women have been excluded in nature discussions, few good role models exist. Where are the female Thoreaus, Muirs, Leopolds? What evidence do we have that the values of women have been incorporated into land management ethics in the past? Women have always been a part of (not apart from) nature and have worked for causes in the environment and the outdoors, but their efforts have not been visible except for a few notable exceptions such as Rachel Carson. The exclusion of women has resulted in a continuing circle of exclusion.

Central to feminist perspectives is the inclusion of the voices of other oppressed groups that have been excluded from the mainstream. Women's lives are diverse. Individuals representing female ways of being have been careful not to force universal generalizations from their personal reflections and have tried to emphasize that each person has a different journey (Gray, 1988). Including a variety of voices (e.g., the voices of people of color, low-income individuals, people with disabilities) is the essence of understanding ways of being related to nature. This inclusion also requires that women be involved in land management decision making as well as in the creation and interpretation of knowledge bases through research. The inclusion of women's voices and the voices of other oppressed groups is necessary to address the difficult environmental and ethical issues that we face.

Ecofeminism and the Treatment of Nature and Women

The convergence of ideas about the treatment of females and the Earth, referred to as ecofeminism, links a feminist consciousness about the Earth with an ecological understanding of feminism. Ecofeminism is likened to a patchwork quilt which may represent many forms (Wirth and Boddy, 1991). For example, for some people ecofeminism is a movement toward developing women- and Earth-centered spiritualities. For others it is a social/philosophical connection. For yet others, it is a grassroots political movement that connects the peace, environmental, and women's movements.

Thus, there is no one form of ecofeminism; all the views share a common commitment to making visible the ways in which women and nonhuman nature are dominated under patriarchy. Ecofeminists embody this commitment by developing practices aimed at ending the exploitation of women and nature. Because both women and nature have been devalued in our society (Merchant, 1980), the analogy of women as a recreational resource and nature as a recreational resource has some validity. The parallel between the emergence of the second wave of the feminist movement in the late 1960s and the commencing of the contemporary environmental movement in the early 1970s is, perhaps, no coincidence.

Issues of power have been paramount in ecofeminism. Since an analysis of power is central to any feminist critique, all forms of criticism within ecofeminism would have to include power. The power that patriarchy attempts to hold over nature is seen as parallel to the power that many men have tried to assert over women. Feminist perspectives have challenged notions of "power over" (e.g., dominance, subordination, power of control) and replaced them with ideas of "power from within" (e.g., ability, choice and engagement, creativity, affecting and transforming). This power from within is then used to affect positive change related to addressing social as well as environmental issues. Ecofeminist perspectives suggest that to empower women will result in the empowerment of oppressed entities including nature.

Ecofeminists contend that the powerlessness of women must be changed so that environmental management addresses all forms of domination on the Earth. Ecofeminism is concerned with the ethics of love, caring, and friendship to balance the current emphasis on rights, justice, and obligation (Cheney, 1987). The differences between women and men as well as humans and nonhumans must be valued, and all must seek the power to find unity within that diversity (Henderson and Bialeschki, 1990-91). Much has been written about ecofeminism in recent years (e.g., Diamond and Orenstein, 1990; Plant, 1989) but a great deal of work remains in applying ecofeminism to better understanding nature-based, human values and managing for a new land ethic.

Environmental Activism

Some women have chosen to put nature-based, human values into action by becoming involved in environmental activism. The relationship between gender differences and activism is highly inconclusive (Mohai, 1992). One of the premises of feminist perspectives and female ways of being, however, acknowledges the need for conscious action if the world is to become a better place in which to live. When women today attempt to change society's domination of nature, they are acting to overturn modern construction of nature and women as passive and subordinate (Merchant, 1980). The work of many female nature writers, spiritualists, and social activists has been consistent in addressing how to live in harmony with the Earth (Schaef, 1981).

As environmental activists, many women have been tackling projects to "fix the Earth" as well as asking questions about issues that cannot be readily answered. Feminist concerns have led to the need for activism. In addition, the activism has allowed for women to have a greater voice in what the world should be like. Social concerns have emerged consciously and unconsciously from cultural norms, social ideologies, religions, and philosophical assumptions which encourage activism based on a feminist focus on action (Merchant, 1980). On both local and global issues, women are continuing to address the environmental needs, such as food production and population control, that are salient and obvious to them (Stranahan, 1993).

Some criticism has been leveled at women as environmental activists because they are having to "clean up the mess men have made of the Earth" (Griffin, 1978). Many feminists believe, however, that something must be done to save the Earth and that female ways of being provide one such model, particularly when the qualities of caring not controlling, harmony not mastery, humility not arrogance, and appreciation not acquisitiveness are presented as nature-based, human values. In essence, all feminist values pertaining to nature reflect a form of environmental activism; the contribution that can be made from these female values can no longer be ignored.

Recommendations for a New Land Management Ethic

Feminist perspectives and female ways of being concerning nature have implications for land managers both personally and professionally. Values inherent to feminist perspectives such as caring, concern for future generations, protectiveness and responsibility toward lives besides our own, gentleness, tenderness, patience, sensitivity, nurturance, reverence for life, aesthetic intuition, and receptivity are important to consider (Anderson, 1991). In this way, female values related to nature pertain to acts of respect and acts of restraint. It is difficult to be enriched with respect and restraint when the dominant culture encourages us to consume and behave as we do and when we live in a world that has largely alienated both men and women from experiencing the natural world from many perspectives. In a similar manner, feminist perspectives can also offer ways for both males and females to embody emerging values in the way that nature is viewed and to encourage socially and environmentally responsible actions in outdoor behavior and management.

Regardless of which feminist perspective is the anchor, the land management implications for female ways of being can be summed up simply in one word—*inclusion*. This inclusion relates to incorporating female values as well as specifically addressing the needs and concerns of women and the employment of females in policymaking situations. The end result will be the inclusion of broader perspectives incorporated into land management ethics.

What would the management of public lands resemble if female ways of being from either or both feminine and feminist world-views were incorporated into the philosophy and management plans? By this incorporation can managers develop new ways of thinking about the ethics of land management? Many activists, theorists, and artists operating from female ways of being stress the advantages of consciously creating new management ethics and plans that embrace and honor the value of caretaking and nurturing—situations that do not perpetuate the dichotomy by raising nature over culture or by raising women over men (Diamond and Orenstein, 1990). Thus, I am not necessarily suggesting that managers replace current land management practices with feminist approaches per se, but I am suggesting that they incorporate the messages that feminist perspectives and female ways of being offer for planning and policymaking. To conceive of the world as only female seems to suggest an essentialism that continues to highlight the differences between males and females. Ideally, Murphy (1988) offered that perhaps we ought to abandon all patriarchal ideologies and transcend sex typing and its limitations altogether.

Land managers wishing to encourage recognition of feminist values and nature may want to consider several aspects evolving from female ways of being. First, philosophically the diversity that exists in the world cannot be ignored. What must be ignored, however, is the concept that diversity and difference imply judgment. Observing diversity in terms of how each part contributes to the whole is an important aspect to consider in intersecting human and nonhuman issues. To operationalize the philosophical notion of diversity requires, for example, that public hearings offer all individuals a chance to be heard and that a gender balance is the target for employee hiring.

A second philosophical view is that managers must acknowledge that any form of oppression is not justifiable. Managers must consider how traditional, dominant views may have silenced some perspectives and views. Female ways of being underline that any form of oppression, such as sexism, racism, or naturism is wrong. The basis of female values and ecofeminism can provide a perspective that will allow land managers to address alternatives and solutions to human and environmental problems. Ecofeminism, for example, is not just a "women's issue" although women have contributed to its understanding. The propositions of ecofeminism have much to offer in analyzing how racism, sexism, culturism, and naturism have resulted in oppression in visible as well as invisible forms.

Third, the values of females and other silenced groups must be given credence in land management planning. Female ways of being have not been predominant in land management ethics because of the powerlessness that many women, and men outside the dominant structure, have felt. Because of this powerlessness, many people have not had an opportunity to express the meaning of their personal nature-based human values. These individuals need to be given ways to express feelings of empowerment through public hearings and opportunities for environmental activism so their views can be heard and implemented.

Changing values are a fourth aspect for land managers to consider from female ways of being. A shift seems to be occurring in the conception of ethics based on moral rights to ethics that make a central case for care, love, friendship, trust, and appropriate reciprocity—values that presuppose relationships to others as central to an understanding of who we are (Warren, 1990). In essence, the emerging female values suggest that all acts should focus on respect, the diversity of human beings, and the life enhancement of all environments. This is a philosophy that might be considered in all aspects of land management through opening channels for communication and by paying attention to "different" points of view.

Fifth, in considering female values, the styles of management in agencies may need to change from that of a conqueror or "power" mentality to one of cooperation and nurturance. These management changes may be accomplished by thinking about such issues as facilitating meetings rather than running them, mediating agreements rather than litigation, considering socially responsible holistic health, and replacing pure objectivity in decision making with intuition and consensual decision making (Russell, 1990). Similarly, when addressing land management issues, the superiority of humans in managing lands and particularly the needs of the dominant culture, should not take priority over nonhuman needs and the needs of those males and females who have previously been voiceless.

Sixth, language may also enter into some of the changes that might occur if female ways of being were acknowledged more completely. For example, language that is sexist/naturist needs to be changed. Discussing nature as if it needs to be conquered or mastered would no longer be appropriate. Language suggesting violence such as "assaults" on mountain peaks needs to be scrutinized for the hidden message of force and power. The use of language in outdoor recreation often sanctions and perpetuates the domination and inferiority of both women and nature (Wirth and Boddy, 1991). Similarly, to refer to the manager as "he" or to talk about "man and nature" serves to exclude women from the possibilities for inclusion.

Involving women in management decisions is a seventh way to acknowledge female values. This suggestion overtly encourages the employment of women in positions of decision making so that women are visible. It is granted that not all women think alike or necessarily think that differently from men due to their socialization, but if females are not given opportunities for decision making, they will never be able to effect change based on their feminine or feminist perspectives or their life situations.

Eighth, female ways of knowing also have implications for how data are collected for making management decisions. A number of feminist researchers (e.g., Belenky, Clinchy, Goldberger, and Tarule, 1986; Harding, 1991; Roberts, 1981; Stanley, 1990) have suggested that female ways of being often are best understood through qualitative data collection. Understanding the nature-based, human values and experiences of women may be better understood by using research and evaluation that is contextual and phenomenological rather than reductionist, value free, and aimed at the control and manipulation of variables. The implication is that land managers will need to examine the benefits of multiple research methods in attempting to explain female ways of being and the experiences of other oppressed groups.

Ninth, one cannot support female ways of being without working for socially responsible change. Change is a way of life; all methods used to create change, however, should be life affirming, consensual, and nonviolent. The basis of interactions as a female way of being relates to new ways to honor the Earth and all the inhabitants of it. Female ways of being suggest that land managers must examine their role in relation to social responsibility so that all actions are life enhancing.

Finally, land managers must acknowledge that environmental activism is at the heart of any management of recreation lands. Land managers may want to see environmental activism as an important element to encourage. Rather than see environmental activism as a threat, it may in fact be one way that change can occur in addressing environmental issues and hearing the voices of many women and men.

Exploring female values related to nature results in many perspectives that can contribute to better land management ethics and practices. Some of these perspectives are old, while others are new and may seem somewhat radical and far-fetched. Female ways of being can provide an emerging voice for discussions about ethics and land management. Feminist perspectives can offer a way to critique, correct, and transform the ways that land managers have traditionally conceptualized the role of women and land management. The explication of the nature-based, human values of women, whether through advocating essentialism or feminism or a combination of these perspectives, can allow us to understand life enhancement through environmental pursuits from broader perspectives. No one perspective will provide all the answers to any human or environmental challenge. With the pressing issues that exist, land managers will need to use as many perspectives as possible, including those of women and feminists.

Literature Cited

Anderson, L. (1991). *Sisters of the Earth*. New York, NY: Vintage Books.

Belenky, M., Clinchy, V., Goldberger, N., and Tarule, J. (1986). *Women's ways of knowing*. New York, NY: Basic Books, Inc. Publishers.

Card, C. (Ed.). (1991). *Feminist ethics*. Lawrence, KS: University Press of Kansas.

Cheney, J. (1987). Ecofeminism and deep ecology. *Environmental Ethics, 9*, 115-145.

Diamond, I. and Orenstein, G. (Eds.). (1990). *Reweaving the world*. San Francisco, CA: Sierra Club Books.

Dustin, D. (1992). The dance of the dispossessed: On patriarchy, feminism and the practice of leisure science. *Journal of Leisure Research, 24*(4), 324-332.

Eichler, M. (1980). *The double standard*. New York, NY: Saint Martin's Press.

Estes, C. (1992). *Women who run with the wolves*. New York, NY: Ballantine Books, Inc.

Fox, K. (1992). Choreographing differences in the dance of leisure: The potential of feminist thought. *Journal of Leisure Research, 24*(4), 333-347.

Gilligan, C. (1982). *In a different voice*. Cambridge, MA: Harvard University Press.

Gray, E. (Ed.). (1988). *Sacred dimensions of women's experience*. Wellesley, MA: Roundtable Press.

Griffin, S. (1978). *Woman and nature: The roaring inside her*. New York, NY: Harper & Row Publishers, Inc.

Harding, S. (1991). *Whose science? Whose knowledge?* Ithaca, NY: Cornell University Press.

Held, V. (1990). Feminist transformations of moral theory. *Philosophy and Phenomenological Research, 1*, 321-344.

Henderson, K. and Bialeschki, M. (1990-91). Ecofeminism: Recreation as if nature and woman mattered. *Leisure Information Quarterly, 17*(1), 1-5.

Henderson, K., Bialeschki, M., Shaw, S., and Freysinger, V. (1989). *A leisure of one's own*. State College, PA: Venture Publishing, Inc.

Kaza, S. (1989, January). "Feedback loops that work." Paper presented to the Ecological Restoration Management Annual Meeting. Oakland, CA.

King, R. (1991). Caring about nature: Feminist ethics and the environment. *Hypatia, 6*(1), 75-89.

Merchant, C. (1980). *The death of nature: Women, ecology, and the scientific revolution*. San Francisco, CA: Harper & Row Publishers, Inc.

Mitten, D. (1992). Empowering girls and women in the outdoors. *Journal of Physical Education, Recreation, and Dance, 63*(2), 56-60.

Mohai, P. (1992). Men, women, and the environment: An examination of the gender gap in environmental concern and activism. *Society and Natural Resources, 5,* 1-19.

Murphy, P. (1988). Sex-typing the planet: Gaia imagery and the problem of subverting patriarchy. *Environmental Ethics, 10,* 155-168.

Ortner, S. (1974). Is female to male as nature is to culture? In M. Rosaldo and L. Lamphere (Eds.). *Women, culture, and society.* Stamford, CA: Stamford University Press.

Plant, J. (Ed.). (1989). *Healing the wounds: The promise of ecofeminism.* Philadelphia, PA: New Society Publishers.

Roberts, H. (Ed.). (1981). *Doing feminist research.* London, UK: Routledge and Kegan Paul.

Ruether, R. (1983). Sexism, religion, and the social and spiritual liberation of women today. In C. Gould (Ed.), *Beyond domination: New perspectives on women and philosophy* (pp. 107-122). Totowa, NJ: Rowman and Allanheld.

Russell, J. (1990). The evolution of an ecofeminist. In I. Diamond and G. Orenstein (Eds.), *Reweaving the World* (pp. 223-230). San Francisco, CA: Sierra Club Books.

Salleh, A. (1984). Deeper than deep ecology: The ecofeminist connection. *Environmental Ethics, 6,* 339-345.

Schaef, A. (1981). *Women's reality.* Minneapolis, MN: Winston Press, Inc.

Simpson, C. (1991, July). "Women outdoors: New Zealand study." Paper presented to the World Leisure and Recreation Association, Sydney, Australia.

Stanley, L. (Ed.). (1990). *Feminist praxis.* London: Routledge.

Starhawk. (1982). *Dreaming the dark: Magic, sex, and politics.* Boston, MA: Beacon Press.

Stranahan, S. (1993, May/June). Empowering women. *International Wildlife,* pp. 12-19.

Warren, K. (1990). The power and promise of ecological feminism. *Environmental Ethics, 12,* 125-146.

Wirth, D. and Boddy, P. (Interviewers). (1991). The quilt of ecological feminism: An interview with Karen Warren. *Woman of Power,* (issue *20*), 64-68.

Yerkes, R. and Miranda, W. (1985). Women outdoors: Who are they? *Parks and Recreation, 20*(3), 48-51, 95.

Section III

Part B

PERSONAL AND PROFESSIONAL
PERSPECTIVES

IN THE OPEN: WILD PLACES AND THE AMERICAN CHARACTER

CHAPTER 13

CHRIS MADSON
Wyoming Wildlife Magazine
Cheyenne, Wyoming

For more than a decade, I had a small poem thumbtacked to the bulletin board over my typewriter. It was the work of a twentieth-century American poet whose name I'm embarrassed to say I no longer recall—Vachel Lindsay, maybe, or Archibald MacLeish. I can't remember. Nor do I remember the title or the first line, either of which could be tracked in *Granger's Guide to American Poetry*. This would be no special problem if some ham-fisted colleague of mine hadn't lost the poem itself during our last office move. Now there is a good chance I will go to my grave with just the one line in my brain. It's enough to drive an otherwise stable personality into deep psychological difficulties.

Just the one line. "Or if there is a thing we can mean by freedom," it went, "that is land, not men." The poem went on to ruminate on the passing of the American frontier, "like sunlight," as I remember, "fading in the grass."

It's something the American culture seems to have missed. Much of what we accept as our history reads more like a creation myth than a measured recitation of fact. Bravery, hard work, sacrifice, the intervention of God—these, we believe, are the attributes that made this nation great. I'm a dyed-in-the-wool American myself; I can trace parts of my lineage back to the Revolutionary War and out across the Western frontier. I believe that Americans have been brave, strong, and disciplined, that they have sacrificed themselves and their loved ones willingly in the cause of empire building.

What I don't see is how these traits explain our unique circumstances as a people. Other peoples have been brave, strong, disciplined; others have sacrificed themselves and their loved ones in noble causes. In fact, the history I've read is replete with examples of bravery, strength, endurance, and sacrifice that outshine almost anything we have done. And yet, many of these cultures never enjoyed the wealth, comfort, or influence Americans have enjoyed ever since the first Europeans committed themselves to the New World. There must be another variable at work, something that explains why this culture has risen to its position in the history of human development.

I believe my unknown poet laid his hand on that variable—the land. The freedom we have enjoyed on this continent has always rested on a foundation of open country. In some ways, I suppose my view of the matter harks back to Frederick Jackson Turner's famous 1893 essay, "The Significance of the Frontier in American History" (1920). In that address,

Turner reacted to a report from the U.S. Bureau of the Census in which the superintendent stated that his agency could no longer identify a frontier in the nation's pattern of settlement. Turner wrote that "this brief statement marks the closing of a great historic movement. . . . The existence of an area of free land and the advance of American settlement westward, explain American development."

It's become fashionable among historians to debunk Turner's thesis, and I must admit that many of his observations seem quaint, sometimes paternal, and even a little racist by modern standards. Still, the thread underlying Turner's essay seems sound to me. The influence of wilderness and sheer open space on the American character has been profound, and even in this day of urban sprawl and population explosion, it plays a part in the way we think and feel about the nation and each other.

The roots of this influence reach back to the moment Columbus gathered a crew for his first western voyage. From that time through the end of the nineteenth century, a selective process was at work in the settlement of the continent. As I've grayed at the temples, I've occasionally found myself wondering how I would have responded to Major William Ashley's *St. Louis Gazette* advertisement, "To Enterprising Young Men . . . to ascend the river Missouri to its source, there to be employed for one, two, or three years." Ashley's call to the western fur trade was the beginning of a great adventure in boundless country, to be sure. When I was twenty, I was nearly sure I would have signed on; now, at 43, I'm nearly sure I would not. The fur trade was an excellent way to see the wilderness—it was also an excellent way to end up dead.

America was explored and settled by people who were willing to take up such challenges. It was often more than accepting a personal risk. It usually meant leading one's wife and children into danger, and it nearly always meant abandoning family ties, friends, familiar country and customs, even a native language. For many people the decision to come to America was irrevocable—once they had given up their land and spent the money for the trip, they had little choice but to go. For all these reasons the price of passage was high, and the people who accepted it were highly motivated, either because of circumstances they were trying to escape or, more often, possibilities they were trying to capture. Either way, American immigrants have

probably never been a cross section of the societies from which they came.

So what sort of person decided to make the trip? In his history of the Oregon Trail, *The Plains Across*, John Unruh (1979) has pointed out that the emigrants to the West were generally middle class—it took a little money to prepare for a trip of that magnitude. This has probably been true of most American pioneers, regardless of the era. There were criminals and indentured servants among the early colonists, certainly, but the majority had enough money for passage, some tools, and provisions. They seemed to be steady citizens who, for one reason or another, were profoundly disaffected with European politics, religion, economics, or all three.

Most historians cast the first waves of immigration in political, religious, or economic terms, but I think an argument can be made that geography was at least as powerful a motivator; that is to say, issues of land. America was largely beyond the reach of European politics as King George III ultimately found out when he pressured colonists to pay for military protection they felt they could provide on their own. Even before independence, the New World had enough room to afford a degree of tolerance that was impossible in Europe. Space allowed the Puritans, Quakers, and followers of the Church of England to establish their own communities and to follow their own religious tenets with no outside interference. By the early seventeenth century, this patchwork of religion had led people to question whether any human should be persecuted for his or her religion. In 1636 Roger Williams bought a tract of land from local Native Americans (a radical concept in itself) and established the colony of Rhode Island, separating the rule of church and state for the first time in Western history. At about the same time, plantation owners to the south began building an enclave of moral tolerance for the institution of slavery.

It would be nice to think that such freedoms could have developed in the Europe of the time, but without the physical space to separate societies with violently different precepts, there was no way to avoid conflict. The broad-minded society that drafted the Declaration of Independence and the U.S. Constitution simply would not have existed without huge tracts of open country.

That space was very much on the minds of the citizens of the infant nation. Pioneers had been moving beyond the Appalachians for decades before independence in the face of dire threats from local Indians, the French, and frequently their own colonial governments as well. One of the first acts of the new nation was to establish the Northwest Territory from land ceded to the U.S. by the British. The wilderness between the Ohio River, the Mississippi River, and the Great Lakes was to be surveyed and offered free of charge to settlers. When an area gained enough population, the people there could apply to the federal government for statehood. As early as 1783 the French minister in Philadelphia could see what was brewing in the American imagination: "The Americans," he wrote, "in pushing their possessions as far as Lake of the Woods, are preparing for their remote posterity a communication with the Pacific." The U.S. had already begun to pursue what came to be called its Manifest Destiny. In the century that followed, the main theme of American history was to be the acquisition, settlement, and exploitation of open country.

Recent historians hasten to point out that while the "frontier" was being opened the nation faced other issues, particularly slavery and the question of Southern secession. It's interesting, however, that even in this matter new land loomed large as part of the problem and attempted solution. With the addition of western states, Southern slave holders were concerned that they would lose their political advantage in Congress and might also see their style of agriculture contained in the Southeast. Henry Clay's Missouri Compromise sought to ease tensions on both sides of the issue by dividing the West into free and slave territory. The subsequent Compromise of 1850 ceded more land to each side in the conflict over slaves. For two generations these attempts to give room to each view successfully postponed the inevitable conflict. And when the South finally decided to withdraw from the Union, it was the issue of loss of southern territory, not slavery, that galvanized the North into action.

It's difficult to separate politics from the marketplace, especially in America. While the size and nature of the American landscape shaped much of our political history, they were shaping our economy as well. The great land giveaway that began in the Northwest Territory in 1787 continued with the Homestead Act of 1862. The Surface Mining Act of 1872 essentially followed suit, granting minerals on federal land to the discoverer for pennies. Water

rights in the West, as precious as gold in places like California's Imperial Valley, were similarly given away to the earliest applicants. A few politicians like John Quincy Adams suggested some sort of sale of land to American citizens, seeing the demand for unsettled real estate as a good source of income for the government. But even in Adams' time the tradition of free natural resources was too strong to fight. It was based on two tenets of the frontier ethic—the inexhaustibility of the land and the concept of "first come, first served." The ongoing debates over issues like public-land grazing and multibillion dollar water "development" in the West shows that this frontier ethic continues to exert a powerful influence on our business and political dealings. Even in this "information age," the health of the American economy continues to depend largely on the extraction of natural resources, some of which are nonrenewable, most of which can't renew themselves as fast as they are being sold.

If the history of our politics and economy weren't enough to prove our intimate relationship with the land, our art, literature, and collective myths certainly would be. We have been engaged in a love-hate relationship with the American wilderness ever since the Puritans touched Plymouth Rock. They first crystallized the struggle to settle America as a holy confrontation between the forces of Light and Darkness. That role as a divine champion on Earth has been extended to the struggle to move other people off the land as we moved in.

Almost as soon as the lines were drawn in the battle between Civilization and Wilderness, a few people struck up a more amiable relationship with the new continent. In 1624, lawyer Thomas Morton abandoned the Plymouth colony and took up residence with a few immigrant friends and the Massachusetts and Wampanoag Indians. "Millions of Turtle doves," he wrote later, " . . . sweet crystal fountains, and clear running streams . . . Fowles in abundance . . . Nature's masterpiece—If this land be not rich, then is the whole world poore."

It was the second great theme in the American relationship with the land, one that gained currency as more people became acquainted with the wilderness and there seemed an increasing likelihood that we would gain some sort of dingy triumph in our confrontation with it. As the centuries passed, the frontiersman became an icon, defining the strength and self-reliance we've strived to cultivate in ourselves.

Among the earliest examples is Natty Bumpo, James Fenimore Cooper's (1993) wilderness pragmatist, who routinely saves urban damsels and dandies alike from the threats lurking in wild places, all the while deploring the settlement of the frontier and the resulting loss of frontier values. The character has been a staple of novels, film, and folk stories ever since.

Henry David Thoreau was probably the first serious American philosopher to grapple with the issues of wildness and the American character, but a long line of intellectuals followed him. By the time the Bureau of Census announced the official end of the frontier in 1890, the nation was well on its way to recognizing the cataclysmic changes it had worked on the face of the continent and, in the process, on ourselves.

I don't think we ever laid the issue of the lost frontier to rest. What with two world wars, a catastrophic depression, and a generation of nuclear confrontation, the twentieth century has provided its own unique distractions. Now we approach the end of another century, the beginning of another millennium, a superpower trying to figure out how to fight greed, poverty, and the lust for power in far-off countries. For the first time since Teddy Roosevelt, we find ourselves with the time to look at ourselves, and we find the same problems waiting.

A government of the people can work in two circumstances. One, and perhaps the best, is a small community of like-minded citizens built on the blueprint of the New England town meeting. The key is homogeneity, fundamental agreement on matters of religion, politics, morality, and ultimate goals. Disagreements in such communities are more often about means than ends.

The United States was built on a much different foundation. By historic accident, we started out as a pluralistic society. Tolerance was and is the key. It allowed us to hang together in spite of differences in culture, background, economic interests, and even goals. It gave us the chance to combine two disparate things—representative democracy and empire.

As I see it, the concept of frontier is the only idea that can hold a large, pluralistic, democratic society together. Except in a community of saints, tolerance often requires space—enough room to separate idealists who can't find common ground. Wealth helps, too. If minorities can earn enough to be comfortable, they are more likely to work inside a system than depose it. In the absence of actual wealth, opportunity may serve the same purpose.

Frontier provides both of these. Most of history's great pluralistic societies—Rome, the great Mongol empire of the Middle Ages and the Muslim empire that followed, Renaissance Spain, and modern Britain—all thrived on frontier and withered for the lack of it. Like these societies, we consider ourselves a chosen people, somehow immune from the pressures that laid earlier cultures low, and, like these societies, we overestimate our uniqueness.

As I consider some of the most divisive issues in late twentieth-century America, I see a growing hunger for the lost frontier. We decry violence in our society even though violence has been one of our defining characteristics throughout our history. What has changed? I get the impression that we're used to having violence out on the fringe of society, either on a physical frontier or at a boundary between two more or less homogeneous communities. It's been us against them for generations, "them" being people of different language, different color, different customs, or economic status. We took steps to segregate these people whenever possible so that, when a violent confrontation arose, we had no problem recognizing "them."

One of the troubling aspects of violence in this generation of Americans is that it comes right into the neighborhood after us. Random drive-by shootings, husbands murdering wives, mass murders at the local post office or school, reclusive neighbors who turn out to be serial killers—we can no longer depend on the security of community. I don't pretend to fathom the complex roots of this phenomenon, but I get the sense that part of it is a matter of territory. As we continue to subdivide the continent, we find less and less room to accommodate differences. We're more and more irritated by malcontents and nonconformists. People who are emotionally on the fringe of society have fewer and fewer chances to move physically to the fringe. Those of us who would stay and those of us who would go all miss the frontier.

We pay more lip service to the rights of minorities, but we seem to do a poorer job of incorporating them into mainstream American culture. Ethnic groups seem more inclined to cling to their own languages and communities; younger generations seem less inclined to embrace or even acknowledge their parents' values and ambitions. Why? Could it be that the passing of Manifest Destiny leaves us without an alternative?

America's middle class, long regarded as the economic and moral backbone of the nation, seems to be under siege. The political Right has blamed this phenomenon on bloated government; the Left has accused capitalists. Thomas Jefferson would probably have attributed the problem to the movement away from the soil, the passing of the largely self-sufficient farmer working cheap land and surrounded by an embarrassment of natural wealth—the loss of frontier.

As these and other social problems press in on us, I think we will have no choice but to deal at last with Frederick Jackson Turner's (1920) passing of the frontier. It will be difficult because our feeling about wild country is still a compound of the two views of our forefathers—on the one hand, that wild country should be subdued for moral as well as economic reasons and, on the other, that wild country can open our eyes and heal our souls.

Literature Cited

Cooper, J. (1993). *The deerslayer*. New York, NY: Oxford University Press.

Turner, F. (1920). *The frontier in American history*. New York, NY: Henry Holt & Company, Inc.

Unruh, J. (1979). *The plains across: The overland emigrants and the Trans-Mississippi West, 1840-60*. Urbana, IL: University of Illinois Press.

LESSONS FROM THE CINNAMON MARE

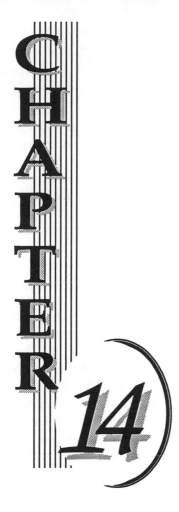

BOB BUDD
Red Canyon Ranch
Lander, Wyoming

For what it's worth, I'm a cowboy. I have no doctorate in philosophy, but I have known a few good old philosophers in my lifetime. All their lives they maintained that too much of that philosophy just got in the way of common sense, and then all of a sudden they got old enough to hold court within earshot of young pups like me. Just like that, each of them was transformed into some kind of buckaroo Socrates. And, lucky for me as I see it now, I actually listened to what the old-time cowboys had to say to me. Maybe someday, if I use enough common sense, I'll be able to sit around and act wise even if I'm not.

Yesterday I rode the cinnamon mare. She's new to the ranch, and to me. That makes us even. The last two days she's been walking the corral fence. Despite the cold, I knew that she and I both needed to be outside. Some days I do better with the cinnamon mare than I do with people. Other days, I leave the cinnamon mare alone. She is a lady, and there are times she's best left to walk the fence. Some days she listens to me, and some days I listen to her. Ours is a cautious relationship.

I seem to listen best to the land when I am on horseback. It may be the sense of terrain conveyed from muscle and sinew, as the horse moves through open country. Certainly, much of my sensitivity is tied to the constant signals of a horse's ears, and its greater sense of what is out there, behind the trees, in the rocks, beneath the land. The greater part of sensitivity, though, is more likely the complete vulnerability you feel when life is largely held in the hands of nature, and an animal which outweighs you five or six times over. The old saying goes that if horses knew how puny we were, they'd stomp us to death. For whatever reason, most choose to allow us to feel those things we could not otherwise understand.

Today, the red rocks are chuckling. A warm wind blows from the northwest, and molten snow plummets over the rim, cascades of silver, black stains etched into red sandstone where thousands of trickles have come before. In that spot below the rim, there are two springs. One is a short-lived spring recharged annually by snowmelt. The other is a deep, geothermal pool which gushes from the earth at thirty gallons each minute. Surely, there is some connection over geologic time and a logical explanation for the occurrence of both. I am content just to know they are there.

Along the creek snow and ice are breaking up. I'll not have to chop ice for the mare come morning. In the willows a moose lies in the shadows less than three hundred yards from the house. She moved in this winter, the first one the old-timers have seen on the creek in a decade. I am hopeful she will stay for the summer too, but I'm not optimistic. More willow and water may keep her close, and as long as the beaver don't back water into the corrals, or take more willow than the creek can stand to lose, they'll keep the water table up. There are new cuttings above and below the house this day, and as much as I like the beaver, the level of activity causes me concern. Sometimes it seems the beaver have a poor sense of balance, and I fear they will eat themselves into oblivion, or leave the creeks devoid of shade and places for birds to nest and hide. But, on the whole they are a welcome sight, a sign of health and vitality on the creek, a signal that balance can be achieved on this piece of land.

In the uplands the mare adopts a leggy trot. I settle into her rhythm and let her move in the direction she chooses. She doesn't like mud or ice, I've found, and I try to follow her line by looking behind me. Some wet day I'll thank her for this track across higher ground. In the junipers on the rim we excite a little bunch of deer, and they sneak around the twisted trees like cats peeking at us as we pass through their domain. This is the first herd of deer I've seen all winter, and it gives me peace to know they have not disappeared entirely, as gossip in town maintains. We cut a single lion track on the rim. Lions and the cinnamon mare share disdain for mud. The mare's disdain for lions is one-sided.

In the uplands I look for water—seeps, springs, and little potholes out of the sun's direct stare. This pasture is still filled with grass, mostly bluebunch and needlegrass, and it will make good feed for the cattle which will arrive in early spring. The cows will use it for ten days, maybe twelve at the most, and for that period and the rest of the year, it will be home to others. The price of this land has exceeded its value for grazing now. Just over the ridge houses light up the night sky. People haul water to these mansions in pickup trucks, and while deer may adapt, the lions do not. The water I seek will not

sustain a household, but if we nurture and protect the source, it will help disperse 600 cows and their calves for the brief period they will spend on this piece of land. We might save snowmelt in a hole in the ground and tap the spring only so long as the cattle are here. By midsummer, it will be parched and dry.

Far below, in the alluvial wake of time, the meadows along the creek are beginning to show traces of green beneath the receding line of snow. It might be my eyes for they are anxious. As the mare catches her breath, I study the ditches, easy to pick out by snow trapped in the shadow of the banks. These ditches, carefully following contours of the alluvium, were dug with draft horses and slip. In an ancient gulch bleached remnants of a wooden flume glow silver. The land speaks of a single mistake in judgment, an effort to carry water down the slope too fast. The ancient flume speaks of a steward's touch, and now, grass and silt on top of the flume have nearly reclaimed the boards. In the center of the silvery flume runs a single pipe, a more modern solution of conveyance, but one no less a means of saving land than the solution created a century past. The early owners learned quickly of this land, for from that one point as far north as I can see, there are no more gullies or flumes. Ditches branch far above the lower meadows, and they move slowly down the slope. There is a lesson I must remember about this soil; mistakes are not forgiven in short order.

The importance of water has been ingrained in my mind since I was a boy. Whether chopping ice on a cold morning or chasing a head of water through the mud on sultry summer days, I seem to have inherited four generations of understanding the vitality of hydrogen and oxygen, properly mixed. The power of water is never lost on the cowboy. Slow, soaking rains bring joy and contentment. A good snowpack tempers the difficulty of deep powder and ice on the meadows. Perhaps that is why so many of us have a fly rod nestled in a cotton sleeve behind the seat of the pickup.

Cowboys think of water always.

Yesterday water was not so prominent in my mind. The wind was less than charitable, howling down the canyons, driving snow through every crack in the barn. The wild cats were huddled on my saddle blankets savoring the warmth, and they hissed at me for invading their space and removing their bed. The cinnamon mare stayed in the corner of the shed until she was certain I'd brought oats, and even then she came to me with a great sense of personal sacrifice. The cinnamon mare wears her heart on her sleeve.

Mule deer formed dense, immobile shadows beneath the willows in the creek bottom. A small group of elk were nearly invisible beneath the red rocks, their white breath the only clue that they lay waiting for the sun to track south across the morning sky. Even the chickadees were fluffed into balls deep in the hawthorn and sumac. A single track spoke of a cottontail hidden in the woodpile. Another belonged to a bobcat holed up at the opposite end from its prey. Yesterday, all of us living here looked at the land for the shelter it gives us.

My family and I find shelter on this piece of ground, but we are not alone. We know that, and we understand that must be true. We welcome the communion. The place where we live is sheltered, with clean water, but it is not the "best" place in the valley. The best place on this ranch can only be framed by the needs and desires of the user. When a meadowlark sings from a fence post, he is certain he has found the very best place on the land, or he wouldn't sing. But his singing is no more claim to the land than human claims manifested in law, and all of the laws in the world will not make the meadowlark sing if he is not content. Nor is the meadowlark exclusionary, for in the wake of his shrill aria countless other birds manifest their own sense of joy. There is the slap of a beaver tail on the water, the howl of the coyote, the motherly bawling of a cow, and the irreverent squeals of my own children. If we can learn to share the land and to care for the needs of others, material and spiritual, we can begin to see the land as a part of ourselves and not a prize to be won.

Ownership is important. Whether by fee title or spiritual bond, ownership is critical to stewardship. But with ownership must come respect and responsibility. If spiritual ownership ends at the moment rapture passes, then spiritual ownership is not enough. The test of ownership lies in loving the land as much when it is covered in ice and snow, or blown desolate with drought, as when meadows are capped by waves of wildflowers. Most of this ranch is owned by the people of the nation, but that must not change or alter the way I view this piece of ground. To succumb to such would render me incapable of caring for the land as a whole. Most of us rarely admit such, but the land may own us more than we own the land.

In finding shelter on this piece of land, my family and I accept the responsibility of sharing it with other creatures. Whether trained in ecology or immersed in it by reality, as is the rancher, most of us on the land understand the minutiae to which we are reduced by countless other forms of life upon which we depend. My children are the sixth generation on the land, but yesterday, as we watched a bobcat dance in the snow, I wondered how many generations of these cats have shared the land with one of our own. How many more generations of bobcats and cowboys might share this piece of ground?

As I rest in the saddle, I can feel the land undulate beneath the mare, but I sense more than rock, sinew, and chinook. At the heart of wondering lies the soul of our own value system. What gifts can we truly offer to those whose wide eyes sparkle beneath broad brimmed hats, or those whose eyes watch us from the shelter of the red rocks? I believe we strive to offer a better place than that which we found, a place where life and vitality are no less, and maybe even greater. Perhaps therein lies the reason I toil and fret over the landscape on which I live. The true measure of the gift lies not in the value of the land. The important thing is how we choose to value land.

To a cowboy the single most important value in the land is its ability to sustain native grasses, forbs, and shrubs. Year after year. Cash values may exponentially surpass the true reward of bluebunch seedlings, but so long as springtime brings a flush of green to yellow-gray sagebrush hillsides, cash values dim and fade. My greatest measure of success lies not in how I use the grass, but in how I am able to leave it each year and in the amalgamation of years I am able to care for the land. Grass is much less important to the cowboy for its economic value than for the spiritual rendering it leaves in us all. Purely economic, as bankers tend to be, grass properly managed means sustainable business over the long haul. Purely ecological, as most ranchers would prefer to be, grass tells us how the land senses our touch long before other signs of joy or despair become evident. Grass provides the basic habitat for lives not human. But, in sensual reality, it is plants, and especially grass, which rejuvenates our souls.

The cinnamon mare is anxious for her head, and I give it, for my own head is drifting beyond the scope of my sight. As the mare picks her way from red rock to snow covered slopes of phosphoria and limestone, I sense some of the gifts left to me by the old cowboys. I am saddened that I was never able to tell them that I finally understand some of the knowledge they tried to share. The filly is anxious, as I have been, as my own children often seem. For once I feel my own patience rising. In its grandeur and immensity, the short ride from one side of the canyon to the other is more than I can possibly comprehend, and yet, if I am to be successful in living with this piece of ground, I must do more than simply comprehend. I must begin to understand, and in doing so, I must also take the time to tell of what I've learned, or think I might have learned. Most of all, I must realize that the land will change over time, and that nothing I might try can overcome the power of the land itself. It is not my place to conquer the land. My opportunity lies in adapting to change and evolving with realities presented by things I cannot understand.

Most of what I know of the land and of the values which reside within myself I have learned on the land. On good days the land lives within me, and I am able to give myself back. Now I think that is what my parents sought so desperately to share with me. And when I was patient enough to sit and listen to those older than me, I was offered grains of knowledge earned in a lifetime of rides on cinnamon mares. The land was not always kind. Tears of those broken by a piece of ground stain my fingers yet, and I still taste the salt of their pain on my lips. When I worry about the land and my care for it, it seems I can see every set of eyes blown dry by wind both hot and cold. I am frightened by what the land can do to mortality; even those most indomitable have been withered when they chose to fight. And yet, I see most often the nurturing, patient eyes of those who have made the land the ultimate guide of their enterprise in life. These are the men and women from whom I hope to learn. These are the people whose spirit rises in me on the truly good days.

The filly is into her element now. Her trot rises and falls as if she is adrift on a favorable current. I find my thoughts there. A hundred rides rush back to me. Three hundred miles away, Bob Wright is pointing out a bobolink, a titmouse, a waving stand of sedge amidst whitecaps of sage. Stan Flitner's eyes burn azure in the shimmering heat of Red

Gulch, and I see him pointing out every single new plant, nearly falling off his horse to see that it is true, that his care for the land has created such response. Mildred Miller stands regally next to me. She is confident and serene as she explains the harsh realities of making a living with the land. I feel the bitter cold in the midnight hour, engine off and only moonlight as Gary and Nancy Espenscheid pour out their excitement about caring for the land holistically. My father's hand is on my shoulder, and he whispers to me to watch; more than 200 bighorn ewes and lambs graze within reach of the shelter we have found in the rocks. My father's father is alive again, and he is leading me into the willows to find a fifteen-petal rose, a single strange variant he noticed in nearly four square miles of rose bushes and willows. Bill Hancock is sitting on the board seats in the sale barn, and the history of the land and its people pours out above the excited clatter of the auctioneer. Ron Vore stands waist deep in a beaver pond, casting deftly, chuckling. Pearl Spencer wanders another red canyon with me. Ninety years from birth, nearly a century of this piece of the world, she still reveres living things with the anxiousness of a child. Now nearly blind, she seems to discern wildflowers by scent, a voice on the breeze. My sense of the land is mine, and mine alone, but there are so many others living within my definition of the land that it transcends human reality. My challenge is to help carry on the tradition of stewardship ingrained in generations of ranchers, and to share those values with others who will listen. This is not easy work. I have barely begun to understand the cinnamon mare.

Often I am asked if other ranchers feel this way about the land. Some do not. That is evident. But the ranchers I have known for a lifetime have taught me these values. Some of my learning has been active, as sharp as the sting of a lariat across the shoulders. Most has been passive and interactive. Above all, the land teaches humility and acceptance. Very few of the ranchers I know enunciate their feelings for they have learned to hold these matters closely. When you allow others to view the soft underside of your values, you open them to ridicule or challenge by others. It is easier to gallop into a biting wind than to be chastised or denigrated for beliefs which shape your life. I talk of the land and its influence on the soul with many cowboys, and always, there is a soft calm which must precede and characterize the discussion. Speaking of the land is not taken lightly when soil, water, and vegetation frames life's failures and dreams.

A nasty wind drives us from the ridge behind the house, and the mare drifts easily back toward the ranch. She isn't anxious, nor is she reluctant. It's been a good day, but we are both ready to be home. At the barn, her back is dark, streaked with sweat beneath the saddle. Steam curls into the blue light of evening. The mare nickers when I step from the barn, and I rub her down slowly, a luxury for both of us. She closes her eyes and rubs her hard forehead against my shoulder, then nips at my elbow. She's earned her oats this day, but I linger. Instead of filling the bucket and letting her clean it herself, I feed her handfuls at a time. The mare lingers too, it seems, playing me for attention. In the quiet, reflected light of winter evening, I am content with this land, with this place I call home.

The aroma of dinner drifts down the hill, and in the frigid stillness, every word from mother to son is amplified. A three-foot tall man steps off the porch, casts a nine-foot shadow across the snow, and then he is immersed in a drift as deep as his chest. The cinnamon mare looks his way and nickers. Her ears are up now, and the boy slogs through the snow, carrot ensconced within a red mitten. The mare nickers again. I will never understand the magic which exists between horses and small children, but maybe I am not meant to understand such things. My friend Tony Malmberg says it is quite simple. When a little kid catches a horse or gives him oats, it's because the kid likes the horse. When bigger cowboys do it, they want something from the horse. The carrot is gone, and my own mortality is intact.

The boy leads the mare into the corral; she resting her very nose on the snow so that he can remove the halter. His shadow has been absorbed by sunset, but he remains nine-feet tall. We start our journey to the house, and as much as I long to reach down and hold him, I resist. Halfway, his legs grow weary, and he asks me to carry him. My own legs are light and strong. I will never forget this evening—this place, this feeling. In the darkness behind me, the mare nickers again. The boy is sound asleep in my arms.

As I watch her dark shape move down to the creek, I wonder if this place is special somehow to the cinnamon mare. Does she sense her contribution to the boy who sneaks her carrots from the kitchen? In the depth of winter, we lean on one another, and we learn the land together. Her ancestors were here long before my own, but this piece of ground has brought us together. I wonder if there is a place on the ranch where the cinnamon mare finds her own sense of place. I suspect there are many.

My own sense of place is not centric, and cannot be so. For me to focus on a single place would be to ignore all other pieces of the landscape. In winter I am drawn to south-facing slopes where sunlight is gathered. In the heat of summer deep glades of aspen provide escape from the same blistering sun. Every day there is a new place on this ranch to be discovered and felt. Most of them are not new at all. I may have failed to pay proper attention, or maybe that one day, the land chose to show me its heart. In living on this land, and caring for the soil, plants, and creatures both wild and domestic, my sense of mortality is heightened by the reality that I will never know the land as well as some might wish or claim. The reason ranchers continue to grow grass and cattle in the face of vertical acceleration of land prices is because they cannot imagine a life where every day is the same. A cowboy likes the land. It matters not whether conditions produce mesquite and sideoats grama or tall grasses which brush the bottoms of the stirrups. While no two days or pieces of ground can ever be the same, there is constancy in being on the land, an incredible connection with life's diversity that drives us into the day. Every morning holds new fortune, some good, some not so good, but no two are ever the same.

A fire crackles in the living room. Outside, not a single light blinks, save countless stars. The moon is reclusive. On the wall of my office hangs a map of the ranch and the land beyond those borders. My eye is drawn to the other side of the continental divide, to a place where my family has ranched for six generations. Buried bones are all that remain of the early ones, though their names are affixed to creeks and mountains. That is not enough to mark a family's passing. In every generation hence has come grim optimism, a desire to hold and nurture the land around us, to let it fall asleep in our arms. It would be easy to declare those homesteads and ranches somehow sacred, to say that they would be treated with the same degree of love and attention my great-great grandfather felt. But to do so would be to err as much in retrospect as arrogant declarations of immortal superiority would be today. How can we possibly choose a most important place if we truly see the land as the vast amalgamation of life which it truly represents?

My interaction with this land is successional. If I can be a source of energy to coax living diversity in a positive direction, to retain nature's treasures, then my time will be well spent. My attachment to the land is not permanent, nor is it temporary. It is both. In sharing this land with cinnamon mares, cows and their calves, golden-eyed bobcats and darting bluebirds, I must seek balance every day. In handing this piece of land to my children, I offer opportunity, not immortality. Most of all, every day, I try to accept and teach the responsibility which rests in the grasp or gentle embrace of my life's work. From the moment the sun blooms over the Nugget Sandstone until it blushes and hides behind Limestone Mountain, I try to think and act for tomorrow, and appreciate the day at hand.

I make mistakes. Some I make more than once. But the land is patient with me, and I believe it senses my intent, just as the cinnamon mare senses the heart of my child. Somewhere between geologic time, mortality, and the longevity of a wonderful mare lies reality.

———————————●———————————

Six months ago, the cinnamon mare and I shared a day in the stillness of winter, as if time stood still. Like the night sky, my thoughts were crystalline, sharp, and patient. The next morning would bring new learning, new opportunity, and new life. But the next morning brought no rain, and there was none after that. Now folks say it is the driest year ever. Thick red dust coats every millimeter of our lives. The hot wind drives it beneath the doors and through the windows. Grasses which should be hidden in their sheaths are headed out, withered and spent. The cows are anxious, and the meadows are tanned. The first day of summer is still more than a month away.

This morning, I'm riding the roan filly, Muffin. She is bigger than the cinnamon mare, and she glides across the land with a feminine grace that belies her youth. She doesn't know this land yet, but she learns quickly, and remembers well. Maybe she is lucky not to have been here in the cold winter for she has no frame of reference from which to complain. Today she is my favorite of all the horses in the pen.

More than one hundred species of birds are here for the summer, among them tiny wrens which flit about, then turn their tail feathers to the blue sky when they perch on the log pile outside the kitchen window. In their zest for life they remind me of my mom. Today the wrens are birds most special. Yesterday a drumming ruffed grouse held my favor.

On Greenough Mountain a trio of pronghorn fawns bursts out of the sagebrush and spook the Muffin filly, then scatter into three racing plumes of dust. Their mother stamps her feet at me and wheezes through her nose. They are my favorites, too.

Even a single plant captured my attention, though I never saw it over the course of the day. One sego lily in a tiny vase above the sink, a fragile white whisper brought from my three-year-old son to his mother. It is a gift of the land through the fingers of a child. Neither flower nor boy will remain the same, but my own memory of this single day will not wane. Even in the heart of drought, the land has rekindled my soul.

The Perspective of Outfitters and Guides

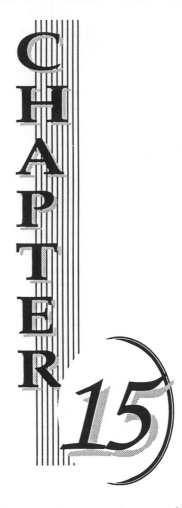

CHAPTER 15

Doug Tims
America Outdoors
Boise, Idaho

Early explorers were outfitters and guides seeking the unknown and acquiring a knowledge of the lands and waters while striving for survival. This was often viewed as a battle, pitting humans against nature. But as our numbers have increased, and the amount of natural resources has remained constant, our view has evolved into one of seeking a better understanding of our role in nature, not one of battling against it. Current trends in outfitter and guide values and behaviors reflect this transition. Most outfitters are adopting a value added approach to the services they offer the public. Traditional outfitter and guide operations are expanding to a more varied spectrum of services.

America Outdoors, the professional trade association of the outfitting industry, was formed in 1990. America Outdoors includes the traditional outfitting services offered by packers and boaters, but also includes biking, hiking, skiing, fishing, guest ranches, skill training, and interpretive and educational services. America Outdoors has quickly become the source for individual outfitters and regional and state outfitter organizations to obtain the necessary skills to be professional service providers. America Outdoors' mission is to conserve and enhance quality outdoor experiences on America's

lands and waters. This mission recognizes a web of connection between protection of our wildland base, a public that values nature, and the public's need for a cadre of caring, professional service providers.

The Professional Guide Institute (PGI) is affiliated with America Outdoors. The PGI, formed in Idaho and the Northern Rockies, is reaching out to outfitters and guides nationally. The PGI's mission is to "identify, enhance and disseminate the natural interpretive and educational resource of the outfitting industry so that outfitters and guides can offer the highest quality experience to the public" (Professional Guide Institute Mission Statement, n.d.). The institute connects guides to their origins and mission and prepares them for the future by offering a fourfold curriculum:

1. Our Wildlands Heritage—the ethical, historical, cultural, legislative and managerial underpinnings of public lands, wilderness, parks, and wild rivers.

2. Backcountry Leadership—the communication and group skills to improve the outdoor experience.

3. Wildlands Interpretation—the details about flora, fauna, geology, and ecosystems.

4. Outfitter Operations—the critical skills, practices, equipment, and fiscal management (Professional Guide Institute Curriculum, n.d.).

Through a five year strategic plan, the PGI is working to become fully functional by 1996, with an array of courses that can be taken through video/workbook correspondence courses and through programs offered at local, state, and national outfitter gatherings.

The current industry trend is moving away from conflict and confrontation with land managers and other user groups to an emphasis on common goals and values, partnerships, and efforts to build understanding among user groups (see Wondolleck, Chapter Twenty-Three, in this volume). Participation and growing expertise in land management planning processes is the future. The Limits of Acceptable Change process has been embraced as a tool to provide input into management decisions. An unexpected, but valuable result of involvement in land management planning efforts, has been a heightened understanding of other user groups' perspectives and the evolution of an enhanced network of interested parties on resource issues.

An industry program called Partners Afloat and Partners Astride is a tool increasingly used to get agency managers, outfitters, and other user groups together in the field to discuss issues and resolve differences. A how-to kit including a video and pamphlet has been developed to assist in the implementation of Partners Afloat and Partners Astride. The program's purpose is to improve understanding and communication among groups who have a common interest in an area or activity, to foster an attitude of partnership, and to highlight common goals and values.

This program is changing the traditional perspective that the most difficult unresolved issues are characterized by differing values. In tackling difficult resource use issues together in the backcountry, agency managers, outfitters, and other user groups have become increasingly aware that it is not the values per se that are different, but the perspectives of the values that are different. Sitting in a meeting room, each group holds its own internal view of where other's values lay. Around the campfire, however, or on the bow of a raft, sharing the experience and the resources that make the experience possible leads to common perspectives and to an understanding of common values.

Facilitating Hard-to-Define Values

Nature-based values are an integral part of the culture of the outfitting and guiding community. They are woven into the fabric of experience that results when people interact with nature on a guided backcountry adventure. I now explore how outfitters and guides view these values, and their relevance to our ethics. While there has been no formal study of these values by the outfitting and guiding industries, their existence and importance are reinforced on a regular anecdotal basis through observation of, and interaction with, participants on backcountry outings. The values that outfitters and guides emphasize in experiences offered to the public include recreation, refuge, preparedness, an opportunity for challenge and risk, skill development, service, aesthetics, creativity, and awareness.

Recreation

Recreation is the most common value expressed by people on a guided trip. Recreation is viewed as an opportunity to get away from the everyday environment, away from one's routine, and to re-create a less stressful, more natural state of mind or perspective. In the Wilderness Act (1964) Congress stated that outfitter and guide services may be allowed, contrary to the act's general prohibition of commercial activities in wilderness, "to the extent necessary for activities which are proper for realizing the recreational or other wilderness purposes of the areas." This use of recreation as the named activity, followed by other unnamed purposes, is similar to the public's initial view of a trip into natural settings. The named purpose of their trip may be recreation, but they find that a wilderness activity, or any nature-based activity, has other purposes as well. Congress identified other purposes as scenic, scientific, educational, conservation, and historical. Outfitters and guides have an excellent opportunity to add to the recreational value of the public's immersion in nature by using the experiential learning opportunity to expand their knowledge, understanding, and appreciation of the cultural, historical, scientific, and conservation values of their natural surroundings.

Some outfitters intentionally design their trips to offer more opportunities for value added experiences.

Others see them happening, yet strongly resist structuring the trip to enhance the opportunities because they see structure as the antithesis of a nature-based trip. In either case, the values added to recreation in natural settings can range from a simple slowing of one's internal clock to a more life changing experience, as was the case for Ely on a trip in Idaho's Selway-Bitterroot wilderness area.

Ely was one of twelve wilderness visitors camped on Tango Bar, the remnant of a 500-year-old flood that deposited tons of rock, gravel, and sand below a sharp bend in the Selway River. The bar is now anchored by several-hundred-year-old cedars and ponderosas, bordered on one side by the river and on the other by a heavily forested north facing slope. The slope is a dense stand of Douglas fir, moss and ferns—a biologically diverse enclave of the coastal type, located hundreds of miles inland from the Pacific Ocean. It is also where I often draw an outline of Idaho in the sand and explain to our wilderness guests how geologic forces created this part of America.

"I stepped out of my tent last night, and as I looked up at the canopy of stars in the sky, my soul expanded," Ely explained. She was a linguist by profession and had earlier shared with the group at our orientation meeting that, although a native of Ohio, she had spent the last sixteen years in Australia working with and studying the language of the aborigines in the outback. I pondered her choice of words for a day, and over coffee on the last morning of the trip I asked what she meant.

"I was intrigued by your presentation at Tango Bar on geology and wilderness," she explained. "You used all natural tools to paint a picture in the sand of where we are. Your discussion of humans as a part of nature made me think about my place in nature, too. As I sat there in the still of the night, gazing up at the stars, I sensed how I fit into a larger universe. My view of myself, who and what I am and how I am connected to the natural world, expanded." Certainly, Ely had found more than recreational value in the wilderness trip.

Refuge

Refuge is another commonly expressed value of a guided nature-based trip. An examination of outfitter and guide literature and accounts of guided trips will find references to "escaping" to a place that is different from the ordinary—a getaway or a counterbalance to the stress of one's normal environment. Edward Abbey (1975) expressed this sense of refuge through one of the many colorful characters in *The Monkey Wrench Gang*:

> 'The wilderness once offered men a plausible way of life,' the doctor said. 'Now it functions as a psychiatric refuge. Soon there will be no wilderness. Soon there will be no place to go. Then the madness becomes universal. And the universe goes mad.'

Abbey puts the value of refuge in the context of necessity for the nation's sanity. Individually, refuge is also often seen as a reward for enduring the demands and stresses of a more crowded urban environment.

Preparedness

Preparedness is another value of a nature-based, wildlands experience, particularly in the case of persons from an urban environment. Often one hears guided, backcountry visitors refer to the rut or routine of their everyday lives. In order to venture from the routine, visitors must prepare. Anticipation of a future backcountry trip requires that they attempt to experience the trip in their minds. They plan and prepare, trying to balance their existing knowledge and experience with what they anticipate will be encountered. Preparation includes attempts to identify the areas where knowledge, and experience are lacking. They often do research to overcome these shortcomings, or they rely on the skill, knowledge and experience of those who will lead them. The value of preparedness is important because it forces people to focus on the future, to prepare, to predict the results of their own behavior.

The outfitted visitor's struggle to prepare, to deal with the unknown, creates an opportunity for the skilled guide to expand the visitor's understanding of natural surroundings. Rick's College biology professor and Yellowstone National Park outfitter Richard Clark refers to this opportunity as the "thawed" period in a "freeze, thaw, freeze" cycle that backcountry visitors go through. As trip participants arrive, they are comfortable with their knowledge of the world around them and resistant to new ideas. Clark's trips are highly participatory. As the visitors adjust to the unknown world of packing and caring for their own horse, even kicking "horse apples" around the meadow to disperse the droppings, they are in a "thawed" stage. That is when Clark expands their thinking with stories of Chief Joseph and the Nez Perce who preceded them through the park. Clark has his guests ponder their own view of the world in the light of that Native-American world-view. He then challenges them to think of their role in protecting the environment so that their great-grand-children can have the same experience in the same surroundings in the future. Toward the end of the trip, as everyone becomes familiar with the routine of a backcountry horse trip, they begin to "freeze" again, and the opportunity to influence them fades.

Challenge and Risk

The opportunity for challenge and risk is a value that is readily seen in more obvious risky adventures—a class five river trip, or a two week hunt for big game in remote, difficult terrain. What is less obvious is the challenge and risk faced by those who take what many people might perceive to be small or minor departures from the norm. Small, but very real challenge and risk, is what Faye, a sixty-three-year-old woman, and her two grown daughters found on a trip into the Frank Church–River of No Return wilderness area. When she arrived in Stanley, Idaho, to begin the trip, Faye appeared frail, but up to the challenge. She handled the rigors of river camping well. On the third night, her group camped at Shelf Camp, two miles from Loon Creek Hot Springs, a popular hiking destination for river travelers.

At four-thirty in the afternoon, after setting up camp, she approached me about accompanying the rest of the group on the hike to the springs. "How far is it?" she queried. "About a mile," I responded.

Two hours later she returned and pulled me aside.

> 'You lied to me!' she said 'That hot springs were much farther, and you knew it! Why didn't you tell me they were two miles each way?'

> 'I knew what a special place the hot springs is and that the trail was good and level,' I replied. 'I was afraid if I said two miles, you might not go, so I fibbed a little and said only one mile. Now that you've been there and back, was it worth it?'

The anger faded from her face as she recalled the scenic hike along the creek and the warm, sooth-ing waters of the hot springs—a special time and place she had shared with her daughters. My intent was to allow the wilderness to challenge an aging urbanite. She met the challenge and experienced the rewards of pushing beyond her preset notions of limits to succeed in risking the unknown.

I did not know until two years later how an event that seemed routine to me had become a special part of the lives of Faye and her daughters. Her daughter sent me a personal note requesting that I remove Faye from my mailing list. She had succumbed to cancer. The note expressed thanks for the experience with their mother in Idaho's wilderness, a memory their mother had cherished, and that her daughters would carry with them for the rest of their lives. That extra mile, at Faye's age and level of experience walking in the backcountry, was a major challenge to her. We should not easily dismiss the importance of small risks and challenges for people who do not readily or often take them.

Skill Development

Nature-based experiences offer the opportunity to learn new skills. People are skilled when they can use their hands synergistically with their minds. When we were farmers and ranchers, we developed our skill levels through the demands of day-to-day work. Now that most of us work at a desk, we do not always have that opportunity. An outfitted, backcountry experience offers the opportunity. Having to think through the process of how uncommon tasks are accomplished is of value.

Some acquired skills have special significance due to their connections to unique elements of the American character. Aldo Leopold said:

> *Wilderness areas are first of all a series of sanctuaries for the primitive arts of wilderness travel, especially canoeing and packing. I suppose some will wish to debate whether it is important to keep these primitive arts alive. I shall not debate it. Either you know it in your bones, or you are very very old.*
>
> Leopold, 1949, p. 193

Reacquiring the primitive skills of handling a paddle or tying a knot connects people to their heritage. Recognizing the connection between current activities and historical practices is a nature-based value. The visitor learns through instruction that the paddle stroke being used is the same stroke used by Lewis and Clark, or that the style of packing is the same style used by the Spanish and Kit Carson.

Service

Service is another value that outfitters and guides nurture in the trips they offer. Service involves two operations:

1. recognizing a human need, and
2. administering to the need.

Typically, the busy pace of our lives does not allow much time for either one. A natural outcome of a shared backcountry trip is a sense of community, or bonding, among the participants. This leads to a desire to serve one another. The trip is an exercise in service—recognizing need and administering to it. Backcountry trips allow urbanites to come together with others, to share new experiences, and to face new challenges and risks. Such trips stimulate a renewed sense of community—a common goal of programs like those of Outward Bound and the National Outdoor Leadership School.

Aesthetics, Creativity, and Awareness

Aesthetics and the stimulation of creativity are also important parts of backcountry experiences. Why does one find mountains, trees, streams, lakes, meadows, and canyons beautiful? Does it have something to do with our genetic makeup, imprinted eons ago? The recognition of beauty, combined with a sense of community, stimulates one to communicate one's perceptions to others (see Susan Driver, Chapter Sixteen, in this volume). When one experiences the elements of one's environment more closely, when one sees the world in its natural state, one connects more completely with it. Ely found that connection in her experience under the stars. She found that she fit into the natural world. The more one perceives the elements of the world in which one lives, the more humane one may become. In this regard, no one value stands alone. One of the many facets of nature-based experiences is that they are often manifested as a warmness, a feeling of peace and contentment, or a spirituality that is generated from within.

The Role of Outfitters and Guides in Promoting a Land Ethic

There are two necessities for sustaining outfitting and guiding as a profession. One is the natural resources that are our lifeblood—clean, free flowing streams, and quality wildlife habitat. The second is a public that values nature and the experiences they have in nature and the people who afford them the opportunity to experience nature. These two necessities are connected in our social and political system. Without public support, wildlands protected through the political process will vanish.

Leopold (1949) said:

Unless there be wilderness-minded men scattered through all the conservation bureaus, the society may never learn of new invasions until the time for action has passed. Furthermore a militant minority of wilderness-minded citizens must be on watch throughout the nation, and available for action in a pinch. (p. 200)

This link between public support for wildlands and our future is part of the outfitter and guide land ethic. Outfitters continually work to build and maintain a constituency among the American public in support of wildlands protected in their natural condition.

One way is through political action. The battles for protection of wild places are supported by those close to the land and by those who have been energized by a guided wildlands experience. Congress and conservation groups know this and regularly call on outfitters and guides for support. Congressman George Miller (Democrat, California), former chairman of the House Natural Resources Committee once said to me, "In Congress, we can tell to the day when outfitters activate their mailing list supporting wild and scenic or wilderness designation." A personal letter from home from those who have fully sensed and valued the resource is powerful politically. In a sense, then, outfitters and guides are keepers of the flame for conservation of wild places.

Also integral to our land ethic is leadership by demonstration and example. A leadership role in minimum impact practices is essential. Explaining why guides set a camp the way they do and demonstrating proper stock handling and containment procedures are important tools to educate the public. Practicing and demonstrating a caring land ethic heightens esteem for guides by the guided public who appreciate the guide's skills, knowledge and demonstrated respect for the land.

As our population expands, there may be a time when protected lands and waters might be viewed as more valuable for other more extractive or consumptive uses. Almost six billion people on planet Earth are consuming wood fiber and other natural resources at a steady rate. If that population grows dramatically in the future, how will the natural resources preserved in parks, wild rivers, and wildlands be valued? For their consumptive value? Or for their spiritual value?

The relevance of nature-based spiritual values to our land ethic is that it should be in our hearts and in our interest to protect lands in their natural state, to work responsibly with the public to understand, enjoy, and preserve the land. Outfitters and guides are links to pioneer skills and knowledge, purveyors of the public's opportunity to experience discovery and exploration in wildlands, and guardians of elements of America's cultural heritage.

At a time when traditional resource-based industries are declining, the importance and value of outfitting and guiding is growing in rural communities. Nature-based, nonextractive activities can be a key component in the future of some rural economic development. The small community of Riggins, Idaho, on the Salmon River is an example. In 1978, the community had no outfitters and relied on a sawmill as its primary source of jobs. The mill burned in 1980 and was not replaced. Today, fourteen outfitters, some who are former loggers, contribute to the recreation-based economy of a town now calling itself "The Whitewater Capital of the World." Eighty percent of Idaho's resident outfitters live in and contribute to the economies of rural communities with an average population of 451 people.

Current Problems and Challenges

The debate over humankind's relationship with nature is ongoing. The role of outfitters and guides places them in the middle. On the one hand, outfitters' and guides' support for the protection of wildlands in their natural condition places them at odds with those who would use such lands for more consumptive or extractive purposes. On the other hand, the outfitters' and guides' commercial interest in taking people into wildland settings makes them a visible and easy target for those who want less or no commercial activity there.

Problems and challenges are also arising out of the outfitters' and guides' success. Protected wildland systems—wilderness, wild and scenic rivers, wildlife refuges, national parks—are much larger than originally envisioned. Larger systems were secured with the political support of a broad coalition of wildland users, including outfitters and guides. Without that support, a smaller, more "pure" system with little human use would likely have been the result.

While legislation protecting these larger systems recognizes the appropriateness of the historical and established uses represented by that broad coalition, there is a tendency, as time passes and institutional memory of the political agreements creating the protected areas fades, for managers and others to characterize some historical uses of wildlands as "inconsistent" or "nonconforming." Traditional users see this change in terminology as an indication of a changing, more hostile view of their chosen activity. Some are concerned that this may lead to unnecessary restrictions or even elimination of legislatively protected uses. As an outfitter and guide, I see this as a breaking of trust and a devaluation of my role in securing and conserving wildlands.

The challenge to outfitters, guides, and managers is to be cautious in how they characterize one another's roles. Long-term support for a larger, protected wildland system will be enhanced if we can nurture a positive, collaborative relationship between diverse users and managers of our wildland resources. Our views should reflect the common ground we share. We share a right to use natural areas, we share a responsibility to protect them, and we share a commitment to keeping the public connected to and supportive of wildlands.

Changing demographics have potentially serious implications for the future of outfitters and guides and the future connection of the public to nature-based experiences. As the nation becomes more urban and the population ages, will fewer people seek nature-based experiences and values? Will access to virtual reality experiences piped into homes through the information superhighway supplant the public's need for real experiences? Will these trends lead to a disconnection from the values of lands in their natural condition and result in future Congressional reconsideration of protected status? Will outfitters, guides, and managers succeed in maintaining Leopold's "minority of wilderness-minded citizens" who are "on watch throughout the nation" and supportive of wildlands?

There is a tendency to extrapolate growing use of wild areas near urban centers to remote areas. However, the concern that outfitters, guides, and managers are "loving to death" the same natural settings they are trying to preserve is not valid in the backcountry. America's wilderness system, particularly the large Western units, is in excellent shape and improving. In 1990 the Moose Creek Ranger District removed eleven tons of trash from a wilderness ranger station left from the days when the accepted practice was to dump agency garbage in the nearest ravine. Miles of old telephone wire rendered unnecessary by radio systems have been removed from the backcountry. The use of camp structures has been minimized. In Idaho, caches are no longer used—replaced by lightweight, portable equipment that can be taken in and out each season. Most of this was accomplished through cooperative agreements between users and managers.

One source of conflict over values and uses of public lands can be traced to an attitude of ownership. This attitude exists in frequent users of the resource and in people who live nearby. This includes outfitters and guides and agency managers and staff with a long history of working in an area. They tend to lose sight of the fact that ownership of these lands rests with the American people. This attitude is reflected in the common term "outfitter camp," when in reality the camp is reserved for short periods of time for the public that uses outfitter services. Another example is the term "Forest Service land." In fact, it is national forest land, owned by the American people. The people, through Congress, empower the Forest Service to manage their forests.

Problems and challenges related to how we value and use our natural areas are inherent in America's political system. Change in our legislative, legal, and administrative treatment of natural areas is constitutionally designed to be slow. We are in a several decade transition period when shifting public attitudes about use of public forests and wildlands are not being reflected in new legislation that articulates a definitive change of direction. Congress, for example, has spent decades giving rural communities that are dependent on timber from public forests assurances that the practice will continue. At the same time, Congress has given environmental groups numerous tools to stop the practice. The battle that is raging toward some new direction has left professional managers, as well as traditional users, in limbo. Moreover, demands that managers comply with numerous complex legislative mandates—endangered species, clean air and water, reform of relationships with commercial users and concession operators—has not been accompanied by budgets and personnel authorizations to fulfill those mandates.

Conclusion

We are, in sum, evolving toward a new relationship with the world around us. As messy and chaotic as that seems, and as uncertain as we are about what that relationship will look like, we can take heart in the thought that it is being carried out in an atmosphere of heightened, not lessened, environmental sensitivity. Multiple use is a timeworn philosophy with considerable baggage from past conflicts. Therefore, in many cases, it seems to encourage an "I've got the right to be here" attitude, and not "If I am to be allowed the privilege of being here, I must act responsibly."

A new ethic of responsible, shared use, recognizes that to continue to manage, work on, and use the public lands, we must demonstrate the ability to respond to the heightened environmental sensitivity and changing ethics and needs of the American public. Responsible, shared use gives all of us an opportunity to enjoy the public lands, but in doing so we must demonstrate a willingness to modify our activities in a way that honors the full range of values the land represents (Tims, 1991).

Literature Cited

Abbey, E. (1975). *The monkey wrench gang.* New York, NY: Avon Books.

Leopold, A. (1949). *A sand county almanac and sketches here and there.* New York, NY: Oxford University Press.

Professional Guide Institute Curriculum. (no date). Boise, ID.

Professional Guide Institute Mission Statement. (no date). Boise, ID.

Tims, D. (1991). Visions for the '90s: Responsible, shared use. *American Forests*, May/June, 17-21.

Wilderness Act. (1964). U.S. Public Law 88-577. In *Status at Large, 78*, 890-96.

Values of Nature for Artists and Artists' Interpretations of These Values for Society

CHAPTER

16

Susan Driver
Fort Collins, Colorado

This chapter considers how artists interact with, use, and benefit from nature. Though the focus is on painters and sculptors, much that is written here can be expanded to musicians and writers. The first and major part of the chapter considers the ways in which artists are inspired by nature and use nature for different purposes. The second part describes a few of the fundamental elements of visual art (line, color, and light) that are also common elements of nature and which elicit similar physiological and psychological responses in humans. The chapter ends with a brief review of "ecological" art and a comment about how public land managers can help maintain the benefits people receive from art that is inspired by nature.

Uses of Nature by Artists

Throughout time artists have expressed culture through words, music, the decoration of utilitarian and ceremonial objects, and the arrangement and decoration of buildings and other structures. As civilizations have evolved and dissolved, artists'

views of nature have also changed. What they have seen in nature has been a product of what they have been looking for, what they have believed, and what they have interpreted through their hearts.

Throughout history nature has been a source of symbols, metaphors, decorations, and rules for artistic organization. Artists looking at nature have elevated the commonplace to a thing of beauty. They have made the beautiful more beautiful in some cases and have focused on features of nature that have aroused deep feelings of terror, horror, joy, peace or awe. Nature or events in nature—sunrise, sunset, storm—have been subjects for commemoration. Artists have looked to nature for a feeling of connection with all life, and as a source of subject matter through which they can express themselves or see themselves more clearly. Artists also use nature for income as their nature-inspired expressions find markets. Finally, artists use nature to help educate—and even to protest—environmentally harmful actions. Each of these uses of nature by artists will be described briefly.

Nature as a Source of Symbols

Cave drawings and early pictographs symbolized animals that were important as a source of food or clothing, a metaphor, a model of certain behaviors, an ideal, or a spirit (Smeets, 1982). The art of indigenous people, however, includes not only symbols of life forms, but designs in which abstract ideas become personified allegories. Thus, a coyote in some Native-American art might symbolize a coyote, the coyote spirit, or the allegory of cosmic spiritual-physical transformation. Symbols for mountains, feathers, the four directions, birds, other animals, and dancers are woven into Native-American rugs. Pottery is decorated not just for visual effects but also to represent traditional respect for the spirit(s) behind that object and its place in the balance of life forces that comprise the "great unknown." Nature is a source of symbols that represent beliefs about life. These beliefs govern personal conduct, rituals, and group interrelations, and form the framework for a persona—a spiritual orientation to life.

Early Christian art took the form of church paintings, architecture, mosaics, carvings, and decorated texts where the use of nature as a source of symbol and metaphor was common. While Christian art was planned to lead people to God and salvation, it was replete with symbolism to open the mind to another level of reality and the Christian view of the meaning of life. The butterfly was a symbol of the resurrection of Christ; the dove represented the Holy Ghost; and the fish represented Christians. The shape of the church itself and the colors used also held symbolic meanings well-known to the initiated.

In one way, it can be said that all paintings or photographs of nature are only symbolic of something real. But the choice of subject, its treatment, and its emotional tone—stormy and dark, or light and pastel colored—is often a reflection of subconscious or unconscious workings. Ansel Adams said, "A great photograph is a full expression of what one feels about what is being photographed in the deepest sense, and is thereby, a true impression of what one feels about life and its entirety" (Fichner-Rathus, 1986, p. 142). I would add that visual art at some subconscious level often represents the artist's feelings about something else such as a time in his or her life present or past, something repressed or desired.

Nature as a Source of Decoration, Patterns, and Design Principles

Everywhere within nature are forms which serve as patterns for sculptors, architects, craftspersons, commercial artists, and fine artists. Ivy leaves, acanthus leaves, flowers in their infinite forms, the designs of snow, dendritic patterns, and the magnified photos of human biology (cells, neurons and the chains and links of DNA) are only a few of nature's varied forms found in the decorative arts of our environment. The patterns or shapes are used for their visual beauty and for the contribution they make to the whole form. Imagine an abstract tree form in a quilt or the repeated pattern of leaves around the border of a rug.

A broader application of the use of natural forms can be found in the work of James Hubbell, an architect, designer, builder, poet, and painter who worked with metal, stained glass, and tile. In the fashion of the Spanish architect Antonio Gaudi, Hubbell took the flowing and curving natural forms in nature as inspiration for his buildings and other art works. His buildings are mixtures of brick, stained glass, free-form strengthened concrete, and rock. They curve, arch, drop, and blossom with unexpected decorations that add to the graceful organic feel of the structures (Rigan, 1979).

Innate in natural forms is a certain organization, simplicity, unity, legibility, harmony, coherence, balance, accent and rhythm, all of which should have counterparts in good art of any kind. Charles Ephraim Burchfield painted cool, simplified landscapes. His early works were romantic fantasies. Then he shifted to the Midwestern scene and back to fantasy in his later years. He tried to paint life, recreated through the medium of design and organization. In 1945 he said:

The inner structure [of a picture] must be the result of the close study of nature's laws, and not of human invention. The artist must come to nature, not with a ready-made formula, but in humble reverence to learn. The work of an artist is superior to the surface appearance of nature but not its basic laws.

Novak and Blaugrund,
1980, p. 190

Nature Art as an Elevation of the Commonplace

The commonplace in nature—reflections in water, fallen leaves, the inside of a flower, patterns and colors in rocks, a sparkling spider web, weeds growing out of rocks where growth should be impossible, a moonlit snow covered corn field—can be captured by a vigilant eye. Admiration of the aesthetics and mental reflections on these commonplace settings of nature can elevate the human spirit. Frequently, the artist will capture and interpret scenes or aspects of a scene not commonly noticed. Viewing the artist's interpretations, the observer can sense the artist's thoughts and feelings about this once commonplace subject and add his or her own interpretations of it.

Nature as a Source of Beauty and the Sublime

Gustave Corbet said, "The beautiful is in nature, and it is encountered in the most diverse forms of reality. Once it is found, it belongs to art or rather, to the artist who discovers it" (Fichner-Rathus, 1986, p. 2). The beauty of nature can be seen in the photographic realism of Edward Weston and Ansel Adams. It can be seen in the color filtered realism of the Impressionists who sought to paint changing light. The beauty of nature can be seen in Albert Bierstadt's magnificent nineteenth-century paintings of the new frontier, the Rocky Mountains, and Yosemite Valley. The landscapes that win the "Arts for the Parks" competition each year stand out as twentieth-century examples of interpretations of natural beauty that are not just elevations of the commonplace, but occasionally reach toward the magnificent.[1]

Occasionally nature takes on a sublime face, such as when one responds with strong emotions to a sunset, a sunrise, an experience in or above the clouds in a mountain range, a storm, a fog, or a moonlit night view. One also responds this way to art, music, sculpture, poetry, or paintings that make one stop and catch one's breath. The styles may vary in the art one responds to from photographic

realism to impressionism to abstract expressionism to something else. In reality one is responding to the artist's experiences. As Tolstoy said, "Art is not a handcraft, it is the transmission of feelings the artist has experienced" (Fichner-Rathus, 1986, p. 14). Thus, the artist not only represents but helps create the sense of the sublime.

Nature as a Subject for Commemoration

Many scenes captured by American landscapists cannot be seen in nature any more. Development has replaced the natural scenes. In one sense those paintings and photographs commemorate what is gone. While painting several places of quiet beauty near my home, I have been saddened by the thought that the scenes will likely give way to "progress." Painting, music, and photos can capture time, a fleeting moment, a park opening, or the process of developing a community park. The 75th anniversary of Rocky Mountain National Park was commemorated with a traveling art exhibit of paintings of the park with the dual purposes of celebrating the park as well as promoting environmental awareness (Cuba, 1991).

Nature as a Source of Transcendence

For many people, including artists, nature can be a place for reconnecting with the essence of life—a place of worship, an opening up to another dimension, and for other deep psychological experiences. Hubbell put it this way: "It is from nature we have come. We are the descendants of the stars and polliwogs" (Rigan, 1979, p. 53). In the same place he also wrote the following:

> From each hill and rock
> I hear a song
> Life adrift within
>
> All parts are mine
> Earth and river
> Field and tree
> Interlaced with man
>
> Song of wind wrapped in sea
> of rain and stars
> Sprinkled in the sand.
>
> Mud and Life and I Together
> Quiet worship bring. (p. 79)

---

[1]The "Arts for the Parks" competition is sponsored by the Academy of the Arts, Inc., P.O. Box 1158, Jackson Hole, Wyoming, 83001 (1-800-555-2787).

Hubbel seems to find being outside and open to interaction with nature deeply satisfying and connecting. Perhaps he would define life around us as a unified system of interrelated equals. The life in the atoms in the hill and rock has a consciousness that speaks to itself in the atoms of our bodies when we quiet our hearts and minds to listen.

A Colorado artist, Steve Elliot, expresses similar feelings of oneness with nature and reports an added dimension to his work. He finds in nature a sensation of "returning to the essential reality; it takes us into our beginnings; it [Wyoming] is open, spacious, generous—like home" (1994).

In the catalog for Rocky Mountain National Park's 75th Anniversary Exhibit, artist Leona Sophocles states, "My love of the land is my religion. My God or Goddess is Mother Earth. My paintings are my celebration and glorification of her" (Cuba, 1991, p. 73).

A young English sculptor, Andy Goldsworthy, who works in and with nature, looks at, pokes, and feels items in nature until an idea begins to form for a sculpture. Examples of his art include a string of bright orange birch leaves threaded together by their own stems, floating on a pond breaking up reflections of sky and trees; poppy petals covering a small granite boulder that sits in its niche among larger boulders; an arch of carefully stacked slate; and a series of two-and-one-half foot snowballs rolled with different materials, frozen, and transported to a museum. He photographs his creations as they grow, reach their peak, and decay. Of his work he says,

At its most successful, my 'touch' looks into the heart of nature. . . . When I work with a leaf, rock, or stick, it is not just that material in itself, it is an opening into the process of life within and around it. . . . Although it is often a practical and physical art, it is also an intensely spiritual affair I have with nature: a relationship.

Friedman and Goldsworthy, 1991, p. 164

Elliot, the Colorado landscapist mentioned above, describes painting outside as:

Similar to a meditative experience . . . pressures of changing light and time limitations trigger a visceral Zen-like response. The experience of seeing, smelling, feeling, hearing,

and thinking is passed on to the canvas with the pressure of each stroke, the selection of each color. The painting becomes an experiential interpretation of life.

Elliot, 1994.

Strangely enough, when Elliot gets the painting home he finds in the picture something he "wasn't aware of being conscious of at the time—something unexpected—improbable."

Others claim to use nature only as a starting point for the creative experience. A famous American expressionist landscape artist, Wolfe Kahn, uses nature as a starting place for simple forms, light, tonal relationships, structure, and flow of color. He usually finishes his paintings inside, developing the stark and the simple in the painting started outside. He states,

To me the interest is in the struggle to make the thing become a scheme rather than an illustration. Sometimes I don't know what the image will be until the end. I want spontaneity to dictate what happens. . . . The picture is the by-product of a more compelling and private process of handling materials . . . . The making is tied to a process of capture, of penetration and reclamation: the artist is claiming a particular place as his own, in a sense, as his home in the world. . . .

Nixon, 1991, p. 3

Nature Arts as a Source of Income

The nature-based arts, and all the arts for that matter, provide a profit to enterprising top artists. Society benefits not only from the availability of the art and the enrichment it provides, but also from the support of industries that make the basic materials: the galleries, printers, framers, decorators, agents, and governments that tax them all. Fads and tastes in art vary from coast to coast. Successful artists know their art, their market, and marketing techniques. Reiss, in the *Arts Management Reader* (1979), points to the growing economic importance of the arts. Managers of urban and hinterland natural areas could possibly use information from his book to guide the development of art-based income generating programs.

Nature as a Source of Therapeutic Line, Color, and Light

Every natural area from seaside parks, canyon lands, and magnificent mountain parks, to planned city open spaces, has its specific character of lines, color and light. These fundamental dimensions of how humans perceive nature are experienced and translated by artists into the art forms they express. In this way, lines, color, and light also become the fundamental elements of the visual arts.

Lines

Lines are found in nature and art where one form overlaps another, where one color joins another, and where light clearly separates bright from dark. They delineate or contour objects depending upon the color and light that is inherent in the scene being depicted. Our eyes are drawn to the sharp contrasts formed. Our eyes follow lines that are said to create strong "movement"— winding roads, the shapes of mountains, tall buildings, bridges, flat regions. Henri (1984) speaks of our "spiritual sight" that should look for the "spirit line" in things. In contemporary parlance, we could use the words "right brain" or intuitive sight which recognizes the essential energy, weight, or dance of an object.

As an artist, teacher and "nature lover," I believe we seek out lines, color, and shades of light in our environments and art that help nurture and create mental and physical balance in our lives. When I worked in a cooperative artists gallery, I frequently asked people about their favorite painting. Their responses were as varied as the people; "It's so peaceful," "I like the subject matter," "I like the colors," "It reminds me of. . . . " They seldom answered, "I like the lines in it." Yet, lines do form a part of the composition of nature and its psychological impact.

Color

Color and light are so interrelated in painting that it is hard to think of them separately. Without light there is no visible color. The amount of, and quality of, the light—warm (yellow, orange, and red to warm white) or cool (hazy, bluish to lavender, bluish green, and blue gray)—can create the atmosphere of a painting or an outdoor experience.

Colors affect us physiologically and psychologically. For example, an artist friend said she didn't like winter pictures because they looked so cold, so wintry. She liked and thrived on warm colors—vibrant pinks, yellows, yellow greens and orange reds.

The changing colors of the days and seasons in nature and the colors of our interior environments affect us more than we know. We are each aware of the soothing effects of the colors of nature, especially the blues and greens. In a similar way, color therapy (i.e., using colored lights or settings to help treat emotional problems) is offered in some mental health settings (Heline, 1987).

Light

While color and light are highly interrelated, artists are sensitive to all forms of light. They use light to set a mood and focus on particular subjects, and viewers of visual art are affected by this use of light. More generally, it appears that different types of light affect human well-being, with natural light having optimal effects.

For thousands of years, we humans spent the major part of our days outside. Our eyes developed not only as information gatherers to help us get around, but as receptors that activate our nervous system and thus affect emotional responses (Hyman, 1990). Liberman (1991) suggests that humans should be outside to receive full spectrum light at least one hour a day. Full spectrum means natural light which includes the frequencies of all the colors made possible by visible light. If Liberman is correct, we make maintaining our health difficult by spending so much time inside with insufficient and unbalanced lighting. Our bodies get too much orange and yellow light from florescence and not enough blue, red, and purple. From incandescent bulbs, high in reds (normal in yellows), we get little green, blue-green, and blue. Thus, a possible benefit of natural areas in cities is the opportunity they provide for people to be outside where they can experience the lights and colors lacking in their interior environments.

Paintings act as organizations of frozen color and light. In their interactions of line, color, and light, paintings create visually vibrational "music" that speaks to those who "hear," through their eyes, the feelings and experiences of the artist who created those paintings. Just as people respond psychologically and physiologically to lines, color, and light in nature, so do they to the lines, colors, and light of paintings that represent natural scenes. Artists skilled at using lines, color, and light for expressive purposes need not copy nature to transmit its joy and peace and harmony.

Nature Art and Land Ethics

Ecological Art

Are pictures of oil slick covered wildlife, clear-cut mountain slopes, and pollution filled rivers art? Perhaps not, but these and similar types of "art" can be an early warning system for society. As McLuhan said, "The artist picks up the message of cultural and technological challenge decades before its transforming impact occurs" (1994). A new field called "ecological art" has arisen to help educate people about the results of human disregard for the environment.

Joseph Beuys was an early pioneer in ecological art. His work was called social sculpture. As an artist shaman he tried to integrate the spiritual, mystical, and irrational with the casual and rational to awaken a participatory dialogue of reform. He fervently hoped his art work would become a "humus of concepts and ideas" and the basis for real change (Adams, 1992, p. 30). The following is a description of one of his works:

> In his famous work 'Coyote' of 1974 he tackled white America's disrespect and lack of appreciation for both the Native-American peoples and wild nature in the form of the coyote, an Indian image of cosmic spiritual–physical transformation. 'The spirit of the coyote is so mighty,' announced the artist, 'that the human being cannot understand what it is, or what it can do for humankind in the future.' During a week of nights and days spent together with a coyote in the Renè Block Gallery in New York, Beuys tried to make contact with this essential spirit of the coyote and performed a cyclic sequence of actions, involving a number of representative materials and props: his felt and the coyote's straw (which were exchanged many times); a flashlight, as an image of energy; a triangle chime, which he

> struck on occasion, as 'an impulse of consciousness' for the coyote; contrasting recorded sounds of a confused roar of a turbine, to represent a more chaotic wild energy, as well as human civilization's dominating technology; brown gloves, to represent the freedom and flexibility of the human hand, in contrast to the specialization of animal extremities; and a daily stack of Wall Street Journals, to represent 'the tyranny exerted by money and power' and 'the diminished and destructive interpretation of money and economics, an inorganic fixation based solely on the production of physical goods.' In the action it could be said that the coyote reclaimed the objects representing the civilized world.

> Adams, 1992, p. 32

Adams (1992) also recorded that,

> While working on what is probably still the world's largest ecological sculpture, '7,000 Oaks,' Beuys stated his feeling that trees today are far more intelligent than people. In the wind that blows their leaves he sensed the essence of suffering human beings, as trees, too, are sufferers.

> Adams, p. 30

Helen and Newton Harrison have been ecological artists since 1970. Their work creates opportunities both in art galleries and in the halls of government to encourage conversation about ecological problems and to work toward their solution. In the case of *The Lagoon Cycle*, they began with a controversial lagoon area, and produced "numerous images, texts, performances, and books between 1972 and 1983" (Adcock, 1992, p. 38). In the texts, they integrated a "story," a dialogue between two mystical alter egos—the "Lagoonmaker," an enterprising market-oriented analytical problem solver (symbolizing human civilization), and "the witness" representing nature. The art is the framed display of plan, maps, diagrams, and descriptions with the story's dialogue interwoven.

One of the Harrison's more ambitious undertakings was a proposal to divide the North American continent into bioregional entities with supranational powers. The project was called the Great Lakes Proposal, which included the drainage basin of the Great Lakes. They took up the issue in 1976. In 1986 they were asked by various environmental groups to rework the proposal. The purification of the Sava River in Croatia and Serbia was another project. This project solution went to the Croatian water board and was even supported by the World Bank (Adcock, 1992).

A desire to do something with art for animals prompted Lynn Hull, an artist who lives and works in Wyoming, to create "art for animals." She carved glyphic images into rocks mostly on private land to serve as pockets or small trenches to hold water or snowmelt for animals and birds. She was concerned with the way eagles and other birds of prey are being electrocuted by power transmission lines in parts of Nebraska. Her solution was a series of alternative raptor roosts she placed out in the landscape—sculptures made of materials she found nearby. All of these and other designs were made with the help of wildlife biologists (Gablik, 1991).

Many other artists who are concerned about the environment are using diverse artistic methods to point out what is being done and its connectedness to human endeavors. Some seek to make us more aware of the web of life, and to remind us that we are members, not masters, of the biosphere. Patricia Johanson's *Endangered Garden* for the city of San Francisco upgrades a part of the sewage system and creates an ecological park friendly to native wildlife (Johanson, 1992).

Suzi Gablik (1992) concludes that:

> *In the past we have had art which acted as a mirror (reflecting the times); we have had art used as a hammer (social protest); we have had art as furniture (something nice to have on the walls); and we have had art as an inner search for the self.* (p. 51)

While ecological art might be "used as a hammer," it is also helping educate us about the need to be good stewards of Mother Earth.

Artistic Needs to Protect Nature

The simplest way to relate this discussion to the need for an expanded land management ethic is to say that nature needs to be protected if its representations by artists are to continue. We humans seem to have a need for beauty wherever we find it, on public lands or elsewhere. Given the high demand for and appreciation of nature-related art, artistic use of the public lands clearly should be an important part of the ongoing discussion of hard-to-define

values and benefits. In this regard, it should be noted that while the mainstream of art since 1945 has been concerned with ideas and innovation, nature has remained the primary subject for many artists and writers. With proper stewardship, nature will continue to be a significant source of artistic inspiration.

Literature Cited

Adams, O. (1992). Joseph Beuys, pioneer of radical ecology. *Art Journal*, 26-34.

Adcock, C. (1992). Conversational drift, Helen Mayer Harrison and Newton Harrison. *Art Journal*, 35-45.

Berry, T. (1992). Art in the ecozoic era. *Art Journal*, 46-48.

Cuba, S. (1991). A park for all seasons. *Southwest Art*, 69-74.

Elliot, S. (1994). Personal communication (telephone conversation).

Fichner-Rathus, L. (1986). *Understanding art.* Englewood Cliffs, NJ: Prentice Hall.

Friedman, T. and Goldsworthy, A. (Eds.). (1991). *Hand to earth: Andy Goldsworthy sculpture 1976-1990.* Leeds, UK: W. S. Maney.

Gablik, S. (1991). The ecological imperative. *Art Journal*, Summer, 49-51.

Heline, C. (1987). *Healing and regeneration through color.* Marina del Rey, CA: DeVorss.

Henri, R. (1984). *The Art Spirit.* New York, NY: Harper & Row Publishers, Inc

Hyman, J. (1990). *The light book, how natural and artificial light affect our health, mood and behavior.* Los Angeles, CA: Tarcher.

Johanson, P. (1992). Endangered garden. *Art Journal*, Summer, 21.

Liberman, J. (1991). *Light: Medicine of the future.* Santa Fe, NM: Bear & Company.

McLuhan, M. (1964). *Understanding media: The extensions of man* (1st MIT Press ed.). Cambridge, MA: MIT Press.

Nixon, B. (1991). Lovers of the land. *Art Week*, September 26, 3.

Novak, B. and Blaugrund, A. (1980). *Next to nature: Landscape paintings from the National Academy of Design.* New York, NY: Harper and Row Publishers, Inc.

Reiss, A. (1979). *The arts management reader.* New York, NY: Marcel Dekker.

Rigan, O. (1979). *From the earth up.* New York, NY: McGraw-Hill.

Smeets, R. (1982). *Signs, symbols and ornaments.* New York, NY: Van Nostrand Reinhold.

Private Forest Landowners and an Emerging Land Management Ethic

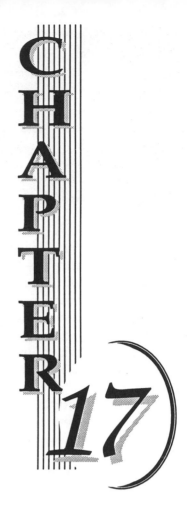

Mark Rey
American Forest and Paper Association
Washington, DC

Introduction

The values that bind private forest landowners and managers to the land they own or manage are similar to many of the hard-to-define nature-based values featured in this text. A commitment to good land stewardship goes beyond simple pride of ownership. Moreover, landowners who have undergone specialized training have an intellectual and emotional relationship with the land. Their training in resource management undoubtedly included the works of Muir and Leopold both in the development of technical expertise and, more importantly, in shaping moral convictions. Thus, many private forest landowners and managers bring with them a moral imperative to land stewardship. The same strong sense of place that motivates a wide variety of people to express an affinity for the land is also common to landowners and managers. They often identify closely with the tracts for which they have a stewardship responsibility, deriving both the satisfaction of a job well done and nature-based spiritual benefits.

Over the last several decades, private forest landowners and managers have demonstrated responsible environmental stewardship in many ways. For example, in the 1930s local cooperatives for forest protection flourished as individual and corporate ties to the land became more pronounced. During the 1940s, the start-up and development of the National Tree Farm program was a way for private landowners to express and publicize their strong commitment to land stewardship. This was closely followed by the formation of intellectual cooperatives to advance forest research for developing better land management techniques. These cooperatives involved universities, government, and, most important, private and corporate forest landowners in a collaborative effort. Following these cooperative efforts, many corporate landowners began to promote land stewardship to others—primarily small, private landowners throughout the 1950s and 1960s. These cooperative programs reached their apex in the late 1970s, and they continue today.

Notwithstanding these strong spiritual ties to the land and the moral values reflected in private land stewardship efforts, the general public has recently come to question both the sincerity and environmental quality of private stewardship of forest lands. With greater urbanization of our population there has been an erosion of both a broadly felt tie to the land and a native understanding of natural processes. Many people have lost their sense of attachment to the land, even though at some level they still embrace many of the hard-to-define values discussed in this text. Moreover, the conflict over the management of public lands—lands that all people feel they own—has spilled over onto all lands, with private land management being viewed by the general population as being driven almost solely by the desire for financial gain. Finally, it is inevitable that usurpers and careless practitioners have created a negative image in the minds of an American public generally disassociated from day-to-day land stewardship, but nevertheless aware of the problems caused by poor land management practices.

This conflict has created a strong desire on the part of private landowners (industrial owners as well as individuals) to communicate more directly with the public and to convey a stronger sense of land stewardship. In so doing, landowners are not merely trying to convey to the public that they "get it." Rather, they are attempting, in part, to illustrate the spiritual value of the land to them by *publicly* committing to a course of land stewardship.

Efforts to Better Understand the Public's Views and Expectations About the Stewardship of Private Lands

To better understand why the public is generally unaware of the values held by private landowners and managers regarding environmental stewardship, in 1992 the forest industry contracted Market Strategies, Inc. to conduct a research effort. The study involved three iterative research sets to assess public attitudes about the stewardship record of private landowners and managers, and of public expectations about what more acceptable stewardship might entail.

Methods

Market Strategies, Inc. conducted the first research set in April 1992. The effort involved a comprehensive qualitative study of how the public perceives forest resource owners and managers. The objectives of this portion of the study were to:

1. identify key policy issues for forest landowners over the next decade;

2. analyze the gaps in perception (if they exist) between forest landowners and others important to the public debate on forest stewardship and, where evident, basic areas of agreement; and

3. provide a basis for better communication with the public as a whole.

From May through September 1992, Market Strategies, Inc. conducted a series of interviews with forest industry leaders, leaders of environmental groups, and federal regulators and legislators. These core interviews were supplemented by additional direct interviews and a continuing dialogue with academics and media representatives, as well as an analysis of public opinion trends and background research on the current literature related to land stewardship issues.

The second research set involved modified focus group sessions conducted by Market Strategies, Inc. throughout the country during late 1993 and early 1994. The small group research format involved two message evaluation sessions in five locations. There were 25 participants per session, making the total universe of involved parties in excess of 250. The target audience was selected to reflect:

1. demographics associated with attentiveness to politics and public policy; and

2. an ideologically balanced, high-income, college and postgraduate educated population ranging from 25 to 45 years of age in a gender-balanced sample.

The research objectives were to:

1. determine the extent to which the public accepts or rejects several basic policy propositions related to forest management practices;

2. determine the persuasiveness of selected messages supporting or opposing these policy propositions; and

3. recommend message strategies and tactics to reposition the public's current perception of forest landowners.

In each session, participants responded to a preexposure questionnaire, participated in the session, and responded to a postexposure questionnaire. Group discussion was encouraged following each formal session.

To evaluate the public's current perceptions about private forest land stewardship, the policy propositions evaluated were chosen to reflect basic tenets of private landowners and forest managers. They included the following:

1. Private forest landowners should be allowed to manage their land and trees as they see fit, as long as they adhere to current environmental laws and regulations.

2. U.S. forest products companies recognize the existence of forest management problems and are committed to correcting these problems and practicing responsible management.

3. The federal and state governments should provide incentives for private forest land owners to grow and harvest trees.

4. U.S. forest and paper companies should be allowed to harvest trees on public lands.

5. Responsible forest management is compatible with wildlife conservation and recreational uses such as camping, hiking, fishing, and other forms of outdoor recreation.

The messages supporting these propositions were rated on a 0 to 100 scale, with 0 being not at all persuasive and 100 being very persuasive. Forty-five messages supporting the industry's policy propositions were used, compared to 28 messages opposing the policy propositions. Participants were asked to evaluate the persuasiveness of each pro and con argument. Following the results of this research, several messages were found to be more persuasive than others. Additionally, the results suggested several behavioral changes associated with how forest landowners presently practice land stewardship (Market Strategies, Inc., 1993, 1994).

The public's reaction to these behavioral changes, as well as further development of the more persuasive messages, were tested by Market Strategies, Inc. in a third research set in March, 1994. In this phase of the effort, traditional survey research conducted nationally was done to better frame landowner responses to the erosion of public support for private forest land stewardship.

Findings

The first set of interviews identified significant gaps between forest landowners' perception of themselves (and their stewardship record), and the perception of environmental activists, regulators and legislators. In sum, forest landowners (at least those in the industrial sector) believe they:

1. are technologically advanced;

2. hold a position of leadership in forest stewardship;

3. have done a good job in environmental performance; and

4. have the technology to balance economic needs and environmental demands, as long as these demands are based on reason.

Most landowners surveyed acknowledged that there is still work to do, but shared a general feeling that forest landowners have not received due credit for their progress and abilities. While by definition, the environmental movement is not viewed as the enemy there is a strong feeling that environmentalist attacks are unfair and motivated largely by self-preservation and organizational promotion (Market Strategies, Inc., 1994).

Environmental group leaders take an opposite position on virtually every key point. They believe private forest stewardship in the United States is inadequate. Private forest landowners lag behind in employing the most sensitive and advanced environmental requirements. Their goal is to frustrate, rather than support, environmental protection, and they will have to be forced into a position of environmental responsibility (Market Strategies, Inc., 1994).

Regulators and legislators are, to varying degrees, in the middle of this spectrum. On the one hand, they acknowledge that they are often forced into creating unnecessary legislation and then enforcing it with regulations that go well beyond the scope of reasonable environmental protection. On the other hand, among forest landowners they see an element of society that tends to resist effecting environmental change (Market Strategies, Inc., 1994).

The academics surveyed by Market Strategies, Inc. (1994) tended to have a more balanced view of the environmental performance of private forest landowners and managers. They are not harsh critics of that performance, but they see increasing legislative, regulatory, and public pressures driven by environmental concern, and they observe a segment of society (i.e., forest landowners) that can't seem to get its story across.

One of the most striking elements of the findings of the study done by Market Strategies, Inc. (1994) is the existence of a significant perception gap that has risen out of two fundamentally different assessments of the nature of the problem. Much of the landowning community believes the problem is one of communication, while the environmental movement contends that it is a behavioral problem—one that will require private landowners to make substantial changes in the way they do business in the future. There is clear support for demonstrable change from legislators and regulators who, while not unsympathetic to many forest landowners' positions, find it increasingly difficult to resist the broadly based political momentum for change generated by the environmental community.

The second stage of the research conducted by Market Strategies, Inc. (1994) provided some general public perceptions of the forest industry and land managers. The results suggest that the landowning community is not high profile or well-defined in the public mind. The public has a generally mixed view. Few are openly hostile, and few are intensely positive. The generally positive feelings about forest landowners are really a function of the lack of any hard negatives. For example, most people cannot articulate the reasons why they like or dislike America's forest and paper companies. Thus, the industrial component of the forest landowning community is not perceived to be a corporate "villain." On the other hand, the industrial portion of the forest landowning community (and perhaps the community as a whole) suffers from a general negativity that afflicts most businesses and industries. The public has developed a pervasive cynicism about the motives behind much of private sector America's behavior. The forest industry's credibility is not bankrupt, but it is low enough that it diminishes the persuasiveness of its communications on all public policy issues and in debates.

This research indicates that the strongest prostewardship message supporting the industry's

commitment to responsible forestry is the concept of partnerships and alliances with unbiased third parties. Two messages related to third-party certification were the most persuasive:

1. third party certification sends a message of openness and accessibility which serves to enhance landowner credibility; and

2. the counterintuitive nature of third-party certification appears to cut through the skepticism and cynicism of the public at large.

Interestingly, the notion of partnerships in third-party certification was more persuasive than additional governmental involvement in the regulation of private forest lands. This may be a reflection of the general skepticism of government at all levels (Market Strategies, Inc., 1994).

The policy propositions generally lost ground after exposure to both the pro and con messages. This follows, given the average persuasiveness ratings of the two sets of messages. It indicates, however, that the simple notion of better communication, as opposed to behavioral change, is one that will not reinstill in the public a strong sense of the stewardship values that landowners bring to their responsibilities.

The third research set done by Market Strategies, Inc. (1994) was designed to follow-up some of the ideas learned and formed from the second research set. Specifically, the objective was to test some of the more persuasive messages and to better evaluate what type of third-party alliances the public would find most sincere and persuasive. Also important was the need to isolate the type of third-party relationship that the public views as important and the public's perception of how well forest landowners have performed with respect to different land values.

The most significant finding from this research set is that the public has no fixed view about the nature of a third party alliance. It seems that the public is content that forest landowners would involve some independent, outside observer in evaluating its land stewardship activities. The public has no firm conclusions about what these third parties should do, or who they should be, other than that they should be technical experts. And, in this regard, environmental groups are not viewed as technical experts (Market Strategies, Inc., 1994).

This research set also uncovered a large gap between what the public views as the important land stewardship values and the perception of how well landowners are performing. The public views the provision of forest recreation by private landowners as something that is done well but is, nonetheless, not terribly important. The commitment to replanting trees and conserving forest resources is viewed to be both more important and something that forest landowners are perceived to be doing well. Unfortunately, the provision of forests for future generations and the protection of lakes, streams, and wildlife habitat are viewed to be critically important to the public, but they are viewed as areas where forest landowners are not doing a very good job. This indicates that these areas are the most pertinent for both behavioral changes and additional communication initiatives.

The Development of a Sustainable Forestry Initiative

Benefiting from the commissioned research done by Market Strategies, Inc. on public perceptions of private forest stewardship, the forest industry has developed a set of forest principles wrapped around a commitment to sustainable forest management. The rationale underlying this initiative corroborates the supposition reflected in many chapters of this text that much of our human concern for sustaining natural ecosystems while reasonably providing for human needs is rooted in our fundamental sense of connectedness to the land that sustains us.

Principles for Sustainable Forestry

America's managed forests make a vital contribution to the nation and to the world by providing economic, consumer, environmental, and aesthetic benefits indispensable to our quality of life. A vital forest-based economy provides wood and paper products and employment, while ensuring a viable tax base. Accomplishing sustainable forestry on private land requires a partnership among landowners, contractors, and the companies that purchase wood.

Members of the American Forest and Paper Association (AF&PA) therefore support on their lands—and all others—sustainable forestry practices. Moreover, AF&PA members support efforts to protect private property rights and the ability of all private landowners to manage their forest lands in a sustainable way. This support stems from the AF&PA memberships belief that forest landowners have an important stewardship responsibility and obligation to society. In keeping with this responsibility, the members of the AF&PA support the following principles:

SUSTAINABLE FORESTRY

I. To practice sustainable forestry so as to meet the needs of the present without compromising the ability of future generations to meet their own needs by practicing a land stewardship ethic which integrates the reforestation, managing, growing, nurturing, and harvesting of trees for useful products with the conservation of soil, air and water quality, wildlife and fish habitat, and aesthetics.

RESPONSIBLE PRACTICES

II. To use in its own forests, and promote among other forest landowners, sustainable forestry practices that are both economically and environmentally responsible.

FOREST HEALTH AND PRODUCTIVITY

III. To protect forests from wildfire, pests, diseases, and other damaging agents in order to maintain and improve long-term forest health and productivity.

PROTECTING SPECIAL SITES

IV. To manage its forests and lands of special significance (e.g., biologically, geologically, or historically significant) in a manner that takes into account their unique qualities.

CONTINUOUS IMPROVEMENT

V. To continuously improve the practice of forest management and also monitor, measure, and report the performance of our members in achieving our commitment to sustainable forestry.

Sustainable Forestry Implementation Guidelines

The following guidelines are intended to provide measures by which to evaluate our membership's performance in complying with the AF&PA Sustainable Forestry Principles. On January 1, 1996, compliance with the Sustainable Forestry Principles and Implementation Guidelines became a condition of continued membership in AF&PA.

The performance measures are written in the future tense to reflect the underlying premise of the Sustainable Forestry Principles—continuous improvement. While AF&PA member companies are committed to continuous improvement and assessment, these principles and guidelines also recognize the sustainable forestry efforts in existence throughout the U.S. forest products industry today.

AF&PA members recognize that to maximize the effectiveness of these guidelines, they must be tailored to the unique forest conditions at the regional, state, or site level. For this reason, AF&PA member companies, individually or collectively, at the site, state, or regional level, may adopt performance measures different from those listed here so long as they are *fully consistent* with or exceed the spirit and intent of these objectives.

Implementation Guidelines for the Practice of Sustainable Forestry on AF&PA Members' Forests

Objective 1. Broaden the practice of sustainable forestry by employing an array of scientifically, environmentally, and economically sound practices in the growth, harvest, and use of forests.

Performance Measures:

a. Each AF&PA member company will define its own policies, programs, and plans to implement and achieve the AF&PA Sustainable Forestry Principles and Guidelines.

b. AF&PA members will, individually, through cooperative efforts, or through AF&PA, provide funding for forest research to improve the health, productivity, and management of all forests.

Objective 2. Promptly reforest harvested areas to ensure long-term productivity, sustainable yield, and conservation of forest resources.

Performance Measures:

a. AF&PA members will reforest after final harvest by planting or direct seeding within two years, or by planned natural regeneration methods within five years.

b. AF&PA members will foster the development of processes at the state level to report the overall rate of reforestation success.

Objective 3. Protect the water quality in streams, lakes, and other bodies of water by establishing riparian protection measures based on soil type, terrain, vegetation, and other applicable factors, and by using Best Management Practices (BMPs) in all forest management operations.

Performance Measures:

a. AF&PA members will meet or exceed all established BMPs, applicable state water quality laws and regulations, and the requirements of the Clean Water Act for forestland.

b. AF&PA members will establish and implement riparian protection measures for all perennial streams and lakes and involve a panel of experts at the state level to help identify goals and objectives for riparian protection.

c. AF&PA members will, individually, through cooperative efforts, or through AF&PA, provide funding for water quality research.

Objective 4. Enhance wildlife habitat by developing and implementing measures that promote habitat diversity and the conservation of plant and animal populations found in forest communities.

Performance Measures:

a. Each AF&PA member company will define its own policies, programs, and plans to promote habitat diversity.

b. AF&PA members will, individually, through cooperative efforts, or through AF&PA, provide funding for wildlife research.

Objective 5. Minimize the impact of harvesting on visual quality by shaping harvest units to blend into the terrain, by restricting clear-cut size and/or by using harvest methods, age classes, and judicious placement of harvest units to promote diversity in forest cover.

Performance Measures:

a. Each AF&PA member will define its own policies, programs, and plans to minimize the impact of its forest harvesting on visual quality.

b. AF&PA members will develop and adopt, in each state where they operate, appropriate targets for managing the size of clear-cuts. Where the average size of clear-cut harvest areas exceeds 120 acres, AF&PA member companies will reduce the average size to no more than 120 acres, except when necessary to respond to forest health emergencies or other natural catastrophes.

c. AF&PA members will adopt a "green up" requirement, under which past clear-cut harvest areas must have trees at least three years old or five-feet high at the desired level of stocking before adjacent areas can be clear-cut or more comprehensive methods that provide age, habitat and aesthetic diversity.

Objective 6. Manage company lands of biologic, geologic, or historic significance in a manner that takes into account their special qualities.

Performance Measure:

a. AF&PA members will identify special sites and manage them in a manner that takes into account their unique features. AF&PA members may choose, or continue, to involve organizations with expertise in protecting special places to provide guidance in how these lands can best be managed to maintain their unique character.

Objective 7. Contribute to biodiversity by enhancing landscape diversity and providing an array of habitats.

Performance Measures:

a. AF&PA members will increase support for research to improve the science and understanding of landscape management, ecosystem functions, and the conservation of biological diversity.

b. AF&PA members will continually incorporate the knowledge gained through research, science, technology, and field experience for conserving biological diversity.

Objective 8. Continue to improve forest utilization to maximize the efficient use of forest resources.

Performance Measure:

a. AF&PA members will employ appropriate technology, processes, and practices for ensuring efficient utilization of trees harvested.

Objective 9. Continue the prudent use of forest chemicals to improve forest health and growth while protecting employees, neighbors, the public, and sensitive areas, including stream courses and adjacent lands.

Performance Measure:

a. AF&PA members will meet or exceed all applicable label requirements, laws, and regulations concerning the use of fertilizers, herbicides, and other forest chemicals.

IMPLEMENTATION GUIDELINES FOR THE PRACTICE OF SUSTAINABLE FORESTRY BY AF&PA MEMBERS IN THE PROCUREMENT OF WOOD AND FIBER FROM LOGGERS AND OTHER LANDOWNERS

Objective 10. Broaden the practice of sustainable forestry by further involving nonindustrial landowners, loggers, consulting foresters and company employees active in procurement and landowner assistance.

Performance Measures:

a. AF&PA members will encourage landowners by selling them timber to reforest and use BMPs by providing these landowners information on the advantages of these practices.

b. AF&PA members will work cooperatively with logging and state forestry associations, appropriate agencies and others in the forestry community to further enhance the professionalism of loggers by establishing state groups where none exist and cooperating with existing state groups to promote the training and education of loggers in:

- awareness of AF&PA Sustainable Forestry Principles;
- logging safety;

- BMPs—including road construction and retirement, site preparation, stream side management, etc.;
- regeneration and forest resource conservation;
- OSHA and wage and hour rules;
- awareness of responsibilities under the Endangered Species Act and other wildlife considerations;
- transportation; and
- business management—including employee training, public relations, etc.

As a means of demonstrating AF&PA members' commitment to continuous improvement in sustainable forestry, state groups will be encouraged to have ongoing training and education programs for loggers, employees involved in procurement and landowner assistance, contractors, and suppliers in place by January 1, 1996.

c. AF&PA will collect information from its members, state groups, and other sources to report annually:

- the number of landowners which received information about regeneration from contractors, company employees, and others;
- how many of these landowners made an informed decision to apply BMPs and to regenerate the forest after harvest;
- the number of loggers which completed each year's training and education programs; and
- the percentage of wood delivered by loggers who have completed logger training and education programs.

d. AF&PA members will ensure that their commitment to the Sustainable Forestry Principles is communicated throughout all levels of their company, particularly to mill and woodland managers, wood procurement operations, and field foresters.

e. AF&PA members will support and promote efforts by consultant foresters, state and federal agencies, state groups, and programs like the American Tree Farm System, to educate nonindustrial landowners and encourage them to apply principles of sustainable forest management on their lands.

f. Each AF&PA member will clearly define and implement its own policies, programs, and plans to ensure that mill inventories and procurement practices do not compromise their adherence to the Sustainable Forestry Principles.

Implementation Guidelines for AF&PA Member Companies for Public Reporting and Involvement in the Practice of Sustainable Forestry

Objective 11. Publicly report performance and continuous improvement towards achieving commitment to sustainable forestry.

Performance Measures:

a. AF&PA members will report annually to AF&PA on their compliance with AF&PA Sustainable Forestry Principles and Implementation Guidelines.

b. AF&PA will issue an annual report to the public on its membership's performance regarding compliance with and progress on sustainable forestry, including a list of all companies complying with the AF&PA Sustainable Forestry Principles and Implementation Guidelines.

c. An advisory group of independent experts will assist in the preparation of the annual report including validation of conclusions and an assessment of reported progress.

Objective 12. Provide opportunities for the public and the forestry community to participate in AF&PA membership's commitment to sustainable forestry.

Performance Measure:

a. AF&PA members will support and promote appropriate mechanisms for public outreach, education, and addressing public concerns related to forest management, such as: toll-free numbers; environmental education; and/or private and public sector technical assistance programs.

b. AF&PA members will establish an appropriate procedure at the state level to address concerns raised by loggers, consulting foresters, employees, or AF&PA members with practices which appear to be inconsistent with the AF&PA Sustainable Forestry Principles and Implementation Guidelines.

c. AF&PA members will establish a national forum of loggers, landowners, and senior industry representatives, including CEO representation, that will meet at least twice annually to review progress toward the AF&PA Sustainable Forestry Principles and Implementation Guidelines. The results of each meeting will be reported to the Forest Resources Board of Directors.

AF&PA PUBLIC POLICY GOALS FOR SUSTAINABLE FORESTRY ON ALL PRIVATE AND PUBLIC LANDS IN THE UNITED STATES

1. *Increase Forest Growth, Quality, and Productivity by Practicing Sustainable Forestry.* AF&PA members will support a national goal of sustainable forestry which seeks to increase growth and timber quality of all forests, to ensure there is the volume and quality of domestic timber resources available to meet public needs now and in the future. To accomplish this goal AF&PA members will continue to:

   a. increase the productivity of the forests they own and manage;

   b. encourage the establishment of forests on marginal agricultural lands that could more profitably be managed for forestry;

   c. work with the Forest Service and state agencies to strengthen growth, productivity, and timber quality monitoring programs; and

   d. support federal, state, and local programs and policies that encourage retention and expansion of the productive forestland base and promote long-term forestry investment.

2. *Define and Work to Implement Ecosystem Management on Federal Lands.* AF&PA members will work with Congress and public agencies to appropriately define and implement active ecosystem management on all National Forest System and Bureau of Land Management lands in order to regain stability in land management de-

cision making and facilitate accomplishment of land management goals. This effort must be complemented by improved accountability for meeting the goals. Priority attention should be given to public forests with forest health problems in the implementation of ecosystem management principles.

3. *Reduce the Risk of and Suppress Wildfires.* AF&PA members will support forest fire protection programs that minimize losses of all resource values from wildfire. AF&PA members will use on their lands, and promote on all other lands, appropriate methods, including prescribed fire, to reduce forest fuels, improve regeneration success and wildlife habitat, and minimize the potential for catastrophic wildfire. When prescribed fire is used, sound smoke management guidelines and regulations will be followed.

4. *Promote and Utilize Integrated Pest Management.* AF&PA members will use on their lands, and promote on all other lands, the principles of integrated pest management in the selection and implementation of pest control programs, including the selective and safe use of pesticides.

5. *Encourage Forest Health and Productivity Research.* AF&PA members will support research on wildfire, pests, diseases, and other damaging agents affecting forest resources and other values. AF&PA members will encourage research and monitor the work of other scientists studying the potential impact of climate change, atmospheric pollution, and cumulative effects on forest health and productivity.

6. *Encourage Continuing Education.* AF&PA members will support continuing professional education in state-of-the-art techniques for integrating the management of all forest resources. AF&PA members will educate all employees involved in forest management about their company's plans, policies, and programs to implement the AF&PA Sustainable Forestry Principles and Implementation Guidelines.

7. *Recognize Excellence.* AF&PA members will recognize and promote excellence to encourage improved environmental performance by those engaged in forestry operations.

8. *Protect the Ability of All Private Landowners to Sustainably Manage their Forest Land.* AF&PA members will work with Congress, state legislatures, and federal, state, and local agencies to ensure that laws, regulations, tax structures, and policies promote, rather than compromise, the ability of private landowners to sustainably manage their forest land.

Conclusion

It is too early to tell whether the change in behavior manifested in the Sustainable Forestry Principles will help the public better understand the values held by private landowners and land managers relative to environmental stewardship. However, the development of this initiative has, for many of us, reaffirmed our own sense of connectedness to the land. In this regard, private landowners and managers recognize as well as anyone our ultimate dependence on the health and vitality of Nature to ensure a continuous flow of benefits, however hard or easy to define, to humankind. Our ongoing challenge is to work cooperatively in both the public and private sector to sustain such benefits for the sake of this generation and generations to come.

Literature Cited

Market Strategies, Inc. (1992, 1993, and 1994). "Research study on public perceptions of forest resource owners and managers." Chicago, IL. Unpublished paper.

Section III

Part C

INTERNATIONAL PERSPECTIVES

"DREAMING" DOWN UNDER: THE CULTURAL POLITICS OF PEOPLE AND "COUNTRY"

JIM BIRCKHEAD
School of Environmental and Information Science
Charles Sturt University
Albury, NSW Australia

Australia is the only country in the world with a continuous cultural history of 60,000, possibly more, years.
Hawthorne and Klein, 1994

In this chapter I explore some dimensions of an emerging land management ethic in Australia—an ethic increasingly informed by Aboriginal meanings and values about the land or "country." This ethic, interwoven as it is with Aboriginal spirituality or "The Dreaming," while hard to define for non-Aborigines, is, nevertheless, finding its way into government policy, national park management plans, environmental sciences courses, media, and popular imagination. It, like other indigenous traditions around the world, bespeaks of a reverence for the land, the "Earth our mother," and brings with it a strong ethical imperative and practical obligation "to care for country."

Increasingly, the relatively young settler culture of Australia is looking to, or appropriating, the culture of the first people for more viable ways to feel about and care for this now badly degraded country and for a greater sense of legitimacy and identity in this part of the world on the doorstep of Asia (Lattas, 1990). After all, 206 years of colonial presence is inconsequential compared to more than 60,000 years of Aboriginal occupancy.

Although Australia is one of the most ethnically diverse, multicultural societies in the world, representing a myriad of culturally specific land ethics, the dominant emerging debate is between the settler culture and the colonized Aboriginal and Torres Strait Islander cultures. Similarly, other diverse perspectives and values (e.g., environmentalist, ecofeminist, ecotourist, lesbian/gay, antihunting animal liberationist, hunters, timber cutters, property developers, miners, and New Age) bounce off and incorporate, or contest, core indigenous values and meanings. And although Aboriginal and Torres Strait Islander people comprise only 1.43 percent of the Australian population (some 228,000 people in the 1986 census count), their rights and claims are now enshrined in legislation, becoming central to the agendas of conservation agencies, and debated daily by politicians and the media. I focus, therefore, on aspects of this main debate. This is a difficult task as there is presently no stable viewing platform or stasis in the dizzying flux of dialogue and unfolding events.

My perspective is that of an American-born, naturalized Australian anthropologist, who has been working since 1976 at the dynamic interface where Aboriginal and non-Aboriginal conservation and land management values articulate, often contentiously. As a member of the Johnstone Centre of Parks, Recreation, and Heritage and coordinator of its Indigenous Land Management Program Area, I am involved with these issues in a number of ways; namely, in the education and training of Aboriginal national park rangers; in critically considering the policy question of Aboriginal involvement in park and protected area management (especially Aboriginal ownership, residence in, and joint management of parks); in the long-term evaluation of an Aboriginal and Torres Strait Islander community ranger program based on traditional ecological knowledge as taught by elders (on Cape York in far north Queensland); and in assessing the ecological and cultural impacts of indigenous hunting in a number of remote parts of Australia. Each of these areas revolves around the meaning of land or "country" to Aboriginal people, and the place of Aboriginal people in Australia's emerging identity as an Asian/ Pacific nation. My intent in this chapter, then, is to explore how Australia is expanding and enhancing its dominant "whitefella" park and protected area management regime by officially incorporating Aboriginal values and people into existing structures at both state and commonwealth levels.

The Land of Oz in Question

Australian national culture and identity today, perhaps more so than in any other Western nation, are contested (Rudder, 1992). The popular image of the ruggedly masculine, bronzed, friendly and confident bush bloke saying, "G'day mate," or "throw another shrimp on the barbie," belies the underlying Australian quest to redefine our national identity as the twenty-first century approaches.

Much of our purported alienation and uncertainty of who we are no doubt derives from the ever increasing dissonance between our well-worn images of "The Australian Dream," and present and emerging realities. The contradictions scream out and are palpable. Who is this laconic, easy going, white, male, blond-haired Aussie "Crocodile Dundee" of tourist adverts and beer commercials? What mythic time and space does he inhabit in "The Lucky Country" (Horne, 1988)? Such monocultural, male bush myths fail to sustain us in the inclusive 1990s, nor do they accurately reflect our demography, residential patterns, origins, relationship to the land, aspirations or anxieties.

Both visitors to and residents of Australia today are swamped by other free floating images and discourses, reflecting a contested politics of difference—"Melbourne, third largest Greek city in the world"; Sydney, host to the largest annual Gay and Lesbian Mardi Gras in the world; Australia, the "clever country," successfully competing in the global economy; a reemerging Aboriginal nation; a vigorous politics of sexuality, reproduction and feminism; an incipient but strong "green" movement. Thus, while Mick Dundee may serve as an appealing icon of the fair dinkum Aussie, he belies the pervasive cultural, ethnic, and lifestyle diversity of Australian society and its extreme urbanity.

With respect to ethnic diversity, Australia is one of the most pluralistic societies in the world. The statistics are convincing. As summarized by Pettman:

> In 1947 Australia's population was only 7 million. By 1988 it was over 16 million, an increase due largely to the postwar immigration program. This program has been massive, and has drawn on increasingly varied sources of migrants, so that today Australia is second only to Israel in the numbers and range of its migrant population. . . . In 1980 the total percentage of immigrant populations was 21.6 for Australia, 4.7 for the United States, 6.5 for Great Britain, and 15.2 for Canada. . . . (1992, p. 35)

The diversity of immigrants' homelands is a notable feature as well, "with migrants from 100 nationalities and ethnic groups making the long journey to Australia" (Collins, 1993, p. 106). Thus, it is reasonable to conclude that: "An Australian might still be a man or woman from Snowy River, but he or she might also be a man or woman from Italy or Turkey, Ireland, Lebanon or Cambodia" (Whitlock and Carter, 1992, p. 101). The fair dinkum Aussie myth is further challenged by the fact that the typical resident of multicultural Australia is more likely to be a city or suburban dweller than a bush man or woman "on the land." For although we seem to feel that "the 'Australian spirit' is somehow intimately connected with the bush" (Ward, 1992, p.

180), few people live there. Indeed, Australians, despite their outback mystique, are "the most urbanized people in the world; . . . 85 percent of the people live in a city or a large town" (Birch, 1993, p. 257), with more than 80 percent of the population living in six coastal cities and their adjacent satellite settlements (Spearritt, 1992).

To make matters worse, much of this empty land is now badly damaged and degraded; not a verdant, fertile heartland, but an eroded, defoliated, saline and sour country. Two hundred and six years of whitefella stewardship of these fragile ecosystems poorly understood by Europeans has had disastrous effects. William Lines succinctly and pointedly tallies up the ravages of these years of settler land management:

> But the changes initiated by 200 years of European occupation utterly confounded the integrity of the continent's natural cycles, evolved over 200 million years of evolution and a further 60,000 years of Aboriginal presence. Enlightened civilization introduced a level of biological instability unmatched in the world. Since the first British settlement, Europeans have destroyed over 70 percent of Australia's original woodland and forest. Agricultural and pastoral activities have degraded two-thirds of all arable land and one-half of all grazing land. Land deterioration already costs hundreds of millions of dollars each year in lost agricultural output and imperils future production. Of Australia's 7750 million square kilometers only the desert areas of Western Australia contain no degraded land. Extinction threatens one-third of Australia's mammals, most of them unique to the continent, and over 2,200 native plant species, 10 percent of the total, including nearly one-quarter of all eucalyptus species. In 200 years European technology, warfare, culture and political economy have swept across the Australian landscape as an expression of manifest destiny, changing forever the face of the land. Nowhere else on Earth have so few people pauperized such a large proportion of the world's surface in such a brief period of time. In under 200 years, a natural world millions of years in the making, and an Aboriginal culture of 60,000 years duration, vanished before the voracious, insatiable demands of a foreign invasion. (1991, p. 12)

Alienation, dissonance, and despoiled country aside, Australia, as suggested before, is also reinventing itself politically, constitutionally, legally, and symbolically. At present a number of key identity questions are on the agenda. But the central concern underlying present day Aussie postcolonial soul searching, and integral to most aspects of national and cultural reinvention, is the place of Aboriginal and Torres Strait Islander people in the emerging Australian republic and in our psyche. Aborigines until recently were shadowy figures on the margins of Australian society and consciousness, "distant ancestors who had overstayed their time on Earth" (Reynolds, 1987, p. 128).

Terra Nullius—Positioning Aborigines

Not so long ago, Aborigines occupied the "savage slot" in popular and scientific imagination—Stone Age remnants on the verge of extinction (Trouillot, 1991). A voluminous literature portrayed them as quintessential "others," notable for their absence of significant markers of civilization. They "did not know the wheel, had no written languages, and no implements except spears and throwers, wooden sticks, stone axes and boomerangs" (Berndt and Berndt, 1968, p. 1). Thus, for all intents and purposes, this "Great South Land," "Terra Australis Incognita" was in 1788 "Terra Nullius," land belonging to no one, a "wasteland and unoccupied" (Treaty 88 Campaign, 1988, p. 2). To the British colonizers this "untouched continent" was "an emptiness waiting to be filled" (Brady, 1994, p. 41), to "be carved up" (Spearritt, 1992, p. 1), tamed and civilized. And because this "uncanny," wild and menacing place of settler lore was "uninhabited," and therefore "peacefully settled" by brave and hearty pioneers, there was no need, as with our antipodean neighbors in Aotearoa (New Zealand), to make either treaty or compact with the "invisible" inhabitants of this "empty land."

The continent, of course, was not empty, but was home to some 750,000 to one million people. As contemporary Australians now accept from the archaeological and historical evidence, and see through more enlightened eyes, this "empty land" was fully occupied from coast to coast, from fertile flood plain to parched desert. The land was intimately known, personified, and owned, every square foot of it accounted for through intricate Dreaming stories.

This was no wilderness or wild country, but a humanized cultural landscape. And given the fact of Aboriginal ownership and occupancy of the country we now call Australia, the term "invasion" is increasingly being used in preference to the more benign "settlement" to describe the events of 1788. Regardless of semantics, an ever growing oral and revisionist history has set the record straight by documenting the rapid decimation, decline, removal, and marginalization of Aboriginal people across the continent. The valiant resistance and ultimate survival of Aboriginal people depicted in books and films has put an end to the myth of peaceful settlement (see Reynolds, 1987; Rintoul, 1993; Rutherford, 1988).

The Land Is Us

"Blackfellas" and "whitefellas" characteristically understand and relate to the land or nature in quite different ways. In short, Aborigines speak of "country," particular places to which people belong, and are linked through Dreaming stories going back thousands of years. The relationship is spiritual as well as physical, ordained at the beginning of time and creation—a nurturing "Earth as mother." On the other hand, land for the settler cultures was and is a commodity to be conquered, bought and sold, farmed and mined for profit; an attitude also sanctioned during the Creation. "And God said, Let us make man in our image, after our likeness: and let them have dominion over the fish of the sea, and over the fowl of the air, and over the cattle, and over all the Earth, and over every creeping thing that creepeth upon the Earth" (Genesis 1:26).

Recent thinking about sustainability, biodiversity, reconciliation, and Australian nationalism is seeking a rapprochement between Aboriginal and European land ethics and cultures; a push "to reflect on, point to, and map out. . . . a land management future more in tune with the nature of this country as understood by its traditional owners. . . ." (Birckhead and Smith, 1992-93, p. 5). Settler Australians are looking increasingly to the country's first people for wisdom about the "nature" of Australia and for a greater sense of belonging and spiritual connection to this "uncanny" land (Brady, 1991).

For newcomers, there is indeed an awesomeness about the Australian landscape, a primordial essence, the timelessness of a vast, sparsely settled land, a spiritual resonance. The lone self seems paltry and transient beneath the brilliant burning stars of a chilly central Australian desert night, a deafening silence pounding in one's ears. The endless white sand beaches of Cape York in tropical far north Queensland, framed on one side by azure blue water and by lush, ancient rain forested mountains on the other, also instills a sense of timeless awe and of the temporal insignificance of the human moment.

Yet, behind the awe this "wild" land can be frightening and foreboding to the unknowledgeable. Venomous snakes and spiders, intense desert heat and tropical cyclones, the quiet presence of lurking crocodiles, cycles of flood and drought, and the ever present specter of bushfires can inspire uneasiness and anxiety in most of those who cling to the fringes of the continent in city or suburb. But, these are the perceptions of newcomers to this country, with recent ties to the land of two hundred years or less—strangers in a strange land.

Indeed, those who read the landscape this way position themselves as separate and "other" to it, as spectators gazing in. As Stephen Muecke posits: "There is no landscape without a sense of otherness; landscape has to be seen or experienced, in the way a tourist does" (1992, p. 166). He notes further that "perceptions of landscape depend on difference, therefore, and on displacement." This being the case, he argues that "for the indigenous person, there is really no such thing as the landscape. . . ." Citing specific Aboriginal narratives about "country" he notes that:

What is noticeable about Aboriginal narratives is the complete absence of a specular *version of the landscape. Narration is not interrupted by descriptive passages. Such perspectives are the obsession of the newly arrived, for whom, as we well know, the landscape was necessarily Other—as negative, as empty, as feminine, and whatever other metaphorical displacements of that position as might be called forth by the occasion. To know this country is to walk around it along tracks put down by the ancestors, participating in ceremony. . . . (pp. 167-168)*

Veronica Brady captures well a long enduring settler mood of melancholy, estrangement from nature, and spiritual void:

> Witness the fear of the land in much of our writing in the 1880s. Marcus Clarke, for example, argued that the 'dominant note' of the Australian landscape is a 'weird melancholy' and to this day most Australians see the center of Australia as a 'Dead Heart.' Others may see the Center as an uncanny place, like a mother who will never give birth: the stillborn. Refusing to commit ourselves to it, to the mystery of space, we clung to the fringe of ourselves as we cling to the fringes of the continent, or like Mr. Bonner in Patrick White's Voss, we see Australia as the 'country of the future' in material terms, that is, of buildings, bridges and roads, expanding productivity, large bank balances and large needs.
>
> We find no place for our spirit in the land but rather desolation, like Sturt arriving at Lake Blanche in the Centre where he had hoped to find an inland sea. One of his party reported his reaction: 'The Captain feels most dreadfully chagrined. The scene is the climax of desolation; no trees, no shrubs, all bleak, barren, undulating sand. Miserable! Horrible!' Sturt himself described it as a 'country not to be understood.' European eyes here saw only, in Marcus Clarke's words, 'the scribblings of nature learning to write.' (1991, p. 41)

For indigenous Australians, on the other hand, the late Wandjuk Marika, of the Rirratjinqu Clan conveys some of the meanings of "country": "The land is not empty, the land is full of knowledge, full of story, full of goodness, full of energy, full of power" (Melbourne Festival Program, 1994). The land, then, is for Aboriginal people a nurturing mother, the "country" to which one belongs and is sustained by, as opposed to the bad, devouring, rejecting mother of whitefella fear and obsession (Anderson, 1992).

Eddie Kneebone (1991), an Aboriginal educator, speaks of an at homeness in the universe in *Creation Spirituality and the Dreamtime*:

> Aboriginal spirituality is the belief and the feeling within yourself that allows you to become a part of the whole environment around you—not the built environment, but the natural environment. . . . Birth, life and death are all a part of it, and you welcome each. Ab-

original spirituality is the belief that all objects are living and share the same soul or spirit that Aboriginals share. Therefore all Aboriginals have a kinship with the environment. The soul or spirit is common—only the shape is different, but no less important. . . . (1991, p. 89)

In Aboriginal "deep" cosmology even the vast void of the universe is personified and given meaning in kinship terms, contrasting with whitefella's alienation and aloneness in space. As Kneebone reflects:

> We look up and see the stars shining above and we say: 'They are the bright suns and around them there are planets—possibly with people we will never see.' The Aboriginals looked up at night and they didn't see the stars—they never saw stars. They only saw the campfires of their ancestors on their journey. The bright stars were the ancestors who were not long gone; the dimmer stars were the ancestors further on their journey.
>
> They imagined that the ancestors sitting around their campfires were looking back and seeing the campfires of the living, physical Aboriginals at their own campsites. The Aboriginals looked up and really believed that their eyes could meet.
>
> So for me, Creation Spirituality, as Mathew Fox talks about it, is like the Dreamtime in the way that it brings the entire cosmos into our lives, making it a part of us, and us, a part of it. (1991, pp. 93-94)

So, the contrast in land ethics is clear; 60,000 years of indigenous belonging to "country" as opposed to 206 years of settler culture, tenuously clinging to the fringes of the continent, trying to feel grounded and at home in this strange land down under. What is represented here is the clash of two deeply engrained world-views or cosmologies; an indigenous view which places:

> no species at the center of creation—'Everything comes out of the Earth by Dreaming; everything knows itself; its place, its relationship to other portions of the cosmos'—and a settler 'human-centered' cosmology which readily breeds a 'nihilism of despair.'
>
> Rose, 1992, pp. 219-220

Yet, many whitefellas love the land and are feeling increasingly at home in this place. The environment, threats to it, and new ways to relate to it are discussed and debated almost daily in the media. People increasingly are planting native species in their gardens and finding beauty and value in Australian flora and fauna. Camping, boating, fishing, hunting, and bush walking draw people from cities to nature and the pristine beauty of national parks and nature reserves. And underlying our quest to connect with nature is the growing desire to share and experience Aboriginal meanings of place and country, to lessen the distance between self and landscape. How to expand existing land management ethics to include indigenous knowledge, values, practices and people will now be considered.

"Two-Way Dreamtime": Caring for "Country" Today[1]

The 1990s have been a dynamic time in Australian history, a time during which Aboriginal people have emerged from out of the shadows and become visible and central to national dreams and identity. But it is early, and the real momentum is only just building. As Native Title claims are heard and Aboriginal people gain control over large tracts of land, including national parks, management of "country" increasingly will be governed by Aboriginal knowledge and practices.

This emerging common ground, or "two-way" interface between cultures, seems to be a fertile space for innovation; for expanding, even revolutionizing, dominant Western land ethics and management cultures. Surely the inclusion of Aboriginal ethics, knowledge, and people in protected area management could only expand and enrich current land management practices. Yet this is a contested and contentious ideological and cultural space, often revealing a wide chasm between Euro-Australian notions of conservation and Aboriginal notions of country, a clash between the ethic that "the land is us" and that land and nature are "other" (See Birckhead and Smith, 1992-93).

National parks in Australia, traditionally based on the Yellowstone model of a wilderness preserve which is not inhabited on a permanent basis, reflect this idea of nature as "other," a "wilderness," fenced off, out there removed from everyday life (Foster, 1992-93). As Holmes Rolston, III emphasizes with respect to leisure and "wild" nature: "Both we and nature must be unoccupied—we from our work and nature from our works" (1991, p. 394). National parks, then, as wild places, are cherished and valued as pilgrimage sites along whitefella dreaming tracks, sacred spaces for the renewal of the human spirit; places for time-out from the "paramount reality of everyday life" (Berger and Luckmann, 1966).

These views are anathema to Aboriginal people with their wholistic and inclusive views of nature, the-land-is-us ethic. Our separation and dichotomies do not hold sway in Aboriginal cosmology. Fabienne Bayet, an Aboriginal research assistant, emphasizes that:

> *The concept of wilderness as nature without any trace of human interaction, dehumanizes the indigenous peoples living within that landscape. ... To indigenous peoples the land is no distant wilderness. The whole of Australia is an Aboriginal artifact. The whole of the continent has been affected by Aboriginal people living out their Dreaming obligations.* (1994, p. 28)

These semantic debates about the meaning of wilderness tie in closely to questions of prior ownership, political power, and economic development. Namely, "Wilderness in Australia is, by definition, traditional Aboriginal land" (Brown, 1992, p. 21). Parks, gazetted for their wilderness and conservation values, displaced Aboriginal people and their management regimes from country which is anything but wild. Deborah Bird Rose shows that for Yarralin people in the Northern Territory, "the wild" is seen as "damaged or spoilt country," a man-made and cattle-made wilderness where nothing grows, where life is absent, where all the care, intelligence, and respect that generations of Aboriginal people have put into the country have been eradicated in a matter of a few short years. Rose goes onto explain that:

> *The inescapable irony, and the hurt for many Aboriginal people, is this: the country Europeans would want to see as 'untouched wilderness' is the country that Daly Pulkara and others regard as properly cared for. This 'properly cared for,' or 'quiet country,' is country in which those who know how to read the signs see human action of the most responsible sort.* (1988, p. 386)

---

[1]"Two-Way Dreamtime" is the title of a jazz rap number by singer, Dig, from "Dig Deeper: Directions in Groove," Polygram Music Publishing Australia, Sydney, 1994.

"Wilderness," then, is a whitefella ideological construct, and when enshrined in national parks and conservation legislation, acts as a "second wave of dispossession" for Aboriginal people "which denies their customary inherited right to use land for hunting, gathering, building, rituals and birthing rites" (Bayet, 19894, p. 29). As Stevens cynically suggests, the result of this state of affairs is:

> . . . *the creation of parks where wilderness is artificially contrived, wilderness created with bulldozers and fences, forced migration and resettlement.*

Therefore:

> *It is too often with good cause that indigenous peoples have regarded national parks with suspicion and fear.* (1986, p. 3)

Indeed, "Aboriginal people are very clear in the value they ascribe to 'country'" (De Lacy and Lockwood, 1992, p. 2) and their rightful place in Australia. Aboriginal people owned, knew intimately, were part of, and managed land for many millennia before being dispossessed by the invaders. People now often find themselves excluded from full use and management of national parks which they in effect created and once managed. Aboriginal people now want to redress this situation and regain ownership and control of country, some of which may lie within national park boundaries. They want to care for and use "country" in Aboriginal ways, for cultural, social, and economic development and independence. Thus, in this emerging scenario:

> *The indigenous people of this country will be the custodians of the ecological heritage of the nation. They will become part of the national economic life and they will no longer be pariahs and Fourth-World citizens in their own land. . . .*
>
> Pearson, 1994, pp. 7-8

However, as land managers, black and white, contemplate together this innovative land management future, based heavily on Aboriginal custodianship and traditional ecological knowledge, a number of questions and concerns must be addressed about the "desires to affiliate with indigenous people and to call upon their knowledge and experiences" (Jacobs, 1994, p. 305). Basic to this enterprise is how land managers conceptualize and define Aboriginal land ethics and knowledge, and Aboriginal people themselves for that matter. These concerns are as much matters of cultural politics, political history, ideology, and discourse as they are of ecology, natural history, and park management. How land managers and policymakers view Aboriginal people and their ecological wisdom is very much influenced and structured by the popular cultural formations of the times. Discourses, "anthropological, romantic, and racist" (Muecke, 1992), vie for our attention as Aborigines are still being depicted as being somewhere between noble and ignoble savage. These modes are mostly premised on essentialist notions which locate Aboriginal deep ecology in the genes, an instinct, part of "their essential racial difference," unchanged from the primordial past (Muecke, 1992). Questions of authenticity and continuity of tradition loom large in essentialist understanding and readily instill anxiety in joint management arenas. As non-Aborigines are looking to 60,000 years of indigenous wisdom as a corrective to 206 years of a rapacious environmental ethic, they want to ensure that it is the "real" thing.

On a more general level, the nature, accessibility, and transferability of an Aboriginal land ethic and traditional ecological knowledge becomes an issue (Lewis, 1993). As I have shown previously, an Aboriginal land ethic, in general, can be considered as quite a singular ethic of "the land is us" and "caring for country." But, it is more than an abstract principle or value. As Anderson (1992) explains:

> *Issues about country are always social issues. There is no global, abstract, sentimentalized or externalized view of landscape, something which is at the root of much of our thinking about land. For Aboriginal people, land is humanized, it's social, it's read in social terms. Shipton's Flat, a particular area of country that I know well, is Johnny Walker. It is the Friday family, there's no difference at one level between that group and that bit of land and we've got to recognize that.* (p. 82)

This social embeddedness of knowledge is often overlooked by romantic, New Age "ecospiritual revisionists" intent on quickly and painlessly absorbing and appropriating an Aboriginal the-land-is-us ethic (Jacobs, 1994). As I have written elsewhere with respect to our possibly misguided efforts to incorporate Aboriginal traditional knowledge and practice into our park management programs:

While such knowledge and practice certainly exist, it is not found as a refined entity or commodity which can be extracted from its context, processed and packaged quickly and unproblematically. Indeed, our consultants did not find knowledge of fire, wildlife, plants, bush tucker and cultural sites there for the plucking. To reiterate, then, there is no fixed and frozen corpus of orthodox knowledge and practice 'out there' removed from human interaction and interpretation, like so many artifacts for the taking. Knowledge and practice are tied to rights of ownership, part of an appropriate community cultural transmission, inextricably bound to the Tjukurrpa (Law and Dreaming) and related considerations of secret/sacred, male/female, young/old, kinship ties, and so forth. . . . In short, control and access are crucial issues here.

Birckhead, 1992-93, p. 302

Winona La Duke notes with respect to American Indian and other indigenous traditions that:

What is happening is that our culture is taken out of context and certain parts of it are sold or just extracted. It's like mining. . . . To me, that's appropriation of our culture. It's the same thing as expropriating our wild rice or our land. And it's one of the last things we have.

Jacobs, p. 306

Sadly, much of this knowledge in Australia has become fragmented and attenuated, with the past dispersal of Aboriginal people from their country to which their knowledge was tied. People often find themselves now in country on whose behalf they cannot speak with authority. By commodifying and taking knowledge out of context we also lose sight of the link between knowledge, practice, and livelihood. While it might give New Age people a warm feeling to think about Aborigines as the ultimate conservationists living in an ongoing Dreamtime, clearly Aboriginal material and economic needs must be met.

Australia is, nevertheless, forging ahead with various two-way management strategies and concepts. The political, cultural, policy, and discursive climate is now right for the Aboriginalization of various aspects of mainstream land management. From local level conservation and development initiatives such as Aboriginal "community rangers" (see Birckhead and Wallis, 1994) to Aboriginal own-ership and joint management of national parks, the momentum is building.

National park and protected areas are key sites for the infusion of Aboriginal land ethics and practices. Australia, incredibly, has some 530 national parks, eight World Heritage Areas, and a further 28.3 million hectares of areas protected in other parks or conservation reserves (Wescott, 1991). Some 5.3 percent of Australia is set aside for national parks and nature reserves, with individual states and territories ranging from 46.8 percent as reserves in the Australian Capitol Territory to 2.1 percent in Queensland (Birch, 1993, pp. 216-217).

Many of these parks and protected areas impinge upon or include Aboriginal land in their domains, a point of some contestation where Aboriginal rights have not been adequately negotiated. This reflects the enduring conflict between conservation practices and Aboriginal use of "country." Increasingly, World Heritage managers and conservation agencies are attempting to narrow this ideological and cultural gap.

Aboriginal ownership and joint management of parks has been a reality for many years, especially in the Northern Territory. Other such parks now exist in Western Australia and are proposed for South Australia, New South Wales, and Queensland. There are now, in fact, some thirty proposals for joint management of protected areas under consideration (De Lacy, 1994).

Opinions vary widely as to the benefits or detriments of such arrangements. Some see joint management as tokenistic, and as a smoke screen for incorporating Aboriginal people further into the bureaucratic processes of the state. As John Cordell reflects:

. . .judging from Kakadu and Uluru, Aboriginal involvement in protected area management is on the verge of degenerating into Smokey Bear–style ranger training, in which the role of traditional owners is simply to add an interpretive and marketable ethnic element to running the parks. . . . Is the Uluru and Kakadu model equitable for indigenous peoples? Have two hundred years of dispossession been reversed? Is it really 'no worries, mate'? Or, in deconstructing the political economy of national parks in Australia, are we seeing the lengthening and tightening of green fingers around black lands? (1993, pp. 110-113)

But Aboriginal elder and member of Uluru board of management, Tony Tjamiwa, tells a different story:

> *I work long way away, at Mututjulu, and I want to talk to you about our national park, and how our park management is running straight. . . . In our park, Aboriginal Law is in the front guiding the way. The board of management doesn't get pushed around, they look after Aboriginal Law.* (1992-93, p. 7)

The "truth" no doubt lies somewhere in between, is changing by the moment, and is very much a matter of interpretation. But if the increasing number of people I meet who are making the decision not to climb "the rock" in deference to Aboriginal spiritual values are any indication, then perhaps an Aboriginal land ethic is slowly seeping into "whitefella" consciousness, transforming, if ever so slightly, our sense of landscape to a sense of "country."

Literature Cited

Anderson, C. (1992). Identifying groups for negotiations about land. In R. Hill (Ed.), *Cross cultural management of natural and cultural heritage* (pp. 74-85). Cairns, Queensland, Aust: Cairns College of Technical and Further Education.

Bayet, F. (1994). Overturning the doctrine: Indigenous people and wilderness—Being Aboriginal in the environmental movement. *Social Alternatives, 13,* 27-32.

Berger, P. and Luckmann, T. (1966). *The social construction of reality.* New York, NY: Anchor Books.

Berndt, R. and Berndt, C. (1968). Australian Aborigines: Blending past and present. In *Vanishing peoples of the earth* (pp. 114-131). Washington, DC: National Geographic Society.

Holy Bible (c), King James Version. Genesis 1:26

Birch, C. (1993). *Confronting the future: Australia and the world—the next hundred years.* Ringwood, Victoria, Aust: Penguin Books.

Birckhead, J. (1992-93). Traditional Aboriginal land management practices at Charles Sturt University: The cultural politics of a curriculum innovation. In J. Birckhead, T. De Lacy, and L. Smith (Eds.), *Aboriginal involvement in parks and protected areas* (pp. 297-306). Canberra, Australian Capital Territory: Aboriginal Studies Press.

Birckhead, J. and Smith, L. (1992-93). Introduction: Conservation and country—A reassessment. In J. Birckhead, T. De Lacy, and L. Smith (Eds.), *Aboriginal involvement in parks and protected areas* (pp. 1-5). Canberra, Australian Capital Territory, Aust: Aboriginal Studies Press.

Birckhead, J. and Wallis, A. (1994). An evaluation of the Cairns College of TAFE "Community Ranger" program: Final report. Albury, New South Wales, Aust: The Johnstone Center of Parks, Recreation, and Heritage.

Brady, V. (1991). Called by the land to enter the land. In C. Hammond (Ed.), *Creation spirituality and the dreamtime.* Sydney, New South Wales, Aust: Millennium Books.

Brady, V. (1994). *Caught in the draught.* Sydney, New South Wales, Aust: Angus and Robertson.

Brown, A. (1992). Wild place: Aboriginal place—A review essay. *Aboriginal Law Bulletin, 2* (56), 20-21.

Collins, J. (1993). Migrant hands in a distant land. In G. Whitlock and D. Carter (Eds.), *Images of Australia* (pp. 103-128). St. Lucia, Queensland, Aust: University of Queensland Press.

Cordell, J. (1993). Who owns the land? Indigenous involvement in Australian protected areas. In E. Kemf (Ed.), *The law of the mother—Protecting indigenous peoples in protected areas* (pp. 104-113). San Francisco, CA: Sierra Club Books.

De Lacy, T. (1994). The Uluru/Kakadu model—Anangu Tjukurrpa. 50,000 years of Aboriginal law and land management changing the concept of national parks in Australia. *Society and Natural Resources, 7*, 479-498.

De Lacy, T. and Lockwood, M. (1992). Economic valuation of natural areas. In M. Lockwood and T. De Lacy (Eds.), *Valuing natural areas: Applications and problems of the contingent valuation method* (pp. 1-16). Albury, New South Wales, Aust: The Johnstone Centre of Parks, Recreation and Heritage.

Foster, D. (1992-93). Applying the Yellowstone model in America's backyard: Alaska. In J. Birckhead, T. De Lacy, and L. Smith (Eds.), *Aboriginal involvement in parks and protected areas* (pp. 363-376). Canberra, Australian Capital Territory, Aust: Aboriginal Studies Press.

Hawthorne, S. and Klein, R. (1994). *Australia for women: Travel and culture*. Melbourne, Victoria, Aust: Spinifex Press.

Horne, D. (1988). *The lucky country*. Ringwood, Victoria, Aust: Penguin Books.

Jacobs, J. (1994). Earth honouring—Western desires and indigenous knowledges. *Meanjin, 53* (2), 305-314.

Kneebone, E. (1991). An Aboriginal response. In C. Hammond (Ed.), *Creation spirituality and the dreamtime* (pp. 87-94). Sydney, New South Wales, Aust: Millennium Books.

Lattas, A. (1990). Aborigines and contemporary Australian nationalism. In J. Marcus (Ed.), *Writing Australian culture: Text, society and national identity* (pp. 50-69). Social Analysis.

Lewis, H. (1993). Traditional ecological knowledge: Some definitions. In N. Williams and G. Baines (Eds.), *Traditional ecological knowledge: Wisdom for sustainable development* (pp. 8-12). Canberra, Australian Capital Territory, Aust: Centre For Resource And Environmental Studies, Australian National University.

Lines, W. (1991). *Taming the great southland: A history of the conquest of nature in Australia*. Sydney, New South Wales, Aust: Allen and Unwin.

Muecke, S. (1992). *Textual spaces: Aboriginality and cultural studies*. Sydney, New South Wales, Aust: University Press.

Pearson, N. (1994). A troubling inheritance. In P. Poynton (Ed.), *Aboriginal Australia: Land, law and culture* (pp. 1-9). Race and Class.

Pettman, J. (1992). *Living in the margins: Racism, sexism and feminism in Australia*. Sydney, New South Wales, Aust: Allen and Unwin.

Reynolds, H. (1987). *Frontier: Aborigines, settlers and land*. Sydney, New South Wales, Aust: Allen and Unwin.

Rintoul, S. (1993). *The wailing: A national black oral history*. Melbourne, Victoria, Aust: William Heinemann Australia.

Rolston, H. (1991). Creation and recreation: Environmental benefits and human leisure. In B. Driver, P. Brown, and G. Peterson (Eds.), *Benefits of leisure* (pp. 393-403). State College, PA: Venture Publishing, Inc.

Rose, D. (1988). Exploring an Aboriginal land ethic. *Meanjin, 47* (3), 378-387.

Rose, D. (1992). *Dingo makes us human: Life and land in an Australian Aboriginal culture*. Cambridge, UK: Cambridge University Press.

Rudder, G. (1992). Advertising and Australian nationalism. In A. Shiell and A. Stephen (Eds.), *The lie of the land* (pp. 36-37). Melbourne, Victoria, Aust: National Centre for Australian Studies, Monash University.

Rutherford, A. (Ed.). (1988). *Aboriginal culture today*. Sydney, New South Wales, Aust: Dangaroo Press.

Spearritt, P. (1992). The lie of the land. In A. Shiell and A. Stephen (Eds.), *The lie of the land* (pp. 1-6). Melbourne, Victoria, Aust: National Centre For Australian Studies, Monash University.

Stevens, S. (1986). *Inhabited national parks: Indigenous peoples in protected landscapes*. East Kimberley Working Paper No. 10: Canberra Centre for Resource and Environmental Studies, Australian National University.

Tjamiwa, T. (1992-93). Tjunguringkula Waakaripai: Joint management of Uluru National Park. In J. Birckhead, T. De Lacy and L. Smith (Eds.), *Aboriginal involvement in parks and protected areas* (pp. 7-11). Canberra, Australian Capital Territory, Aust: Aboriginal Studies Press.

Treaty 88 Campaign. (1988). Aboriginal sovereignty—Never ceded. In S. Janson and S. Macintyre (Eds.), Making the bicentenary (pp. 1-2). *Australian Historical Studies* (Special Issue).

Trouillot, M. (1991). Anthropology and the savage slot: The poetics and politics of otherness. In R. Fox (Ed.), *Recapturing uëthropology: Working in the present* (pp. 17-44). Santa Fe, NM: School of American Research Press.

Ward, R. (1992). The Australian legend. In G. Whitlock and D. Carter (Eds.), *Images of Australia* (pp. 179-190). St. Lucia, Queensland, Aust: University of Queensland Press.

Wescott, G. (1991). Australia's distinctive national parks system. *Environmental Conservation, 18* (4), 331-340.

Whitlock, G. and Carter, D. (Eds.). (1992). *Images of Australia*. St. Lucia, Queensland, Aust: University of Queensland Press.

CURRENT ENVIRONMENTAL ISSUES IN URBAN WESTERN EUROPE AND THEIR RELEVANCE TO A NEW LAND MANAGEMENT ETHIC

ROGER SIDAWAY
Research and Policy Consultant
Edinburgh, Scotland

CHAPTER 19

Introduction

This chapter considers current environmental issues in Western Europe which are likely to be relevant to the development of a new land management ethic in the U.S. It illustrates how hard-to-define values play a key role in structuring the debate over environmental issues within the developing political institutions of the European Union (EU). The chapter concentrates on the highly urbanized parts of Western Europe, mainly lowland areas in which the countryside has a largely symbolic value to society and in which any direct expression of the spiritual value of nature has been suppressed in recent generations. The chapter analyzes environmental values as they are represented in social institutions rather than at the level of the individual. The principal examples are drawn from Britain and the Netherlands with reference to the changing institutions of the EU. These areas provide a marked contrast to the Scandinavian countries described by Reunala in the next chapter. With the removal of woodland cover from much of Western Europe, the forest traditions have all but disappeared except for place names whose meanings are long forgotten save a few archaic figures of speech. However, in the more rural parts of Germany, France, and alpine Europe these traditions live on.

Similarities and Differences Within a Common Tradition

There are at least as many similarities as differences between the European and North American continents. Both contain considerable ethnic and religious diversity, share a common scientific culture, and play prominent roles in the global village of entertainment and media discourse. Within the world of leisure there are the commonalities of the dominance of television and video entertainment, a trend towards exercise, fitness and healthy living, and the commodification of leisure which has led to increasingly active participation in outdoor recreation.

Urban Living and Rural Nostalgia

Continent to continent, the differences in geographical scale may not be as large as supposed, although the major climatic habitat types (e.g., the mountain ranges) are probably more fragmented in Western Europe. These relatively remote areas are popular for recreation and tourism but do not have the cultural significance of wilderness as they do in the U.S. As Western Europe houses more people in a smaller area, any remaining wild areas are more accessible to more people. Meanwhile, greater attention is paid to the accessible areas closer to home which show many signs of human intervention but are nevertheless considered "natural."

In the fertile lowlands, a thriving agribusiness sector has transformed the land, and the agricultural population has declined (to less than 5 percent in Britain). There has been an increasing movement of population into rural areas, but the direct contact that most rural dwellers have with such relics of nature that remain in the landscape is no greater than that of their urban counterparts. Although this chapter concentrates on the dominant urban culture and its perceptions of nature, it is well to remember that in the upland areas, and around the Mediterranean regions, Western Europe still contains a relatively large peasant population. These rural areas remain relatively stable and conservative, as the weight of their tradition proves resistant to change. The rural communities remain a significant political force within the EU. These people and their land reinforce the urban dream that the countryside is, or should be, unchanging when compared to the turmoil of the rapid social, economic, and technological changes surrounding them. The countryside is therefore seen as a welcome haven of peace and quiet compared to the city.

This bucolic myth has been around for a long time, and its history has been skillfully analyzed by Raymond Williams (1975). He showed how each supposedly halcyon era was preceded by another perhaps 50 years earlier, each having a slightly different emphasis in the perceptions of the scenery, a rural way of life, or the role of the rural economy. The perpetuation of the bucolic myth helps to explain why countryside images are used in advertising and why the affluent migrate to their rural retreats in former agricultural dwellings, houses in former market towns, or suburban estates tacked on to the traditional villages. Certainly the values of these exurbanites are evident in their "not in my back yard" reactions to change.

In England, in particular, there is a romanticized nostalgic view of rural areas. It has its historical precedent in the Victorian response to rapid industrialization:

> *Progress, as the nineteenth century understood it, had become inimical to the vision of England as a green and pleasant land. Progress was creating a black and unpleasant land. The Victorians reacted to this tragic anomaly with contradictory attitudes . . . they continued to plunder nature in the interests of science, progress and money; and they demonstrated their affection for it by stuffing their houses and gardens with nature, and decorating their industrial products with loving images of it. How these contradictory attitudes came to be resolved was by swamping the whole subject of nature with nostalgia. . . . The advantage of nostalgia is always to have it both ways.*
>
> Mullins, 1985, p. 136

People, Politics and the State

It is perhaps in the political institutions of the two continents that some of the most marked distinctions need to be drawn. Representative democracy may be a common element, but it differs both in levels of participation and in its institutions. Both continents share a popular cynicism about politics and politicians, but it may be the case that while the voting levels in European elections are higher, there may be more active participation in local democracy in the U.S. at the local government meeting or in the Parent-Teacher Association.

The role and function of the state have been called into question more openly and rapidly in Western Europe. In an attempt to recreate "enterprise culture," the New Right in Europe has borrowed notions of deregulation from Reaganism and has set about reducing the role of the state with a vengeance. The vogue for privatization is perhaps most advanced in Britain with not only many public utilities and transportation networks being sold to private owners, but major sections of the Civil Service are also being moved into a twilight zone of management buy-outs and diminished public accountability.

The environmental agencies have not been immune to this exercise. The state Forestry Service (the Forestry Commission) has been forced by the present British government to sell areas of national forest, and it was threatened with privatization of its organization and assets. But just as in the seventeenth century when public outcry at the sale of royal forests eventually brought them into public ownership, so public protests have (temporarily at least) halted this privatization, although the piecemeal sale of forests continues. The opposition to privatization came from the timber industry concerned about its future supplies of raw material and from recreation organizations concerned about the loss of public access to forests sold to private owners. Meanwhile, any initiative to increase the conservation of environmental resources by land purchase has passed to nongovernmental organizations. Bodies like the Royal Society for the Protection of Birds in Britain and Natuurmonumenten in the Netherlands have become significant rural landowners while their membership and political influence has also increased dramatically in recent years.

The "withering" of the state is most pronounced in Britain where the antibureaucratic, antiplanning sentiments are strongest and are so frequently directed at the political and administrative institutions of the EU. Yet while national governments preach a rhetoric of decentralization, they practice the centralization of power. In recent years substantial areas of both national and local government have been removed from the scrutiny of parliament or locally elected councils and placed in the hands of "quasi-autonomous nongovernmental organizations" (QUANGOs), funded and controlled by national governments. The board members, commissioners or trustees who ostensibly direct these QUANGOs are accountable only to the government ministers who appoint them.

The Struggle for Power

Ironically, the main reason why the institutions of the EU are largely unaccountable to democratically elected representatives is that effective power resides with national governments who appoint the Council of Ministers and the Executive Commission. National governments oppose the development of federal institutions which might be responsible to the elected European Parliament and which might delegate functions to the regions, many of which have strong cultural identity, such as the Basque country, Catalonia, Scotland, and Wallonia. This power struggle helps explain the lack of collective political will to deal with economic and social problems that affect the community as a whole, such as unemployment, let alone matters of foreign policy.

Environmental policy is a notable exception. In the early days of the community, perhaps when the significance of these issues was not realized, the Council of Ministers gave the Commission limited responsibilities for "harmonizing" policy including agriculture and environmental issues. While the Commission can issue directives that are mandatory on the Member States, the details of implementation are largely a matter of national discretion.

Within the EU there is debate about reflecting a wider range of values within environmental policy and practice, but the context of that debate is the rival philosophies of the market and ecology, the continuing political struggle over the respective powers of national governments and potential federal institutions, attempts to standardize policy throughout the Union, and the aspirations of cultural minorities.

Current Environmental Issues

Protecting Landscape and Nature

Although some legislation to protect nature had been enacted in most countries of the EU within the first 25 years of this century, the protection of natural resource areas has taken markedly different forms. Belgium, Denmark, the former West Germany, Luxembourg, and Britain have given greater emphasis to landscape protection (i.e., measures to control development within cultural landscapes which may or may not be largely in private ownership). These countries, together with the Netherlands, have well over 10 percent of their land area designated for landscape or nature protection (Bischoff and Jongman, 1993). Although 25 percent of Britain is protected in this way, Scotland, the birthplace of John Muir, has no national parks.

The degree of protection afforded to designated areas varies considerably in each country, as do the criteria by which these areas are selected. However, it is probably fair to say that the protection of cultural landscapes is both an older tradition and based on a holistic concept of "natural beauty" which included wildlife and nature. Although attempts to use scientific, or quasi-scientific, techniques of landscape evaluation have been pursued on both sides of the Atlantic, the actual methods used to define scenic areas have been subjective, albeit applied in a consistent manner (Sidaway, 1990). In Britain they have been biased towards the scenic grandeur of the romantic cultural landscapes of England's Lake District, Wales' Snowdonia, and the western Highlands of Scotland while ignoring, for example, the subtleties of open landscape in eastern England and the southern uplands of Scotland. The values of cultural elites have been reinforced by professionals paying scant regard to broader public opinion. The battle over countryside aesthetics has been a furious one, the only consensus being over what constitutes intrusions, disfigurements, and eyesores.

The single-minded nature conservation perspective has its own critics. Barkham (1988) argues that a preoccupation with scientific rationality accompanied by a loss of passionate emotion has marginalized nature conservation to the status of a special interest group. Tracing the history of the movement in Britain over the last fifty years, he claims that its achievements have been largely symbolic—a network of national parks and nature reserves surrounded by the wholesale destruction of seminatural habitats in the wider countryside. "Nature conservationists have gained their just deserts and no more." He considers this is in part because of the philistine values of a society which may favor environmental protection in principle but which " . . . has been urbanized for so long that the majority have been profoundly out of touch with 'wildness' for generations" (Barkham, 1988).

Nevertheless, as the EU moves relentlessly towards standardization, more progress is likely to be made over nature designations with their seemingly objective criteria based on species assemblages and migratory bird populations which lend themselves to measurement or estimation. The failure to provide adequate criteria for landscape and other cultural values is likely to result in the dominance of nature and the neglect of humanity. This trend is already evident in the following themes.

Bringing Back Nature

It would be premature to claim environmental policy as a success story for the EU when the Common Agricultural Policy (CAP) is seen to be instrumental in promoting the loss of habitat and the removal of nature. Widely recognized as an attempt to maintain rural populations, financial support for agricultural production also has resulted in increased mechanization in the most productive areas. Major landscape features have been lost with consequent detrimental effects on wildlife while the pollution of water tables has increased dramatically through excessive application of fertilizers. Other dramatic developments with adverse ecological effects have been the increases in coastal tourism and the conversion of indigenous forests to plantations of exotic species.

However, the CAP problem could be turned into an opportunity if land is taken out of agricultural production and converted into areas devoted to nature conservation. Leading this initiative are the Dutch whose outstanding agricultural efficiency has contributed to one of the least natural landscapes in Europe. The engineering logic and skills they applied to winning land from the sea are now being devoted to "bringing back nature," but based on the premise that in a highly developed countryside one knows what nature is.

In Britain most of the areas that have been earmarked for landscape or nature protection are far from natural, indeed even the wilder areas are usually described as "seminatural." These landscapes are usually relics of former agricultural systems such as the English hedgerow. The hedgerow story is full of ironies. Many were planted in the eighteenth and nineteenth centuries as landowners used the Inclosure Acts to dispossess the peasantry from common land. More recently, farmers received financial payments from the Ministry of Agriculture to remove hedgerows in the name of agricultural efficiency. Now they can be protected by law.

If there are problems with the word "natural," there can surely be no difficulty with "native species." This, however, is where the environmental equivalent of political correctness comes in. The selection of trees for planting is no longer a question of practical silviculture but one of ecological purity. Part of the tradition of "landscape improvement," which dates back several centuries, was the collection of exotic species from many parts of the world. Private estates, which were planted in the eighteenth and nineteenth centuries, provided the experimental plots from which the foresters of the early twentieth century selected more productive species. Trees from the Pacific Northwest suited the British climate, and Sitka spruce has become ubiquitous in British monocultural plantations. But to the purist there are problems with earlier introductions such as the sycamore introduced by the Romans or even the common English elm introduced before England separated from the continental landmass. There is no consistent logic to the argument as to why any particular period of history or any geographical boundary should be preferred to any other.

As English rapidly becomes the lingua franca of the EU, the Dutch have taken liberties with English usage to coin the phrase "nature development" which incorporates two concepts that conflict in English culture. Their definition of the term nature is more elastic, too, as nature areas in the Netherlands include plantations, albeit of broad-leafed species, which would be considered unnatural in Britain. Yet the British pioneered an earlier form of nature development. Faced with a timber shortage after the two World Wars, marginal agricultural land, mainly in the western uplands, was bought by the Forestry Commission and converted into plantations. Almost invariably the pioneer species were exotic conifers. However, their "alien" nature and the ruthless two-dimensional geometry of plantation design offended the landscape aesthetics of the English. Rolt's description of a "dark and deadening blanket of alien conifers" comparing the plantations to a "vegetable concentration camp" is not an unusual reaction (Rolt, 1977). Indeed he is continuing a tradition started 150 years earlier by William Wordsworth who attacked the planting of Scotch firs and larches which "disfigured" the Lake District.

Plantations in the British uplands clash not only with aesthetic sensibilities, but they also conflict with another important cultural value, that of "freedom to roam"—the ability to walk at will in any direction in open countryside. Rolt also complains about the foresters' fences "so wantonly blocking ancient tracks and footpaths" as well as the "arbitrary rule by a hand utterly unmoved by any tenderness or reverence for the lovely natural folds and curves of the landscape" (1977, p. 60).

Perhaps it is an inherent trait of "nature developers" that they lack "tenderness or reverence" to earlier cultural traditions. Evans (1993) refers to the recent removal of "weed" tree species from formal landscapes designed in the eighteenth century as acts of "botanical cleansing" in the name of "historical correctness." Another recent example is the destruction, in the name of ecologically sound "critical forestry," of an avenue of trees steeped in historical tradition at Sparenswoud near Hilversum in the Netherlands. Or there is the definition of nature that excludes people and sets aside nature areas with no public access for recreation in the name of the "precautionary principle" (Taylor, 1991). Such clashes of ideology can bring about the severest of conflicts. Yet, only as recently as 1969, the Union for the Conservation of Nature defined conservation as the "rational use of the environment to achieve the highest quality of living for mankind." Even now the debate continues in many voluntary conservation organizations as to whether "their" nature reserves should be open for public enjoyment, as John Muir (1898) advocated, so as to increase knowledge and awareness of conservation, or whether they should be immune from further human influence.

Public Access and Appropriate Recreational Use

It could be argued that attitudes towards public access for recreation on private land give an indication of the extent to which land is seen as a common resource. Within Western Europe the arrangements vary between:

1. general rights or traditions of access on forested or uncultivated land (freedom to roam);

2. public rights to use paths or tracks across private land on foot, horseback, or by vehicle;

3. payment to landowners to use private land or water for particular forms of recreation; and

4. various combinations of these arrangements.

The most marked contrast is between those European countries where the first or the third of those categories predominate. In Norway and Sweden, which have relatively little cultivated land, general rights of access are part of the cultural heritage. In the more intensively cultivated and more densely populated countries, such as France and the Netherlands, private ownership takes precedence over limited public rights (Scott, 1991).

Whatever the arrangements may be, they are under increasing pressure from changing recreational demands, from concerns about the impacts on habitats and species, and from resistant landowners. Recreational interests have become politically organized to protect or extend their access rights. The situation is particularly polarized in Britain and the Netherlands. Although the conflict is usually described as recreation versus nature, there are often deeper undercurrents between walkers and landowners, between recreation and nature developers, and between different recreation activities.

Three types of argument can be used to exclude recreational use from nature areas or to restrict it to a group of "appropriate activities." These can be arguments of principle, of biological impact, or of social impact. Arguments of principle might distinguish between machines or vehicles and nature, thereby excluding motor vehicles or mountain bikes. Evidence of damaging impacts is not necessarily clear-cut, for while one mountain bike in adverse conditions can have noticeable effects, many more feet trampling over a longer period can be cumulatively more damaging. However, these arguments are frequently used to mask the sensibilities of one user group on another. Occasionally the arguments are widened to include "noisy" or "intrusive" sports. But the characteristic feature of such disputes is that existing users (e.g., walkers) are concerned about the social characteristics of a new and challenging group such as mountain bikers or motorcyclists. Carolyn Harrison (1991) describes how an elite set of values, which she terms the "countryside aesthetic," dominate outdoor recreation in Britain. This analysis has wider implications for any study of the social institutions and the way in which they recognize hard-to-define values.

Conclusions on European Problems

RESOURCE PROTECTION

The debate over establishing criteria for designating areas to protect landscape and nature within Europe is part of a wider debate about the limits of science. Attempts to use objective and/or scientific criteria to assess landscape quality are at least temporarily in abeyance while use of science to legitimate the selection of nature conservation areas is also in question. In the latter case the criteria may be objective and even quantitative but they are conventionally or arbitrarily selected nevertheless.

BRINGING BACK NATURE

Nature, native, and natural appear to be equally difficult to define, and certainly the terms are not applied consistently throughout Europe. If nature protection has been concerned with conserving historic features, and thus has been open to accusations of rural nostalgia, nature development may give rise to similar anomalies. But despite any definitional or semantic difficulties, the practice could prove popular in many European countries as long as it is not associated with the total exclusion of recreation. Opinions vary as to whether nature can exist without humanity.

PUBLIC ACCESS AND APPROPRIATE RECREATION

Any discussion of appropriateness masks a deeper seated debate about access and social equity. Values such as "appropriate" behavior are set by dominant groups in society, and if the political institutions which control access do not consciously provide for minorities, the values of the dominant group prevail.

Problems Common to the Two Continents

Are there parallels between what is happening in rural America and urbanized Western Europe, and are there lessons to be transferred across the Atlantic? There are certainly common trends in taste and behavior. The trends identified in the introductory chapter to this volume—heightened demand for recreation opportunities, changes in lifestyle and lifestyle management, concerns about environmental quality, distrust of government, and deregulation—are all evident in Western Europe. They may take somewhat different forms and some aspects may be accentuated from country to country, but there are many broad parallels.

The Role of Science in Evaluation

At the most general level there is the common problem of how society deals with social and environmental change and how to incorporate new values or restore old ones in public policy decision making. The brief consideration of three contemporary problems of natural resource management in Western Europe presented in this chapter suggests some obvious parallels with the U.S. For example, the attachment to the rural way of life on the part of the affluent exurbanite or the support given to the peasant farmer which stems from long-standing cultural values is as powerful as any recent political dogma. These values are poorly expressed by science although they feature prominently in many conflicts over conservation and development.

The problem of putting a value on the invaluable has been confronted many times. Rolt (1977) is among those who have been concerned about the relation between people and nature and/or the intangible aspects of landscape. An engineer fascinated by nature, Rolt (1977) tried to resolve the internal contradictions in his own thinking. He was attracted by medieval thinking of the world as a cosmos and humanity's place in it, more so than any subsequent scientific view of the universe. But he concluded that "the pursuit of truth is an endless journey into undiscovered country" and that any scientific laws are only partially true and so are frequently proved invalid by the next generation of scientists. In effect, he is among those who suggest that evaluation is an eternal problem that is never satisfactorily resolved; it merely reflects changing values—a true dilemma (Rolt, 1977).

Indeed, science today is in something of a quandary as it loses many of its certainties and is engaged in territorial disputes with the arts, religion, and philosophy. Nowhere is this better illustrated than in the current debate about conservation and whether it has a mystical or scientific basis. Many see science overstepping its bounds in attempting to quantify or explain matters that are not its proper concern.

For most of us the problem isn't that the official scientific view is bad or wrong. The trouble is what it leaves out. It has nothing useful to say about love, beauty, purpose, mind or meaning. And these things matter to people far more than the physical aspects that can be measured by scientists or economists.

Schwarz, 1986

And as Kidel and Rowe-Leete argue,

. . . Some cultures have never set human consciousness apart from nature in quite the same way. (1986)

Fraser Harrison, meanwhile, living in one of the smaller rural communities whose surroundings have been radically changed by contemporary agriculture, comments on the inadequacy of contemporary thinking in dealing with conservation problems:

. . . despite this wealth of new knowledge, we no longer know how to respond emotionally and philosophically to nature. We lack an aesthetic which, on the one hand accommodates the awful fact that nature is being killed off, and on the other, expresses once more our age-old sense of spiritual and imaginative identification with it.

Harrison, 1986, pp. 8-9

Thus it may well be that the problem we are examining is not amenable to scientific investigation and research.

Incorporating Hard-to-Define Values in Land Management

As there is no exact equivalent of the federal lands in Western Europe, the problem of how hard-to-define values could be incorporated into a land management ethic is not being addressed here. There are attempts to find a new paradigm within the general rubric of sustainability. Attempts are being made to apply and refine this concept, and some of them make a conscious effort to include cultural as well as natural values. "Different disciplines have contributed their own perspectives to sustainability. The economic and ecological domains are most generally recognized. It is believed that the concept also has significant social and cultural dimensions" (Countryside Commission, 1993).

Holland and Rawles (1993) argue that judgments of value are always open to challenge, that rather than values being "things that we reason *from,*" they are "what we reason *towards*—things that we work out or discover through a process of critical discussion" [their emphasis]. They argue that nature (which in Europe might be defined by the degree of human intervention) might provide a better focus for conservation than the health of the land or the defense of natural capital. Their justification is that it is the relationship with nature (rather than features of nature) which provides the very content of existence.

> *Nature embodies the history of life on Earth and carries so much of our history with it. By keeping in touch with nature we are keeping in touch with our history. This does not so much show that nature is good as explain why we find it important. . . . At the same time, conservation has as much to do with conserving the future as conserving the past. It is not, however, simply about preserving the potential for future exuberance, but about preserving the future as a realization of the potential of the past . . . [his emphasis]. The rationale of conservation is not to be gleaned from a mere synthesis of subjective interests but rather established through a process of critical debate. . . . Conservation is about negotiating the transition from past to future in such a way as to secure the transfer of maximum significance.*
>
> Rolt, 1977

The Appropriate Level of Decision Making in a Representative Democracy

Is the top down perspective the right one? Perhaps there are elements of an older order that provide superior perspectives. Older traditions of European forestry carried a certainty that traditional forest practices were right, practices that are now being rediscovered as "sustainable forestry." But they were often practiced within the tight community of the commune which managed the forest around the village. The village elders making decisions on the commune's behalf might seem autocratic and undemocratic, but, placed in a more democratic framework, the disciplines of working within consensus on a local scale might produce a broader and more appropriate set of values. Certainly bottom up approaches have their attractions in many parts of Europe compared to the top down domination of self-interest groups purporting to act in the national interest.

Among the environmental agencies, the U.S. Forest Service in particular has strived to involve the public in its decision making, but there are few similar initiatives in Europe. The professional can perform a number of roles as information provider, researcher, facilitator, or arbiter. Perhaps the professional should represent the public interest by being more concerned with the process of decision making and its fairness to the parties involved rather than in being the expert decision maker. Should one not have faith that the requisite values will find their own spokespersons?

Conclusion

Many parts of Western Europe are highly urbanized and changing rapidly, but although their inhabitants have little direct contact with nature, their need for nature remains. It may take the form of visiting the countryside for recreation or purchasing commodities which use rural nostalgia as part of their marketing. In other words, the cultural relationship takes many different forms, and no one group has the prerogative to define nature. Any such attempt to secure exclusive domination by a narrowly focused biocentrism is likely to conflict with other vital values. The need for access to nature is as valid as the need to protect habitats, species or special areas; the degree of access has to be negotiated.

The key to greater understanding is to recognize that nature is a human construct that helps define our relationship to our history and our future. That relationship, whether it is expressed as nature, conservation, or sustainability, is a relationship between cultural interests. The form that it takes at any point in time is a temporary stage in a continuing process of redefinition. We therefore need to pay close attention to how such a definition is derived and devise social institutions that help different cultures or groups in society negotiate new definitions. This need to democratize decision making is particularly acute in Western Europe. There are more innovative forms of decision making being developed in the U.S. and in Europe we need to consider how we can apply some of the principles of "alternative dispute resolution." Such reform is more likely to come about from the grass roots than by innovation at the top.

The implications of what is happening in Western Europe for the development of a new land management ethic in the U.S. relate to broad principles rather than detailed content. In a multicultural pluralistic society, it may be unrealistic to strive for a single all-encompassing ethic. It may be more realistic to seek, instead, a general approach which allows for cultural variation, which incorporates urban as well as rural values and can be adapted at local and regional levels. It has to cover the backyard as well as the nationally prestigious pristine areas, and it has to be applied in both public and private domains. This means it is the process of how the ethic is derived, who is involved in its formulation, and the philosophies that it embraces that are as important as the ethical content itself.

Literature Cited

Barkham, J. (1988). Developing the spiritual. *ECOS*, 13-21.

Bischoff, N. and Jongman, R. (1993). *Development of rural areas in Europe: The claim for nature*. The Hague, Netherlands: Scientific Council for Government Policy.

Countryside Commission. (1993). *Sustainability and the English countryside*. Position statement. Cheltenham, UK: Countryside Commission.

Evans, P. (1993). Weedkillers. *The Guardian, 3*. 12. 93, 14-15.

Harrison, C. (1991). *Countryside recreation in a changing society*. London, UK: TMS Partnership.

Harrison, F. (1986). *The living landscape*. London, UK: Pluto Press.

Holland, A. and Rawles, K. (1993). Values in conservation. *ECOS, 14*(1), 14-19.

Kidel, M. and Rowe-Leete, S. (1986). The wilderness that baffles modern man. *The Guardian, 29*. 1. 86.

Muir, J. (1898). Wild parks and forest reservations of the west. *Atlantic Monthly, 81*:15-28.

Mullins, E. (1985). *A love affair with nature: A personal view of British art*. Oxford, UK: Phaidon.

Rolt, L. (1977). *Landscape with canals: An autobiography*. London, UK: Allen Lane.

Schwarz, W. (1986). What sanctuary from science. *The Guardian, 28*. 10. 86.

Scott, P. (1991). *Countryside access in Europe: A review of access rights, legislation and provision in selected European countries*. An unpublished report prepared for the Countryside Commission for Scotland.

Sidaway, R. (1990). Contemporary attitudes to landscape and implications for policy: A research agenda. *Landscape Research, 15*, 2, 2-6.

Taylor, P. (1991). The precautionary principle and the prevention of pollution. *ECOS, 12*(4), 41-46.

Williams, R. (1975). *The country and the city*. St. Albans, UK: Paladin.

Cultural and Spiritual Forest Values in Scandinavia

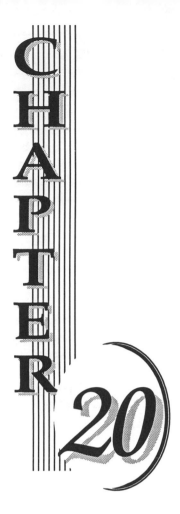

Aarne Reunala
Finnish Forest Research Institute
Helsinki, Finland

Introduction

This chapter describes the importance of forests in Scandinavia, especially in Finland, Norway, and Sweden. In these scarcely populated countries forests have always been, and still are, a major economic resource which has been used in a multitude of different ways. Cultural forest traditions are rich, and a foreigner easily feels the special value given to the forests. Scandinavians' relationship to their forests is described with the aid of a three-level classification:

1. archetypal forest values, common to all humanity;

2. cultural forest values specific to a certain culture—in this case, Scandinavia; and,

3. psychological, individual forest values.

From my experience, this classification scheme helps land managers and others better understand the deep importance of intangible forest values.

Scandinavia

By Scandinavia one generally means the five Nordic countries: Denmark, Finland, Iceland, Norway and Sweden. This chapter, however, is limited to the three most forested countries—Finland, Norway, and Sweden—where people's relationship to nature is very similar because of an abundance of northern boreal forests and relatively scarce population. The land area of these three Scandinavian countries is larger than France and Germany combined, but their population amounts to only 18 million. There are fifteen to twenty times more forest per inhabitant in Scandinavia than in Central Europe. Scandinavians have always depended on forests, and they have gained a livelihood from them in innumerable ways.

Finland is the most forested and most forest dependent of the three countries. Old eastern (Boreal-Siberian) forest traditions, beliefs, and attitudes are more prominent than in its neighboring countries to the west. Northern Sweden is much like Finland, but southern Sweden is, historically and culturally, closer to Central European agricultural traditions. Besides forest traditions, Norway is characterized by its orientation to the sea, fishing, and high, treeless mountains. For Norwegians nature means mountains, forests, and sea.

Although I try to cover the three countries objectively, the reader should recognize that Finland is my principal focus. Especially in Southern and Middle Sweden, one can hardly find the positive attachments to forests that I describe later, because for hundreds of years farming, not the forests, has been the principal source of livelihood for the population. Traditional attitudes toward the forest are, therefore, negative because forests have threatened to "take back" the painfully cleared fields (Kardell, 1990a).

In Finland, Norway, and Sweden forests can be seen everywhere. More than two-thirds of Finland's and Sweden's land area is covered by forests. In Norway the percentage is lower, 27 percent, because of the abundance of treeless mountains. Forests are mainly coniferous, of two principal species: Norway spruce (picea abies) and scots pine (pinus silvestris). Hardwoods, mainly silver birch (betula verrucosa), and ten to fifteen other species like alder, ash, aspen and maple grow most often in small groups or as scattered single trees among spruce and pine stands. In southern Sweden, as in Denmark, hardwood forests of oak and beech are also found. On average, hardwoods comprise 10 to 20 percent of stands.

From south to north, variation between forests is considerable. In the north and on the mountains forests are limited by treeless tundra. Trees grow much slower, and forests are less dense than in the south. In the north, 120 to 200 years is needed for the growth of large-sized timber whereas in the south 70 to 100 years is enough (Kuusela, 1990).

Forest Use History

About 10,000 years ago hunters and fishermen occupied the land bit by bit after the retreating glaciers. Forests were used, besides hunting, for all necessities of life: firewood, construction wood, berries, material for clothes, shoes, tools and weapons. When commerce developed, furs were the first exchange product in order to get valuable goods like salt and jewelry.

Farming was introduced to Scandinavia over 5,000 years ago, but it was only during the first millennium that permanent agriculture and animal husbandry began to have practical importance. Most fertile forests were cleared for cultivation, and forests were used as pasture for domestic animals, mainly cows and horses. Forest pasturage ended only in the twentieth century with the emergence of modern agriculture. Nowadays many people miss the traditional pastured forest landscapes with crooked trees and good visibility because of lack of brush layer. Many people still remember the beautiful forest paths of their childhood and accuse the forestry practices for their disappearance. They don't know that the real cause is the absence of pasturing cattle.

Along with permanent agriculture, an even more ancient form of culture, swidden cultivation, or slash and burn cultivation, remained part of forest use on less fertile soils and in remote regions. The forest was burned, and the soil was used for cultivation while it was productive. The land then was left for nature to reforest. With the help of swidden cultivation, permanent habitation spread all over Scandinavia. On good soils, burning was beneficial for the regeneration of forest ecosystems in the same way that forest fires have regularly regenerated boreal coniferous forests. On less fertile soils, repeated burning resulted in a loss of fertility and poor stands which prompted many nineteenth-century foresters to express concern about forest destruction. Swidden cultivation ended only in the beginning of the twentieth century when increasing timber prices made it unprofitable (Raumolin, 1987).

Tar, especially important for ship building, was produced by burning pine wood in a specially constructed pit. Finland and Sweden became Europe's main producers because of the abundance of suitable raw material. In Sweden, following German traditions, mainly old pine trees and stumps were used as raw material with relatively small effects on the forest ecosystems. In Finland, on the other hand, middle-aged and young pine trees were burned resulting in forest deterioration. Tar was Finland's main export product in the seventeenth and eighteenth centuries. The history of tar ended along with the end of wooden ship building. Tar burning is now only a historical curiosity, kept alive only for historical and tourism interests.

Besides tar, wood was used for the production of charcoal and potash which tended to degenerate into overuse and forest destruction. Iron industries were important users of charcoal, and around the industrial sites charcoal was by far the most important forest product. The oldest forest legislation in Scandinavia aimed at restricting the population's local use of forests in order to protect the interests of the iron industry and its need for charcoal.

Throughout history the use of wood for domestic needs has been extremely important and varied. Buildings were constructed of timber and roofs were covered with wooden shingles. Wood was the most important domestic fuel and is still generally used in rural habitations. Wood was used for fences, furniture, tools, dishes, shovels, ladles, scoops, bowls, and baskets. Wooden torches were used as a source of light. Sleighs and carts were made of wood. Birch bark was used for boxes, baskets, shoes, and inner soles of leather footwear. In particularly severe famine years flour was made of pine bark.

The use of wood was so varied and important that it would not be an exaggeration to speak of the "Scandinavian Wood Age" which ended with the advent of industrialization in the twentieth century (Gunnarson, 1988; Kardell, 1990a; Liie, 1923; Persson, 1977; Reunala and Heikinheimo, 1987). It was only in the 1950s that industrial use of wood surpassed in volume the domestic use of firewood and construction wood.

Forest Use After Industrialization

At the end of the nineteenth century, developing timber industries began to change patterns of forest use. Because of rising timber prices, forests were now cut for timber sales, and swidden cultivation and tar burning ended. Timber fellings and transport offered much needed work to rural people and timber sale revenues allowed farmers to modernize their agriculture. A standard of living never before seen was now accessible to an increasingly larger rural population. One consequence of increasing timber prices was the development of modern silviculture and its many organizations.

The number of people employed in forestry reached its peak after World War II and has since decreased gradually. The economic importance of forestry and forest industries has, however, remained strong. The relative growth of timber prices assured a steady increase of income in the rural regions until the abrupt fall of prices after 1991. Forest industries remain among the most important export industries amounting to 40 percent of Finland's export revenues. The corresponding figure for Sweden is 16 percent.

Timber felling for forest industries has increased steadily in the twentieth century. After World War II, new technology was introduced and mechanization of forestry advanced rapidly. A forest was a factor of production which had to be used as effectively as possible in order to increase the material wealth of society. Timber growth was enhanced with increasing investments in forest improvement. Artificial regeneration, soil preparation, and herbicides and fertilizers were widely used. Infrastructure was improved by forest road building and drainage of peatlands. After the middle of the 1970s, the intensity of forest operations slowed down as a consequence of economic crisis and improved timber balance. The emerging environmental criticism against intensive forestry had an effect. From the viewpoint of nature-based values, intensive forest management did not differ during the first half of the twentieth century. Its main objective was the same—production of valuable timber. Methods and machines were more effective in the latter half of the twentieth century.

Industrialization, urbanization, and an improving standard of living also brought new values with them; namely, nature recreation and nature protection. Traditionally, hunting, fishing, and berry picking had been normal practices for many rural families. Often they were also pleasurable practices. It was only with a higher standard of living, more free time, and an increasingly urban population that these old forest activities began to be thought of as "recreation." Nowadays, hunters number in the hundreds of thousands, and more than half of Scandinavian families go berry and mushroom picking in the forests.

A small upper class has spent their summer holidays in specially constructed summer houses since the end of the nineteenth century, but it was only the economic growth after World War II that made summer houses accessible for middle and working class families. Urban Scandinavian families want to experience the simple life close to nature during their holidays. In their summer houses Scandinavians can feel the life of their ancestors and practice the same simple activities like gardening, cutting wood, and building fires that were so important to their forefathers. Summer houses are an escape from stressful urban life, but above all, they are a cultural tie to the life of past generations. The number of summer houses has increased steadily in recent years.

There are many other forms of forest recreation. Developed originally as a necessity, cross-country skiing is the most popular winter sport in Scandinavia. Orienteering, where one employs way-finding skills similar to those used by former rural generations, is a popular summer sport. Backpacking has its supporters, especially in Norway. Special recreation forests have been established around big cities since the 1960s. They are important and popular, but, in the last few years, visitor numbers have stabilized and even declined in some places (Kardell, 1990b). In general, the need for special recreation forests is not as great as in many other countries because there is a tradition of free access to all forests.

The first national parks were established in Scandinavia at the beginning of the twentieth century. Foresters were active and successful in promoting remarkable areas for protection. The harmony between forestry and nature conservation ended in the 1960s when the new international environmental movement emerged. New environmentalism not only demanded new protected areas, but also claimed that principles and practices of modern forestry led to the destruction of natural forest ecosystems. Since there is a limit to growth, forestry should also be more careful in its efforts to intensify production. For almost thirty years, conflicts between production and protection values of forests have been regular issues on the public scene.

Besides its environmental dimension, criticism of forestry practices has almost always had a cultural/emotional dimension. Intensified timber production has been felt not only as a threat to natural forest ecosystems but also to cultural and spiritual values attached to forest landscapes and earlier "real" forests. A cultivated forest is not felt to be a "real" forest in Scandinavia (Reunala and Heikinheimo, 1987).

Archetypal Forest Values

Intangible forest values are difficult to grasp. In the following discussion I divide them into three classes: archetypal values, common to all humanity; cultural values, typical to a certain culture; and psychological values, which vary individually.

Forests have been essential for the existence and economic well-being of Scandinavians, but at the same time people have, by looking at nature, grasped something about the meaning of life. Forests and trees are powerful symbols of life, "archetypes" in Jungian terminology (see Schroeder, Chapter Five, in this volume).

Lennart Meri, a well-known anthropologist who is, at present, the President of Estonia, has described how the belief in a World Tree probably originated. Scandinavian mythology tells the same story. In ancient times people wondered how the sun, moon, and the stars could hang up in the sky without falling down. When one had a stone in one's hand and opened one's fingers, the stone fell out. Why didn't the sky and the stars fall? The evident answer was that something supported the sky, and it was, wise men said, a huge pole or a huge tree. Nobody had seen it, but it was in the mythical center of the Earth. In Scandinavian mythology, the holy ash tree was called *Yggdrasil* (Reunala, 1987).

From this original image of the World Tree which is spread all over the world were born innumerable beliefs and customs, in which the tree and wood have a good, protective function. Some customs, like dancing around the Maypole, or Finno-Ugrians' habit of building their dwellings as miniatures of the universe, with a ceremonial pole in the center of the hut, had a kind of religious function of strengthening the good order of the universe. In many other customs, trees, wood, and branches were used to protect people in the same manner as the World Tree protected the universe. Special memorial trees and other sacred trees protected the household and brought good luck. If a broken branch fell from a house tree, somebody in the family was soon to die. A farmer might leave a tree to protect the land's fertility in the middle of a burned clearing. Wooden objects, foliage, and branches were used in spells for curing diseases, protecting people and domestic animals, bringing good luck in hunting and fishing, and arousing affection. There was a kind of sacred unity between people and trees.

Traces of these old habits are still seen in Scandinavia. Some years ago in eastern Finland an old woman told me that in her childhood it was a custom to paint some parts of cows with tar every spring when the animals were let out to pasture in the forest for the first time after winter. It was believed that the tar protected the cows from snakes. Tar is prepared from wood, so it was immediately evident to me that I was being told a true story of an extremely old protective World Tree myth and belief. I had a strong feeling of history speaking.

What is also remarkable is that World Tree customs are not only history but also everyday reality even in urban Scandinavians' lives. People just don't think about it. A Maypole is still raised at Midsummer festivals, and Midsummer and Easter bonfires are burned. Midsummer fires are big events in many cities, even in the Scandinavian capitals of Helsinki, Stockholm, and Oslo. The original purpose of fires was protection from evil spirits and disease. The Christmas tree is a relatively young World Tree symbol, which originated in Germany in the seventeenth century and spread to Scandinavia in the nineteenth century. The Midsummer birch, at the house entrance, has the same role as the Christmas tree; confirming and protecting the course of the year. The use of a birch whisk in the sauna and willow branches at Easter are heirs of the old healing spells. The well-known saying "touch wood" probably has its origin in the World Tree beliefs. (At least the meaning of the saying is the same as in all World Tree customs; to protect a person from a possible misfortune.) A common feature of all these present customs is that they are practiced ritually every year, even if people do not know or question the meaning of them. The customs are continued because one has always done so (Gunnarsson, 1988; Liie, 1923; Persson, 1977; Reunala, 1987).

World Tree customs are spread all over the world, but they are probably more common in Scandinavia than in other Western countries. For example, an ancient ceremony after bear hunting in which the skull of the bear was hung on a tree in order to send the bear's spirit back to heaven was still practiced in Finland at the end of the nineteenth century—the last remaining place of this custom in Europe. The bear-skull tree was, of course, a symbol of the World Tree, uniting heaven and Earth (Pentikäinen, 1994).

A study made by a Japanese research group (Kitamura, Shidei, Isida, Sugahara, and Akasaka, 1986) seems to confirm the importance of these old myths and beliefs in Scandinavia. Researchers asked how people felt about forests and trees, and, especially, if they felt a kind of spiritual unity with them. Comparisons were made between a sample of persons from Finland, Germany, France, and Japan with the result that in Finland people's closeness with trees, forests, and even stones, was somewhat stronger than in other countries. The majority of Finns felt, for example, that there are spirits in trees and other natural objects.

Cultural Forest Values

The fact that forests have throughout history been a major source of livelihood in Scandinavia has deep significance for Scandinavian forest attitudes and values. Forests are felt to be a national property, like insurance that gives security in an uncertain world. Their existence is highly valued because they have provided a livelihood for every generation. This feeling was expressed by a Finnish nineteenth-century author who said that without forest cover human life would not be possible in these northern conditions (Reunala and Virtanen, 1987).

Another important factor which explains forest feelings and attitudes in Scandinavia is that there exists a traditional common right of access to all forests. Everybody is free to walk, ski, pick berries and mushrooms, and even stay overnight in any forest, with the condition that no damage is done and the owner is not disturbed. Free access exists not only in publicly owned forests but also in forests owned by private families or industrial companies. This free access strengthens the feeling that forests are common national property, important for everybody.

The existence of this customary right shows how wide and deeply rooted forest traditions are in Scandinavia. Common right of access to privately owned land is especially important because only about 25 percent of the forest area is in public ownership. When all forests are open for recreation, the need for specially managed recreation forests is not as important as in many other countries and, therefore, good recreation opportunities can be offered with little investment. Because of the abundance of forests, recreational use is frequently so dispersed that it does not cause inconveniences to the owner. It is worth mentioning that two-thirds of Scandinavian forests are owned by private families, at one time by farmers, but nowadays most often by ordinary urban families who have inherited forest property.

It is hard to say what is an "economic" and what is a "spiritual" value when a long history of varied forest use has resulted in a kind of feeling that forests are important for people's very existence (Opetusministeriö, 1993). This could be called a spiritual value and is a part of Scandinavians' forest experience. Ten years ago there was a wide publicity campaign in Finland organized by the forest industries, the main message of which was condensed in the slogan "Finland lives from the forest." Opinion polls showed afterwards that nine out of ten Finns agreed with the slogan.

That forests are important can also be called a cultural value because it is based on economic and cultural history. Every Scandinavian learns, both at home and at school, that forests are important. History speaks to Scandinavians in their forests. It is a history of past generations' lives and their struggle for a better future.

The strong cultural traditions attached to forests are easy to see in all art forms. Scandinavian music, literature, painting, cinema, architecture, and popular arts all reflect the importance of forests. A literary critic summarized Finnish literature by saying that it has only one theme: from forest to town. Of course, forests are not a rare theme in other countries' arts either, but in Scandinavia, especially in Finland, it is something central, representing the very essence of life in these northern countries (Osuuskunta, 1962; Reunala and Virtanen, 1987; Sörlin, 1983).

In Scandinavia there is only one traditional cultural minority, the Lapps. There are about 20,000 Lapps living in the northernmost parts of Norway, Sweden, and Finland. Their traditional economy is based on reindeer husbandry, fishing, and hunting (even if most of them are now integrated into the main population in the sense that they live in permanent residences, and many have ordinary rural and urban professions). Lapps have their own language which only recently has been developed into a written form which can be used at schools in teaching the language.

In the Lapps' relationship to nature one can still find archetypal myths and images. Nature is full of spirits. All living and nonliving objects, like stones, mountains, and streams have their own spirit. They are feeling beings and can communicate with humans. This communication means communion, belonging together. "The forest is part of me," says a Finnish Lapp, "as necessary a part as my ability to speak or to think. Without the forest, I would not exist" (Aikio, 1994).

Lapps do not think that they own the land or the forest in the same way that other Scandinavians speak about land ownership. By "their" forest the Lapps mean quite a large area around their house where they are used to hunting and fishing. Legal ownership doesn't have much to do with the area they feel is theirs. They do not say that they "own" this area; they "are one with their forest."

Lapps have always used nature for their livelihood; therefore, they do not appreciate strict nature conservation, which forbids all human activities. They have always lived with nature, used it, and respected it. The forest is their companion. It can be used with respect, but not as a one-dimensional object of utility. The relationship between Lapps and nature can be described as a kind of symbiosis.

Lapps do not have special, holy places in the forest, which should be specially protected in forest management. Nature spirits are everywhere; hence spiritual values should be taken into account in all forests. It is, however, the opinion of some Lapps that their traditional knowledge is not transferable to the main Scandinavian culture. Therefore, in order to respect spiritual values, the only solution is to let Lapps themselves take care of forest management (Aikio, 1994). This is not easily done, because the majority of the area inhabited by Lapps is owned by the State and managed by national Forest Services.

The mythical way of experiencing nature is not shared by all Lapps because their cultural identity has been so strongly influenced by the dominant Scandinavian culture. Keeping with traditional cultural values is only one survival strategy of minorities. Many Lapps have tried to integrate themselves into the majority and its culture, but many have also fallen into cultural disintegration and rootlessness.

Psychological Forest Values

In people's experiences of nature there is something general that is basically similar all over the world, something special that is culturally defined, and something completely unique and individual, because as all individuals differ so do their nature experiences and values. There seem to be several kinds of psychological values attached to the forests.

First, forests belong, in anthropologists' terminology, to a so-called "outer circle," an environment which is outside the permanent habitation. The world is divided in two: a familiar home and its surroundings and the unfamiliar, unknown, exterior world away from home (Anttonen, 1994).

When people have had difficulties in their everyday familiar environment, they have sought escape in the exterior world which in Scandinavia is the forest. People have escaped the law in the forests. They have escaped enemies during war. But it has also been common to escape to forests when family life or social life has been unhappy and stressful. One of the central themes in Finnish traditional folk poetry is the lonely, rejected person who in his sadness goes alone to the forest and cries to the trees, his only friends (Järvinen, 1984).

In Scandinavian literature and poetry forests are most often described as pleasant places, where people feel free from the obligations and stresses of society. Ordinary people today, when describing their forest experiences or a weekend at their summer house, invariably say how free and relaxed they were in the forest, and how they replenished their strength and energy there. A weekend in the countryside is a kind of spiritual and physical revival.

These positively felt experiences can have two sources. They can be motivated by a desire to escape the stressful everyday environment. When life is difficult at work or at home, it is good to get away for a while and have some rest. Any place outside the inner circle is good. It may be a forest or it may be a trip to any place far away from home. But forests are not only places in which to escape; they also are places that attract people because of their naturalness with little or no human influence. When stressful situations are caused by humans, it is good to be able to get away from them, to rest in nature. There one is close to eternal, archetypal symbols of life, which, according to Jung, give a reassuring feeling of life's deepest essence.

The forest also has a strong "pull" in the sense that it is a powerful symbol of mother. It is no coincidence that we use expressions like "mother forest," "mother nature," or "being in the lap of the forest," or "rape of the forest" (Brudal, 1992; Hägglund, 1994; Lugassy, 1970; Reunala, 1987; Siltala, 1987). Jungians speak about the universal archetype of the mother, a dualistic symbol which is either good and protecting, or frightening, even devouring her children.

During our psychological development we are all condemned to lose the protection of our mother in order to become independent individuals. Individuation is stressful, therefore there remains, somewhere in our deepest soul, more or less strongly, an unconscious desire to get back to the eternal paradise, the original state of relaxed well-being in the lap of our parents, or, as some psychoanalysts say, in the womb, which was the real paradise for us now lost forever (Chasseguet-Smirgel, 1985; McDougall, 1989).

A recent study (Reunala, 1994) confirmed that three out of four Finns feel the forest is a womb-like environment. The forest is seen to be a lost paradise, a protective place, where one can feel safe, free, and relaxed. The study was simple. Finns were asked to describe their feelings in the forest with a set of adjectives, some of which were neutral, others of which were chosen from psychological and psychoanalytical literature, describing infant feelings in the lap of one's parents or in the womb. Seventy-five percent of Finns chose the lap and womb adjectives to describe their forest feelings. For the remaining 25 percent, the forest was, on the contrary, a place that aroused anxiety and even fear. For the majority of Finns, and probably the majority of Scandinavians, forests are not only culturally important environments, but also powerful environments, touching a person's deepest unconscious desires.

Another psychological dimension is quite simple and comes from the studies of environmental psychologists; namely, that familiarity of environment is important (Ittleson, Proshansky, Rivelin, and Winkel, 1974). We all get attached to places where we live. Our personal development is attached to certain places, which, therefore, have a personal value for us. We have "our" forests, "our" hills, "our" streets, "our" houses. Places come to represent a part of our identity. If somebody changes or destroys our places, we get angry because we feel it is an attack on our identity. Or we get sad if it is something inevitable that makes our past places disappear. In Scandinavia where forests are such a prominent part of the environment, innumerable memories and feelings are attached to forests.

Once I met a professor who remembered how wonderful it was when she went berry picking as a child with her parents on a beautiful open hill. How disappointed and sad she was years later when she came back and the hill had disappeared because thick forest had grown over the hill. Her childhood environment, a clear-cut hill with an abundance of wild raspberries, didn't exist anymore. Normally, in Scandinavia, disappointments have been the other way around: forests full of memories have disappeared because of cuttings.

Conclusion

To summarize, Scandinavians have strong cultural traditions and values attached to forests because forests have been so important to their life. These traditions are strongest in Finland and in the remote forested regions of Sweden and Norway and least significant in agriculturally rich southern Sweden.

Beneath the cultural layer, there is a layer of primitive beliefs which sees "nature" as an all-encompassing living entity of which people are but a small part. These archetypal forest traditions and values are universal. They are probably a more prominent part of normal, everyday life in Scandinavia than in other Western countries and are most prominent in the Lapp culture.

The economic value of forests is simple to understand. Timber has value, as does wild game, berries, and other commodities. Intangible values are much more difficult to grasp. It is my impression that while timber production will likely remain the main value of Scandinavian forests in years to come, foresters need to try harder to understand the cultural history of forest use and try to respect it in forest management.

Literature Cited

Aikio, E. (1994). *Pohjoisen alkuperäiskansalaisen metsä*. Summary: Forest of Nordic Natives. Manuscript. Finnish Forest Research Institute.

Anttonen, V. (1994). *Erä- ja metsäluonnon pyhyys*. Kalevalaseuran vuosikirja 73. Suomalaisen kirjallisuuden seura. Helsinki, Finland.

Brudal, P. (1992). *Naturopplevelse, identitet och psykisk sunnhet*. Manuscript. Asker.

Chasseguet-Smirgel, J. (1985). *The ego ideal. A psychoanalytic essay on the malady of the ideal*. London, UK: Free Association Books.

Gunnarsson, A. (1988). *Träden och människan*. Rabén and Sjögren.

Hägglund, T. (1994). *Luonnon ja mielen metsä*. Kalevalaseuran vuosikirja 73. Suomaiaisen kirjallisuuden seura. Helsinki, Finalnd.

Ittelson, W., Proshansky, H., Rivlin, L., and Winkel, G. (Eds.). (1974). *An introduction to environmental psychology*. New York, NY: Holt, Rinehart and Winston.

Järvinen, I. (1984). *Metsän kasvot*. Suomen Luonto 1/1984.

Kardell, L. (1990a). *Svenskens syn på skogen*. Sveriges Skogsvårdsförbunds Tidskrift nr 6.

Kardell, L. (1990b). *Talltorpsmon i Åtvidaberg*. Förändringar i upplevelsen av skogen mellan 1978 och 1989. Sveriges Lantbruksuniversitet, Institutionen för skoglig landskapsvård. Rapport 46.

Kitamura, M., Shidei, T., Isida, M., Sugahara, S., and Akasaka, M. (1986). *Untersuchungen uber die Bewohnersstellungnahme fur Wald und Umwelt*-im Vergleich zwischen Finnland und Japan.

Kuusela, K. (1990). *The dynamics of boreal coniferous forest*. Sitra 112. Helsinki, Finland.

Liie, H. (1923). *Mennesket og traerne*. Groendahl and Soens Boktrykkeri, Kristiania.

Lugassy, F. (1970). *Contribution à une psychosociologie de l'espace urbain*. La relation habitat-forêt: Significations et fonctions des espaces boisés. Publications de Recherches Urbains, Ministère de l'Equipement et du Logement. Paris, France.

McDougall, J. (1989). *Theatres of the body*. London, UK: Free Association Books.

Opetusministeriö. (1993). *Metsän tulevaisuuskuvia*. Maanantaiseuran julkaisuja 6, Helsinki, Finland.

Osuuskunta, M. (1962). *Metsään mentiin*. Helsinki, Finland.

Pentikäinen, J. (1994). *Metsä suomalaisten maailmankuvassa*. Kalevalaseuran vuosikirja 73. Suomalaisen kirjallisuuden seura. Helsinki, Finland.

Persson, O. (1977). *Träd och människor.* Skogek. Stockholm, Sweden.

Raumolin, J. (Ed.). (1987). Special Issue on Swidden Cultivation. *Journal of the Finnish Anthropological Society, 4,* 183-279.

Reunala, A. (1976). *Miksi metsien hoidosta on niin vaikea keskustella asiallisesti?* Metsä ja Puu N:o 6-7, s. 4-8.

Reunala, A. (1987). Metsä arkkityyppinä. Summary: Forest as an Archetype. In A. Reunala and P. Virtanen, *Metsä suomalaisten elämässä* (pp. 415-426).

Reunala, A. (1994). *Turvallisuuden tunne metsän henkisenä arvona.* Kalevalaseuran vuosikirja 73. Suomalaisen kirjallisuuden seura. Helsinki, Finland.

Reunala, A. and Heikinheimo, M. (1987). *Taistelu metsistä.* Voimaperäinen metsätalous Suomessa ja muissa maissa. Kirjayhtymä. Helsinki, Finland.

Reunala, A. and Virtanen, P. (Eds). (1987). *Metsä suomalaisten elämässä.* The Forest as a Finnish Cultural Entity. Monitieteellinen seminaari 18-19.12.1986. Silva Fennica Vol. 21 N:o 4.

Siltala, P. (1987). Metsän turvallisuus. Summary: Security of the Forest. In A. Reunala and P. Virtanen. *Metsä suomalaisten elämässä* (pp. 405-414).

Sörlin, S. (1983). *Sinnenas skog.* Författarna, Falköping.

Section IV

Public Land Management
Concerns and Directions

When we see land as a community to which we belong,

we may begin to use it with love and respect . . .

That land is a community is the basic concept of ecology,

but that land is to be loved and respected is an extension of ethics.

Aldo Leopold (1949)

BEYOND CONSERVATION AND PRESERVATION IN AMERICAN ENVIRONMENTAL VALUES

CHAPTER 21

ED GRUMBINE
Sierra Institute
University of California Extension
Santa Cruz, California

Introduction

How Americans feel about their relationship with nature has always been contentious. The first settlers brought a certain amount of cultural baggage from Europe that immediately set them against both the wildlands and native peoples of North America. By the turn of the twentieth century, with westward expansion complete, the Native Americans subdued, and the first fragments of a public domain established, arguments swirled around what uses the new federal lands might best serve. As conservation evolved into environmentalism during the 1960s and '70s, the main body of U.S. environmental laws were passed, state and federal bureaucracies grew to implement policies, and debate over the government's role in regulating private interests grew.

It is not surprising, therefore, to find that public land management has a history of conflict and competing claims over general goals and specific practices. John Muir did not agree with Gifford Pinchot. Private enterprise has always fought against government rules and regulations. Those who favor transforming nature with few restrictions continue to argue with those who prefer less development.

The legacy of America's ambivalent attitudes toward resolving environmental conflicts remains. Two broad competing visions of public land management, representing two values sets, appear on center stage today. In the first vision, nature is conceived as supplying commodity and amenity resources for human use. Faith in human problem solving through efficient use of technology is expressed. Better stewardship of nature, legal reform, and more sophisticated use of science in management are all invoked as solutions to environmental problems. This vision of management has its U.S. roots in the wise use conservation advocated by Pinchot during the first half of this century. It is represented in varying degrees today by the Wise Use Movement, advocates of sustainable development, and, to some extent, supporters of ecosystem management.

The second vision of public land management challenges wise use conservation by posing a new land ethic based on certain limits to the human use of wild nature. This vision is founded, in part, on the wilderness preservation movement as embodied by Muir. Many supporters advocate ecocentrism which acknowledges that nonhuman living beings and ecosystems share equal standing with people—human concerns do not automatically trump other species. Sufficiency replaces efficiency as a management goal. This values set and corresponding vision of human/nature relations remains a minority view in American culture.

These two visions do share some common ground. Supporters of both argue for legal reform and better application of science to environmental problems. Fundamentally, however, wise use conservation and its variations and biocentric/ecocentric management visions differ in both core values and management goals.

My purpose in this chapter is to examine each of these broad visions of nature, explore their ethical underpinnings within the evolving history of American public land management, and evaluate the contribution each might make to resolving current and future environmental problems.

The Wise Use Conservation Vision

From its inception in the late 1890s through today, the main problem that wise use conservation has addressed is how to maximize the efficient use of nature to meet human needs. There are several implicit values upon which this vision is based. First and foremost is anthropocentrism, the belief that humans are privileged over all the rest of life on Earth (Devall and Sessions, 1985; Fox, 1990). Closely allied with anthropocentrism is resourcism—the belief that nature gains value only as people transform it into goods and services for humans (Grumbine, 1992). It is under these two assumptions that nature becomes "natural resources"—economics and efficiency are the twin standards by which this transformation is measured and the results are labeled "progress."

Gifford Pinchot is widely credited with crystallizing the wise use image of conservation and bringing it to the forefront of policy during the administration of Teddy Roosevelt. Pinchot was clear in his definition of wise use: "The first great fact about conservation is that it stands for development" (Pinchot, 1987, p. 261) and "[conservation is] the one great central problem of the use of the earth for the good of man" (p. 322). The goal of conservation quickly came

to be defined as "the greatest good for the greatest number for the longest time" (Pinchot, 1987, pp. 325-326). That Pinchot's views were enthusiastically endorsed by Roosevelt, codified by Congress with the passage of the Multiple Use Sustained Yield Act in 1906, and formed the bedrock beliefs of many public land managers some nine decades later, speaks to the nerve in American environmental values that Pinchot touched.

Questioning Pinchot's dictums, however, provides an exercise in critical thinking. Who defined what happiness was and how much was enough? How was satisfaction of the greatest number to be determined? How long was the long term? Pinchot defined happiness strictly in terms of material wealth, placed no limits on its acquisition, did not address issues of numbers, and stated clearly that benefits should accrue only to "the people who live here now" (Pinchot, 1987, p. 261).

But Pinchot must be seen as a forceful spokesman for wise use conservation, not a target. He gave voice and form to the dominant environmental values of his era. Anthropocentrism and resourcism remain intact today not because of Pinchot but due to the fact that:

1. they represent core values in all modern industrial societies, and

2. they are supported by corollary beliefs that further define a wise use relationship with nature.

Modern societies all depend on a conception of nature that considers reality as relatively fixed, all problems as soluble, upholds rational science as the only true source of knowledge, and believes humans to be rational actors whose behavior is ultimately predictable (Ehrenfeld, 1978; Toulmin, 1990). For Pinchot, as for the majority of Americans since the late nineteenth century, nature has been constructed to be in a state of relatively unchanging harmonious balance, with scientists and managerial experts wielding technology toward predictable resource outputs as measured by board feet or recreational visitor days. Professionals and the lay public hold this image of nature in common. This is a major reason why wise use conservation has held sway for so long.

The reforms of the Progressive Era certainly offered an antidote to the exploitation of America's native landscapes and ecosystems. Pinchot wanted to end the destructive cut-and-get-out practices of the frontier. With westward expansion being challenged, Americans had the opportunity to reenvision their relationship with nature. But it was yet too early to unseat resourcism. What Americans opted for instead was Pinchot's conception of humans as wise, scientific managers of natural resources.

The Preservation Vision

Even as Pinchot and his supporters seized the time, there was another response to environmental degradation in America. With roots in the ideas of Henry David Thoreau and George Perkins Marsh, the nascent wilderness preservation movement sought not to use nature so much as to protect it. Led by John Muir, the preservationists valued America's wild places for spiritual encounters with nature. The new national parks and forests symbolized a harmonious balance between wilderness and civilization and could provide respite for citizens caught up in the rising industrial environment.

Muir was a complex character, a pantheist who rejected anthropocentrism. He was one of the first Americans to suggest explicitly that "the universe would be incomplete without man; but it would also be incomplete without the smallest transmicroscopic creature that dwells beyond our conceitful eyes and knowledge" (quoted in Fox, 1981, p. 53). Muir's activism infused the preservation movement with a moral rather than a materialistic tone. The fight to save nature was for Muir and his followers part of the "eternal conflict between right and wrong" (quoted in Fox, 1981, p. 107).

Yet Muir also embodied some of the conflicts Americans faced as they attempted to work with nature in North America. Though he fought long and hard to protect the Sierra Nevada, Muir supported the building of the railroad into Yosemite Valley and the construction of the Tioga Pass road. He authored many impassioned pages against the development of wilderness but wrote relatively little about how people might use nature in a nonexploitative manner outside of parks and preserves.

Muir's greatest contributions to American environmentalism were his pantheism and political acumen. Of these two gifts, however, only his policy savvy was widely adopted. This occurred for several reasons which also illuminate common ground between wise use conservation and wilderness preservation. Both Pinchot and Muir believed that nature

existed in a balanced steady state that, when disturbed, would eventually readjust to its original pristine condition. For wise use conservationists, this balance could be manipulated for an endless flow of forest products, the scientific harvesting of which would not degrade ecosystems. For preservationists, nature's ongoing steady state could produce parks as protected paradises where primitive vignettes of wild America could be experienced by visitors. Neither faction was concerned much with ecological relationships between protected parks and managed lands. For both movements, federal control was the best path to these goals.

Conservation and preservation also depended implicitly on separating people from nature. For the former, nature was a vast storehouse whose secrets could be unlocked through scientific discovery. For the latter, people were always visitors to wildlands, never living in them. Muir's pantheism aside, philosopher Warwick Fox (1990) is correct when he points out that conservation and preservation share anthropocentric roots. Pinchot and Muir may have wrangled over whether humans stood with or above the rest of life on Earth, but history reveals that multiple use is closely allied with wilderness preservation at a deep level—public lands management, whether for commodities or amenities, places humans first.

The Evolution of Environmental Values

Westward expansion and the destruction of native peoples and landscapes was but the first of four great environmental events in U.S. history. The second important event, the rise of conservation and preservation, grew out of the first. American environmental values have continued to evolve since. The third U.S. environmental watershed, the 1960s and 1970s era of environmental lawmaking, did little to change the two streams of environmentalism philosophically or politically. But it did foster an increased awareness of ecological issues and brought them into the mainstream of all sectors of American society (Fox, 1981).

The fourth defining event in U.S. environmental history, the biodiversity crisis, has only recently been perceived. The biodiversity crisis is the awareness that the accelerating loss of species across all ecological scales may be reaching some critical threshold (Grumbine, 1992; Noss and Cooperrider, 1994). This awareness has yet to affect profoundly public policy or environmental values, but the prospects for fundamental change are great. Americans may now have the opportunity to move beyond conservation and preservation and possibly even anthropocentrism and resourcism. To understand the potential of the biodiversity crisis to reframe American values, both the biological and social consequences of extinction and habitat loss must be explored.

The Biodiversity Crisis

The biodiversity crisis exists across all levels of ecological organization. Global warming and ozone depletion threaten diversity at the biosphere level. Entire groups of organisms (e.g., birds and amphibians) are declining worldwide. Regionally, groups of organisms are also threatened. Over 30 percent of North American freshwater fishes are in decline (Williams et al., 1989). In the former West Germany, 25 percent of all known invertebrates are threatened (Wilson, 1993). Ecosystem-level destruction is also widespread. Nineteen percent of all U.S. ecosystem types have been reduced to critical levels (Noss, Scott, and La Roe, 1994). With habitat destruction so ubiquitous, it is not surprising that species and populations are also faring poorly. Estimates of species loss over the next decade range from 2.5 to 15 percent of all life forms on the planet (Primack, 1993).

Unfortunately, the legacy of wise use and preservation has left little land protected. As of 1992, less than 5 percent of Earth's terrestrial surface was under some type of protected status (World Resources Institute, 1992). And this statistic reveals little about important ecological measures such as the kind, number, and amount of ecosystem types represented in existing reserves.

Social Consequences

As the biodiversity crisis has become more evident, science and policy debates have intensified (see Grumbine, 1994a). Within ecological science, a new world-view that recognizes "flux" over "balance" in nature has emerged (Botkin, 1990; Pickett, Parker, and Fiedler, 1992). While in the past, scientists (and Pinchot and Muir) characterized nature as orderly and in homeostatic equilibrium, the new model considers natural systems to be dynamic, full of uncertainty, and changing at different space–time scales. Nature is episodic, not in balance, and these changes are difficult and sometimes impossible to predict.

Developments in environmental policy analysis show intriguing similarities to this new model of nature. Policy theorists are moving away from technical rational analyses that lead toward single "correct" solutions to policy problems. Problems are increasingly seen as context-dependent where knowledge of the policy arena and organizational structure and behavior are as important as scientific input.

Both the science of ecology and policy analysis are actively reframing cognitive maps that better fit recent learning of how nature works and how humans behave. But no new policies have been adopted as yet that are effective at slowing down the rate and scale of the biodiversity crisis. In fact, industrial development, population growth, and resource consumption are still expanding (see Brown, Flavin, and Kane, 1992). These trends are causing a domino-like chain reaction in American environmental politics:

1. the safety net of laws is being stretched thin;

2. the Administration, Congress, and the public lands agencies react slowly and, more often than not, attempt to defend the status quo;

3. environmentalists appeal and/or litigate over biodiversity issues and win; and

4. further policy implementation grinds to a halt as protracted lawsuits lead to legal decisions that are unacceptable to those in power.

Both the loss of biodiversity and the inadequate political response to the crisis are contributing to widespread reexamination of the appropriate relationship between people and nature. Collectively, it appears that more U.S. citizens are asking for less development (Dunlap, 1991; Steger, Pierce, Steel, and Lovrich, 1989). But it is far from clear whether this general proenvironment sentiment will translate into decisive political action.

Because of the tension today between new learning and maintaining the status quo, it is difficult to ascertain the future course of American environmental values. But so far, several trends are clear. The first trend, the Wise Use Movement, seeks to perpetuate and even to increase the development of nature. The second trend, sustainable development, updates conservation to fit modern scientific and management techniques. The third trend, ecosystem management, is less easy to characterize. Some forms of ecosystem management adopt Pinchotian values, but others seek to reframe management based on the value of protecting ecological integrity. This second kind of ecosystem management places humans on equal footing with nonhuman beings, very close to a fourth trend, ecocentrism. Each of these trends is reviewed briefly below.

The Wise Use Movement

The Wise Use Movement (WUM) is a caricature of the wise use of Gifford Pinchot (see Echeverria and Eby, 1994). A loose conglomeration of over 250 groups, the WUM seeks to turn back the clock to frontier times when natural resources were perceived as unlimited. Supporters wish to replace public land management with privatization. The movement's manifesto, *The Wise Use Agenda* (Arnold, 1988), includes the following goals: open access to minerals and oil in all U.S. protected areas; logging of all old-growth forests; reducing the protections offered by the Endangered Species Act; elimination of wetlands development restrictions; and more.

The WUM is spearheaded by several conservative and charismatic leaders including Ron Arnold of the Center for the Defense of Free Enterprise and Charles Cushman of the Multiple Use Lands Alliance. But the majority of its membership is a grassroots and diverse group of loggers, miners, developers, farmers, county politicians, and others.

It is not evident how influential the WUM will be. The grassroots membership has yet to organize effectively its power nationally. So far, the movement's focus has been on organization and fund raising along with several political issues including opposition to the reauthorization of the Endangered Species Act, weakening state and county land use regulations in the western U.S., and fighting against reform of the 1872 Mining Law. But it is clear why the WUM has appeared during an era of increasing loss of biodiversity and environmental regulations.

The movement represents the last stand by the most radical utilitarian members of society to maintain their nonsustainable lifestyles (Grumbine, 1994b). WUM positions are based on fear of losing access to resources that extractive industries depend on and losing commodity-oriented jobs. WUM supporters comprehend natural ecosystems as embedded within a laissez-faire economy with the primary goal of generating private profits.

As a policy option and value system, the WUM has nothing to offer the future. This is evident by comparing the movement's immediate goals (e.g., opening national parks to exploitation) with what most U.S. citizens prefer (increased levels of environmental protection). But the WUM also suffers from dependence on a cornucopia model of nature that simply does not fit the current situation if sustaining biodiversity and human economies is a goal. Nor does the individualistic, frontier mentality of the WUM fit well in a world where the frontier closed a century ago.

Sustainable Development

The sustainable development ideal first appeared in the *World Conservation Strategy* of the International Union for the Conservation of Nature (1980). The most influential exposition of the concept, however, is the Brundtland Report, *Our Common Future*, where sustainable development is defined as "meet[ing] the needs of the present without compromising the ability of future generations to meet their own needs" (WCED, 1987, p. 43).

The values behind sustainable development are closely related to the values behind wise use conservation. This is clearly seen in the Brundtland Report:

> *sustainable development does imply limits—not absolute limits but limitations imposed by the present state of technology and social organizations . . . both [can be] managed and improved to make way for a new era of economic growth.*
>
> WCED, 1987, p. 8

Sustainable development focuses exclusively on human needs, assumes that scientific uncertainty is unimportant, and implicitly suggests that current political arrangements are sufficient to carry us into the future.

Sustainable development will not solve the biodiversity crisis or allay the tensions that result from environmental deterioration and rising social inequity.

Applying more science and technology to environmental problems in part caused by conceiving success in terms of predictable, efficient manipulation of nature adds insult to injury. As philosopher Bryan Norton has observed, economic determinism and developmental boosterism may be successful politically, but they are anathema to working with nature over the long term (Norton, 1991). There is little reason to believe that the same values that have contributed to current problems, updated with the latest technological and managerial expertise, can take us very far.

Ecosystem Management

Hope as well as caution surrounds the recent development of ecosystem management. The concept has grown out of the biodiversity crisis, the new ecological view of nature, and a critique of narrowly focused attempts to manage the health of single species through the Endangered Species Act and other laws (see Grumbine, 1992, 1994c). With the species approach to management deemed a failure and a recently expanded model of nature which includes ecosystems and landscapes as well as species and populations, ecosystem management is being promoted as the path toward more sustainable land management.

But ecosystem management has not yet been uniformly defined or consistently applied. As might be expected, defining a new kind of management relationship with nature brings into focus the basic values of the groups participating in the debate. Defining ecosystem management, at least in the short term, is a political act. Currently, there are two broad visions of ecosystem management and competing claims over which definition will carry environmental policy into the future (Grumbine, 1994c).

Representative of one vision, current Forest Service policy has affinities with both wise use conservation and sustainable development. One Forest Service definition portrays ecosystem management as sustaining "the patterns and processes of ecosystems for the benefit of future generations, while providing goods and services for each generation" (USDA Forest Service, 1993). In what is the most complete treatment of the concept, Jensen and Bourgeron (1994) suggest that ecosystem management "requires a balance between human desires

and the biological and physical capacities of ecosystems." Another Forest Service document states that "Sustaining ecosystems for people is the ultimate objective for adaptive ecosystem management" (Bormann et al., 1994). These statements suggest that these versions of ecosystem management are simply treating commodity and amenity production within a broader ecological context—to maintain life support systems for humans. The old idea of balance appears in new forms; yet current ecological theory suggests that such ideas of balance cannot be derived from the study of ecosystem processes (see Pickett, Parker, and Fiedler, 1992).

The recent political history of ecosystem management also gives pause. The Clinton Administration's treatment of the northern spotted owl has shown that timber targets still carry inordinate weight over ecosystem concerns (Yaffee, 1994). Full funding for the Administration's plan for Pacific Northwest forest watershed analyses by Congress has not been forthcoming. And no economic study has been attempted that portrays the costs of more management with less in the owl forests.

Yet it is difficult to judge government versions of ecosystem management by initial definitions and recent political acts. The concept is still evolving. Are the above problems indicative of the ongoing sway of resourcism or the difficulty in moving from one management paradigm to another?

There is an alternative definition of ecosystem management that is supported by many academic conservation biologists and policy analysts who have published peer-reviewed papers on the subject (for references see Grumbine, 1994c). In this version, maintaining ecological integrity is proposed as the organizing principle of ecosystem management. Ecological integrity means managing to protect total native diversity (species, populations, ecosystems, landscapes) and the ecological patterns and processes that maintain diversity (Norton, 1992). Five specific management goals are frequently cited:

1. Protect viable populations of all native species.

2. Represent, within protected areas, all native ecosystem types in functional assemblages.

3. Maintain ecological patterns and processes (wildfires, nutrient cycles, etc.).

4. Manage over periods of time long enough to maintain the evolutionary potential of species and ecosystems.

5. Accommodate human use of nature within the above constraints.

The goal of ecological integrity explicitly considers all human use of nature as flowing from ecosystems only after basic patterns and processes are maintained and restored. It is encouraging to note that this vision of ecosystem management can also be found in some Forest Service documents. Kaufmann and his colleagues (1994) state explicitly that ecosystem capability:

> *must be integrated into the decision-making process* before *[emphasis added] we can compare human demands with the sustainable capacity of the system.*

If ecosystem management is to take hold and flourish, the relationship between the new goal of protecting ecological integrity and the old standard of providing natural resources for humans must be reconciled. This is a values and political question that does not depend exclusively on science for resolution.

Biocentrism and Ecocentrism

Present as a minority tradition in American environmental values since the time of Thoreau and Muir, biocentrism is the belief that all life forms have "equal right to live and blossom" (Naess, 1973). Biocentrism, literally "life-centered," presents an alternative to "human-centered," anthropocentrism by recognizing that humans are but one species among many and without special privileges vís-à-vís the rest of life on Earth. Biocentrism expands into ecocentrism as individual beings are acknowledged to be in relationship with each other and embedded in ecological communities, patterns and processes. The fence between nature and culture is reduced. Nature is not so much an object to be manipulated for material resources as it is a source of life to be approached with respect and humility. Both biocentrism and ecocentrism see nature as full of relationships, interacting webs, and individuals-in-community rather than autonomous, isolated (human) actors who are superior.

Supporters of these values are usually identified as part of the deep ecology movement (see Devall and Sessions, 1985; Fox, 1990). Much has been written about deep ecology in the academic and popular literature in environmental philosophy (see Fox, 1990 for references). But the movement itself is less concerned with philosophy and ethics and more concerned with people experiencing an ecological self where identification with nature grounds human action. Supporters of deep ecology believe that bringing nature into decision making not only expands one's locus of concern beyond the (merely) personal and social, but also may foster a dramatic social transformation away from the industrial world-view which has segregated people from nature and created the biodiversity crisis.

It is here that links between ecological integrity as a management goal to reduce the biodiversity crisis and ecocentrism as a social practice are apparent. Because people are dependent on healthy, functioning ecosystems, nothing short of maintaining ecological integrity can protect human communities over the long term. As the biodiversity crisis has deepened, managers have begun to admit that traditional resource management values are inadequate; in some cases they are even suggesting that the conservation/preservation vision is part of the problem (see Society of American Foresters, 1993). Though ecocentrism is certainly not required to support ecological integrity goals, it does offer a close match to these goals compared to anthropocentrism, resourcism, and the conservation/preservation traditions they have spawned. The hope contained in ecosystem management for native diversity is that adjusting management goals to reduce extinction and habitat destruction will not only reduce the present biodiversity crisis but also provide the opportunity for people to forge a new relationship with nature.

Beyond Conservation and Preservation

Human values evolve slowly, yet periods of crisis and social upheaval cause rates of change to quicken. And while change may occur slowly, the effects of the biodiversity crisis cannot be avoided. Consider the key sign "biological diversity." In the new ecological world-view, "biological" no long refers only to specific life forms but expands to include the ecological patterns and processes that living beings have evolved within, adapted to, and depend on. "Diversity" admits the many as well as the few—contextuality, individuality, complexity along with simplicity, the particular and the global, the cultural and natural. A diverse world is changeable, less predictable, uncertain, and fundamentally full of wildness. Providing an alternative to both conservation and preservation, social critic Max Cafard (1992, p. 17) points out that nature has ". . . no resources. Only sources and the return to sources."

It is here that the language, ideology, and politics of commodities and amenities might evolve into that of sustainable ecosystems with the policy goal of protecting ecological integrity. Maintaining ecological integrity includes human use without excluding nonhuman beings and their vital needs. It requires that "sustainable" be made more specific as diverse peoples in many places begin to discover how to live within the constraints of local ecological conditions. Including the needs of all living species, ecosystems, and landscapes directs people away from the technocratic potential in ecosystem management toward a more inclusive accounting of the vital needs of all of Earth's life forms.

The transition away from traditional resource management toward ecosystem management for native diversity, from endless material growth toward sustainable ecosystems, and from anthropocentrism toward some more inclusive value system will be difficult. An ecological world-view, whatever its ethical basis, challenges the most fundamental values of most Americans. U.S. citizens have always based their expectations on an unchanging, endlessly productive nature, precise management prediction and control, short-term decision making, and the sanctity of private property. All of these are being challenged today—nature is increasingly seen as uncertain, management is experimental at best, the long-term view is becoming essential, and private property is anachronistic. It is no wonder that supporters of the Wise Use Movement advocate environmental values from a time when life was perceived as less complex.

For the long term, however, there is no alternative to protecting the sources of life—healthy ecosystems. When issues of equity in politics and policy expand outward from the human community to embrace the ecological community, American environmental values will have left wise use conservation and wilderness preservation far behind.

Literature Cited

Arnold, R. (Ed.). (1988). *The wise use agenda*. Bellevue, WA: Center for the Defense of Free Enterprise.

Bormann, B., Brookes, M., Ford, D., Kiester, A., Oliver, C., and Weigand, J. (1994). *A framework for sustainable-ecosystem management* (Vol. V) (General Technical Report PNW-GTR-331). Portland, OR: USDA Forest Service.

Botkin, D. (1990). *Discordant harmonies: A new ecology for the twenty-first century*. New York, NY: Oxford University Press.

Brown, L., Flavin, C., and Kane, H. (1992). *Vital signs 1993*. New York, NY: W. W. Norton & Company, Inc.

Cafard, M. (1992). The surre(gion)alist manifesto. *Upriver Downriver, 15*, 14-19.

Devall, B. and Sessions, G. (1985). *Deep ecology*. Layton, UT: Peregrine Smith Books.

Dunlap, R. (1991). Trends in public opinion toward environmental issues: 1965-1990. *Society and Natural Resources, 4*, 285-312.

Echeverria, J. and Eby, R. (1994). *Let the people judge: Wise use and the private property rights movement*. Washington, DC: Island Press.

Ehrenfeld, D. (1978). *The arrogance of humanism*. New York, NY: Oxford University Press.

Fox, S. (1981). *The American conservation movement*. Madison, WI: University of Wisconsin Press.

Fox, W. (1990). *Toward a transpersonal psychology*. Boston, MA: Shambhala.

Grumbine, R. (1992). *Ghost bears: Exploring the biodiversity crisis*. Washington, DC: Island Press.

Grumbine, R. (1994a). *Environmental policy and biodiversity*. Washington, DC: Island Press.

Grumbine, R. (1994b). Wildness, wise use, and sustainable development. *Environmental Ethics, 16* (3), 227-249.

Grumbine, R. (1994c). What is ecosystem management? *Conservation Biology, 8* (1), 27-38.

International Union for the Conservation of Nature (IUCN). (1980). *World conservation strategy*. Geneva, Switzerland: IUCN.

Jensen, M. and Bourgeron, P. (Eds.). (1994). *Volume II: Ecosystem management: Principles and applications. Eastside forest ecosystem health assessment* (General Technical Report PNW-GTR-318). Portland, OR: USDA Forest Service.

Kaufmann, M., Graham, R., Boyce, D., Jr., Moir, W., Perry, L., Reynolds, R., Bassett, R., Mehlhop, P., Edminster, C., Block, W., and Corn, P. (1994). *An ecological basis for ecosystem management* (General Technical Report RM-246). Fort Collins, CO: USDA Forest Service.

Naess, A. (1973). The shallow and the deep, long-range ecology movement: A summary. *Inquiry, 16,* 95-100.

Norton, B. (1991). *Toward unity among environmentalists.* New York, NY: Oxford University Press.

Norton, B. (1992). A new paradigm for environmental management. In R. Costanza, B. Norton, and B. Haskell (Eds.). *Ecosystem health* (pp. 23-41). Washington, DC: Island Press.

Noss, R. and Cooperrider, A. (1994). *Saving nature's legacy: Protecting and restoring biodiversity.* Washington, DC: Island Press.

Noss, R., Scott, J., and La Roe, E. (1994). *Endangered ecosystems of the United States: A preliminary assessment of loss and degradation.* Washington, DC: USDI Fish and Wildlife Service.

Pickett, S., Parker, V., and Fiedler, P. (1992). The new paradigm in ecology: Implications for conservation biology above the species level. In P. Fiedler and S. Jain (Eds.), *Conservation biology* (pp. 65-88). New York, NY: Chapman and Hall.

Pinchot, G. (1987). *Breaking new ground.* Washington, DC: Island Press.

Primack, R. (1993). *Essentials of conservation biology.* Sunderland, MA: Sinauer Associates.

Society of American Foresters. (1993). *Task force report on sustaining long-term forest health and productivity.* Washington, DC: Society of American Foresters.

Steger, M., Pierce, J., Steel, B., and Lovrich, N. (1989). Political culture, postmaterial values, and the new environmental paradigm: A comparative analysis from Canada and the U.S. *Political Behavior, 11,* 233-254.

Toulmin, S. (1990). *Cosmopolis: The hidden agenda of modernity.* New York, NY: Free Press.

USDA and others. (1993). *Forests ecosystem management: An ecological, economic, and social assessment.* Washington, DC: USDA and others.

USDA Forest Service. (1992). *Ecosystem management of the national forests and grasslands* (Memorandum 1330-1). Washington, DC: USDA Forest Service.

USDA Forest Service. (1993). *Subregional/regional ecological assessment.* Portland, OR: USDA Forest Service Regional Office.

WCED (World Commission on Environment and Development). (1987). *Our common future.* Oxford, England: Oxford University Press.

Williams, J., Johnson, J., Hendrickson, D., Contrarar-Balderas, S., Williams, J., Navarro-Mendoza, D., McAllister, D., and Deacon, J. (1989). Fishes of North America endangered, threatened, or of special concern: 1989. *Fisheries, 14* (6), 2-20.

Wilson, E. (1993). *The diversity of life.* New York, NY: W. W. Norton and Company.

World Resources Institute/UNEP/UNDP. (1992). *World resources 1992-1993.* New York, NY: Oxford University Press.

Yaffee S. (1994). *The wisdom of the spotted owl: Policy lessons for a new century.* Washington, DC: Island Press.

Nature, the Human Spirit, and the First Amendment

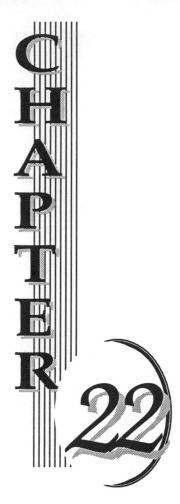

Jennifer Friesen
Loyola Law School,
Los Angeles, California

Shall she not find in comforts of the sun,
In pungent fruits and bright, green wings, or else
In any balm or beauty of the earth,
Things to be cherished like the thought of heaven?
Divinity must live within herself:
Passions of rain, or moods in falling snow;
Grievings in loneliness, or unsubdued
Elations when the forest blooms; gusty
Emotions on wet roads on autumn nights;
All pleasure and all pains, remembering
The bough of summer and the winter branch.
These are the measures destined for her soul.

Wallace Stevens, 1971

Introduction

As so beautifully exemplified by Wallace Stevens' most famous poem, *Sunday Morning*, language chosen to express a passionate relationship to nature often evokes duties and ecstasies that are also the province of religion. Throughout this volume, authors have described nature as sublime, as a miracle, as a source of reverence, wonder, mystery, and awe. A felt obligation toward the Earth may be described as a sacred trust, a devotion. We may say that we seek communion with nature, hoping for a spiritual awakening or renewal; we may even be derided as nature worshippers. Professor Joseph Sax describes preservationists as "secular prophets, preaching a message of secular salvation" (Sax, 1980).

In poetry and in everyday speech expressions such as these, whatever else they are, are the stuff of metaphor. They do not necessarily imply that human beings' hard-to-capture aspirations toward nature include religion, as that term is customarily used. What is clear is that public landscapes are capable of evoking deep feelings, whether they are described as spiritual, ethical, emotional, aesthetic, cultural, or existential. For those who find themselves in a state of deep alienation, as many do in the late twentieth century, these feelings toward the land are a poignant reminder that we still believe that we can be redeemed by love.

Nevertheless, because the words "spirit" or "spiritual" crop up so often in our groping attempts to describe the intangible benefits that we are after, it is helpful to explain why a public land ethic that designs for this, among other human needs, conforms to laws that separate church and state.

We are unaccustomed to hearing the word "spiritual" in public or political discourse, outside of its conventional envelope of religion. Some may automatically equate these two concepts, although they are not at all synonymous. First, therefore, I draw some distinctions between religion and spirituality. Spirituality includes both the sacred and the secular. As I understand the proposal under study, the Forest Service does not aim to teach or promote religion. Rather, spirituality is used broadly to express, for example, a longing for transcendence through connection with something infinitely larger and more permanent than ourselves; a reverence and wonder for something we can never reduce to mere data; or renewal of the human spirit, a mysterious sense of well-being in the world. Second, although the law has had no occasion to define the meaning of "spiritual" outside the narrow context of religion, it has never defined religion so sweepingly as to include such emotions or philosophies as these. Third, secular government policies that happen incidentally to benefit religion are not unconstitutional.

In the main part of my chapter I address the technical aspects of the law of religion that supports my conclusions. First, however, I would like briefly to summarize, in a nontechnical way, how moving toward an ethic that promotes nature-based values fits into our existing political and legal culture. Certainly, land managers will want to pursue that goal in a way that both honors our religious and cultural pluralism *and* stays within the bounds of the Constitution. Both justice and law require that public institutions show equal respect for everyone's religious (or nonreligious) tradition by acting only for what

might be called "public reasons." Public reasons are reasons that "could be accepted by individuals from a diversity of faiths or no faith at all" (Solum, 1990).

Given the fact of pluralism in American society—probably a permanent division of political, moral, and religious belief—government cannot hope to take any action that promotes any particular vision of the good without creating controversy. Nevertheless, it can justify policies that it makes if these policies are actually based on principles that have firm roots in the political culture. It would not matter that public and religious reasons supporting the same policy overlapped. For example, a legal prohibition on murder is not improperly motivated by religion, because a consensus in the political culture condemns the arbitrary killing of human beings, even though a deeper foundation for such a law may be found in the Ten Commandments.

Ample public reasons justify implementation of the broader land management ethic advocated throughout this text. These reasons include logic and common sense, knowledge of facts established by science, ethical values that can be derived from the public political culture of society, and existing law. For example, no one would contend that government acts unconstitutionally when it advocates a conservation ethic; this, in fact, is an element of the Forest Service Mission Statement. Other Acts of Congress, in different contexts, assign to federal land managers the duties of safeguarding social well-being and cultural values. Moreover, it is well-settled that the government may legitimately exercise its powers to advance aesthetic values as part of public welfare. Significantly, the Supreme Court has said:

> *The concept of public welfare is broad and inclusive. The values it represents are spiritual as well as physical, aesthetic as well as monetary.*

Berman versus Parker, 1954

To recognize citizens' higher values regarding nature and to provide opportunities for discovery, learning, and related experiences on public lands, fits well within the recognized powers and responsibilities of government. It is also consistent with—though an expansion of—a current policy shift away from a historically heavy emphasis on commodities and toward an increased emphasis on recreation and wildlife. The reasons for advocating a conservation ethic may shift from a narrow interest in the creature comforts one can harvest from public lands to the emotional well-being to be found there, but this is a change in emphasis rather than substance. Moreover, given what is now known, the survival of the species and the whole biotic system in which it co-exists may depend on inculcating this ethic. No stronger statement of public welfare can be imagined.

Another public reason for a more inclusive land management ethic is the widely shared belief that it is important to protect the cultural integrity of people—including "mainstream" Americans—whose identity depends in part on the preservation of natural sites or places steeped in cultural meaning for them. Respect for cultural diversity is another legitimate reason, derived from our shared political culture, for incorporating a variety of noncommodity values into land management planning.

All of these reasons, and others, are documented in the pages of this volume with more eloquence and expertise than I can bring to them here. My task, rather, is to show that nothing in our constitutional framework prevents the implementation of a deliberate policy to manage federal lands in such a way as to facilitate the satisfaction of these deep human needs. The government does not cross the boundary between church and state when it teaches that our ultimate interconnectedness impels a protective and respectful ethic toward public lands, or when it facilitates the use of the land by private citizens to realize complex, nature-based values that they already hold or that they discover there.

The Constitutional Separation of Church and State

The hypothetical legal question I address is this: if the government adopts land use policies that emphasize noncommodity human values, including "spiritual benefits," would these policies pose a realistic risk of officially promoting, or "establishing," religion contrary to the Constitution? The second and distinct question is whether or not specific legal protections for the cultural and religious practices of Native Americans on federal lands improperly establish religion, or must this situation be treated as a special case under the Constitution.

The Basic Premises: Establishment and Free Exercise Clause

The legal premises that constrain government's choices in matters of religion derive from the first amendment to the U.S. Constitution as interpreted by the Supreme Court. The text of the first amendment contains two references to religion addressed to government: "Congress shall make no law respecting an establishment of religion, or prohibiting the free exercise thereof." The primary concern here is with the first prohibition, the establishment of religion clause.

It is often said that the two religion clauses taken together are meant to impose on the government a duty of neutrality toward religion: roughly speaking, the government must pursue its secular goals so as not to endorse religion officially nor deliberately to inhibit it. In practical application, the meaning of neutrality has not been obvious. Judicial opinions are full of catch phrases about what the prohibition on religious establishment "means," but this standard rule is as clear as any: government may not promote or affiliate itself with any religious doctrine or organization, may not discriminate among persons on the basis of their religious beliefs and practices, may not delegate governmental power to religious institutions, and may not involve itself too deeply in a religious institution's affairs (County of Allegheny versus American Civil Liberties Union, 1989).

What the Law Views as Religion

Neither of the injunctions of the first amendment comes into play at all unless government policy improperly promotes something that the law would call "religion." And although it may seem surprising, a precise judicial definition of "religion" does not exist.

For most of the nation's history, the definition was probably not controversial. The eighteenth-century concept was that of a *duty* toward a supreme, or supernatural entity. Thus, James Madison called religion "the duty which we owe to our creator, and the manner of discharging it" (Madison, 1964, p. 84). At the end of the nineteenth century, the Supreme Court still conceived of religion strictly in these theistic terms, declaring that "the term 'religion' has reference to one's views of his relations to his Creator, and to the obligations they impose of reverence for his being and character, and of obedience to his will" (Davis versus Beacon, 1890). In the modern era, the Supreme Court has on rare occasions backed away from the notion that religious belief invariably includes belief in a Supreme Being, once suggesting that organized, but nontheistic belief systems such as Taoism and Buddhism were religions protected by the Constitution (Torasco versus Watkins, 1961). Nevertheless, the Court has avoided creating a more precise definition.

Respect for religious freedom and deference to social goals pursued by government explain this judicial restraint. In order to assure a generous scope to individual freedom, courts have been wary of creating a bright line rule for what constitutes religion, either in the free exercise or the establishment cases. Most lower courts that have wrestled with a definition have been forced to do so only in free exercise cases. These are disputes in which individuals seek relief from a general rule or policy, asserting that their religion makes it impossible or immoral for them to comply (e.g., their religion requires that they ingest peyote despite criminal laws that prohibit it). If a claimant asserts a right to engage in conduct that he or she calls religious, but which is not generally recognized as religious, a court may be "called upon to ponder the imponderable and define the indefinable and determine whether plaintiff's beliefs and practices constitute a religion" (Jacques versus Hilton,1983).

Establishment cases, the main focus here, are brought instead by interested third parties who claim that the government has illegally favored religion, or has favored one form of religion over another. In these cases, the court must examine the policy pursued by the government to decide whether it primarily reflects a secular goal, with any benefits to religion being merely incidental. In the overwhelming majority of reported cases that have found an improper establishment, the government has become entangled somehow with recognizable, traditional religious beliefs.

In short, nothing resembling a public land management ethic designed to respond to or to reawaken human needs for these kinds of experiences in natural settings has ever been tested against the first amendment. Nevertheless, we can project from past trends what a court's likely response would be.

Religion Is Not Synonymous with Spiritual Experience

First, the law does not equate "spiritual benefit," as it is used in this text, with religious worship, just as authors of the text do not. Rather the intent appears to be to respond to, and perhaps to inculcate in the public, an ethical vision of the natural world. Those who share this vision believe that the health of American culture, perhaps even its survival, will be better off if more people discover, or rediscover, the sense of well-being that closeness to nature can create.

Of course, there is nothing radically new in linking an ethical vision of the sanctity of life to the caretaking of the Earth. For example, Albert Schweitzer's view was that:

> *A man is ethical only when life, as such, is sacred to him, that of plants and animals as that of his fellow men, and when he devotes himself helpfully to all life that is in need of help. Only the universal ethic of the feeling of responsibility in an ever-widening sphere for all that lives—only that ethic can be founded in thought. The ethic of the relation of man to man is not something apart by itself: it is only a particular relation which results from the universal one.*

Schweitzer, 1933, pp. 158-159

The Supreme Court has on occasion drawn a clear distinction between religion on the one hand and secular philosophy or ethics on the other. In the famous case of *Wisconsin versus Yoder,* the Court contrasted the religious convictions of the Amish people regarding the education of their children with the secular and personal philosophy of Henry David Thoreau. In a lower court decision the court refused to define as religion an organization called MOVE, which the court called a "social philosophy," and a "quasi-back-to-nature social movement" (Africa versus Commonwealth of Pennsylvania, 1981). However sincerely professed, purely moral philosophy is not "religion" entitled to governmental protection nor does the first amendment's Establishment Clause forbid government policymakers from pursuing a philosophic vision that comports with other legal restraints on their power.

To contrast, one rare judicial opinion did condemn, as "establishment," government sponsorship of a nontraditional but clearly religious practice. A lawsuit filed by parents sought to stop public high schools from teaching a course called the Science of Creative Intelligence/Transcendental Mediation. The textbook for the course was developed by Maharishi Mahesh Yogi, a Hindu monk. Each student was required to acquire a mantra, or chant, by attending a ritualized ceremony, at which the teacher of the course made lengthy offerings and chants to a "deified" and divine guru. The court held that these activities denoted a religious, not a secular, activity, and that the school could not constitutionally make the course part of the official curriculum. This was the first appellate court decision that had ever concluded that "a set of ideas constitutes a religion over the objection and protestations of secularity by those espousing those ideas" (Malnik versus Yogi, 1979). The distinctions are obvious between this instance of government intervention and the proposal here. Policymakers do nothing improper—quite the contrary—when they write their policies to promote a multicultural, protective ethic by users of public lands, so long as the government does not give actual religious beliefs or practices special or favored treatment.

Like Thoreau's philosophy, much of what motivates a public demand or a government choice to reorient federal land policy to maximize "spiritual benefits," along with other benefits, does not contradict any of the traditional legal definitions of religion. Clearly, the purpose and effect of such a choice is not to exercise a duty that flows either from a Supreme Being or other system of divine or revealed norms. Members of various disciplines agree that human beings have emotional needs and desires for an experience of nature that is deeper or higher than what is captured by notions of recreation or economic sustenance. However, the land is valued, not on the basis of a single belief system, but on the basis of many, even in the absence of any belief system. Research can attempt to locate the roots of people's nature-based values in psychology, in culture, and in ethics. But there can be no agreement, and there need be none, on whether such needs are religious in their origin or nature. Indeed, they may be described as pragmatic, given the link between human attitudes of biophilia and the survival of the planet as we know it.

Secular Purposes Commonly Overlap with Religious Tenets

Further, assuming for the sake of argument that this land management ethic was said to reflect ultimately religious attitudes toward nature, that alone would not make it a religious program. Government policies do not become religious simply because they advance causes—for example, opposition to war or the enactment of humanitarian economic programs that some citizens would vote for because of their own religious beliefs. That is, the government does not violate the Establishment Clause simply because its secular goals happen to coincide with the concededly religious interests of some group. As Justice O'Connor has stated:

> [I]t is inevitable that the secular interests of Government and the religious interests of various sects and their adherents will frequently intersect, conflict, and combine. A statute that ostensibly promotes a secular interest often has an incidental or even a primary effect of helping or hindering a sectarian belief. Chaos would ensue if every such statute were invalid under the Establishment Clause.
>
> Wallace versus Jaffree, 1985

The Establishment Clause does not forbid government activity that is actively supported by the most orthodox of conventional religions so long as that activity is not itself unconstitutional. One federal judge made this point with the observation: "The Biblical and clerical endorsement of laws against stealing and murder do not make such laws establishments of religion" (Malnik versus Yogi, 1979). Thus, even though private environmental attitudes may well be shaped by religious beliefs, the government does not endorse these beliefs unconstitutionally by protecting species or preserving wilderness.

No ruling of the Supreme Court has suggested that government acts improperly when it promotes realization of "spiritual benefits" such as those envisioned here, unconnected with a traditional religious practice ordered by the government. Again, a simple contrasting example can be found in the cases that disapproved, as a violation of the Establishment Clause, government ordered "moments of silence" for public schoolchildren. The reason that the court disapproved was not that reflection as such is religious, but that evidence showed that state officials clearly intended these moments for prayer.

Incidental Benefits to Members of Religious Sects

Existing land management policies do not—and could not lawfully—exclude users that seek subjective religious benefits so long as their conduct coincides with the existing uses allowed. For example, hiking, singing, prayer, meditation, and "reflective or contemplative recreation" (Sax, 1980) might be within these uses in a wilderness area, but not the construction of shrines or other significant alterations of the environment. When activities are compatible with the dedicated uses of the land, and if the government does not treat believers any differently from nonbelievers, then the government has not improperly "endorsed" religion.

Some of the experiences within the spectrum of values that an expanded land management ethic might facilitate could also be true religious experiences, fitting the traditional definition. No one knows whether any meaningful proportion of them would be identified as religious by the individuals concerned. It is unlikely that this will ever be known, even if there were inoffensive methods of research that would elicit truthful responses. But suppose the direct result is that more (true) religious experiences will be enjoyed by private citizens on federally managed land. Would that make the land management ethic a forbidden "establishment" of religion?

Again the law is clear that government policies do not "establish" religion simply because they are adopted with the knowledge that religious believers, along with nonbelievers, will benefit from them. The Supreme Court has been explicit in saying so, even when it is clear the benefits sought by these private seekers were thought to be religious in the traditional sense. Thus, Justice O'Connor, after deciding in the 1988 *Lyng* case that Native Americans had no constitutional right to stop forest development that would destroy places sacred to them, wrote that:

> *Nothing in our opinion should be read to encourage governmental insensitivity to the religious needs of any citizen. The Government's rights to the use of its own land, for example,*

> *need not and should not discourage it from accommodating religious practices like those engaged in by the Indian respondents.*
>
> Lyng versus North Indian Cemetery Protective Association, 1988

And in another controversial opinion in which the Court decided that sacramental users of peyote had no constitutional right to be exempted from a general statute forbidding drug use, Justice Scalia also wrote that the legislature could—even should—create an exemption to accommodate their religious needs:

> *A society that believes in the negative protection accorded to religious belief can be expected to be solicitous of that value in its legislation as well. . . . But to say that a nondiscriminatory religious-practice exemption is permitted, or even that it is desirable, is not to say that it is constitutionally required.*
>
> Employment Division versus Smith, 1990

Both of these well-known cases ultimately ruled that the government must have constitutional authority in order to grant any particular religious accommodation. (Both, incidentally, may have a short shelf life due to hostile Congressional reaction within the last two years.) But the land management approach under discussion here presents a completely different situation. Here the working assumption is that the government is willing to take the psychological or broad spiritual needs of land users into account in implementing its plans. The question is not what the government must do, but what it may do within the confines of its constitutional authority.

Many confirmations of the principle that government need not be hostile to religion can be found in the opinions of the Supreme Court, but a recent one illustrates the use of government property by an organized religious group. A public school allowed community groups access to school premises after school was out for social, civic, and recreational meetings and entertainments. The school board refused permission to a church to exhibit, for public viewing, a religious film dealing with family and child-rearing issues. The Supreme Court held that the refusal was an unconstitutional discrimination against the church, and added that giving permission would not be an establishment of religion:

Under these circumstances ... there would have been no realistic danger that the community would think that the District was endorsing religion or any particular creed, and any benefit to religion or to the Church would have been no more than incidental.

Lamb's Chapel versus Center
Moriches Union Free School
District, 1993.

By taking into account the philosophical, psychological, moral, cultural, and even spiritual roots of environmental values, public land managers would be, commendably, seeking to respond to diversity, not to impose orthodoxy. At most it appears that the government would be doing what Justice O'Connor approved in *Lyng*: making a place in the landscape for the spiritual needs and desires of the people who come to it.

The Special Case of Native-American Access to Public Lands

Native Americans hold a unique position when it comes to the their cultural or religious needs for what is now government owned land. It is beyond question that Native-American tribal and other groupings do not ordinarily separate religion from culture as European descendants do. Their spiritual and cultural connection with the land is all of a piece. Second, even though they were forced by the dominant political and legal view to isolate a ceremonial use of land as religious, Native Americans are unique in this matter. To put it simply, the government does not own anyone else's "churches." Yet whenever advocates of Native-American interests have proposed special accommodations that take into account these historic facts, they have been challenged with legal arguments that any special treatment of their ceremonials would unconstitutionally favor one religion over others. I believe that the law is otherwise. Because of the unique relationship between the federal government and Native-American tribes, as well as the documented history of deliberate suppression of Native-American religious and cultural practices, the federal government would not violate the Establishment Clause by giving certain protections to Native Americans not given to any other religious group.

Established first amendment doctrine, as well as cases particular to the Native-American context, supports this conclusion. As I noted earlier, the Constitution generally imposes government neutrality toward religion. At the same time, neutrality is not rigid, and government "accommodation" of one's religious practice is sometimes required, or permitted, in order to relieve a government-created burden on a person's free exercise of religion. Accommodation explains why Amish parents won the right to educate their children at home for religious reasons despite a mandatory public school attendance law (Wisconsin versus Yoder, 1972). In addition, certain voluntary government accommodations of religious needs do not violate the Establishment Clause, even if the same actions would not be required. An example might be the government providing chaplains and places of worship for prisoners or soldiers cut off by the state from other opportunities for worship (School District of Abington versus Schempp, 1963).

As the Court affirmed recently, accommodation does not authorize favoritism toward one religion over others, but it can sometimes justify treating those who share a particular belief differently from those who do not (Board of Education of Kiryas Joel Village School District versus Grumet, 1994). Taking deliberate steps to lift government-created burdens on Native Americans' use of public lands for religious and cultural practices could be treated as a permitted accommodation rather than a forbidden establishment, even without the powerful additional arguments based on the federal government's unique relationship with these sovereign peoples.

In the *Lyng* sacred lands case, government attorneys argued that it would be illegal favoritism—giving one religion an unfair benefit at public expense—to halt the building of a planned road. The Native-American plaintiffs in that case had made a completely credible claim that the planned development would destroy their religion by degrading pristine sites essential to its practice. The Court ruled that the plaintiffs' rights to the free exercise of religion did not prevail over the government's right to use its own land. But it did not rule that a voluntary decision by the Forest Service to halt the road in order to preserve sacred sites would have violated the Establishment Clause. The Court's comment is worth repeating at this point:

Nothing in our opinion should be read to encourage governmental insensitivity to the religious needs of any citizen. The Government's rights to the use of its own land, for example, need not and should not discourage it from accommodating religious practices like those engaged in by the Indian respondents.

Lyng versus North Indian
Cemetery Protective Association,
1988

Lyng has been much criticized by advocates, scholars, and politicians for refusing to honor the plaintiffs' free exercise claim (Ward, 1992). In fact, Congress afterward added the property at stake in the case to the Siskiyou Wilderness, permanently blocking completion of the road and protecting the endangered sacred sites (P.L. 101-612, 1990). Commentators have suggested that Congress could go further by setting national standards to stop the degrading of sacred sites, and to ensure privacy necessary for Native-American ceremonies on lands now under the control of the United States government. It could do so without offending the Establishment Clause if it acted for reasons of religious accommodation, or for the nonreligious goals of preservation of cultural diversity by assuring a future for Native-American traditions (Ward, 1992).

These traditions include practices that may be thought of as religious, but it is wrong to assume that Native-American religions can be conceived of, and treated, as separate from other traditional cultural practices and beliefs. As Native-American advocates and scholars have long maintained, culture and religion are integral and inseparable, and both require the use of natural environments. In fact, a major bill seeking to facilitate both religious and cultural practices of Native Americans is presently pending in Congress. Senator Inouye's Native American Cultural Protection and Free Exercise of Religion Act of 1994 (S.B. 2269) repeatedly stresses the purpose of the law to protect traditional native cultures, of which religious practice is only an aspect. For example, one of the bill's proposed Findings of Congress states that "the European concept that religion is an activity or belief that is separate from all other aspects of daily life, or that religious is separable from culture, is a concept that has no application in the traditional cultures of Native Americans" (Sec. 101, 2).

If passed, the proposed Act (S.B. 2269) would guarantee Native Americans access to federal lands at all times for "traditional cultural, ceremonial or religious purposes" (Sec. 102). The right of access would include the right to gather natural substances and products for traditional cultural purposes. Upon request of a tribe or traditional leader, public land managers could also temporarily close portions of federal land to general public use in order to protect the privacy of traditional cultural, ceremonial, or religious activities.

The bill's drafters openly criticize the *Lyng* and *Smith* cases discussed above as "chilling and discriminatory" to Native-American traditional cultures; they recognize the necessity of sacred places, plants, and animals to Native-American cultures, including religions; they note that "lack of sensitivity to, and understanding of" these cultures has resulted in lack of a coherent, protective policy; and they record that the practice of Native-American cultures and religions has historically been intruded on, interfered with, and sometimes banned by federal authorities, with devastating and continuing effects. The urgency of the problem is revealed in the final report of the Senate Committee on Indian Affairs which notes that there are currently over 44 Native-American sacred sites that are threatened by tourism, development, and resource exploitation (Senate Report 103-411, 1994).

In connection with a 1993 version of S.B. 2269, the Senate Committee on Indian Affairs received extensive expert testimony on how the religion clauses related to the bill's religion-specific provisions. Three prominent law professors testified that the proposed Act did not create the danger of government favoritism or endorsement that the Constitution prohibits (Hearings on S.B. 1021, 1993). In sum, they stated that unique circumstances make its relatively modest accommodations necessary to restore neutrality by lifting existing burdens on religious liberty, burdens not shared by other religions. These burdens can be attributed in large degree to government acts, including the government's ownership of holy places. As Professor Milner Ball testified, if the United States owned the National Cathedral, it seems unlikely the Establishment Clause would be used to forbid a temporary closure of the sanctuary to tourists during sacred services.

Another unique circumstance calling for correction is the documented history, unparalleled in degree, of governmental (and clearly unconstitutional) suppression of Native-American cultures and religions, accompanied by aggressive government-sponsored attempts to promote Christianity among Indian peoples. It is well-established in the law of race relations, for example, that affirmative action to remedy government inflicted injury is constitutional.

Finally, the professors testified, the Act (S.B. 2269) is necessary to protect Native Americans' culture, inseparable from their religions, and is therefore mandated by the United States' historic trust relationship with Native American nations. Their conclusions are supported with dozens of pages of legal arguments and authoritative opinions. Among them are two recent cases in which different federal courts of appeal concluded that the federal government did not violate the Establishment Clause by extending protection only to tribal religions, though such a preference would be prohibited if extended to other religions (Peyote Way Church of God, Inc. versus Thornburgh, 1991; Rupert versus United States Fish and Wildlife Service, 1992).

The sponsors of the Native American Cultural Protection and Free Exercise of Religion Act have taken to heart Justice Scalia's suggestion in the *Smith* case that religious accommodations are best left to the political process. Federal land managers would surely be aided by a well-drafted, national policy. Even without one, some have put much thought and effort into how best to honor requests in connection with Native-American ceremonial uses. As Louis Redmond points out (see Chapter Nine in this volume), neutrality is not always indifference since federal land managers already engage in religious and cultural accommodations on occasion such as the arrangements necessary for the Sun Dance. The constitutional arguments marshalled in support of Congressional intervention support the continuation and expansion of such arrangements. For Native-American religious practitioners, as for no other, nature-based spiritual experiences depend on natural settings largely in the control of federal authorities.

Conclusion

At this stage, the precise ways in which changes in land management philosophy would create changes in management practices at the implementation level need to be studied. Education and dialogue should increase understanding of, and sensitivity to, the diverse nature-based values that contribute to the psychological essence of human life, but the final outlines of any new strategies to incorporate them are, necessarily, not yet written. Better means of research might identify what environmental factors within managers' control favor or obstruct the realization of these values. Managers might then wish, more systematically than at present, to give a higher priority to whatever programs, including educational ones, that seem to promise this type of benefit over competing demands for the same land, staff, and funds. In some cases, they might simply agree to take newly discovered obstacles, possibly themselves, out of the way. We can probably assume that indirectness, silence, and the absence of outside stimulation are the minimum necessary conditions for spiritual reflection (see Magary, Chapter Twenty-Six, in this volume), but we are still learning what would best create the space needed for the sense of well-being and connectedness that we seek.

Whatever its source, existing knowledge supports the notion that these deep human needs and desires exist, and that they spring from a rich spectrum of values. A better understanding of such values by officials should lead to a climate and a landscape in which these private choices can flourish. We also know that they may conflict in practice, calling for a neutral agent to make decisions of priority and allocation. In this most delicate endeavor, the government must seek always to be responsive to its human constituency. But there is also a proper place for leadership. The peace and the rapture that we seek in public lands cannot long survive without commitments from both the public and public servants to the ethical vision that is the inspiration for this text.

Literature Cited

Madison, J. (1964). A memorial and remonstrance on the religious rights of man. In J. Blau (Ed.), *Cornerstones of Religious Freedom in America* (84-90). New York, NY: Harper & Row Publishers, Inc.

Sax, J. (1980). *Mountains without handrails: Reflections on the national parks.* Ann Arbor, MI: University of Michigan Press.

Schweitzer, A. (1933). *Out of my life and thought: An autobiography* (C. Campion, Trans.). New York, NY: H. Holt and Company.

Solum, L. (1990). Faith and justice. *Dapple Law Review,* 39:1083.

Stevens, W. (1971). Sunday morning. In H. Stevens (Ed.), *The palm at the end of the mind: Selected poems and a play.* New York, NY: Alfred A. Knopf, Inc.

Ward, R. (1992). *The spirits will leave: Preventing the desecration and destruction of Native-American sacred sites on federal land.* Ecology Law Quarterly, 19:795, 810, 814.

Judicial Opinions Cited

Africa versus Commonwealth of Pennsylvania, 662 F. 2d 1025, 1029 (3d Cir. 1981).

Berman versus Parker, 348 U.S. 26, 33 (1954).

Board of Education of Kiryas Joel Village School District versus Grumet, 114 S. Ct. 2481 (1994).

County of Allegheny versus American Civil Liberties Union, 492 U.S. 573 (1989).

Davis versus Beacon, 133 U.S. 333 (1890).

Employment Division versus Smith, 494 U.S. 872, 890 (1990).

Jacques versus Hilton, 569 F. Supp. 730 (D. NJ. 1983).

Lamb's Chapel versus Center Moriches Union Free School District, 113 S. Ct. 2141 (1993).

Lyng versus North Indian Cemetery Protective Association, 485 U.S. 439, 453-54 (1988).

Malnik versus Yogi, 592 F.d 197 (3d Cir. 1979).

Peyote Way Church of God, Inc. versus Thornburgh, 922 F.d 1210, 1216-17 (5th Cir. 1991).

Rupert versus United States Fish and Wildlife Service, 957 F.d 32, 34-35 (1st Cir. 1992).

School District of Abington versus Schempp, 374 U.S. 203 (1963).

Torasco versus Watkins, 367 U.S. 488 (1961).

Wallace versus Jaffree, 472 U.S. 38, 69-70 (1985).

Wisconsin versus Yoder, 406 U.S. 205 (1972).

Acts and Bills Cited

Hearings on S.B. 1021, Sept. 10, 1993, Senate Committee on Indian Affairs.

Religious Freedom Restoration Act of 1993, P.L. 103-141, 103rd Congress (1993), codified at 42 U.S.C. §§ 2000bb—200bb-4.

S.B. 1021, Native American Free Exercise of Religion Act (1993).

S.B. 2566, P.L. 101-612, 101st Congress (1990).

S.B. 2269, Native American Cultural Protection and Free Exercise of Religion Act of 1994, analyzed, with do pass recommendation, in Senate Report 103-411 (1994) (Senate Committee on Indian Affairs).

Incorporating Hard-to-Define Values into Public Lands Decision Making: A Conflict Management Perspective

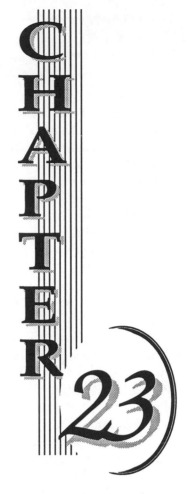

Julia Wondolleck
School of Natural Resources and Environment
The University of Michigan
Ann Arbor, Michigan

Tradition has it that the Great Spirit created the Sioux at what is today known as Devils Tower National Monument in Wyoming. Designated in 1906 as the first national monument, this 865-foot high volcanic monolith is, in the 1990s, the site of what has become a new chapter in the evolving saga of public lands conflicts. Plains Indians have for centuries revered Devils Tower as a sacred site, seeking religious visions there and offering sage and tobacco prayer bundles to the Great Spirit. They have difficulty restraining their anger at the monolith's more recent pilgrims, those who seek the thrill of climbing its volcanic face, leaving climbing bolts and urine stains in their wake, and whose noise and disruptions make it hard for the Native Americans to hear the Great Spirit. The climbers, in turn, are disgusted by the prayer bundles scattered about the site. As one climber comments, "As far as I'm concerned, prayer bundles are a bunch of trash, and I'm very offended to have them hanging around the monument." He argues further that, "the Indians don't climb that rock which I own as an American citizen." Francis Bacon, an Arapaho Indian advocating protection for Devils Tower and other sacred sites, retorts that, "all hell would break loose if I went to climbing the Washington Monument or the National Cathedral."[1]

This conflict is but the tip of the iceberg of a set of resource management disputes that will increase in frequency in coming years. As once abundant public resources become more scarce in the face of mounting demands, age-old as well as New Age values are beginning to clash more often with those given legitimacy in the economic and legislative priorities of twentieth-century America. This conflict is symptomatic not only of the consequences of a growing resource scarcity, but it also is evidence of the inadequacies of the administrative processes that are followed when making resource allocation decisions (Wondolleck, 1988). Part of the reason such conflicts persist and are so pervasive is that the ways in which resource management decisions are made either ignore these hard-to-define values simply because they are so hard-to-define or, conversely, because they try to seek "the right answer" in balancing competing values when there simply is no such "right" answer that systematic technical analysis will uncover. While Gifford Pinchot established a widely regarded scientific approach to managing public lands at the turn of the century (Hays, 1959), the systematic technical analysis

---

[1]See "Tribes, climbers clash over Devils Tower," in *The Ann Arbor News*, November 10, 1994, p. D4.

which is at the heart of this approach falls short in those increasingly prevalent situations where "right" answers are elusive. In addition, from the perspective of traditional approaches to resource decision making these kinds of conflicts tend to be viewed as irreconcilable. When resource managers believe that no solutions could possibly exist in the face of such conflicts, they have little reason to even try to find them.

Most people will agree that spiritual values are qualitatively different from economic or political values and, consequently, should not be subjected to the same scientific assessment as are the more readily quantifiable resource values. The question that arises, then, is how might these values best be represented in decision making? In this chapter, I argue that a different approach to decision making might better manage these conflicts by more effectively incorporating a greater diversity of hard-to-define values into public lands decisions. I describe the characteristics of different public land disputes and the ways in which traditional public land decision-making processes fail when trying to grapple with complex, multiparty disputes. I then discuss the consequences of these shortcomings and conclude by proposing an alternative conception of the role of land managers in these situations, one that may accommodate more creatively the different communities of interest with a stake in how public lands are managed.

How Resource Allocation Decisions Are Traditionally Made

Other chapters in this text attest to the diversity of values that define our public lands. These values reflect a full range of needs and emotions, from the readily quantifiable commodities of timber and rangeland, to others that can never be quantified and that are personal and frequently spiritual in nature. While disputes involving hard-to-define values certainly capture public attention and seem counter to the image of professional land management, these situations in fact exhibit many of the same characteristics as other resource allocation disputes. They pit seemingly irreconcilable values in what appears to be a win/lose confrontation. They involve organized interest groups that advocate for their interests in whatever forum is available. The stakes are great for

all involved, providing incentives for vigorous, unyielding debate. Even when legitimized and empowered through legislative mandates or court rulings, it is not obvious how the nonquantifiable factors should be measured in decision making. Which values should be given greater weight? Conventional technical and scientific analyses alone can seldom shed light on the most appropriate course of action and, as a result, the issue persists, awaiting a resolution that is both meaningful and acceptable to those involved.

Land managers are understandably ill at ease when encountering situations where they must make decisions involving hard-to-define values. These values are often unfamiliar and not well understood by the land manager. They frequently have meaning only in the context of an individual's mind or heart, and this meaning is at times evolving. Consequently, traditional modes of acquiring and incorporating public input can seldom inform the decision maker adequately. It is virtually impossible for a resource manager following traditional administrative processes and scientific methods of analysis to understand sufficiently and act on such values when making decisions. Even though they must make a decision in a particular case, it is unclear how the land manager should go about including, assessing, and accommodating these values. They were not trained to deal with issues such as these when they received their professional education and training in forestry, wildlife biology, or related land management topics. These hard-to-define values do not fit within the traditional paradigms of professional land management, and hence present a challenge even to those resource managers with training in the social sciences.

Current administrative decision-making processes are not helpful when either the resource manager or the individuals or organizations holding these hard-to-define values try to incorporate them into decision making. These processes are not sufficiently informative or convincing, are tremendously divisive and, because of these two failures, seldom lead to enduring decisions that can be implemented (Wondolleck, 1988). These processes foster an adversarial system in which natural resource disputes are perpetuated, not resolved. Examining how decisions are made lends insight into why many values become lost in these processes and result in protracted conflicts that, in many cases, may simply be unnecessary.

The Process Is Not Sufficiently Informative or Convincing

In theory, land management decision-making processes appear straightforward and rational. In essence, what is asked of a land manager is that he or she obtain the necessary information and data, assess it thoroughly, develop reasonable alternatives, and assess these alternatives in selecting the most appropriate one. In practice, this analysis is inadequate to the task of incorporating hard-to-define values. It is not obvious how to weigh these values in decision making or what types of alternatives would adequately accommodate them.

The conventional systematic, technical analysis conducted by resource managers is essential to making informed decisions, yet it alone can seldom provide sufficient information with which to make decisions in these cases. Critical assumptions must be made in selecting which alternatives should be studied and in bounding the subsequent analysis within various parameters. These subjective aspects of decision making cannot be subsumed sufficiently within objective technical analysis. And while the rigorous process of analysis may satisfy agency officials that all pertinent information has been considered and convince *them* that the decision reached is the most appropriate, this same process, time and time again, fails to satisfy or convince other affected groups or individuals. If the objective of this process is solely to reach a decision, it is successful. However, if the objective is to be decisive—to make decisions that are accepted and supported rather than immediately contested and undermined—the process fails.

Inevitably, many groups have preconceived notions about what an appropriate decision should be long before any studies or analyses are completed. The decision-making process does not convince these groups either that their preconceived notions were wrong or that the decision reached is right. The process does not provide the opportunity for mutual inquiry among stakeholders so that all involved, including the resource managers, can better understand the issues at stake and the merit of a variety of alternatives. The process does not convince these affected groups that the critical assumptions and value judgments that ultimately dictate which decision will be reached are the most acceptable. It

gives them little opportunity to amend, support, or reject their early notions. Instead, the process inadvertently encourages opposition and criticism and, moreover, very often provides a substantive basis for such criticism.

A Divisive Process

As currently structured, public lands decision-making processes are divisive. They promote distrust and polarization between parties, while encouraging adversarial behavior and extreme position taking. Ultimately, this negative dynamic ensures opposition to whatever decisions are made. Although conflict over many public land management proposals is inevitable, the process by which decisions are made provides inadequate mechanisms for anticipating this conflict and trying to resolve the differences among affected parties. As a result, the process frequently exacerbates conflict and inhibits accommodation of the interests at stake. A wise strategy for individuals and organizations enmeshed in such conflicts is to question the validity or reasonableness of their opponent's interests while distorting the magnitude of their own needs. Seldom are incentives or opportunities provided for conflicting parties to try to collaborate in order to build understanding of each others' concerns and needs, thereby providing the foundation for determining if a creative outcome that satisfies each interest might be found. The official approach to making decisions seldom encourages groups to try to solve what is quite often a *mutual* problem. Instead, the process provides incentives for those involved to try to "win" the battle. Hence, national forest plans are appealed repeatedly, endangered species management decisions are contested, and seemingly everyday administrative decisions swell into festering disputes that frequently end up in the courts.

While often characterized as such, public land management conflicts are not generally rooted in the actions of capricious agency officials. The problem is not that the agency decision maker selects the wrong alternatives to study, evaluates them using the wrong criteria, or assigns the wrong values to different outcomes. The problem is that there is seldom one right answer to these questions. Because the process is structured to develop the most technically correct decision when such a decision does not exist, it ensures that decisions will be opposed. The stakes are just too great to expect otherwise. Further, the distrust that has been engendered by this approach to decision making has, over time, cast a dark shadow over almost any decision. Many individuals and organizations do not believe that resource managers will adequately and appropriately represent their interests, and this belief, well-founded or not, colors their assessment of the validity of whatever decision is eventually made.

In short, the consequence of these traditional decision-making processes is often heightened conflict, misunderstanding, animosity, and distrust. And as resource managers insulate themselves behind the cloak of technical expertise and objective analysis, they become further isolated from the individuals whose information, ideas, and support are essential to acceptable and workable decisions. This process puts the resource manager in the middle, not only as a source of information and analysis on which to base decisions, but also as the target of criticism and emotion about the decisions eventually rendered. While these issues are undeniably difficult to resolve under any circumstances, they are nonetheless common problems shared by all members of society. By forcing resource managers to shoulder the burden for dealing with these issues alone, traditional decision-making processes fail to instill a sense of responsibility for facilitating effective public choices among divergent groups instead allowing them to criticize freely the efforts of land managers.

These endless conflicts are not inevitable. To better manage such disputes, decision making must be structured to deal with the difficult underlying characteristics that define these issues. More appropriate ways must be found to be articulate and act on the diverse values involved in decision making (Wondolleck, 1985). In many cases, it is possible to accommodate a full range of interests and values in an effective decision-making process. To do so requires that decision-making processes be more effective at acknowledging, understanding, and involving the diversity of interests with a stake in the management of these lands so that, when possible, a credible, acceptable common ground might be achieved (Carpenter and Kennedy, 1988; Susskind and Cruikshank, 1987). In the case of nontraditional and hard-to-define values, new methods need to be developed and new opportunities need to be provided for these values to be more meaningfully articulated and integrated into decision making. At times this common ground is found when stakeholders better understand the needs of the varying groups involved and the realm of possible decisions available. At other times, the dialogue that ensues leads to acceptable compromises among the parties, creating common ground where one did not previously exist. The innovative experiments of a number of different resource managers provide some insight into how managers might at least begin *trying* to do so (Wondolleck and Yaffee, 1994).

Doing Better at Accommodating the Diversity of Public Land Values

At the heart of public land management is the challenge of making resource allocation decisions in the face of competing demands. Time and experience have illustrated that relying solely on conventional technical analysis, regardless of how thorough and systematic, does not sufficiently inform decision makers about what should be done nor does it convince those affected that the appropriate decision has, in fact, been reached. Where does that leave the resource manager? How might these decisions be made more effectively in the face of seemingly irreconcilable demands?

Efforts by some resource managers to work collaboratively with groups adhering to seemingly incompatible values have uncovered the reality that divergent groups often have more in common than they would have thought. Hence, there is greater room for building understanding and a larger set of opportunities to discuss new and different ways of accommodating a diverse set of interests than most involved parties assumed was possible at the outset of their interactions. Seth Diamond, a Forest Service employee on the Lewis and Clark National Forest in Montana, provides a good example of the possibilities inherent in reframing our understanding and approach to these situations. He found himself in the midst of a heated conflict between his agency, ranchers, environmentalists, and others over management for the endangered grizzly bear. He responded to this situation with a very different approach than that dictated by traditional administrative procedures. As he put it:

the grizzly bear has the ability to stimulate great interest. Let's transform it into something positive—to grizzly bears, ranchers, environmentalists, and the general public. Let's do something positive and use it to bring people together.

see "The Beartree Challenge" case in Wondolleck and Yaffee, 1994

The result has been an ongoing, collaborative management partnership among these diverse interests. Traditional adversaries have found that they *can* work together in solving this problem that they share. They have found viable ways of restoring and protecting grizzly bear habitat while protecting the interests of the adjacent ranching community. However, their collaboration would not have been possible had the problem not been framed as one that they all shared responsibility for addressing, or had the opportunity not been provided by Diamond to bring all interests together to begin working constructively on the problem.

Is it possible to view efforts to integrate other hard-to-define and nontraditional values into public land decision making in similar terms? To make something positive out of what seems to be a crisis situation? Perhaps here, too, there is promise in viewing the situations as opportunities; opportunities to build bridges rather than walls, and to try a different course towards understanding, problem solving, and accommodation rather than continued adversarial confrontation.

Individuals seeking a better way to make resource management decisions when diverse values are at stake have been experimenting with collaborative efforts with nonagency groups throughout the United States. For example, on a ranger district in Alaska's Tongass National Forest, innovative district staff have been diligently seeking new ways to incorporate traditionally underrepresented and diverse communities of interest into that forest's management activities. In one case, they are involving the local native Alaskan community in restoring and preserving sacred sites within the forest, with the native community itself providing the interpretation and education for both agency staff and interested public visitors. Efforts such as these provide promising models for how interactions between seemingly incompatible interests can promote understanding and creativity, building the productive working relationships that are essential when seeking solutions that accommodate a diversity of interests.

Precedent setting cases such as these are the notable efforts of one or more individuals who realized the need for change and committed themselves to finding a more accommodating path. These individuals have been open-minded in their approach and have encouraged those whose help they enlisted to be willing to try to conceive a workable solution. At the heart of these successful efforts is an emphasis on building understanding between parties, providing at long last the opportunity to talk face-to-face in a way that shatters old stereotypes in a way that the needs and concerns of the multiple interests can truly be understood and acted on. These approaches take the agency out of the middle and disperse responsibility more broadly for the difficult analysis and choices to be made. In contrast to the more traditional approaches to decision making, these more recent interactions combine technical analysis with stakeholder collaboration with the objective of problem solving rather than truth seeking.

Conclusion

Arguments can be made at both the moral-ethical and the strategic–political levels for why traditional approaches to decision making are inadequate given the increasing diversity of values at stake in public lands management. While earlier chapters have framed the argument concerning normative responsibilities, for those who remain skeptical there are quite compelling strategic and political reasons for pursuing this common ground. The past two decades have illustrated how persistent these conflicts can be, straining critical relationships between land managers and their diverse constituencies, burning bridges that are essential for effective land management, and providing political officials with untenable choices (Yaffee, 1994).

The particular debate surrounding conflicts between traditional land uses and the hard-to-define values is more often than not based on the assumption that the decisions to be made are either/or in nature, that we simply cannot have both. It is worth probing whether or not the arguments truly need to be framed in these terms and consequently if the decision-making process is appropriately structured for the task at hand. If these conflicts were approached in a different way, might it be possible to accommodate a broader set of land uses in a more meaningful way? Perhaps efforts to include the diversity of values at stake do not need to be thought of in win or lose terms. The greatest chance we have for promoting win/win solutions is to approach these situations in a different manner, trying to understand flexibly and creatively and to accommodate all communities of interest before jumping to the conclusion that to do so is impossible (Fisher and Ury, 1981). One way to determine whether or not a common ground exists among the diversity of values, including those that are spiritual or otherwise hard-to-define, is simply to try. We should not presume impossibility before first attempting to find possibilities.

The chapters in this text illustrate the spectrum of hard-to-define values that comprise a legitimate part of the meaning of public lands. But understanding that such values exist and acknowledging their legitimacy does not qualify resource managers to represent those values in decision-making processes. Regardless of how open-minded and sensitive they are, resource managers cannot merely consult this text and suddenly become expert representatives of these values. However, they do need to recognize the existence and legitimacy of hard-to-define values and ensure their consideration. The question is *how* to provide opportunities for these values to be articulated and accommodated in decision making by those who can appropriately do so?

One way can be found in the hopeful initiatives of resource managers who have recognized that there *are* ambiguous truths, and who consequently understand the need to begin reframing the issues and the manner in which they are considered by providing opportunities for the collaborative involvement of those whose values are at stake in seeking appropriate and workable solutions (Wondolleck and Yaffee, 1994). To do otherwise will most certainly direct the debate along well-traveled, yet poorly chosen paths where conflicts thrive. The adversarial interactions and mistrust that get promoted by this conflict will continue to plague efforts to develop credible and stable land management decisions. Surely it is worth trying to pursue a more promising path than to continue along old ones that have been proven both insufficient and ineffective.

Literature Cited

Carpenter, S. and Kennedy, W. (1988). *Managing public disputes: A practical guide to handling conflict and reaching agreements*. San Francisco, CA: Jossey-Bass.

Fisher, R. and Ury, W. (1981). *Getting to yes: Negotiating agreement without giving in*. Boston, MA: Houghton Mifflin Company.

Hays, S. (1959). *Conservation and the gospel of efficiency*. Cambridge, MA: Harvard University Press.

Susskind, L. and Cruikshank, J. (1987). *Breaking the impasse: Consensual approaches to resolving public disputes*. New York, NY: Basic Books, Inc.

Wondolleck, J. (1985). The importance of process in resolving environmental disputes. *Environmental Impact Assessment Review, 5* (4), 341-356.

Wondolleck, J. (1988). *Public lands conflict and resolution: Managing national forest disputes*. New York, NY: Plenum Publishing, Corp.

Wondolleck, J. and Yaffee, S. (1994). *Building bridges across agency boundaries: In search of excellence in the U.S. Forest Service*. A report prepared for the USDA Forest Service, Pacific Northwest Research Station.

Yaffee, S. (1994). *The wisdom of the spotted owl: Policy lessons for a new century*. Washington, DC: Island Press.

TECHNOLOGY AND THE EVOLUTION OF LAND ETHICS

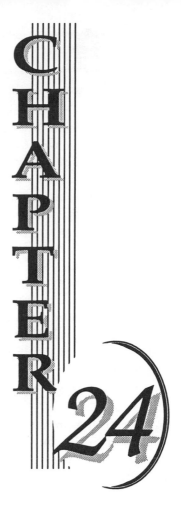

TONY BALTIC
Rocky Mountain Forest and Range Experiment Station
USDA Forest Service
Fort Collins, Colorado

*Recreational development is a job not of
building roads into lovely country, but
of building receptivity into the still unlovely human mind.*

Aldo Leopold, 1966

Introduction

Aldo Leopold's conception of conservation, which he called "the land ethic" (Leopold, 1966, pp. 237–264) and outdoor recreation within that larger context, is an idea that has been widely acclaimed. Yet Leopold's vision has not become reality as attested to by ongoing environmental crises and conflict that surround the debate over appropriate land management practices. This text is an attempt to identify and better understand the principles behind Leopold's vision that can guide management practices, and, in turn, enhance the potential for his vision to become reality. With that in mind, this chapter examines the relationship between technology and a land ethic, a relationship that Leopold considered critical.

The "unlovely human mind" is Leopold's metaphor for humanity's poorly developed land ethic.

Leopold implied that a land ethic evolves in a learning process through human interaction with the natural environment and that management technologies (recreation development in this case) facilitate this process. Indeed, Leopold believed that the evolution of a land ethic is the ultimate goal of all land management and that progress toward this goal is directly linked to how management technologies are applied. A narrowly conceived land management technology may not only retard the evolution of a land ethic, as Leopold suspected, but also could contribute to the development of a dysfunctional ethic. If our seemingly intractable environmental crises and conflicts are a manifestation of such dysfunction, the relationship between technology and a land ethic is a critical consideration for land managers.

The authors in this volume have construed nature-based values related to the human spirit as essential elements in a new land management ethic. This represents a continuing evolution of the principles that inform natural resource management. This chapter focuses on an expanded view of the concept of technology in the context of an expanded view of a land management ethic. The analysis contrasts current narrow views of technology with more expansive ones. Working definitions of a land ethic and technology are followed by an examination of their relationship and the consequences that can flow from this relationship. Finally, implications for agencies involved in research, planning, and management of the public lands are explored.

Definitions

Ethics, which relate to moral principles or values, are not subject to rigorous investigation under the dominant scientific paradigm. Ethics are considered to be reflected in people's preferences. These preferences are taken as given, assumed to be ethical, and are treated as demands to be identified and considered under the management that derives from the dominant scientific paradigm. Unresolved issues, such as seemingly irreconcilable demands, are seen as technical problems that can be objectively adjudicated based on quantitative and trade-off analyses. Questions concerning the origin and evolution of values are never raised. The underlying dichotomous and possibly dysfunctional nature of societal demands on nature is never investigated. This narrow treatment of values in the natural sciences and resource management may contribute to a narrow conception of land ethics throughout a culture while exacerbating the environmental and social crises we are experiencing.

Land ethics are those learned values that guide humans in their experience of and relationship with the land. A narrow view is reflected in a relationship that is hierarchical. It is an ethic that focuses on differences between humans and the land where land tends to be viewed, in Leopold's words, as "a commodity belonging to us." An expanded view is reflected in a relationship that is an identity. It is an ethic that focuses on the sameness of humans and the land where the land tends to be viewed as "a community to which we belong" (Leopold, p.

xviii). The expanded view is characterized by cultural connectedness to the land because intrinsic values relating humans *with* the land are fundamental values. In the narrow view, these values may be present, but separate from and subordinate to, instrumental values attributed *to* the land by humans.

Technology is the totality of the means employed to provide for human sustenance and well-being. The narrow view understands technology only as the hardware, objects, or physical transformations involved. An expanded view would include systems of thought and ways of gaining, organizing, and utilizing knowledge. The key here, as in the expanded view of a land ethic, is *connectedness*. Knowledge, process, tool, and artifact are interrelated. In an expanded view, an entire economic system, such as a market economy, is a technology, not just its artifacts and physically manipulative components. Nonconventional or non-Western ways of knowing and living would also be viewed as technologies under the expanded view; for example, the methods and techniques of mystical traditions (Capra, 1975, 1982) and the life ways of aboriginal cultures (Green and Smith, 1986; Lewis, 1992; McNeely and Pitt, 1985; Nelson, 1993; Norberg-Hodge, 1991).

Parallels between narrow and expanded views of a land ethic and technology are shown in Figure 24-1. The narrow view in both is object oriented while the expanded view in both is system oriented. This observation is important to understanding the consequences and implications of the special relationship between a land ethic and technology.

FIGURE 24-1. DEFINING VIEWS

LAND ETHIC	SCOPE OF VIEW	TECHNOLOGY
Utilitarian ⇐	Narrow ⇒	Objects/tools/physical manipulations
Community ⇐	Expanded ⇒	Connectedness of knowledge, process, and artifact

The Technology/Land Ethic Relationship

Human sustenance and well-being which include the religious and spiritual realms are fundamental human goals. Because human life is embedded within the natural environment, we must accept as fact that we derive sustenance and well-being through our experiences in and relations with the natural environment. An understanding of human sustenance and well-being thus requires an interpretation in terms analogous to Leopold's land ethic. A world-view, or social paradigm, held in the collective conscience of a culture defines our purpose in life and gives meaning to notions of sustenance and well-being. This collective conscience is "mother culture," our cultural connection to the land, and every individual in a culture is susceptible to her influence and direction (Quinn, 1993). It is our land ethic, and it guides human experience of and relations with the natural world in pursuit of sustenance and well-being.

While a land ethic guides us toward these ends, technology is the means to achieve the ends. Thus, technology mediates and facilitates our experience of and relationship with the natural world, and the appropriate technology is dictated by the guiding hand of a land ethic. But the relationship between a land ethic and technology is not strictly linear because our experiences and relationships in the natural world constitute a learning environment that tends to be shaped by a technology that in turn is shaped by the evolution of our land ethic.

Any investigation into this relationship must begin, however, by looking at the origin of a land ethic. In large part it is instinctual. It involves the unalterable tendency of the human mind to make complex and specific responses to environmental stimuli without involving reason. It is the result of the human mind evolving in concert with the rest of the natural world over the eons. Edward Wilson called it "biophilia" and defined it as "the innate tendency to focus on life and lifelike processes" (Wilson, 1984, p. 1). Vice President Al Gore in *Earth In The Balance* described it as part of the "basic architecture of the human body" that determines how we experience the world. It is the part of the human brain that evolved to enable us to re-

late to the world through a "sense of context and spatial proportion," a "consolidating" instinct in that it seeks to conserve the world and to protect it against unintended consequences (Gore, 1993, pp. 213-214).

We have learned from the fields of natural philosophy, psychology, and sociology that another aspect of human instinct is an innate tendency toward self-expression while striving for personal freedom and growth. These two aspects of instinct interact to constitute the "human spirit," the coming together of human instinctual conceptions of "self" and "other" (Schroeder, 1991).

The source of a land ethic can also be traced to the innate human capacity to reason. This involves human perception of the physical world through the interaction of our physical senses and capabilities for abstract thought. This influence is characterized by our conceptual reduction and physical transformation of the natural world.

To summarize: a land ethic, which evolves through a learning process and has an evolutionary origin that imparts to humans a biologically prepared readiness to learn (Kellert and Wilson, 1993) defines human purpose in life and gives meaning to the notions of human sustenance and well-being and guides human experience of and relationships with the natural world. Technology, the means dictated by the guiding ethic to provide for human sustenance and well-being, mediates and facilitates human experiences and relationships in the natural world and has a tendency to shape the learning environment. This environment in turn shapes and influences our land ethic by affecting the relative expression of the human spirit and human reasoning in the learning process. Thus, we see a circular system of cause and effect (Figure 24-2) in which technology occupies a critical position in a complex feedback loop.

FIGURE 24-2. LAND ETHIC/TECHNOLOGY FEEDBACK LOOP

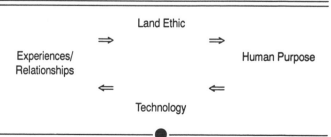

Consequences of the Technology/Land Ethic Relationship

If technology is viewed and applied expansively, human experiences and relationships in the world will reflect a symbiotic and harmonious interaction among human instinctual conceptions of "self" and "other" and human reasoning capabilities. A healthy human spirit and a land ethic based on community are nurtured. If technology is viewed and applied narrowly, human experiences and relationships in the world will be incomplete and will reflect a repression of the human spirit by human reasoning capabilities perhaps conflicting within the human spirit. The land ethic will tend to be narrow, exhibiting characteristics of a dysfunctional family, and the human spirit itself may become diseased (see discussion of anomie and alienation by Roberts, Chapter Four, in this volume).

The Narrow View

Under a narrow view of technology, systems of thought and ways of knowing that tap into the instinctual are subordinate to and segregated from those that tap our reasoning capabilities, or they are ignored altogether. This reasoning-based view is narrowed even further by seeing technology as simply tools and artifacts separate from the knowledge and processes to which they are connected (e.g., utilizing the hard technologies of resource extraction in the absence of ecological knowledge). In its most dysfunctional form, a technology of objects and manipulation can become an ethic in and of itself. The functioning of the Western market economy in theory and practice is used to illustrate feedback dynamics (Figure 24-2, see page 265) that produce consequences associated with a narrow technological view.

The market economy is a technology focused on material well-being and quantitative mechanisms, and in the U.S. it circumscribes the cultural technological view. It is often described as the "dominant social paradigm" which would suggest that it has even become the embodiment of an American land ethic. This has resulted in feedback consequences analogous to what John Platt called "social traps":

> . . . situations in society that contain traps formally like a fish trap, where men or organizations or whole societies get themselves started in some direction or some set of relationships that later prove to be unpleasant or lethal and that they see no easy way to back out of or to avoid.

> Platt, 1973, p. 641

Platt (1973) explicitly referred to our market economy when he discussed "unexpected locked-in behavioral patterns" in our experiences and relationships in the world that arise from the accumulation of immediate and small material reinforcements. Platt (1973) asserted that the "locked-in" nature of a social behavioral pattern is not inherently good or bad; it simply facilitates providing for human sustenance and well-being. In this respect, a market economy has proven to be an efficient technology for providing our material sustenance. The "unexpected" patterns of locked-in behavior that Platt (1973) referred to, the tendency toward "either escalation or elimination past some point of no return," are the result of a narrow technological view that produces only a narrow range of reinforcements. As Gore put it:

> By enhancing some senses more than others, by magnifying some abilities more than others, and by heightening some potentials more than others, technologies can profoundly alter how we perceive, experience, and then relate to the world.

> Gore, 1993, p. 214

The senses, abilities, and potentials that are enhanced, magnified, and heightened by an exclusively material technological vision are inevitably those that are utilitarian in nature. This alters human perception, experience, and relationships in the natural world in unexpected ways that are more lethal than unpleasant, alterations that lead to the escalation of environmental damage and social displacements and the elimination of natural diversity (Brown, 1991, 1993; Wilson, 1985, 1993). Platt (1973) referred to such consequences as the "invisible fist" of the market to draw a contrasting analogy with the short-term positive material reinforcements of the "invisible hand." The dynamic that locks in the production of these negative results in the long term is the tendency of the feedback loop (Figure 24-2) to become a self-maintaining system analogous to what Platt (1973) called an "invisible chain of transactional relationships" (p. 647). We continue in behavioral patterns designed only to capture material reinforcements even though these reinforcements become "less and less rewarding and in fact punishing," what Platt (1973) referred to as "sliding reinforcers," because material benefits are the only kind of reinforcements we can conceive of coming out of an exclusively material technological vision. As Platt wrote, we persist "in the hope that the results will sometime again be as good as they once were" (1973, p. 644).

Gore (1993) suggests that a fundamental alteration to the human spirit results when manipulative technologies become unquestioned rules governing relationships. Because "feelings represent the essential link between mind and body, between our intellect and the physical world," human beings find that they have to function in the world as "disembodied intellects." The resulting "cleavage between mind and body, intellect and nature, has created a kind of psychic pain" which in turn causes a "feverish hunger for distraction," that distraction manifesting itself in our societal addiction to the consumption of the Earth (Gore, 1993, pp. 218-223). In this way, a disease of the human spirit becomes a catalyst for further social trap consequences.

At about the same time Platt (1973) was developing social trap theory in behavioral science, a similar development was taking place in management science. Jay Forrester (1975) applied the principles of "system dynamics" from the study of complex physical systems to develop a theory of "counterintuitive behavior" in social systems. Forrester's description of counterintuitive behavior is analogous to Platt's social trap phenomenon:

Orderly processes are at work in the creation of human judgement and intuition, which frequently lead people to wrong decisions when faced with complex and highly interacting systems.

Forrester, p. 211

Forrester modeled the dysfunctional consequences of such behavior first in an examination of urban dynamics (Forrester, 1969) and later from a larger global perspective (Forrester, 1973).

Both Platt's conceptualization of social traps and Forrester's conceptualization of counterintuitive behavior were attempts to explain how bad results can accrue from a technology based on goals that are believed to be inherently positive. While Platt and Forrester have contributed to a better understanding of social trap dynamics by placing them in a systems context, their models are still incomplete because they exclude the spiritual values that are at the core of land ethics. Unfortunately, Western perceptions of spiritual values are antithetical to the rational, objective technological perspective that dominates the culture. Platt (1973) explicitly articulated this attitude in excluding these values from any role in his model. Their conspicuous absence from Forrester's model suggests a similar cultural bias. Thus, both of their approaches to escaping and avoiding social traps perpetuate a fundamental conceptual roadblock to an expansive vision of technology and, in turn, land ethics.

Constrained by this a priori bias, the Platt (1973) and Forrester (1969, 1973, 1975) models simulate solutions that are better characterized as technical fixes. They are simply the restructuring of present technological means. Social trap consequences are known as "externalities" in the jargon of economists and are understood as physically or materially induced stresses. Technical fix approaches are attempts to redistribute or "internalize" these stresses to those individuals, groups, institutions, or systems judged responsible for their creation through some form of prescriptive government or extragovernment action, policy, structure, or law. The logic is that the problem should be fixed or borne by the responsible parties. For example, stresses related to the loss of wildlife habitat may be converted to stresses on local extractive economies through preservation policies or laws. Such approaches may be necessary in the short term, but they are not sufficient because they do not address the underlying systemic dysfunction. The stresses persist and tend to diffuse, spawning more coercive prescriptive "solutions" which in effect become part of the trap.

The technical fix approach suffers from what Alfred North Whitehead (1929) called the "fallacy of misplaced concreteness." Herman Daly and John Cobb interpreted this as the fallacy perpetrated "whenever thinkers forget the degree of abstraction involved in thought and draw unwarranted conclusions about concrete reality" (Daly and Cobb, 1989, p. 36). Abstraction itself is a technology. It is the process of separating, subtracting from, and simplifying concrete reality as a means to gain knowledge of that reality to support decision making. Under the influence of a narrow technological view, nonmaterial parts are misplaced in this abstracting process while the material parts are reconstituted as the whole of concrete reality. Of course, this is misplaced concreteness because the knowledge base is incomplete. When critical decisions or systems based on this false whole generate external stresses, because of feedback from the misplaced parts, the process is reiterated inevitably generating the same results. For example, the stresses related to habitat loss may appear on the surface to be induced by the material dependencies of an economy, but they are fundamentally the result of economic abstractions that lead to the practical structuring of economies in ways that neither recognize nor explicitly provide opportunities for the realization of spiritual well-being. This induces an unrecognized psychological stress in the economy that is converted to stresses on wildlife habitat when people attempt to fill this void by seeking more material reinforcement. Denying the economy this material resource to relieve the stress of habitat loss simply shifts the stress back to the economy which is incapable of internalizing alternatives to material inputs, thus exacerbating the original psychological stress. The intensified stress on the economy is further redistributed among individuals, groups and institutions, settling on those with the least economic leverage as prescribed by the structural design of the economy. Yet another technical fix might be designed to shift the stress away from one of these recipients if they are judged to be undeserving of the stress. Not only is the fundamental problem of misplaced concreteness in economic abstractions not addressed, but also technical fixes become a part of the vicious cycles that are characteristic of social traps.

The Expanded View

Under an expanded view of technology, systems of thought and ways of knowing and living that tap into the instinctual, share fundamental connections with human reasoning capabilities. Tool and artifact are circumscribed by the knowledge base and processes within which they function, and the distinction between technology and a land ethic is well-understood. Unfortunately, an expanded view is not dominant in any part of the developed world today. And in the undeveloped world it appears that the movement toward development is so influenced or controlled by dominant views in the developed world that any progress toward an expanded view, or in

building on existing expansive traditions, is painfully slow, if not stalled or even regressing (Korten, 1990; Mander, 1991; Norberg-Hodge, 1991; Quinn, 1993). Perhaps, then, the only consequences of an expanded view are those posited by advocates for change. For example, recognizing that the nonmaterial needs of humanity have been left out of the conventional view of development, the International Foundation for Development Alternatives (IFDA) proposed a more expansive view of development:

> *Some still consider that development refers to things and can be reduced to capital accumulation, economic growth and economic restructuring. But development fundamentally refers to human beings, the whole man, the whole woman. It is a human experience synonymous with the fulfillment of individual mental, emotional and physical potentiality. The society, its economy and polity ought to be organized in such a manner as to maximize for the individual the opportunities for self-fulfillment. There is development when people and their communities act as subject and are not acted upon as objects, assert their autonomy, self-reliance and self-confidence, when they set out and carry out projects. To develop is to be or become, not to have.* (IFDA, 1980, pp. 9-10)

Wilson expanded on this nonmaterial component of well-being in his description of biophilia by explicitly including the existence of an innate human bond with other species in the notion of development:

> *. . . to explore and affiliate with life is a deep and complicated process in mental development . . . our existence depends on this propensity, our spirit is woven from it, hope rises on its currents.* (1984, p. 1)

Leopold considered development as "true sustained yield" and placed ecological principles above the material (Flader, 1987). Leopold distinguished between "economic biology" which he asserted emphasizes the sustained production of commodity resources, thus giving competitive advantage to "useful" species, and "true sustained yield" which recognizes the necessity to preserve the health of the entire biotic system because "no man can say where utility begins or ends" (Flader, p. 17). His articulation of a land ethic embraced the concept of a true sustained yield:

*A land ethic . . . reflects the existence of an eco-
logical conscience, and this in turn reflects a
conviction of individual responsibility for the
health of the land. Health is the capacity of
the land for self-renewal. Conservation is our
effort to understand and preserve this capacity.*

Leopold, 1966, p. 258

Leopold believed that this conscience and conviction
initially "must come from within," as the result of
the flowering of "love, respect, and admiration for
land," and then evolve in symbiosis with the more
intellectual human processes (Leopold, 1966, pp.
210, 261-263).

Daly (1991) pioneered the intellectual expansion
of the concept of development through his work in
making ecological principles a central focus in economic analysis. His leadership has inspired the discipline of ecological economics which is generating
"new ways of thinking about the linkages between
ecological and economic systems" (Costanza, 1989).
Daly's most recent work with theologian John B.
Cobb (1989) probed even more deeply into the systemic origins of social traps and sustainability by
linking economic, ecologic analyses with characteristics of the human spirit to synthesize a practical concept of "community."

Human beings are learners. The most important
consequence of an expansive technological vision is
that it enables individuals and whole societies to focus on this ultimate human purpose. Although the
Platt (1973) and Forrester models take a systems
approach, they do not question the narrow technological view that sees and treats humans primarily
as consumers. Material reinforcements monopolize
the human learning environment, and consumption
becomes the focus of human purpose. Because of
ecological limits and conflicts with human spiritual
needs, such a focus on consumption is bound to become degenerative. Technical fixes that address the
degenerative symptoms don't change this fundamental condition and only aggravate the situation because they are coercive forces external to the individual that tend to proliferate. Learning, on the
other hand, is inherently generative. An expansive
technological view creates a positive learning environment that reinforces motivations to learn and
create that are internal to the individual.

Peter Senge, a protege of Forrester, has written
a remarkable book, *The Fifth Discipline: The Art
and Practice of the Learning Organization* (1990)

that builds on Forrester's "systems thinking" by embracing an expansive technological view while laying
a conceptual foundation for tapping into the full
range of innate human preparedness to learn. While
humankind's material world is an important component of this model, Senge argues that learning involves our "higher aspirations beyond food, shelter,
and belonging" that "enhance our capacity to create"
(1990, pp. 5, 14). He also insists that learning requires skills that can be developed through practice
and outlines five "disciplines" or "component technologies" that define these skills (pp. 6-10). Each of
these disciplines are innovative in the ways they interact and incorporate human reasoning capabilities.
Senge's conception of "systems thinking," which he
identifies as the cornerstone discipline, is more complete than conventional definitions. However, the
discipline Senge calls "personal mastery" is perhaps
the most revolutionary. According to Senge, this is
the "spiritual foundation" of learning, the roots of
which "lie in both Eastern and Western spiritual traditions, and in secular traditions as well" (p. 7). Personal mastery embodies two underlying tasks: "continually clarifying what is most important to us" and
"continually learning how to see current reality more
clearly." Those who become highly proficient at these
tasks develop a "special sense of purpose" (pp. 141-
143). Senge describes these tasks in great detail, but
they fundamentally involve the integration of reason
and intuition in our emotional development, which he
implies is perhaps more important than our physical
and intellectual development. One might say that in
contrast to the technical fix approach that requires
prescriptive mechanisms to "internalize externalities," the learning approach relies on individual systems thinking to "externalize internalities"; that is, to
stimulate those qualities and values that derive from
the human spirit and give one her or his sense of connectedness to the world. Senge believes that this
sense of connectedness is the most significant result
of the learning process and represents a fundamental
shift of mind he calls "metanoia" (pp. 12-13).

While one can only find hypothesized consequences of an expanded view in the world of the developed and developing nations, there are real consequences of the expanded view to be observed in the
so-called "primitive" world. Primitive is a universal
reference by dominant societies all over the world to
the cultures of indigenous peoples which still function
within at least 3,000 native societies worldwide

(Mander, 1991). The reference is derogatory in the sense that these cultures are considered below the dominant cultures on a scale of social evolution. These perceptions are understandable and even logical coming from the narrow view of technology. The error comes with equating the minimum material comforts of indigenous cultures with an inferior quality of life. The historical, anthropological, and archaeological evidence is quite the contrary. Not only are many aspects and qualities of life in these cultures admirable and desirable even by modern, narrowly viewed standards, but they have also displayed a remarkable stability over time (Kopper, 1986; Sahlins, 1972). Further, while these cultures are not perfect (Diamond, 1989, 1993), there is no evidence of the culturally dichotomous and dysfunctional relationships that exist in modern societies. Indeed, their stability attests to this (Alcorn, 1991; Booth and Jacobs, 1990; Dasmann, 1991; Green and Smith, 1986; McNeely and Pitt, 1985; Nelson, 1993; Oldfield, 1991; Quinn, 1993).

The fundamental misperception, however, lies in the belief that aboriginal cultures lack a technological basis. Technological societies value their technological prowess highly and are even willing to learn and apply alternative technologies from other societies. Unfortunately, the concept that disqualifies aboriginal cultures as technological in the judgment of dominant cultures is the very component of their technological view that sees the connectedness of all things and results in a land ethic of community, the component that embodies the values and processes that derive from the nature-human spirit interface. The presence of community, missing from the evolution of a technological society's land ethic, is the reason that aboriginal cultures appear to have avoided social trap phenomena (Mander, 1991). If one recognized these alternative life ways and paths to knowledge as the technologies they truly are, one might be willing to explore how they could inform our own technological and scientific view.

Senge (1990) cited indigenous practices several times in his discussions of the five component technologies for learning. Analysts from other disciplines have also recognized and documented the technological nature of indigenous cultures, including their spiritual component, and the potential for traditional conservation technologies to inform and improve Western science and technology (e.g.,

Birckhead, De Lacy and Smith, 1991; Booth and Jacobs, 1990; Green and Smith, 1986; Johannes, 1989; McNeely and Pitt, 1985; Nabhan and St. Antoine, 1993; Nelson, 1993; Oldfield and Alcorn, 1991; Williams and Hunn, 1982).

Implications of the Technology/Land Ethic Relationship for Land Management and Planning

Land management agencies in the U.S. have been profoundly affected by social trap phenomena as they result in public lands conflicts (Crowfoot and Wondolleck, 1990; Wondolleck, 1988) and associated legislative fallout (Le Master, 1984). In fact, the consequences of social traps contributed to the establishment of these agencies dating back to Gifford Pinchot's Forest Service and the beginnings of the conservation movement (Wilkinson and Anderson, 1987). The conservation concept as instituted in these agencies and environmental laws has been steadily expanding in the U.S. (Nash, 1989). This evolution is continuing. For example, a new management policy called "sustainable ecosystem management" that is more responsive to ecological principles has recently been adopted by several federal agencies including the USDA Forest Service (Kaufmann et al., 1994; Robertson, 1992).

However, such initiatives must be part of a larger strategy whose goal is the genesis of an expanded land ethic. If not, their effects will be reduced to a technical fix, only intensifying the symptoms of social dysfunction, because the present narrow land ethic will continue to produce human demands that are incompatible with ecological integrity. Land management agencies have a unique opportunity and responsibility to understand and act on their role in this genesis because they have become the primary intermediaries between modern society and its experience of and relationship with the land.

Agency Role in the Genesis of an Expanded Land Ethic

A land ethic cannot be prescribed. It can only evolve through a learning process embedded in human experiences and relationships in the natural world. Fortunately, the innate human capability for this learning is the essence of a human dimension of ecosystems. Technologies that facilitate and enable this human preparedness to learn must be the focus of a larger strategy that encompasses the biophysical emphasis of ecosystem management. Further, an expanded view of technology that addresses human learning capabilities involves the integration of the human spirit with human reasoning.

Many of the policy directives needed to support a larger strategy are already in place. The USDA Forest Service provides a good example. The first element of the Forest Service Mission Statement (USDA Forest Service, 1993a) calls for the development of a conservation ethic and the agency's *Mission/Issue Guidebook* (USDA Forest Service, 1993b) identifies spiritual and human values as important issues in the new ecosystem management approach. Another important supporting directive is the Forest Service Guiding Principle to select the most appropriate technologies (USDA Forest Service, 1993a). Perhaps the key directive is in how an agency defines its service to people. People absolutely must be identified and treated as learners if an expanded land ethic is the ultimate goal. Current agency policies treat people as "customers" (e.g., USDA Forest Service, 1993a) which reinforces a narrow land ethic. Given a set of supporting policy directives, the job then becomes one of defining and integrating the policy elements in a planning and analysis process to develop a comprehensive management strategy.

Implications for Planning and Analysis

The land management planning and analysis process has traditionally focused on independent functional analyses for commodity production and purely financial objectives. However, agency researchers have recently broadened their technological view to focus more on ecological principles in response to the new policy of ecosystem management. For example, a significant component of research is now organized to understand ecosystem relationships, and research in the area of management science is now focusing on resource interactions (see FS-RM-4852). Further, ecosystem conditions and responses that were once treated exclusively as constraints or explanatory variables, or ignored altogether in land management planning analyses, are now often found in the objective function of optimization models and on the output side of production functions (see FS-RM-4803). In the research area of amenity resource valuation one of the current research initiatives is the "clarification and development of alternative valuation paradigms and value concepts" (see FS-RM-4851). There has also been an increased emphasis on interdisciplinary research and planning.

Researchers are now confident they can design a coarse "ecosystem principles filter" for decision analysis models that will identify the biophysical dimensions of ecosystems that need to be protected or restored in order to preserve biological integrity to a large degree (Kaufmann et al., 1994, pp. 9-11). Fine filter analyses that extend this protection will soon be possible with the development of more advanced techniques that include biophysical objectives such as spatial optimization modeling (Hof, Bevers, Joyce, and Kent, 1994; Hof and Joyce, 1992, 1993).

Incorporating ecological knowledge more centrally into the analysis is necessary, but it is not sufficient. The technological view must also be extended to address the human dimensions of ecosystems. While the new policy of sustainable ecosystem management has acknowledged this human dimension, it has so far been narrowly defined in terms of the difficulties encountered in attempting to integrate the biophysical capabilities of ecosystems and human needs. For example, Kaufmann et al. have suggested that, "because the physical and biological capabilities of ecosystems are limited in flexibility, convergence requires shifts in social and economic needs to comply more with ecosystem capabilities" (1994, p. 2).

The "analytical engine" that drives one of the leading proposals for a decision support system (DSS) that addresses the human dimension is a conventional supply-side approach that relies on trade-off analysis (Driver, Kent, and Hof, 1994). The supply of biophysical attributes needed to secure a certain level of ecological integrity is formulated as an ecosystem principles filter. The range of human demands and needs is assessed to determine the supply of biophysical attributes it requires. The biophysical requirement of the human dimension is passed through the ecosystem filter to "determine which economic and social needs can be met while sustaining ecosystems" (Kaufmann et al., 1994, p. 11). The trade-offs will effectively come from the range of human demands. The proposed DSS does incorporate innovative public involvement techniques to mitigate the consequences of the trade-offs. However, the principal result is typical of a technical fix approach, the redistribution of social trap consequences.

Analyses with an exclusive supply-side focus are incapable of fully addressing the human dimensions of ecosystems. An expansive technological view must include a demand-side analysis as an equal and interactive component of the analytical engine in decision support systems. Whereas the natural sciences take the lead in the supply-side analysis, the social sciences must take the lead in the demand-side analysis. However, both analyses must be collaborative and integrated. Demand-side analysis is *not* the inventorying and accounting of human demands and biophysical supplies required to meet those demands. That is an information system typically used as input into supply-side trade-off analyses. Demand-side analysis is the scientific inquiry into the nature and source of human demands. Integrated with supply side analysis, it supports the development of management strategies to facilitate human learning. The demand-supply dynamic (Figure 24-3) is a complex system of feedback loops, analogous to and embedded in the land ethic/technology dynamic (Figure 24-2, see page 265). What is supplied and how it is supplied can have

---

FIGURE 24-3. EMBEDDED DEMAND/SUPPLY FEEDBACK LOOP

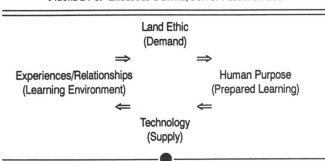

---

a profound influence on the learning process and in turn the nature of human demands. That learning process involves feedback between the innate human capacity to learn and the learning environment. Because innate reasoning capabilities and the instinctual characteristics of the human spirit combine

to prepare humans for learning, both must necessarily be included within the scope of the demand analysis. The ultimate goal is to design a management strategy for facilitating a learning process that leads to a society of learners creating their own expansive land ethic, thus avoiding the vicious cycle of dysfunction that results from social traps.

There has been much research on both human cognitive and affective learning and knowledge in the field of human judgment and behavioral decision theory that can be applied in demand-side analyses for land management planning (see Hammond, McClelland, and Mumpower, 1980; Slovic, Fischhoff, and Lichtenstein, 1977). Perhaps a point of departure for a demand-side analysis approach could involve the work of Mihaly Csikszentmihalyi (1990) who introduced a new theory of human well-being which he called "flow." Flow is a peak mental state that is more the result of a process of learning and creating than any material end. Csikszentmihalyi (1993) theorized that the experience of flow can expand beyond isolated peak experiences and that the human spirit plays an important part in such evolution. "To transform the entirety of life into a unified flow experience, it helps to have faith in a system of meanings that gives purpose to one's being" (Csikszentmihalyi, 1993, p. xv).

A new theory about human preparedness for learning through interactions with the natural environment called the "Biophilia Hypothesis" (Kellert and Wilson, 1993) could also inform the demand-side analysis. It has been hypothesized that human coevolution with the natural world has resulted in a "biologically prepared complex of learning rules" that enable "higher-order cognitive functioning" (as reflected in land ethics), but only when stimulation is provided through direct experiences of and relationships with the natural environment (Kellert and Wilson, 1993, pp. 31-33, 110-112).

Senge's systems approach (1990) which focuses on learning processes and recognizes a prominent role for the human spirit, could serve as a model for integrating the demand- and supply-side analyses.

Perhaps the deepest insights for both demand-side and supply-side analyses could come from scientific investigations into experiential knowledge. This involves traditional ecological knowledge, ways of knowing, and management practices of aboriginal cultures. Milton Freeman, who helped organize the

Working Group on Traditional Knowledge, Conservation, and Rural Development, of the International Union for the Conservation of Nature and Natural Resources (IUCN) has suggested that:

> . . . *both Native systems and western science rest on the same foundation—namely empirical evidence. Both systems place value on the systematic accumulation of detailed observations and the abstraction of norms from disparate data sets. At this point, however, the two systems begin to diverge. The Native system assesses deviation from the norm in a qualitative sense.*
>
> Mander, 1991, p. 259

This qualitative sense involves the spiritual values discussed in this text. Freeman is just one of many scientists and managers who are beginning to recognize the scientific legitimacy of this qualitative sense and of traditional Native paths to knowledge in general (Birckhead, De Lacy, and Smith, 1991; Booth and Jacobs, 1990; Feit, 1986; Freeman, 1984, 1986; Green and Smith, 1986; Johannes, 1989; McNeely and Pitt, 1985; Nabhan and St. Antoine, 1993; Nelson, 1993; Oldfield and Alcorn, 1991; Williams and Hunn, 1982). If land management agencies truly do value a multicultural organization as essential to their success (e.g., USDA Forest Service, 1993a), they need to integrate aboriginal knowledge into their science and management, not just aboriginal artifacts into their museums.

Implications for Management

The management philosophy and strategy that reflects an expanded technological view will be very different from current ones. Instead of creating outputs or products fashioned from biophysical supplies for customers to use, land managers will optimize opportunities for experiences and relationships with the natural world for learners who create their own benefits. The benefits can derive from the immaterial as well as the material, from off-site, as well as on-site, experiences and relationships with the ultimate benefit being the generative process of learning itself. And the ultimate creation of learners is an expansive land ethic, the result of a feedback dynamic (Figure 24-3) Senge (1990), calls a "virtuous cycle" (p. 81).

The full range of human cognitive and affective learning capabilities must be allowed to function in

the learning process. If any of these are obstructed, either through neglect or inappropriate technologies that impede or impair the learning process, management becomes prescriptive. Thus, nonmaterial or spiritual values must be explicitly considered in any management strategy. And land managers become learners in this process along with the people they serve. Further, learning is not just the taking in of information from external sources nor is it limited simply to adapting to circumstances, what Senge (1990) calls "survival learning" (p. 14). These kinds of learning are necessary but not sufficient. They can be characterized as "adaptive learning," and "must be joined by 'generative learning,' learning that enhances our capacity to create" (Senge, 1990, p. 14).

Land managers' greatest responsibility and opportunity may lie in their role as facilitators and mediators in the direct relationships and experiences of people with the land. In modern societies, outdoor recreation provides the primary opportunity for this direct interaction. In fact, a shift in management emphasis from commodity extraction to outdoor recreation is already taking place within land management agencies. This shift has been supported by a growing body of applied research that has documented the beneficial consequences of nature-based leisure (Driver, Brown and Peterson, 1991). This research has focused on physiological and psychological benefits to individuals such as restoration from stress and satisfaction of aesthetic preferences. There has been much less applied research into the social benefits and essentially none with respect to land ethic development. However, hypotheses like Wilson's "biophilia" and Csikszentmihalyi's "flow" suggest that benefits derived from human experiences of and relationships with the natural world can influence the very structure of human behavior and institutions.

The implications of such hypotheses for a culture whose only meaningful direct relationships with the land are derived through recreating on it are far-reaching. Leopold's intuitive recognition of these implications predated the articulation of these hypotheses by several decades. Leopold believed that "to promote perception is the only truly creative part of recreational engineering" (Leopold, 1966, p. 290). Unfortunately, recreation management is a technology that has been treated very narrowly under traditional land management practices. For example, the "ultimate goal" of the Forest Service's National Recreation Strategy is "customer satisfaction" with a major emphasis on "recreation quality" (Super and Cordell, 1990, pp. 814-815). This goal and emphasis is driven by the public's "recreation preferences" which are assumed to be fixed before these customers even "come to our Forests" (Super and Cordell, 1990, p. 816). The major means, referred to as accomplishments, of the National Recreation Strategy are "new and better interpretive and informational signs, improved maps showing recreation opportunities, formation of a national scenic byways program, and the development of partnerships that share the costs of improving or expanding facilities" (Super and Cordell, 1990, p. 814). This is the language of recreation as commodity and is reinforced by the current trend toward more user fees for outdoor recreation on public lands.

In contrast to this is an expanded view of recreation management best exemplified by Leopold's vision of human–wildland encounters. According to Susan Flader, Leopold's biographer, "Leopold saw the importance of developing a metaphysic, an aesthetic appreciation . . . leading to ecological understanding . . . to love and respect and finally a land ethic" (Flader, 1987, p. 17). Under an expanded view, outdoor recreation management would be part of a larger conservation initiative. Instead of customer satisfaction, the goal would be an American land ethic. Instead of emphasizing recreation quality, the emphasis would be on experiences and interactions. Instead of the process being driven by the idea of preferences, it would be driven by the idea of learning. Instead of signs, maps, byways, and facilities, the major accomplishment would be the generative learning of people whose ultimate creation is an expanded land ethic. Specific actions in support of this overall strategy would include a major expansion and upgrading of the wildland trail systems, expanded interpretive staff, a major expansion of the wilderness system to include all 233 of the nation's ecosystems (Davis, 1984), a re-evaluation of the very meaning and management of wildlands in relation to humans (Alcorn, 1991; Botkin, 1990; Grumbine, 1992), and strategies to provide urban residents more direct opportunities to learn ecological principles and to acquire a better understanding of how society draws its sustenance, both material and immaterial, from the land. Access to private lands could be included in this recreation strategy through agricultural extension and private forestry program agreements. This approach would better serve Leopold's conception of recreation than would the current commodity oriented approach. In fact, a new agency approach to managing amenity resources called Benefits-Based Management (Lee and Driver, 1992), which is in the evolutionary and developmental stages, has moved beyond this narrow view and has the potential to be built upon to establish an expansive management technology.

An expanded conception of a recreation management technology may also be incompatible with user fees (Cockrell and Wellman, 1985; Schultz, McAvoy and Dustin, 1988). Aside from the arguments that cite the nonexclusive and nonrival nature of the benefits derived from outdoor recreation, and that the sum total of revenue generated from user fees may be spectacularly trivial compared to the hypothesized social benefit, a land ethic, unlike customer satisfaction, cannot be bought and sold in the marketplace. Indeed, an ethic is an intangible reality, one that is too often misplaced in our money economy (Daly, 1991). As Leopold wrote,

> *An ethic may be regarded as a mode of guidance for meeting ecological situations so new or intricate, or involving such deferred reactions, that the path to social expediency is not discernible to the average individual.* (1966, p. 239)

An ecological conscience is not a consumer good. Recreation quality is amenable to exchange in the market but meaningful experiences and interactions with nature may not be. In describing the consciousness-stimulating results of such experiences and interactions as a benefit of habitat preservation, Byron Norton argued that, "Novel and unexpected encounters with species can jar sensibilities and can begin the processes of value transformation. . . . However, . . . treated as a consumptive 'commodity,' a species does not provide occasions for value transformation" (Norton, 1987, p. 266).

Individual preference is the foundation of market economics but an individual's perception of nature may be distorted by it. For example, Driver and Rosenthal (1984) found that people sometimes perceive an outdoor recreation experience to be of "higher quality" simply because they have to pay more for it. Finally, signs, maps, byways, and facilities can readily be thought of as products and assigned a commodity value in exchange without altering the public perception of their true underlying use value. However, charging fees to support trail, staff, and wilderness expansion could severely distract the perception or value transformation that these means are intended to stimulate in the learning process. Outdoor recreation, in this context, should not be a competitor for scarce resources, but a facilitator in helping to guide wise public allocation of scarce resources.

Conclusion

Vice President Gore (1993) observed that the ultimate dichotomy of the "dominant social paradigm" is the separation of human experience in the world from the human spirit. He viewed the human spirit as a "kind of inner ecology that relates perception, emotions, thinking, and choices to forces outside ourselves" and suggests that the implication is that we need to foster a new "environmentalism of the spirit" (pp. 241-242). This entails a reconnecting of the intellect with the physical world leading in turn to a reconnection of mind with body, thinking with feeling, facts with values, and knowledge with morality. Gore (1993) argued that the catalyst for this change should be to "make the rescue of the environment a central organizing principle for civilization" just as the commitment to democracy and free markets has served as the central organizing principle in the struggle for the ideas of freedom and human rights. Gore emphasized that this new principle is "consistent in every way with democracy and free markets" and is simply a "larger conception of how democracy and free markets enhance each other" (pp. 269-277).

Gore's "environmentalism of the spirit" is analogous to an expanded land ethic and embodies in a meaningful way the hard-to-define human values. His prescription for fostering this ethic, a reconnecting strategy, is analogous to an expanded technological view which also embraces the human spirit. Finally, Gore's suggestion that the catalyst for this fostering effort can come from government, the means by which we organize our collective lives, is well-taken. In the expanded view of technology, a governmental system of organization is a technology. Government can foster an expanded land ethic through making this social organizing technology more expansive. This should not be confused with governmental attempts to institutionalize specific behaviors through prescriptive or punitive laws and legislation. Our objective should be to facilitate, not dictate, relationships. As Ishmael said, "People need more than to be scolded, more than to be made to feel stupid and guilty. They need more than a vision of doom. They need a vision of the world and of themselves that inspires them" (Quinn, 1993, p. 243). Give people the opportunity to create this vision for themselves, to learn by using the appropriate technologies, and they will. Land management agencies, not legislatures, have the central role in such a strategy because they are the public organizations that deal directly with the land and through which the public has its most direct contact with the land.

Literature Cited

Alcorn, J. (1991). Epilogue: Ethics, economics, and conservation. In M. Oldfield and J. Alcorn (Eds.), *Biodiversity: Culture, conservation, and ecodevelopment* (pp. 317-349). Boulder, CO: Westview Press, Inc.

Birckhead, J., De Lacy, T., and Smith, L. (1991). *Aboriginal involvement in parks and protected areas* (Australian Institute of Aboriginal and Torres Strait Islander Studies Report Series). Canberra, Australia: Aboriginal Studies Press.

Booth, A. and Jacobs, H. (1990). Ties that bind: Native American beliefs as a foundation for environmental consciousness. *Environmental Ethics, 12*, 27–43.

Botkin, D. (1990). *Discordant harmonies: A new ecology for the twenty-first century*. New York, NY: Oxford University Press.

Brown, L. (Ed.). 1991. *The World Watch reader on global environmental issues*. New York, NY: W. W. Norton & Company, Inc.

Brown, L. (1993). *State of the world 1993*. New York, NY: W. W. Norton & Company, Inc.

Capra, F. (1975). *The tao of physics*. Berkeley, CA: Shambhala Publications, Inc.

Capra, F. (1982). *The turning point: Science, society, and the rising culture*. New York, NY: Bantam Books.

Cockrell, D. and Wellman, D. (1985). Against the running tide: Democracy and outdoor recreation user fees. In J. Wood (Ed.), *Proceedings of the National Outdoor Recreation Trends Symposium II* (pp. 193-205). February 24-27. Myrtle Beach, SC.

Costanza, R. (1989). What is ecological economics? *Ecological Economics, 1*(1), 1-7.

Crowfoot, J. and Wondolleck, J. (1990). *Environmental disputes: Community involvement in conflict resolution*. Covelo, CA: Island Press.

Csikszentmihalyi, M. (1990). *Flow: The psychology of optimal experience*. New York, NY: Harper & Row Publishers, Inc.

Csikszentmihalyi, M. (1993). *The evolving self: A psychology for the third millennium*. New York, NY: HarperCollins Publishers.

Daly, H. (1991). *Steady state economics* (2nd ed.). Covelo, CA: Island Press.

Daly, H. and Cobb, J., Jr. (1989). *For the common good: Redirecting the economy toward community, the environment, and a sustainable future*. Boston, MA: Beacon Press.

Dasmann, R. (1991). The importance of culture and biological diversity. In M. Oldfield and J. Alcorn (Eds.), *Biodiversity: Culture, conservation, and ecodevelopment* (pp. 7-15). Boulder, CO: Westview Press, Inc.

Davis, G. (1984). Natural diversity for future generations: The role of wilderness. In J. Cooley and J. H. Cooley (Eds.), *Natural diversity in forest ecosystems: Proceedings of a workshop* (pp. 141-154). Nov 29-Dec 1, 1982. Athens, GA: Institute of Ecology, University of Georgia.

Diamond, J. (1989). Overview of recent extinctions. In D. Western and M. Pearl (Eds.), *Conservation for the twenty-first century* (pp. 37-41). New York, NY: Oxford University Press.

Diamond, J. (1993). New Guineans and their natural world. In S. Kellert and E. Wilson (Eds.), *The biophilia hypothesis* (pp. 251-271). Covelo, CA: Island Press.

Driver, B., Brown, P., and Peterson, G. (Eds.). (1991). *Benefits of leisure*. State College, PA: Venture Publishing, Inc.

Driver, B., Kent, B., and Hof, J. (1994). A planning and analysis process for including social and biophysical considerations in sustainable ecosystem management. In W. Covington and L. DeBano (Technical Coordinators), *Sustainable ecological systems: Implementing an ecological approach to land management* (pp. 281-291). (Gen. Tech. Rep. RM–247). USDA Forest Service, Rocky Mountain Forest and Range Experiment Station. Fort Collins, CO.

Driver, B. and Rosenthal, D. (1984). "Public responses to user fees." Paper presented at the Conference on Fees for Outdoor Recreation on Lands Open to the Public. Jan 1-3. Durham, NH.

Feit, H. (1986). James Bay Cree Indian management and moral consideration of furbearers. In *Native people and renewable resource management* (pp. 49-62). The 1986 Symposium of the Alberta Society of Professional Biologists.

Flader, S. (1987). Aldo Leopold and the evolution of a land ethic. In T. Tanner (Ed.), *Aldo Leopold: The man and his legacy* (pp. 3-24). Ankeny, IA: Soil Conservation Society of America.

Forrester, J. (1969). *Urban dynamics*. Cambridge, MA: MIT. Press.

Forrester, J. (1973). *World dynamics*. Cambridge, MA: Wright-Allen Press.

Forrester, J. (1975). Counterintuitive behavior of social systems. In J. Forrester (Ed.), *Collected papers of Jay W. Forrester* (pp. 211-244). Cambridge, MA: Wright-Allen Press.

Freeman, M. (1984). New/old approaches to renewable resources management in the north. In *Northern frontier development: Alaska/Canadian perspectives*. The Third Annual Meeting of the Western Regional Science Association, Feb. 1984, Monterey, CA.

Freeman, M. (1986). Renewable resources, economics and native communities. In *Native people and renewable resource management* (pp. 29-37). The 1986 Symposium of the Alberta Society of Professional Biologists.

FS-RM-4803. (no date). *Research work unit description: Advanced research in economics and optimization for forest service panning*. USDA Forest Service, Rocky Mountain Forest and Range Experiment Station, Fort Collins, CO.

FS-RM-4851. (no date). *Research work unit description: Valuation of wildland resource benefits*. USDA Forest Service, Rocky Mountain Forest and Range Experiment Station, Fort Collins, CO.

FS-RM-4852. (no date). *Research work unit description: Natural resource assessment, ecology and management science research*. USDA Forest Service, Rocky Mountain Forest and Range Experiment Station, Fort Collins, CO.

Gore, A. (1993). *Earth in the balance: Ecology and the human spirit*. New York, NY: Plume.

Green, J. and Smith, J. (Eds.). (1986). *Nature, people, and renewable resource management*. The 1986 Symposium of the Alberta Society of Professional Biologists. April 29-May 1, 1986. Edmonton, Alberta.

Grumbine, R. (1992). *Ghost bears: Exploring the biodiversity crisis*. Covelo, CA: Island Press.

Hammond, K., McClelland, B., and Mumpower, J. (1980). *Human judgement and decision making: Theories, methods, and procedures*. New York, NY: Praeger Publishers.

Hof, J., Bevers, M., Joyce, L., and Kent, B. (1994). An integer programming approach for spatially and temporally optimizing wildlife populations. *Forest Science, 40*(1): 177-191.

Hof, J. and Joyce, L. (1992). Spatial optimization for wildlife and timber in managed forest ecosystems. *Forest Science, 38*(3), 489-508.

Hof, J. and Joyce, L. (1993). A mixed integer linear programming approach for spatially optimizing for wildlife and timber in managed forest ecosystems. *Forest Science, 39*(4), 816-834.

International Foundation for Development Alternatives (IFDA). (1980). *Building blocks for alternative development strategies, a progress report from the third system project: IFDA Dossier*. Nyon, Switzerland.

Johannes, R. (Ed.). (1989). *Traditional ecological knowledge: A collection of essays*. Gland, Switzerland: International Union for Nature Conservation.

Kaufmann, M., Graham, R., Boyce, D., Moir, W., Perry, L., Reynolds, R., Bassett, R., Mehlhop, P., Edminster, C., Block, W., and Corn, P. (1994). *An ecological basis for ecosystem management* (Gen. Tech. Rep. RM–246). Fort Collins, CO: USDA Forest Service, Rocky Mountain Forest and Range Experiment Station.

Kellert, S. and Wilson, E. (Eds.). (1993). *The biophilia hypothesis*. Covelo, CA: Island Press.

Kopper, P. (1986). *The Smithsonian book of North American Indians: Before the coming of the Europeans*. Washington, DC: Smithsonian Books.

Korten, D. (1990). *Getting to the 21st century: Voluntary action and the global agenda*. West Hartford, CT: Kumarian Press, Inc.

Lee, M. and Driver, B. (1992). *Benefits-based management: A new paradigm for managing amenity resources*. Paper presented at The Second Canada/U.S. Workshop on Visitor Management in Parks, Forests, and Protected Areas. University of Wisconsin–Madison. May 13-16, 1992. Madison, WI.

Le Master, D. (1984). *Decade of change: The remaking of the Forest Service statutory authority during the 1970s*. Westport, CT: Greenwood Publishing Group, Inc.

Leopold, A. (1966). *A sand county almanac: With essays on conservation from Round River*. New York, NY: Ballantine Books.

Lewis, H. (1992). The technology and ecology of nature's custodians: Anthropological perspectives on aborigines and national parks. In J. Birckhead, T. De Lacy and L. Smith (Eds.), *Aboriginal involvement in parks and protected areas* (pp. 15-28). Australian Institute of Aboriginal and Torres Strait Islander Studies Report Series. Canberra, Australia: Aboriginal Studies Press.

Mander, J. (1991). *In the absence of the sacred: The failure of technology and the survival of the Indian nations*. San Francisco, CA: Sierra Club Books.

McNeely, J. and Pitt, D. (Eds.). (1985). *Culture and conservation: The human dimension in environmental planning*. Dover, NH: Crown Helm.

Nabhan, G. and St. Antoine, S. (1993). The loss of floral and faunal story: The extinction of experience. In S. Kellert and E. Wilson (Eds.), *The biophilia hypothesis* (pp. 229-250). Covelo, CA: Island Press.

Nash, R. (1989). *The rights of nature: A history of environmental ethics*. Madison, WI: University of Wisconsin Press.

Nelson, R. (1993). Searching for the lost arrow: Physical and spiritual ecology in the hunter's world. In S. Kellert and E. Wilson (Eds.), *The biophilia hypothesis* (pp. 201-228). Covelo, CA: Island Press.

Norberg-Hodge, H. (1991). *Ancient futures: Learning from Ladakh*. San Francisco, CA: Sierra Club Books.

Norton, B. (1987). *Why preserve natural diversity?* Princeton, NJ: Princeton University Press.

Oldfield, M. (1991). Introduction to part one: Biodiversity and culture. In M. Oldfield and J. Alcorn (Eds.), *Biodiversity: Culture, conservation, and ecodevelopment* (pp. 3-6). Boulder, CO: Westview Press, Inc.

Oldfield, M. and Alcorn, J. (Eds.). (1991). *Biodiversity: culture, conservation, and ecodevelopment*. Boulder, CO: Westview Press, Inc.

Platt, J. (1973). Social traps. *American Psychologist, 28*, 641-651.

Quinn, D. (1993). *Ishmael*. New York, NY: Bantam Books.

Robertson, F. (1992). *Ecosystem management of the national forests and grasslands* (1330-1 policy letter). Washington, DC: USDA Forest Service.

Sahlins, M. (1972). *Stone age economics*. New York, NY: Aldine Publishing.

Schroeder, H. (1991). The spiritual aspect of nature: A perspective from depth psychology. In T. More, M. Donnelly, A. Graefe and J. Vaske (Eds.), *Proceedings of the 1991 Northeastern Recreation Research Symposium* (pp. 25-30). (Gen. Tech. Rep. NE–145). Radnor, PA: USDA Forest Service, Northeastern Forest Experiment Station.

Schultz, J., McAvoy, L., and Dustin, D. (1988, January). What are we in business for? *Parks and Recreation*, 52-54.

Senge, P. (1990). *The fifth discipline: The art and practice of the learning organization*. New York, NY: Doubleday.

Slovic, P., Fischhoff, B., and Lichtenstein, S. (1977). Behavioral decision theory. *Annual Review of Psychology, 28,* 1-39.

Super, G. and Cordell, K. (1990). Managing for changing recreation needs on national forests: A viewpoint. In J. O'Leary, D. Fesenmaier, T. Brown, D. Stynes and B. Driver (Eds.), *Proceedings of the National Outdoor Recreation Trends Symposium III* (pp. 813-816). March 29–31, 1990. Indianapolis, IN.

USDA Forest Service. (1993a). *Forest Service Manual* (FSM 1020). Washington, DC: USDA Forest Service.

USDA Forest Service. (1993b). *Forest Service Mission/Issue Guidebook*. Washington, DC: USDA Forest Service.

Whitehead, A. (1929). *Process and reality*. New York, NY: Harper & Row Publishers, Inc.

Wilkinson, C. and Anderson, M. (1987). *Land and resource planning in the national forests*. Covelo, CA: Island Press.

Williams, N. and Hunn, E. (1982). *Resource managers: North American and Australian hunter-gatherers*. Boulder, CO: Westview Press, Inc.

Wilson, E. (1984). *Biophilia: The human bond with other species*. Cambridge, MA: Harvard University Press.

Wilson, E. (1985). The biological diversity crisis: A challenge to science. *Issues in Science and Technology, 2,* 20-29.

Wilson, E. (1993). *The diversity of life*. Cambridge, MA: Belknap Press.

Wondolleck, J. (1988). *Public lands conflict and resolution: Managing national forest disputes*. New York, NY: Plenum Publishing Corp.

Adapting Management Frameworks to Better Account for Hard-to-Define Values of Public Lands

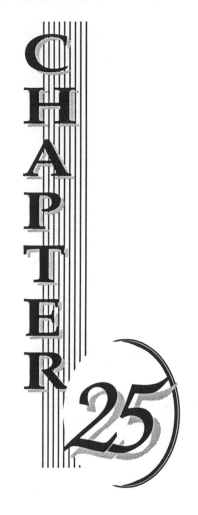

Daniel Stynes
Department of Park, Recreation, and Tourism Resources
Michigan State University
East Lansing, Michigan

George Peterson
Rocky Mountain Forest and Range Experiment Station
USDA Forest Service
Fort Collins, Colorado

Introduction

Public land management agencies (PLMAs) are charged with managing the public estate to serve a multitude of uses, groups, and values. PLMAs use a variety of management frameworks to organize and guide this complex task. Some of these frameworks are institutionalized in the form of laws, policies, administrative rules, or standard operating procedures. Other frameworks are more informal, and some are simply personal preferences or management styles of individuals or organizations. Benefit/cost (B/C) analysis, the recreation opportunity spectrum (ROS), limits of acceptable change (LAC), and management by objectives (MBO) are examples of well-known management or decision-making frameworks, as are public involvement and broader political processes.

Frameworks play important roles in both defining and solving management problems. Management frameworks help in organizing and structuring the process of defining problems, gathering information, identifying and evaluating alternatives, and making decisions. Frameworks suggest the key players, the relevant information to focus on,

and, in many cases, how this information should be organized to address the problem.

While we generally think of management frameworks as providing guidance, they can also misdirect attention. Inappropriate, outdated, or incomplete frameworks may misguide management decisions by omitting or misrepresenting key variables, relationships, values, or stakeholder perspectives. Frameworks can misdirect attention and distort the importance of one set of problems, variables, publics, or values at the expense of others. Like any tool, a given management or decision-making framework may be abused, poorly applied, or extended to problems to which it is not well-suited. What is a useful and valid framework to one person may be seen as quite inappropriate to another. To a considerable extent our perspective on a particular problem and many of our values are embedded in the frameworks we choose.

The ability or inability of existing management frameworks to handle certain hard-to-define values is our concern here. Frameworks frequently direct our attention to specific values and particular representations of these values. In highly structured analytical frameworks like B/C analysis, values are made explicit so that it is clear which values have been considered or not considered, how each value has been represented, and what role or weight each receives in a given management decision. In other types of frameworks, like public involvement processes and advisory groups, values are implicitly represented by various participants. By definition, hard-to-define values are generally implicit, leaving considerable room for interpretation of whether, how, or how well such values have been taken into account in a given decision.

We initially approached this chapter thinking of fairly specific management and decision-making frameworks like B/C analysis, public involvement procedures, the ROS system and the like. These frameworks each provide an explicit or implicit way of incorporating certain values in public land management decisions. Our task was to extend these frameworks to better account for hard-to-define values and multicultural perspectives. As we listened to the other participants at the workshops organized to plan this text, it dawned on us that most of the frameworks we were considering were already part of a particular cultural perspective (i.e., the public land management and supporting research professions). Objections voiced by "outsiders" were often as much with the frameworks themselves as with the handling of particular values within these frameworks.

Frameworks are not value neutral. Frameworks implicitly embrace a set of currently held values. Indeed, one important role of frameworks is to emphasize and foster a particular set of values. Embedded within B/C analysis are values of efficiency, consumer sovereignty, the market system, and formal analytical processes. Public involvement frameworks embody the values of a democratic system, informed citizenry, and political process. ROS, LAC and other carrying-capacity related frameworks embrace values of sustainability and conservation. These embedded values are often widely shared, at least within the organizations and individuals embracing a particular framework, so that they are rarely questioned from within. Across cultures and disciplines, however, there is considerable diversity and disagreement over frameworks. Battles between environmentalists and developers, economists and sociologists, Republicans and Democrats, and Marxists and Capitalists are as much over frameworks as over

any particular values. When two groups are having difficulty communicating, they often have not agreed on a common language or perspective.

Public Land Management Agency Paradigms

The term "paradigm" was introduced by Kuhn (1962) to describe how research is guided and directed by an agreed upon set of concepts, theories, and methods. Brown and Harris (1992) note how the idea extends readily to particular cultural world-views (Dunlap and van Liere, 1984; Pirages, 1977) and to public land management organizations (Behan, 1990). The paradigm under which a particular PLMA operates is defined by the legislation, mission statements, organizational structures, management frameworks, values, and individuals that guide the agency. Management frameworks and values both define and are defined by the organization's dominant paradigm. Important elements of the dominant PLMA paradigms in the United States are stewardship, professionalism, scientific management, a land ethic, efficiency, and public participation in decisions. Spiritual and other hard-to-define values that do not receive extensive attention within PLMAs tend to fall outside of, or in some cases conflict with, one or more elements of the dominant paradigm.

Two alternative ways to increase consideration of these hard-to-define values is to link the values more clearly to existing paradigms or to adopt new land management paradigms that better reflect and support these values. These two approaches are apparent in the chapters of this text with some authors suggesting marginal adjustments in existing approaches, while others argue for entirely new paradigms (see Grumbine, Chapter Twenty-One, in this volume). As Brown and Harris (1992) point out, competing paradigms exist within PLMAs like the U.S. Forest Service and, to varying degrees, these competing paradigms seek to change or overthrow the accepted or official ones.

The values and paradigms embodied by public land management organizations are, however, only part of the picture. PLMAs are made up of individuals who, along with the organization itself, function within a particular cultural, social, and political context. Individual managers bring their own values, world-views, decision-making styles, and cultural backgrounds to their jobs. Decisions and approaches taken by any given individual in the organization will reflect both organizational and personal values. Collective decisions are more likely to reflect the common organizational paradigm, although these too will be influenced by the mix of individuals that are involved. One of the arguments for work force diversity is to capture a broader range of perspectives, styles and values within the organization.

Publics: Another Set of Paradigms and Values

The public in "public land management" dictates that the values of a wide range of individuals, organizations, and stakeholder groups be considered in land management decisions. Part of the changing management paradigm of PLMAs over the past 20 years has been the added importance of public involvement. This paradigm shift involves changes in procedures and frameworks, as well as a change in philosophy (Sample, 1993). While public involvement serves a variety of purposes from informational to cooptive (Heberlein, 1976), the role that directly concerns us here is the use of public involvement as a vehicle for injecting additional value information into public land management decisions. Public participation procedures are one of the primary vehicles PLMAs use to deal with hard-to-define values, as "easier-to-define" values can often be captured within existing analytical frameworks.

Part of the complexity of public land management is the number and diversity of groups with interests in how public lands are managed. These groups have traditionally been defined to include related federal, state and local agencies, special commodity and environmental interest groups, and individual stakeholders. They hold somewhat distinct values relative to management issues, but perhaps, more important, they approach the issues from quite distinct perspectives. Each perspective suggests a somewhat different management or decision-making framework, which in turn dictates what values are relevant and how they are represented. Objections are frequently raised when values arising from a one-world-view or perspective are forced into a framework that is seen as incompatible.

Cultural diversity presents a relatively new set of issues for PLMAs. Historically, minority groups have not been well-represented within public land management professions (Mohai, Stillman, Jakes and Liggett, 1994) or in public participation forums (Burch, 1976; Force and Williams, 1989). Managing lands to account for cultural diversity therefore poses new challenges for PLMAs (McDonough, 1991). Differences in values and cultural paradigms or worldviews are further compounded by differences in languages and in communication and negotiation styles. How can PLMAs better communicate value information across cultures in order to understand and reconcile values that are represented within completely different world-views? Many groups with particular interests in the spiritual values of public lands fall outside of the dominant culture (e.g., Native Americans and deep ecologists).

Communicating Value Information: Four Layers of Influence and Decision Making

Before discussing management frameworks themselves, it will be helpful to place values and frameworks within their organizational and cultural context. Management frameworks can be positioned between the individuals and organizations that interpret and use them and the governmental institutions and culture that in part define them. Working from the inside out we can identify roles for the individual land manager, the land management organization, broader government institutions of which PLMAs are a part, and finally the social and cultural milieu. As PLMAs attempt to incorporate hard-to-define values in their management decisions, all of these layers should be considered. We therefore review each, in turn, before addressing specific management frameworks.

PLMA personnel. Public land managers bring their own values to their job, as well as a particular cultural background and communication style. Based on their backgrounds and activities outside the workplace, PLMA employees will hold certain values and will be more or less able to understand and/or represent the values of particular cultural or special interest groups. PLMA personnel are not a perfect representation of society at large and never will be. While the transition from a white male-dominated agency culture is broadening the representation of many values in PLMAs, other values will always be over- or underrepresented simply because of what attracts people to the land management profession and the professional training these people receive.

The stereotype of public land managers as rugged, independent outdoorsmen remains reasonably valid. Diversity efforts have added more outdoorswomen to PLMAs, but women and minorities that are attracted to PLMAs are likely to share most of the organization's basic values—interest in the outdoors, public service, love of nature, usually a dislike for big cities, and so forth. The professional training of foresters, wildlife biologists, and land managers in general reinforces and builds on the set of values that attracts people to these professions in the first place. The professional training imparts a strong scientific and analytical orientation. Land managers are taught to believe in the benefits of silviculture, wildlife management, environmental interpretation, and other practices.

Current efforts in PLMAs to diversify the work force will improve the ability of land management organizations to understand the orientations, history, behavior, and values of different population subgroups. Programs to train existing personnel to be more aware of and sensitive to the values and cultural backgrounds of coworkers and the public also contribute. Training in communication skills generally, and cross cultural communication in particular, is also needed.

PLMA organizations. The values of an organization are embodied in the policies, structure, rules, and formal and informal procedures that define the organization and its management paradigm. Public land management paradigms are an outgrowth of the society in which PLMAs exist and will, therefore, partially reflect the dominant social paradigm and value system. To the extent that minority values and cultural perspectives are not well-represented in the dominant social paradigm, they are also likely to be absent or underrepresented in PLMA frameworks.

PLMA values may also diverge from the dominant societal values due to the special training, responsibilities, and organizational culture of public land managers. PLMA organizational values include stewardship, a scientific orientation, and a land

ethic. In contrast to the general public, PLMAs are more likely to espouse values of public versus private land ownership, of conservation versus development, and of scientific versus laissez-faire management. Some hard-to-define values are more clearly understood as hard to include within the PLMAs organizational value system and management frameworks. For example, the values involved in the disruption of sacred areas are no more difficult to define than the value of a board foot of timber unless one insists on adherence to a system of market-determined prices for defining value.

PLMAs are often required by law or executive orders to use particular frameworks, to favor certain values, or to ignore others. Communication problems are particularly difficult when PLMAs attempt to deal with a public whose world-views do not fit readily with the organization's. While mainline environmental and commodity groups have generally chosen to work within the PLMAs' frameworks, other groups have not. Deep ecologists, "tree huggers," animal rights groups, and religious cults frequently challenge the frameworks themselves.

There are several ways that PLMAs can improve their understanding and consideration of hard-to-define values. The first way is to carefully articulate the organization's own values and to understand where these values may differ from those of various groups with whom they are communicating. Second, land management organizations should constantly be evaluating their policies, rules, procedures, and management frameworks to assure that relevant values, whether easy or hard-to-define, are represented as fully and accurately as possible. Fairly representing all relevant values will generally require that a multiplicity of frameworks be used since any single framework will typically favor one set of values or perspectives over another.

Government. The three branches of government define the mission of PLMAs and a set of parameters in which they must operate. Legislation defines both broad and specific values that PLMAs must consider, while also providing explicit or implicit direction on the kinds of frameworks to be used. Executive orders and decisions guide how the missions of PLMAs are to be carried out, often suggesting priorities among values and approaches. The courts evaluate the degree to which agencies properly interpret and implement legislation. Many of the analytical frameworks used by PLMAs can be traced to specific legislation or judicial decisions (e.g., the frameworks that structure environmental impact and public participation processes). In other cases, a philosophy or set of priorities within a particular administration may emphasize certain frameworks or values over others.

The social, cultural, and political environment. The ultimate source of values and frameworks for communicating value information is, of course, the broader social/cultural/political milieu in which PLMAs, their employees, and all groups exist. We should not overlook the important roles that educational and religious institutions, along with the mass media, the arts, and the market system play in communicating value information. The preponderance of largely analytic, scientific, biological, and economic frameworks within PLMAs reflects in part the dominant culture of our society, and what that society expects from public agencies, and the land management professions in particular.

Two Management Decision-Making Frameworks

For our purposes, decision-making frameworks may be divided into two types which we will call:

1. analytic, and
2. interpretive.

These two types of decision frameworks roughly parallel the quantitative/qualitative paradigms for knowing (see Stynes and Stokowski, Chapter Thirty-Seven, in this volume) and may similarly be distinguished along eight dimensions:

Analytic	Interpretive
1. reductionist	holistic
2. analysis-synthesis	direct synthesis
3. explicit	implicit
4. rational	interpretive
5. cognitive	affective
6. separate facts and values	values embedded
7. objective	subjective
8. quantitative	qualitative

Examples:

Analytic	Interpretive
1. Benefit-cost analysis	political process
2. Benefits-based management	public involvement
3. ROS, EIS, LAC	personal leadership
4. goals-achievement matrices	intuition, group consensus

Analytical Frameworks

The management, planning, policy analysis and decision-making literature is replete with analytical frameworks that attempt to either describe, explain, or inform management decisions. MBO, PPBS, systems analysis, and B/C analysis are some of the best-known general frameworks employed by public agencies. Public land management agencies employ these general frameworks as well as others that are tailored to more specific kinds of decisions. PLMA management frameworks include general federal accounting stances (NED, RED, etc.), and approaches to planning and environmental impact assessment. More specific frameworks exist for particular problems and decisions, like those related to recreation carrying capacity problems (ROS, LAC). Many of these frameworks are institutionalized in one form or another within laws, policies, administrative rules, standard operating procedures, or training programs.

Analytical frameworks embody scientific management traditions. Complex problems are addressed by dividing the problem into smaller pieces, examining the pieces separately, and then reassembling them into an overall solution. Analysis is explicit, objective, rational, and usually quantitative. Facts are distinguished from values and the role of distinct values is made reasonably explicit in the analysis (often via formal weights).

The general approach to capturing hard-to-define values within analytical frameworks is to first define and measure these values and then to incorporate them within the framework. The approach is outlined by Driver, Brown and Peterson (1991, p. 6) in the context of capturing the benefits of recreation:

1. specify the benefit,
2. measure it, and
3. determine its worth.

The final step is necessary to incorporate the benefit within a particular value framework such as B/C analysis.

Interpretive Frameworks

Interpretive frameworks generally address problems in a holistic manner. A solution is directly synthesized via a relatively unstructured, indeterminant and often nonrepeatable process. Values are implicit rather than explicit. Feelings and intuitions, intentionally excluded from most analytic processes, play as important a role as facts and formal analysis within interpretive frameworks. The resulting decision and the process for obtaining it are subject to quite distinct interpretations, hence the label "interpretive." Interpretive frameworks rest on nonpositivist, phenomenological, and postmodern epistemologies (Rosenau, 1992).

Public involvement processes are good examples of interpretive frameworks that are widely used by PLMAs to identify values and to consider the views of diverse publics. Public involvement frameworks provide one of the key links between PLMAs and the public. They therefore constitute particularly important vehicles for communicating value information between agencies and the public. Public involvement mechanisms are, however, not the only interpretive framework used by PLMAs. A host of informal problem-solving and decision-making structures within PLMAs can be classified as interpretive frameworks.

While analytic and interpretive frameworks are somewhat mutually exclusive in approach, they are frequently used together. Analytic frameworks inform more interpretive decision processes and interpretive frameworks (e.g., public involvement) often inform or control analytic ones. Analytic frameworks seldom make decisions, although they frequently play key roles in decision making. Public decisions generally require that some individual or group interpret and integrate information from many sources, usually combining formal and quantitative analysis with intangible, political, personal, and other factors to arrive at a decision. Different managers and organizations have distinct preferences for analytic and holistic frameworks and choose an appropriate mix of the two for a given decision.

Handling Hard-to-Define Values

Almost by definition, hard-to-define values are more readily incorporated into interpretive frameworks than analytic ones. Analytic frameworks require that we first define and measure these values so they may be included explicitly in the analysis. Interpretive frameworks impose no such preconditions. Within interpretive frameworks, values remain implicit, leaving open questions like whose values and what values have been considered. These judgments are left to potentially quite distinct interpretations of different individuals.

Incorporating hard-to-define values within analytic frameworks generally involves coming up with better definitions, measures, or surrogates for these values (i.e., making them less hard to define). Simply defining and measuring a value is not enough. There must also be an acceptable and consistent way of including the value within a given framework. For example, economic frameworks like B/C analysis require that benefits and costs be measured in dollars so that they may be combined and discounted over time.

Using the analytic-interpretive dichotomization of decision-making styles, we may advance three approaches for better incorporating hard-to-define values within public land management:

1. *Refine existing analytic frameworks* by developing better definitions and measures of hard-to-define values and ways of integrating these into existing analytic frameworks. This has been the traditional scientific approach to broadening the range of values that are formally considered.

2. *Refine existing interpretive frameworks* to involve a broader range of people and represent a wider range of perspectives, values, and communication styles. Consideration should be given to who is involved in various stages of management decision making, as well as how they are involved. Work force diversity, training in interpretive decision-making techniques, and modifications to public involvement and organizational decision processes are examples of changes that are currently underway in PLMAs.

3. *Develop new frameworks* that may be based on different management or behavioral assumptions and reflect different land management perspectives. These may be new analytic frameworks, new interpretive frameworks, or better frameworks for integrating or combining the two.

Applying the Ideas—the Case of Spiritual Values

In the interest of providing more concrete examples and recommendations, the authors turn to the class of hard-to-define values that have been called "spiritual" values. We first make suggestions for refining existing analytical and interpretive frameworks to better account for these values. Following this, we propose some possible places to look for new and integrative frameworks.

Refining Analytical Frameworks

We can continue to work within existing scientific and scientific management traditions to more fully consider a broader range of values in public land management. To incorporate spiritual values within existing analytical frameworks, we must better define the nature of spiritual values, develop means of measuring them, and then somehow capture these values within given analytical frameworks in an acceptable manner.

There are several ways that the spiritual dimensions of public lands could be captured within existing frameworks. Existing management frameworks each imply somewhat distinct conceptualizations of the spiritual dimension and hence different measures of it. For example:

a. Multiple use management frameworks suggest defining spiritual values in terms of particular types of uses. Spiritual uses may range from the concrete (burial grounds) to more abstract uses (sacred areas).

b. Frameworks focusing on serving groups suggest incorporating spiritual values through a special category of users.

c. Benefits-based management frameworks suggest associating spiritual values with a set of benefits from public lands.

d. The ROS system of managing for various experiences suggests capturing spiritual values as a dimension of nature-based experiences.

e. Resource inventory and management frameworks suggest treating spiritual values as an additional category or dimension of natural and cultural resources.

There are a number of alternative ways of formally measuring spiritual values within each of these conceptualizations. The point the authors wish to make here is that each conceptualization arises from a different framework or perspective on public land management. By defining spiritual values within a given framework we assure that they can be accommodated within that framework.

Analytical frameworks cannot, however, either individually or collectively fully capture the spiritual dimension. Analytical approaches are by nature reductionist, attempting to extract the most essential elements for a particular analysis. In this case, the underlying values are adapted to the analytical framework rather than vice versa. In doing so, reality is always simplified and much of substance may be discarded. This can be particularly so when frameworks developed to handle particular types of information are adapted or extended to handle information of a different sort. Good scientific models and management decisions rest on good choices of what to focus on and what to discard, ignore, or assume away. Such choices apply to spiritual values in the same way as to economic, environmental, or any other class of values.

What distinguishes the spiritual dimension and many other hard-to-define values is that many of these values are implicitly holistic concepts that therefore defy reductionist treatments. Compounding the problem is that spiritual values are also very personal and deeply held. Where many readily accept the Dow Jones average, interest rates, unemployment, or gross national product as measures of the performance of our economic system, most individuals are reluctant to accept partial treatments, simplifications, or someone else's interpretations of their spiritual values. Some simplification, scientific interpretation, and collective agreement seem to be prerequisites to considering spiritual values within any analytical framework. This will lead some to reject the application of any analytical framework to spiritual matters.

Refining Interpretive Frameworks

Although they are certainly as pervasive and influential in decision making as the more structured, analytic frameworks, interpretive decision frameworks are more difficult to define formally. The nature of interpretive frameworks precludes very precise statements about how to refine them. Problems, decision processes, and values are never as clear or uniformly understood as analytical frameworks.

Decisions in public organizations today seldom appear as discrete steps taken by a high-level individual or committee at a single point in time, although this is the perspective from which one tends to analyze them. Decisions are more likely to emerge from a highly amorphous and gradual process with many subdecisions made at lower levels both inside and outside the organization (Mandell, 1984). Values similarly are reflected in many ways at different steps in management and decision processes.

A distinguishing feature of interpretive frameworks is that values tend to be treated as inseparable from the actions and behaviors that reflect them. Identifiable interpretive frameworks generally capture some portion of a much broader decision process; for example, the political process surrounding a decision, public involvement mechanisms, informal decision structures within organizations, or a particular individual's brainstorming process. Decision makers may be individuals, small groups, or large public bodies. While the specific frameworks relevant to each are varied, they share a common set of elements that suggest better ways to capturing hard-to-define values. These may be summarized under:

a. Who is involved?

b. How?

c. Why?

The subjective nature of interpretive frameworks makes decisions on who is involved and how critical. To the extent that each individual or group brings distinct values and interpretations to a problem, a decision is incomplete if all relevant groups are not somehow represented. Individuals and groups may be involved either directly or indirectly. Direct involvement requires that an individual be the decision maker or be part of a decision-making group. Indirect involvement means that someone in the decision-making group represents an individual's or group's viewpoints. In our democratic political process, individuals are directly involved through voting, letter writing, and the like, and indirectly involved through their representa-

tives or spokespersons in legislative bodies, advisory committees, and in PLMAs themselves.

Direct involvement of distinct perspectives may be enhanced by work force diversification, and broader involvement of groups with distinct value orientations in advisory bodies and other public involvement mechanisms. Given the infinite variety of perspectives on any given issue, no finite set of individuals can adequately represent all viewpoints. Expanded cross-cultural and diversity training for PLMA personnel can improve their ability to understand and perhaps to represent the views and values of groups that may lack direct representation in any given matter. Communication and sensitivity training can also help PLMA personnel to better understand and communicate with groups who have different land management perspectives, values, or communication styles.

As important as who is involved in PLMA decisions is how they are involved and why. Distinct involvement mechanisms and communication frameworks are required to capture the values and perspectives of different groups. Organizations need to consider the world-views, perspectives, and communication styles of the public to involve them effectively. In most cases, people are asked to make inputs based upon the agency's framing of the issues and to use communication vehicles that the organization has established. A host of refinements to public involvement come from simply looking at public involvement from the perspective of different groups including those that traditionally have not been involved.

The traditional methods of bringing diverse groups together for involvement sessions is useful to promote understanding between groups and to help resolve conflicts. The goal of understanding a particular group's values and perspective, however, is likely better served by sessions with just that group. Focus group sessions or interactions in which the stakeholder group itself determines the setting, framework, and agenda are recommended. Goals of understanding and partnerships are also better fostered by a wide range of continuing involvement vehicles. The distinction in marketing between making a sale and building a relationship with customers or clients suggests other refinements to PLMA public involvement programs (Levitt, 1983).

Just as in the case of analytic frameworks, spiritual values pose some unique problems for interpretive frameworks. Many spiritual values are mystical and are not readily communicated across distinct cultures. Individuals may be either unwilling or unable to express these values and experiences. Even when spiritual values are expressed and heard, there is no guarantee they will be understood sufficiently to incorporate them properly in a decision. The solution to this dilemma is to obtain agreement about decisions and actions without having to define, understand, or incorporate the spiritual values per se. Interpretive frameworks recognize that values may not be expressible and that many values are intimately connected with the actions or symbols that foster or represent them.

New and Integrative Frameworks

A more radical approach to the hard-to-define values problem is to develop completely new frameworks within which any given class of values may be more faithfully and fully represented. The cultural, historical, institutional, and legal foundations of current PLMA frameworks suggest that refinements are more likely than revolutions. Recent "new initiatives," including frameworks based on marketing, ecosystem management, and sustainable development can all be seen as variations on existing frameworks. The vast changes associated with public involvement in decisions is perhaps the clearest "new" framework or paradigm within PLMAs in the past 30 years. Of the emerging frameworks being discussed today, privatization seems to involve the greatest shift in how public land management decisions would be made and what values they might reflect.

Wicker (1985) proposes four strategies for expanding our conceptual frameworks:

1. play with ideas,
2. consider contexts,
3. tinker with assumptions, and
4. clarify and systematize the conceptual framework.

New frameworks can also emerge by integrating and combining several existing frameworks in ways that are faithful to each component. In the research realm, the effort to combine the frameworks of economics and psychology to better capture wild-

land values is a good example (Peterson, Driver and Gregory, 1988). While less progress has been made than one would like to see, efforts to integrate economic, social, and environmental values within environmental assessments point to other potential new frameworks for making public land management decisions.

Perhaps the most neglected area of integration lies between the analytic and interpretive paradigms themselves. Value information is brought to bear on public decisions through a complex mix of analytic and interpretive vehicles. Most people tend to favor either an analytic (left brain) or interpretive (right brain) mode of thinking. Each has advantages in different situations. The best decisions likely draw somewhat from both analytic and interpretive perspectives, yet our understanding of how to combine the two and in what proportions in any given situation is weak.

The scientific orientation of PLMAs has generally favored the clear separation of facts and values. The relationships between the formal analyses that PLMAs carry out and the personal, emotional, and interpretive aspects of management decisions remain relatively obscure. The problem of how to reconcile hard-to-define values with those that are defined and measured seems to require some bridging of the gap between analytic and interpretive frameworks. Computer simulations that combine formal models with qualitative information in a highly interactive format may be one way to do this (Hollings, 1978).

Conclusions

There is no single road to better incorporating hard-to-define values in public land management decisions. An important first step is to recognize the important role that management frameworks serve in PLMAs and the ways that various values and perspectives are represented or not represented within these frameworks. Progress will come from refining the existing frameworks and being open to new ones. As no single framework can adequately represent all viewpoints in all situations, a variety of frameworks encompassing both analytic and interpretive types seems necessary. The problem is not simply choosing the right framework for a given problem, but of enlisting multiple frameworks for any given decision.

PLMAs need to be particularly careful about forcing hard-to-define values into frameworks where they do not fit or of asking diverse groups to adopt frameworks that are inconsistent with their worldviews or value perspectives. Many hard-to-define values are not so much hard to define, as hard to agree on, hard to communicate, or hard to fit into a particular framework. Frameworks that limit the range of ways that values may be expressed inherently limit the range of values that can be explicitly considered. Values are just as evident in emotional responses to natural environments as in market transactions, yet the former are frequently discounted as irrational (Vining, 1991), while the latter are readily accepted as valid indicators.

Public involvement processes have helped inject a much broader range of value information into PLMA decisions. Refinements to public involvement procedures promise even more in the future. Problems remain in how to assess the reliability, validity, and relative importance of the various inputs. Particularly problematic is how to reconcile alternative interpretations and how to combine quantitative and qualitative types of information.

Clearly we need rules, frameworks, theories, philosophies, religions, world-views or whatever to make sense of our experience. PLMAs should continue to develop new frameworks and to refine and adapt the analytic and interpretive frameworks they currently use. The greatest danger in frameworks is forgetting that they are always simplifications of reality, and any given framework is only one of an infinite number of possibilities. The representation of many distinct perspectives on public land management requires many different frameworks.

Neglect of some values and interests in the past can be linked to an excessive attachment to one or two frameworks (e.g., B/C analysis as the dominant analytic framework and the public hearing as the dominant interpretive framework). Perhaps we are too quick to institutionalize particular frameworks in legislation, administrative rules, and training programs. This produces specialists, procedural manuals, and requirements that tend to restrict the development and use of alternative frameworks. Frameworks take on a life of their own, striving all too often to be *the* way of seeing and doing things rather than one of many ways. Whether inten-

tional or not, frameworks tend to exclude particular values and perspectives just as clearly as they include others. Specialists who become too attached to a single framework frequently are not able to see or understand that there are other perspectives.

We therefore urge a proliferation of frameworks—analytic, interpretive, and combinations of the two. Managers should draw from a broad range of possible frameworks and be able to analyze problems using several different ones. PLMA training should focus on the distinct perspectives afforded by different frameworks and provide experience in developing and adapting frameworks to solve a particular problem. Exposure to a wider range of frameworks will help managers and analysts better understand the frameworks and perspectives that others might bring to the table. From such shared understandings may come new frameworks capable of embracing a wider range of perspectives and values.

Literature Cited

Behan, R. (1990). Multiresource forest management: A paradigmatic challenge to professional forestry. *Journal of Forestry, 88*, 12-18.

Brown, G. and Harris, C. (1992). The U.S. Forest Service: Toward the new resource management paradigm? *Society and Natural Resources, 5*, 231-245.

Burch, W., Jr. (1976). Who participates: A sociological interpretation of natural resource decisions. *Natural Resources Journal, 16*(1), 41-54.

Driver, B., Brown, P., and Peterson, G. (Eds.). (1991). *Benefits of leisure*. State College, PA: Venture Publishing, Inc.

Dunlap, R. and van Liere, K. (1984). Commitment to the dominant social paradigm and concern for environmental quality. *Social Science Quarterly, 65*,1013-1028.

Force, J. and Williams, K. (1989). A profile of national forest planning participants. *Journal of Forestry, 87*(1), 33-38.

Heberlein, T. (1976). Some observations on alternative mechanisms for public involvement: The hearing, public opinion poll, the workshop and quasi-experiment. *Natural Resources Journal, 16*(1), 197-212.

Hollings, C. (Ed.). (1978). *Adaptive environmental assessment and management*. New York, NY: John Wiley & Sons.

Kuhn, T. (1962). *The structure of scientific revolutions*. Chicago, IL: University of Chicago Press.

Levitt, T. (1983). *The marketing imagination*. New York, NY: The Free Press.

Mandell, M. (1984). Strategies for improving the usefulness of analytical techniques for public sector decision making. In L. Nigro (Ed.), *Decision making in the public sector* (pp. 289-310). New York, NY: Marcel Dekker.

McDonough, M. (1991). Integrating the diversity of public values into ecosystem management. In D. LeMaster and G. Parker (Eds.), *Ecosystem management in a dynamic society* (pp.133-138). West Lafayette, IN: Department of Forestry and Natural Resources, Purdue University.

Mohai, P., Stillman, P., Jakes, P., and Liggett, C. (1994). *Change in the USDA Forest Service: Are we heading in the right direction?* (General Technical Report NC-172). St. Paul, MN: USDA Forest Service, North Central Forest Experiment Station.

Peterson, G., Driver, B., and Gregory, R. (Eds.). (1988). *Amenity resource valuation: Integrating economics with other disciplines*. State College, PA: Venture Publishing, Inc.

Pirages, D. (Ed.). (1977). *The sustainable society*. New York, NY: Praeger.

Rosenau, P. (1992). *Postmodernism and the social sciences*. Princeton, NJ: Princeton University Press.

Sample, V. (1993). A framework for public participation in natural resource decision making. *Journal of Forestry, 91*(7), 22-27.

Vining, J. (1991). Environmental values, emotions, and public involvement. In D. LeMaster and G. Parker (Eds.), *Ecosystem management in a dynamic society* (pp. 26-35). West Lafayette, IN: Department of Forestry and Natural Resources, Purdue University.

Wicker, A. (1985). Getting out of our conceptual ruts: Strategies for expanding conceptual frameworks. *American Psychologist, 40*(10),1094-1103.

A Few Observations on Design for Spiritual Values

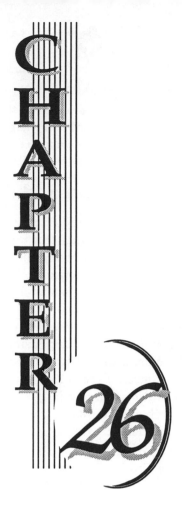

Frank Magary
Lake Tahoe Basin Management Unit
USDA Forest Service
South Lake Tahoe, California

Administration

To promote perception is the only truly creative part of recreational engineering. . . . The bulk of all land relations hinges on investments of time, forethought, skill, and faith rather than on investments in cash. As a land user thinketh, so is he.

Aldo Leopold, 1966

First, let me save hundreds of words: "hard-to-define, nature-based values" in this chapter will simply be "spiritual" values, even at the risk of supplanting the vague with the inaccurate. Attempts to define the spiritual/religious beyond a "set of symbolic forms that relate man to the ultimate conditions of his existence" may not be especially fruitful (Bellah, 1964, p. 358). Richard Rorty argues at some length that even the present distinction between "spiritual" and "natural" should be dropped (1979, p. 353).

I take the position that government cannot clearly nurture, much less promote spiritual values; that our government has been utilitarian, or consequentialist, since its eighteenth-century founding. If the public demands spiritual landscapes, the government will have to be careful to cultivate them by utilitarian means. As will be stated later, the prob-

lem is ontological: do the government's management schemes subsume, "enclose," the spiritual quest? I would not like to think so.

There is some danger that the assumptions necessary to accommodate spiritual values would be seen as a prescription by the federal government for "what is good" spiritually. If not carefully done, opponents would, and should, seize upon that.

At issue is not private, but public landscape. On public lands the government becomes, in spite of itself, involved in how clients *act* on the landscape and with what clients *need* from the landscape. Of these two, the former seems simpler, with a plain duty already well-established to prevent damage to the land or to mediate conflicts that affect the land.

Apart from that, we are left with the fact that government manages the places where spiritual experiences occur. Organized religions create the spaces that suit them, which they can control, and which they share only on their own terms. The government has to make a space that the public feels free to fill with its own spirituality.

Identification and Allocation

Can administrators identify lands as "spiritual" reserves? At first glance this may seem harmless, especially for lands already allocated to wilderness-like uses. But self-consciousness about spirituality accompanies this. If such a landscape is not managed with a light touch, the possibility of a spiritual experience becomes less likely, not more. Even to name and set something "aside" is a form of control, and advising the visitor serves to clamp the control down tighter. Percy (1954) has observed how administration and publicity about the Grand Canyon blocks the possibility of the visitor having an *original* experience:

> *Why is it almost impossible to gaze directly at the Grand Canyon . . . and see it for what it is . . . ? It is almost impossible because the Grand Canyon, the thing as it is has been appropriated by the symbolic complex which has already been formed in the sightseer's mind . . . formulated—by picture postcards, geography books, tourist folders, and the words* Grand Canyon. *How can the sightseer recover the Grand Canyon? . . . in any number of ways, all sharing the stratagem of avoiding the approved confrontation of the tour and the Park Service. This dialectic of sightseeing cannot be taken into account by the planners because the object [of it] is nothing more than the subversion of the efforts of the planners.* (1954, p.48)

Percy goes on to describe ways of subverting the administration by approaching the canyon from unusual routes, or at unusual times, to avoid the "symbolic complex." But he slyly notes that if a sensitive ranger found out about this technique and began to tell people about it to "help" them enjoy their experience, even more indirect and ingenious ways to experience the canyon would have to be found.

Management Presence

A few people may tell themselves, "Okay, now I'm going to have a spiritual experience." But others will find it simply happens. It can only be studied phenomenologically which is definitely outside the orbit of the objective/empirical tradition in which land management agencies work. The experience, it seems, is rarely controlled even by the individual doing the experiencing. Managers hope that their clientele is happy, too, but they don't manage directly for happiness—they know by instinct that it can't be summoned up directly, but that it arises in the course of pursuing other goals. Managers should pursue "spiritual management" with the same indirectness and subtlety that they would use to encourage "happiness" in their customers.

Even if a design for spirituality exists, it will be difficult to find out whether managers are practitioners of it. Feedback about success is going to be fuzzy because somebody's inner change may not be expressed even to intimates, much less the government. Survey methodologies are not well-suited to delving into spiritual experiences. Popularity is a slippery measure. Would managers have to use academically disreputable methods (e.g., summit registers that often contain fervent spiritual observations)?

Ecosystem Management

Perhaps the answer lies in land areas that are large and hard-to-define. Ecosystem management seems destined to use ecological considerations to supplant more than a few established political claims that call for productivity on lands that won't stand up to continued production. The National Forest System, formerly split between wilderness on the one hand and productive timber and range on the other, may turn out to have large tracts that don't fit either category. Already altered beyond the definition of wilderness, they are not productive enough for sawlogs and cows—or scenic spectacle.

Ecosystem management will involve choices, desired conditions of pattern and composition of vegetation; choices will be negotiated with members of the public. Land managers will not, as before, ask them what kind of campground or visitor center they would like. Land managers will not cite clear-cut "purposes." Rather, for the first time, they will ask citizens to design the landscape of home.

People may, if they are inclined, find these landscapes to be good "spiritually." There is much to be said for a land that is not "designated"; that does not exist "for" something, "for some people," but is simply, in repose, itself.

Certainly we are approaching a turning point in the vision of what public lands are. The original concept of custodianship—that lands were ultimately to be given over to private ownership—has evolved toward seeing public lands as the "commons" in a way that Native Americans would understand. Ecosystem management contains within it the notion that rather than being cultivated for instrumental reasons, the landscape may be allowed to be itself.

A difficult synthesis lies before land managers. They are forsaking the old transcendent (human-dominating-the-landscape) mode. Yet, those managers who are active, inquisitive, questing descendants of Europeans are instinctively resistant to the alternative "immanent" version that nature's claims are absolute. Tribe suggests a fusion "of *becoming* as the synthesis of accepting and subduing" nature (1976, p. 82). Here is where a multicultural influence is needed; the Asian traditions and Native-American traditions would be a rich source.

Capacity and Size

The earliest known tourism was spiritually based. The Japanese visited certain landscapes believed to have spiritual presence (Higuchi, 1983). Now the sheer numbers of people climbing Mt. Fuji guarantee that the real outcome is going to be a social experience. But Asian art never associated spirituality with crowds: Hokusai's *Thirty-six Views of Mt. Fuji* does not include jostling multitudes.

America, then, is not pioneering in the matter of inquiring into spiritual landscapes. But managers have the chance to avoid the mistake of making a package from the experience (possibly lack of space has driven the Japanese to it). The hard-to-define aspect of this should possibly include the land area itself, which, whether "set aside" or not for spiritual fulfillment, would have to be large relative to the amount of use. Not only does this principle protect the visitor from disturbing influences, but, perhaps more important, insures that rational administrative ordering would not be necessary. It is a truism of design that the more intense the use, the more "hardening" and control have to be evident; that, as noted above by Percy (1954), is inimical to the experience.

Silence and absence of outside stimulation can be assumed as a safe, minimal working hypothesis. As in "Pascal's wager:"

we don't lose much if we're wrong, but if we don't choose this starting point, we've probably lost the game before it begins. This is a good start, then, for managing from outside the "brackets" of spirituality:

Immensity is within ourselves. It is attached to a sort of expansion of being that life curbs and caution arrests, but which starts again when we are alone. As soon as we become motionless, we are elsewhere; we are dreaming in a world that is immense. Indeed, immensity is the movement of motionless man. It is one of the dynamic characteristics of quiet reverie.

Bachelard, 1969

The Search for Meaning in the Landscape

The "end of nature" has been widely anticipated, a generally despairing view that nature now exists *inside* the human context: *we* incorporate *it* in an era when no land, no thing is uninfluenced by humankind. Could this become our dominant metaphor? The history of the Forest Service (including its political context) contains much thinking like this. Yet there is resistance and denial even in the face of overwhelming physical evidence of human domination. What are the (sometimes) frenzied advocates of wilderness after, anyway?

The resistance is based on the almost universal tendency in late twentieth-century America that everything is eventually:

. . . commodified, as consumer culture makes of places and experience a product to be marketed and consumed. Nature is no longer process, much less the foundation of existence, but only the latest style on display.

Helphand, 1993

Surrounded by our materials and artifacts, we have become a playful, yet despairing, society in which we all pitch in to enjoy the goods while maintaining an ironic, distant view of the whole thing.

And why should we not? Kierkegaard (1966) thought irony was the beginning of wisdom: if the phenomena of modern life (government, corporations, the church) are taken seriously, they are conceded to have a certain reality, an *essence*, one of the building blocks we must use to make a life with meaning. Irony detaches essence from these things enabling us to stand apart, to free our minds.

Kierkegaard would have been surprised to find that in the following century irony would become the dominant mode of thought. Now we use it to become defensively detached from everything; we need the ironic stance even to protect us from each other. Kierkegaard (1966) was right: we need it for our freedom, but we are left feeling jaded and without belief. *Nature is the only "essence" that resists this process.* The person whose faith has been shaken in all human things can sometimes find what looks to be the real and the true only in nature.

Thus the land manager finds that she or he is responsible for the very ground of being itself. Tribe (1976), pursuing this line, notes:

> *the paradox that the world beyond man can define his greatness rather than engulfing him in terror only if some dimension of that world remains forever beyond his grasp . . . once the world is seen as man's playground and ultimately his mirror, nothing remains outside himself against which to test his uniqueness or his strength.* (p. 82)

If the Forest Service could sometimes resist the universal commodification of nature—which could be part of a program to define "nature-based, hard-to-define" landscapes—this would do much to restore trust in the agency. Even strident critics would be agape that a government agency could bring about such a staggering ontological reversal.

Design

> *Landscape Architects . . . are not primarily in the business of making places look good, [but] in the business of helping human beings feel more human, by translating the often inchoate rhythms, values, and aspirations . . . into material realities . . . by helping us see who we are, [designers] strengthen our sense of being.*
>
> Yi-Fu Tuan, 1978

Is it contradictory to talk of design in the present context? Perhaps no design, or very little of it, is required. But some of it is unavoidable. Even wilderness, where the "works of man" are not allowed, has a physical design component in trailheads, signs, bridges, brochures, maps—and a relational design component in the capacities, land uses, circulation patterns, the naming of features (defining

what is important) and even in the choice of which areas are to be the subject of land managers' design art.

Spiritual landscapes do not have to be, like wilderness, "untrammelled by man." If deliberations about ecosystem management begin to reveal that certain vegetative patterns are ecologically productive and pleasing to human sensibilities as well, land designers needn't fear replicating them.

Nature is almost universally seen as eternal. Not only its processes (which *are* eternal) are seen that way, but also the present manifestations of the processes. It is an important clue for our inquiry that nature is almost always perceived by the public as being far more "eternal" than it really is. What science knows to be a historical process of continual change is seen intellectually by the public as flux, but emotionally as stasis. A stand of large trees is an eternal feature, to be revered, perhaps in the same way as the Cathedral of Chartres. Bachelard (1969) notes the "immediate immensity" of old forests:

> *We should have to know how the forest experiences its great age; why, in the reign of the imagination,* there are no young forests . . . (emphasis added) *I feel that fields and meadows are [temporally] with me, and with us. But forests reign in the past.* (p.188)

Land managers should yield gracefully to this because it will not change. An "older" landscape will seem to the public to be more "spiritual," and nothing in the politics of preservation has ever contradicted this.

What human-designed things belong in the spiritual environment? On what basis is a fiberglass picnic table or toilet building inappropriate? As a beginning, I offer that:

> *the spiritual landscape can contain only those elements which have been absorbed thoroughly into the culture as appropriate to the context.*[1]

Most elements perceived to fit will have, unsurprisingly, something of the eternal about them. They will seem unrelated to the here-and-now, the styles, fads, and fancies of everyday life.

---

[1] Hall (1977) clarifies what the costs and benefits are of living in a fast-moving, "low-context" world in his discussion of "high context" and "low context" cultures. Many of the artifacts that make our culture flexible and varied remain, in effect, unassimilated, alien to us.

Everyone responds powerfully to a relict spiritual landscape. Suddenly coming upon petroglyphs in the desert may be unforgettable. But even human-made objects no more "eternal" than last Tuesday must at least contain a timeless quality. One finds clues of how to do this by observing how objects over time accrete value and gain authority if they are *still in process* (rusting, bleaching, weathering), being shaped by the very elements we experience (cold wind, hot sun) at the time one sees them. One sees the character of surfaces. Weathered plastic is not even a conceptual category.

What land managers add to the spiritual landscape by design will be seen inescapably as symbolic. Some meanings may be unintended, clinging to an object from its more usual context. On an obvious level, motorized travel and high-tech artifacts are correctly perceived as extensions of another world into that landscape. Less obviously, even minor modifications may carry meanings that the inhabitant of the landscape doesn't want. An interpretive sign in a specific location, for example, "says" something and has "content," perhaps innocent-seeming. But its *meaning* is that unseen administrators have taken control of the experience of that place.

Form

We have traditional guides such as the notion that horizontal masses suggest repose and stability and that vertical ones imply elation or aspiration. This will not commonly be translated into physical design, because we're not building a temple to anything. Yet, nature provides these elements; they can be sought out and used as part of the scheme.

If there are social conflicts about what is "significant" or what "belongs," the safe answer may be to have nothing human-made. Mount Shasta, a noted spiritual landscape, was shared by several tribes and was a church to each. Whether consciously intended or not, the ethic of the Native Americans—Wintus, Karuks, Pit River, and Shastas—to leave the spiritual site unaltered may have been a response to the problem that there were many tribes but only one Mount Shasta. "Purification has been a requirement . . . of an individual's preparation for an approach to the mountain . . . behavior and activities on Mt. Shasta should leave the mountain in an unaltered state" (Theodoratus and Evans, 1991). This is a partial answer to the problem of groups with differing values.

Craftsmanship

Land designers should do good work and use noble materials. The basis for the design program, however minimal, should be an *enlightened materialism*; not the decidedly unspiritual use of materials to provide convenience and comfort, or to symbolize prestige or power, but a genuine reverence for materials. Whether it be a sculptor with stone, or a boatbuilder with wood, any craftsman or artist reveres the material. Those looking for a spiritual landscape will be turned off by the expedient or the cheap. In the 1930s managers designed more creatively using native stone and timbers to produce Stonehenge-like campsite tables. Significantly, this work was done in a era when all outdoor recreation was thought to confer moral benefits on the clientele.

Certain designs have a timeless look: the national park "Cascadian" architecture had this strength, the eternal look, as though the glaciers had retreated leaving only a ranger station. Ingredients of eternalness: *mass* (connection to earth?) and *unprocessed natural materials*. "Those things fit best into the landscape which enhance its coherence, render the landscape comprehensible, contribute to order, and add to a sense of harmony" (Gussow, 1979, p. 9). Prefabricated things that are emblematic of other places and of processes alien to the understanding sought are likely to get in the way.

Integrity

Whatever ineffable value managers may find in a "hard-to-define, nature-based" landscape must clearly saturate the *entire* landscape, avoiding the stage-management of the linear, controlled-sequence-of-views spirit of design. Control can be benign and subtle, as in a Japanese garden, or "managed" in the Forest Service way for balance of utility and esthetics, or totally controlled, as at Disney World. But it is dubious whether control applies at all to the present inquiry. Gussow (1979) has it right:

> *A scenic resource is the landscape we see,* all *of it, not merely some predigested, preselected, prearranged, arbitrarily focused view . . . a scene is something we are part of, to which we relate, not as spectators . . . but as participants in events.* (p. 8)

Relationship with land also deepens with familiarity. A changeless (in the human timespan) landscape—integrity over time—may encourage the deep relaxation and receptivity that people need. One can afford to love wilderness, for example, because of the political security—permanence—of the wilderness allocation.

Spatial Relationships and Circulation

Is the notion of "pilgrimage" a necessary one? Some sort of real or symbolic *ordeal* seems to be involved in many spiritual pursuits, and anyone can summon up examples from Native American, Christian, or Muslim thought. Minimally, one can't get too spiritual next to one's car. The Shangri-la of legend was approached by trekking over the mountains, not by landing at Shangri-la International.

The shaping of a landscape for spiritual experience, if that can be done, would have to be carried out with full awareness that space is experiential and connected as much to effort and accomplishment as to linear distance. Yi-Fu Tuan is lucid on this point:

> *An explanation for the wide use of time to measure distance is the fact that units of time convey a clear sense of effort. The useful answer to questions of distance tells us how much effort is needed—what resources of energy are required....* (1977, p. 129)

Høeg (1993) describes the Inuit concept of sinik (sleeps), the number of overnights a journey requires is:

> *... not a fixed distance, because the number ... can vary, depending on the weather and time of year.... Sinik is not a distance, not a number of days and hours. It is both a spatial and a temporal phenomenon ... a union of space and motion and time that is taken for granted by Inuits but that cannot be captured ... by any European language.* (pp. 307-308)

A certain *indirectness* in things will discourage an overt goal orientation. While many observers have pointed out evidence that human origins in the savanna landscape of Africa may have instilled a taste for a tree-studded but open-to-view landscape, forests may promise not only a higher capacity, but mystery. Bachelard (1969) comments that:

> *We do not have to be long in the woods to experience the always rather anxious impression of 'going deeper and deeper' into a limitless world. Soon, if we do not know where we are going, we do not know where we are ... this is a primary attribute of the forest.* (p. 185)

Later, Bachelard quotes from Marcault and Therese Brosse (*L'education de demain*):

> *Forests, especially, with the mystery of their space prolonged indefinitely beyond the veil of tree trunks and leaves, space that is veiled for our eyes, but transparent to action, are veritable psychological transcendents.*

Plainly, the polarity is between the clean, "readable" landscape and the dense, mysterious one. One suggests purpose and reassuring order, the other, mystery, anxiety, and uncertainty. Designers have to be careful here because the professional bias is strongly toward the former.

Students of landscape perception have noted that first they "make sense" of the landscape, showing a preference for "coherence" and "complexity" (Kaplan, 1979, p. 245). This may tie back to a survival instinct, being able to read the environment to evaluate the chances of getting what one needs from it. These elements lend themselves to methodology, and one finds them or their surrogates present in most methods of landscape evaluation. The Forest Service's methodology until recently was almost entirely based on formal elements of composition; the human as observer, not a participant.

Beyond the formal, however, is a significant dimension that Kaplan (1979) called "mystery" (p. 244). Mystery balances the elements (not *compositional* visual elements) of inquisitiveness toward the new and fear of the unknown. Space can be "inferred" and "anticipated," but, significantly, the contents of that space are not required to be novel or surprising. It is the successive revelation of the known in new patterns, at a pace controlled by the observer who *enters* the scene—not simply views it. As Kaplan (1979) notes, "For a creature readily bored with the familiar, yet fearful of the strange, such an arrangement must be close to ideal" (p. 244). Kaplan's (1979) mystery is "intriguing but not threatening"; he does not include the spiritual connotations of the word. Yet, this state of receptivity—alertness, with calm—is often cited as a precondition of spiritual experience.

Signs

Signs give direction, reducing ambiguity (and mystery). Direction should perhaps always contain its opposite, *indirection*. In earnest efforts to make things clear, humans forget that the human mind is unparalleled at filling in the whole picture from a fragmentary context, a quality that truly distinguishes the humans from information processors such as computers.

Rather than labeling and directing, people could be allowed to be free to *perceive the relationship of natural features* as their guide. "At the bottom of the drainage, turn and go up the stream." The powers of perception are sharpened, precisely the aim. Perhaps experiment with ambiguous signs? Wordless signs, symbols. An aspen leaf carved into a heavy boulder at a trail junction. One could create a guidebook with nothing but line drawings and sketch maps to stimulate exploration rather than defining and limiting. The accompanying text would depict ecotypes with a little discourse on how each developed over time. Let the getting there be up to the seeker. The existential experience of freedom, according to Percy, (1954) is:

> *(1) an openness of the thing before one—instead of being an exercise to be learned according to an approved mode, it is a garden of delights which beckons to one; (2) a sovereignty of the knower—instead of being a consumer of prepared experience, I am a sovereign wanderer, a wanderer in the neighborhood of being who stumbles into the garden.* (p. 60)

Social Versus Contemplative

Design for these two basic motives would be inherently contradictory. Nature is sometimes a backdrop for intensive social experiences such as the Rainbow Family gatherings well-known to land managers. Solitude in a crowd may be possible if one understands and subscribes to what the others are up to (a Zen monastery), but the clientele for spiritual landscapes will not automatically be so in tune with one another. A group, by definition, is exclusive to those not a part of it and that can be distracting to others. Feeling either annoyed or "out of it" drags one back into daily life. Moreover, the group itself feels oppressed if "wanna-be's" intrude. (The tribal ceremonies at Panther Meadow on

Mount Shasta, according to Theodoratus and Evans (1991) have been interrupted by curious New Agers, some of whom have dropped crystals in the sacred springs.)

Social interference may exist even in the absence of other people if the others have left a mark on the landscape. Some "new" spiritual values incorporate artifacts, such as the New Age medicine wheels built near Sedona, Arizona, on the Coconino National Forest.

Lifestyle is an issue in the socially fractured end of the twentieth century. All "seekers" will not be middle-class, buttoned-up members of respected conservation organizations. Some of the clientele will be fond of ingesting hallucinogens or running naked through the woods. Others will dispel mystery and solitude by wandering with cellular telephones and electronic global positioning (GPS) devices harnessed to their chests. These examples (which could be multiplied beyond number) constitute an argument for a landscape of generous size.

Gender

Design will have to take into account cultural differences between the sexes, a subject that needs much more inquiry. Women, for example, may not have the same motivations as men.

> *. . . Women move out of the way . . . they have smaller cachement areas. They are weavers, gaze-averters, arm-closers, seeking anonymity when alone and quiet corners to talk in when they have companions. They walk shorter distances . . . and come in groups.*
>
> Kay, 1993

> *. . . Bowing [to the earth] is a gesture of respect, of mutuality . . . surrendering means stripping down, taking away every veil, every obstacle between ourselves and the earth. It means losing ourselves in the otherness of a place . . . to open ourselves to every small and ordinary thing for the larger purpose of knowing its truth . . . if we go out to find, not to impose, the landscape touches us and we it. Only then is a sense of place born.*
>
> Ehrlich, 1991

Much more needs to be said about this: women's need for physical security; the lesser tendencies of women to "conquer" and impose their will; the differences when women experience nature with other women and with men; the distinctive character of all male groups in the outdoors. A common plaint of academic inquiry applies: "we need more research."

Water, Weather, and other Ephemera

Water has always been rich in association. Land management planners should not hesitate to think that watery features contribute strongly to spiritual landscapes. Every kind of water—waterfalls, mist, crystalline pools, deep water, white water, whirlpools, still water, oceans—has been used as a metaphor for some kind of spiritual realization. Water attacks all the senses; visual, tactile, acoustical, taste, and sometimes, olfactory. Reflections of parts of the landscape in water deconstruct the landscape forms as commonly perceived enabling new perceptions to occur. Many nature photographers have observed this.

The advent of rain, thunderstorms, mist, and fog require a slowing down as well as a loss of control over our rationally planned experience. Land management planners can't design the weather, but they can choose the location. A case can be made that bad weather enshrouds the landscape in mystery, some insecurity ("I say, Holmes, these appear to be the footprints of a gigantic hound . . ."), and may repel the merely pleasure bent.

Happy accidents, like yellow cottonwood leaves falling into a stream and whirling down for miles, contribute. Land management planners may be a long way, however, from having sensibilities finely honed enough that they design them into the landscape.

Avoiding Featurism

Nothing really precludes an inspirational experience in Yosemite Valley or at Old Faithful, but the rest of the multitudes have come to see the biggest, the deepest, the highest, the most dangerous, and so on—a bad beginning to spiritual inquiry. But since managers can't save features for the exclusive use of spiritual seekers, spiritual landscapes need more of John Burroughs' inspiration to look to the particular and the local and (heretically) less from John Muir who encouraged the cultivation of scenic spectacle. Burroughs, who is now as much ignored as Muir is lionized, would have had us look toward cultivating

quieter, less dramatic country that gets little attention from feature and/or creature seekers.

Design should aim to attract people whose presence (at least) is not inconsistent with the achievement of spiritual goals. Land management planners should avoid creating magnets for "active-expressive" or "social comfort-seeking" recreationists (Burch, 1965; Burch and Wenger, 1966). These motivations involve calling attention to oneself or importing elaborate material life-support systems. (Recreational vehicles, high-tech backpacking equipment, and portable computers may all be social indicators of the wrong kind.) Bachelard is onto this, warning against the:

> . . . spectacle complex, in which pride of seeing is at the core of consciousness of a being in contemplation . . . I should like to liquidate, as it were, the spectacle . . . which could harden certain varieties of poetic contemplation. (p. 190)

Interpretation

We feel that when all possible scientific questions have been answered, the problems of life remain completely untouched. Of course, there are then no questions left, and this itself is the answer . . . . There are, indeed, things that cannot be put into words. They make themselves manifest. They are what is mystical.

Wittgenstein, 1961

Land management's interpretive tradition concentrates on pure content and warms it up with some sentiment. Managers seldom advise the public that:

> . . . to see—that is, to discover—is not an act of interpretation, of transfixing with preconceived ideas what is before us; rather, it is an act of surrender . . .

Ehrlich, 1991

For the present purposes at least, managers should be "against interpretation" (Sontag, 1961). In our context this means avoiding the usual focus on content at the expense of appreciating—or, simply revealing—form. If "nature" is substituted for "art," Sontag's (1961) statement loses no force:

> *In a culture whose already classical dilemma is the hypertrophy of the intellect at the expense of energy, interpretation is the revenge of the*

intellect upon art . . . [and] the world. . . . The world, our world, is depleted, impoverished enough. Away with all duplicates of it, *until we again experience more immediately what we have.* (p. 17, emphasis added)

Land management's theme is experiential. And in the same way Sontag (1961) tried to do for art, managers should ask, *how does the wild landscape do its work?*

Even enlightened interpretation is going to view nature as having "something out there" that we have to "get." Rolston locates this perception deep in "the hinterlands of our minds, a hidden persuader that silently shapes an ethic," going on to ask whether "living well is not merely getting [from nature] what I value but . . . a negotiating of my values in a neighborhood of worth" (1989, p. 115).

Knowledge, as Luipen and Koren (1969) remind us, is "not a relationship between two different realities, but the subject himself involved in the world" (p. 61). Does this leave solitary people wandering around and no naturalists? It does not. Luminous perception may occur jointly with others: realizing intersubjectively that this is so for us both. This "interpreting for each other" is unrecognized by agencies whose drift must always be toward the objective and the empirical (this is so because I said so), and toward "processing" large numbers of people. Nyberg (1992) comments:

> *When the interpreter tells his reality, he does not share it on an equal footing. Rather, he tells it so that it is to be someone else's reality. It is an act of epistemological violence, not simply saying 'my reality is better than your reality,' but 'my reality is reality.' All else is illusion or delusion.*

Sontag would add ". . . ultimately, having an experience becomes identical with taking a photograph of it" (1994, p. 40).

And so one is left with the impoverishment, ironically noted by Percy, that

> *. . . there is no sense of impoverishment . . . due altogether to the eager surrender of sovereignty by the layman so he can take up the role not of the person but of the consumer.* (p. 54)

To the wall that separates people and nature, managers add a brick.

We would do well to remember the way packaged knowledge:

> *. . . rumble[s] in the gut . . . too much refined food. If you always eat out you can never be sure what's going in, and received information is nobody's exercise . . . . Here is some advice. If you want to keep your own teeth, make your own sandwiches . . . .*
> Winterson, 1985, p. 95

Some of the foregoing remarks may have seemed rather cool toward the arts of administration, design, and interpretation. But they are so only in proportion to claims made by these fields that may come to extend over the realm of spiritual experiences.

The example of Wilderness is a good one. A Forest Service designer, landscape architect Arthur Carhart, recognized as far back as 1916 that physical design and rational ordering had certain inherent limits. Because administrators agreed with him, the first Wilderness came to be. I have tried to argue that interpretation has its own limits. Restraint exercised by public agencies toward spiritual things, the willingness to provide a space—but not to fill it—is analogous to the silences that are essential in music.

Literature Cited

Bachelard, G. (1969). *The poetics of space*. Translated by Maria Jolas. Boston, MA: Beacon Press.

Bellah, R. (1964). Religious evolution. *American Sociological Review, XXIX*, 358-374.

Burch, W., Jr. (1965). The play world of camping: Research into the social meaning of outdoor recreation. *American Journal of Sociology, LXX* (5), 604-612.

Burch, W., Jr. and Wenger, W. (1966). The social characteristics of participants in three styles of family camping. Pacific Northwest Experiment Station Research Paper PNW-48. USDA Forest Service.

Ehrlich, G. (1991, September). Legacy of light. *Harper's*, p. 24.

Gussow, A. (1979). Conserving the magnitude of uselessness: a philosophical perspective. In G. Elsner and R. Smardon (Eds.), *Our national landscape: Applied techniques for the analysis and management of the visual resource* (pp. 6-11). Pacific Southwest Experiment Station General Technical Report PSW-35. USDA Forest Service.

Hall, E. (1977). *Beyond culture*. Garden City, NY: Anchor Press/Doubleday.

Helphand, K. (1993). Reading the contemporary landscape. In review of *The culture of nature: North American landscape from Disney to the Exxon Valdez*. Landscape Architecture supplement. Book Reviews and Bookstore, Fall.

Higuchi, T. (1983). *The visual and spatial structure of landscapes*. Translated by Charles S. Terry. Cambridge, MA: MIT. Press.

Høeg, P. (1993). *Smilla's sense of snow*. Translated by Tiina Nunn-ally. New York, NY: Farrar, Straus & Giroux, Inc.

Kaplan, S. (1979). Perception and landscape: Conceptions and misconceptions. In Gary Elsner and Richard Smardon (Eds.), *Our national landscape: Applied techniques for analysis and management of the visual resource* (pp. 241-248). Pacific Southwest Experiment Station General Technical Report PSW-35. USDA Forest Service.

Kay, J. (1993). Women, land, design: Vaulting the garden wall. *Landscape Architecture, 83*, (8), 38.

Kierkegaard, S. (1966). *The concept of irony, with constant reference to Socrates*. (Lee M. Cape, Trans.). London, UK: Collins.

Leopold, A. (1966). *A sand county almanac: With essays on conservation from Round River*. New York, NY: Ballantine Books.

Luipen, W. and Koren, H. (1969). *Existential phenomenology*. Pittsburgh, PA: Duquesne University Press.

Nyberg, K. (1992). Some radical comments on interpretation: A little heresy is good for the soul. In Gary Machlis and Donald Field (Eds.), *On interpretation: Sociology for interpreters of natural and cultural history*, (rev. ed.) (pp. 206-211). Corvallis, OR: Oregon State University Press.

Percy, W. (1954). *The message in the bottle*. New York, NY: Farrar, Straus & Giroux, Inc.

Rolston, H. (1989). *Philosophy gone wild*. Buffalo, NY: Prometheus Books.

Rorty, R. (1979). *Philosophy and the mirror of nature*. Princeton University Press.

Sontag, S. (1961). *Against interpretation*. New York, NY: Dell Publishing.

Sontag, S. (1994, July). Sunbeams. *The Sun: A Magazine of Ideas*, p. 40.

Theodoratus, D. and Evans, N. (1991). *Statement of findings: Native American interview and data collection study of Mt. Shasta, California*. Commissioned by USDA Forest Service, Shasta-Trinity National Forests, Redding, CA: Fair Oaks, CA: Theodoratus Cultural Research.

Tribe, L. (1976). Ways not to think about plastic trees. In L. Tribe, C. Schelling and J. Voss (Eds.), *When values conflict: Essays on environmental analysis, discourse, and decision*. Cambridge, MA: Ballinger Publishing.

Tuan, Y. (1978, March). Raw emotion to intellectual delight. *Landscape Architecture*.

Tuan, Y. (1977). *Space and place: The perspective of experience*. Minneapolis, MN: University of Minnesota Press.

Winterson, J. (1985). *Oranges are not the only fruit*. New York, NY: Atlantic Monthly Press.

Wittgenstein, L. (1961). *Tractatus logico-philosophicus* (D. Pears and B. McGuinness, Trans.). London, UK: Routledge and Kegan Paul.

COGNITION AND THE MANAGEMENT OF PLACE

THOMAS GREENE
Department of Psychology
St. Lawrence University
Canton, New York

CHAPTER 27

Introduction

Prior to the last half-century, public land management practices aimed to provide sustainable yields of trees, wildlife, water, and other tangible resources. Given the dominant North American culture of that time, it is not difficult to understand why natural resources were viewed as commodities to be produced or why economic value was adopted as a metric for comparing different resource values and as an index of managerial success. Presumably, managers perceived that these resources were being produced for human consumption, but their value to most citizens was realized only after they were extracted from public lands. Resources were valued not as trees but as lumber, not as streams but as water, and not as wildlife but as trophies or food. In this climate, recreation on public lands also increased, and it became an important management consideration. Recreation was simply added to the dominant management paradigm and measured in mechanical terms like days afield, willingness to pay, and carrying capacity.

Although it may be possible for some people to ski, climb, or paddle while dismissing the surrounding landscape as nothing more than a medium for their activity, many others have also come to value natural settings for their intrinsic character. And unlike the many resource values that accrue indirectly to individual citizens after they purchase products made from distant sources of raw materials, the effects of setting on human experience are immediate and personal. Some of these personal effects are directly observable from behavior (e.g., recreational activities or user counts) and may be fairly concrete and measurable. On the other hand, many of the effects of landscapes on humans are based on personal, intimate relationships between individual persons and settings. Whether these relationships are perceived as aesthetic, nostalgic, or spiritual, they provide a sense of place or of place meaning. Perhaps because these relationships with human meaning and experience are so direct, they are often viewed as deeply important. Ironically, this directness means there are few material artifacts of place relationships to see, count, or otherwise document. For example, a few hundred of my friends and students have completed the following exercise:

'Spirit of place' results from a combination of a landscape, culture, and the personal experiences and psychology of an individual that give a location a 'feel' or personality. For example, sometimes places might be notable to you because of the way they look, sometimes because of people with whom you have shared them, sometimes because of the thoughts you have had there. Please try to think of three places in natural environments that are special for you (in this case, a natural environment can be anything from a city park to a pristine wilderness). What are your three places? Please use a paragraph to explain why each place you listed is important to you.

The resulting narratives typically are anything but mundane. For some, places seem to obtain their meaning from the character of the landscape. For others, places are tied to the memory of an event or a person. Nearly all of the narratives are highly personal, and together they provide a testimonial to the personal significance of place. Sense of place and place attachment are not limited to wild or even natural environments, but I believe they are particularly good examples of land-based values that are important, hard-to-define, and underrepresented in public land management.

Roberts (Chapter Four, in this volume) admirably articulates the richness and importance of place in human experience. Although she makes a plea for new management guidelines, her cause is clearly not to add place as just one more resource dimension to be weighed by managers who are already struggling to balance competing multiple uses. The changes she seeks are revolutionary; nothing less than the establishment of a new management ethic which recognizes the prepotency of intact, unmodified natural areas. Her management proposal is simple and elegant: stop "developing" natural landscapes, close roads, and allow the regeneration of both the landscapes and human contact with "authentic" (unmanaged and natural) settings. Roberts beautifully conveys the richness of place meaning, challenges present management, and offers a simple, parsimonious replacement.

I don't want to resist overdue change, but I wish to provide another perspective on place and management. My goals are more modest, and my suggestions aim at broadening the domain of established management rather than replacing it; that

is, mine is more a proposal for evolution than revolution. Although the roots of the present discussion begin with the same place phenomena, my present interest is in the importance of place in human cognition and affect rather than in spirituality. It would be foolish to argue that cognition is more important than spirit, but sense of place is a cognitive as well as spiritual phenomenon. As such, it represents another way in which human experience is affected by natural environments, while providing another example of a domain that remains poorly defined and poorly understood.

Some would assert that we have arrived at a crisis of management because our culture is dominated by a mechanistic world-view that was created and perpetuated by science and adopted to serve the hegemony of capitalism (e.g., Merchant, 1992). Still, in the present context of our society and government, land must be managed by professionals according to legislated policies. For many areas, the ideal may be to minimize "development" and to reduce human impact by restricting access. On the other hand, picnic grounds, engineered trails, and ski areas already exist and will continue to be part of the public landscape. It may be that land managers have been far too eager to manipulate natural environments, but human trespass on public lands is a reality and passive management simply sends public lands into chaos, placing them at the mercy of special interests and economic expediency.

A Model of Place Relationships

Workable descriptions of place and related phenomena are fairly straightforward. A place results from an interaction between the unique cultural and physical characteristics of a setting and the personality and behavior of an individual in that setting (Steele, 1981). As an individual moves through a setting, he or she acquires knowledge about it and encounters place-related experiences, some of which are memorable. Strong setting/experience episodes acquire special meaning and result in place attachment.

These place experiences are complex, private, and often hard to articulate in objective terms. Of course, simplicity of measurement should not be a requirement for the inclusion of a dimension in management. I share the concern of Mitchell, Force, Carroll, and McLaughlin (1991) and Roberts (in this volume) that place and attachment-centered values are underrepresented in land management decision making. Figure 27-1 represents a simple diagram of place relationships. The model includes a third setting component not presented by Steele: the managerial setting. This addition is necessary because managers moderate or regulate the opportunities for visitor/setting interactions on public lands. Note also the bidirectional arrow between setting and person which emphasizes that this relationship is interactive or transactional. That is, place takes its meaning from individuals who are themselves partly defined by the places they inhabit. Even a fairly common location may acquire deep personal meaning if it is the site of salient life events, but distinctive physical settings and culturally important locations are more likely to provide the context for important places. Although such abstract descriptions may support a general under-

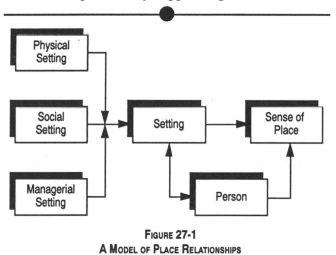

FIGURE 27-1
A MODEL OF PLACE RELATIONSHIPS

(adapted from: *The Sense of Place* by F. Steele, 1981)

standing of places, they fail to capture their deeply personal significance. In our culture, the meanings one takes from certain special places resemble one's feelings for one's most intimate friends. Places become inextricably tied to life events and the people with whom one has shared them. Like friendships, one's personal relationships with important places are difficult to abstract from their experiential context, operationally define, and describe with graphs or summary statistics. My love for the high plains of my home state of Wyoming is not shared by my

New York–raised children, and I am certain that they have special affections for landscapes and locations that I will never fully comprehend. Thus, place-centered experiences result in consequences that are personal, highly valued, and sometimes perceived as spiritual or religious. Place experiences remain hard to define and even more difficult to measure.

Place as an experiential dimension reflects the interplay between an individual and a physical, cultural, and managerial setting. Its transactional nature requires that managers recognize that place experiences will be unique for each pairing of setting and person. And yet, the context of the present discussion is the management of place on public lands. Although every human/setting interaction is strictly unique, I doubt that managers are capable of responding to each idiosyncratic person/setting relationship. So I now focus on just two aspects of place: aggregate summaries of place experiences, and the contribution of the physical setting to the salience and memorability of places.

Identifying Personal Places

The National Environmental Policy Act of 1969 requires public involvement in land management decision making. In this regard, public stakeholders should have an opportunity to document the importance of sense of place as a characteristic of the experiential landscape. Although theoretically fundamental to the experience of place, the contribution of individual personalities and life histories may be difficult to integrate into management practice. Indeed, if place experiences are completely idiosyncratic, they cannot be aggregated statistically or philosophically. On the other hand, certain locations may be more likely to be adopted as places. When a landscape demands attention, it will have increased probability of becoming a part of a place. In other words, place experiences will tend to accumulate around locations that are remarkable, and positive place experiences may be particularly salient. At a broad level, a rich understanding of the spectrum of place-related experiences of an area's users should help managers develop a more complete, more sensitive understanding of their management challenges.

At my university we have established a first year program that places all first year students in contained residential living groups and requires them to take a yearlong team-taught common course with others in their "college." In the fall 1994 course, two other faculty members and I used the personal place exercise found at the beginning of this chapter with our first year college students. The students (and faculty) completed the three personal place narratives, selected one, revised it as a short script, and then videotaped its presentation. During a subsequent overnight stay in a lodge in the Adirondacks the class shared the videotaped narratives. Of course, some students were more articulate, some more theatrical, and some more reserved, but I was struck by the sense that almost all of the narratives were at the same time revealing and entirely voluntary. It seems that when most of us talk about our places, we know that we are revealing something personal, but it is a valued opportunity to express our individuality rather than an intrusion on our privacy. Without wishing to overinterpret this exercise, that night in the Adirondacks was one of the experiences that the residents of the first year program still regard as an occasion that began building an unusual sense of community and good will.

It might be possible to analyze the content of these essays and present some tentative summary (with apologies to anyone who finds this hopelessly reductionistic). One recent small sample of the personal place narratives revealed the following breakdown of themes:

aesthetic sensations	16
isolation/seclusion	10
being with friends	6
vacation spot	6
closeness to nature	5
physical activity or sport	5
childhood memories	5
being with relatives	5
relaxation/reflection	4
belongingness/comfort	4
a "first" experience	2
sense of power	2
euphoria	1

Perhaps a systematic approach to content analysis will reveal individual variations in place attachments that can be meaningfully categorized. If so, place-related behaviors and attitudes can be fruitfully discussed as manifestations of personality. For

example, several authors propose that certain individuals exhibit personality types that make them more sensitive to places and their meaning (e.g., Mitchell, Force, Carroll, and McLaughlin, 1991; Steele, 1981; Williams and Roggenbuck, 1989). In one investigation of forest landscapes, Mitchell, Force, Carroll, and McLaughlin (1991) distinguished between "use-oriented" visitors and those who are more "attachment-oriented." Whereas use orientation resulted in a focus on activities and activity-based experiences, attachment orientation indicated an emotional bond with the setting. Accordingly, attachment-oriented users had a greater need to return to a specific site. Apparently because of their place attachment, they were more likely to demonstrate stewardship (cleaning up, making minor repairs) in their adopted environments. Those with a stronger attachment are probably more sensitive to managerial changes as they occur in a landscape, some of which may result in their dissatisfaction. Thus, the reactions of attached users may be particularly sensitive barometers of the changes that will eventually affect many users (Mitchell, Force, Carroll, and McLaughlin, 1991; Steele, 1981; Schreyer and Knopf, 1984).

A second promising method of obtaining individual place information is visitor employed photography (Cherem and Driver, 1983). Hikers were asked to photograph anything they wished on a hiking trail using inexpensive cameras which were distributed at trailheads. Visitors often photographed similar scenes with certain consensus photographs appearing in the records of more than 10 percent of the visitors.

Place as a Dimension in Management

There are still only a few relevant studies of place by recreation researchers (e.g., Fishwick and Vining, 1992; Mitchell, Force, Carroll, and McLaughlin, 1991; Steele, 1981; Williams and Roggenbuck, 1989). Why is place so late in emerging as an issue in the assessment and management of natural settings? Perhaps the roots of this oversight lie in historical accident, perhaps in differences in epistemology, or perhaps in the pragmatics of productive research and management. For example, it seems to be only a historical accident that most of the behavioral scientists who have written about place have restricted their inquiries to residential environments.

Whether urban or natural environments are the subject, many examinations of place are also phenomenological, and thus at odds with the empiricism that dominates behavioral science (Low and Altman, 1992). On the other hand, one reservation about systematic place investigations might also come from those who recoil from "cold" empiricism or misguided attempts to quantify a spiritual experience (Relph, 1993). Of course, a final explanation for the lack of systematic attention to place is that it simply is difficult to measure. It is possible that the experiences of place are so private and so idiosyncratic that they defy objective investigation (Low and Altman, 1992).

Just as there may be several reasons why place has not been a common dimension for assessment and management, I can imagine several distinct reasons for including place in these activities. One line of reasoning is admirably articulated by Roberts (Chapter Four, in this volume) when she stresses the importance of place as a component of personal identity and spiritual understanding. To the extent that current management practices regard the land as a commodity for the use (and abuse) of humans, a familiar consequence may be the "scars" that result from the destruction of natural environments. Roberts makes the important point that attempts to "hide" these scars with cosmetic manipulations of appearance are deceptions that attempt to substitute inauthentic places for genuine, evolved ecosystems. This inauthenticity is just one source of a spiritual estrangement between humans and nature that she believes has led to a loss of regional identity and personal meaning.

Methodological arguments are also important. Perhaps the reductionism of traditional scientific methodology as adopted by land managers divorces us from the context of our environments. Approaches which simplify in order to quantify are limited in their ability to characterize deep and complex individual relationships with place (Fishwick and Vining, 1992). Art and literature are subject to variations in observational skills and articulation by the reporter (Shami, 1991), but these and other qualitative or phenomenological inquiries are necessary for a complete understanding of place experiences. Perhaps the most important function of this text will be to provide a voice for those who properly demand inclusion of phenomenological and spiritual issues as part of an

expanded land management ethic. The spirit or meaning of place represents an instance in which the rich texture of human experience seems pitifully underrepresented by simple quantification.

Thus, I believe that a second mandate for inclusion of place as a dimension in management stems, not from a rejection of behavioral science, but from a desire to incorporate a level of analysis that may have been overlooked. I neither advocate substituting this understanding of place for the phenomenological initiative nor do I dispute the need for a new management ethic. This more concrete and limited cognitive perspective may be useful for managers. In this regard, I assert that:

1. the dangers of managing land as a commodity for human use are real, but the alternative to some form of management is chaos and environmental destruction;

2. the methods of behavioral science should be included among the tools for land and recreation management;

3. empirical evidence supports place as an important, underrepresented concept in understanding environmental attitudes, cognition, experiences, and management; and

4. place has promise as a dimension in the assessment and management of natural landscapes.

Returning to Figure 27-1, (page 303) we see three primary sources of a sense of place: characteristics of the physical setting, characteristics of the social setting, and characteristics of the individual perceiver. There is no reason to suppose that any one of these dimensions is primary. In fact, researchers emphasize that these components are complex, with dynamic connections that defy simplification into cause-effect relationships (e.g., Low and Altman, 1992; Steele, 1981). These components of place differ in their level of concreteness and accessibility to investigators. A critical point is that their nexus (that point at which place and meaning are established) exists primarily in memory.

Settings and Place Cognition

Clearly the experience of "place" is not simply a function of its physical attributes. On the other hand, a place experience is not just an accidental product of a particular time and person. If it were, the dimensions of place would be entirely idiosyncratic and beyond the reach of management. Apparently, some physical and social settings are just so potent that they are more likely to evoke a particular response in a variety of people. Further, even when social interactions or other life events initiate place experiences, they can be associated in memory with a physical setting. And such associative links may be more likely in some settings than others. The question becomes, "Are there important characteristics of locations in natural environments that make them candidates as 'places'?" The simplest answer might be that in order to become a place, a particular setting must be remembered, and this remembered location needs to be associated with some sort of emotion or affect.

Human Cognition and Memory for Places

How does one remember and find one's way back to desirable places? How does one avoid places one has learned are dangerous? The cognitive mapping and way-finding literatures provide a rich source of possibilities. There are at least two, and perhaps three, distinct literatures. One was developed by urban planners with an eye toward making cities and buildings more comprehensible and more pleasant. The second is more interested in an abstract understanding of the nature and structure of human spatial memory. Behavioral geographers may represent a third perspective that is more theoretical than that of planners but is more clearly tied to knowledge of actual environments than is typical of cognitive psychologists.

Kevin Lynch (1960) is the best known of the planners. In *The Image of the City*, Lynch simultaneously established a field of inquiry, a methodological approach to data collection, and a vocabulary for describing features of cognitive maps. Based on his analysis of sketch maps of cities drawn from memory, Lynch identified five categories of features that could be used to describe and analyze cognitive maps: paths, edges, districts, nodes, and landmarks. *Paths* are shared travel corridors such as streets, walkways or trails. *Edges* are limiting or enclosing features that tend to be linear but do not function as paths, such as a seashore or wall. *Districts* are larger spaces of the

cognitive maps that share a common "feel" or character. *Nodes* are major points where behavior is focused, typically associated with the intersections of major paths or places where paths are terminated or broken. Finally, *landmarks* are distinctive features, usually visible from a distance, that people use for navigation.

Lynch (1960) studied and wrote about cities, but the vocabulary of cognitive mapping can easily be applied to wilderness paths, mountain landmarks, and impenetrable edges created by cliff faces or wetlands. According to Lynch, those features of a setting that contribute to its memorability can be grouped under the term "legibility," and Lynch believed that legibility was important in creating a pleasant, livable city. Garling, Lindberg, Carreiras, and Book (1986) provided a somewhat more detailed analysis, suggesting three characteristics of easily remembered environments: differentiation, degree of visual access, and the complexity of the spatial layout. *Differentiation* is the degree to which parts of the environment are unusual or distinctive; *visual access* is the degree to which the environment is easily seen from the outside; and *complexity* of the spatial layout is the amount of information that must be comprehended to move through a particular environment. Anyone who has ever been lost in a remote forest will probably agree that the experience is profoundly troubling and will appreciate the value of way-finding cues like paths and landmarks.

Of course, not all paths or landmarks are remembered. Perhaps this simply reflects limitations in the capacity of human memory, a topic more typically of interest to cognitive psychologists than planners. For many memory tasks, humans seem to benefit from strategies that organize complex information into a smaller number of meaningful "chunks." It might prove quite difficult to memorize the letters *reptginkleinagnaph*; certainly more difficult than memorizing the same letters ordered into the three meaningful words *raging pink elephant*. People also seem to divide spatial information in a manner similar to "chunking" (Allen, 1981; Allen and Kirasic, 1985; Holding, 1992). Although the criteria for inclusion in a chunk or cluster may differ, good candidates are landmarks that are near to each other and are similar in character, or those that become associated as part of meaningful events. In landscapes, it is possible that this amounts to a rediscovery of what Lynch (1960) termed "districts." In a natural trail environment, Gustke and Hodgson (1980) identified the related information dimension of discontinuity, noting that people seem to pay particular attention to those locations where a trail moves from one landscape type into another. Between these known clusters or districts lie areas in which knowledge is less precise. Figure 27-2 helps illustrate some of the issues. Landmarks within the same cluster (say, points A and B) are judged to be closer to each other than to other, equidistant points (such as H) outside their cluster (Hirtle and Jonides, 1985; Holding, 1992; McNamara, Hardy and Hirtle, 1989). (As an aside I should mention that recent findings also reveal that the estimated distance between point A and point B on a cognitive map is not necessarily the same as the distance from point B back to point A [Foley and Cohen, 1984; Lee, 1970; Sadalla and Staplin, 1980]. This result may be less remarkable to those who are all too familiar with the phenomenon when it occurs on a mountain trail than it is to experimental psychologists whose map prototype seems to be a city grid.) Finally, each cluster may be represented by a *reference point*, a sort of "best example" that symbolizes all the locations within the cluster (Couclelis, Golledge, Gale, and Tobler, 1987; Sadalla and Staplin, 1980). In Figure 27-2 hypothetical reference points are shaded. One might imagine a world of well-known clusters or districts within which mutual associations are strong and distance estimates are fairly accurate.

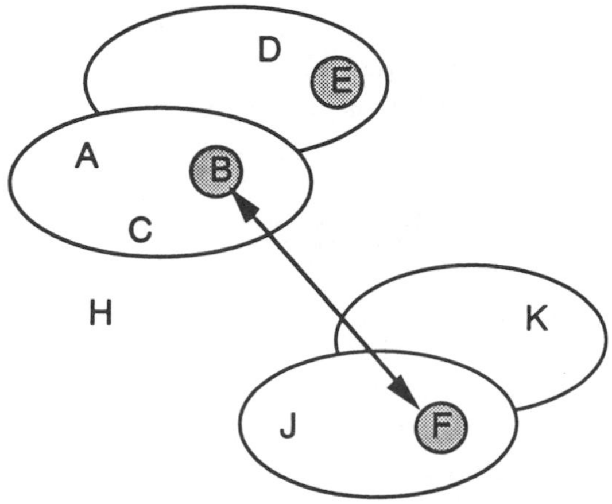

Connections also exist between districts as indicated by the arrow, but the actual connections may be primarily between reference points.

Cognitive research seems to be heading for a striking convergence with what has been primarily a phenomenological understanding of place. It seems that one's spatial memories are tied to a limited number of distinctive, affectively charged locations. How might researchers learn of these emotions or attitudes? They could construct some sort of questionnaire and compile the responses, but they might lose the spatial nature and richness of place experience. Instead, it may be useful to use one of several cognitive mapping techniques. Sketch maps (see Figure 27-3), very much like those Lynch (1960) pioneered, are one option. The procedure would first ask users to sketch a map of an area. Upon completion, participants would be asked to annotate their maps indicating why certain features appeared. Scenic vistas and challenging hills might be predictable, but visitors might disagree on whether a bridge over a brook is pleasant or unsightly. Presumably it is these rich and idiosyncratic differences in perception

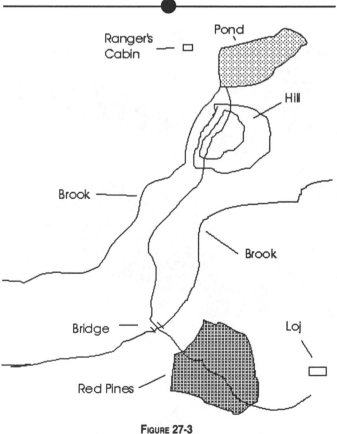

FIGURE 27-2
EXAMPLE OF A COGNITION MAP OF "DISTRICTS" WITH LANDMARKS AND HYPOTHETICAL REFERENCE POINTS.

FIGURE 27-3
EXAMPLE OF A SKETCH MAP THAT USES COGNITIVE MAPPING TECHNIQUES

and attitude that are most likely to offer insights that are not obtainable from standard management assessment practices.

A second technique would acquire a different sort of data. In this case, visitors would receive an accurate base map and would be asked to draw colored lines around the areas of a trail to indicate degrees of pleasantness, familiarity, danger, variety, or almost any other characteristic. If aggregate data are sought, these maps could be digitized and computer compiled to represent average ratings of some quality like pleasantness or challenge. As part of our campus planning I have used this computer mapping technique to compile maps of pleasantness, daytime danger, nighttime danger, and familiarity with the campus. It would be as easy to ask about remoteness, wildness, or comfort. Although we wrote the software to compile these maps, we export the file to a Geographical Information System (GIS) for more sophisticated analysis and presentation. The data the maps provide are rich, and occasionally overwhelming, but they are easily integrated into existing GIS systems (see Figure 27-4).

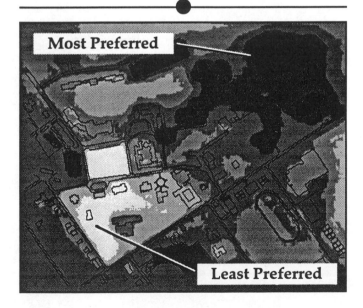

FIGURE 27.4
EXAMPLE OF A DIGITIZED, COMPUTER COMPLIED PREFERENCE MAP

These cognitive mapping techniques share a common problem: they rely on participants who are already familiar with the environment of interest.

For example, this reliance on veteran users would make these cognitive techniques inappropriate substitutes for the present systems for visual landscape assessment because first-time visitors are an important group. On the other hand, by tapping memory, researchers can move closer to an understanding of the acquired affections and attitudes that characterize place experiences. What dimensions should be investigated? Visual preference, remoteness, or variety are likely candidates because they represent the cognitive manifestation of dimensions that are already part of management concern.

Another dimension is psychological ownership. In a Ghost Ranch, New Mexico, office building is a small display dedicated to Georgia O'Keefe. Referring to a distant mesa, O'Keefe remarks that she has painted it so often she feels a sense of ownership. This quality has taken many names. It may be termed "territory" (Altman, 1975) or "kinship" (Mitchell, Force, Carroll, and McLaughlin, 1991), or drawn as a distinction between the landscapes of "insiders" or "outsiders" (Relph, 1993). Altman is among the most successful in articulating the notion that territory serves not only as a physical domain subject to boundary regulating defensive behaviors, but also as an important component of personal identity or self-definition. Ownership may be a desire to lay a purely intellectual claim to a place, to understand it through an informal scholarship of place. A visitor who acquires a detailed knowledge of an area's history, its flora and fauna, and the names of its features has laid a framework for meaning as well as knowledge. Although some territorial attachments must be sacrificed to the common good (Mitchell, Force, Carroll, and McLaughlin, 1991; Schreyer and Knopf, 1984), the needs of attachment-oriented visitors have probably been shortchanged.

Summary

Although it is less concrete than many other characteristics of natural landscapes, there is ample evidence that sense of place is a significant part of the experiences of visitors. Place is experienced as a deeply important, even spiritual, quality of a setting. Places are most likely to be:

1. *Distinctive*. This discussion has long been part of the USDA's visual assessment system.

2. *Memorable*. Related to distinctiveness, memorability has been a common planning dimension for more than three decades (e.g., Lynch, 1960).

3. *Affect Generating*. Some places are the source of powerful associations—sometimes idiosyncratic, sometimes cultural. The associations may be based on characteristics such as landscape aesthetics, historic associations, or wildness. Relevant information may come from sources as varied as published works of poetry or fiction, traditional surveys, or laboratory studies of biophilic responses to natural scenes.

4. *Psychologically Owned*. An opportunity to form a psychological sense of a special, unique relationship with an area.

In practice, many of these dimensions are already part of landscape inventories, but they are not explicitly assessed as components of place. The key to their successful integration is recognition of their importance to the understanding of place and the use of a palette of techniques including personal narratives, questionnaires, and cognitive mapping techniques which allow managers to inspect personal and previously overlooked relationships.

Literature Cited

Allen, G. (1981). A developmental perspective on the effects of "subdividing" macrospatial distance. *Journal of Experimental Psychology*: *Human Learning and Memory, 7*, 120-132.

Allen, G. and Kirasic, K. (1985). Effects of the cognitive organization of knowledge on judgments of macro–spatial distance. *Memory and Cognition, 13*, 218-227.

Altman, I. (1975). *The environment and social behavior*. Belmont, CA: Wadsworth.

Cherem, G. and Driver, B. (1983). Visitor employed photography: A technique to measure common perceptions of natural environments. *Journal of Leisure Research, 15*, 65-83.

Couclelis, H., Golledge, R., Gale, N., and Tobler, W. (1987). Exploring the anchor-point hypothesis of spatial cognition. *Journal of Environmental Psychology, 7*, 99-122.

Fishwick, L. and Vining, J. (1992). Toward a phenomenology of recreation place. *Journal of Environmental Psychology, 12*, 57-63.

Foley, J. and Cohen, A. (1984). Working mental representations of the environment. *Environment and Behavior, 16*, 712-713.

Garling, T., Lindberg, E., Carreiras, M., and Book, A. (1986). Reference systems in cognitive maps. *Journal of Environmental Psychology, 6*, 1-18.

Gustke, L. and Hodgson, R. (1980). Rate of travel along an interpretive trail: The effects of environmental discontinuity. *Environment and Behavior, 12*, 53-63.

Hirtle, S. and Jonides, J. (1985). Evidence of hierarchies in cognitive maps. *Memory and Cognition, 13*, 208-217.

Holding, C. (1992). Clusters and reference points in cognitive representation of the environment. *Journal of Environmental Psychology, 12*, 45-55.

Lee, T. (1970). Perceived distance as a function of direction in the city. *Environment and Behavior, 2*, 40-51.

Low, S. and Altman, I. (1992). Place attachment: A conceptual inquiry. In E. Altman and S. Low (Eds.), *Place attachment* (pp. 1-12). New York, NY: Plenum Publishing Corp.

Lynch, K. (1960). *The image of the city*. Cambridge, MA: MIT Press.

McNamara, T., Hardy, J., and Hirtle, S. (1989). Subjective hierarchies in spatial memory. *Journal of Experimental Psychology: Learning, Memory and Cognition, 15*, 211-227.

Merchant, C. (1992). *Radical ecology*. New York, NY: Routledge.

Mitchell, M., Force, J., Carroll, M., and McLaughlin, W. (1991). Forest places of the heart: Incorporating special places into public management. *Journal of Forestry, 4*, 32-37.

Relph, E. (1993). The reclamation of place. *Orion*, 32-36.

Sadalla, E. and Staplin, L. (1980). An information storage model for distance cognition. *Environment and Behavior, 12*, 183-193.

Schreyer, R. and Knopf, R. (1984). The dynamics of change in outdoor recreation environments—some equity issues. *Journal of Park and Recreation Administration, 2*, 9-19.

Shami, S. (1991). Sense of place: An empirical measurement. *Geoforum, 22*, 347-358.

Steele, F. (1981). *The sense of place*. Boston, MA: CBI.

Williams, D. and Roggenbuck, J. (1989). Measuring place attachment: Some preliminary results. Paper presented at the session on outdoor planning and management, NRPA Symposium on Leisure Research, San Antonio, TX.

MULTISENSORY LANDSCAPE AESTHETICS

CHAPTER 28

WARREN BACON
Pacific Northwest Region
USDA Forest Service
Portland, Oregon

Aesthetics is often thought to be only visual in nature, but the aesthetic impulse should be understood to include all the senses—touch, smell, taste, sound, and sight. When aesthetics is integrated with ecology, it requires the addition of knowledge and appreciation of a healthy ecosystem and how we humans fit into it. Though the ability to appreciate beauty is strongly linked to culture and varies from individual to individual and group to group, there are cross-cultural commonalities in the perception of beauty. In other words, beauty is not totally in the eye of the beholder. There are some physiological bases of aesthetics. Most common preferences for aesthetics, however, stem from a tradition of landscape painting and aesthetic theory that began in seventeenth- and eighteenth-century Europe.

Experiencing the various senses is aided by an individual's getting into an aesthetic mode psychologically. The aesthetic mode is a mood, a feeling, or an emotion. For the aesthetic mode to occur, a certain psychological distancing from the routines of everyday life is necessary. Being immersed in nature appears to help facilitate the psychological distancing process.

The aesthetic mode tends to have two extremes. One is the dream-like immersion of the senses. The other is the critical or intellectual enjoyment of the "object(s)" that trigger the senses. Young children tend to inhabit the space between the two. One environment that tends to facilitate this in-between state is the "nook." Particularly satisfying are special outdoor places—a cave, a hollow in a tree, or a tree house. For a child nestled there, time seems to come to a complete stop, and the senses are characterized by a complete immersion. Young children live in a world of wonder, and, far from being insensitive to beauty, they have special access to it.

Delight of the Senses

Since distancing oneself from the rigors of the everyday world is essential to the aesthetic experience, it is not surprising that the potential of the proximate senses has been undervalued. Yet the senses of touch, smell, taste, sound, and sight add immensely to the vitality and beauty of the world.

Touch

Humans can go through life completely blind and deaf and entirely devoid of the senses of smell and taste. But they cannot survive without the functions provided by touch. Proper workings of the digestive and eliminative organs are dependent on the skin being stimulated, particularly in the very young. Touch is essential to survival and growth, yielding a pleasure little diminished by age.

One's deepest sense of well-being may come from touch: the coolness of a stone in the shade, the roughness of a cobbled walk, a stroll beneath a row of trees sensing the alternating warmth and coolness of sun and shade, touching the bark of a nearby tree, or dipping one's feet into the warm sand at the beach. Touch is the critical element for exploring and appreciating the world. For children, touch is the primary mode of learning about their environment.

Adults can also explore the world through touch, and by leaving trees, shrubs, herbaceous plants, rotting logs, rocks and small critters intact they can enhance this sense in themselves and in others. As a tactile part of the immediate environment, such restraint is even more important for other forest visitors who have limited sight or no sight at all.

Most tactile sensations are experienced indirectly through one's eyes. Though only a small part of one's physical environment is experienced through the sense of touch, the overall tactile impression is quite strong. Seeing and the tactile sensations are closely related, and there are times when one cannot be sure which is playing the primary role. Nature has a strong appeal because of the extent and complexity of its tactile impressions. A single plant may have rough bark, smooth waxy leaves, and satiny petals. A small section of the forest floor may expose moss among the ferns, fruiting bodies on an old rotting log, and numerous critters among the duff.

As with most senses, the tactile sense is activated by contrasts: heat and cold, rough and smooth, light and heavy. The range of appreciation may be narrower than for sight because touch is more closely bonded to the moods and emotions of the basic psychological processes.

With over 80 percent of the population now living in urban areas, people are rapidly losing "touch" with nature. Children still enjoy jumping into piles of leaves, wiggling their toes in the sand, and rolling down a snow bank, but adults often limit their enjoyment of nature by simply looking at it.

Smell

Smell imparts many aesthetic pleasures, yet it is frequently underappreciated. Until deprived of it one is often unaware of how much the sense of smell contributes to the quality of one's life. But think about how one delights in the fragrance of spring flowers, the clean smell of fall rains, or the smell of sage after a brief shower. Distinctive odors make a place seem real in a way that visual images do not. The Russian novelist Tolstoy describes the excitement he felt as a child after a spring thunderstorm:

> *On all sides crested skylarks circle with glad songs and swoop swiftly down. . . . The delicious scent of the wood . . . the odor of the birches, of the violets, the rotting leaves, the mushrooms, and the wild cherry is so enthralling that I cannot stay in the brichka.*
>
> Tolstoy, 1961, p. 74

The fragrances from the rural countryside are often commented on with pleasure—the smell of burning wood as the farmers settle down for their evening meals, or the odor of fresh new mown hay. As Yi-Fu Tuan concludes:

> *Scents capture the aesthetic, emotional quality of place. In middle latitude deciduous forests, it may be the smell of spring, understood as the smell of life; in the boreal forests, the smell of pine needles and fir cones; in certain parts of the Great Plains, the fragrance of sage; in New Mexico, pinon and juniper basking in the hot sun; in Australia, eucalyptus; on sea coasts, cool ozone-tinted air with a whiff of seaweed; in hot deserts, the slightly acrid odor of intensely heated soil and rock; and so on. People who speak of preserving natural landscapes usually have only their visual character in mind. Yet not only a silhouette but an aroma is destroyed when an old deciduous forest is chopped down and replaced by fast-growing conifers. An olfactory geography does not come naturally to us. For this reason, when we have learned to appreciate nature's extraordinary range of aromas and are ready to write an olfactory geography, we will have demonstrated a higher level of aesthetic sophistication.*
>
> Tuan, 1993, p. 69

Taste

Taste is strongly related to touch. "Eating is touch carried to the bitter end," said Samuel Butler. In nature one tastes the salt in the ocean spray, the dryness of the desert air, the dampness and humidity of the rain forest. Barring poisonous plants, tasting things in nature can add a delightful dimension to the aesthetic mode (e.g., the twigs of the black birch, the leaves of the mint plant, and the fruit of the blackberry, raspberry, salmon, and huckleberry bushes).

Sound

Most people consider loss of sight a far worse calamity than loss of hearing. But a world without sound begets a sense of deadness. Life involves movement and most movement creates sound.

City dwellers who often tire of the hustle and bustle of the urban setting seek the peace and quiet of nature. But nature is often not quiet. It is peace that is important. In nature, one hears the roar of the waterfall, the rustle of leaves, the chirping of birds. Absolute silence is intolerable. And much as people eulogize dramatic sounds like the call of the loon, it is the background noises of all the little clicks and flutters that envelope one in nature that add depth to one's experiences.

Sound can evoke deeply felt emotions even more than sight. However, the necessary distancing to reach an aesthetic mode is more difficult in a world of human sound than in nature. Many human sounds are highly distractive to achieving an aesthetic mood. But in nature one has little trouble savoring the isolated symphony of sounds—the chirping of birds, the lapping of waves on the shore, or the distant sighing of the wind. Then there's the sense of mystery when acoustical space exceeds the visual space, such as in a deep woods or a dense tropical forest where the presence of unseen animals can only be experienced by hearing their cries.

Part of the attraction of sound, such as the lone bird call across a lake, is the silence that immediately precedes and follows it. Silence alone can be deadly but in our frantic noise-filled world momentary silence can be highly desirable—a life-restoring experience in its own right.

A common sound in nature is wind on vegetation. Where there is little wind and little vegetation, silence prevails. The great deserts of the world often fall silent. Under the intense white heat, when nothing stirs except an occasional dust devil, one may hear only the thump of one's own heart. The great ice caps can be even more awesome and still.

Nature, of course, can also be full of sound and fury—the roar of a storm with an occasional peal of thunder. It can start quietly. A needle leaf northwestern forest can be eerily quiet. But that all changes as the wind starts to blow, gently at first producing a quiet whisper, then louder and louder as millions of needles twist and turn in their dance of the storm.

Sight

Sight tends to be valued more than all other senses. All senses give one a world to relate to, but the visual world has the greatest definition and scope. It is both sensual and intellectual. It is sensual not only because of its colors and shapes but also because of its textures or tactile quality. One can almost feel what one sees.

Reality as composition is a most salient visual experience. Composition is three-dimensional space defined by objects which in themselves are three-dimensional. One lives among objects located at various distances in space which can be seen both close at hand and at great distances. Sight is the distance sensor for humans as smell is for many other animals. Color is particularly important to one's visual aesthetics.

While color vision is a property of human perception shared with other primates, people tend to take it for granted. Color vision varies from individual to individual. Everyone is color blind to some degree. Some people are more sensitive than others to certain colors. Most people are content with the color capabilities they have:

however, we now realize that even the most philistine person, to enjoy the world, must have a sensitivity to color. People are more aesthetically inclined than they know or are willing to admit. However, individuals and cultures differ widely in their capacity for and style of appreciation. Age, predictably, makes a difference. Young children are drawn to vivid primary colors. A wider range of color awareness and a greater liking for the subtler tones come with age and education. As for the preferences of different cultures, Brent Berlin and

Paul Kay note that all cultures have three basic color terms—black, white, and red—and that the more advanced the cultures are materially and politically the more terms they possess; and this means that among the riches a culture gains as it becomes more complexly structured is a more brightly and subtly colored world.

Tuan, 1993, p. 103

Ecology

The idea of ecological aesthetics adds another dimension, the knowledge and appreciation of a healthy sustainable ecosystem and how we humans fit into it (Gobster, 1995). An ecological aesthetic asks for expanding one's thinking about how one "sees" the landscape and one's place in it. In the visual aesthetic the pursuit of pleasure is primary, and pleasure can be derived from viewing the landscape irrespective of its ecological integrity. In contrast, pleasure in an ecological aesthetic comes from knowing about the landscape and knowing it is ecologically "fit." This ties aesthetics to ecology and ethics, as expressed in Leopold's land ethic:

> *A thing is right when it tends to preserve the integrity, stability, and beauty of the biotic community. It is wrong when it tends otherwise.*

Leopold, 1949, pp. 224-225

This change in focus also broadens our idea of aesthetic perception from a process that is visual, immediate, and largely pleasure-oriented to one that uses all our senses and our intellect. Ecological aesthetics, for example, involve appreciating how "esthetic indicator species" (Callicott, 1983) like the Kirtland's warbler, eastern timber wolf, and northern spotted owl are sustained in an intact ecosystem. These features imbue the forest landscape with deep symbolic meaning, while the composed view is often appreciated only at face value.

Person/landscape interactions and outcomes are perhaps the most significant parts of an ecological aesthetic. Having an ecological aesthetic requires that one experiences the landscape as an active participant—relating to it as a living entity rather than watching it passively as if it were a picture or other art object. It is through these interactions that one develops "dialogues" with oneself and with the landscape that help one, as Spirn suggests,

know oneself and one's place in the world. Although "snapshot" experiences of pretty landscapes may temporarily lift one's moods, extended dialogues with nature restore one psychologically and allow opportunities for inner change (Kaplan, 1993).

Multisensory Landscape Aesthetics and Psychologically Deep Nature-Based Experiences

It seems reasonable to suggest that there would be no psychologically deep, nature-based, human experiences without the types of multisensory landscape aesthetic experiences just described. It also seems reasonable to suggest that settings which vary in naturalness, remoteness, social encounters, control, regimentation, and ease of access offer different degrees of probability of these experiences happening. From a managerial perspective, the multisensory landscape aesthetics question is: how can an array of opportunities be provided for these experiences while also allowing for the provision of other natural resource-based goods and services? The recreation opportunity spectrum (ROS) offers a useful framework for meeting both of these managerial objectives.

The Recreation Opportunity Spectrum

The great outdoors presents a tremendous diversity of opportunities for aesthetic and other hard-to-define, nature-based experiences, and the public demands an equally diverse set of experiences. From pristine wilderness to urban settings, people look to the outdoors to satisfy their needs. In doing so, they attempt to match their desires, abilities, and expectations to a particular activity and setting. The ROS has been designed to facilitate that matching process (Driver, Brown, Stankey and Gregoire, 1987). The ROS is based on the following premises:

- People purposefully choose settings with particular attributes for their recreation activities.

- Recreation-related choices are made with the expectation of achieving particular recreation experiences.

- It is desirable, from a macroplanning perspective, to present a wide spectrum of activity and recreation setting opportunities, ranging from highly developed to primitive, from which people may choose.

- The different types of settings arrayed along the ROS provide both similar and undeniably different opportunities for various types of recreation experiences.

For the purposes of this chapter and this text, I offer two new and different premises for the ROS:

1. The different experience opportunities available in different ROS settings are enhanced because of their synergism with particular "aesthetic experience opportunities" available in those settings.

2. Knowledge and appreciation of a healthy sustainable ecosystem add still another dimension to the aesthetic experience, particularly when one actively relates to that ecosystem.

The ROS framework offers a continuum of possible combinations of recreation settings, activities, and experiential (including aesthetic) opportunities, which, when used, provide a wide array of benefits to recreationists (Driver and Brown, 1978). As implemented in the USDA Forest Service and in other agencies in the United States and abroad, the ROS is comprised of six or seven classes or "zones" that differ somewhat in the types of recreation opportunities that can be realized there. Each of those zones will now be reviewed briefly, including consideration of the types of "aesthetic experience opportunities" available.

PRIMITIVE AND SEMIPRIMITIVE

As operationalized in many land management agencies, the ROS has one primitive and two semiprimitive (nonmotorized and motorized) classes. These primitive and semiprimitive settings are primarily unmodified natural- or near natural-appearing environments. They are often characterized by dramatic scenery and abundant wildlife offering a high probability of engaging and enjoying all of the senses. There are usually few encounters with other people, and the sights and sounds of human activity are usually distant or not audible. This makes the necessary psychological distancing for an aesthetic mode to occur highly probable. Being totally immersed in

a highly diverse natural setting makes ephemeral elements of light, wind, water, and wildlife integral to the symphony of aesthetic experiences. Add to this the aesthetic (or kinesthetic) sense of movement through space on skis, horseback, or watercraft. Where the use is motorized, such as in a semiprimitive motorized zone, users must stop and turn off the equipment before aesthetic modes can begin to occur. Even superficial visual experiences are unlikely while the equipment is moving because so much attention must be given to keeping the vehicle on the trail or primitive road. Some of these settings offer the opportunity to experience an ecosystem with limited disturbance by humans, though some of the more popular settings may be heavily impacted.

Roaded Natural: The predominant aesthetic experience enjoyed in this zone is viewing the landscape through car windows. Though this is a limited aesthetic as far as all senses are concerned, the importance of it should not be discounted. Driving for pleasure is one of the leading recreation activities, and it is continuing to grow in popularity. In addition, there are opportunities for people to get out of their cars to hike, go on interpretive walks, stroll through visitor centers, and frequent special archaeological and historical exhibits which engage the other aesthetic senses. There are also often remote parts of roaded natural areas where people can build their own camps, hunt, fish, and participate in other activities where the senses of the aesthetic may come into play.

Roaded Modified: This zone probably offers the fewest opportunities for aesthetic experiences. The setting is usually a highly modified natural environment from timber harvests, mining, or other extractive activities. The scenic attractiveness of this setting tends to be fairly low on the scale of human preferences. Logging or mining activities often create considerable noise and dust. People may seek out hidden special places along streams or small lakes to get away from the activity or sight of microsite aesthetics being realized—enjoyment of gurgling water, a campfire, a sunset, and the stars twinkling at night.

Rural: Rural environments, though culturally modified, often have a lot to offer the aesthetic senses—old wooden farm houses with large front porches, brightly colored barns, post and rail fences, the smell of wood smoke in the air, newly mown hay, and the sound of sheep bleating in the pasture (see Bruns and Stokowski, Chapter Twenty-Nine, in this volume).

Urban: Cities offer many different character subtypes in providing opportunities for psychologically deep, nature-based, human experiences. Some tease aesthetic senses—cobble stone streets with ornate historic structures, city parks, zoos, golf courses, and other green spaces, a charming waterfront with boats moored tightly. After dark, many parts of the city take on new charm when bathed in brightly colored lights.

URBAN/RURAL SUBCLASSES

There is a tendency for many people to think that the psychologically deep, nature-based experiences on which this text focuses can only be realized in natural settings that are relatively free of noticeable human activity. While those types of settings might be optimal for many people, they are not the only settings where aesthetic experiences take place. In this regard, the role of urban green spaces in providing opportunities for psychologically deep, nature-based, human experiences seems particularly important. In the aggregate, readily available and frequently used urban natural areas probably contribute more psychologically deep, nature-based experiences to the lives of the citizenry than any other type of natural area. To assess the role of these areas in providing opportunities for nature-based, multisensory, aesthetic experiences, the following subclasses of the urban and rural ROS classes are offered.

Nature Dominant: This zone is an area where an element or complex of the natural environment remains intact, can be rehabilitated, or is of a size or has other characteristics where at least some sense of remoteness or isolation can be experienced. This may be created through visual shielding from external sights and sounds as well as distance. Recreational activities focus on the natural environment and are generally self-determined and self-scheduled. Examples would include nature preserves, wildlife viewing areas, green ways, and undeveloped portions of parks.

Natural/Facility Accommodation: This zone is a park-like area with varying mixes of natural and human-made elements. Facilities are readily apparent with a high degree of comfort and convenience but should blend harmoniously with the natural environment. Visitors may expect to see large numbers of other people but still have opportunities for low interaction. Structured recreational programs may be offered, but opportunities also exist for some degree of self-scheduling. Examples would include minimally developed portions of parks, open spaces, botanical gardens, and historical/cultural parks.

Facility Dominant: This zone is an activity focused area where human-made elements are primary. Facilities are mainly designed for user comfort and convenience but should complement the site. Visitors may find little shielding from external sights and sounds and will encounter high social interaction. Activities are largely externally programmed and regulated. Examples would include highly developed portions of parks, ball fields, courts, and swimming pools.

The *nature dominant* areas might offer the best opportunities for multisensory aesthetics to come to life depending on how well the external sights and sounds are screened out, how many encounters with other people are occurring, and how attractive the scenery is. In *nature/facility accommodation* areas, well-designed botanical or Japanese gardens may tickle the aesthetic fancy in terms of scenic attractiveness like a fine painting. In *facility dominant* areas, the visual aesthetic sense may be all that comes into play and that in only a critical evaluation sense.

Undeveloped settings in and near cities generally offer the most readily available opportunities for aesthetic and deeper psychological nature-based experiences. One of the reasons for suggesting the subsettings of rural and urban is to inventory and examine all the possible setting options which provide or come close to providing "micro" semiprimitive experiences.

MANAGING THE AESTHETIC LANDSCAPE

Managing landscapes for multisensory aesthetics involves taking inventory of existing characteristics, analyzing character variations, setting goals for future opportunities, and establishing mitigation objectives. Processes for mitigating visual impacts have been quite successful in both the Forest Service's visual management system (VMS) and the Bureau of Land Management's system. The Forest Service system recently has been refined to incorporate landscape character, a better constituent analysis, and other improvements. It has been renamed and focuses primarily on the sense of sight. After a brief description of that new scenery management system (SMS), I suggest an amendment to it which integrates the other senses of the aesthetic.

In the Forest Service, the art and science of scenery management using the SMS adopts the following concepts to operate within an overall integrative ecosystems approach. First, past, present, and potential landscape character is described for each land type or land type association. Second, past and present levels of scenic integrity are identified, and the present levels are mapped. They are described in terms of six different degrees of existing human alteration of the natural appearing landscape or deviations from valued cultural landscapes. Third, information about constituents or the using public is collected to determine preferred travel ways and special places, landscape character, and scenic integrity. Fourth, this constituent information is translated into landscape visibility elements of viewer concern levels, distance zones, view sheds, preferred landscape character and scenic integrity. Fifth, landscapes are categorized into scenic classes, derived from a combination of inherent scenic attractiveness and landscape visibility. Scenic classes establish the value of National Forest landscapes as scenery for comparison with other uses of National Forest resources, such as timber, range, minerals, or wildlife habitat. Sixth, with an adopted forest plan, landscape character goals are established after considering constituent preferences and analyzing existing landscapes and their origins, possible landscape character themes and variations, and the overall desired future condition of the ecosystem. In addition, scenic integrity objectives are established in an adopted forest plan from constituents' preferences, scenic classes, and values of other National Forest resources.

The following is a suggested supplement to the SMS that would better incorporate the other senses of the aesthetic discussed in this chapter.

Landscape Character is defined as the overall visual impression or physical appearance attributes of a landscape that give it an identity and sense of place. It is usually described in terms of its vegetative patterns, rock formations, landforms, water forms, and, where they exist, structures of distinctive and/or historic character. Included are ecologi-

cal processes such as disturbance regimes, successional stages and age class distribution. These same attributes may be used to describe the landscape character which existed in the "past," one that "currently" exists, or a desired "future" character.

Here I suggest adding opportunities to experience the other senses: sound, smell, taste, and touch that existed in the past, currently exist, or may be possible in the future. Examples include:

- native vegetation with berries that are good to eat (e.g., huckleberries, salmon berries, etc.);
- habitat of native wildlife species that have particularly colorful sounds;
- native vegetation that has particularly fragrant spring flowers;
- mix of vegetative species that have both coarse and fine textures adding the tactile dimension through sight;
- vegetative species which add both sound and sight (e.g., quaking aspen); and
- opportunities to experience ecological processes.

The addition of opportunities to experience the other senses is particularly important in the development of variations on character themes. Within the biological parameters of each character theme are several possible variations. They are often expressed in terms of creating or maintaining specific plant successional stages, large tree character, diversity of age classes, or natural-appearing open spaces. The variations should include not only these different scenic attributes but also those possibilities for sound, smell, touch, and feel. Practices for good ecosystem management such as prescribed fires, standing dead trees, and downed woody material should be in view and possibly interpreted to help speed up the expectations for ecological aesthetics.

Inherent Scenic Attractiveness measures the scenic importance of a landscape based on human perceptions of the intrinsic beauty of landform, rock form, water form, and vegetative patterns. People value all landscapes, but they regard those having the most positive combinations of visual variety, unity, vividness, mystery, intactness, coherence, harmony, uniqueness, pattern, and balance as having the greatest potential for high scenic value.

While the scenic aspects and, in particular, visual variety will normally be the most critical, it is important to recognize the opportunities to experience the other senses.

Constituent Information for scenery management is an inventory and analysis of user expectations, desires, preferences, acceptable levels of quality, behaviors, and values. The inventory produces information useful in developing statements about desired or preferred landscape character and scenic condition. Numerous tools are available, but they often include constituent surveys, visitor observations, and public participation.

Landscape Visibility refers to one's ability to see and perceive landscapes. It is a function of many essential interconnected considerations including:

1. context of the viewers,

2. duration of view,

3. degree of discernible detail,

4. seasonal variations, and

5. number of viewers.

Sometimes there may be only small numbers of people viewing certain landscapes but they have a high concern for scenic quality. When associated with other experience-based opportunities related to spirituality and introspection, these landscapes have even higher importance and value. In these kinds of situations the possibility of users coming into touch with all the senses (aesthetic mode) is much greater. Therefore, the need for more sophisticated management of landscapes in primitive and semiprimitive settings is greater.

To analyze many aspects of discernible detail and duration of view, landscapes seen from roads, trails, and other travel ways are subdivided into distance zones as discussed below. (Note that in primitive and semiprimitive settings the viewer is usually in the foreground, so that distance zone is important for senses other than sight.)

1. Immediate Foreground: 0 to 300 feet

   At an immediate foreground distance, people can distinguish individual leaves, flowers, twigs, bark texture, small animals (chipmunks and songbirds), and can notice movement of leaves and grasses in light winds. They can also receive other sensory messages at an immediate foreground distance, such as sounds of small animals, bird calls, wind whispering through leaves and grasses, and pungent odors or sweet smells. Texture is made up of individual leaves, needle clusters, bark patterns, and twig patterns. Details are important.

2. Foreground: 300 feet to 1/2 mile

   At a foreground distance, people can distinguish small boughs of leaf clusters, tree trunks and large branches, individual shrubs, clumps of wildflowers, medium-sized animals (squirrels and rabbits), and medium to large birds (hawks, geese, and ducks). At this distance, people can also distinguish movement of tree boughs and treetops in moderate winds. At a foreground distance, people receive other sensory messages, such as sounds of medium-sized animals, bird calls, a moderate wind whistling through branches, and smells of the forest. Texture is largely made up of boughs, large branches, and visible portions of trunks. Individual forms are dominant.

3. Middle ground: 1/2 mile to 4 miles

   Middle ground is usually the predominant distance zone at which National Forest landscapes are seen, except for regions of flatlands or tall, dense vegetation. At this distance, people can distinguish individual tree form, large boulders, fields of wildflowers, small openings in the forest, and small rock outcrops. Tree forms typically stand out vividly in silhouetted situations. Form, texture, and color remain dominant, and pattern is important. Texture is often made up of repetitive tree forms. In steeper topography, a middle ground landscape perspective is similar to an aerial one. Because the viewer is able to see human activities from this perspective in context with the overall landscape, a middle ground landscape having steep topography is often the most critical of all distance zones for scenery management.

4. Background: 4 miles to horizon

   At a background distance, people can distinguish groves or stands of trees, large openings in the forest, and large rock outcrops. Texture has disappeared and color has flattened, but large patterns of vegetation or rock are still distinguishable, and landform ridge lines and horizon lines are the dominant visual characteristics. As a result, the landscape has been simplified. The role of background in providing scenic quality lies mainly in its capacity as a contrasting softened backdrop, a pleasantly distant vista, or a strikingly beautiful focal point.

Of all the distance zones, our immediate environment is often experienced in multiple modes. What is close at hand can be touched, smelled, heard, and seen. With distance, however, one by one of these senses begin to drop off. First, touch and taste, then smell, then hearing, and finally only sight remains. An evaluation mode of the aesthetic tends to predominate rather than more emotional sensing. Psychological distancing is more difficult in the immediate environment because one tends to be overcome by the senses' power to stir the emotions, and also because several senses come into play making it more difficult to concentrate on effect.

Summary

In this chapter I have attempted to interpret various senses of the aesthetic: touch, smell, taste, sound, and sight and the importance of achieving a psychological distancing from human activity in order to experience the aesthetic mode. I have introduced the concept of ecological aesthetics which not only involves all the senses noted above but the depth of one's intellect as well. Pleasure is derived from knowing how all the parts relate to the ecosystem as a whole. Two management frameworks, the recreation opportunity spectrum and the scenery management system, should have more depth and meaning when catering to all of the senses. Last there would likely be no psychologically deep, nature-based human experiences without the multisensory aesthetic experiences described in this chapter. These multisensory aesthetics facilitate the deeper, nature-based experiences such as spirituality, introspection, and transcendence.

Acknowledgments

I would like to thank Don Exenberger of the Oregon State Department of Parks and Recreation for his contributions to the section on Urban/Suburban subclasses and B. L. Driver for his assistance with the entire chapter.

Literature Cited

Callicott, J. (1983). Leopold's land esthetic. *Journal of Soil and Water Conservation*, 329-332.

Driver, B. and Brown, P. (1978). The opportunity spectrum concept and behavioral information in outdoor recreation resource supply inventories: A rationale. In *Integrated inventories of renewable natural resources* (pp. 24-31). General Technical Report RM-55. Fort Collins, Colorado, USDA Forest Service Rocky Mountain Station.

Driver, B., Brown, P., Stankey, G., and Gregoire, G. (1987). The ROS planning system: Evolution, basic concepts, and research needed. *Leisure Sciences*, 9(3), 203-214.

Gobster, P. (1995, February). Aldo Leopold's "Ecological Esthetic": Integrating esthetic and biodiversity values. *Journal of Forestry*, 6-10.

Kaplan, S. (1993). The role of natural environment esthetics in the restorative experience. In P. Gobster (Ed.), *Managing urban and high-use recreation settings*. General Technical Report NC-163. USDA Forest Service.

Leopold, A. (1949). *A sand county almanac and sketches here and there*. New York, NY: Oxford University Press.

Tolstoy, L. (1961). *"The Hunt" in childhood*. New York, NY: Vintage Books.

Tuan, Y. (1993). *Passing strange and wonderful: Aesthetics, nature, and culture*. Washington, DC: Island Press/Shearwater Books.

SUSTAINING OPPORTUNITIES TO EXPERIENCE EARLY AMERICAN LANDSCAPES

CHAPTER 29

DON BRUNS
Colorado State Office
USDI Bureau of Land Management
Lakewood, Colorado

PATRICIA STOKOWSKI
Department of Recreation, Park and Tourism Sciences
Texas A&M University
College Station, Texas

Throughout the conversation, both of us had occasionally glanced out the window. . . . So striking was the view that it had almost seemed like a participant in the conversation.

T. Conover, 1991

Increased urbanization and an accelerating pace of life characterize the American experience in the latter half of the twentieth century. A national system of interstate highways reinforces an image of a homogenous, "sterilized" countryside where every new mile looks much like the last. Most of rural America disappeared long ago from the view of most people who increasingly find themselves traveling freeway routes more out of necessity than by choice. Indeed, speakers at the 1993 National Rural Tourism Development Conference in Rapid City, South Dakota, reported that while most people now live and work in urban areas, only a small fraction prefer to do so. A recent Western Governors' Association report refers to a 1985 Gallup Poll which found that, given the opportunity, nearly half of American adults would move to towns under 10,000 people or to rural areas (Murphy and McGinniss, 1992). More and more, Americans are experiencing a profoundly greater sense of detachment from the land. Out of this context a new sense of appreciation for rural America,

the change of pace it affords, and the Early American Landscapes (EALs) it presents, has developed.

We employ the term, Early American, rather broadly. EALs are rural areas of the country where a mix of the land and its cultures combine to create an experience of bygone places and times. EALs are fully functioning, coherent, working landscapes of community and country that represent an earlier way of life. EALs share in common a resistance to modernization and urbanization. Much of the community's original architecture is still intact, and, more importantly, many residents are still making a living doing what they always did; they have not yet been driven out of town by escalating real estate speculation. For example, farmers and ranchers continue to conduct business in hardware and machinery stores, tack and saddle shops, and the like. One gets the feeling that people live there because they like the country; for them, country is where they live, not some place to escape to on evenings and weekends.

Time is an important dimension of EALs. In these landscapes the pace of life is often slower than in the urban "fast lane." Resistance of most EAL features to passage of time is definitive; old wooden doors and screen doors (instead of plate glass and aluminum security doors with cushy door closers) welcome customers into Main Street shops, and shop floors creak with our steps. Some EALs have cobblestone or brick streets, and old-fashioned street lights in others have not yet been replaced by the piercing glare and annoying hum of mercury vapor lights. Others have unpaved streets.

EALs are not intended to, nor should they be understood to, refer exclusively to Colonial America. Included are a wide variety of homesteads, farms, ranches, villages, and the adjacent countryside of small-town America, including remnants of ethnic and Native-American settlements. For example, in the West, EALs include remaining wide-open spaces of the western ranching frontier. In other regions, EALs may also include southern plantation environments, small Midwestern farming communities, logging communities in the Pacific Northwest, small coastal or Great Lakes fishing villages, or colonial New England countrysides. The EAL concept is national in scope, but identification of EAL distinctives depends upon regional and local contexts.

An EAL cannot be defined merely as an assemblage of biophysical and cultural features. Neither are they silent museums of the past (i.e., buildings and facilities), nor memorials to people who once lived there (i.e., visitor centers and exhibits), nor even living histories (i.e., interpretive and educational programs). Each has an element of real culture, not merely the artifact. They are real places, substantially unchanged, that have resisted the cultural and technological transformation of modern society, retaining a coherent biophysical and sociocultural landscape.

EALs involve adjacent countryside as well as main street aesthetics. They include traditional cultures themselves, their use of the land, and the character of business retail shops. They also include personal benefits of living in (for residents) and stepping back into (for visitors) a simpler time.

Most distinguishing is the element of authenticity, defined as the degree to which the original character of the community's culture and its surrounding landscape still lingers. This authenticity is reflected in each landscape's capability to transport its visitors back in time experientially to an earlier way of life that has distinctives of both country and community.

Important benefits are being realized both by residents living within EAL communities and also by guests and visitors. Local residents observe that, because these landscapes are vitally important to their lifestyle and quality of life, forgoing potential economic and social advantages of alternate urban or suburban living with the benefits of living in an EAL has been more than worth it. At the same time, urban and suburban visitors maintain that their own way of life has been so seriously compromised that the benefits which EALs afford them, even as occasional guests, are doubly important to their own well-being. Distinctive EAL characteristics and the benefits they provide are therefore intrinsically important to people regardless of where they live.

In this context, what is most significant about EALs is the need for greater awareness that such landscapes do exist and that they are being lost at an accelerating rate. This loss is being accompanied by a significant loss of benefits which EALs provide to visitors and, perhaps more important, to local residents and their quality of life.

This chapter discusses EALs within the context of the value which an increasingly urbanized society ascribes to them. This value is implicit in people's desire to experience EALs. We suggest measures that EAL providers must take to ensure the continued existence of these valuable landscapes. Recognition and sustainable maintenance of these emerging hard-to-define values requires a lasting attitudinal shift on behalf of all managing partners, including local residents, their governments, tourism attraction and service providers, and land managers. This shift must embody a shared set of attitudes for greater cooperation among all local and regional decision makers that manifests itself in a willingness to support EALs in achieving their desired future through long-term, collaborative management partnerships.

Theoretical Basis

The term "sense of place" refers to the idea that people have "some positive, affective sentiments for certain natural, cultural, social and historic environments, and these sentiments are sometimes elevated into communal meaning" (Stokowski, 1991, p. 1).

Places like EALs are not only settings for behavior, but also they are valued for the way they link the land with community, history and culture (Relph, 1976; Tuan, 1977). Lee (1972) suggests that an understanding of place meanings would help land managers develop suitable interpretation and sensitive visitor management. Williams and Carr (1993) note that agencies must understand "the collective meanings various groups attach to places they use for recreation" (p. 219). For example, visitors have been observed to have an "environmental disposition" for relating to specific kinds of places (Schreyer, Lime and Williams, 1984), and an individual's value of a specific recreation setting encompasses both "functional and symbolic meanings" (Schreyer, Jacob and White, 1981). Place attachment involves some form of bonding to special settings, either because they offer highly valued kinds of experiences or because they have symbolic meaning or specific personal emotional appeal (Williams and Roggenbuck, 1989).

EALs tend to be large and really are not specifically defined within the personal context of individual users. Therefore, people may or may not experience a feeling of place attachment to any given EAL. EALs are objectively defined by the presence of distinctive biophysical and sociocultural features and at least some sense of a surviving culture itself, whether or not there exists any subjective personal attachment. That people often do develop attachments towards certain specific EALs suggests that EAL management has both cognitive and affective aspects (see Roberts, Chapter Four, and Greene, Chapter Twenty-Seven, in this volume).

The EAL concept is also based on the notion of sustainability of dependent natural and cultural elements. What makes each EAL distinctive is its own special mix of the biophysical and sociocultural landscape. At least two aspects of sustainability are significant. The first is that the early American character of any landscape is exhibited both in affected natural resources (i.e., biophysical systems) and in the affected towns, communities, and residents (e.g., sociocultural systems). Sustaining the distinctive character of EALs, then, means sustaining the distinctiveness of resources and society, and land and community.

The second aspect of sustainability is the interdependence of these biophysical and sociocultural systems. If one is neglected, the other is imperiled.

This idea of mutual interdependence is strongly related to the ecosystem ideal: ecosystem sustainability is as much an issue of sustaining the cultural integrity and viability of dependent communities as it is of managing natural resources to retain their health and productive character. Rural communities are dependent on healthy natural resources, but it takes healthy communities to care adequately for the land. Sustaining the quality of EAL-dependent features over time directly involves the simultaneous maintenance of distinctive natural features, cultural patterns, fully functioning societies, and their quality of life. Generally, local communities are most in touch with the sociocultural side of the equation while natural resource agencies are usually most in touch with issues related to maintaining the distinctive character of the surrounding natural resource base. Nonetheless, sustaining EALs requires integration of both views.

There is increasing agreement about the importance of EAL experiences to the quality of life for local residents and to recreation visitor satisfaction. Yet few guidelines exist for interpreting how changes to local communities and natural resources, recreation, and tourism industries may together affect future benefit achievement. Sustaining EALs, and the continued delivery of the benefits they provide, requires that ecotourism partners know what specific attributes are most highly valued by both local residents and visitors. It also requires an assessment of specific kinds of benefit opportunities EALs provide to individuals, households and communities, local and regional economies, and the environment. And it requires establishing the nature of the relationship between EAL attributes and benefit opportunity production.

Not Just Another Landscape: EAL Distinctives

What are the most important characteristics of EALs? In *Guidelines for Evaluating and Documenting Rural Historic Landscapes*, the National Park Service includes eleven characteristics for "reading a rural landscape and for understanding the natural and cultural forces that have shaped it" (McClelland, Keller, Keller, and Melnick, 1984, pp. 3-6). The National Park Service defines landscape characteristics as:

the tangible evidence of the activities and habits of the people who occupied, developed, used, and shaped the land to serve human needs; they may reflect the beliefs, attitudes, traditions, and values of these people.

Of these criteria, four deal with processes which have shaped the land:

1. land uses and activities,
2. patterns of spatial organization,
3. response to the natural environment, and
4. cultural traditions.

The remaining seven criteria involve observable physical features:

5. circulation networks,
6. boundary demarcations,
7. vegetation related to land use,
8. buildings, structures and objects,
9. clustered facilities,
10. archaeologic [and historic] sites, and
11. small-scale elements.

EAL distinctives, however, go beyond processes and features. More profound than these plainly observable elements within the EAL-dependent natural and cultural landscapes are the unique opportunities they provide for people to realize enduring benefits. Since these areas are typically rural and "off the beaten path," they provide people with opportunities for discovery. In his book, *Leisure Travel*, Plog (1991) relates the popularity of trips which rediscover forgotten and overlooked areas to many people's felt need to rediscover their rural roots:

The big winners have been rural regions and off the beaten track destinations . . . where travelers can experience an atmosphere less crowded and more relaxed than at more popular resorts. Local people often are not as hurried or stressed and [are] more willing to engage in conversation with strangers. These interchanges can become unintentional therapy for these leading edge travelers because they can drop many of their psychological defenses established over the years to protect themselves in their competitive work environments. (p. 130)

Plog (1991) identifies highways and byways as significant conduits to that rediscovery experience. He points out that everyone, even those who did not come from small towns or rural America, has a heritage tied to rural life. Plog notes that the pressure-cooker lifestyle of urban living fuels a desire to explore visible history in the search for core personal values:

These travelers have found that they enjoy getting out into the heartland of a nation, particularly in their own country, to discover more about what holds it together in an age when so much of society seems to be falling apart. A new sense of self-discovery and of meaning can come from getting closer to people in less densely populated areas, where the value systems are more stable and daily life is less hurried and more predictable. (pp. 129-130)

Emerging Values Illustrated

Scenic byways illustrate the degree to which EALs are valued, the threats to their existence, and the management challenges and opportunities they represent. The popularity of pleasure driving in the U.S. led the 1985 President's Commission on Americans Outdoors to recommend the establishment of "a network of green ways across America." Scenic byways are just one way in which that recommendation is being implemented. Behind the scenic byway concept lies the felt need of an increasing number of Americans to rediscover the wide diversity of biophysical and sociocultural landscapes from an earlier America that still exists. EALs are one of the principal touring attractions of the nation's outstanding scenic and historic byways.

Examples help to illustrate the significance of EALs to local communities and visitors alike. Kick-off ceremonies for the Bureau of Land Management's (BLM) National Back Country Byways Program in Mesquite, Nevada, found a delegation of journalists with the American Society of Travel Writers involved in a byway tour. At one stop along the tour, these guests—most of them urban residents and some who had never even heard of the public lands the BLM manages—had the opportunity to hear local ranchers recount the benefits of country living. The ranchers shared personal joys of working on the open range and raising a family in a small community substantially removed from the hectic pace and problems of city life. You could have heard a pin drop. After the stop, a reporter from Chicago said, "That was beautiful; you should have taped it!"

In Colorado, the Gold Belt Tour Back Country Byway follows historic narrow gauge railroad grades and wagon roads linking the gold rush town of Cripple Creek with Front Range gateway communities. Byway designation, and particularly the passage of a limited-stakes gambling initiative in Cripple Creek, has provided substantial economic benefits to certain entrepreneurs. Greater numbers of visitors are discovering an opportunity to drive the byway and journey into a distinctive past. Local volunteers have joined forces to interpret the historic railroad and its associated ranching and mining culture, and a local paleontology partnership is developing a dinosaur discovery center along the byway to promote appreciation of nationally significant dinosaur fossils.

These actions, however, have resulted in a more than twofold increase in byway traffic and infrastructure development. Associated EALs are changing. While the external physical appearance of historic structures in the town of Cripple Creek remains intact, the "Wild West" character of their interiors has been replaced with modern gambling parlors. Some believe that their authenticity has been lost. In addition, local residents along the byway route are concerned about increased road dust and traffic congestion. Others report vandalism and an associated loss of privacy in their once quiet neighborhoods and country homes.

Excellent progress has been made to address these issues through a broadly based local byway organization, appointed and empowered by all elected and appointed governing officials along the byway. A 38-member steering committee engages five local communities and their governments, the recreation tourism industry, and land managers in a collaborative planning exercise of self-determination. This balanced, grass-roots organization developed a consensus vision of desired future conditions for communities along the byway, and for how they see the byway's helping to meet those conditions. It further crafted objectives to achieve that vision and wrote a management plan with detailed implementing actions. Having built this shared commitment to their common future, the committee has agreed to continue its collaborative work by managing to implement the plan design.

Another example of communities seeking ways to sensitively maintain their distinctive character of EALs and culture is provided by Stowe, Vermont.

Stowe undertook an extensive community planning effort in 1987 to articulate community vision and shared values. Residents, local government officials, business leaders, and resource managers realized that the EAL qualities of the area were being compromised by Stowe's growth into a four season destination resort. The Stowe approach resulted in informed partnerships with participants dedicated to ideals expressed by a local planner:

> *We must aggressively manage new patterns of growth which meet our needs while respecting and perpetuating those attributes of our communities that give them a sense of place.*
>
> Federspiel, 1992, p. 103

Another Colorado example illustrates the value people ascribe to EALs. Initial attempts at building a recreation tourism partnership to designate one portion of the upper Colorado River corridor a scenic byway failed because local residents feared losing their EAL. Because of the area's close proximity to the Vail ski area and the Interstate 70 freeway corridor, a sharp increase in local traffic seemed inevitable. Residents feared increased traffic, dust, and noise would compromise the peace and quiet of their country road. Residents were also concerned that insensitive urbanites would not respect their property, and they feared interruption of rural lifestyles. Although local community partners on a segment of the river further upstream did eventually reach consensus about their desire for another scenic byway (and it eventually won the approval of the Governor's Scenic and Historic Byway Commission), the controversial segment never did get off the ground.

Management Implications

Increasingly, local communities and their governments, private sector service providers and public land managers are discovering the critical need for greater recognition of EALs and the values assigned them by visitors and local residents alike. At issue is the entire sociocultural and biophysical setting within each EAL which must not be viewed simply in terms of its recreation tourism producing capabilities. It is critically important that the benefit opportunities produced by EALs be defined broadly enough to address the value-added conditions realized by local residents and visitors alike. A local perspective for identifying EALs helps capture the value which local residents ascribe to their own land-scapes: many of the values meaningful to local residents are the same ones sought by visitors. If misunderstood, these values may all too easily be compromised by well-intentioned efforts of enterprising outsiders or, worse yet, locals themselves.

From the visitors' perspective, providers need to consider an entire range of leisure-based recreation and tourism through which these landscapes may be experienced. Managers are discovering that traditional outdoor recreation concepts are inadequate to capture key EAL values being held in highest esteem. Tourism market segmentation research, for example, confirms the importance of looking beyond recreation activities to the characteristics of different types of leisure travel outings. For example, Longwoods International's "Travel USA" found that "Touring" vacations, rather than "Ski Resort" and "Outdoors" trips (i.e., outdoor recreation activities) are Colorado's most popular market segments. Longwoods noted that the distinguishing characteristic of touring "is its emphasis on sightseeing through areas of scenic interest, and upon a variety of cultural and recreational experiences" (Siegel, 1990, p. 13). So, there is both the more passive touring dimension and the more active recreational aspect of the visitors' EAL experience.

The benefits approach to leisure (BAL) also encourages managers to look beyond traditional recreation and tourism concepts in considering important EAL features. Benefits-based management (BAL applied to management) expands managers' emphasis from inputs to outputs by focusing on value added to people's lives. Benefits are defined as desired beneficial experiences, improved conditions or the prevention of worse conditions. Four broad categories of benefits have been identified, including: benefits to individuals (both psychological and physiological), benefits to social groups (individual households and communities), benefits to local-regional economies, and benefits to the environment itself. To capture important contributions of EALs, natural resource agencies, tourism attraction and service providers and host communities need to decide collaboratively which value-added benefit opportunities will be targeted for delivery within each EAL. These are defined in the form of explicitly stated management objectives which all partners jointly agree to provide (Driver, Brown, Peterson, and Bruns, 1991, pp. 12-13).

Natural resource managers, private-sector recreation tourism industry partners and host community residents and governments are all gaining a new perspective on the importance of EALs. A growing number of these providers are convinced that opportunities for visitors to both emotionally and cognitively experience desired benefits on a sustained basis are highly dependent on how the land and its visitors are managed, the type and extent of accommodating facilities and services provided, the character of community infrastructure support services, the quality of those services, and the manner in which they are delivered. While resource managers have typically focused on the land itself—and tourism partners on delivering desirable amenity services—EAL management involves the entire community infrastructure and service delivery system. Since land managers, the tourism industry, and local communities are not the sole-source providers of client benefit opportunities, collaborative management partnerships are required to sustain EALs.

A Protection-Maintenance and Promotion-Development Paradox

The paradox is that, while greater numbers of people are coming to work, live and play in EALs in order to enjoy the benefits offered, their desire to enjoy EALs is putting at risk, and sometimes actually destroying, the very features and attractions being sought. Those who value EALs the most are, unhappily, often the same ones causing their character to erode: urban masses desiring the leisure and recreation benefits that these out-of-the-way places provide and a growing number of urban refugees wanting to make their home in rural America. This occurs because defining and distinctive characteristics both of EAL community and countryside continue to be compromised by unfocused and, at times, unconstrained tourism promotion and development; indeed, all promotion, development and use of any EAL potentially threatens the exact qualities for which people initially value them. In other instances, ongoing modernization and technologic advances within the more traditional commodity or extractive industries compromise distinctive EAL characteristics. These external forces frequently fail to value, and thus protect, EAL distinctives. Either unknowingly or uncaringly, they end up destroying EAL character qualities.

This threat poses a significant challenge. Many local communities, proud of their rural and cultural heritage and associated lifestyles, are faced with realities of a shrinking economy. Wanting to maintain their heritage and the lifestyle it affords, many consider adventure travel recreation and tourism promotion and development to be an attractive strategy for community revival. However, these approaches can bring about new, nonconforming land uses, upset a communities' traditional economic base of support and, ultimately and unwittingly, destroy the very EALs being valued the most by communities and residents alike. These communities need to exercise a measure of caution to avoid being carried away by the prospect of tourism benefits without considering the reality of their costs. Each community needs to ensure maintenance of its distinctive natural and cultural EAL heritage if it is to retain a sufficient measure of individual, social, economic, and environmental benefits for its residents.

Lest EAL communities think they can escape either this threat or challenge, the authors offer a word of caution. It is only a matter of time before presently unknown EALs are discovered by newcomers who want to visit or live there. Each EAL community struggles with the desires of some residents to promote the community and the desires of others to maintain the distinctive characteristics that make it special. Thirty years ago when Steamboat Springs, Colorado, (then known as "Ski Town USA") was about to boom with rapid development of a downhill ski resort at the big mountain, the community went through this struggle. John Fetcher, longtime resident of the valley, wrote a letter to the local paper's editor expressing the sentiments of many: "Each of us," he wrote, "when we drive over the pass, wants to be the last one let into the valley."

The Future of EALs Depends on Collaborative Partnerships

A central theme of this chapter is that without collaborative management partnerships, distinctive and endangered EALs will continue to be degraded and eventually lost by unplanned use, promotion and development. Through such partnerships,

however, not only EALs but also the benefits they produce may continue to be realized on a sustainable basis.

Sustaining EALs requires that all affecting providers recognize that maintaining these landscapes and their hard-to-define values depends on building sustainable management partnerships. While the sharing of common interests and a common future may be the initial motivation for involvement, the goal of sustained delivery of the value added to people's lives can only be accomplished through collaboration. Increasing acceptance of the value-added, collaborative partnership ideal, coupled with reciprocally sustaining interdependent natural and social systems, is part of a major paradigm shift occurring across the American recreation and leisure fields.

> *Since tourism is a community affair, acting on tourism ideas requires that local government, the commercial sector, many nonprofit groups, and your community's citizenry all be solid participants in the tourism development process.*
>
> Richardson, 1991, p. 43

Securing the involvement of all affecting providers into perpetuity requires building a shared infrastructure of attitudes and ideas among current participants. Developing this shared "infrastructure of attitudes, ideas and beliefs" is essential. That phrase, coined by the authors of a report for the Western Governors' Association (Murphy and McGinniss, 1992, p. 66), underscores a critical need for all players in each community to mutually recognize the significance of their rural EALs and agree to a future vision and a subsequent course of action *before* any promotion and development actions are initiated. This understanding must be developed among each provider contributing to (or potentially detracting from) EAL distinctives.

In practice, this shared ideal may not always be achieved. First, the basic partnership commitment itself may be missing. Then, land managers may proceed with a traditional natural resource focus not fully integrated with the sociopolitical infrastructure (the ecosystem management framework may hold some promise here). Conversely, tourism industry partners may not recognize their dependence on either the community's support service infrastructure or adjacent public lands for many, if not most, of their most popular tourism products.

Moreover, while the accelerating rate at which EALs are being lost to rural America has been instructive to many local communities, some small-town residents and their governing officials certainly do not yet fully grasp the degree to which their own lifestyle and economic stability depends upon maintaining the distinctive character of indigenous or historic natural resources, economies, cultures and lifestyles. Thus, effective EAL partnerships must embody at least five essential dimensions, each of which is multifaceted.

First: Structure

First is the EAL structure; partnerships must be representatively balanced. Balanced collaborative partnerships involve three key sectors: public land managers, local community residents and their governments, and private sector recreation tourism associations, attractions and service industries. Too often, not all of the players are at the table when decisions are being made about an EAL community's future. The involvement of all affecting providers must be invited, and representatives must be empowered to achieve their collective goals. A mutuality of commitment, spanning all players and time frames, is essential. This must involve all entities who will affect the future existence of each EAL and it must span the entire life of each EAL initiative.

Insistence on a balanced EAL partnership structure expands, rather than narrows, the scope of public involvement in the community decision-making process. On the one hand, it balances the voice of special interests with those of local residents; at the same time, it balances development and promotional interests with those interested in maintaining and protecting the status quo. The beauty of balanced partnerships is that they moderate loud voices and allow more quiet voices to be heard, all in the interest of building community consensus towards identifying a common desired future. Each partner shares in this responsibility to ensure that no one is disenfranchised from the public involvement process and that no special interests profit at the expense of others.

Second: Function

The second essential dimension of EAL partnerships is their function; they must involve all affecting providers in an exercise of genuine collaboration. A collaborative approach is needed to help dispel the "sole source provider" myth. While several public land

management agencies and individual private sector recreation tourism businesses have traditionally viewed themselves as meeting all of their own visitor or client service needs, very few actually function that way; each implicitly depends on the services of other providers within the community, irrespective of how closely they actually work together.

Partnerships have become the "buzzword" of the 1990s, yet few are truly collaborative. While most natural resource agencies have moved beyond autocratic, top-down management styles wherein field managers are the sole decision makers, most public land managing agency partnerships are still more interactive than collaborative. Many managers are still in the "driver's seat," controlling decisions, and stakeholder involvement often is, unhappily, sought for the primary purpose of helping implement internally crafted agency goals, objectives, and management decisions.

By way of contrast, each genuinely collaborative partnership "emerges from the community, honors a full spectrum of values and assumes that everyone is responsible for the community's success. There's no one leader, and no one is excluded from the table" (USDA Forest Service, 1993, p. 1). Thus, public officials empower one another and their stakeholders as equal partners in developing jointly a management plan which forecloses all independent and advance decision making.

True collaboration occurs when providers and stakeholders proactively enlist each other's involvement as equals in a process that determines and manages their shared future. Collaboration of this nature encourages partners to remain open to the collective identification of issues, a vision, products and implementing management actions. Within the true collaborative model, each public official's role shifts from being a "controller" to that of "facilitator." In such an environment, public officials are discovering that their vital new role includes:

1. promoting the sharing of information,

2. encouraging a frank exchange of views among all interests,

3. helping to identify opportunities for joint problem solving, and

4. making clear how the collaborative partnership reaches its decisions (USDA Forest Service, 1993, p. 7).

This massive paradigm shift is truly earthshaking for public institutions as well as for private businesses and the local citizenry. Many public officials are nervous about sharing their decision-making authority with other community providers; some recreation tourism business entrepreneurs appear to be less than eager to extend their accountability beyond the corporate board room to their host communities and beyond fiscal matters to address critically important social and environmental concerns. Yet, without collaboration, there will be no expanded community involvement, no broad-based community ownership, and ultimately no joint accountability among all providers who serve and affect host communities.

Third: Scope

A third essential dimension of effective EAL partnerships is the scope of systems addressed. Critical to the success of each partnership is its need to ensure simultaneously the interdependent sustainability of biophysical and sociocultural systems. Natural resource providers are fond of making the point that ecosystem planning begins with ensuring healthy natural systems. While it is true that productive natural resource capacity drives healthy societies and economies, the opposite view can be defended equally well. One cannot maintain a productive natural resource base if communities using the land and having the responsibility to care for it are not themselves in good health. Each system requires the other.

Deciding where the lines of EAL influence fall therefore requires adopting a community perspective that is more inclusive than just that portion of the landscape lying on public lands or in any one community. Recreation tourism businesses and associations must be engaged as responsible members of the EAL communities they serve, and the involvement of citizen stakeholders within those communities must be secured. Representatives from each of the three key sectors must be empowered to determine collectively the future character of their community. The character issue must address the local resource, facility, and service infrastructure within affected villages, towns, and cities, attributes of adjacent public lands and the goods and services they provide, and the nature of private sector recreation tourism industry services.

Creative methods are needed to enable partners from each sector to contribute staff, expertise, and skills. At a minimum, each collaborative partnership needs to find a core team of full-time professionals to staff the collaborative partnership. This should include a local government community planner, a recreation tourism industry professional, and a public land management practitioner to maintain balance among all affecting providers.

For this to work, representatives from each of these three key sectors need to develop greater sensitivity to ways in which decisions regarding their own traditional area of responsibility affect the other sectors. Public land managers, for example, need to develop greater awareness of how biophysical resource management actions impact specific sociocultural elements within EAL communities (e.g., the quality of life and livelihood of local residents, private sector recreation tourism businesses, and the capability of local governments to function responsively). At the same time, both on-site and off-site recreation tourism industry service providers need to cultivate greater understanding of how continued efforts to sell more trips and to increase client visitation affect the EAL character of both sociocultural systems, the character of public lands, and the capability of all affecting providers to sustain their delivery of desired EAL recreation leisure benefits. Likewise local governments need to cultivate a greater awareness of the impact which infrastructure modernization and development have on residents' quality of life and on the capability of both recreation tourism industries and public land managers to continue providing desired benefits to residents and outside guests.

Fourth: Content

Content is the fourth essential dimension of EAL partnerships. They must include a vision of the community's future, a plan design to achieve that future, and a cooperative management strategy to implement that design. EAL partnerships must not begin with goals and objectives developed by local governments or land managers. To do so would be to continue the old autocratic and interactive modes of public agency decision making wherein public officials make controlling decisions that determine management ends and, only then, search out partners to help achieve them. Before any kind of meaningful goals and objectives can be developed, all providers and stakeholders must be drawn together as partners to develop a consensus vision of their common future. Unless all partners can first agree on a common future, resulting goals and objectives cannot be embraced, and results are more likely to resemble dissonance than harmony.

Inventorying Community Attitudes

Managing partners must make a concerted effort to understand public perceptions and attitudes right from the start. At a minimum, these studies should address community lifestyles and quality of life issues. Adequacy of the existing EAL infrastructure and supporting services also needs to be assessed. If possible, partners should determine how both residents and visitors feel about EAL-dependent recreation opportunities—including activities, settings within which they occur (addressing physical, social and managerial attributes) and, most important, specific benefits that visitors take with them and those which accrue to host community residents. Both resident and visitor preferences for desired future EAL conditions and the recreation leisure benefits they produce need to be assessed. Even without formal research, partners have enough collective expertise to begin evaluating immediately how the community feels about its distinctive EAL features and benefits thereby provided.

Visioning

Collaborative EAL partnerships begin with:

> *trust building: people educate one another, explore their differences and discover common ground. Together, they envision a future that's compatible with their values and create an action plan to help get there.*

> USDA Forest Service, p. 1

The visioning process is undergirded by the collective identification of issues and problems and an inventory of attractions and services. Just to begin the visioning exercise requires a significant attitudinal shift among all partners that adopts a community perspective and a willingness to be taught by and to teach one another. The visioning process itself can be instrumental in building community consensus.

Visioning leads to the identification of important EAL features of country and community.

These are nonnegotiable EAL elements that must not be compromised. They include elements of the countryside (including public lands) and the community infrastructure, and they involve distinctive products of aesthetics, culture, and economy. Especially important are recreation and tourism products and the community's EAL marketplace niche which supports chosen community ideals. These may include maintaining social solidarity and cultural integrity or pursuing recreation and tourism as an economic diversification strategy. Visioning, therefore, also implies limits, including both the type and amount of promotion and development that can be accommodated while still maintaining distinctive EAL characteristics. These limits must be incorporated in explicit terms in management prescriptions contained within the plan design.

Plan Design

Plan design follows issues and problem identification, attraction and service inventories, and the visioning process. The EAL plan design consists of goals, objectives, and management prescriptions and should, at a minimum, be developed for desired products—both those provided on public lands and within adjacent communities; EAL infrastructure protection, enhancement, and development; EAL visitor service delivery, including interpretation and facilities; marketing and promotion; funding and financing; an implementing collaborative management strategy; and monitoring and evaluation (see Figure 29-1).

Product Definition. This is an exercise that determines major quality of life issues for residents, defines benefit opportunities to be provided visitors, and directly influences the nature of resulting adventure travel industries. It therefore prescribes the character of EAL countryside and community infrastructure and resource attractions to be maintained, visitor services to be delivered, and support facilities to be developed.

Visitor Service Delivery. Visitor services include facilities and interpretation, and both services should be closely aligned to the products identified above. This is particularly important for interpretation. Too often, interpretation is only partially linked with management: off in some remote corner, naturalists tell visitors about all kinds of esoteric ecological interrelationships unrelated to the real reasons they come. Actually, interpretation is a

Step 1: Identification of Issues And Problems
- Community Attitudes Inventory
- Issues Identification with all Partners

Step 2: Community Attractions and Services
- Natural Resources
- Cultural Resources and Local Cultures
- Recreation Resources
- Hospitality Resources
- Attractions
- Adequacy of Lodging, Restaurant and Transportation Service

Step 3: Visioning Process
- Community Values/Attitudes Inventory
- Desired Future Community: Lifestyles and Quality of Life Issues
- Identification of Product "Niche"
- Management Goals and Objectives

Step 4: EAL Products
- Public Land and Community Resource Protection, Enhancement and Development
  - Maintenance of Resource Quality
  - Recreation Attractions
  - Monitoring and Protection
- Infrastructure Protection, Enhancement and Development
  - Accommodations
  - Transportation/Traffic
  - Restaurants
  - Medical/Police/Fire

Step 5: Visitor Services, Facilities and Interpretation
- Visitor-Guest Services
- Interpretive Plan
- On-site Support Facilities

Step 6: Marketing and Promotion
- Identify Markets
- Establish General Marketing Strategy and Techniques
- Establish a Promotion Program

Step 7: Funding and Financing
- Types and Sources of Funding/Revenue
- Budget/Funding Program
- Fund Leveraging
- Financial Projections

Step 8: Implementing Collaborative Management Strategy
- Partnership Management Roles
- Cooperative Management Agreement(s)

Step 9: Monitoring and Evaluation
- Implementation Assessment
- Visitor/Customer Reassessment

powerful visitor services tool and is perhaps nowhere more important than in long-term maintenance of EAL quality. The following marketing narrative identifies at least two additional, unconventional arenas where interpretation is needed to "provoke," "relate," and "reveal" important EAL relationships to visitors.

Marketing. The tourism industry typically uses the term "marketing" to address sales strategies. Land managers use it in almost the opposite sense to talk not about selling but about matching people up with places that provide their desired beneficial experiences. The mutuality of partnership relations calls for a special kind of promotion which provides definitive enough information to enable visitors to make informed choices between competing destinations. This application of interpretive principles is essential for communicating meaningful, understandable, and interesting content in marketing messages. This approach implies a willingness to send potential visitors to other communities if their products are better suited to those visitors' needs and preferences. Invariably, this becomes a major test of the collaborative partnership because it requires service partners to be honest enough with their clients to let them know exactly where they can obtain benefits they desire, even if it means a personal business loss. This is the embodiment of the "truth in advertising" concept in real marketing.

Front-line land managers and community recreation providers cannot do the job of promoting responsible visitor use ethics alone. They also need the help of private sector recreation tourism marketing experts and the use of creative interpretive techniques. These messages must be developed up front and be tailored to the characteristics of each EAL. Land managers and communities must cooperatively engage the understanding and commitment of all visitors to be responsible stewards. User ethics messages should inform visitors about expectations that local community residents, land managers, and other visitors already on-site have for their behavior.

Evaluation and Monitoring. Research is needed both to identify qualitatively EAL values and to determine quantitatively the significance of their contribution to individual experiences and to the communities sense of well-being. Research is also needed to determine the extent to which planned actions being implemented are achieving their intended effect. (A

word of caution: researchers must be careful to respect the values of residents and visitors and must avoid judging them subjectively.)

IMPLEMENTING A COLLABORATIVE MANAGEMENT STRATEGY

EAL organizations that neglect developing a strategy to implement collaborative management have no way of ensuring that their plan design will actually be implemented. Otherwise good collaborative plans may exclude this step, fearing that the partnership will break down when it comes down to deciding which providers need to act and what specific actions need to be taken. Other plans may fail because of a fear of committing to a definite course of action, or of not wanting to foreclose management options.

If the partnership accountability relationship is fully developed around both a vision and explicit objectives, partners can easily agree on actions needed to implement the plan design and the role of each partner in implementing them. Reaching agreement about what needs to be done is relatively easier than developing consensus about who will do it. Nonetheless, distinctive EAL characteristics cannot be ensured without a commitment of funding and staffing from affecting providers.

Fifth: Duration

A fifth essential dimension of EAL partnerships is their duration. Partners must stay involved beyond the planning stage, and the partnership itself must endure beyond plan completion through implementation. The idea is sustaining partnerships for sustainable EAL values. Even if a strategy is included as outlined above, nothing will happen unless all effecting providers actually enter an enduring collaborative management agreement. This agreement engages partners within all three primary contributing sectors in an ongoing, collaborative working relationship, and it commits all providing partners to assume responsibility for implementing management prescriptions for biophysical and sociocultural EAL environments appropriate to their role.

Facing up to the Consequences

The process discussed above is not self-regulating. All partners must decide how to manage cooperatively both recreation tourism development and promotion. In *Leisure Travel*, Plog (1991) identifies the progression of tourism attractions from being unknown, uncharted areas (e.g., EALs) to being well-known and well-developed destination resorts. The challenge is to arrest this progression, to maintain targeted distinguishing EAL characteristics. The partnership vision and plan design must ensure that these areas are neither overpromoted nor overdeveloped to the point that they lose their distinctive EAL characteristics.

Plog (1991) describes what happens when this fails to occur. He uses the terms "allocentric" and "psychocentric" to identify the differing psychographic profiles of visitors. Allocentric visitors enjoy visiting new, uncharted, "nontouristy" areas—what we, the authors, have been calling EALs. But as these areas are promoted as *the* places to go, and as they are discovered by increasing numbers of people and developed with a greater number of amenities, they gradually lose their appeal to the allocentric visitor.

Having lost their unique, nontouristy character, these areas become recognized as popular tourism destinations and appeal to the psychocentric visitor, who Plog describes as preferring familiar destinations which are less adventurous and which provide heavy support facility developments and shops. With enough "success," these areas eventually lose their appeal, even to the psychocentric visitor. The point is that a mutual commitment about the nature of all recreation tourism benefits and how to maintain them over time must be made early in every collaborative EAL partnership. Unless influenced by a well-coordinated partnership strategy, the trend from allocentrism to psychocentrism is virtually certain (see Figure 29-2).

Plog's (1991) analysis is relevant for EALs. In many of the nation's outstanding EALs, well-financed but indiscriminate tourism promotion and development are overwhelming dependent natural and cultural landscape features. Flashy "lure pieces" are designed with a central goal of enticing as many visitors and tourism dollars as possible. Accompanying

this wholesale promotion of out-of-the-way rural areas is often an equal push to modernize and expand supporting infrastructure to accommodate the "successful" promotion efforts. These efforts are a poor substitute for thoughtful marketing plans designed to help potential visitors find the exact areas that can satisfy their specific leisure preferences.

To the extent that communities, tourism industry partners, and land managers allow or, worse yet, even help facilitate this erosion of EAL-dependent natural and cultural distinctives, the potential for generating significant leisure benefits is being lost. In some areas the loss is occurring at an alarming rate. Realization of this loss gives a sense of urgency to the need for building cooperative management partnerships among communities, the tourism industry, and land managers to ensure long-term EAL sustainability.

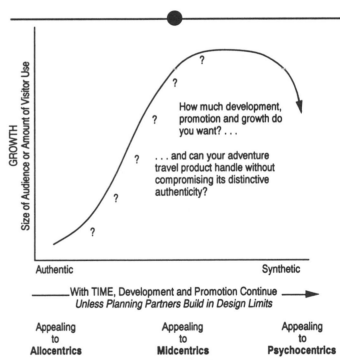

FIGURE 29-2
RECREATION TOURISM DESTINATION GROWTH AND DEVELOPMENT CURVE: THE ALLOCENTRISM-PSYCHOCENTRISM SCALE

(adapted from Plog, Stanley C. (1991). *Leisure travel: Making it a growth market... again!* New York. NY: John Wiley and Sons, Inc., pp. 77-82)

Some Words of Warning

While some communities believe that growth is the solution to declining traditional commodity production, others have found that it is just the beginning of even greater problems. Some have drawn an important distinction between "growth (increasing or adding to what you have) and development (enhancing and strengthening what you already have)" (USDA Forest Service, 1993, p. 3). David Korten, with the People-Centered Development Forum, points out that people-centered development visions contrast with growth-centered visions in that they emphasize quality of life rather than material consumption, needs of everyone in the community rather than the wants of the monied, economic returns to households rather than the corporation, community cooperation rather than individual competition, and locally regulated market economies rather than unregulated global market economies. Korten adds that these decentralized economies favor local production for local markets, local ownership, local diversification, self-reliance in basic needs, financial and environmental conservation and saving, internalized social and environmental costs, taxed and regulated removal of basic resources, and free access to information and technology (USDA Forest Service, 1993, p. 4).

This view corresponds with the rural values espoused in EALs. Such rural values, according to a Western Governors' Association report:

> . . . are a marketable commodity that is worth something . . . combining America's best traditions of both communitarianism and individualism. In a phrase adapted from Wendell Berry, they represent the very humble but absolutely necessary capacity to think locally and to act locally, in contrast to urban values where the thrust is to think globally and act locally.
>
> Murphy and McGinniss,
> 1992, p. 66

In a paper presented at a conference entitled "New Era for Public Lands, the Points West Lecture Series for the Center for the New West," Mary Chapman (1993), a fifth-generation rural Coloradan, warns that:

> an immigration of telecommuters and other 'urban refugees' . . . has weakened community consensus and in some cases paralyzed local government decision making.

She also notes that consequently heightened environmental concerns tend also to undervalue local community concerns (Chapman, 1993, pp. 3-4). Of Chapman's "findings," five underscore how important stable local communities are to the maintenance of important EAL values:

1. Environmental preservation does not equate with economic prosperity; economic diversity does.

   While this view pits the environment against local economic concerns, we believe both are critically important to EAL communities. This reflects the interdependency between biophysical and sociocultural systems identified above.

2. Take away traditional public lands industries and you take away the very stability and economic base which rural communities need in order to diversify their economies.

   Failure to recognize the stabilizing influence of traditional land uses in rural economies invariably destabilizes rather than strengthens their economies. Except for the really big recreation tourism destinations, local economies can only hope to diversify (not supplant) traditional economies with leisure-based developments.

3. Diminish traditional public land industries and the cultures that have grown up around them, and you take away one of the chief attractions of the rural West—its people.

   This point is at the heart of the EAL ideal. Communities failing to recognize their traditional cultures, land uses and lifestyles as EAL attractions will end up destroying one of the principal reasons both residents and visitors value them. However, not all newcomers share this perspective, particularly those who espouse what Chapman calls the "green is gold" idea. Aaron Harp, a University of Idaho rural sociologist, observes that, "The ranchers, miners, and loggers view themselves as an indigenous culture, as second wave natives. To them, newcomers are carrying out a cultural genocide" (Grappling with growth, 1994, p. 16).

4. The assumption that amenity-based uses such as recreation and tourism are less

damaging to the environment than traditional land uses is an assumption that is not validated.

To illustrate, Chapman asks communities whose traditional economies are sagging if condos or mountain bikes are less environmentally damaging than cattle, or if the displacement of service workers by inflated real estate markets in booming recreation tourism communities is to be preferred over traditional economies, noting that some recreation tourism developments "are not environmentally sustainable either."

5. The assumption that amenity-based industries such as tourism and recreation can fill the economic and cultural gaps in the rural West simply does not hold water.

Chapman cites studies that indicate, because of the low wages paid tourism industry service workers, that it takes three tourism jobs to replace one timbering or mining job and two tourism jobs to replace one agricultural job, adding that displaced locals can often not easily shift from one industry to the other.

According to Kurt Culbertson, environmental consultant with Design Workshop in Aspen, Colorado, no amount of planning will prevent development and growth of the West's privately owned valleys (Grappling with growth, 1994, p. 7). Actually, communities are finding that even large sums of money spent on contracted studies and plans cannot ensure attainment of their desired futures. The USDA Forest Service's report (1993) of a national collaborative planning workshop notes that "People are realizing that they don't need 'experts' to make all their decisions. If communities are to do the work and make the sacrifices needed to achieve their dream, it must be their dream." Indeed, a fundamental tenet of this chapter is that no one else can do this job in lieu of local people acting in their own best interests as partners, working hand-in-hand. The mayor of Portland, Oregon, observed that "People need the chance to prove they have the wisdom, imagination and courage to find solutions." At the Forest Service's collaborative workshop, someone else remarked, "Collaborative planning is not a science, it's an art. Don't wait for an expert to come to town; just jump in" (USDA Forest Service, 1993, p. 2).

Some Tools for Collaborating Partners

Sustaining EALs presents significant challenges to elected and appointed government officials. Nonetheless, a number of tools have been used by local governments to respond to these challenges. Now, through collaborative partnerships, elected and appointed government officials can more judiciously apply these tools with greater confidence towards attainment of the community's desired future, knowing that they are supported by the local citizenry, private sector recreation and tourism service industries, and public land managers. Here are a few of the tools that are being used (Grappling with growth, 1994, pp. 9-10):

1. Moratorium:

   Temporary deferments of all land use decisions allow time to develop a strategy and plan for responding to growth initiatives. On the downside, moratoriums can fuel speculation about outcomes of certain developments with the unintended result of accelerating development on other lands not covered by the moratorium.

2. Limit on Permits Allowed:

   A numeric limit on the number of development permits allows building to proceed at a periodic rate (e.g., annual) that is within both the plan design and collaborative partners' comfort range. On the negative side, these limits only forestall an inevitable compromise of EAL values since they deal only with the rate and not with the degree of development desired. Such marketplace limits also tend to inflate artificially property values and, among those investing in those inflated prices, creates a long-term moral obligation to keep these limits in place indefinitely.

3. Zoning:

   Land use prescriptions either set upper limits on allowable types of development and development densities or impose other area-specific use and development constraints. In some communities this is still the hated "Z" word; in others, people are becoming increasingly open to its use to maintain distinctive EAL features. Zoning embodies the notion that EALs contain certain nonnegotiable elements that must not be compromised. Land use prescriptions, however, must be carefully crafted to ensure maintenance of all essential biophysical and sociocultural elements. For example, maintenance of desirable EAL aesthetics (e.g., meadow or cultivated field) in too small a geographic unit may not be possible with zoning.

4. Performance Zoning Standards:

Componentized achievement prescription sets an overall numeric upper sum of individual scores that represents how well development proposals meet established social, environmental, and economic evaluative criteria (impacts on natural resources, public health and safety, conformity with existing neighborhoods, carrying capacity, etc.). This approach assumes that the collective effect of any one development is more significant than the sum of its parts, and it implies that proponents failing to meet some criteria can make up for it by exceeding others. This new zoning twist cannot ensure that all nonnegotiable elements of EALs are sustained.

5. Phased Development Plan:

Development conditioned by essential support services requires having a supporting infrastructure already in place (water, sewer, emergency services, schools . . .) before developments are approved. This tool may be most effective when used in combination with zoning. It allows the community to determine where and when development occurs. Exaction fees allow the community to make developers pay their own way.

6. Exaction Fee:

Development conditioned by proponents paying their own way charges developers up-front fees for essential support services and infrastructure development. This tool

shifts the financial burden from residents to developers: it allows EAL communities, not developers, to maintain control.

7. Set Asides:

Development conditioned by proponents setting aside land to be held in public ownership requires developers to dedicate a certain percentage of planned development acreage as open space and to meet other infrastructure needs. Combined with an EAL ethic, this would allow communities to keep certain nonnegotiable EAL elements intact.

8. Real Estate Assessment Tax:

Amenity fund-raising assessment imposes a certain percentage tax on all real estate transactions to help fund desirable amenities and services to maintain desired quality of life standards for residents and newcomers alike. This tool can be effectively used by communities to help maintain the integrity of nonnegotiable EAL elements.

Even the prospect of using these tools to restrict development within the private sector raises a sense of dread among some community planners and local officials. Their concern is avoiding violation of U.S. Constitutional prohibitions against taking private property without compensation, an action generally referred to as "takings."

Ed Ziegler, Executive Director of the Rocky Mountain Land Use Institute at Denver University, notes that local governments using the kinds of tools outlined above to extract from developers funding or set asides must meet the test of two U.S. Supreme Court decisions (Grappling with growth, 1994, p. 17). In *Nollan versus California Coastal Commission*, the high court found that when extractions seek public benefits, the benefits and the exaction must be related (beach access and building height, it determined, were not related). In the case of *Dolan versus City of Tigard*, it found further that exactions must not be disproportionate to project size (paving of a plumbing supply store parking lot and dedication of associated floodplain property to a storm drain system were, it determined, disproportionate).

Ziegler explains that communities usually have more authority than is realized, "You can take private property; you just have to do some reasonable planning." He observed that a simple reduction in property market value, or profit obtained from it, as a result of local government regulation does not constitute a taking, but that, by one of the court's standards, landowners must prove they have no economically viable alternative use. Ziegler says, "Too many communities accept the big lie that they can't downzone because they will take someone's property."

Implementing an Ethic of Place

EALs and the experiences they foster form the basis for what Charles Wilkinson (1990) calls an "ethic of place":

> *An ethic of place ought to be a shared community value and ought to manifest itself in a dogged determination to treat the environment and its people as equals, to recognize both as sacred, and to insure that all members of the community not only search for, but insist upon, solutions that fulfill the ethic.* (p. 75)

He draws a contrast between the philosophic debate over homocentrism (which he defines as "the belief that things ought to be interpreted according to human values") and biocentrism ("the idea that animals and land systems have an independent right to exist entirely separate from any relationship to human beings"). Inherent in both views is the notion of social value. An ethic of place is inherently personal and related to one's own social value system. In the broad view, EALs are made special and sensible because they embody various degrees of bio- and homocentrism.

Additionally, the authors would argue that the sustainable maintenance of EALs across this nation also requires the successful integration of a third dimension into this ethic of place, and that is "culturalcentrism." The resulting ethic would simultaneously respect the land itself (biocentrism), extant early American cultural landscapes (culturalcentrism), and social values applied to both the land and its cultural landscapes (homocentrism).

There is a delicate synergy here: land managers must continue learning to value local and regional quality of life issues and learn what it takes to maintain them. Local and regional tourism partners must care enough to get involved, and then learn how to keep the values they and their community partners depend on. Local communities and governments must do both. All must continue to develop a greater understanding of the social value of EALs and their dependent biophysical and sociocultural systems, as well as a greater stewardship ethic for the collaborative management of both.

Maintaining the integrity of EALs on a sustainable basis, and the public benefits they afford, requires that local communities, land managers, and recreation tourism industry partners accelerate their efforts to address explicitly EAL values. None can afford to allow important and distinctive ecologic and cultural values—both of which are integral to all EALs—to be compromised by their desire to promote economic stability and growth within affected local communities.

> *Migration data on the rural West suggest that the 'local character' which has built up around traditional public lands industries such as ranching may be providing more incentive for retirees, small business and telecommuters to relocate than the surrounding physical environment. Unlike those relocating in 'gateway' towns or ski resort areas, these people and small businesses moving into the 'average' towns of the rural West say they are doing so for reasons that are at least as cultural as they are environmental. They like the sense of community, the low crime rates, the work ethic, the 4-H bake sales, the county fairs, the rodeos, and even things like livestock being moved on county roads to and from the public lands.*
>
> Chapman, 1993, p. 3

Literature Cited

Chapman, M. (1993). "Observations—From the back of the pumpkin truck." Paper delivered at the University of Colorado Natural Resources Law Center conference entitled New Era for Public Lands, the Points West Lecture Series for the Center for the New West. Boulder, CO.

Conover, T. (1991). *Whiteout: Lost in Aspen*. New York, NY: Random House.

Driver, B., Brown, P., Peterson, G., and Bruns, D. (1991). *The benefits-based approach to leisure policy analysis and service delivery: What is it and why is it needed?* Background Paper No. 1 for Leisure Benefits Application Workshop. Estes Park, CO.

Federspiel, G. (1992). Maintaining small town character in a modern resort community. In A. Gill and R. Hartmann (Eds.), *Mountain resort development: Proceedings of the Vail conference* (pp. 100-103). Burnaby, BC, Canada: The Centre for Tourism Policy and Research, Simon Fraser University.

Grappling with growth. (1994). Denver, CO: *High Country News*, pp. 7, 9-10, 16-17.

Lee, R. (1972). The social definition of outdoor recreation places. In W. Burch, N. Cheek and L. Taylor (Eds.), *Social behavior, natural resources and the environment* (pp. 68-84). New York, NY: Harper and Row Publishers, Inc.

McClelland, L., Keller, J., Keller, G., and Melnick, R. (1984). *Guidelines for evaluating and documenting rural historic landscapes*. National Park Service, National Register Bulletin 30.

Murphy, R. and McGinniss, G. (1992). Rural culture and values. In *Small towns: Culture, change and cooperation* (pp. 63-81). Salt Lake City, UT: Western Governors' Association.

Plog, S. (1991). *Leisure travel: Making it a growth market—again!* New York, NY: John Wiley & Sons.

Relph, E. (1976). *Place and placelessness*. London, UK: Pion Ltd.

Richardson, S. (1991). *Colorado community tourism action guide*. Boulder, CO: Colorado Center for Community Development, University of Colorado at Denver and The Center for Recreation and Tourism Development, University of Colorado at Boulder.

Schreyer, R., Jacob, G., and White, R. (1981). Environmental meaning as a determinant of spatial behavior in recreation. In J. Frazier and B. Epstein (Eds.), *Proceedings of the Applied Geography Conferences, 4,* 294-300.

Schreyer, R., Lime, D., and Williams, D. (1984). The influence of past experience on recreation behavior. *Journal of Leisure Research, 16,* 34-50.

Siegel, W. (1990). *Travel USA: Colorado's opportunities in the U.S. pleasure travel market.*

Stokowski, P. (1991). *'Sense of place' as a social construct.* Summary paper of presentation delivered at the 1991 Research Symposium of the National Recreation and Park Association Congress, Baltimore, MD.

Tuan, Y. (1977). *Space and place: The perspective of experience*. Minneapolis, MN: University of Minnesota Press.

USDA Forest Service. (1993). *Report of the national workshop: The power of collaborative planning*. FS-553. Washington, DC.

Wilkinson, C. (1990). Beyond the mythic west. In *Beyond the mythic west* (pp. 75-79). Salt Lake City, UT: Peregrine Smith Books.

Williams, D. and Carr, D. (1993). The sociocultural meanings of outdoor recreation places: Implications for managing the wildland-urban interface. In A. Ewert, D. Chavez and A. Magill (Eds.), *Culture, conflict and communication in the wildland-urban interface*. Boulder, CO: Westview Press.

Williams, D. and Roggenbuck, J. (1989). *Measuring place attachment: Some preliminary results*. Paper presented at the NRPA Leisure Research Symposium. San Antonio, TX.

MANAGING FOR DIVERSITY IN HERITAGE VALUES

CHAPTER 30

MARTHA LEE
School of Forestry
Northern Arizona University
Flagstaff, Arizona

JOSEPH TAINTER
Rocky Mountain Forest and Range Experiment Station
USDA Forest Service
Albuquerque, New Mexico

Introduction

Americans have paradoxical feelings about history. It is a subject that one must take in school, similar in appeal perhaps to algebra, yet Americans travel overseas in large numbers to visit historic sites. As a technologically creative society, Americans denigrate the past, yet each year in record numbers they go to places like Mesa Verde and the Smithsonian. People casually discard that which is outdated, yet every antique dealer knows that they are susceptible to claims that an item is old. Many cannot recall when the Civil War took place, while Civil War reenactments are a favorite item of television reporting. While this dualism may appear puzzling on the surface, it is our perspective that it reflects a genuine interest in the past that is held at an emotional rather than an intellectual level. Americans do want to understand, or at least feel, the power of history. Those people who study and teach about the past have just not learned effectively how to reach that deep interest.

Heritage management is concerned with sites and cultural landscapes in which people perceive diverse values. While one value, historical significance, has dominated our (land management's) con-

ception of heritage management, it is becoming clear that this is but a part of a spectrum of values. Our (land management's) concern with historic values has inhibited recognition of the remainder of this spectrum. In this chapter we examine some of the values that are assigned to historical and cultural sites. We begin by showing how the conceptual framework of historic preservation inhibits our ability to discern why people value heritage properties in different ways.

The perceptions of the past and of the values of heritage sites are influenced overwhelmingly by the Western modes of thought in which land managers are raised and in which they are professionally trained. These modes of thought are enshrined in the philosophical tradition that has come to be known as *empiricism* (in Great Britain) or as *positivism* (on the European continent). Empiricist/positivist thought has until recently dominated professional discourse. The laws and regulations governing historic preservation, as we will show, were drafted in an empiricist/positivist framework, and that framework continues to guide the management and use of heritage sites. The empiricist/positivist perspective on the past leads land managers to perceive only a limited set of uses for these sites and to regard these as the normal and natural uses. When alternative uses emerge that are not foreseen in the current framework, they inevitably provoke discord and misunderstanding and are regarded by many as inappropriate.

We hope to facilitate an expanded view of heritage and cultural resource management in three ways. The first is to exhort land managers to recognize that their ideas of historic site management have been conditioned by the empiricist/positivist view of knowledge and meaning. The second is to help land managers understand the limitations of empiricist/positivist thought. The third is to illustrate some of the uses of heritage sites and cultural resources that are recognized by an expanded concept of heritage management. We conclude the chapter with illustrations of land management agencies that are managing for heritage resource diversity.

The Epistemological Framework

Empiricists and positivists assert that knowledge derives from "primitive" terms or statements whose meaning is intuitive because they come directly from sensory experiences. In early developments of this view, Locke and Hume " . . . held that every idea must either originate directly in sense experience, or else be compounded of ideas thus originating" (Quine, 1963, p. 38). Since knowledge has its roots in sensory experience, proponents hold that claims to knowledge must be either direct reports of experience or observation, or statements that can be derived from such reports. Imre Lakatos (1968) has stated this view most forcefully:

> . . . *factual propositions and their . . . consequences constitute knowledge: the rest is rubbish.* (p. 319)

The empiricist/positivist perspective has a fundamental implication: if meaning and knowledge come only from sensory experience, then the source of both is *within* the phenomenon being observed. The qualities of phenomena that give rise to meaning are therefore *intrinsic*, and the knowledge to be derived is *immutable* (Tainter and Lucas, 1983, p.

712). "This school," wrote Hill and Evans (1972), "holds to the metaphysical notion that all phenomena . . . have meanings or significance inherent in some sense within themselves" (p. 233).

Criticism of empiricist/positivist thinking is to be found in a large and distinguished literature which is not appropriate to review here (see, for example, Tainter and Lucas, 1983, pp. 712-714). Among the more salient points established in this literature are the following:

1. The empiricist/positivist view assumes that experiences are, or can be, objective. Today it is widely recognized that the idea of objective or value-neutral observation is a myth. One's socialization in a cultural milieu, one's professional training, and the theories to which one subscribes fundamentally influence one's sensory experiences (Feyerabend, 1962; Kuhn, 1962).

2. The empiricist/positivist view that meaning derives from objective experience leads to the condition that Feyerabend (1962) critically calls "meaning invariance" (p. 30) where new theories must always preserve the previous meanings of terms. The vast experience of historical linguistics readily shows the fallacy of this notion.

3. The empiricist/positivist position cannot account for historical changes in scientific frameworks, and it implies that they should not occur. In this regard the empiricist/positivist approach fails unequivocally on both historical and methodological grounds (Feyerabend, 1962; Kuhn, 1962; Lakatos, 1968).

4. The empiricist/positivist position cannot justify any proposition that transcends sense experience. It thus provides no basis for developing generalizations.

5. Most fundamentally, the empiricist/positivist perspective is contradicted by anthropological theory and experience. Anyone familiar with how systems of symbolism vary cross-culturally, where in different cultural contexts the same objective phenomenon can take very different meanings, will know that meaning is not inherent in phenomena. It is assigned by the human mind. The mean-

ings that can be assigned to any phenomenon are as varied as human culture itself (Tainter and Lucas, 1983, p. 714).

Empiricist–positive thought has influenced many disciplines, including history (Collingwood, 1956; Fain, 1970; Meineke, 1972) and archaeology (Hill and Evans, 1972). It has also strongly influenced the public perception of science (Ziman, 1968). From all of these avenues, elements of empiricist/positivist thought have emerged in the laws and regulations of historic preservation.

The Legal Framework

The National Historic Preservation Act (NHPA) of 1966 (as amended) gives the primary direction to heritage preservation in the United States. In the preamble to this act Congress found that:

1. the spirit and direction of the Nation are founded upon and reflected in its historic heritage;

2. the historical and cultural foundations of the Nation should be preserved as a living part of our community life and development in order to give a sense of orientation to the American people; . . . [and]

3. the preservation of this irreplaceable heritage is in the public interest so that its vital legacy of cultural, educational, aesthetic, inspirational, economic, and energy benefits will be maintained and enriched for future generations of Americans. . . . (16 U.S.C. 470, Section 1[b]).

Congress organized the national historic preservation program around the newly established National Register of Historic Places which was intended to list " . . . districts, sites, buildings, structures, and objects significant in American history, architecture, archaeology, engineering, and culture" (16 U.S.C. 470, Section 101[a][1][A]). The Secretary of the Interior was directed to establish criteria for properties to be eligible for inclusion in the National Register.

These regulations, issued as Title 36, Code of Federal Regulations, Part 60 (36 C.F.R. 60) have a venerable history. They are based on standards first released by the National Resources Board in 1934, rewritten by the National Council for Historic Sites and Buildings in 1949, and revised by the National

Trust for Historic Preservation in 1956 (Finley, 1965; Hosmer, 1981; Mulloy, 1976; Schneider, 1935; Tainter and Lucas, 1983). Our thinking about the value of historic sites has changed little since the early 1930s. As presently formulated, historic properties eligible for the National Register of Historic Places are those:

a. that are associated with events that have made a significant contribution to the broad patterns of our history; or

b. that are associated with the lives of persons significant in our past; or

c. that embody the distinctive characteristics of a type, period, or method of construction, or that represent the work of a master, or that possess high artistic value, or that represent a significant and distinguishable entity whose components may lack individual distinction; or

d. that have yielded, or may be likely to yield, information important in prehistory or history (36 C.F.R. 60.4).

The empiricist/positivist influence in the laws and regulations of historic preservation is clear, and it is pervasive. Both 36 C.F.R. 60.4 (discussed above) and a related regulation, 36 C.F.R. 800.10, state that "The quality of significance . . . *is present in* . . . " (emphasis added) properties that are intact and meet one or more of the eligibility criteria. Conversely, a property listed in the National Register may be removed if its significant qualities are "lost or destroyed" (36 C.F.R. 60.15). It is evident that the professionals who wrote these regulations thought of historical, archaeological, and architectural significance as something intrinsic to historic properties, waiting only to be discerned. Emotional, inspirational, or spiritual values were not recognized to be aspects of historic properties. Since the value of historic sites, under empiricist/positivist reasoning, is considered to be those things that are intrinsic to such sites, these latter values do not merit recognition. Accordingly, many historic preservation professionals consider the uses of sites that arise from spiritual or other emotional motivations not to be legitimate uses. When such uses nevertheless arise, as they inevitably do, the stage is set for misunderstanding and conflict. Since those who value heritage resources emotionally will continue to express those values through their uses of sites, it is necessary for land managers to expand their conception of legitimate values of heritage sites.

A heritage professional working in the context of current laws and regulations is, probably unknowingly, likely to have an empiricist/positivist view of the value of historic sites. Such a professional will assume that sites have historical, scientific, or architectural values that are natural and inherent. The alternative view is that historic sites do not hold *inherent* historical, scientific, or architectural values. These values are assigned by individuals and society, through use, language, or other cultural relevance. The variability of cultural meaning opens a universe of realizations. If sites can be assigned the values of scientists and professional land managers, they can also be assigned the values of societal subgroups and of the public at large: emotional, aesthetic, inspirational, or spiritual.

The values that can be assigned to historic sites are nearly unlimited. They are constrained only by the diversity of human feelings about the past. The following examples illustrate the diversity of some of the use claims of heritage resources that land managers may expect (if they have not experienced them already). These uses are evolving and, as will be shown, surprising new ones are emerging.

Alternative Uses of Heritage Sites

Perhaps the best illustration of alternative uses of heritage sites and of how the public assigns meaning and significance to them, comes from the British site of Stonehenge. These uses and values have been catalogued by Christopher Chippindale, who notes:

> *Stonehenge sets a puzzle that has never been solved. For centuries the people who have gone to see it have found it a mirror which reflects back, more or less distorted, that view of the past which the onlooker takes there.*
>
> Chippindale, 1983, p. 6

Thus Stonehenge has been taken to signify imagined pasts as diverse as independent British ingenuity or wished for Classical ancestry. It is imputed to ancient Druids and used by contemporary ones. It is a manifestation of ancient geometry or one of the Earth's acupuncture points. Stonehenge either manifests an ancient cosmic consciousness or is the setting for a masonic mystery play running continuously since 3373 BC. According to one school of writing, it was built to attract spaceships. A young mother once took her handicapped child to lie on the stones at the summer solstice when the ancient forces are thought to work best.

American heritage managers may never experience anything like the long-running Stonehenge free festival (advertised in 1974 as a gathering of "love and awareness"), but the public perceptions that they do experience differ only in degree. Some American heritage sites are becoming surrogate Stonehenges. There is a growing literature, including a guide to sites and to the proper rituals to conduct at them (Joseph, 1992). We include here two examples of such activities, though it appears they are widespread.

Chaco Canyon, an area of concentrated prehistoric Pueblo settlement in northwestern New Mexico, was a gathering spot for the 1987 Harmonic Convergence. To some, it:

> *. . . is a holy place of mystic earth power*

where:

> *. . . today's receptive visitor should be no less fortunate [in having a mystical experience] than the mysterious Anasazi. . . .*
>
> Joseph, 1992, p. 245

The recommended ritual includes placing corn pollen and quartz crystals at cardinal points within Casa Rinconada, a great kiva. Properly done, the ritual allows one to " . . . stride into the future with confidence and the blessing of the Ancient Ones" (Joseph, 1992, pp. 246-247). Yet contemporary spiritual needs will sometimes conflict. In recent years, a group of spiritual seekers interred the cremated remains of one of their members in the kiva floor. Because the Navajo religion prohibits any interaction with the dead their discovery made it impossible for Navajo workers to enter the structure.

An experience of a different kind can be had at Cahokia, a Mississippian Period center in East St. Louis, Illinois, and the largest archaeological site north of Mexico. It was another locus of the Harmonic Convergence. Cahokia is implicitly " . . . associated with ultimate power . . ." (Joseph, 1992, p. 148). The ritual involves ascending Monk's Mound, the great center of Cahokia. From here one immerses oneself in visions of Cahokia's mystical past.

Here, " . . . the high meeting ground between Mother Earth and Father Sky . . . ," is the place " . . . to banish depression, to purge psychic, emotional, even physical toxins . . . ," and to gain many other benefits (Joseph, 1992, p. 149).

Diversity in Values Assigned to Cultural Resources

One of the dominant motives for leisure and recreation travel is a desire to more deeply understand, experience, and appreciate other cultures, both past and present (Lynch, 1972; MacCannell, 1976). Evidence for this position is the millions of visitors drawn each year to heritage sites such as Cahokia, Chaco Canyon, the Serpent Mounds in southern Ohio, Pipestone National Monument in Minnesota, and the Bighorn Medicine Wheel in Wyoming.

Visitors come to cultural sites to find personal meaning as well as to learn about the past. Preliminary results of a study of visitors to three Anasazi cultural parks in the Southwest found that people were drawn to the parks in order "to get a perspective on the present through an understanding of the past," to "grow and develop spiritually," to "feel isolated," and to "be in a calm atmosphere" (Lee and Stephens, 1993). Other motives related to learning and teaching children about native peoples were also important to cultural park visitors.

Visitors are drawn to heritage sites to take advantage of the powers attributed to these sites by earlier native cultures. Tourism and the search for power and spirituality are closely linked. The literature on tourism contains an ongoing discussion of the similarities between pilgrimages, a largely spiritual journey "born of desire and belief" (Morinis, 1992, p. 1) and tourism (Cohen, 1992; Smith, 1992).

In his book *Sacred Places*, James Swan (1990) provides numerous examples of people from all over the world seeking out the sacred sites of ancient inhabitants in their search for enlightenment, restored health, visions, miracles, personal insight, and peace. The nature of these places varies, including natural features such as spectacular mountains, hot springs and caves, as well as the remnants of past cultures such as burial mounds, medicine wheels, petroglyphs, pictographs, and ancient dwellings.

In addition to being drawn to ancient cultural sites, there are those who seek to understand native cultures on a more contemporary level by immersing themselves in the day-to-day lives of native peoples. In the western United States, for example, tourists travel to reservations in an attempt to more intimately experience Native-American life. Many tourists attempt to "play" at being Native American, seeking what they may stereotypically view as a simpler, less complicated life (Laxson, 1991). Ethnic tourism can, however, result in conflict and concern among Native Americans. In an effort to take economic advantage of such interest, some tribes allow tourists to view some of their dances and ceremonies. While Native Americans may appreciate tourist dollars, they do not appreciate the dehumanizing aspects of being looked upon with curiosity as tourist attractions (Laxson, 1991; Smith, 1989). Native-American "wanna bes" adopt and imitate Native-American beliefs and practices and may unknowingly desecrate sacred sites and inhibit their use by Native Americans (Leerhsen, 1991; Swan, 1990). There is growing concern among members of some Native-American tribes about what Haederle (1994) describes as a "theft" of Native-American practices.

While a discussion of Native-American values and beliefs is presented elsewhere in this text (see Redmond, Chapter Nine, in this volume), one particularly relevant point related to heritage values is the relationship and connection between Native-American beliefs and the land (Swan, 1990; Ward, 1992). The religion and culture of most Native Americans is tied to specific geographic places. According to many Native-American beliefs, people are placed on the Earth:

> *in precisely the proper places; each tribe must live symbiotically with the other creatures, the plants, the rocks, the soil, the air and water, and the spirits or gods that share those places.*
>
> Ward, 1992, p. 800

While all of a particular tribe's lands may be sacred, there are special places that are more sacred than others. These special places may be where gods originated or where they live; where people or sacred animals were born; or where individuals communicate with spiritual forces (Ward, 1992). For example, the four sacred mountains of the Navajo mark the boundaries of Dinetah, the Navajo sacred homeland. The San Francisco Peaks in northern Arizona, which mark the southwestern boundary of Dinetah, are also sacred to the Hopi who believe that the kachinas, emissaries from the gods, reside there (Swan, 1990; van Otten, 1982; Ward, 1992). Despoiling or altering the character of sacred sites, many of which are found on public lands, destroys the sacredness of the site to Native Americans, and Ward (1992) suggests that given the connectedness between sacred sites and Native-American culture and religion, such devastation may destroy their religions.

Since early times, Pacific Northwest coastal native people have cherished the giant cedar, hemlock, and Douglas fir trees, not just for canoes and long houses, but for spiritual communion. To the Lummi, Skagit, Nooksack, Duwamish, Snoqualmie, and other tribes in the area, the groves of huge cedar trees, found primarily on lands managed by the U.S. Forest Service, are sacred ground (Swan, 1990).

With increasing lumber prices has come pressure to log these groves of virgin timber. Recreationists seeking relief from urban life are coming to these forests in growing numbers, prompting development of roads and overnight facilities. In an attempt to satisfy increasing demands for lumber and recreation, the Forest Service announced plans to harvest approximately 40 percent of the old-growth cedar on the Mount Baker–Snoqualmie National Forest in Washington and to build new roads for increased recreation access to the forest.

Led by the coastal Lummi tribe, 14 tribes of western Washington opposed the plan. They said logging these trees would destroy sacred places which collectively contribute to their most sacred possession, *skalalitude*, which in the Salish language means "a sacred state of mind where magic and beauty are everywhere" (Swan, 1990, p. 42).

Public land managers face significant challenges in their attempts to manage for such diverse values and to accommodate the sometimes conflicting uses of heritage sites. Besides recognizing and accommodating Native American uses of heritage sites, managers must also deal with nonnatives such as those described earlier, those who seek to not only learn about but also to emulate and adopt Native-American practices, and those who seek out sacred sites for other spiritual purposes.

The diversity of values attached to heritage sites and the complexity of management issues involved in accommodating that diversity are well-illustrated in the southwestern United States. The Southwest is a particularly significant landscape for New Age

pilgrims who yearly come by the thousands to the red rock country of the Sedona Ranger District of Arizona's Coconino National Forest. The pilgrims come to the "vortexes," sources of power and energy found among the red rock formations, and to form "medicine wheels," circles of rock up to 200 feet in diameter (Leerhsen, 1991). New Age believers have adopted wheel building from Native Americans as a focal point for prayers and ceremonies. Native-American sacred sites are being marred and even destroyed by increased use by New Age believers for their rituals (Brown, 1991). Native Americans oppose this disrespect for their beliefs, and Forest Service managers object to the disturbance of the natural features of the landscape and spend many hours taking apart these wheels (Leerhsen, 1991).

This conflict among New Age believers, Native Americans, and land managers embodies the complex array of values and concerns associated with managing heritage sites on public lands. This same diversity of uses and value expression is manifest in how we as Americans revere and experience the remnants of this nation's historic past.

Returning to the Past: Historic Resource Values

Part of who we are as a nation includes numerous clashes and struggles over conflicting beliefs and values. Many of the remnants of and monuments to these conflicts are preserved on public lands as national battlefields, war memorials, and national monuments. Names such as Gettysburg, the Alamo, and Little Bighorn evoke strong, sometimes conflicting, emotions in those who visit, study, and re-create the events that took place there.

While there exists ample documentation of the popularity and interest in such historic sites and the conflicts that can occur over the meaning of such sites, as illustrated by events that have occurred at the Little Bighorn battlefield site (Linenthal, 1991), little research has focused on the diversity of values assigned to these heritage sites by visitors. To assume visitors are interested only in learning about past events being memorialized is overly simplistic. The Vietnam War Memorial, for example, evokes a diversity of responses among those who visit: a sense of pilgrimage, a worshipful attitude, emotional catharsis, and ritual acts such as wearing Vietnam military paraphernalia, searching for names, and leaving flowers (Coombs, 1989). While historic sites and the interpretation and experiences provided by land managers most certainly have educational value to visitors and participants, a nonempirical approach to historic resource management suggests we need to explore some of the emotional, inspirational, patriotic, and spiritual values assigned to such sites.

A growing number of people are trying to capture and express a sense of the past by participating in "living history" experiences. Living history includes the simple demonstrations of old-time skills, with farmers, weavers, blacksmiths, and tradespeople pursuing their crafts in real or simulated historical settings such as colonial Williamsburg, Virginia or Plymouth, Massachusetts, as well as participation in reenactments of historic events— the voyage of Christopher Columbus, the pioneer treks to settle the western United States, and battles fought during the American Civil War. Places and lifestyles are created with often meticulously researched buildings, furnishings, and costumed role players. Visitors ask questions about period life, role players take on the identity of actual people, and create life during a prior period in history (Crowley, 1993; Sussman, 1989; Turim, 1991). Living history events are designed to educate, entertain, and immerse visitors and participants in another time and place and are visited by millions of people yearly (Sussman, 1989).

One type of living history that provides opportunities for participants to intimately experience history is battle reenactments. Enactment participation embodies the variety and depth of motivation and values realized from using and experiencing historic resources. For purposes of illustration we focus on Civil War battle reenactments although reenactments are held at numerous other historic sites throughout the United States.

There is a long history of reenactments of Civil War battles, beginning soon after the war ended. Early reenactments were attempts to reconcile Northern and Southern hostility, and they later became a way to revive the past. During the 1950s a distinct Civil War subculture began to emerge. A growing number of people sought to "experience" the war and its time period. There were those interested in living history, battle reenactors, relic hunters, collectors, and "war gamers" who played complex and lengthy board games that reproduced Civil War battles. Today more than 40,000 people participate in battle reenactments each year (Linenthal, 1991; Lord, 1988).

Authenticity is a critical component of today's reenactments. Reenactors pay substantial sums of money to acquire authentic clothing, from "caps to underwear" (Lawliss, 1991). A small industry of craftsmen has grown up to meet the needs of Civil War reenactors and hobbyists (Lord, 1988).

Reenactors must not only look authentic, but they must have the right attitude toward reenactments. True reenactors are obsessed with detail: some even fight barefoot, in ragged clothes to imitate Southern soldiers in a battle fought later in the war; others fall where a soldier fell and reproduce his wounds when possible (Linenthal, 1991; Potter, 1991).

What motivates reenactors, who come from a variety of situations and occupations, to go to such lengths to re-create the past? What values and benefits are realized from such obsessive participation? Interviews with Civil War reenactors reveal three reasons: a desire to return to the past, to gain a deeper appreciation for the history of that period, and a sense of ancestral pride (Lawliss 1991; Linenthal, 1991; Lord, 1988).

A desire to return to an earlier time, to experience what it was like to live in another period draws reenactors, as does a desire to live a more primitive lifestyle, even for a short period of time (Lord, 1988). Civil War reenactors can experience firsthand what it was like to be a soldier, a nurse, a bugler, a Yankee, a Confederate, or any number of supporting cast members.

The desire to gain a greater appreciation for history reflects the resurgence in interest in the Civil War that has occurred throughout America in recent years (Lord, 1988). Reenacting battles is a way of coming to feel what it was like to fight in the Civil War without anyone getting hurt. A sense of patriotism is evident among participants who feel reenactments are a way to honor and show respect for those who actually sacrificed, fought, and died (Linenthal, 1991; Lord, 1988).

A sense of ancestral pride is a motive expressed by reenactors who had relatives who fought in or were in other ways affected by the war. Reenacting the lives and deaths of family members is a way of honoring their memory (Lord, 1988).

We do not suggest that these are the only feelings that motivate reenactors. Nor are these feelings unique to those who re-create Civil War battles. Reenactments are becoming more and more popular as people seek to learn about, relive, venerate, and preserve the past. People are drawn to the past for a variety of reasons. They seek to re-create and experience history on a variety of levels. Managers of historic resources, like those of other heritage resources, must try to balance the desires of these diverse groups.

Management in Support of Heritage Resource Diversity

In 1984 the First World Congress on Cultural Parks was held at Mesa Verde National Park in Colorado. Some 350 delegates from 52 countries attended this landmark gathering on preserving cultural heritage (Swan, 1990). A number of the participants represented native peoples of the world and, while they had many cultural differences, all the native representatives agreed that they shared one common serious problem: those lands which they considered sacred were in jeopardy due to the diverse demands of modern society. The greatest obstacle to preserving sacred places, according to these participants, was a lack of understanding among modern people as to how or why these places were so special (Swan, 1990).

The concern and frustration expressed by the indigenous participants at the Congress and the diverse values attached to heritage resources described earlier in this chapter suggest two challenges for public land managers that are particularly relevant to our discussion:

1. Heritage resources hold a diversity of values for native and nonnative people: economic, spiritual and life-defining values; healing, enlightenment, educational and learning, curiosity, ancestral pride, veneration, and numerous others. These special values may be strongly held by disparate groups of people and can even lead to conflict among those who seek to express them.

2. Many of the special places, whether cultural or historic in nature, are located on federal lands. This implies, in most cases, that ac-

cess is available to a variety of users and visitors and that these lands may be managed under multiple, even conflicting management objectives.

Recognition of the diversity of values and facilitating the expression of those values while preserving and protecting the resources that engender those values is indeed a worthy but seemingly impossible task for public land managers, given the complex cultural, political, economic, managerial, and social issues involved. In this final section, we illustrate some of the ways managers of heritage resources are responding to these challenges. Cooperation among land managers, Native Americans, local governments, and others involved with heritage resources is an overriding theme in the cases we present. The examples focus on some of the innovative ways managers and others are working together to facilitate expression and understanding of the diversity of values associated with heritage resources while trying to protect and preserve those resources.

Education through interpretation is an important way that land managers can help heritage resource visitors understand the significance of those sites, not only historically and to the native peoples who may still use those sites, but also to help visitors find meaning and value in their own lives. One way managers can do this is to use interpretation to return visitors to the past or to a simpler time and help them become aware of cultures and values other than their own. A number of national forest services have developed information brochures and other materials to help visitors "experience" history and culture. Some examples include:

A brochure titled 'Traveling Through Time,' published by California's Six Rivers National Forest, describes the Native-American tribes who lived within the forest boundaries over the past 6,000 years and the subsequent exploration and settlement of the area by fur traders, gold miners, ranchers, and homesteaders.

The Inyo National Forest developed an interpretive tour of a former gold mine where visitors are invited to close their eyes and 'visualize how life was for those who lived and struggled here.' The brochure includes pictures and descriptions of life at the camp during the late 1800s.

A beautifully designed brochure titled 'Traces of the Past,' published by the Pacific Southwest Region of the Forest Service and the California State Office of the Bureau of Land Management, focuses on cultural resources in California including those resulting from the activities of Native-American peoples, ranching / homesteading, mining, and logging. The brochure includes a section on how to protect cultural heritage.

Cooperation between land managers and native peoples in interpreting cultural heritage is critical. The Miwok tribe of California works closely with the National Park Service and California State Department of Parks and Recreation to accurately interpret for tourists the traditional and modern life of native peoples. Miwok elders, ceremonial, and tribal leaders work with park rangers, interpreters, and archaeologists to develop educational materials for the public (Evans, 1986). Indian Grinding Rocks State Historic Park contains the site of an old Miwok village with thousands of bedrock grinding mortars. It has a museum/culture center where Miwok create and display their arts and crafts, and several Miwok structures including a roundhouse built for traditional dances. Miwok dances, games, and demonstrations are held in the park and participating families come from throughout California to attend. Miwoks restrict access to the park for private and traditional ceremonies.

There are other state parks in California that interpret both past and present Native-American culture and provide an atmosphere where tourists, local residents, and Native Americans can participate in cultural activities (Evans, 1986). This type of cooperation between federal and state land managers and Native Americans can provide economic and cultural benefits to tribes and opportunities for non-Natives to learn about and uniquely experience Native-American culture.

The U.S. Forest Service's "Passport in Time" (PIT) program was established in part to protect heritage resources and to provide individuals and families with an opportunity to learn about and experience cultural and historic resources on public lands. This program solicits volunteers to work under the supervision of U.S. Forest Service and university archaeologists on environmental and historical research projects on national forests (USDA Forest Service, 1994). Volunteers may or may not need special skills and can work on a variety of projects (e.g., archaeological excavations, historic structure reconstruction projects, and compiling oral histories). Some of the 1994 projects (USDA Forest Service, 1994) include:

- looking for artifacts at an old military post in the Chiricahua Mountains in southeastern Arizona;

- excavating Native-American sites occupied around 500 BC on the Kisatchie National Forest in Louisiana;

- labeling, cataloging and preparing artifacts from a ranger district office on the Deschutes National Forest for accessioning to the Oregon State Museum of Natural History; and

- participating in an interpretive reenactment of a Civil War skirmish at Cheat Summit Fort on the Monongahela National Forest in West Virginia.

The cooperative efforts between the Forest Service, university archaeologists, and citizens benefit everyone involved. Land managers gain assistance in protecting and interpreting heritage resources, and volunteers learn and experience cultural and historic resources on a very intimate level.

Part of the uniqueness of visiting historic and cultural sites is being able to walk among remnants of the past, feeling that one has been transported back in time. While managing agencies can encourage and facilitate these engrossing experiences, the landscapes outside the site boundaries can diminish or even destroy that ability to "feel" the past. The sight of a television relay tower or shopping mall located near the park boundary strongly detracts from historical site experiences.

Managers of a number of historic battlefields in the eastern and southern U.S. concerned about impacts from encroaching commercial development work with state and local officials to establish zoning ordinances to prevent or restrict harmful development around national battlefields. To more permanently protect battlefield sites, the Park Service works with private organizations such as the Nature Conservancy and the Trust for Public Lands to purchase land and scenic easements adjacent to Park Service units (Harrison, 1990).

A Final Challenge

Heritage professionals have in recent years confronted expanded uses of historic and cultural sites. Because of the unconscious socialization that professionals receive in the empiricist/positivist view, they have tended to see history, archaeology, and architecture as intrinsic values of such sites. The emergence of new values causes conflict between heritage managers and the public and among segments of the public. Yet to recognize that heritage sites are *assigned* values is figuratively to open Pandora's Box—to allow a potential flood of alternative uses, and a cacophony of divergent claims. Archaeologists are alarmed that the scientific values of heritage sites, once paramount, are being downplayed. Recreational users are eager to participate in professional studies, yet also seek inspiration from the past. Native Americans resent some New Age uses of sites and it may occur to New Agers to challenge the constitutionality of preferring Native-American religions. These conflicts reflect divergent interests within American society over nature, culture, and the human spirit. A resolution of such issues must emerge from that level. Heritage professionals, while awaiting the outcome of that process, should seek to recognize their own unconscious values and work to foster broader understanding of diverse heritage values in management decisions.

Acknowledgments

We would like to express our thanks to the many people who assisted us in preparing this chapter. Mark McCallum, John Nadolski, Jill Osborn, Peter Pilles, Linda Reynolds, Ken Wilson, and Jerry Wylie provided case studies and other useful information. Patricia Stokowski, Maria Teresa Garcia, and Dolores LaChapelle read the draft and made suggestions that led to significant improvements. We are grateful as well to Bev Driver, Dan Dustin, and Gary Elsner for the opportunity to participate.

Literature Cited

Brown, J. (1991). "Evolution of national forest outfitter/guide management: A case study of the Sedona Ranger District." Unpublished professional paper. School of Forestry, Northern Arizona University, Flagstaff, AZ.

Chippindale, C. (1983). *Stonehenge complete*. Ithaca, NY: Cornell University Press.

Cohen, E. (1992). Pilgrimage and tourism: Convergence and divergence. In A. Morinis (Ed.), *Sacred journeys: The anthropology of pilgrimage* (pp. 47-61). Westport, CT: Greenwood Publishing Group, Inc.

Collingwood, R. (1956). *The idea of history*. New York, NY: Galaxy.

Coombs, J. (1989). Celebrations: Rituals of popular veneration. *Journal of Popular Culture*, (Spring), 71-77.

Crowley, C. (1993, May/June). Out of the Maine stream. *The Saturday Evening Post*, 82-84.

Evans, N. (1986). The tourism of Indian California: A neglected legacy. *Annals of Tourism Research, 13*, 435-450.

Fain, H. (1970). *Between philosophy and history*. Princeton, NJ: Princeton University Press.

Feyerabend, P. (1962). Explanation, reduction, and empiricism. In H. Feigl and G. Maxwell (Eds.), *Minnesota studies in the philosophy of science*, Volume III (pp. 28-97). Minneapolis, MN: University of Minnesota Press.

Finley, D. (1965). *History of the National Trust for Historic Preservation, 1947-1963*. Washington, DC: National Trust for Historic Preservation.

Haederle, M. (1994, May 14). Homage or hokum: Wanna bes are intruding on Native-American ritual. *The Arizona Republic*.

Harrison, R. (1990). Protecting U.S. national parks: Innovative measures for challenging times. *Environment, 32*(1), 18-19.

Hill, J. and Evans, R. (1972). A model for classification and typology. In D. Clarke (Ed.), *Models in archaeology* (pp. 231-274). London, UK: Methuen.

Hosmer, C., Jr. (1981). *Preservation comes of age: From Williamsburg to the National Trust, 1926-1949*. Charlottesville, VA: University Press of Virginia.

Joseph, F. (Ed.). (1992). *Sacred sites: A guidebook to sacred centers and mysterious places in the United States*. St. Paul, MN: Llewellyn Publications.

Kuhn, T. (1962). *The structure of scientific revolutions*. Chicago, IL: University of Chicago Press.

Lakatos, I. (1968). Changes in the problem of inductive logic. In I. Lakatos (Ed.), *The problem of inductive logic* (pp. 315-417). Amsterdam, the Netherlands: North Holland Publishing Company.

Lawliss, C. (1991). Reenacting the Civil War. In *The Civil War sourcebook: A traveler's guide* (pp. 286-289). New York, NY: Harmony Books.

Laxson, J. (1991). How "we" see "them": Tourism and Native Americans. *Annals of Tourism Research, 18*(3), 365-391.

Lee, M. and Stephens, D. (1993). *The assessment of visitor experiences at three cultural parks: Progress report*. Flagstaff, AZ: School of Forestry, Northern Arizona University.

Leerhsen, C. (1991, June). Wheels of misfortune. *Newsweek, 26*.

Linenthal, E. (1991). *Sacred ground: Americans and their battlefields*. Urbana, IL: University of Illinois Press.

Lord, L. (1988). The search for what defines us. *U.S. News and World Report, 105*(7), 50-59.

Lynch, K. (1972). *What time is this place?* Cambridge, MA: MIT Press.

MacCannell, D. (1976). *The tourists: A new theory of the leisure class*. London, UK: MacMillan Publishing.

Meineke, F. (1972). *Historicism: The rise of the new historical outlook* (J. Anderson, trans.). London, UK: Routledge and Kegan Paul.

Morinis, A. (1992). Introduction: The territory of the anthropology of pilgrimage. In A. Morinis (Ed.), *Sacred journeys: The anthropology of pilgrimage* (pp. 1-28). Westport, CT: Greenwood Publishing Group, Inc.

Mulloy, E. (1976). *The history of the National Trust for Historic Preservation, 1963-1973*. Washington, DC: Preservation Press.

Potter, E. (1991, May). Why not relive the Civil War. *Money, 165-66*.

Quine, W. (1963). *From a logical point of view: 9 logico-philosophical essays*. New York, NY: Harper and Row Publishers, Inc.

Schneider, J. (1935). *Report to the Secretary of the Interior on the Preservation of Historic Sites and Buildings*. Washington, DC: U.S. Department of the Interior.

Smith, V. (Ed). (1989). *Hosts and guests: The anthropology of tourism* (2nd ed). Philadelphia, PA: University of Pennsylvania Press.

Smith, V. (1992). Introduction: The guest in quest. *Annals of Tourism Research, 19*, 1-17.

Sussman, V. (1989). From Williamsburg to Conner Prairie. *U.S. News and World Report, 107*(4), 58-62.

Swan, J. (1990). *Sacred places: How the living earth seeks our friendship*. Santa Fe, NM: Bear & Company, Inc.

Tainter, J. and Lucas, G. (1983). Epistemology of the significance concept. *American Antiquity, 48*, 707-719.

Turim, G. (1991). Beyond the line of fire. *Americana, 19*(2), 10.

USDA Forest Service. (1994). PIT traveler. *Passport in time newsletter, 4*(2), 3-8.

van Otten, G. (Ed). (1982). *Respecting a mountain: Proceedings of the Arizona Humanities Council*. Northern Arizona University, Department of Geography 1982 Forum on the development of the Arizona Snow Bowl on the San Francisco Peaks, Arizona.

Ward, R. (1992). The spirits will leave: Preventing the desecration and destruction of Native-American sacred sites on federal land. *Ecology Law Quarterly, 19*(4), 795-846.

Ziman, J. (1968). *Public knowledge: An essay concerning the social dimension of science*. Cambridge, UK: Cambridge University Press.

Additional Reading

Hume, D. [1739] (1961). *A treatise on human nature*. New York, NY: Dolphin.

Locke, J. [1690] (1950). *An essay concerning human understanding*. Oxford, UK: Oxford University Press, Inc.

Hard-to-Define Values and Persons with Disabilities

Leo McAvoy
Division of Recreation, Park and Leisure Studies
The University of Minnesota
Minneapolis, Minnesota

Greg Lais
Wilderness Inquiry, Inc.
Minneapolis, Minnesota

This chapter addresses nature and the human spirit as they relate to persons with disabilities. The nature-based values of persons with disabilities garnered from the literature are presented to help managers better understand the value sets these visitors bring to the resource and some of the associated values that may be especially important to persons with disabilities. There are a number of management challenges related to the continued and expanded provision of opportunities for persons with disabilities to experience the values that add a deep psychological essence to life. These are presented with recommendations on how managers can provide opportunities for persons with disabilities to participate fully in nature-based activities.

Nature and Persons with Disabilities

We especially, with all our motor and sensory constraints, need activities which focus on the limitless, not the limitations. We need beauty to counteract the grit in our lives. We need novelty and discovery. We need wilderness.
Corbet, 1992, p. 30

This quote by Barry Corbet (1992) expresses the important role that nature plays in adding to the essence of life for many persons with disabilities. Mr. Corbet is an outdoor recreation enthusiast, editor, and a T12-L1 paraplegic. (This is a method of describing the location on the spinal column where an injury or trauma occurs: C = cervical, T = thoracic, and L = lumbar. The number indicates the specific vertebrae where the trauma is located.) He used this quote as an introduction to a special edition of the *Spinal Network EXTRA* devoted to wildlands and other undeveloped natural areas. Persons with disabilities are journeying to public and private lands to experience the psychological essence of natural landscapes and undeveloped recreation activities. They are canoeing, rafting, sailing, car camping, going on interpretive hikes, going to visitor centers, hang gliding, snorkeling, hunting, fishing, rock climbing, kayaking, dog sledding, and driving for pleasure. They are also enjoying the benefits of personal gardens and plantings, city parks, and other local natural areas. Some (Corbet for one) would say persons with disabilities receive unique spiritual benefits from the natural landscape. Others, including many with disabilities, would say that persons with disabilities do not receive unique benefits. Rather, they receive the same benefits as everyone else.

Whatever the case, persons with disabilities are now demanding a place at the table when natural resource allocation decisions are made. They are also demanding access to these natural resources. Providing this access is a challenge facing those involved in resource management, a challenge that will increase as the population of the United States ages and becomes increasingly aware of the benefits of nature and their rights as citizens to have access to these natural areas.

Section 504 of the Rehabilitation Act of 1973 (PL 93-112), as amended in 1978, required accessibility to all facilities and programs funded by the federal government. The Americans with Disabilities Act (ADA, PL 101-336) of 1990 extended that mandate to all public facilities and programs regardless of funding sources. The passage of the ADA also prompted many governmental agencies to place a renewed emphasis on accessibility. These two pieces of legislation require public land management agencies at all levels, as well as local agencies and private businesses that serve the public, to make reasonable accommodations to enable persons with disabilities to meet the essential eligibility requirements to gain access to and participate in public services and programs. There are a number of guideline manuals available that explain terms like "reasonable accommodations" and "essential eligibility requirements" for specific types of agencies or businesses (McGovern, 1992). These terms and specific guidelines for accessibility are addressed later in this chapter.

Definitions: Disability, Accessibility, and Integration

Disability. Who are these people who are regarded as disabled? In the passage of the (ADA), the U.S. Congress determined that an individual with a disability is one who has a mental or physical impairment which substantially affects one or more of the major life activities, a record of such an impairment, or is regarded as having such an impairment. The major physical life activities are those an individual does in the course of a day, such as walking, hearing, seeing, speaking, dressing, eating, manipulating objects, and driving. The cognitive activities include understanding, problem-solving, and remembering.

This broad definition includes the disabilities most people would recognize—paralysis, spina bifida, cerebral palsy, deafness, blindness, and Down's Syndrome. It is important to remember that this definition is based on function rather than on the label of a medical diagnosis. The definition is based on function over condition. This means that a person who has had a triple bypass may experience an impairment in the ability to walk; a person who has arthritis may experience an impairment in the ability to manipulate objects; and a person with limited vision may experience an impairment in the ability to read directional signs. These are all impairments in the functions of daily living. Therefore, a person with any of these functional impairments should be considered to have a disability.

When one sees the word "disability" or the word "disabled," the usual image created is that of a person with a mobility impairment in a wheelchair or a person with a visual impairment using a guide dog or a white cane. But the ADA has a much broader definition of disability. Other conditions covered by the definition in the ADA include persons with mental illness, emotional illness, mental retardation, drug addiction, and alcoholism.

The number of people in the United States who are considered to have a disability depends to some degree on how disability is defined. The estimates run from 32.5 million (LaPlante, 1988) to 37.3 million (Kraus and Stoddard, 1989), to the 43 million figure used by Congress in passing the ADA. Whichever figure is used, a significant proportion of our population is limited in the ability to perform selected functions. This number is likely to increase as our population ages.

Accessibility. Accessibility in the past has usually been defined in the context of physical access to buildings or facilities. The Uniform Federal Accessibility Standards (UFAS) define accessible as " . . . a site, building, facility, or portion thereof that complies with these standards and that can be approached, entered, and used by physically disabled people" (ATCBC, 1988, p. 3). This means that accessibility includes not only physical access, but also people that have to be able to use the facility once access is gained.

The ADA has sharpened the definition to include program accessibility in addition to facility accessibility. As stated in a recent guide for universal design and programming published by the USDA Forest Service, "To be truly accessible, programs and facilities must offer the person with a disability an opportunity to achieve experiences similar to those offered others" (USDA Forest Service and PLAE, Inc., 1993, p. 9). As an example, a land management agency that provides physical access to an interpretive exhibit by eliminating steps and providing hard surface travel routes should also provide access to the interpretive program. This may be done by placing signs and displays so seated people can easily view them, using large print and contrasting colors in signs, and by incorporating tactile and participatory elements on signs and in exhibits to enhance other forms of communication for people with visual limitations and/or learning disabilities.

Integration. Integration is a process by which persons with and without disabilities are involved in mutually beneficial activities. Integration includes both physical and social integration. Social integration seeks to develop acceptance for mutually beneficial relationships between individuals with and without disabilities (Lais, 1987). The goal of social integration is to ensure that persons with disabilities are accepted as full members of the community, permitted to participate in the activities of life enjoyed by others, and are able to participate alongside their peers who do not have disabilities (Schleien, McAvoy, Lais and Rynders, 1993). A major tenet of the ADA is the philosophy that services, programs, and activities be provided in the most integrated setting possible. The most integrated setting is one which enables interaction between people with and without disabilities.

Outdoor recreation is increasingly recognized as an excellent medium to achieve social integration, a major goal of persons with disabilities. Social integration is the process of perceiving commonalties that facilitate peer relationships. This process is primarily a function of awareness through personal contact. Resource managers, outfitters, interpreters, rangers, and others provide the resource and the activities for personal contact to occur, usually structuring them to encourage positive interactions. Because these activities accelerate the process of social integration, outdoor recreation is a good medium for the process.

Integration is closely related to the human spirit/spirituality emphasis of this text. Spirituality is a kind of integration, the discovering of one's place in the greater whole. Social integration has a spiritual dimension because it is concerned with the sense of interpersonal intimacy, social support, and the deepening of relationships.

Nature-Based Spiritual Values

Benefits of Nature for Persons with Disabilities

A few years ago, researchers from the University of Minnesota conducted a series of interviews with persons with and without disabilities who had participated in an integrated wilderness trip conducted by a nonprofit organization, Wilderness Inquiry, Inc.. Those with disabilities included persons with cerebral palsy, spina bifida, and head injuries which limited mobility and communication. The participants were asked to reflect on the "spiritual" dimension of their canoe trip into northern Minnesota's Boundary Waters Canoe Area Wilderness. In that study (Stringer and McAvoy, 1992) one person with a disability said:

> *I think everyone has to find spirituality in a different way. I have to be in the out-of-doors setting where things become real clear. The clarity is uncanny, because, maybe because of the pace? And, maybe because the setting that we're in is really simple, yet complex. There's a profound power out there, Mother Nature, or whatever people label it, that is totally unconquerable. That's where my soul is. That's where I come alive. I mean, if there's a God, that's where I feel closest to that God. That's where the peace comes from, that inner peace.* (p. 17)

This quote represents the importance that some persons with disabilities place on the nature-based values discussed in this text. They are the same values that persons without disabilities expressed in this study. Persons with disabilities have had limited opportunity to experience the out-of-doors because of the stereotypic attitudes of service providers that limited opportunities, overprotectiveness of well-meaning family and caregivers, lack of role models, and a lack of appropriate equipment. Resource managers often just didn't think "handicapped folks" would want or be able to do things like fish, hunt, hike, camp, canoe, or kayak. The natural environment was deemed to be too dangerous and inaccessible to persons with disabilities. Social forces and legislative mandates have been changing this attitude over the past two decades. Persons with disabilities are now demanding to be full participants when decisions are made about resource allocation and management because they want to be full participants in all the benefits and values of nature-based recreation.

A strong rationale has been developed in the literature for nature-based programs and opportunities which include persons with disabilities. The effects documented in the literature on participants with disabilities center on the psychological, social, and mental health benefits of contact with nature (McAvoy, Schatz, Stutz, Schleien, and Lais, 1989; McAvoy and Schleien, 1988; Robb and Ewert, 1987; Robb, Havens, and Witman, 1983; Schleien, McAvoy, Lais, and Rynders, 1993). These benefits include increased self-concept, self-esteem, and self-fulfillment, personal growth, increased leisure skills, increased social adjustment and cooperation, enhanced body image, and positive behavior change.

Research on integrated outdoor experiences where persons with and without disabilities participate together has indicated positive attitude and lifestyle changes, willingness to take risks, and higher feelings of self-efficacy (McAvoy, Schatz, Stutz, Schleien and Lais, 1989; Stark, 1981). This same research has documented the benefits that accrue to persons without disabilities on these integrated programs, including: increased understanding of the capabilities of persons with disabilities, more positive attitudes about persons with disabilities, and increased tolerance of differences among people. A recent longitudinal study of the benefits of integrated outdoor recreation experiences confirmed many of the above results and also found that participants reported improved sensitivity to the needs of others, an increased sense of priorities, and an increased respect for nature (Anderson, Schleien, Lais, Seligman, and McAvoy, 1993). The participants in this latter study who had disabilities reported that the wilderness environment appeared to intensify and focus individual

efforts producing a dramatic impact on group development and enhanced social integration of group members. The wilderness setting appeared to be crucial in helping groups form and perform together. The theme of "the wilderness" seemed to permeate the journal entries and interview transcripts that were analyzed for this study.

A group often left out in typical consideration of the "disabled" are mentally challenged persons. The mentally challenged are included in the definition of disabled in the ADA, and mentally challenged persons are capable of realizing all of the benefits of contact with nature that are gained by other population groups (McAvoy and Schleien, 1988). Mentally challenged persons often have difficulty in areas of daily living—interacting with peers in a socially acceptable manner, accepting themselves as worthy of respect and human dignity, and engaging in constructive psychomotor, cognitive and affective activities without inordinate frustration, conflict, and failure. Contact with the outdoors has been shown to have positive impacts on these areas. Research on integrated outdoor education and recreation programs has indicated a number of benefits that accrue to participants who are mentally challenged including cognitive gains in environmental concepts, increased levels of social interaction between persons with and without disabilities, increased peer acceptance, a decrease in socially inappropriate behaviors, and an increase in learning lifelong outdoor leisure skills. It appears that the outdoor environment helps contribute to these positive results by offering a stimulating environment with a high degree of predictability due to a low density of human population, low levels of noise and movement, and a slow rate of change (Schleien, McAvoy, Lais, and Rynders, 1993).

Nature Enhancing the Human Spirit of Persons with Disabilities

Few studies have squarely addressed the issue of the spiritual values that persons with disabilities attach to natural environments. However, two studies give us some indication about these values. Lais, McAvoy and Fredrickson (1992) asked a sample of 80 persons with disabilities from across the country who had visited units of the National Wilderness Preservation System what their motivations were for visiting the wilderness. The highest response (93 percent) was "to experience scenery/natural beauty." The next most frequently stated responses were "to experience nature on its own terms" (81 percent) and "to experience a personal challenge" (78 percent). When asked the high points of their wilderness trip, the top response was "scenery or location." Comparing the responses of persons with disabilities with the responses of persons without disabilities found in large national studies, persons with disabilities seemed to interact with nature for the same reasons as those without disabilities.

In a qualitative case study (quoted earlier) of 13 persons with and without disabilities who had participated on an integrated wilderness canoe trip sponsored by Wilderness Inquiry, Inc. of Minneapolis, Stringer and McAvoy (1992) found that subjects were able to describe some of the spiritual benefits or values related to interaction with the natural environment in a group context. These included:

1. The shared or common spirit between and among people:

   The interaction with a group of people living in nature without the usual constraints and obligations of everyday life often creates an unusual closeness that contributes to a sense of shared spiritual bond between people within the group, and a shared bond with the land.

2. Realization of a power or authority greater than self:

   The vastness, beauty, complexity and majesty of natural places encourages for some a consideration of a deity or other more religious aspects of spirituality, or a more transcendentalist approach of seeing the symbols of a deity in nature.

3. Clarity of inner (or self) knowledge:

   The absence of distractions and obligations and the pace of nature encourages introspection and a clearer picture of who we are, where we are going.

4. Inner feelings of peace, oneness, and strength:

   Time in nature often results in calmness, quietness, tranquillity, contentedness, and equilibrium.

5. Awareness of and attunement to the world and one's place in it:

   The subjects in the study found that time in the wilderness encouraged thinking in new ways about the self, the world around oneself, one's place in the world, and how one fits in the universe.

6. The way in which one relates to fellow humans and to the environment (especially in relation to service):

   Time in the wilderness created moments of intense feeling or emotion prompted by interactions with the natural environment and with others in the group. These intense emotional experiences and feelings created a sense of connectedness to people and to nature resulting in desires to serve others and to protect or preserve the natural environment.

7. Ineffability:

   Participants in this study (and in other studies asking people to describe spiritual benefits) often reported that the spiritual effects of contact with nature cannot be expressed or described in language, they are too great and too deeply held to be described by words.

Most participants in this study indicated that their opportunities to experience spirituality were greatly increased and enhanced while in the wilderness.

The spiritual benefits that contact with nature provides persons with disabilities may best be understood through the words of those who find a special kind of spiritual renewal in such contact, particularly through participation in outdoor recreation activities in majestic outdoor spaces. In the special edition of *Spinal Network EXTRA* noted previously, a number of people with disabilities eloquently expressed these benefits. Richard Holicky (1992), a C5-6 quadriplegic, explains the benefits of a river trip:

> *I still compare and long for things to be the same as before March 5, 1989, the day of my injury. Not much is. But sitting in a boat, getting pushed around by the current, hanging around a campfire with friends—that hasn't changed much. Two old stress-management saws: Rule 1—don't sweat the small stuff. Rule 2—it's all small stuff. Often I lose perspective and forget that anything is small*

stuff, more so since my injury when rain or snow or cold or steps seem to be anything but small stuff. Seeing rainbows from the water, looking up canyon walls 900-feet high, ducking under 6-foot standing waves or baking under the sun while viewing snow-capped mountains lets me dismiss much of the small stuff and think much more about the universe and my place in it. (p. 32)

Janet Zeller, an accessibility coordinator for the USDA Forest Service, and an incomplete C6 quadriplegic, recounted her experiences on a canoe trip in Maine, the first time back on the water after the onset of her disability:

I was back to feeling the quiet of the lake, listening to the loons at night as the sun goes down, the sounds of the night, living with the land—it was something that I had sadly missed. It was that place in my soul that needed to be refilled. And it was. At the end of that week I could say that I felt less disabled than I usually do. And it certainly was not because there were fewer barriers. It was the wilderness, that peace you can't get anywhere else.

Zeller, 1992, p. 45

Mark Schultz has experienced chronic complications from diabetes including blindness, two kidney transplants, a below the knee amputation, and some hearing loss. He had been trying to get back to wildland areas since he became disabled but found it difficult. The first time he was able to access the wilderness with the support he needed was when he participated in an integrated canoe trip on the St Croix National Scenic Riverway separating Wisconsin and Minnesota conducted through an outfitter (Wilderness Inquiry):

I can see a little bit, so I'm going down the St. Croix aware of the large amount of space that was there. To me it felt like the sky had opened up and we were going into a big panoramic scene. Everybody was talking about what was around me, hawks, trees, fish in the water. I could feel the sun glistening on the water. I felt like the world had opened up. That's the big feeling I had then. That's what gave me the inspirational feelings. Being in the canoe and feeling movement, having movement again.

Schultz, 1990

These personal testimonials speak to spiritual and aesthetic values and benefits to be found in nature and in nature-based activities by persons with disabilities. For these people the natural environment encourages a sense of freedom from socially imposed status hierarchies and limitations allowing for more personalized development and actualization. Undeveloped natural areas provide an opportunity for being "transported" away from day-to-day reality, offering a fresh perspective on the issues in our lives. These natural areas do this for everyone, including persons with disabilities. The fact that this happens with persons with disabilities is not unique. Persons with disabilities, after all, are people. What is unique is the place from which persons with disabilities start. Their day-to-day reality is different from those who do not have a disability. The realities of a disability, and the societal attitudes that place limits on those with disabilities, make contact with nature and wildlands just that much more precious. It isn't that persons with disabilities find unique benefits in nature. It is just that they often thought they would not be able or allowed to partake of those benefits. Maybe that is why the benefits seem a bit more precious to them. The beauty, the pace, the natural rhythms and time frequencies provide opportunities for introspective thought, the contemplative reflective experience described by Sax (1980) in his book *Mountains Without Handrails* (which had nothing to do with disabilities). These opportunities are not often found in the fast paced urban world.

Horticultural and Adventure Therapy

The restorative capacities of contact with nature addressed in other chapters in this text are described in detail by Rachel and Stephen Kaplan in their text *The Experience of Nature: A Psychological Perspective* (1989), and in more recent papers by the Kaplans in a symposium on the role of horticulture in human well-being (Kaplan, R., 1992; Kaplan, S., 1992). The Kaplans and other authors hold that contact with the natural world is essential to the well-being of most people. Some of the restorative capacities of contact with nature are especially relevant for persons with disabilities and have been utilized as the basis for two treatment approaches, horticultural therapy and therapeutic adventure programs. Horticultural therapy uses gardening and the care of plants to enhance a number of interpersonal and intrapersonal skill areas for persons with disabilities, in particular persons in institutional settings such as rehabilitation hospitals and clinics (Rothert and Daubert, 1981). This may include, for example, persons who are inpatients in rehabilitation facilities immediately after the onset of a disability, elderly persons recovering from a stroke, or cancer patients recovering from surgery. Horticultural therapy has been found to promote healing in hospitals (Ulrich, 1984; Verderber, 1986), and nature-related activities have enhanced health in cancer patients (Cimprich, 1990). Since many persons with disabilities cannot travel to remote wilderness areas to experience the spiritual benefits that nature provides, the "nearby nature" concept described by the Kaplans is even more important for them. Contact with nature in the form of house plants, personal and community gardens, yard trees and plants, city parks, and nearby natural areas can provide opportunities for tranquillity, peace of mind, focus of concentration, relaxation, and a personal uplifting of the human spirit for persons with temporary or permanent disabilities.

Therapeutic outdoor adventure programs utilize nature-based resources as the setting for treatment of psychological and social illnesses. Camping and other nature-based activities including rock climbing, canoeing, rafting, skiing, and biking are utilized as a therapeutic modality. Part of the mental healthcare system, these programs are often sponsored by institutional or outpatient organizations. The clientele may include psychiatric patients, the mentally ill, chronic schizophrenics, the chemically dependent, persons with autism, or the emotionally disturbed. Research has suggested a number of benefits from therapeutic adventure programs including reduced symptomatology and enhanced ability to function in the community (Driver, Peterson and Easley, 1990). Recently researchers and authors have stressed that these programs have not been studied with the necessary rigor to prove direct benefits from contact with nature (Gillis, 1992; Kelley, 1993) and that these programs cannot cure all the ills of society. Rather, these programs and the land base where the activities occur can only add a piece to the overall therapeutic goal of helping a person reach mental health. A land-based experience in a therapeutic program avoids the contaminating effects of institutional care

which often results in antisocial attitudes and an undermining of the patient's care and development. Perhaps one of the more appropriate uses of these programs is to assist in patient/client psychological evaluation (Kimball, 1990). Observing how a person reacts or adapts to the demands and challenges of an outdoor experience can greatly aid in diagnosis or in evaluation of a person's strengths and weaknesses.

Challenges To Management

Accessibility, Experience, Integrity, and Resource Preservation

The primary challenges to management regarding the provision of opportunities for nature-based spiritual values and experiences for persons with disabilities concerns the issues of accessibility, maintaining the integrity of the experience, and resource preservation. Murphy and Datillo (1989) described the often stated perception that there is an inherent conflict between preservation of environmental quality and the provision of access (for persons with disabilities) to natural environments. They go so far as to say that the Wilderness Act of 1964 and the more recent legislative mandates for accessibility to all public lands and facilities are in direct conflict. If one is to provide access to wilderness for persons with disabilities, the wilderness must be altered, developed, and, perhaps opened to motorized vehicles.

Lais, Ellis, and Galland (1990) have argued forcefully that wilderness values need not and should not be compromised by providing inappropriate development and special provisions to allow persons with disabilities the use of internal combustion engines to gain access. They also claim that persons with disabilities are currently using wilderness areas and that wilderness travel can be an appropriate and enjoyable form of recreation for persons with disabilities. The access versus preservation issue is especially highlighted in the wilderness discussion, but the issue of access and environmental preservation goes beyond wilderness and is an important issue in most natural settings open for public use.

The recent passage of the ADA has focused the issue and the discussion about access and preservation of the undeveloped aspects of natural environments. Public land managers are often confused about what is feasible or even required in providing accessible programs and services. They often do not fully understand the current policies of their respective agencies regarding access and resource protection. As an example, Lais, McAvoy, and Fredrickson (1992) surveyed 304 wilderness managers in all federal wilderness management agencies and found that wilderness managers' understanding of existing individual agency policies on access and resource protection varied greatly within and between agencies.

Both persons with and without disabilities want some natural areas to be preserved in a pristine condition so that the integrity of the natural experience is maintained and the signs of humans are minimal. Neither group wants nature to be paved. Nature experiences should be as pristine for integrated groups as for everyone else. Many persons with and without disabilities advocate that nature not be so controlled and so accessible that the integrity of the natural experience is lost. Persons with disabilities want the nature experience to be every bit as challenging and pristine as it is for others. No one wants areas designated just for "the handicapped." Persons without disabilities have a right to undeveloped areas as do persons with disabilities. Persons with disabilities want to recreate and experience natural areas in integrated social groups (families, friends) that include persons without disabilities. If most natural areas are developed to make them easily accessible (paved walks everywhere) then persons without disabilities will not want to visit these areas, and they will become de facto "handicapped only" areas. The way out of this access/integrity/preservation dilemma is to plan and manage a spectrum of natural areas providing a range of access levels and to design access so that it is not an intrusion on the natural experience.

Guidelines for Universal Access

Two federal agencies have taken lead roles in developing guidelines for making natural environments and programs accessible and yet preserving the naturalness of the setting: the USDA Forest Service and the USDI National Park Service. The National Park Service Office on Accessibility has provided leadership and technical assistance to park management agencies for a number of years. In an interagency effort headed by the Forest Service National Accessibility Program, the *Universal Access to Outdoor Recreation: A Design Guide* (USDA Forest Service and

PLAE, Inc., 1993) has been published and is available for distribution. This publication (hereafter referred to as the *Design Guide*) is a comprehensive set of philosophies and specific guidelines for designing and retrofitting outdoor recreation facilities and programs to make them accessible while preserving the integrity of the natural environment. Much of the information in this section is adapted from material in the *Design Guide* to which the reader is urged to refer for a detailed discussion of the subject.

Universal design is a program and facility design and retrofit approach that accommodates the broadest possible spectrum of people through a single design. It is an approach that accommodates everyone including persons with disabilities. An example of the application of universal design would be a common accessible ramp in lieu of stairs at the entrance to an interpretive display in a park. Such a ramp can be used by a wide range of people including those with disabilities. It can be used by persons with no obvious impairment, those with temporary impairments like a sprained ankle or a sore back, by people who have difficulty with balance or in seeing steps because of visual problems, or a person using a wheelchair. It eliminates the provision of separate facilities or programs for the disabled and instead stresses the accommodation of all ability levels in an integrated setting and approach.

The *Design Guide* is based on the recreation opportunity spectrum (ROS) planning and management concept (Clark and Stankey, 1979; Driver and Brown, 1978; USDA Forest Service, 1990). The ROS is based on the premise that quality outdoor recreation experiences are best provided through a diversity of opportunities and that outdoor recreation lands provide certain types of opportunities based on the setting. People choose the setting that best suits their desired recreation experience. Those seeking primitive types of opportunities will choose a primitive setting, and those seeking a developed opportunity will select a more developed setting. The current ROS guidelines for the Forest Service list six categories of settings. The *Design Guide* has collapsed those six into four categories:

1. urban/rural areas,
2. roaded natural areas,
3. semiprimitive areas, and
4. primitive areas.

The *Design Guide* approach ties the level of expected access to a particular outdoor recreation environment to its placement on the ROS. Urban/rural areas are highly developed, and one would expect easy access. Roaded natural areas are less developed and one would expect moderate access. Semiprimitive areas are rarely developed, and one would expect difficult access. Primitive areas have few if any modifications to accommodate visitors, and one would expect access there to be most difficult.

A major premise of the approach in the new *Design Guide* is that there is a direct correlation between customer expectation and level of access. Some sites are going to be more accessible than others. This is in line with one of the major foundations of accessibility legislation that development for accessibility is not required if it would fundamentally alter the nature of the experience. This helps to solve the usual dilemma of resource managers trying to figure out how they can provide access while preserving the naturalness of the resource. In this way a range of access is provided from highly developed access to no development for access. Highly developed facilities will be completely accessible, those less developed less accessible, and wilderness areas where there are no modifications solely for the purpose of access.

A land manager may ask, "How does all of this information help provide opportunities for nature-based spiritual experiences for persons with disabilities? How does it help me decide if I should provide more development so access can be gained by persons with disabilities? How can I provide access and yet protect the resource from inappropriate development?" When faced with the question of developing or not developing for access, the recreation land manager usually has the choices of:

- modifying the site to achieve the desired level of accessibility according to customer expectations;

- or, preserving (not modifying) a site or a part of a site and changing the level of accessibility to a different ROS classification (for that site or part of a site only).

The land manager has two sets of guidelines to reference when making a decision as to the appropriateness and standards of types of development to provide access in the natural environment. The Architectural and Transportation Barriers Compliance Board (ATBCB) in 1991 published the *Americans With Disabilities Act: Accessibility Guidelines for Buildings and Facilities* (ADAAG). ADAAG guidelines apply to the built environment only. Development and retrofitting of buildings, visitor centers, and parking lots must be according to the guidelines in ADAAG. No comparable standards currently exist for outdoor recreation environments like campgrounds, recreational trails, picnic areas, or beaches. The new *Design Guide* offers guidelines for development and retrofitting of these types of areas in the outdoor environment, but the guidelines have not yet been formally accepted and codified by the ATBCB. The *Design Guide* guidelines are expected to be accepted by the ATBCB in the near future.

The *Design Guide* describes three criteria that determine the appropriate action when faced with decisions regarding accessibility:

1. *Customer Expectations of the Site.* When people go to a highly developed campsite or interpretive display, they expect a high level of accessibility similar to facilities in urban areas. When people go to a rustic, relatively undeveloped facility, they expect fewer amenities, a more natural landscape, and less accessibility. When people go to a primitive area, they expect few if any amenities and difficult access.

2. *Degree of Structural Modifications to the Site.* The level of accessibility at a site should be consistent with the level of development at the site. Highly developed sites with a high degree of structural modification should provide a high degree of access. Sites where structural modifications are rare may provide more difficult access.

3. *Natural Features.* Persons with disabilities are attracted to natural sites for the same reasons as everyone else, the natural beauty and majesty of natural systems. They do not want the natural beauty of a site destroyed in the process of making those features more accessible. Site modifications that destroy the fundamental nature of the outdoor experience are not mandated by law and are not wanted by persons with or without disabilities.

The *Design Guide* gives details of the application of the above guidelines. (The reader is encouraged to refer to the *Design Guide* for specific information.) Some overall principles that should guide manager decisions in these situations are:

- to provide the level of access that corresponds to the classification of the site (or the portion of the site) on the ROS;

- to attempt to provide full access to the spaces and elements of a site that are basic to the recreation experience being offered (e.g., parking area, restrooms, picnic units, and water hydrants in a picnic facility); and

- to notify visitors of the levels of access of the site and portions of the site so the visitors can decide if those portions of the site are appropriate for them.

Recommendations for Managers

The following are recommendations on how managers can provide opportunities for persons with disabilities to participate fully in nature-based experiences that lend deep psychological essence and spiritual meaning to their lives.

Do Not Make Assumptions. One of the worst things a manager can do in trying to provide nature-based experiences for persons with disabilities is to assume that the manager knows what these persons want and can do. Research and experience indicate that persons with disabilities are just as varied in their choices for environments, and their ability to access those environments, as the rest of the population. Some have limited desire to experience the outdoors. They prefer to stay in an urban environment with all its attendant development and amenities, as do many persons without disabilities. Other persons with disabilities (like some in the aforementioned personal stories) are literally climbing mountains and going to extremely remote and rugged places. Do not assume that persons with disabilities want all natural areas modified so that access is easy. Lais, McAvoy, and Fredrickson (1992) surveyed wilderness managers and studied persons with disabilities who had visited the National Wilderness Preservation System (NWPS). Wilderness managers in that study estimated that approximately 17,000 people with disabilities visit the NWPS annually, and they visit in the same ways

and for the same reasons as people without disabilities. They also found that the majority (76 percent) of the respondents with disabilities do not believe that the restrictions on mechanized use stated in the Wilderness Act diminish their ability to enjoy the wilderness. They do not want wilderness areas developed to provide easy access.

A key point for managers is to remember that one of the reasons persons with disabilities go to public lands is for the spiritual, as well as recreational and therapeutic, value of the place. The opportunity to feed the human spirit is as important for persons with disabilities as it is for any other population or more so.

Seek Input from Persons with Disabilities. Managers do need to confer with persons with disabilities when making policy decisions regarding access and preservation. This may come in the form of advisory committees, surveys or focus groups, or from contacting representatives of various advocacy groups for persons with disabilities in the community. Managers do have to be careful to contact a number of people in this process. Beware of getting information from a limited number of self-proclaimed experts who say they speak "for the disabled community." There are a number of professional organizations that work with persons with disabilities in outdoor programs that can be of help, as can national advocacy groups with local chapters (see Schleien, McAvoy, Lais, and Rynders 1993 for a list of resource organizations). Managers should tap the resources within their communities that can help in understanding the needs and capabilities of persons with disabilities. Many communities have centers for independent living, local advocacy groups, rehabilitation facilities, and others that can provide information.

Managers should be careful of people with another agenda using the issue of access and the disabled as an opportunity to make a political statement or advance a political agenda that has little to do with access. The access/disability issue has been used in some areas to provide development and access for others, rather than for those with disabilities. Persons with disabilities are perfectly willing and able to speak for themselves regarding these issues.

Promote Social Integration Rather than Special Permits and Waivers. The ADA states that programs and services shall be provided in the most integrated setting possible. The most integrated setting is the one which enables interaction between people with and without disabilities to the maximum extent feasible. Separate or different programs and services specifically for persons with disabilities are only acceptable in the event they are necessary to provide equally effective benefits and services. Individuals with disabilities may not be denied the right to participate in "regular" outdoor recreation opportunities and programming even if there is a separate program. Programs are not required to guarantee successful participation, but they must offer equal opportunity for participation.

Managers should look at the natural environment as a wonderful medium for the promotion of social integration. They should use outdoor facilities as an opportunity for everyone to interact with nature together regardless of ability level. The nation's parks and outdoor resources have long been regarded as a symbol of the egalitarian basis of this culture and they should be utilized to make that egalitarian dream a reality for people with disabilities. Access to these majestic and peaceful places should be a regular part of the maintenance of a healthy life and should not require special permits. Managers are encouraged to avoid issuing special permits and the waiver of fees for persons with disabilities based on stereotypes. Not all persons with disabilities are poor. If special permits are to be granted they are to be based on reality rather than stereotypes.

Make Primary Activities and Elements Accessible. Managers should move to make primary activities and elements necessary to the nature-based experience accessible without damaging the natural qualities of the resource. This means using the ROS to establish appropriate levels of accessibility. An element is defined in the *Design Guide* as an architectural or mechanical component of a building, facility, space, or site (USDA Forest Service and PLAE, 1993). These basic activities and elements may include parking areas, informational signs, restrooms, trailheads, fishing piers, picnic areas, and interpretive displays. Managers should also move to install telecommunications devices for the deaf (TDDs) in ranger stations and facility offices.

Base Essential Eligibility Requirements on Fact. In order to participate in a program, service or activity, an individual must be able to meet essential eligibility requirements for use, enjoyment of, or participation in, programs. The purpose of essential eligibility requirements is to establish whether or not an individual can participate in an activity based on her or his ability to perform the basic eligibility criteria of the activity.

The ADA does not state what constitutes essential eligibility in every program or service provided throughout the United States. This will only be determined over time through case law. However, if managers proactively embrace a common sense approach they will not only lessen the chance of lawsuits, but they will also implement better customer service.

The concept of essential eligibility is something most managers already do. The goal of developing essential eligibility guidelines is to provide managers and visitors with the information they need to make accurate, objective assessments when deciding if their abilities are appropriate for an activity. This means managers must articulate guidelines for participation that are based on functional components and that are applied equally to everyone. Managers should be sure that the essential eligibility requirements for travel in or use of an area or program are based on fact and not on stereotypes. These requirements should be established based on functional criteria that are demonstrable and rational. Instead of disqualifying a person from a raft trip simply because she or he uses a wheelchair, the manager must apply functional guidelines for participation in the activity such as the ability to remain floating in a personal flotation device with one's head out of the water if the raft is overturned. The manager must identify the basic eligibility criteria of the experience provided and then determine whether the individual can perform those functions.

The eligibility guidelines must be based on commonly accepted standards for recreation resource management as a whole. We suggest that these guidelines be based on safety, quality, and cost-effectiveness. Safety is a primary concern, and ADA recognizes the primary importance of safety, provided the assessment of safety is based on fact, not stereotypes or fear. As an example, if a managing agency prohibited persons with disabilities from kayaking through a challenging set of rapids because of safety concerns, the managing agency had better be able to defend that action based on facts and not on stereotypes of what persons with disabilities are supposed to be able to do or not do.

Some persons with disabilities may be highly skilled in kayaking, have appropriate equipment, and the support necessary to participate in this activity safely. Managers need to provide quality opportunities and services to visitors whether or not the visitor has a disability.

The ADA recognizes that the process of making a program or facility accessible should not substantially alter the nature of the activity. Managers must make sure that they do not detract from the quality of the nature experience or agency service. Cost-effectiveness is a concern of everyone. Managers are concerned with providing the highest safety and quality at the lowest possible cost. The ADA directs managers to make reasonable accommodations for persons with disabilities to meet the essential eligibility requirements for participation in programs, services, and activities. Reasonable accommodations are such that they would not fundamentally alter the nature of the services provided by the program. When an accommodation would result in a substantial economic or administrative burden, or would result in a fundamental alteration of the nature of the service, a manager may refuse to make accommodation. Examples of reasonable accommodations would include auxiliary services like sign language interpreters, assistive listening devices, large print materials; removing architectural barriers like curbs, steps, inaccessible restrooms; and providing accessible transportation if transportation is part of the activity.

Develop Consistent Guidelines and Policies. Managers should develop guidelines and consistent policies across sites within a system and across systems of land management agencies. These should be guidelines regarding accommodations, special permits, facility modifications, and policy modifications that refer to use by persons with disabilities. Managers should be encouraged to facilitate resource use by persons with disabilities that is consistent with the goals of resource preservation. Managers should work with persons with disabilities, outfitters, and other programs that use the resources in the development of these guidelines.

Managers should develop guidelines that are consistent across agencies. Federal agencies are moving to develop such a set of uniform guidelines as indicated in the new *Design Guide* developed by the USDA Forest Service and PLAE Inc. (1993). As an example of policies not being uniform, the Na-

tional Park Service (NPS) has allowed the use of motorized wheelchairs in NPS wilderness areas by persons with disabilities while their use has been prohibited in wilderness areas managed by the Forest Service. This inconsistency has caused confusion about which policies are in effect among some managers of these agencies (Lais, McAvoy, and Fredrickson, 1992).

Provide Training. Managers should receive training to increase their general awareness of disability issues and specific awareness of policies, guidelines and practices regarding the use of natural areas by persons with disabilities. Private parties that offer service to the public on public lands (concessionaires and outfitters) should also be trained in making services and facilities fully accessible to persons with disabilities. At least three training programs are currently available to assist managers in this training:

1. The University of Minnesota and Wilderness Inquiry, Inc. in Minneapolis have worked with the Forest Service to design a training program on universal design for facilities and programs.

2. The Indiana University in Bloomington has worked with the National Park Service to develop a training program making facilities and programs accessible.

3. The Wilderness Inquiry, Inc. has worked with the Forest Service and America Outdoors to develop a training program for concessionaires, outfitters, and others in resource management and program administration.

Provide Program Opportunities and Program Adaptation. One of the major challenges for persons with disabilities gaining access to undeveloped public lands is that of mobility. Some areas are just too rugged for a person to gain access in a wheelchair, on crutches, or other prosthetic devices. Persons with disabilities and a number of adventure travel organizations overcome this obstacle by using water as a travel medium. Canoes, boats, kayaks, rafts, and dogsleds allow persons with mobility impairments to gain access to some of America's most pristine and rugged landscapes. The water allows access without the need for leg mobility. Horses can provide access to other areas for some. Managers should try to provide information for visitors about local water-based programs that can provide access for a wide range of people.

All people should participate in programs in as normal a manner as possible. There may be some instances when programs need to be adapted to make them accessible to as wide a range of abilities as possible. If a program is adapted, the following are some guidelines for successful and appropriate adaptations (Schleien, McAvoy, Lais, and Rynders, 1993):

- Adapt only when necessary. Do not underestimate the ability level of participants. A simplified version of an activity may not be required.

- View adaptations as temporary and transitional. Sometimes adaptations are a poor substitute for the real thing. A visitor center may not be able to provide access to an adjacent marsh because of unstable terrain and a lack of funding to build a boardwalk. Instead, a model of the marsh is provided in the accessible visitor center building. As soon as funding can be obtained, the boardwalk should be built to allow access to the marsh for everyone.

- Adapt on an individual basis. Treat all persons as individuals and make special arrangements on an individual basis.

- Adapt for normalization. If a modification is necessary, keep it as close to the standard version as possible. Promote social integration by making people aware of similarities rather than differences.

- Adapt for availability. Try to have the adaptation be as close to the real thing as possible and as close to the conditions the person with disabilities will encounter at other sites and programs.

Realize the Potential of Information and Marketing. Managers and agencies should develop better and more comprehensive information about what is available to persons with disabilities who may want to use agency lands for the spiritual benefits described in this text. Information should be readily available that describes the level of access of all areas and sites managed by specific agencies so persons with disabilities can make informed decisions about where to go and what to do on-site. The marketing of these opportunities can make ar-

eas available for a broader spectrum of the population, including persons with disabilities.

Utilize Cooperative Agreements with Outfitters and Programs. Managers can work with outfitters and other cooperating businesses and organizations to offer integrated, accessible services to visitors. Information about these integrated or accessible opportunities should be available and distributed by the managing agency. This can greatly expand the range of services available to everyone including those with disabilities.

Conclusion

A key aspect of the ADA and other social forces related to public services and public lands is the concept of integration. Persons with disabilities do not want to be served separately from the rest of society. "Trails for the handicapped" are undesirable because persons with disabilities want to participate with others in a full range of land-based recreational and cultural experiences. Land managers would do well to remember that persons with disabilities participate in natural environment-based activities not only for the therapeutic benefits, but also for the same reasons as do persons without disabilities. Those reasons include a feeling of connection with the natural world.

Literature Cited

Anderson, L., Schleien, S., Lais, G., Seligman, D., and McAvoy, L. (1993). *Integration through adventure: Results of a three-year longitudinal study* (Grant No. H128J00034). Washington, DC: U.S. Department of Education.

Architectural and Transportation Barriers Compliance Board (ATBCB). (1988). *Uniform federal accessibility standards*. Washington, DC.

Architectural and Transportation Barriers Compliance Board (ATBCB). (1991). *Americans with Disabilities Act: Accessibility guidelines for buildings and facilities*. Washington, DC.

Cimprich, B. (1990). *Attentional fatigue and restoration in individuals with cancer*. Unpublished doctoral dissertation, University of Michigan, Ann Arbor, MI.

Clark, R. and Stankey, G. (1979). *The recreation opportunity spectrum: A framework for planning, management, and research*. Portland, OR: USDA Forest Service, Pacific Northwest Forest and Range Experiment Station.

Corbet, B. (1992). Going wild: Your guide to outdoor adventure. *Spinal Network EXTRA, Spring, 30*, 31, 44-49.

Driver, B. and Brown, P. (1978). *The opportunity spectrum concept and behavior information in outdoor recreation resource supply inventories: A rationale*. Fort Collins, CO: USDA Forest Service, Rocky Mountain Forest and Range Experiment Station.

Driver, B., Peterson, G., and Easley, A. (1990). Benefits perceived by past participants in the N. O. L. S. Wind River Wilderness Course: A methodological inquiry. In *The use of wilderness for personal growth, therapy, and education* (pp. 52-62) (General Technical Report RM-193). Fort Collins, CO: Rocky Mountain Forest and Range Experiment Station, USDA Forest Service.

Gillis, H. (1992). Therapeutic uses of adventure-challenge-outdoor-wilderness: Theory and research. In K. Henderson (Ed.), *Coalition for Education in the Outdoors Research Symposium Proceedings* (pp. 35-47). Cortland, NY: Coalition for Education in the Outdoors, State University of New York College at Cortland.

Holicky, R. (1992). Is there wilderness after quadriplegia? *Spinal Network EXTRA*, Spring, 32.

Kaplan, R. (1992). The psychological benefits of nearby nature. In D. Relf (Ed.), *The role of horticulture in human well-being and social development: A national symposium* (pp. 125-133). Portland, OR: Timber Press, Inc.

Kaplan, R. and Kaplan, S. (1989). *The experience of nature: A psychological perspective*. New York, NY: Cambridge University Press.

Kaplan, S. (1992). The restorative environment: Nature and human experiences. In D. Relf (Ed.), *The role of horticulture in human well-being and social development: A national symposium* (pp. 134-141). Portland, OR: Timber Press, Inc.

Kelley, M. (1993). The therapeutic potential of outdoor adventure: A review with a focus on adults with mental illness. *Therapeutic Recreation Journal, 27* (2), 110-125.

Kimball, R. (1990). The Santa Fe mountain school. In J. Miles and S. Priest (Eds.), *Adventure Education* (pp. 11-15). State College, PA: Venture Publishing, Inc.

Kraus, L. and Stoddard, S. (1989). *Chartbook on disability in the United States*. Washington, DC: National Institute on Disability and Rehabilitation Research.

Lais, G. (1987). Toward fullest participation: Suggested leadership techniques for integrated adventure programming. In *Bradford Papers Annual 2*, (pp. 55-64). Bloomington, IN: Department of Recreation and Park Administration, Indiana University.

Lais, G., Ellis, W., and Galland, J. (1990). Access to wilderness by persons with disabilities. In D. Lime (Ed.), *Managing America's enduring wilderness resource* (pp. 243-249). St Paul, MN: Minnesota Extension Service, University of Minnesota.

Lais, G., McAvoy, L., and Fredrickson, L. (1992). *Wilderness accessibility for people with disabilities: A report to the President and the Congress of the United States on section 507 (a) of the Americans with Disabilities Act*. Washington, DC: National Council on Disability.

LaPlante, M. (1988). *Data on disability from the National Health Interview Survey, 1983-1985: An InfoUse Report*. Washington, DC: U.S. National Institute on Disability and Rehabilitation Research.

McAvoy, L., Schatz, E., Stutz, M., Schleien, S., and Lais, G. (1989). Integrated wilderness adventure: Effects on personal and lifestyle traits of persons with and without disabilities. *Therapeutic Recreation Journal, 23* (3), 51-64.

McAvoy, L. and Schleien, S. (1988). Effects of integrated interpretive programs on persons with and without disabilities. In L. Beck (Ed.), *Research in interpretation: Proceedings of the 1988 National Association of Interpretation Research Symposium* (pp. 13-26). San Diego, CA: Institute for Leisure Behavior, San Diego State University.

McGovern, J. (1992). *The ADA self-evaluation: A handbook for compliance with the Americans with Disabilities Act by parks and recreation agencies*. Arlington, VA: National Recreation and Park Association.

Murphy, W. and Datillo, J. (1989). Wilderness preservation and accessibility for people with disabilities: A discussion. *Therapeutic Recreation Journal, 23* (3), 19-26.

Robb, G. and Ewert, A. (1987). Risk recreation and persons with disabilities. *Therapeutic Recreation Journal, 21* (1), 58-69.

Robb, G., Havens, M., and Witman, J. (1983). *Special education . . . naturally*. Bloomington, IN: Indiana University.

Rothert, E. and Daubert, J. (1981). *Horticultural therapy at a physical rehabilitation facility*. Glencoe, IL: Chicago Horticultural Society.

Sax, J. (1980). *Mountains without handrails: Reflections on the national parks*. Ann Arbor, MI: University of Michigan Press.

Schleien, S., McAvoy, L., Lais, G., and Rynders, J. (1993). *Integrated outdoor education and adventure programs*. Champaign, IL: Sagamore Publishing, Inc.

Schultz, M. (1990). [Personal benefits of a Wilderness Inquiry, Inc. integrated wilderness trip]. Unpublished raw data.

Stark, G. (1981). *Wilderness Inquiry II: Six perspectives on a common experience*. (Wilderness Inquiry, Inc., 1313 5th Street, Minneapolis, MN 55414).

Stringer, L. and McAvoy, L. (1992). The need for something different: Spirituality and wilderness adventure. *Journal of Experiential Education, 15* (1), 13-20

Ulrich, R. (1984). View through a window may influence recovery from surgery. *Science, 224*, 420-421.

USDA Forest Service. (1990). *ROS primer field guide*. R6-REC-021-90. Portland, OR.

USDA Forest Service and PLAE, Inc. (1993). *Universal access to outdoor recreation: A Design Guide*. Berkeley, CA: PLAE, Inc.

Verderber, S. (1986). Dimensions of person-window transactions in the hospital environment. *Environment and Behavior, 18* (4), 450-466.

Zeller, J. (1992). Is there wilderness after quadriplegia? *Spinal Network EXTRA, Spring*, 32

Additional Reading

Peer, L. (1992). What wilderness means to a high quad. *Spinal Network EXTRA*, Spring, 32.

Belief, Wholeness, and Experience: Sensitizing Professional Land Managers to Spiritual Values

Herb Hammond
Silva Ecosystem Consultants
Winlaw, British Columbia, Canada

Stephanie Judy
Silva Ecosystem Consultants
Winlaw, British Columbia, Canada

Introduction

We have spent the last 15 years working on the ground, doing land use evaluation and planning with indigenous people and rural communities—with people who say, unequivocally, "This land is our home . . . This land is sacred to our people . . . This stream, this forest, this fish, this tree is essential to our way of life." We have used our expertise to help people protect the land and its values.

In this process we have learned a lot. We are happy to share what we have learned, with the caveat that it is the result of our personal experience and not a set of scientific findings or precise definitions. Most aspects of protecting spiritual values cannot be defined scientifically because spiritual values are not quantifiable but part of an interconnected whole.

We are speaking from the viewpoint of university-trained professionals who work every day with people whose spiritual values dominate their method of land use. These are also people—let's not kid ourselves about this—whose land has been degraded, in many cases beyond reclamation, by other people who have "managed" it either for them or in spite of them.

We have not, by and large, found academic approaches very helpful. We have found it helpful to listen, to be humble, and to believe what the people tell us. We have found it helpful to know and respect who we are (a scientist and a writer, skilled in collecting, analyzing, and interpreting data), and to respect the people with whom we are working. To work *with* these groups we have had to learn some humbling lessons about the limits of our own knowledge and experience. We have become sensitized to a much wider range of values than we learned about in academic situations.

One thing we have learned is that hard science, data, objectivity, and rational analysis are not enough. We have learned to take a "soft" approach: to respect not only the diversity of the land we consider, but also the diversity of human thought and culture. We have learned that our university-trained style of categorizing and analyzing is not the only way. We have learned that demanding a precise definition of every term can be counterproductive and that demanding hard evidence to substantiate every issue is missing the point. We have learned to leave room for doubt and also for truth, especially the kinds of truth that are not reachable by linear or numerical means.

How can land management professionals learn to care for spiritual values? Given our experience, we cannot assume a hard-nosed, academic approach to this topic. No academic has yet defined spiritual values unequivocally. Similarly, we cannot define exhaustively every concept we use and support every assertion with research. We can only tell you what we have found to be true and what we think would help others in our situation.

In our experience, caring for spiritual values means that we must understand the land and think about our plans for it in ways that are often labelled nonlinear or wholistic. Knowing the label for this mode of thought, however, does not mean that we succeed in achieving it. To do this, most of us must change our way of thinking. The first step in change is awareness; hence, our concern in this chapter is with ways of sensitizing professional land managers to spiritual values.

The principles and examples offered are drawn primarily from our direct experience in ecosystem-based planning where a central objective is to care for the spiritual values of indigenous people and rural communities, groups, and individuals who are living *with* an ecosystem "from the inside," perceiving it as a web of interconnected life and energy of which humans are only a part. We have found that achieving such an objective is not a simple task for most conventionally-trained North American land managers—those who are trained and paid to understand an ecosystem "from the outside," perceiving it as a resource with economic values that must be managed or manipulated in some way by professionals who have been trained to do so. That very training, however, may leave a land manager poorly prepared to understand and care for noneconomic values, particularly those that are categorized as "spiritual" or "hard-to-define."

John Sallenave, senior policy advisor with the Canadian Arctic Resources Committee, has experienced this challenge in the context of environmental impact assessments (EIAs):

> *In essence, EIAs are reductionist in their approach, breaking down each study into various biophysical components, which are then measured and evaluated independently from one another and from the human components.*

> *This process of compartmentalizing biophysical components is inconsistent with the aboriginal view of the world, which sees all aspects of the environment as equally important. In aboriginal peoples' "holistic" view, biophysical components can be separated neither from each other nor from the human components— the social, cultural, spiritual, and economic aspects of the environment.*
>
> Sallenave, 1994, p. 17

This text addresses a wide range of hard-to-define values. Because we work in the forest and with forest-based communities, we use the forest ecosystem and forest-based spiritual values as our main reference points. What we say, however, applies to other kinds of terrestrial ecosystems as well, and we hope that our experience in land use planning with indigenous people and rural communities in Canada is relevant to many other settings where hard-to-define values exist. We concentrate on land that is considered spiritual, sacred, or home. We do not address visual and landscape design to protect recreational values (golf courses, ski hills, hiking trails) because we believe a large body of material already exists about this, and others can offer better suggestions. We are discussing here spiritual places that are intuited rather than created, appreciated rather than managed.

We know from personal experience that it is possible to become sensitized to diverse spiritual values that relate to the land. At the same time, we believe that there is no way to teach anyone how to analyze or quantify spiritual values simply because such values are not knowable by these means. Conventional prescriptive methods of land management will be forever incompatible with caring for spiritual values, and, indeed, a prescriptive mentality may be unable to grasp the problem itself.

Parallels do exist between principles of ecosystem-based management and principles of caring for spiritual values. Practicing genuine ecosystem-based management means that we learn from the ecosystem itself how human use can be distributed and accommodated (if it can be at all). It means that we understand that the forest sustains us—we do not sustain the forest. Therefore, rather than imposing formulae that reflect human-centered plans for timber quotas or recreation user-days, we focus our planning on the protection and maintenance of forest functioning at all scales through time.

Similarly, if we are caring for spiritual values, we cannot generate formulae that will show us how to do it. We must learn what we can from the cultures and people involved. In doing so, we may well find—particularly where indigenous spiritual values or sacred land are concerned—that we can never fully comprehend the issues. We will certainly never find a formula waiting to absorb hard data and spit out cut blocks, campsites, and ski trails. We will have to operate with sensitivity and compassion while focusing our decision making on protection. *We cannot mitigate damage to spiritual values.*

When we consider the question of how to educate land managers to care for spiritual values, we quickly come up against the problem of evaluation. Conventional methods of measuring learning—grades, test scores, college credits, continuing education (CE) units, or certification—can never represent the acquisition of sensitivity to spiritual values. At best, such measures can only attest that a learner had an opportunity to do so. The only evidence of actual learning is shown in how the learner lives. As David Orr puts it, "Environmental education ought to change the way people live, not just how we talk" (1992, p. 91).

True sensitization to spiritual values is made evident not in the questions we can answer (as on an exam) but in the questions we ask and how we seek the answers. For example, someone who is sensitized to spiritual values will not ask,

"How can I get these people to understand and accept what I'm saying,"

but, "What can I do to understand and accommodate what these people are saying?"

Not, "How can we cover our tracks?"

but, "How can we leave no tracks?"

Not "How much can we take?"

but, "What must we leave?"

Not, "How can we improve on nature?"

but, "How can we plan with nature?"

The ideas expressed in this chapter have grown out of our direct experience, and this opportunity to review the meaning of our experience in caring for spiritual values has reminded us once more of the limits of our own knowledge. In presenting these ideas, we hope we have not trespassed into areas that we know too little about. We do not presume to speak for anyone but ourselves, and especially, we cannot speak for indigenous people.

Principles: What Constitutes Education for Spiritual Values?

What constitutes a viable kind of education for sensitizing land use managers to spiritual values? We can't outline a curriculum leading to a certificate, but we can suggest twelve principles that we believe rest at the core of sensitivity to spiritual values. (Although the principles are numbered from 1 to 12, the order does not represent a sequence or a hierarchy. All of the principles are important, and all overlap and reinforce one another.)

1. *To search for and accommodate natural connectedness.* One should focus on how an ecosystem sustains itself, not on how it "produces" any particular commodity or event such as timber, sport fishing opportunities, or tourism revenue. Fully functioning cultures and societies require fully functioning ecosystems. Cultures are, in fact, subsets of their ecosystems.

Being aware of natural connectedness poses an intellectual hurdle for some. Traditional Western thought patterns lead one to see separations more easily than connections, boundaries more easily than transitions, humans as "masters" of nature rather than humans as part of nature. Ecologist Stan Rowe pinpoints the major defect in Western thought as conceiving of the Earth as resource rather than as source:

The ways that we use and exploit the earth's surface are direct and visible measures of [our] sensitivity to our source. The landscapes of our making match and reflect society's cultural inscapes.

Rowe, 1990, p. 15

Consider for a moment "the landscapes of our making" in North America—the multilane highways, the shopping malls, the suburban residential grids, the fragmented forests. Manipulation of the Earth demonstrates linear, compartmentalized, human-centered thinking. Sensitivity to spiritual values, on the other hand, depends on nonlinear, wholistic, ecosystem-centered understanding.

2. *To focus on maintaining fully-functioning ecosystems at all scales.* Protecting spiritual values involves much more than protecting one tree, one grave site, or one fishing spot along a creek. Protecting spiritual values or any other values means protecting whole ecosystems from a microbial community to an entire drainage basin.

For many, this principle means rethinking the relationship to land and water. It will be necessary to begin thinking in terms of forests rather than commodities, in terms of interactions rather than specific sites. For example, one may learn that a particular boulder along a particular river in an indigenous peoples' territory is a traditional fishing site used for many generations. Protecting that boulder, and maybe a few acres around it, will not protect the value of this site for the people who use it. It is also necessary to protect the river itself, all the way up to its headwaters, in order to protect the purity of the water, the continuity of fish stocks, and the spirits of the river. It is also necessary to protect the aesthetic quality—both what can be seen and what can be heard—along all the trails to and from the site. And it is necessary to enable the people to protect and maintain their culture so that the fishing site is not a museum, but a vibrant, useful, and spiritual part of the whole.

Ultimately, one will find that spiritual sites do not have borders. In order to protect a spiritual site that may appear to be only a few yards square, one must maintain the functioning of a whole landscape. One of the most valuable concepts to be learned from indigenous cultures is that "everything is everywhere." The values inherent in the land are not enclosed in neat boundaries; they are distributed in repeating patterns throughout a landscape. In mapping land use patterns with indigenous people, for example, one is told that hunting happens here . . . and here . . . and over here . . . and also here . . . and here, too. Fishing? Same thing. Here's a good place to fish . . . and here's another one . . . and there are some more here. Berry-picking? Same thing. Sacred places? Same thing. Good timber for building long houses? Same thing. Everything is everywhere.

If everything is everywhere, if everything is interconnected, then what is done in one place will affect what is possible in another. One can't degrade the land for timber here and still expect to gather berries and catch salmon over there. One can't draw a boundary on a map and say, "You keep your spirits on this side of the line, and we'll keep our logging machinery on that side." If everything is everywhere, the result, in terms of planning and using the land, is that every place must be treated in the same way: every site must be protected and maintained as a fully-functioning ecosystem at all times. One can't draw a boundary on a map and say, "It's okay, to maintain ecosystem functioning on this side of the line and compromise it on that side."

Protecting and maintaining fully functioning ecosystems does not mean that additional timber can be cut or any more golf courses built. It does mean that whether one is cutting trees, designing recreational facilities, or protecting sacred land, one needs to know from whom to learn, when to act, where to act, how to act, and what to do. The required knowledge is only partly scientific. Some of the most vital information about protecting ecosystem functioning is often held by the people who truely know the land. This information is held as wisdom—the combination of knowledge and intuition. Protecting spiritual values in particular will be done best by those who are spiritually connected to the land.

In our own work, we have learned that we are more likely to succeed in the effort of protecting fully functioning ecosystems if we are open to the wisdom of local people who are close to the land (whether they are indigenous or nonindigenous). For land managers, sensitivity to spiritual values does not mean adopting someone else's belief system; it means being sensitive to other belief systems and respecting the wholeness of knowledge (or what Sallenave [1994] calls traditional ecological knowledge [TEK]) that others can offer. In incorporating TEK in environmental impact assessments, land managers face, according to Sallenave, three barriers. Developing sensitivity to spiritual values means confronting these barriers directly:

The first barrier to the integration of TEK is perceptual. There is a distinct difference between what aboriginal peoples interpret as 'significant' impacts and what policy makers and proponents of development projects perceive as significant impacts. . . . The chasm between the two perceptions is understandable since the reactions of a society or culture to development cannot be understood outside the context of its particular history (emphasis added); *however, the continued exclusion of aboriginal peoples and their traditional knowledge only exacerbates the problem. . . .*

The second barrier to the inclusion of traditional knowledge in the EIA process is the skepticism within the scientific community about the credibility or reliability of aboriginal information . . . in general, EIA researchers rely primarily on 'hard' data—such as biophysical data. This reliance on 'objective' data is found particularly among scientists on policy or regulatory committees, who tend to dismiss aboriginal knowledge as subjective, anecdotal, and unscientific.

The third, and perhaps most overwhelming, barrier to the inclusion of traditional knowledge is the political obstacle. The decision-making process for EIAs would have to be altered significantly to accommodate the use of TEK, and such alteration may not be politically palatable to policy makers.

Sallenave, 1994, p. 19

3. *To adopt an attitude of acceptance and belief.* Spiritual values must be accepted; they cannot be defined. This does not mean that one literally embraces someone else's spiritual belief, but rather that one accepts that spiritual values exist (even if they cannot be fully defined), that they are expressed differently by different people, and that the people who identify a place as spiritual are the right people to plan its use.

Too often spiritual values are eclipsed by the reductionist idea that if things cannot be quantified, they do not exist. As Rowe (1990) explains it:

The rational mind of science has a terrible failing. If it cannot cope with aspects of experience that are unmeasurable, it declares them meaningless, unimportant. They are unsubstantial epiphenomena. Feelings, the promptings of emotions, are distrusted because no white-coated savant has corked the incontrovertible evidence of them in a test tube. The better humanity becomes at science and its kind of rationality, the less room remains for noncognitive things of the spirit. Values still call society's shots, but they are debased to those values that can live with science and those with which science can live.

Rowe, pp. 89-90

Spiritual values often cannot "live with science" in any simple way. Therefore, developing sensitivity to spiritual values means developing a wholistic way of thinking that combines the rational and the emotional, understanding and belief.

In our experience, the ability to believe begins with trust—trusting one's inner self and trusting one another. Unfortunately, society does not place much value on either self-trust or mutual trust. In many areas of life (education and healthcare are the most obvious examples) one is taught to defer responsibility to experts rather than to trust one's own instincts and observations. (And, of course, in areas where *we* are the experts, we expect this deference in return.) Daily routines are characterized by a lack of trust. Many feel that it's all right to "borrow" supplies from the office; to weasel little extras onto the expense account; to withhold helpful information from opponents, competitors, and even colleagues; to skew statistics to make "our side" look good. This lack of openness means lack of trust. If people do not trust others, how can they believe others? If people do not have the capacity to trust and to believe, they will be unable to understand their own spirituality and to accommodate the spirituality of others.

I (Herb Hammond) have had the experience of standing in a forest with an indigenous Elder who has told me, "This place is sacred to our people." When I hear this, I have two choices. I can say, "I accept that and I'll protect this place in ways that meet your needs," or I can say, "Prove it."

Acceptance, belief, and trust must be principles of education for sensitivity to spiritual values, and this will require that we define "education" very broadly indeed. Gordon Robinson, forester and philosopher, shows us where this kind of thinking can take us:

I believe the most important aspect of life is to gather up all the specific beliefs we have about many kinds of things in many areas of life into an emotional whole, and hopefully, but rarely, into a reasonable whole. We are striving to comfortably sense the oneness of all things.

But this requires verification, and I think that comes from great art, great music, great love. But the ultimate verification comes from wilderness experience—the recognition that everything is in its place.

Robinson, 1990

4. *To trust the heart/brain connection.* It is necessary to understand that wisdom is a combination of knowledge and intuition. Balance reliance on hard data, prescribed methods, and quantitative analysis with an attitude of trust and respect for "soft" traits: imagination, emotion, intuition, appreciation, synthesis, feelings of connectedness and strength. For those educated in the scientific method, accepting intuition is difficult. Often this way of thinking has been "educated" out of many.

For many years, I (Herb Hammond) hiked in the old growth Douglas-fir forests that cloak the Cascade Mountains in Oregon. While I fly-fished in the pure streams and walked from valley bottom to ridge top, I was always clamoring up and over large fallen trees. In forestry school I was taught that these were waste—something to avoid in managed forests. However, my heart told me that these tree bodies performed many important functions. It also told me that this is where the elder tree spirits live.

Science eventually caught up with my heart about the important ecological functions. From water storage and water filtration to soil structure and wildlife habitat, we now know that large fallen trees are indispensable to forest functioning. As for the elder tree spirits, they are my own personal belief.

Heart/brain connections have also been damaged by society's preoccupation with compartmentalizing and specializing. It is not believed that one can understand the whole because one starts with the parts. In forestry the start is timber. In recreation the start is a ski trail or a golf course. In human communities the start is with the individual.

Neither science nor intuition can completely comprehend the whole. Trusting the connection between hearts and brains will lead toward accepting the whole. It may well be that the best contribution that can be made is science, but trusting the heart/brain connection is a reminder that this is not the only, or necessarily the most important, contribution to a plan or to the solution to a problem. Trusting the heart/brain connection helps put science in perspective and maintain respect for other ways of knowing and perceiving.

5. *To emphasize experiential and participatory modes of learning.* According to Alfred North Whitehead:

> *Firsthand knowledge is the ultimate basis of intellectual life. . . . The secondhandedness of the learned world is the secret of its mediocrity. It is tame because it has never been scared by the facts.*
>
> Whitehead, 1967, p. 51

One needs to learn to trust one's own perceptions and observations. One also needs to learn to get out of the offices and classrooms and go see for oneself.

For example, consider the traditional fishing site described in the second principle. A land manager planning to protect this site must actually go there and experience it first-hand with people who understand its significance. After walking to the site and spending time there, any manager who has learned to trust his or her own perceptions and observations will realize that it can't be adequately protected if a main logging road or recreation vehicle (RV) campsite is engineered 150 yards from the stream so that someone standing there trying to fish, trying to be part of the forest, has to listen to noise from logging trucks or televisions in RVs. In addition, the land manager must walk potentially unstable slopes upstream from the fishing site to be sure that it is protected in its landscape context.

This type of experiential learning and planning takes time, but without it, there is only the illusion of protecting spiritual areas. Computer graphics and thick reports are useful, but distant. They are not substitutes for being there, face-to-face with the real situation, learning to understand it and the people who care about it in all dimensions. As environmental educator Carl Reidel (1990), put it:

> *Go and see for yourself. With all due respect to IBM, you must get up from your computer monitor and see for yourself where history is headed. Don't depend exclusively on geographic information systems, fancy simulation models, or CNN to interpret the times . . . . [W]e can only be responsible professionals if we have first-hand experience of the world we teach about or advocate. So go have a look. See for yourself.* (p. 19)

6. *To focus more on the outdoors and nature than on indoors and books.* Academic jargon and intellectual abstractions are inadequate modes for conveying the substance of spiritual values. According to Orr, "Ecological literacy is difficult . . . because we have

come to believe that education is solely an indoor activity" (1992, p. 87). Simply put, the forest is outdoors, not indoors.

This principle may be particularly challenging for managers raised in the dominant North American culture unless they understand something about their own cultural roots. North Americans of European descent have a long history of living at a distance from the forest and from nature. The pattern of European communities imported to North America reflects the values of human institutions: small farms clustered around small villages with the school and church at the center. North Americans of European descent tend to respect institutions; they see themselves as controlling or managing the land; they have traditionally sought education inside a building called a school and spiritual comfort inside a building called a church.

In contrast, many non-European traditional or indigenous cultures respect the natural world; they see themselves as part of the land; they seek both education and spiritual comfort directly from the land. A wide gap in values and world-view is bound to exist between the member of a traditional culture who says, "In order to live as part of the forest, I have learned about life from the forest," and the North American of European descent who says, "In order to manage the forest, I have learned about the forest at school."

The result of the alienation of the dominant European culture from the natural world, according to Rowe (1990), is that:

> [T]he planet, its land and water and air surface, is being beaten and poisoned to death because, compared to people, it is considered to be relatively unimportant. We have developed little feeling for it as a valuable thing. Nature study has barely made it into our school and college agendas and our natural attraction to the world remains uneducated, diffuse and unrefined. (p. 140)

In order to learn how to be sensitive to spiritual values, it will be necessary to move beyond an abstract, text-centered, indoor approach to education, and begin to trust nature to supply directly the necessary concepts, symbols, images, and models. In the absence of such nature-generated modes of understanding, even partial sensitization to forest-based spiritual values is unlikely because academic jargon and intellectual abstractions are inadequate modes

for conveying the substance of spiritual values. The more time and awareness invested outdoors, the more likely one is to learn directly from nature and to become more sensitive towards those who find spiritual values inherent in nature.

7. *To recognize that spiritual values are culturally specific.* Becoming sensitized to spiritual values means learning to act from a sense of social justice and respect for cultural diversity. On the face of it, something has gone terribly askew in our system of education and governance when resource managers, working for the economic benefit of some people, are required to make or defend land use decisions that disrupt or violate areas that are a homeland or a sacred place for other people. Such behavior is possible only where people have been taught to separate their heart from their brain, their compassion from their intellect.

By now, most resource managers realize that spiritual values do not ordinarily carry the economic weight of commodity-based values. Forest-based spiritual values often spring from social or cultural structures that the typical resource manager, as a result of previous education, is poorly prepared to comprehend. In this situation, sensitivity to unfamiliar spiritual values can begin with a simple "what if" exercise of the imagination. How would a land manager feel if some group walked into a church or synagogue in her or his hometown, disrupted the service, and presented a "development" plan that would destroy the building?

Recognizing that spiritual values are culturally specific begins with the principles of belief and trust described earlier and ends with the principle of devolution of power. It means that when one sets out to protect a spiritual value, one asks the people involved to reveal where these values exist, one believes what is told, and willingly devolves the power to manage for these values to the people themselves.

A good statement about the relationship of spiritual to natural values and the importance of spiritual diversity comes from the novel, *The Fifth Sacred Thing*, by Starhawk (1993). In the story, a small human community copes with the effects of global ecological catastrophe by declaring that, in their isolated watershed, four things are sacred: air, water, fire (energy), and earth.

To call these things sacred is to say that they have a value beyond their usefulness for human ends, that they themselves become the standards by which our acts, our economics, our laws, and purposes must be judged. No one has the right to appropriate them or profit from them at the expense of others. Any government that fails to protect them forfeits its legitimacy.

All people, all living things, are part of the earth life, and so are sacred. No one of us stands higher or lower than any other. Only justice can assure balance: only ecological balance can sustain freedom. Only in freedom can that fifth sacred thing we call spirit flourish in its full diversity. (p. i)

8. *To focus on means for devolving power and control.* Land managers kid themselves if they think they can care for some other culture's spiritual values and sacred places on their behalf. Unless it's one's own culture, one can't do it. In the case of many indigenous cultures, land managers will probably never be given enough information to do it right, no matter how patiently they ask and no matter how sincere their intentions.

The words "care for" are used intentionally here in place of "manage." Aside from protecting and maintaining existing ecosystems, one cannot "manage" for spiritual values. Management carries with it the connotation of manipulation, improvement, or change for the better. In contrast, spiritual values simply are. They are not better or worse. All one can do is guard the conditions that perpetuate spiritual values, and this can only be done by devolving (handing on) power to those who know about them.

Devolving power means having power and control *with* others rather than having power and control *over* others. In the case of caring for spiritual values, devolving power means finding out who knows about spiritual places and who cares about them, and only then handing over to that group the power to care for those places for themselves.

Sallenave (1994) concurs with this approach in the context of EIAs, and is mindful of its challenges:

Integrating TEK [traditional ecological knowledge] into the EIA process entails more than a transfer of information from one culture to another: it will require a change in the mind set of policy makers and of many in the scientific

community. If knowledge truly is power, then appropriate decision-making power must be transferred to those at the source of the knowledge to be used. . . . [emphasis added] (p. 19)

The biggest challenge that land managers are going to encounter may be in deciding whom to believe and whose information to trust. Management's first step is to believe and trust the people who are indigenous to the area. If these people can't be found immediately, or if they don't find the manager, management must look for them. If all of the indigenous people have been extirpated, a land use plan must be developed from a consensus of divergent interests. The important point, however, is to emphasize belief and protection, not doubt and degradation.

Professional land managers will still have a role to play in helping individuals and groups care for spiritual places by helping protect upstream or landscape level ecosystem functioning so that land use impacts arising at a distant site do not degrade a spiritual place. Devolving power springs from respect for cultural diversity and results in having access to a source of power much greater than one would have if one hung on to all of it.

9. *To base all learning on a strong sense of place and a strong sense of human community.* Orr (1992) defines the global environmental crisis as "the sum total of violence wrought by people who do not know who they are because they do not know where they are" (p. 102). A crippling disadvantage of many corporate, governmental, and "upwardly mobile" career lifestyles is the rootlessness created by frequent transfers to other assignments in other locations. Complicating this trend for land use managers (even for those who live in a place they love) are governmental and corporate land use patterns that tend to trivialize or ignore the sense of place. The result is a system that puts landscapes into boxes and people into compartments. Problems come in envelopes and leave in envelopes. Neighbors are numbers on a computer screen. Nature is defined by inventories and data bases.

In contrast, members of functioning traditional cultures tend to stay in the place where they grew up, or at least tend to stay focused on their place of origin, even if they are forced to move. People in any culture who possess a strong sense of place know a lot about the place where they live. They know its landforms, weather, vegetation, and inhabitants—animals, humans, and spirits. They know these things not as data in an inventory but as direct personal experience. People who have a strong sense of place are valued and often irreplaceable members of the community where they live, rather than being interchangeable "occupants" to whom bulk mail is addressed.

For many traditional cultures, the sense of place is strongly bound up with spiritual values. As long as society looks at forests as quantifiable resources to be *managed* by prescriptive methods, it will forever fail in any attempts to *care for* spiritual values. If a land use manager does not possess a personal sense of place, it is unlikely that he or she can understand the spiritual values expressed by any other group. If a land manager does not comprehend a sense of place in regard to any area being managed, it is incumbent upon him or her to learn about it from local elders and longtime inhabitants.

Having a sense of place does not guarantee homogeneity in thinking. Indeed, when a group of people—a culture—have place, there is normally a diversity of thinking and an ongoing debate that enriches the culture. The combination of place and diversity of thought is centered about the need for survival, which means people as individuals and groups taking responsibility for the care of each other and of the ecosystem that sustains them. Sense of place and diversity of thinking, and the responsible actions that this combination generates, are vital to caring for spiritual values. A land use manager who demonstrates sensitivity to spiritual values is one who has learned to respect both another culture's sense of place and another culture's diversity of thought.

10. *To learn to apply traditional, common-sense systems first, before calling for research. Design research, if it is needed, in the context of ecosystem-based management and not resource-based management.* One cannot justify postponing a switch from resource-based management to ecosystem-based management until all the research is "in." The basic research is already in. Ecosystems themselves can show how they function, and indigenous cultures from around the world can show how to live as part of an ecosystem. As Orr (1992) puts it:

A sizable part of [university research] is motivated by the fantasy of making an end run around constraints of time, space, nature, and human nature . . . it is time to ask what we need to know to live humanely, peacefully, and responsibly on the earth and to set research priorities accordingly. (p. 126)

By and large, ecosystem-based management can be accomplished using common-sense systems that protect fully-functioning ecosystems while providing some resource benefits. If a system of use protects and maintains ecosystem composition and structures from the landscape level to the patch level, overall ecosystem functioning will be protected. Land use activities that purport to protect ecosystems must be monitored and evaluated on an ongoing basis to ensure that this goal is achieved. There is sufficient evidence, without further research, to reject human activities that do not protect and maintain ecosystem composition and structures at all scales through time.

In the course of investigating spiritual values connected to any particular area, one may find some individuals or groups who already understand the ecosystem and already have a system designed for protecting it and using it that's been working well for generations. For example, many small-scale tourism operations focused on hiking and camping have operated in ecologically responsible ways for years, leaving few, if any, footprints on ecosystem functioning. The same is often true of small-scale logging operations that remove timber through partial cutting. In these situations, the land manager's job is easy if he or she is open enough to believe them and incorporate what they've already been doing for generations into the plan. Aside from slight modifications from time to time, these are not situations that call for elaborate research or the application of experimental findings. Ecosystem-based management becomes a matter of doing the scientific and the traditional together, rather than trying to force the scientific to lead the traditional.

11. *To believe in the wholeness of life, and make both personal and professional decisions in light of this belief.* Land use managers have inherited the legacy of a dominant culture that has refused to consider the consequences

of its actions. Too many North Americans continue to subscribe to vague principles of sustainability while living a disposable, non-returnable, nonreusable lifestyle. According to environmental educator Robert Harrington (1990):

. . . we have been too remote from nature's signals for too long a while. The indications are everywhere, but we can no longer read the language. We have succumbed to too many of our own myths: that we are the most important beings in the universe; that we can dispose of toxic substances in the soil, air and water and they will be forever gone; that our plasticized, artificial world is the real world simply because many of us would like it to be that way; that every other living thing on earth, and the nonliving things as well, can simply be categorized as resources for our use; and that we can take and take from the natural world and give back nothing, neither love nor concern, neither time nor effort, not even a tiny bit of thought or a little conscientious restraint. (pp. 84-85)

Believing in the wholeness of life is an extension of the third principle: adopting an attitude of acceptance and belief—an attitude of trust. One will never be able to explain fully or to quantify the need for wholistic thinking and whole systems. However, whole systems are the only ones that have endured over time.

Spiritual values are the source of wholeness. Thus, one has a chicken-and-egg conundrum. One cannot believe in wholeness without spiritual values of one's own, and one cannot have spiritual values without believing in wholeness. Both wholeness and spiritual values reside in all people, but they require recognition and active acceptance. Being open to their influence is all the education necessary to be whole.

12. *To be receptive to the experience of elders and previous generations, conveyed in whatever form is appropriate to the teacher's or learner's culture.* The last principle circles back to the first. The principle of acknowledging natural connectedness includes recognizing the human inhabitants who live or have lived wisely as part of the ecosystem,

and being willing to learn from their collective experience.

In an indigenous culture, spiritual values related to the land may be conveyed through story, song, dance, vision, ceremony, and daily activities. In a European-derived culture, spiritual values related to the land may be conveyed through artistic expression, contemplation or meditation, outdoor experiences, and literature.

Short-Term Solutions for Current Managers

Caring for spiritual values during land management means nothing short of rethinking and retooling the culture, beginning with the system of education. In the meantime, managers will have to teach themselves which will include incorporating the principles described above as part of land use planning and as part of "in-house" training. Managers must learn to believe in spiritual values and plan the protection and caring use of whole systems. They must trust local people's description of and needs for protection of spiritual values and devolve the power to plan and carry out the protection of spiritual values for those who traditionally hold and honor those values in a particular area. If a manager has influence over the curriculum of an existing institution, he or she can introduce the issue of sensitivity to spiritual values. Managers looking for education should measure programs by their incorporation of the twelve listed principles. Above all, managers should trust their own intuition and observations.

Many land management professionals in quest of new knowledge logically turn to a college or university. However, a cursory survey of course descriptions for conventional postsecondary programs in resource management reveals at best only slight interest in spiritual values as a topic of academic pursuit. (By "conventional programs," we mean programs that focus on linear and quantitative concepts and that teach primarily the techniques required to manipulate ecosystems and extract resources.)

Established institutions can hardly be expected to promote sensitivity to spiritual values, because educational institutions at all levels largely mirror the dominant society's values. According to Harrington:

Of all the areas in which we have been remiss, the area of education is the one which has spun its wheels most deeply into a morass of trivia. Anchored to the trailing edge of culture, the educational system has ignored all signs of decay of the planet and toddled willingly behind the purveyors of the idea that affluence and progress are the same thing. . . . The educational machine, at this point, seems both unaware of the needs of its students and hopelessly shackled to the prevailing commercial mentality. (p. 239)

Individuals and small programs in a variety of universities appear to be trying to incorporate spiritual values into formal education. By and large, however, the North American pattern of schooling at all levels emphasizes quantitative, linear, and analytical modes of thought. These are the ways of thinking that block sensitivity to spiritual values. Cultural biases coupled with the strong influence over curriculum by industry and corporations create substantial obstacles for the individual seeking to be sensitized to spiritual values through existing educational institutions.

Managers should be aware of opportunities for education in spiritual values in the context of land use planning in addition to those presented by conventional institutions and associations. There are many community, indigenous, nonprofit organizations in other parts of the world as well as in North America that offer a variety of programs which address these sensitive issues and provide valuable insights in this area.

Educating land use managers to care for spiritual values cannot be separated from educating them to manage fully functioning ecosystems and to put the health and integrity of the ecosystem above short-term revenue targets of government and industry.

Remaining sensitive to land-based spiritual values also requires maintaining contacts with nature. In this regard, the Society of American Foresters (SAF) provides an interesting insight into career expectations of foresters. According to a career guidance brochure from the SAF, "After a few years of on-the-ground experience and crew supervision, foresters typically advance to administrative positions and spend less time outdoors" (Society of American Foresters, 1988, p. 1). This professional association, it appears, has known all along that "advancement" in forestry means putting oneself at a distance from the forest and its inherent values. It is certainly true in

Canada that the more successful foresters become in their profession, the further they are removed from the forest. Success in forestry means promotion to the head office—in a city! This must change. It is incumbent on land managers to question the inevitability and wisdom of this career design. To become part of the solution, land use managers must speak first for the forest, not for the interests of industry. They must learn to have as much pride in the number of fish, the diversity of bacteria, the quality of water that flows from a forest, and the protection of spiritual values as they have in the number and size of trees or the annual increase in visitor days.

Another alternative for self-study is "bibliotherapy"—reading works by land use visionaries. In-service learning could include a discussion group based on the principles of the "learning circle," facilitated by a local inhabitant familiar with the literature. To be effective, however, such reading must be approached with a receptive heart and must not be a substitute for excursions out of the books and onto the land. In North America, a reading list might include Aldo Leopold's (1949) essay "The Land Ethic," included in *A Sand County Almanac and Sketches Here and There*, and Henry David Thoreau's (1983) *Walden*, James Lovelock's (1988) *The Ages of Gaia*, Gary Snyder's (1974) *Earth Household* and *Turtle Island*, Stan Rowe's (1990) *Home Place*, David Orr's (1992) *Ecological Literacy*, Robert Harrington's (1990) *To Heal the Earth*, and Devall and Sessions's (1985) *Deep Ecology*.

Self-education or in-service training to sensitize managers to spiritual values should also include some reading, introspection, and discussion about the history and actual consequences of our current use of the land. Foresters, for example, need to consider the historical bases of:

a. *silviculture*: Modern silvicultural principles were largely derived from eighteenth century efforts to revive the badly degraded forests of Germany (efforts which have proven to be unsustainable).

b. *clear-cutting*: The currently favored method of timber cutting was not adopted as a result of research that determined it to be ecologically suitable. Rather, it was and continues to be employed as the most efficient way to get the largest volume of trees to a mill in the short term.

c. *employment levels and community stability relative to mechanization and corporate profits:* The relationship of these four factors through time shows that increased corporate control and corporate "success" in the timber industry is tied to steadily increasing levels of mechanization, steadily decreasing levels of employment, and destabilization of rural communities.

Teaching land managers to be sensitive to spiritual values ultimately becomes an ongoing creative endeavor. The most effective path will be the one of self-discovery and self-education rather than waiting for the right course or the definitive set of instructions. Land managers should keep a journal, learn anew or reinvolve themselves in some activity they used to do that will enhance the heart/brain connection—making music, painting, drawing or photographing nature.

Managers should take every opportunity to meet and observe people who use the forest and the natural world in "soft" or noncommercial ways and to spend a weekend with an artist who paints landscapes, a composer who finds inspiration in natural settings, or with crafters who gather natural materials for baskets, furniture, toymaking, or herbal remedies.

It is most important to spend time talking and listening to the forest. Some parts of the forest may be more poignant than others, but any part of the forest is spiritual. Rediscovering first-hand what this means will help land managers to learn and to accommodate effectively the spiritual values of others. At first, this type of experience may be led by an experienced Elder, but eventually the best learning will occur alone. Spiritual values are part of the land, not part of a written plan.

Finally, the best way to appreciate the depth, wholeness, and vitality of spiritual values—and to understand their significance—is to be involved, immersed, with an indigenous or nonindigenous group or community that is actively practicing and protecting these values while relating them to the land.

If land managers are sincere and willing to make such an experience more than a weekend vacation, they will be able to find people who will welcome them to observe and share their life for a period of time. They will be honored by the presence, courage, and respect shown. If one's heart and mind are open, one will realize (as in "make real") a set of values that previously may have been only abstractions. No

workshop, no consultant's report, no indirect means can convey that which can only be experienced first-hand. We would argue that witnessing spiritual values in context (spending time in a community that is actively expressing traditional land-based spiritual values) is cost-effective and probably the only path leading to enough sensitivity to spiritual values so that a land manager can make good decisions for their care and protection.

Time is the real key here. Spiritual values are not expressed on a schedule. When a place is found where spiritual values can be experienced in context, one should be prepared to spend a month in that place. By keeping an open mind and heart, one will come away with new appreciations and sensitivities. Witnessing spiritual values in context is the best way to learn to trust those who know and have traditionally cared for spiritual values in a particular place. Trusting those who know and have traditionally cared for spiritual values is the only effective way to ensure these values endure for those who follow.

A New Mode of Education for Sensitivity to Spiritual Values

Both indigenous and nonindigenous cultures today are attempting to understand and apply aspects of the other's culture in an effort to live better in their own. Many nonindigenous efforts at blending the two cultures appear to be an attempt to jettison Western values entirely while at the same time trivializing, distorting, or coopting indigenous ways. Indigenous efforts, in contrast, seem more often to hold fast to indigenous values, while adopting nonindigenous practices that are useful but not disruptive to the culture.

A good example is the recently completed draft of the indigenous Economics Curriculum (Abrams, 1993), designed by the First Nations Development Institute to be used in tribal college settings. (The curriculum was tested in its pilot form beginning in the fall of 1993 at Sinte Gleska University in Rosebud, South Dakota; Navajo Community College in Shiprock, New Mexico; and Blackfeet Community College in Browning, Montana.) The subject matter is not directly concerned with land use management. However, it is an excellent example because it demonstrates how indigenous people have developed learning experiences to sensitize students to nonindigenous values.

The purpose of the indigenous Economics Curriculum, according to Abrams (1993), is "to provide tribal college students with a culturally relevant economics curriculum for understanding and analyzing western economic theories and models" (p. 8). The curriculum begins with a section on "Assessing Beliefs and Values," including, among others, these objectives:

- Students will become more comfortable with one another in terms of sharing, trust, safe place, inclusiveness, self-confidence in speaking and cooperation.

- Students will assess themselves as it pertains to their knowledge of traditional ways and their place in the community.

- Students will learn basic information regarding culture, history, and tradition from local community sources.

- Students will examine their own lives for examples in which they can describe the clash between traditional and modern world-views. The examples will include one each of the following: political thinking, spirituality, social thinking, technology, and economics (Abrams, pp. 8-9).

Here is a college course in Western economic theory that begins with respectful self-awareness. Abstract definitions and concepts do not come first. The student comes first: the student's relationships to others in the course, the student's knowledge of and place in the community and the culture, and the student's own experience, including explicit spiritual experiences.

Many subsequent objectives listed as major elements in this curriculum would fit comfortably into any conventional Western-style economics course. Others would come as a surprise:

- Students will find examples of the six [economic] concepts inherent within creation stories and songs and determine if these concepts are important or not to the traditional knowledge base.

- Students will conduct process and structural analysis of ceremony so that they can discuss principles, laws, attitudes and values of indigenous peoples.

- Students will successfully apply traditional knowledge to solve an economic problem or issue that is group-defined (entire class).

- Students will identify and select those issues most important or significant to themselves and relate such to seventh generation thinking and concepts.

- Students will develop activities to celebrate their vision and learning (Abrams, 1993, p. 8-9).

The indigenous Economics Curriculum is based on the idea that "economics is everywhere"—in personal life, in relationships, in tradition, in community, in story and song, in ceremony and celebration, reaching all the way to the seventh generation.

As a model for education in any given field, this kind of curriculum is an attempt to educate the whole person for living a whole life in a whole world. Any subject could be approached this way, especially land use management.

How Do We Get from Here to There?

In addition to all of the principles and ways of applying the principles already discussed, one further step is required if the education (or reeducation) of land use professionals is to have any effect. Becoming sensitized to spiritual values and caring for spiritual values in land use planning requires learning by individuals at all levels within an organization. This process of learning must be a symbiotic relationship between field personnel and policymakers. Unless sensitization to spiritual values occurs at all levels, effective recognition and protection of spiritual values is unlikely. Contradictions and misunderstandings between field personnel and policymakers will most likely result in lip service being paid to the protection of spiritual values, while management practices continue to degrade the forest and the spiritual values that depend upon a whole, fully functioning ecosystem.

The principles described in this chapter can provide a good foundation for all to begin to become sensitized to spiritual values. These principles can be incorporated at all levels of education be it in an institution or in the most effective classroom, the forest. The only really effective teachers, however, will be those who make spiritual values a part of their lives—a part of their *whole* being. And the most effective place and way to learn about land-based spiritual values is in a forest from those who know, revere, and are actively practicing such values. There is no substitute for experience in this, or any other learning process.

Working as a forest planner, I (Herb Hammond) found this out first-hand. I once helped Lax'skiik (the Eagle Clan of the Gitksan) gather information about their forest along the Skeena River in north-western British Columbia. Our goal was to develop a wholistic forest use plan for this part of Lax'skiik territory. However, there was a surprise in store for me. For over a week, we lived in the forest, finding most of our sustenance from the forest's bounty. Salmon and various forest fruits, along with the pure water that comes only from old growth forests, nurtured us. The canopy of ancient trees sheltered our tent from the rain and wind. Boughs of trees formed our beds. Once, when I cut my hand, salve from a fir catalyzed an amazingly fast healing process. As the days passed, I realized that I was becoming part of the forest in a way that I had never been before.

However, I also came to realize that the real source of this connectedness came not only from the nourishment and shelter of the forest, but also from our morning and evening prayers to Mother Earth. We cleansed ourselves with sage, sweet grass, and the pure mountain air. We bathed ourselves in silence. The forest spoke to each of us in personal ways. In this quiet time, little was said and each of us was alone, yet together. We, each in our own way, thanked the spirits of the forest for our well-being, and committed ourselves to protect this forest.

In considering the issue of sensitization to land-based spiritual values, our greatest hope is that all people may have this kind of experience on the land with people who know and actively practice such values. One should seek out an opportunity not trying too hard; being receptive to the experience is the most important thing. One cannot force or schedule learning about spiritual values. It will

happen when one least expects it, and often without knowing that it is occurring. If one truly wants to learn about spiritual values, and if one wants to help all of us "get from here to there," one must go to the forest taking an elder or a child and an open heart. The spirits await.

Literature Cited

Abrams, S. (1993). Building our own knowledge: Indigenous economic understandings. *First Nations Development Institute Business Alert, 8* (2), 8-9.

Devall, B. and Sessions, G. (1985). *Deep ecology.* Layton, UT: Peregrine Smith Books.

Harrington, R. (1990). *To heal the earth: The case for an earth ethic.* Surrey, BC: Hancock House Publishers, Ltd.

Leopold, A. (1949). *A sand county almanac and sketches here and there.* New York, NY: Oxford University Press.

Lovelock, J. (1988). *The ages of Gaia.* New York, NY: W. W. Norton & Company, Inc.

Orr, D. (1992). *Ecological literacy: Education and the transition to a postmodern world.* Albany, NY: State University of New York Press.

Reidel, C. (1992). Asking the right questions. *Journal of Forestry, 90* (10), 14-19.

Robinson, G. (1990). Personal communication.

Rowe, S. (1990). *Home place: Essays on ecology.* Edmonton, Alberta: NeWest Press.

Sallenave, J. (1994). Giving traditional ecological knowledge its rightful place in environmental impact assessment. *Northern Perspectives* (Canadian Arctic Resources Committee) *22* (1),16-19.

Snyder, G. (1969). *Earth household: Technical notes and queries to fellow dharma revolutionaries.* New York, NY: New Directions Publishing Corp.

Snyder, G. (1974). *Turtle Island.* New York, NY: New Directions Publishing Corp.

Society of American Foresters. (1988). *Career information question and answer sheet* (brochure). Bethesda, MD.

Starhawk. (1993). *The fifth sacred thing.* New York, NY: Bantam Books.

Thoreau, H. (1983). *Walden.* New York, NY: Penguin Books.

Whitehead, A. (1967). *The aims of education.* New York, NY: The Free Press.

Public Land Management Agencies, Environmental Education, and an Expanded Land Management Ethic

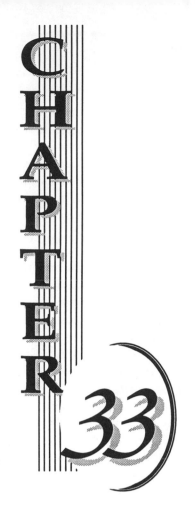

CHAPTER 33

Joseph Roggenbuck
Department of Forestry
Virginia Polytechnic Institute and State University
Blacksburg, Virginia

B. L. Driver
Rocky Mountain Forest and Range Experiment Station
USDA Forest Service
Fort Collins, Colorado

Introduction

The purpose of this chapter is to describe how public land managers can cooperate with environmental educators to promote an expanded land management ethic that will accommodate both the psychologically deep, nature-based human values on which this text focuses and ecosystem sustainability. Because most public land managers are not familiar with environmental education, we begin by providing considerable background information to set the stage for the specific recommendations made later. We define environmental education, describe its purposes, and trace its evolution from the nature-study, outdoor education, and conservation education movements. We also describe typical environmental education program content and comment on what portions of that content public land management agencies can address. We then turn to a discussion of environmental education in the 1990s and describe its methods and measures of program effectiveness. We review the involvement of public land management agencies in environmental education to describe what agencies are involved, how, and why. We conclude by looking to the future and describing the need for greater involvement by public land management agencies in environmental education, especially in promoting an expanded land management ethic based on ecosystem sustainability.

Definition of Environmental Education

Various definitions of environmental education have been encoded into law or have been given institutional standing by the United States or other world governmental bodies. For example, the United States Environmental Education Act of 1970 (PL 91-516) defined environmental education as an educational process dealing with humankind's relationship with its natural and human-made surroundings including the relation of population, pollution, resource allocation and depletion, conservation, transportation, technology, and urban and rural planning to the total human environment. In establishing the goals of environmental education, Stapp (1969) noted that environmental education is aimed at producing a citizenry that is knowledgeable concerning the biophysical environment and its associated problems, aware of how to help solve those problems, and motivated to work toward their solution. Hawkins and Vinton (1973) stated that the ultimate goal of environmental education for students is to develop an awareness of their environment that will lead to a personal sense of involvement and eventually to the shaping of an environmental ethic to guide their behavior.

In addition, various international governmental bodies and professional meetings have recognized the need for and role of environmental education in addressing the worldwide environmental crisis, reducing social inequities, and fostering quality of life. For example, Recommendation 96 of the 1972 Stockholm Conference on the Human Environment called for the development of environmental education as one of the most critical elements of an all-out attack on the world's environmental crisis. This was followed in 1975 by the "Belgrade Charter: A Global Framework for Environmental Education," produced and adopted at the International Environmental Education Workshop in Belgrade, Yugoslavia. That framework stated that the goal of environmental education was to develop an environmentally literate and activist world population within the institutional and cultural milieu of nation states and international bodies by empowering people to action (Schmieder, 1977). The 1977 Intergovernmental Conference on Environmental Education at Tbilisi, (Republic of Georgia), was more specific in its declaration of the objectives of environmental education. This body stated that environmental education should help social groups and individuals:

1. become aware of and sensitive to the total environment and its allied problems,

2. gain a variety of experiences in and acquire a basic knowledge of the environment and its associated problems,

3. acquire a set of attitudes of concern for the environment and motivation for actively participating in environmental improvement and protection,

4. acquire the skills for identifying and solving environmental problems, and

5. have opportunities to participate actively at all levels in working toward resolution of environmental problems (UNESCO, 1978).

Precursors to Environmental Education

Drawing on the work of Stapp (1974), three phases of the conservation movement can be identified within which environmental education has evolved in the United States. They are:

1. concerns about exploitation,

2. needs to manage the public lands, and

3. concerns about environmental quality.

Concerns about Exploitation and the Nature Study and Outdoor Education Movements

From the inception of the U.S. to the end of the nineteenth century, exploitation was the dominant theme regarding humankind's relationship to nature. Then, in response to writers like George Marsh, John Muir, and Gifford Pinchot there was a shift in land-related values, at least among the intellectual elite. This shift was particularly evident during the administration of Teddy Roosevelt. Over 150 million acres of public land were designated as national forests; 80 million acres of potential mineral-bearing land were withdrawn from the public domain; and four big game refuges, five national parks, and several national monuments were created (Stapp, 1974).

About the same time, the nature education movement began. It was led by educators like Wilbur Jackman and Liberty Hyde Bailey who articulated the need for schools to include nature education in their curricula and for instructors to acquire skills in teaching about the environment. Bailey founded the American Nature Study Society in 1908, the society which continues to shape educational efforts and aims to develop appreciation and understanding of nature through firsthand experiences outdoors, support the conservation of natural areas and encourage their use in nature education, and to improve the quality of nature interpretation in schools, parks, literature, and nature organizations (Stapp, 1974).

The nature interpretation program of the USDI National Park Service has its pedagogical roots in the nature-study movement. For example, every park interpreter emphasizes firsthand experiences with real objects of the environment. The belief remains that this approach to "knowing" (i.e., use of all the senses in the context of the whole environment) will inevitably lead to greater concern for, and protection of, the environment. In line with this philosophy, and unlike that of the later environmental education movement, nature interpretation tends to deal less directly with values clarification, motivational interventions, or provision of skills or means to empower people toward action.

After it emerged in the 1920s, the outdoor education movement enlarged the educational philosophy of the nature study movement. It placed great emphasis on firsthand observations and direct learning in the outdoors as the ideal way to learn (Hammerman and Hammerman, 1964). Outdoor educators also saw their profession as much more than simply learning about the environment. They viewed the outdoors as the ideal place to learn much about traditional academic subjects at the elementary and secondary levels as well as to learn the wise use of leisure time and how to best protect the natural environment. Finally, and in part because of the teaching techniques employed (e.g., creative use of questioning, providing manageable challenges), educators believed that being in the outdoors helped students learn more about themselves and gain self-esteem. Thus, outdoor education, in contrast to nature study, took a more holistic view of relevant content and learning objectives, and it directly attempted to empower individuals for personal and social change. However, unlike most current approaches to environmental education, outdoor education frequently placed its learning activities in a recreational context (i.e., students learn important environmental or academic concepts while engaged in activities such as hiking, orienteering, and camping).

Need to Manage the Public Lands and Conservation Education

Recognition of the need to manage the public lands that had been designated as national parks, forests, and wildlife areas gradually evolved from about 1906 to 1930. The U.S. Congress realized that these resources could not simply be locked up, so it created federal agencies to manage them.

Two national disasters in the 1930s—the Great Depression and the Dust Bowl— quickened the

pace toward resource management and recognition of the need for conservation education in the United States. With the Great Depression came considerable poverty and high rates of unemployment. President Franklin Delano Roosevelt turned to the rich natural resources of the United States to help solve problems that accompanied the Great Depression. For example, thousands of men carried out construction and conservation projects on public lands and learned basic resource management concepts while working in the Civilian Conservation Corps. At the same time, President Roosevelt established the Soil Erosion Service (later to become the Soil Conservation Service), the Tennessee Valley Authority, and the Natural Resources Board (Stapp, 1974). These agencies were to be models of resource conservation. With continued waste and depletion of natural resources, heightened by the Dust Bowl, they and other federal and state agencies established various management and educational programs for the public.

The Dust Bowl years illustrated the need to inform the citizenry about wise resource management and conservation practices. Programs for conservation education in public schools flourished. Federal and state agencies employed specialists in conservation education, and these individuals developed instructional materials for the classroom. Thus started the conservation education movement in the United States. The Conservation Education Association (which recently merged with the North American Association for Environmental Education, [NAAEE]) provided direction to the movement. Its goals were to assist youth and adults in:

1. understanding the characteristics, status, problems, and policies regarding natural resources;

2. learning the importance of natural resources to our society's well-being; and

3. developing citizen support for natural resource management.

The conservation education movement has similarities to the earlier nature study and outdoor education fields; one such commonality is the emphasis on learning in the out-of-doors. But the conservation education movement is more problem-oriented, more focused on specific issues of resource depletion and waste, and more ready to recommend wise management as the solution. In its focus on specific resource problems, the conservation education movement is similar to the later environmental education movement. However, the environmental education field takes a much broader and holistic view of the nature of the environmental crisis, looks to solutions other than wise management, and much more closely attends to the process of changing people and institutions to protect and promote environmental quality and quality of life.

Concerns about Environmental Quality and the Environmental Education Movement

According to Stapp (1974), a desire for environmental quality fostered the third and current phase of the conservation movement. This phase came to the forefront in America and much of the industrialized world in the 1960s and '70s. For example, Rachel Carson's (1962) book, *Silent Spring*, provided dramatic evidence that certain short-term technological fixes (e.g., pesticides) come at pervasive, long-term costs to environmental quality. About that time, we also reached the moon, looked back at the Earth, and realized more vividly that we were riding on our own spaceship, a finite planet Earth. This aroused public concern about environmental quality as well as environmental protection.

People concerned about environmental quality recognized that current political, economic, and social institutions did not provide equal opportunity and access to a quality life, including life in a quality environment. The movement recognized that if humans were to have a high quality of life on a sustainable level, and if such quality was to be made available to all socioeconomic classes, humans had to learn to live with and within their physical environment. This would require colossal personal, institutional, and societal change.

The goal of promoting a high quality of life and environmental quality on a sustainable level gave rise to the definitions of environmental education presented at the beginning of this chapter. No longer was the conservation movement with its educational programs simply trying to teach and excite the public about the beauty of nature. No longer was it simply attempting to make people aware of resource waste and depletion. No longer was it simply provoking people to protect and manage re-

sources wisely. The environmental education movement took a general systems view of the problem (see Peterson, Chapter Two, in this volume), and this required a different approach to its solution. The approach focused on the interrelatedness of humans, their culture, and their biological surroundings. Thus, in addition to understanding biological systems and the role of humans in them, an environmentally responsible citizen had to understand the role of human systems in shaping the quality of life. Environmental education recognized that problems related to quality of life and environmental quality emerged in a cultural and social context. This created both a new challenge and expanded opportunities for environmental educators. They now needed to make human ecology an explicit part of environmental protection and sustainability and do so cross-culturally both nationally and internationally.

The target populations of past conservation education efforts were most often children or adolescents, adults engaged in rural enterprises like farming, or families visiting national parks and forests. Environmental education efforts from the 1960s to the 1980s continued to focus on children and adolescents, but the field shifted sharply to where the need was the greatest—urban and suburban populations. Thus, while school curricula in rural America and program activities in nature camps included environmental education, urban problems and urban culture represented an important target group of environmental education. (Today, environmental education continues to enlarge its scope, addressing the needs of elementary through secondary grades; undergraduate, graduate, and adult populations; and the nation's various racial and ethnic populations. Their education is accomplished primarily through in-school curricular materials and teacher education, but this is also supplemented by field trips and by visits from environmental specialists.)

Finally, like the nature study and conservation education movements before it, the environmental education movement fostered awareness, knowledge, excitement, and positive attitudes about resource protection and management. Like the previous conservation education efforts, environmental educators promoted responsible action (and taking responsibility for this action) regarding the environment among their students. Environmental education differed, however, in the effort it gave to helping students recognize and define environmental problems and their solutions in larger ideological and political contexts; in providing the motivation and skills necessary to effect changes in their own lives and in the social and political systems around them; and in empowering people to become agents of change.

From this brief review of the evolution of the environmental education movement in the United States, it can be seen that the movement broadened its focus greatly from 1900 to 1990. That focus is still expanding to include stronger advocacy for an environmental ethic that promotes ecosystem sustainability. We envision and call for an even wider focus that includes those psychologically deep nature-based human values and experiences that contribute substantively to the quality of life of most, if not all, Americans.

Environmental Education in the 1990s

Goals

While some of the idealism of the 1960s and '70s has diminished, the environmental education movement remains vibrant and retains essentially the same goals. The NAAEE now has 2,000 members and four interactive sections: elementary and secondary education, informal education, environmental studies, and conservation education (Disinger, 1993). The passage of the 1990 National Environmental Education Act demonstrated a renewal of the Federal government's commitment to environmental education (the 1970 Environmental Education Act was funded only through 1975 and repealed in 1981) (Marcinkowski, 1990). That act created an Office of Environmental Education within the Environmental Protection Agency (EPA) and charged it with developing, disseminating, and evaluating environmental education programs and curricula; providing demonstrations on how to design and conduct environmental field studies; providing classroom training; sponsoring partnerships, networks, conferences, and exchanges of environmental teachers and scholars to advance the field; and maintaining a library of environmental education documents.

The National Advisory Council on Environmental Education (1993) established today's goals or

values for environmental education: protect the quality of America's natural heritage; educate, foster, and protect public health as it relates to the environment; foster human welfare by nurturing interest in environmental jobs and careers; address such issues of global concern and sustainable development as overpopulation and poverty; and enhance the quality of education through inclusion of environmental education.

Processes of Modern Environmental Education

Disinger (1993) identifies four characteristics of environmental education, and the way they are accomplished that make them ideally suited to enhancing environmental quality and sustainability:

1. its emphasis on interdisciplinary, multifaceted conceptual approaches;

2. its mechanisms for promoting higher order thinking skills;

3. its strategies for increasing four strands of environmental literacy (knowledge, skill, affect, and behavior); and

4. its recognition that more than simple knowledge change is necessary to accomplish behavioral change.

As we have already stated, a basic tenet of the environmental education movement is that environmentally responsible behavior is only possible through understanding interrelationships among human and natural systems. The route to gaining such knowledge is developmental and necessarily interdisciplinary. Thus, the ideal environmental education program spans kindergarten through twelfth grade (and beyond) and includes content on natural systems (e.g., environment, earth, biosphere, abiotic components, biotic components, processes, and biological systems), resources (e.g., distribution and consumption, management and conservation, sustainable development, energy and minerals, water, land and soil, forests, wildlife and fisheries, biodiversity, limits to systems, pollution), and human resources (e.g., humans as part of environment; human adaptation to and influence on environment; population factors; technological systems such as agriculture, settlements, and manufacturing; values and ethics; education and communication; participatory/voluntary action; legislation and enforcement).

Environmental education is inherently well-suited and has formal prescriptions to advance higher-order thinking skills among its students. Such skills include critical thinking, creative thinking, integrative thinking, and problem solving. The processes of environmental education encourage these thinking skills by requiring and developing abilities to synthesize and evaluate data from across the social and natural sciences as well as the humanities. Students work with real or simulated problems and topics adjusted to their developmental levels to investigate, integrate, generalize, and invent solutions.

Environmental education (and the achieving of environmental literacy) is a developmental process, a process that is both progressive and spiral (Marshall, 1993). By progressive we mean that the environmental educator and program materials move the student from awareness to knowledge, to changes of affect, to skill development, and ultimately to behaviors that sustain quality of the environment and quality of life. The spiraling nature of the environmental education process takes the student through the different learning domains multiple times at increasingly complex (and higher order thinking) levels. Without such a progressive and spiraling approach, long-term, environmentally responsible behavioral change is unlikely.

Stakeholders in Environmental Education in the 1990s

Four different professional groups carry the banner of environmental education in the 1990s (Disinger, 1993):

1. professional environmental educators typically working in kindergarten through twelfth grade, and in universities, environmental stations, or environmental education field camps;

2. federal and state resource agencies;

3. nongovernmental agencies and other environmental advocacy groups; and

4. certain private sector entities.

The commitment of formal education agencies to environmental learning has sometimes been questioned (Schafer, 1981), but the enthusiasm, dedication, and growing professionalism of those in the teaching professions who actually do environmental education are at an all-time high. As has been indicated previously, NAAEE has a growing membership from all states and several countries; currently publishes a series of *Environmental Issues Forums*; and has published monographs or reports on the relationship between environmental education and environmental communication, on teacher education for environmental education, on a database for building environmental education activities, on the uses, strengths, and weaknesses of computer-aided environmental education, and on research paradigms for environmental education (Disinger, 1993).

Federal and state agencies have demonstrated great interest in environmental education, although their level of support has ebbed and flowed with changes in their priorities and funding levels. The Fish and Wildlife Service, the National Park Service, the Forest Service, the Soil Conservation Service, the National Oceanic and Atmospheric Administration through its Sea Grant Program, the Department of Energy, the Peace Corps, and the Office of Environmental Education in the EPA provide personnel with environmental education responsibilities, prepare instructional materials for elementary through secondary grade school programs, visit schools or meet the public to provide environmental programs, and/or open their lands to environmental learning activities. The agencies' programs are typically justified as a means to accomplish their mission and to develop public support for themselves and their resource management philosophy. In the past, this was sometimes viewed more as "resource management" than environmental education (Roth, 1978), but increasingly both the agencies and their specialists are taking a more holistic and balanced view of the route to environmental quality and quality of life. This is dramatically demonstrated by the recent Forest Service commitment to ecosystem sustainability.

Environmental advocacy groups such as the National Wildlife Federation, National Audubon Society, Sierra Club, the Izaak Walton League, and Defenders of Wildlife have worked to foster environmental awareness and to preserve and conserve natural resources. Their methods have often included the publication of environmental education materials, many of which are useful in schools as well as for the general public (Disinger, 1993). These organizations quickly respond to environmental threats and can frequently mobilize the public to action much more quickly than can public agencies or classroom teachers.

Finally, more and more private corporations are becoming partners with resource agencies or are providing grants to environmental education groups to sponsor environmental awareness, appreciation, and learning. Sometimes this is done to assure that their side of the environmental issues or controversies are known to the public. At other times they underwrite the cost of an environmental program, such as a nature program on public television, as a community service. Professional societies or their programs, such as the American Forest Foundation or the American Institute of Architects' "Learning by Design" program, acknowledge the importance of a healthy environment to their enterprise and support environmental education efforts (Disinger, 1993).

Predictor Variables

Studies by Sia, Hungerford, and Tomera (1985) and Hines, Hungerford, and Tomera (1986), which looked at the relationship between the standard "predictor variables" of environmental education and the extent of responsible environmental behavior in a multivariate context, along with a host of studies with less complex designs and analysis (e.g., see Klinger, 1980; Marcinkowski, 1989; Ramsey and Hungerford, 1989; Simpson, 1989; Sivek and Hungerford, 1990; Volk, 1989) permit the following conclusions:

- demographic variables have limited usefulness in explaining environmental behavior;

- knowledge of ecology and environmental problems is usually not enough to produce responsible behavior;

- knowledge and concern (respect) for the environment are necessary but insufficient conditions for action; and

- environmental sensitivity, in-depth knowledge of issues, issue investigation skills, citizenship skills (ecomanagement or physical action, persuasion, consumer action, political action, and legal action), and internal locus of control are needed (Hungerford and Volk, 1990).

Shaping the Predictor Variables

KNOWLEDGE AND ATTITUDES

Most of the research efforts conducted to evaluate the success of environmental education interventions have addressed the lowest or most basic levels of ecological thinking and skill development (i.e., the learning of ecological concepts, interrelationships among those concepts, and positive feelings or attitudes about the environment). Iozzi (1984) reviewed environmental education research from 1971 to 1982 and found that 58 percent of the research dealt with the affective domain and 41 percent with the cognitive or knowledge domain. Most of these early studies were descriptive, often simply reporting environmental attitude or value profiles of various segments of the population. Few studies attempted to assess the change in values due to specific educational interventions, and many of these studies lacked scientific rigor.

Nevertheless, on the basis of more than 50 studies, Iozzi (1989) was able to draw the following generally positive conclusions about environmental education efforts to shape attitudes:

- Environmental education is effective in teaching positive environmental attitudes and values when programs and methods designed specifically to accomplish those objectives are used;

- The relationship between environmental knowledge and positive environmental attitudes and values is unclear;

- Positive environmental attitudes and values, once acquired, appear to be long-lasting;

- Development of environmental attitudes and values should begin before kindergarten and be further developed and regularly reinforced as a student progresses through elementary, middle/junior high school, and senior high school;

- The relationship between environmental attitudes and age, socioeconomic status, place of residence, and gender is conflicting and inconclusive;

- Outdoor education is an effective way of improving environmental attitudes and values;

- Various types of teaching methods seem to be effective in improving environmental attitudes and values; and

- The media are powerful sources for influencing environmental attitudes and values.

Volk, Hungerford, and Tomera (1984) completed a national survey of professional environmental educators which asked for an assessment of their success at teaching key ecological concepts and allied principles. Mean ratings on a five-point scale ranged from 3.5 (between moderate to considerable success) for elementary school children to 4.6 (between considerable and complete success) for college students. These findings suggest that environmental education programs do enhance environmental awareness and knowledge.

ENVIRONMENTAL SENSITIVITY

As we have already stated, environmental sensitivity is one of the most important correlates of responsible environmental behavior. Such sensitivity appears to result from an interplay of outdoor experiences (usually at an early age), role models (either familial or nonfamilial) who are empathetic to the environment, and knowledge about the natural environment (Marcinkowski, 1989). Chawla (1992) reports that children develop an empathetic connection with the environment through positive outdoor experiences over extended periods of time in wild or semiwild places, either during solitary play or activities with friends or families. Peters-Grant (1987), Peterson (1982), Scholl (1983), and Tanner (1980) all have reported that environmentally sensitive individuals can be characterized as long-term participants in such outdoor experiences as hiking, hunting, and fishing, usually with a small number of close acquaintances.

These findings point to the important role that families, teachers, communities, and land management agencies that manage public forest and park lands, must play in the environmental education process. Environmental education must provide outdoor experiences in informal settings for parents and their children. Opportunities for these experiences must be made available on a continual basis to permit periodic reinforcement and nurturing of environmental sensitivity. Also, opportunities to visit natural areas for long stays appear to be critically important. Residential nature camps, the family vacation

to national parks, and outfitted or nonoutfitted journeys into wild places are important elements of the environmental education process.

IN-DEPTH KNOWLEDGE OF ISSUES, ISSUE INVESTIGATION SKILLS, AND CITIZENSHIP SKILLS

Little research has been done on whether environmental education students:

1. learn information accessing and processing skills to gain deep understanding of the range of human-environment issues and problems around them,

2. learn problem-solving skills, and

3. learn action skills to improve environmental conditions in their homes and communities.

Professional environmental educators in one national survey (Volk , Hungerford, and Tomera, 1984) felt they had only "very limited" to "moderate" success at helping students understand various solutions for solving specific environmental problems, to develop skills to evaluate the cultural and ecological implications of alternative solutions, and to develop and apply skills to take individual or group action on one or more environmental issues in their communities. Those programs which seem most successful are those which permit and promote active student involvement in a variety of issues, promote involvement in environmental issues throughout the student's developmental career in the elementary through secondary grade curriculum, and permit and reinforce successful change interventions (Volk, 1993). Success at environmental projects is important to build the student's sense of internal locus of control (i.e., the feeling that he or she can make a difference).

Public Land Management Agencies, Environmental Education, and an Expanded Land Management Ethic

The Current Situation

Public land management agencies such as the Forest Service, the National Park Service, the Fish and Wildlife Service, and various state natural resource agencies currently play a vitally important role in environmental education in America. They do this in two primary and formal ways: environmental interpretation programming, and sponsorship of environmental education curriculum materials for classrooms and workshops. To a lesser extent, resource agency specialists accomplish environmental education through visits to schools, residential nature camps and nature centers, and through programming for mass media outlets. Finally, and very important, the public lands are both symbols and havens for Americans to periodically establish, renew, and reinforce their connections to nature and such values as rugged individualism that define the spirit of America. Also, such visits are crucial to developing environmental sensitivity, an important prerequisite to fostering responsible environmental behavior.

ENVIRONMENTAL INTERPRETATION PROGRAMMING

Virtually all of the massive commitment to environmental education by the National Park Service and much of the effort by agencies like the Forest Service, the Fish and Wildlife Service, and the Bureau of Land Management can be classified as nature interpretation. Their environmental learning takes place outdoors, or at least on site, and during leisure time. As such, the agency programming is solidly based in nature study and outdoor education traditions and to a lesser extent in the conservation education movement. While the agencies often state that developing a "land ethic" or an "environmental ethic" is a goal of their environmental education efforts, specific programs are usually far less grand in their scope and objectives. Typically, programming has not had multidisciplinary grounding, the breadth and continuity of reinforcement, in-depth analysis of issues and practice at issue investigation, the commitment to fostering responsible behavior and citizenship, and formalized attempts to empower people to action. The agencies thus have not adopted the environmental education model in its entirety. Nevertheless, much progress has been made.

Roggenbuck, Loomis, and Dagostina (1991) reviewed the results of almost 100 studies of the learning outcomes of visits to parks and forests or participation in environmental interpretive programs. Most such programs were provided by public land management agencies, and most were directed toward park or forest visitors (typically family groups) or toward children. Most sought to entertain and to promote factual learning, and most were successful. For example, park visitors often did learn low-impact camping practices, the important role of fire in ecosystems, or historical or ecological facts about a park. Many studies also showed that students learned such outdoor skills as map reading, using compasses, rock climbing, proper camping procedures, and low impact behaviors in parks and wilderness areas.

Evidence that positive attitude and value learning occurred as a result of agency interpretive programs is far less compelling. Sometimes such change occurred, and at other times the interpretive programs were not successful. As we have stated, past evaluation of environmental education programming suggests that it can be effective at developing positive attitudes but only when the programs are specifically designed and implemented to effect such change. Most interpretive programs are not purposefully planned and presented to effect such a change.

Finally, Roggenbuck, Loomis, and Dagostina (1991) found little evidence of higher levels of concept, schematic, and metacognition learning due to participation in interpretive programs during visits to public forests and parks. This is in part because environmental interpreters have generally not conceptualized their educational efforts at this level of abstract thinking. This kind of learning requires synthesis, creativity, and critical thinking. It represents the kind of learning that the environmental education process is specifically designed to accomplish. It also appears to be a prerequisite to educating for a "land ethic," and Passineau and Roggenbuck (1993) have called for environmental interpreters in land management agencies to adopt a more holistic education paradigm of environmental education.

SUPPLEMENTARY CURRICULUM MATERIALS

Various public land management agencies, especially at the state level, along with partners from the field of education and professional resource societies, have been active in producing supplementary environmental education materials for the classroom and for various youth clubs and organizations. Most notable of these are Project Learning Tree and Project Wild. Both of these programs are solidly anchored in environmental education. They attempt to foster environmental awareness and to teach ecological concepts, the interrelationships between humans and their environment, the role of forests or wildlife in a societal context, in-depth understanding of environmental problems and issues, and skills in creative problem solving, critical thinking, evaluation, and research. In short, the process tries to help the student clarify his or her own values about the environment, teaches them how to think—not what to think—and provokes an evaluation and possible modification of lifestyle (Noy and Brohl, 1990). Project Learning Tree workshops, teacher-training, and student programs are available in all 50 states, all Canadian provinces, and eight foreign countries (Disinger, 1993). Since 1993, more than 380,000 teachers have participated in Project Wild and more than 25 million elementary and secondary school students have been exposed to project materials (Disinger, 1993). Project Wild is now being taught in all 50 states, all Canadian provinces, and five foreign countries.

Future Challenges and Opportunities

We now turn to the changing role of resource management agencies in American society and how environmental education can help accomplish new agency mandates. We address the future by reviewing recent and projected changes in public concerns about the environment, public attitudes about the efficacy of possible solutions to environmental problems, and the role of public land management agencies in such solutions. We then address the expanded land management ethic called for in this text, and describe how environmental education efforts by land management agencies can foster such an ethic.

INCREASED DEMAND FOR ENVIRONMENTAL HARMONY

The commitment of the American people to "environmentalism" grew sharply during the 1980s, despite frequent recessions, a weak economy, and calls by the President to reduce environmental regulations. For example, a national environmental forum survey by Roper (1992) indicated that nine in ten Americans felt that environmentalism was "in," placing it behind only physical fitness and aerobics,

and ahead of such issues as safe sex and patriotism. Between 1982 and 1991, the percentage of Americans who said the environment was one of their top three personal concerns tripled, growing from 7 percent to 23 percent.

Concern for human health was the major motivating force for calls to protect the environment. For example, 63 percent of Americans expressed concern about environmental pollution. About 42 percent and 32 percent, respectively, favored protecting natural resources for future generations, and insuring that natural places and wildlife will always exist. When forced to choose between protecting the environment for human health or for preserving natural places and wildlife, health-related values won by a margin of 73 percent to 21 percent (The Roper Organization, 1992).

When asked what environmental health problems were "one of most serious," survey respondents indicated pollution of lakes, rivers, streams and coastal waters (77 percent), pollution from toxic waste sites (72 percent), shortages of good drinking water (68 percent), air pollution or smog (64 percent), damage to the ozone layer in the atmosphere (62 percent), and adequate landfill space for garbage and trash (58 percent).

The scientific community, and indeed the Forest Service with its recent promotion of an ethic of ecosystem sustainability, has called upon the American people to view specific environmental pollution problems in a broader ecological context (i.e., problems may not be solvable until humans live in harmony with all species and within the biotic and abiotic constraints of spaceship Earth). Given this, the 1992 Roper survey measured public concern over problems that pose primarily an ecological (in contrast to a health) risk. Concerns were high, but perhaps lower than what might have been expected. For example, 46 percent felt that loss of open areas, woods and natural places was one of the most serious problems facing our nation; 45 percent felt the same about global warming and the extinction of some plants, animals and insects; and 42 percent expressed comparable concern over the loss of wetland areas. This finding about resources over which the public land management agencies have direct jurisdiction suggests a need to raise the level of public awareness about the linkages between "land health" and human mental and physical health and the intrinsic values of healthy ecosystems. These concerns about human health, especially our mental health, certainly relate to the psychologically deep, nature-based, human values and experiences on which this text focuses.

SOLUTIONS TO ENVIRONMENTAL AND SOCIAL PROBLEMS

The Roper (1992) survey found that Americans were generally optimistic that environmental problems could be solved, that technological solutions would help protect the environment, and that economic development and environmental protection could go hand in hand. Virtually all respondents felt it was possible to find a proper balance between economic development and environmental quality, and most favored a "conservation" over a "preservation" ethic.

What is perhaps most interesting about these findings for public land management agencies is the support for the conservation ethic and the belief in technological solutions. As we noted earlier, the public appeared less knowledgeable and less concerned about the natural areas, wildlands, wildlife, and natural ecosystems of such agencies as the Forest Service or the Fish and Wildlife Service than it was about air, water, and waste pollution. However, the public's primary ethic about the land and its beliefs about wise use and management seem to be in harmony with those of the nation's major multiple use resource management agencies. This may reflect the greater success of resource agencies in promoting their resource management philosophy than in educating the public about the ecological systems under their stewardship. It may also simply be that the "wise use management" ethic is more pervasive throughout society.

The Roper (1992) data also provide some insight about the extent to which the American conservation ethic is compatible with an ethic of ecosystem sustainability. When asked if the goal to protect resources should be for the sake of nature or for the long-term benefit of humankind, 49 percent of the respondents agreed that plants and animals are "primarily for human use," but another 49 percent disagreed. Among younger, more affluent and better educated adults, most disagreed with the idea that nature exists only for human use. Thus, it appears that a gradual shift toward recognition of the larger ecosystem values of plants and animals will likely occur.

The strong belief in technology is not surprising. It is, after all, the American way. Examples of some of today's emerging and apparently successful environmental solutions include reformulated and lower-polluting gasolines, more fuel efficient and cleaner-burning automobiles, new alternatives to chlorofluorocarbons which deplete the Earth's ozone layer, and the capability to *build* wetlands (The Roper Organization, 1992).

These public survey findings suggest cautious optimism about the likely success of environmental education in fostering an ethic of ecosystem sustainability. The American people are tuned into the environment, they are concerned about environmental problems, and they support regulations to protect the environment. But much remains to be done. Positive attitudes and an expressed concern do not necessarily mean a life lived sustainably, or that threatened ecosystems will be saved. Indeed, the Roper survey has some warning signals to which public resource agencies and environmental educators should attend. For example, while most of the public would like to see federal government spending shifted to environmental programs from other areas, they do not favor net increases in their taxes for environmental protection. Many Americans are not well-informed about the ecological value of such systems as wetlands or about the extent of our ecological problems. Still, a large minority of Americans (48 percent) believe that the 1990s represent the last decade when humans will have a chance to save the Earth from environmental catastrophe. This might indicate readiness to take action; it might also suggest paralysis from fear of failure. In the final analysis, the lack of action to support positive attitudes may be the biggest challenge. The 1992 Roper poll indicated that while 82 percent of Americans are sympathetic to environmental concerns, only 30 percent think of themselves as active environmentalists.

AN ETHIC OF ECOSYSTEM SUSTAINABILITY

LEOPOLD'S LAND ETHIC

Aldo Leopold, America's great conservationist, ecologist, and wilderness philosopher, was perhaps the first public land manager to recognize the need for an ethic of ecosystem sustainability. As he slowly came to this position, Leopold was forging colossal intellectual advances. First, he noted that science can and must inform ethical choice. He believed that ecological knowledge must be brought to bear upon prescriptive questions concerning the interrelations between humans and the larger biotic community (Oelschlaeger, 1991). In his essay "The Conservation Ethic," Leopold explored the dominant view of resource management of his day (and for the most part still the prevailing view of resource managers), and noted the limits of efficiency and utility as the guiding ends of conservation. He wrote:

> *There is as yet no ethic dealing with man's relationship to land and to the nonhuman animals and plants which grow upon it. Land, like Odysseus' slave-girls, is still property. The land-relation is still strictly economic, entailing privileges but not obligations.*
>
> Leopold in Oelschlaeger, 1991, p. 221

In *A Sand County Almanac* (1949), Leopold again noted the limitations of conservation efforts of his time and called for an ecological, biocentric and ethical perspective. For Leopold, humans were not lords over the land, but rather members of the biotic community upon which our survival and the survival of our culture were dependent. This demonstrated our need to respect, love, and care for the land. This required a new land ethic to guide our behavior.

From the writings of Leopold, we have a prescription for a land ethic, and some guidelines on how to move toward individual and cultural acceptance of a land ethic. We know that a land ethic involves knowledge of the land, love and respect for the land, a set of moral principles about proper behavior toward the land, and then acting—as individuals, as institutions, and as a society—according to those principles. In the decades that have passed since Leopold's work, how far have we advanced in our understanding of an ethic of ecosystem sustainability? Do we as a society act according to it? And what is the role and potential of resource management agencies in fostering a public ethic of ecosystem sustainability?

THE VISION OF ECOSYSTEM SUSTAINABILITY

As Leopold noted, cultural adoption of an ethic of ecosystem sustainability will require a dramatic shift in how Americans view the Earth. In sociologi-

cal terms, what is needed is a shift in world-view. Kluckholn (1971) described human-nature relationships, or world-views, in terms of three cultural orientations: cultures who perceive themselves as dominant over nature (utilitarian cultures), subjugated to nature (fatalistic cultures), and in harmony with nature (harmonic cultures). In harmonic cultures, humans are considered to be integrated into the process and elements of nature on equal footing with other natural elements. Machlis (1989) calls this the ecological perspective, a perspective which assumes a connectedness between human values, human behavior, and the environment.

At this time in American culture the human-dominant utilitarian perspective predominates. Dustin, Knopf, and Fox (1993) have stated that building a new relationship with the Earth, one of ecosystem sustainability, will require changes in attitude, values, institutional structures, power, and managerial strategies. But established world-views are highly resistant to change (Simcox, 1993). Public land management agencies in the United States have recently called for a vision of ecosystem sustainability in resource management practices, in institutional philosophy about the meaning of natural resources, and in educational efforts directed at the public. Tenets of this new philosophy include, but are not limited to:

- Understanding the basic processes and functions of the biotic and abiotic environment with an emphasis on sustainability and humans as an integral part of the ecosystem.

- Understanding the role of culture and diversity of culture in shaping how humans change and adapt to their environment in their search for quality of life. Specific environments provide a sense of identity, a sense of place, and a sense of community for the American public. Also, the cultural heritage of Americans of varying ethnic and racial backgrounds provides a rich diversity of meanings, beliefs, values and solutions about an ideal relationship between humans and nature. Dustin, Knopf, and Fox (1993) admonish us to remember that the variety and richness of the human experience is as essential to our cultural health as is genetic variety to the health of any species or species variety to the health of any natural ecosystem.

- Expansion of agency land management ethics to include ecosystem values more clearly articulated by science, philosophy and religion, and the public. Examples of such values include biodiversity, ethnic diversity, aesthetics, intrinsic rights of species, humans as members of, rather than lords over, the community of life on Earth, and recognition and commitment to live within the constraints or limitations of the ecological community.

- Development of a well-grounded, holistic ethic among the public about how humans should interact with the environment. Such an ethic would encompass such past agency efforts as "Leave No Trace," but would reach far beyond it. Education for the "new" environmental ethic would have as its goal the harmonic relationship between humans and their environment (Dustin, McAvoy and Schultz, 1995), but would not prescribe one approach to attaining that goal as ideal. As already stated, diversity in cultural response to the environment is as valuable to long-term sustainability of the Earth as is diversity of ecological processes and systems. The goal would be to motivate all citizens to develop a holistic value system that would provide guidance to all behaviors involving the environment, and to empower them to take necessary personal, social, political, and environmental actions to solve problems of ecosystem sustainability.

A Partnership of the Environmental Education and Land Management Professions: An Ideal Route to Ecosystem Sustainability?

As we have seen, the goals of the environmental education profession and the recent commitment of land management agencies to ecosystem sustainability are essentially the same: develop knowledge, respect, and appropriate behavior toward the environment; recognize the connections of humans to the abiotic and other biotic components of the ecosystem; live within the constraints of ecological systems; recognize environmental problems; develop skills to solve envi-

ronmental problems by social, political, and ecological means; and take actions at the personal, community, and larger institutional levels to solve environmental problems. Some would argue that while the goals are the same, public servants in the land management professions are more constrained in how they can assist and promote actions of ecosystem sustainability beyond the level of the individual.

The environmental education profession has gained valuable insights on how to best educate environmentally: hands-on strategies, multidisciplinary approaches, higher-order thinking skills, and developmental learning. Environmental educators have also learned the best predictors of responsible environmental behavior and environmental activism: environmental sensitivity, respect for and knowledge about the environment, knowledge and skill at using environmental action strategies, high internal locus of control, and feelings of personal responsibility toward the environment. Finally, environmental educators have discovered some of the ways that people gain the necessary sensitivity, skills, and commitment: positive outdoor experiences as children over extended periods of time in informal and wild or semiwild settings with a significant friend or family member; help or involvement with many and varied real environmental issues across the elementary through secondary grade curriculum; and success in achieving desired personal, group, or community change.

Given what environmental educators have learned, what role can public land management agencies play in fostering an ethic of ecosystem sustainability? In what ways are resource agencies ideally positioned to advance environmental education toward ecosystem sustainability? How can resource agencies best utilize their lands, personnel, and expertise to foster a harmonic human/land ethic among their own staffs, partners, and the public at large? We conclude by turning to these crucial questions.

FORM PARTNERSHIPS

Perhaps the most important lesson learned from the last three decades of environmental education is that change in environmental ethics and lifestyle does not come easily. Such change occurs slowly, incrementally, and with much effort. If such change is to be sustained, individuals involved need frequent positive reinforcement, opportunities for success at environmental activism, and organizational and instructional support for environmental responsibility. Any agent of change must be prepared to take the long view, have realistic expectations about the rate of change, and be prepared to form partnerships to nurture lifelong learning. Thus, public land management agencies should not attempt to teach a new ethic of ecosystem sustainability alone. If they do, their efforts will be doomed. Instead, agency personnel must reach out and form partnerships with preschool and day-care center teachers, elementary through secondary grade teachers, professors of philosophy, humanities, and the sciences who teach university core curricula, directors of nature centers, zoos, museums, and art centers, outfitters, guides and tour operators, and representatives of the mass media. The "teaching teachers" model of Project Learning Tree and Project Wild represents one effective way that such partnerships can be implemented. This approach needs to be expanded to include both younger children and adults. It needs to provide opportunities for those who visit and those who don't visit public lands to come in contact with committed teachers of the environment. Finally, the content of these outreach programs needs to be broadened to include not only a focus on forests, wildlife, or water, but also a holistic expression of quality of life lived sustainably in an ecological context—including the qualitative dimensions of human life reflected by the psychologically deep, nature-based values considered in this text.

Nurture Internal Change

We have suggested that the primary land ethic of the bulk of resource management agencies and most of the American public has been one of human domination, utilitarian values, efficiency, wise use, and sustained yield. Accompanying this value system is a strong belief in technological fixes to environmental and societal problems. This world-view can be incompatible with an ethic of ecosystem sustainability (see Baltic, Chapter Twenty-Four, in this volume), but we have also noted that making a shift in world-view (e.g., in the proper relationship between humans and nature) at the individual, organizational, or societal level is very difficult. Thus, even after an agency leader announces a commitment to a new land ethic, there is considerable lag time in adopting and institutionalizing the new value systems required. Built-in organizational checks and balances which protect the old value system must be

changed to accept the new. Employees need to learn the new ethic and come to accept it. This takes time, effort, and environmental education.

Before they can reach out to promote an ethic of ecosystem sustainability, many resource agencies and their personnel must undergo considerable environmental ethical change. Fortunately, the work setting provides many, but not all, of the precursors to effective environmental education. On the positive side, resource managers have lived a life of concern for, and commitment to, the environment. They come to the job day after day, week after week, and year after year. There is time for progressive, developmental, and spiraling learning—learning which gradually leads the participants into deeper and deeper critical thinking and issue awareness. The job provides the employee with frequent and real world issues and challenges regarding values and ethics. Decisions must be made and actions taken. All this provides an ideal setting for intellectual growth, values clarification, and ethical change. What is needed is a nurturing supervisor who shapes the learning tasks, guards against failure in decision making and action based upon the new paradigm, facilitates the learning curve with in-service training where necessary, and shapes the institutional environment to reward adoption of the new ethic.

Barriers to change, however, are also strong. The wise use/utilitarian ethic was inculcated within agency professionals during their training in natural resource schools and has been reinforced on the job. Old habits and viewpoints are difficult to change. Finally, the ethic of ecosystem sustainability is both new and complex, and therefore anxiety producing. For example, the new ethic calls for the consideration of many land management issues within the context of more than one human value system. What is the best answer depends not only on the biotic or abiotic limitations of the ecosystem, but also on the diversity of human value systems which have developed across time to assure quality of life. Responsible environmental decision making in this new ethical context requires considerable on-the-job training for many of today's resource managers.

Utilize Existing Partners

Land management agencies have a variety of partners who directly or indirectly act to provide the

American people with goods and services from public lands. For example, on national forest lands, logging companies harvest timber, ranchers graze cattle, outfitters guide hunting trips, permittees guide the public on river or jeep trips, and concessionaires manage campgrounds. These partners demonstrate through their actions their own ethic about the land and indirectly the agency ethic. Thus, if the agency adopts a new land ethic or promotes a new management philosophy (like ecosystem sustainability), then these partners also must learn and adopt the new approach to land management. Indeed, the partners may be more effective than the agency itself in persuading the visiting public to adopt the new ethic. For example, Roggenbuck, Williams, and Bobinski (1992) found that river guides were much more influential than National Park Service rangers in gaining guest compliance in low impact practices on a whitewater river in West Virginia.

Several characteristics of the agency/permittee relationship enhance the likelihood that environmental education could hasten the adoption of an ethic of ecosystem sustainability among private partners. First, like the agency staff itself, the private partners have a long history of working and spending time in the outdoors. As a result, these individuals likely have considerable sensitivity to the environment. Their very livelihood depends directly on the commodity goods produced on the public lands or on their ability to facilitate enjoyment of the public lands by visitors. It is in their own and their family's best interest to act responsibly with respect to the environments they use and enjoy (see Budd, Chapter Fourteen; Tims, Chapter Fifteen; and Rey, Chapter Seventeen; in this volume).

From the agency perspective, permittees, concessionaires, and tourism promoting organizations typically have a long-term relationship with the government. Thus, there is time for the incremental and hierarchical nature of effective environmental education to unfold. Also, given the stewardship role of the land management agency, it can ask for participation of the private partners in environmental education workshops on a periodic basis as a requirement for the continuation of the permit or concession. Through such workshops the resource agency can utilize repetition, real world examples, and positive reinforcement to teach relevant concepts, enhance in-depth knowledge of environmental

problems and issues, foster concern for the quality of the environment, increase knowledge of action strategies to protect ecosystem sustainability, develop commitment and practice at taking appropriate environmental actions, and provide empowerment for the permittee or concessionaire to actually take environmentally responsible actions.

PROVIDE A SENSE OF WONDER FOR CHILDREN

As we have already noted, environmental sensitivity is a necessary precursor to environmental activism and environmentally responsible behavior. While sensitivity at a cognitive level may develop through environmental education in the classroom, some educators doubt whether the necessary emotional attachment to the Earth can occur there (Roggenbuck, Loomis and Dagostina, 1991). Several authors (e.g., Chawla, 1992; Marcinkowski, 1989) have noted that the necessary "sense of wonder" is most often developed at a very young age (frequently preschool), often with parents, and in a wild or semiwild place. Statements by some of our greatest naturalists support these views. For example, Minnesota naturalist Sigurd Olson recalled his first sense of wonder in *The Singing Wilderness*:

> *My first recollection came one sunny afternoon when Mother led me through a grove of maples in the fall. That day the trees must have been in full color, for the ground was deep in drifting leaves. As we walked through them we were surrounded with color, and when the wind blew we were drenched with it. The whirling masses of red and yellow filled me with excitement, and when we ran through the grove we ran and ran until we could run no more and sank laughing to the ground—color and beauty became a part of my life.*

> quoted in Herman, Passineau, Schimpf and Treuer, 1991, p. 6

Rachel Carson (1962) also recognized the importance of the childhood years for developing respect and love for nature. She attributed her love for nature to childhood explorations of the woods and fields surrounding the family farm in the Allegheny Mountains with the loving encouragement of her mother.

While most Americans today do not grow up amid fields and wood lots, public land management agencies are ideally suited to provide "places of the heart" for children. This is especially the case for those agencies which manage urban forest parks and urban recreation areas. Patches of trees and shrubs in schoolyards or at neighborhood nature centers can also become places of wonder. Resource managers can nurture environmental sensitivity through guarding the existence and health of these microenvironments, assuring the safety of children who play there while protecting the "free play" of children and their special adult friends.

Finally, environmental education specialists and interpretive naturalists at urban and metropolitan parks may become mentors that spark a sense of joy in children for nature. Such mentoring is especially helpful for disadvantaged children, or children whose parents have little time or ability to provide a sense of wonder about the Earth. The mentoring role is especially suitable for effective environmental education because of the frequent and periodic contact between mentor and child over extended periods of time. This permits the developmental and spiraling growth in sensitivity and understanding of the environment. The "problem" of the labor intensive nature of mentoring might be mitigated by implementing the Project Learning Tree model of extending resources (i.e., environmental education specialists could train mentors from the community in the sense of wonder of nature).

Provide Extended Field Experiences for Youth

As we have already seen, considerable environmental education efforts are currently directed at children in the elementary and secondary schools. These efforts typically include the development of curriculum materials, environmental problem solving, and sometimes case studies or environmental actions. Public resource agencies have supported these school programs by providing learning models and materials such as Project Learning Tree, by visiting classrooms or providing field interpretation, or by making their lands available as outdoor laboratories.

Public land managers are thus well-positioned to incorporate an ethic of ecosystem sustainability within school and field curricular materials and programs for elementary through secondary grade students. This should be expanded to include students at the college level. Public land managers must work with their environmental education partners to

bring discussions of ecosystem sustainability to university core curricula so that all university students have opportunities to learn, discuss, and debate human/nature relationships. Resource agencies must work with university instructors to encourage visits to demonstration sites which illustrate management practices supporting an ethic of ecosystem sustainability. This is especially important for those academic programs training tomorrow's resource professionals.

Another environmental education avenue for reaching youngsters, and for which resource agencies are ideally suited, are residential camps on public lands. Job Corps, Youth Conservation Corps, and Young Adult Conservation Corps camps are illustrative. These residential camps typically accept youths of troubled or disadvantaged backgrounds and provide opportunities for development of work-related skills, social skills, and enhanced self-concept. They also provide environmental education and are ideally positioned to teach an ethic of ecosystem sustainability. In residential camps youngsters are in wild nature, and their stay extends for weeks. This provides time for gradual immersion in nature (which enhances environmental sensitivity) and for the progressive nature of effective environmental education to unfold. There is time for familiarization with nature, learning the four strands of environmental literacy (knowledge, affect, skill, behavior), developing higher order thinking skills (critical thinking, creative thinking, integrative thinking, and problem solving), and practicing environmentally responsible behavior. Unfortunately, such residential camps are gradually being phased out by many natural resource agencies, and those that do exist appear to offer shorter and shorter programs. Both of these recent trends reduce the effectiveness of land managers in teaching youngsters a new land ethic.

Intensify Contact with the Visiting Public

Currently, the American people visit public lands in vast numbers, often while at leisure. Most natural resource agencies provide some sort of nature education or interpretive programs for their visitors. But at least three factors reduce the effectiveness of these programs as tools for environmental education. First, only a small percentage of visitors to public lands come into contact with nature interpretation programs. Second, there is no planning for, and little likelihood of multiple and progressive contacts with, the same visitors across time, so any environmental learning is haphazard. Finally, the content of nature education programs most typically provides factual information about the environment, develops support for the resource management agency and its policies, or entertains. Sometimes the programs attempt to develop sensitivity toward, and empathy for, the environment. Rarely do these programs deal with cultural and environmental values, critical thinking skills, problem solving, practice at environmental responsibility, or environmental activism.

While we doubt that the leisure visitor is or should be a prime candidate for environmental education in its fullest sense, we believe that some progress can be made in this area. We have seen that a prerequisite to a life lived sustainably or a life of environmental activism is environmental sensitivity and wonder. This best develops through time—ample time—spent in special natural places. Public land managers are the guardians of many of America's most special places. Resource agencies need to promulgate policies and management actions to encourage visitors to get out of their cars and spend time in contemplation at these special places. They might develop short loop trails, as have Great Smoky Mountains National Park managers in Tennessee and North Carolina, to encourage park visitors to take leisurely strolls along streams, to hemlock stands, or to a pioneer's long abandoned cabin. While such experiences are short, the goal is to encourage many such periodic strolls during a visit to the park.

Another recommendation is to encourage increased lengths of stay. Length of stay is a critical variable in shaping the nature of the leisure experience (Williams and Knopf, 1985), and it is critical to environmental learning in nature. For example, it seems critical to the attainment of the ideal wilderness experience. Sigurd Olson (1956) noted that it took some days before his guests on canoe trips could shed the trappings of urban life, begin to move to ancient rhythms, and feel oneness with our ancestors and the Earth. We believe such feelings of oneness and harmony are conducive to environmental learning and an ethic of ecosystem sustainability. Finally, while we believe that nature inter-

preters on public lands must be cognizant of the leisure frame of mind of their visitors, their programs can—in goal, content, and process—support the teaching of an ethic of ecosystem sustainability. For example, an interpretive walk along a stream through a recent timber harvest might demonstrate conservation practices to protect water quality and quantity, include activities to measure water quality and in-stream biotic diversity, involve questioning, role playing, discussion, and perhaps debate about the advisability of the timber harvest and the success of the conservation practices, and discuss the implications of participants' water and paper use patterns back home for decisions in the forest. Such learning experiences build upon the successful principles and techniques of the environmental education and interpretive professions.

INVOLVE THE MASS MEDIA

Our final recommendation to public land management agencies is that they involve the mass media in promoting environmental education oriented toward ecosystem sustainability. The obvious reason for this is that a relatively small proportion of all Americans actually visit the public lands. A second reason is that a large and growing proportion of Americans gain their knowledge of natural resource issues from the mass media, especially television.

The mass media (including primarily radio, television, and newspapers, but also movies, popular music, and books) can be seen both as sources of information and entertainment and as "manipulators" of information. The mass media not only report about news and issues, but they also determine what news and issues are aired. Resource managers must work with the media to gain coverage of policy statements regarding agency shifts toward an ethic of ecosystem sustainability and of demonstrations of the effect of such an ethical shift in programs on the land. They must also work to make such coverage more educational. They must sell more than just the "sound bite." They need repeated coverage of the topic; philosophical, historical, and environmental reasons for the new paradigm; discussions of timely resource management issues illustrating the new ethic; and public debate about the causes, costs, outcomes, and public benefits of sustainable living. Talk shows and call-in programs can facilitate such public policy debate and learning. But the greatest potential for mass media environmental learning is the information highway of tomorrow, a future where interactive television and computers will be in virtually every American home. Land managers and environmental education specialists must begin planning today to build upon the strengths of the new highway. That information highway will permit frequent contact with the American public, time for individualized and in-depth coverage of topics of mutual interest, opportunity for progressive or hierarchical learning, definition and discussion of land management issues, simulation of the effectiveness of alternative resource allocation solutions, and practice at real or simulated actions to support sustainable living.

Conclusion

We have attempted to show that public land management agencies are uniquely positioned to work more effectively with environmental education professionals to promote a land management ethic oriented both toward ecosystem sustainability and better accommodation of psychologically deep, nature-based, human experiences. We close with the admonition to those agencies that they cannot meet their legislative mandates and internal agency decrees and policy directives unless the public they serve both supports and understands them. This requires an environmentally literate public which not only scores high in environmental concerns in national opinion surveys, but which also understands basic problems and principles of land management.

The real challenge is reflected in the last census of the United States which showed that 85 percent of the American people reside in urban areas. Other surveys and widespread social commentary indicate that American society is becoming increasingly polarized along many lines, including who should own and manage the public lands, and how they should be managed. Environmental education must play a larger role in teaching urbanites about basic principles of land management and in helping prevent and resolve public land management disputes. Educational efforts along these lines must be intensified by all public land management agencies whether urban or rural in nature. These efforts must include considerably more off-site education about the environment in elementary and secondary schools. It must involve cooperation with a multiplicity of part-

ners. And it must involve the news media. Most important, it must be a high and adequately funded priority of all the involved agencies, led by people within those agencies who have the necessary professional expertise and a lasting commitment to effect change.

Acknowledgment

The authors thank Dr. Tom Marcinkowski, Science Education Department, Florida Institute of Technology, Melbourne, Florida, for his helpful review of an earlier version of this chapter.

Literature Cited

Carson, R. (1962). *Silent spring*. Boston MA: Houghton Mifflin Company.

Chawla, L. (1992). Research priorities in environmental education. *Children's Environments, 9*(1), 68-71.

Disinger, J. (1993). Environment in the K-12 curriculum: An overview. In R. Wilke (Ed.), *Environmental education teacher resource handbook* (pp. 23-43). Millwood, NY: Kraus International Publications.

Dustin, D., Knopf, R., and Fox, K. (1993). Building multicultural responsiveness into outdoor recreation management. In A. Ewert, D. Chavez and A. Magill (Eds.), *Culture, conflict, and communication in the wildland-urban interface* (pp. 259-265). Boulder, CO: Westview Press, Inc.

Dustin, D., McAvoy, L., and Schultz, J. (1995). *Stewards of access custodians of choice: A philosophical foundation for the park and recreation profession* (2nd ed.). Champaign, IL: Sagamore Publishing, Inc.

Hammerman, D. and Hammerman, W. (1964). *Teaching in the outdoors*. Minneapolis, MN: Burgess International Group, Inc.

Hawkins, D. and Vinton, D. (1973). *The environmental classroom*. Englewood Cliffs, NJ: Prentice-Hall.

Herman, M., Passineau, J., Schimpf, A., and Treuer, P. (1991). *Teaching kids to love the earth*. Duluth, MN: Pfeifer-Hamilton Publishers.

Hines, J., Hungerford, H., and Tomera, A. (1986). Analysis and synthesis of research on responsible environmental behavior: A meta-analysis. *Journal of Environmental Education, 18*(2), 1-8.

Hungerford, H. and Volk, T. (1990). Changing learner behaviors through environmental education. *Journal of Environmental Education, 21*(3), 8-21.

Iozzi, L. (1984). *Monographs in environmental education and environmental studies #2*. Columbus, OH: ERIC Clearinghouse for Science, Mathematics, and Environmental Education.

Iozzi, L. (1989). What research says to the educator; part one: Environmental education and the affective domain. *Journal of Environmental Education, 20*(3), 3-9.

Klinger, G. (1980). *The effect of an instructional sequence on the environmental action skills of a sample of southern Illinois eighth graders*. Unpublished master's thesis, Southern Illinois University, Carbondale, IL.

Kluckholn, F. (1971). Dominant and variant value orientations. In C. Kluckholn, H. Murray and D. Schneider (Eds.), *Personality in nature, society, and culture* (pp. 342-357). New York, NY: Alfred A. Knopf, Inc.

Leopold, A. (1949). *A sand county almanac and sketches here and there*. New York, NY: Oxford University Press.

Machlis, G. (1989). Managing parks as human ecosystems. In I. Altman and E. Zube (Eds.), *Public places and spaces, human behavior and environment* (pp. 255-275). Vol. 10. New York, NY: Plenum Publishing Corp.

Marcinkowski, T. (1989). An analysis of correlates and predictors of responsible environmental behavior. *Dissertation Abstracts International, 49*(12), 3677-A.

Marcinkowski, T. (1990). The new National Environmental Education Act: A renewal of commitment. *Journal of Environmental Education, 22*(2), 7-10.

Marshall, K. (1993). State-level curriculum guidelines: An analysis. In R. Wilke (Ed.), *Environmental education teacher resource handbook* (pp. 106-134). Millwood, NY: Kraus International Publications.

National Advisory Council on Environmental Education. (1993). *Review draft, national report on environmental education*. Washington, DC: Environmental Protection Agency.

Noy, L. and Brohl, C. (1990). Project Learning Tree as an educational tool for wilderness mangers. In D. Lime (Ed.), *Managing America's enduring wilderness resource* (pp. 131-132). Proceedings of the Conference, Minneapolis, MN, Sept. 11-17, 1989. Published by Tourism Center, Minnesota Extension Service and Minnesota Agricultural Experiment Station, University of Minnesota, St. Paul, MN.

Oelschlaeger, M. (1991). *The idea of wilderness*. New Haven, CT: Yale University Press.

Olson, S. (1956). *The singing wilderness*. New York, NY: Alfred A. Knopf, Inc.

Passineau, J. and Roggenbuck, J. (1993). *Wilderness education in the U.S: Do we teach low impact knowledge, behavior, or a wilderness ethic?* Paper presented at the 5th World Wilderness Congress, International Wilderness Allocation, Management, and Research Symposium, Sept. 24-Oct. 1, Troms, Norway.

Peters-Grant, V. (1987). The influence of life experiences in the vocational interests of volunteer environmental workers. *Dissertation Abstracts International, 47*(10).

Peterson, N. (1982). *Developmental variables affecting environmental sensitivity in professional environmental educators*. Unpublished master's thesis, Southern Illinois University, Carbondale, IL.

Ramsey, J. and Hungerford, H. (1989). The effects of issue and action training on environmental behavior in seventh grade students. *Journal of Environmental Education, 20*(4), 29-34.

Roggenbuck, J., Loomis, R., and Dagostina, J. (1991). The learning benefits of leisure. In B. Driver, P. Brown and G. Peterson (Eds.), *Benefits of leisure* (pp. 195-213). State College, PA: Venture Publishing, Inc.

Roggenbuck, J., Williams, D., and Bobinski, C. (1992). Public-private partnership to increase commercial tour guides' effectiveness as nature interpreters. *Journal of Park and Recreation Administration, 10*(2), 41-50.

The Roper Organization. (1992). *Natural resource conservation—Where environmentalism is headed in the 1990s.* National Environmental Forum, Times Mirror magazines. Conservation Council.

Roth, R. (1978). Off the merry-go-round and onto the escalator. In W. Stapp (Ed.), *From ought to action in environmental education: A report of the national leadership conference on environmental education* (pp. 12-22). Columbus, OH: SMEAC Information Reference Center. ED 159 046.

Roth, R. (1980). Conceptual development and environmental education. *Journal of Environmental Education, 11*(1), 6-9.

Schafer, R. (1981). Education and resource managers: A partnership with a future. In M. Bowman (Ed.), *Teaching natural resource management through environmental education activities* (pp. 3-12). Columbus, OH: ERIC Clearinghouse for Science, Mathematics, and Environmental Education 214 752.

Schmieder, A. (1977). *The nature and philosophy of environmental education.* Trends in Environmental Education. UNESCO.

Scholl, M. (1983). *A survey of significant childhood learning experiences of suburban/urban environmentalists.* Paper presented at the Annual Conference of the North American Association for Environmental Education, Ypsilanti, MI.

Sia, A., Hungerford, H., and Tomera, A. (1985). Predictions of environmentally responsible behavior: An analysis. *Journal of Environmental Education, 17*(2), 31-40.

Simcox, D. (1993). Cultural foundations for leisure preference, behavior, and environmental orientation. In A. Ewert, D. Chavez and A. Magill (Eds.), *Culture, conflict, and communication in the wildland-urban interface* (pp. 267-280). Boulder, CO: Westview Press, Inc.

Simpson, P. (1989). *The effects of an extended case study on citizenship behavior and associated variables in fifth and sixth grade students.* Unpublished doctoral dissertation, Southern Illinois University, Carbondale, Illinois.

Sivek, D. and Hungerford, H. (1990). Predictors of responsible behavior in members of three Wisconsin conservation organizations. *Journal of Environmental Education, 21*(2), 35-40.

Stapp, W. (1969). The concept of environmental education. *Journal of Environmental Education, 1*(1), 30-31.

Stapp, W. (1974). Historical setting of environmental education. In J. Swan and W. Stapp (Eds.), *Environmental education: Strategies toward a more liveable future* (pp. 42-49). New York, NY: Halsted Press.

Tanner, T. (1980). Significant life experiences: A new research area in environmental education. *Journal of Environmental Education, 11*(4), 20-24.

UNESCO. (1978). *Final report, intergovernmental conference on environmental education.* Organized by UNESCO in cooperation with UNEP, Tbilisi, USSR, 14-26 October 1977. Paris, France: UNESCO ED/MD/49.

Volk, T. (1989). Two issue-related approaches to citizenship education. *Councilor, 49*(October), 39-44.

Volk, T. (1993). Integration and curriculum design. In R. Wilke (Ed.), *Environmental education teacher resource handbook* (pp. 45-75). Millwood, NY: Kraus International Publications.

Volk, T., Hungerford, H., and Tomera, A. (1984). A national survey of curriculum needs as perceived by professional environmental educators. *Journal of Environmental Education, 16*(1), 10-19.

Williams, D. and Knopf, R. (1985). In search of the primitive—urban continuum: The dimensional structure of outdoor recreation settings. *Environment and Behavior, 17*, 351-370.

Research Directions

The most beautiful thing we can experience is the mystical. . . . It is the source of all true art and science.

Albert Einstein (1930)

Approaches in the Social and Behavioral Sciences to the Systematic Study of Hard-to-Define Human Values and Experiences

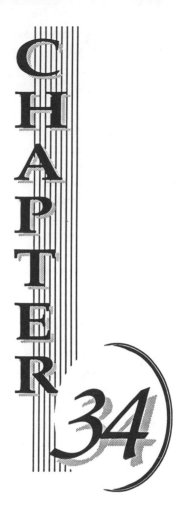

Roger Mannell
Department of Recreation and Leisure Studies
University of Waterloo
Waterloo, Ontario, Canada

Introduction

In this chapter I evaluate the scientific status of that subset of hard-to-define values and experiences that, for lack of a better term, I refer to as "psychologically deep" experiences. Over the years, I have faced the challenge of studying and trying to understand the valued and meaningful experiences that people derive from recreation settings, natural and otherwise, with a variety of social scientific methods. I have also been involved in attempting to translate social science knowledge into policies and management practices. The assumptions underlying my analyses in this chapter are that psychologically deep experiences are an important class of leisure benefits, that recreation providers need to understand the social and psychological nature of these experiences if they are to manage for these types of experiential opportunities, and that social science methods are one legitimate and useful way of coming to know about these phenomena.

Psychologically Deep Experiences

By psychologically deep experiences I have in mind those psychological states that people experience and label as special, out-of-the-ordinary, or meaningful. To assess the feasibility of scientifically studying and managing for psychologically deep experiences, particularly those linked to natural settings, I examine a variety of psychological states that have been identified. A large number of these out-of-the-ordinary experiences have been proposed and studied including: aesthetic, absorbing, flow, peak, leisure, tourism, mystical, spiritual, religious, transcendental, nature, and wilderness experiences. Psychologically deep experiences occurring in natural and built settings can also be considered altered states of consciousness. Altered states, or different modes of experiencing everyday reality, also include psychological phenomena such as creativity, hypnosis, dreaming and meditation (Spilka, Hood, and Gorsuch, 1985). The catchall phrase "altered states of consciousness" has become the accepted term for a loosely knit area in which the focus is on the empirical study of what have often been assumed to be either novel or pathological experiences. Yet investigators in this area seem to share a view that these experiences are normal and valid features of human experience (Lee, Ornstein, Galin, Deikman, and Tart, 1976; Spilka, Hood, and Gorsuch, 1985).

Various types of experiences have been identified and studied by social scientists as special and out-of-the-ordinary. Perusal of the literature suggests that for our purposes the various constructs developed to describe these psychologically deep experiences may be characterized in several ways. First, they vary in terms of the rareness with which they occur in people's experience. Related to this rareness of the experience is the degree to which they are perceived by individuals to be outside their normal daily experiences. Second, psychologically deep experiences differ to the extent that they have a secular or religious connotation.

For example, Csikszentmihalyi (1975, 1990) has described a type of psychologically deep experience that is generally accessible to most people and is characterized by varying degrees of psychological involvement in the activities of everyday life. On the other hand, Maslow's (1968) peak experience has been conceptualized as not only more intense and rare in the experience of the individual, but as a state experienced by a relatively small number of people—those who are self-actualized.

Various psychologically deep experience constructs also differ on the basis of their connection with a set of religious beliefs and values. Intense religious experiences, such as the conversion experience (Dawson, 1990), may have no existence outside of a religious context. However, other psychologically deep and absorbing experiences that have been conceptualized including flow, aesthetic, nature, wilderness, and leisure experiences do not require a set of religious values to be experienced or to be meaningful to the individual.

However, many of these psychologically deep experiences (e.g., mystical, spiritual, transcendental) have both religious and secular counterparts. In the former case, these experiences are conceptualized as

being religious experiences that have meaning only within the context of a particular set of religious beliefs and practices. In the latter case, these experiences are independent of religious values. Similarly, aesthetic, nature and wilderness experiences can, for the most part, be thought of as secular experiences, yet they may have religious overtones and be associated with religious experience for some people. Even leisure experiences, which are for the most part viewed as secular, have been seen as dependent on a religious perspective by some writers (e.g., Pieper, 1952).

Social Scientific Status

By scientific status I have in mind determining what social scientists "know" about these psychologically deep experiences as opposed to other ways of "knowing" such as through religious, philosophical or artistic scrutiny. The social science approach is a scientific approach. Science is the application of the scientific method to answerable questions. The scientific method is here simply viewed as a way of making observations or gathering information in a systematic way involving the use of controlled, systematic inquiry, and a logical and rational approach to explanation.

Answerable questions are questions that can be answered by the use of the scientific method. While this reasoning sounds a bit circular, it simply means that the questions should have answers that can be arrived at by observing what is going on under various circumstances. If the problem cannot be answered through careful, systematic observation or the use of the scientific method, approaches other than science may be necessary. Many areas of human study and knowledge address questions for which science-based disciplines have no answers. Philosophy, art, literature, and religious studies are devoted to exploring not only some of the same questions addressed by the scientific disciplines but also many issues that cannot be dealt with by the scientific approach. Novels are written, pictures painted, philosophical analyses presented, religious and cultural standards called on which provide answers to these questions for many of us.

Purpose

Specifically, in this chapter I briefly review and assess the extent to which social scientists:

1. have shown an interest in psychologically deep experiences and have treated them as legitimate social and psychological phenomena;

2. have used existing social science approaches to explain and relate these phenomena to other aspects of human behavior and experience; and

3. have exposed these phenomena to empirical scrutiny through the development of operational definitions, measurement techniques, and the application of various social science research methods.

I draw from several rich areas of social and psychological inquiry on psychologically deep experiences for this assessment including the study of optimal experiences in daily life, leisure, and touristic experiences, religious, mystical, and spiritual experiences, and nature and wilderness experiences.

Social Science Attempts to Study Psychologically Deep Experiences

Optimal Experiences

A number of constructs, such as peak experience (Maslow, 1968), absorbing experience (Tellegen and Atkinson, 1974) and flow (Csikszentmihalyi, 1975) have been proposed which have special meaning and stand out in the phenomenological experience of the individual. The occurrence of these experiences is seen to both reflect optimal cognitive and emotional functioning and to be important to the well-being of the individual (Csikszentmihalyi and Kleiber, 1991). Maslow's (1968) notion of "peak" experience and Csikszentmihalyi's (1975, 1990) concept of "flow" have been particularly attractive conceptualizations for researchers interested in optimal experiences since they identify a variety of characteristics of phenomenological experiences derived from a wide range of engagements which have been amenable to operationalization.

Maslow (1968) describes peak experiences as "moments of highest happiness and fulfillment" often achieved through the nature experience, aesthetic perception, creative movement, intellectual insight, organismic experience, athletic pursuit, and the like (p. 73). Flow experiences for Csikszentmihalyi (1990) are "the best moments of our lives, are not the passive, receptive, relaxing times" and they "occur when a person's body or mind is stretched to its limits in a voluntary effort to accomplish something difficult and worthwhile" (p. 3). Flow experiences are characterized by a centering of the individual's attention, transitoriness, richer perception, forgetting oneself and becoming totally involved in the activity at hand, disorientation in time and space, and enjoyment and momentary loss of anxiety and constraint. The flow notion differs from peak experience in several ways and recognizes that the experience need not be an "all-or-none" experience and that the degree of flow can vary from modest involvement to intense peak-like involvement (Mannell, 1980).

The theory of flow experiences, in particular, has stimulated substantial theory and research. Csikszentmihalyi (1975) developed a model which has provided insight into how the activities of everyday life come to be invested with meaning and experienced as optimal. In the case of research, innovative research techniques have been used to further study the phenomenon and examine both the conditions in which it occurs and its relationship to mental health and other benefits.

In his original research, Csikszentmihalyi, a social psychologist at the University of Chicago, did extensive interviews with rock climbers, recreational dancers, chess players and surgeons. He identified the characteristics of those experiences which his subjects reported to be their best and most meaningful. These episodes provided absorbing experiences, were challenging, and included those in which the participants lost track of time and their awareness of themselves.

Out of this research Csikszentmihalyi and his colleagues (Larson and Csikszentmihalyi, 1983) have developed the "experiential sampling method" (ESM). Typically respondents carry electronic pagers with them and are randomly signaled throughout the day for a period of one week. Each time the pager emits a signal (an audible beep), the respondents take out a booklet of brief questionnaires (experiential sampling forms [ESFs]) and complete a series of open- and close-ended items indicating their current activity, the social and physical context of their activity, and psychological state.

While the ESF has been varied slightly across studies, the types of variables and scales included have been fairly standard. The ESF includes items that require respondents to:

1. write in the time of the pager signal and the time that they actually filled out the ESF (usually the questionnaire data is dropped if too much time elapses between signal and response);

2. write down what they were thinking about at the time of the signal;

3. write down the main thing/activity they were doing;

4. check on a list whom they were with;

5. rate on Likert scales several items that measure the level of psychological involvement in the activity (e.g., level of concentration, personal skills and challenge, perception of the passage of time);

6. rate mood states on semantic differential scales assessing affect and arousal; and

7. check reasons or motivations for participation (see Larson and Csikszentmihalyi, 1983).

Some researchers have included additional scales or items on the ESF; for example, self-esteem (Wells, 1988), leisureliness (Samdahl, 1988), and willingness to engage in alternative activities (Mannell and Zuzanek, 1991). The reliability of the multiple item mood scales has been shown to be consistently high in most studies reported. In analyses of the psychometric properties of the ESF measures over a week of repeated use, the subjects' responses have been shown to change only slightly from the first to the second half of the study week. Differences between individuals were also found to be stable (Csikszentmihalyi and Larson, 1984; Wells, 1988).

Flow and optimal experiences have been examined with people from different walks of life and differing ages. Optimal experiences in daily life have been studied and related to issues such as self-awareness, feelings of control and freedom, eating disorders, self-actualization and mental health, and the experiences of television viewing, work, school, and being alone.

Leisure and Touristic States

The experience of leisure at its best, for example, "unconditional" (Kelly, 1983) or "pure" (Neulinger, 1974) leisure, has frequently been described as a special and "out-of-the-ordinary" experience.

Leisure and free time live in two different worlds. Anybody can have free time. Not everybody can have leisure. Leisure refers to a state of being, a condition of man, which few desire and fewer achieve.

de Grazia, 1962, p. 5

Touristic experiences have also been seen to have some special quality, to be more than simply an experience accompanying travel or tourist behavior. The ultimate travel experience itself has been compared to a religious experience (Cohen, 1979a) and to be the result of pilgrimage, where the tourist searches for something less tangible than the trip and more rewarding than just being there. The search for this ultimate touristic experience has been described as a quest. MacCannell (1976) refers to it as a quest for authenticity; Cohen (1979b) calls it a quest for center; Meyersohn (1981) suggests it is a quest for meaning; and, Przeclawski (1985) considers it a quest for values. Not unlike de Grazia, Cohen (1979b, p. 194) suggests that these more profound modes of experience are realized by only a select few.

During the last several decades there has been a steady growth in the amount of psychologically oriented leisure research reported. Leisure experiences have come to be seen not only as important but also, perhaps, the primary outcome of recreational behavior. In the early 1970s, Driver and his associates began laying a more systematic social psychological foundation for the study of experiences in outdoor recreation (Driver, 1976; Driver and Tocher, 1970). The traditional view of recreation was based on outdoor activities such as fishing, swimming, hiking, and camping. While this activity approach was seen as useful for descriptive purposes, it left unaddressed the reasons why the recreationist participates in the activity, what satisfactions or rewards are received from the activity, and how the quality of the experience can be enhanced (Driver and Tocher, 1970, p. 10). Research in the outdoor recreation and resource management area has provided a strong impetus for recreation providers to be as concerned with the experiential nature and quality of their services as they are the activities and settings they manage (Driver, Brown, Stankey, and Gregoire, 1987).

Leisure experiences at their best have often been conceptualized as optimal states with the potential to contribute to psychological growth and well-being (Csikszentmihalyi and Kleiber, 1991; Kleiber and Dirkin, 1985; Mannell, 1980, 1993; Tinsley and Tinsley, 1986). Researchers have been successful in measuring these states with qualitative methods (e.g., Gunter, 1987; Henderson, 1990), in the laboratory (e.g., Mannell and Bradley, 1986), with time budget diaries (e.g., Shaw, 1985) and with the experiential sampling method (e.g., Graef, Csikszentmihalyi, and Gianinno, 1983; Mannell, Zuzanek, and Larson, 1988; Samdahl and Kleiber, 1989).

For example, Gunter (1987) asked various groups of people to describe in writing their most memorable and enjoyable leisure experiences. He then analyzed these "stories" to discover if the leisure experiences that stood out in their minds shared similar characteristics. Researchers have also used methods that involve monitoring people's everyday behavior. Shaw (1985) has used the time-budget diary to examine the factors that determine whether individuals define a given situation or activity as leisure or nonleisure during the course of their daily lives. Time-budget research allows the researcher to estimate the amount of time spent by people in various activities including leisure by having them carry around a diary in which they record their activities and time of participation. Shaw added a new wrinkle. During a follow-up interview, after the completion of the time-budget diaries, her research participants, sixty married couples, were asked to classify all the activities they had listed in their diaries as "work," "leisure," "a mixture of work and leisure," or "neither work nor leisure." Shaw found that some activities such as cooking, home chores, shopping, childcare, and travel were more frequently defined as leisure by males than by females. She also found individuals defined the same activity differently at different times. For example, those people in her sample who reported engaging in cooking more than once during the study, defined it as leisure on one occasion and as work on the other 69 percent of the time. Additionally, she had her subjects explain

their choices. Activities labelled "leisure" were characterized by the perception that they had been freely chosen and intrinsically motivated. She also found that enjoyment, relaxation, and a lack of evaluation by other people seemed to accompany those activities her respondents experienced as leisure.

Iso-Ahola (1979) demonstrated with a quasi-experimental approach the linkage between perceived freedom and intrinsic motivation and the perception of an activity as leisure. He had his subjects imagine themselves in a variety of recreational situations that he created. These situations varied systematically according to the amount of freedom the individuals had in choosing an activity, the extent to which their participation was intrinsically or extrinsically motivated, plus a variety of other factors. As have other researchers, Iso-Ahola found that people were highly consistent in the criteria they used to identify leisure and, in particular, he found perceived freedom and intrinsic motivation were critical criteria for what becomes leisure in people's minds and what does not.

Researchers have also gone on-site, into the recreation setting itself, to study the texture of leisure experiences—their quality, duration, intensity, and memorability. For example, moods and enjoyment have been monitored during the course of a day trip to a rural park by having visitors fill out a survey when they entered and then again when they left the park (More and Payne, 1978). Researchers Brandmeyer and Alexander (1986) studied the experiences of men who flew to Florida, paid large sums of money to attend an adult baseball camp, and pretended they were professional baseball players for a week. The researchers attended the camp and closely observed the participants.

I have taken the study of leisure experiences into the psychological laboratory. Here, along with my colleagues, I have studied a variety of social and personality factors that affect how absorbed people become in activities engaged in during free time periods. In these controlled experiments we have been able to examine the impact of a variety of factors such as the amount of freedom of choice subjects have, the level of competition in the setting, and the nature of the rewards available on how involved people get in their leisure and the quality of their experiences (Bradley and Mannell, 1984; Mannell, 1979). In one experiment we were able to show that not everyone experiences greater leisure as a consequence of more freedom of choice. People with certain personality characteristics actually found higher levels of freedom threatening. They were only able to achieve higher quality experiences in more structured and restricted settings (Mannell and Bradley, 1986).

Researchers have also been examining the quality of leisure experiences in the context of people's daily lives using the ESM discussed earlier. These "beeper" studies are allowing us to confirm insights found with other research approaches. The ESM has been used to address a number of leisure-related research questions. Studies have examined the intrinsic satisfactions resulting from participation in recreational activities as compared with non-recreational activities (Graef, Csikszentmihalyi, and Gianinno, 1983), the meaning and quality of experiences derived from leisure activities engaged in by adolescents (Kleiber, Larson, and Csikszentmihalyi, 1986), and the experience of leisure in the context of social relationships (Larson, Mannell, and Zuzanek, 1986). The conditions that foster optimal experiences during leisure (Mannell, Zuzanek, and Larson, 1988; Samdahl, 1988; Samdahl and Kleiber, 1989) and the relationship between the occurrence of these experiences and life satisfaction have also been examined (Mannell, 1993).

Religious, Mystical and Spiritual Experiences

If we were to be intimidated in pursuing a social science understanding of any type of psychologically deep experiences, it would be in the area of religious, mystical, and spiritual experiences. However, to develop a better social science understanding of psychologically deep experiences in natural settings, we can also draw on the extensive theory and research that has treated religious, mystical, and spiritual experiences as social and psychological phenomena. The formal social science study of religious phenomena is as old as the field of sociology which emerged during the nineteenth century. Johnstone (1988) suggests that the stimulus for sociological interest in religion seems to have been the reports of anthropologists during the early and middle nineteenth century who encountered and studied "primitive" societies. While it was not until after the Second World War that the sociology of re-

ligion really took off, early prominent sociologists, such as Emile Durkheim, George Simmel and Max Weber devoted a significant portion of their scholarly energies to analyzing the role of religion in society. Karl Marx, the founding father of conflict theory, also identified and treated religion as any other social phenomenon. His famous comment calling religion the "opium of the people" reflects this approach. The sociology of religion has grown into a major area of inquiry since the late 1960s, and religion is a phenomenon studied like any other social behavior and institution (Johnstone, 1988). Issues studied by sociologists include religious socialization, religion as a social organization, and the relationship of religious institutions with other social institutions.

The psychology of religion and the empirical study of various religious phenomena also have a long tradition within psychology, though the topic has at various times been out of favor. In the heyday of behaviorism, religion came to be considered a taboo topic in psychology. However, early in the century the work of scholars such as William James, G. Stanley Hall, and Carl Jung had alerted others to the importance of understanding the psychological nature of religious phenomena and provided study in this area with scientific respectability. James' (1902) classic treatise, *Varieties of Religious Experience* is still extensively quoted and is influential today. The empirical psychology of religion underwent a renaissance in the mid-1950s. New journals appeared that were exclusively devoted to social scientific research on religion. Among these journals were the *Journal for the Scientific Study of Religion, Journal of Religion and Health, Review of Religious Research* and *Journal for Psychology and Theology*. In addition, empirical research on the psychology of religion began to appear in the mainstream journals of the American Psychological Association (APA). In the mid-1970s, APA Division 36 was formed to represent psychologists interested in the psychology of religion. In recent years, research activity has continued to grow as has the number of texts and collections of readings that have been published.

By asserting that religious, mystical, and spiritual experiences are social and psychological phenomena, researchers have suggested several things. First, the truth or falsity of any religious connotations associated with these experiences cannot be addressed (Spilka, Hood, and Gorsuch, 1985). While the myth of a completely value-free social science has been successfully challenged (e.g., Henderson, 1992), a conscious effort to achieve objectivity must be present in any social science investigation. Second, the social science approach to these psychologically deep experiences can be empirical. Batson, Schoenrade, and Ventis (1993), in their discussion of developing a social psychology of religious experience, clearly identify the problem when they observe that:

> the psychologist must . . . be ready to subject individuals' religious experience to careful, critical scrutiny and systematic investigation . . . however, the problem is this: Is there not a fundamental incompatibility between the requirements of respecting the integrity and complexity of the religious experience and of proceeding scientifically? If there is, then a social psychology of religion seems impossible. (p. 12-13)

To carry out social science studies of these hard-to-define values and experiences, we must overcome the difficulties of applying the scientific method to the "unobservables" of an individual's psychologically deep experiences. Again, Batson, Schoenrade, and Ventis (1993) point out in reference to the psychological study of religion that some critics argue that any study must be limited to observable behavior such as going to church, praying, or marking agreement or disagreement with questionnaire items concerning religious attitudes and beliefs. According to this empiricist view, one can have a science of religious behavior but not of religious experience (p. 17). However, it is possible to develop the study of mystical and spiritual experience that is phenomenological and empirical—phenomenological in its focus on deeply felt and meaningful experiences, empirical in its reliance on empirical observations to test theories.

> As religious experience in all its individuality, transcendence and mystery leaves observable tracks or symptoms, it is amenable to empirical analysis. According to the contemporary view, religious experience, like other experience, leaves publicly observable 'racks' in the life of the individual. The scientist can make much use of these tracks, as long as he or she is careful not to confuse the tracks with the experience that produced them. . . . Just as children learn to recognize the presence of the wind from observable facts—a snapping flag, a displaced hat, or chill on the skin.

Batson, Schoenrade, and
Ventis, 1993, p. 17

Psychologists who study religion have examined a wide range of phenomena including socialization through and into religion, the impact of participation in various types of religious groups and organizations on the individual's behavior, attitudes and experience, the role of religion in conformity and deviance, and the influence of religious beliefs on mental health and well-being. However, of particular relevance to our understanding of psychologically deep experiences in natural settings is the theoretical and empirical work focused on religious experience which includes mystical, transcendental, and conversion experiences. In this work we can find psychological theories, constructs, operational definitions, and empirical measures to contribute to the exploration and understanding of psychologically deep experiences in natural and leisure environments.

Substantial systematic study of religious experiences has been reported during the past decade and a half. For example, Hardy (1979) published an extensive classification of the major defining characteristics of religious experiences derived from a pool of 3,000 reported experiences obtained as part of the research of the Religious Experience Research Unit at Manchester College, Oxford. Psychologists studying religious, mystical, spiritual, and transcendental experiences have also used surveys (Bourque, 1969; Greeley, 1974; Wuthnow, 1978) and qualitative research strategies (Lofland and Skonovd, 1981), including participant observation (Balch, 1980). A variety of types of mystical experience have been identified including "nature mysticism" (Stace, 1960). Standardized scales have been developed and used to measure mystical and spiritual experiences (Hood, 1975; Kass, Friedman, Leserman, Zuttermeister, and Benson, 1991; Rosegrant, 1976).

Researchers have even been able to examine spiritual and mystical experience in laboratory experiments (Hood and Morris, 1981) as well as in quasi-experimental field studies in natural settings (Rosegrant, 1976; Hood, Morris, and Watson, 1990). Hood and his associates have had people in their experiments undergo an isolation tank experience under a variety of experimental conditions. They have not only been able to demonstrate that these artificial conditions of solitude will elicit psychologically deep experiences but that the religious orientation of the participant influences whether these experiences are given a religious interpretation. Quasi-experimental field research in natural environments with the use of questionnaire items and standardized scales has also shown that the interplay of factors in the natural environment and the social setting can trigger the occurrence of religious and mystical experiences (e.g., Hood, 1977; Rosegrant, 1976).

Nature Experiences and Psychologically Deep Experiences in Natural Settings

As with theory and research in other areas dealing with psychologically deep experiences, theories about nature experience are founded on concerns about health and quality of life (Hartig and Evans, 1993). Much recent research interest on wilderness values has focused on the experiences that visitors have in natural environments and the individual-environmental interchanges which occur in the wilderness setting (Pigram, 1993). Hartig and Evans (1993) suggest that in "the nature experience the person has in their experiential focus some part of the surrounding that is either not of human manufacture or that is a surrogate of something not of human origin" (p. 429). They also argue that nature experiences are set apart from "purely religious or philosophical experiences" since the former require some physical referent.

The nature experience is commonly viewed as providing benefits (Driver, Brown, Stankey, and Gregoire, 1987) as a consequence of being a "sort of time-out period," while the built environment is seen as having deleterious or constraining qualities. Hartig and Evans (1993) also argue that explanations about the attraction and benefits of nature experiences start from the idea "that some part of an ability to realize nature experience benefits is, in a sense, built-in" and that the way we are programmed by evolution causes us to perceive and experience natural environments in such a way as to promote relaxation and restoration. The results of empirical work in wilderness and natural areas have been interpreted to support the centrality of appreciation of nature to people's outdoor recreation experiences. Recreationists select specific settings for leisure pursuits with specific benefits in mind (Schreyer and Driver, 1989). The demonstrated attraction of natural settings for leisure is seen as a reflection of this human preference for environments dominated by natural rather than human-influenced elements.

The ability of natural settings to provide opportunities for spiritual experiences as a leisure benefit has been long recognized. In fact, spiritual needs have been assessed by a number of standardized scales developed for the purpose of measuring leisure needs and satisfactions (Driver, Tinsley, and Manfredo, 1991). Also, spiritual experiences are typically considered to be an important part of wilderness experiences (Stringer and McAvoy, 1992). As Stringer and McAvoy point out:

> . . . *personal accounts of philosophers, theologians, environmentalists, experiential educators, and outdoorspersons throughout history have suggested that wilderness adventure experiences offer opportunities to explore the spiritual side of human existence.* (p. 13)

However, spiritual needs and experiences have received little empirical attention as they relate to outdoor leisure environments. McDonald and Schreyer (1991) recently pointed out that while spiritual experiences may occur in a variety of situations and settings, the leisure setting, particularly the outdoor recreation context, has been neglected as a major source of spiritual experience. They argue that very little is actually known about the spiritual characteristics of leisure, and even less attention has been devoted to them from a management/planning perspective.

There are, however, examples of research that demonstrate the feasibility of systematically studying these psychologically deep experiences. For example, Hood (1977) studied factors that triggered spiritual and religious nature experiences among a group of young people on a weekend retreat in a wilderness area with specially developed scales and in-depth interviews. More recently, Stringer and McAvoy (1992) carried out a study designed to explore the spiritual dimension of the wilderness experiences of participants in an adventure trip program. Using pretrip questionnaires, on-site observations, posttrip interviews, and analyses of participants' trip journals, they examined the physical, cognitive, and emotional experiences of the participants. Their data allowed them to identify the personal definitions of spirituality for each individual in the study. While these definitions were found to be different for each individual, they shared many common themes. The participants also felt that the opportunities to experience their spirituality were greatly increased while in the wilderness, and that being in the wilderness enhanced those experiences. Stringer and McAvoy found that a variety of factors in the wilderness setting (e.g., close bonds with other participants, physical activity, time alone, weather, relaxed atmosphere) influenced the occurrence of psychologically deep experiences.

Another approach to understanding the psychologically deep and meaningful experiences associated with nature settings is reflected in the emerging interest in the concept "sense of place" or "attachment to place" (Roberts, Chapter Four, Greene, Chapter Twenty-Seven, and Bruns and Stokowski, Chapter Twenty-Nine, in this volume). These terms refer to the emotional and symbolic ties nature and wilderness users have to outdoor recreation settings. Williams, Patterson, Roggenbuck and Watson (1992) note that such a view has been emerging in environmental psychology and consumer behavior, and they argue that not only may people specialize in the leisure activities they pursue in natural environments, but also may be place specialists with patterns of leisure focused on the experience of place (p. 43). The place perspective reminds us that natural settings and:

> resources are not only raw materials to be inventoried and molded into a recreation opportunity, but also, and more important, places with histories, places that people care about, places that for many people embody a sense of belonging and purpose that give meaning to life. (p. 44)

A recent study by Williams, Patterson, Roggenbuck and Watson (1992) demonstrates that sense of place and the hard-to-define values and experiences associated with it are amenable to empirical study. Data were gathered from people visiting four wilderness areas using brief on-site interviews and a mail-back questionnaire. They found that stronger place and wilderness attachment were associated with a variety of factors; for example, the number of previous visits, living in a rural environment, having a setting as opposed to activity or group focus when visiting the setting, and visiting alone. Place attachment was also associated with a lack of nonwilderness substitutes and lower income and education. Wilderness attachment was associated with factors such as membership in wilderness and conservation organizations, visits to more wilderness areas, and a preference for longer visits.

Conclusion

A review of the above literature suggests that there is substantial overlap and interconnectedness among these psychologically deep experience constructs, the phenomena they represent, and the underlying psychological mechanisms proposed to explain them. The "processes that go on in the mind may be universal—what a person experiences may be similar whether the content is a specific religious ritual or participation in a leisure activity" (McDonald and Schreyer, 1991, p. 181). I have hypothesized that since similar internal psychological processes may "provide the basis for intense religious, aesthetic, nature, sporting, etc., experiences, the setting in which the experience occurs is influential in how the individual labels it" (Mannell, 1980, p. 77). Spilka, Hood, and Gorsuch, (1985) have developed a model of religious experience which shares this notion that religious, spiritual and other intense absorbing experiences are altered states of consciousness based on the same underlying psychological mechanisms but are labelled and defined differently by the person experiencing them based on the setting in which they occur and the values and attitudes held.

Regardless of whether these psychologically deep values and experiences have a common psychological basis or not, the overview provided by this chapter suggests that it is possible to conceptualize, operationalize and subject them to empirical scrutiny. While it is only one way of "knowing," social scientists have had substantial success at making the abstract more concrete and providing their own brand of insight into these phenomena. The further social scientific study of these experiences and values seems warranted and may be useful in our attempts to better provide opportunities for the diverse needs of people who look to natural settings for important experiences, meanings and values.

Literature Cited

Balch, R. (1980). Looking behind the scenes in a religious cult: Implications for the study of conversion. *Sociological Analysis, 41*, 137-143.

Batson, C., Schoenrade, P., and Ventis, W. (1993). *Religion and the individual: A social psychological perspective.* Oxford, UK: Oxford University Press.

Bourque, L. (1969). Social correlates of transcendental experiences. *Sociological Analysis, 30*, 151-163.

Bradley, W. and Mannell, R. (1984). Sensitivity of intrinsic motivation to reward procedure instructions. *Personality and Social Psychology Bulletin, 10*, 426-431.

Brandmeyer, G. and Alexander, L. (1986). "I caught the dream": The adult baseball camp as fantasy leisure. *Journal of Leisure Research, 18*, 26-39.

Cohen, E. (1979a). A phenomenology of tourist experiences. *Sociology, 13*, 179-201.

Cohen, E. (1979b). Rethinking the sociology of tourism. *Annals of Tourism Research, 6*, 18-35.

Csikszentmihalyi, M. (1975). *Beyond boredom and anxiety: The experience of play in work and games.* San Francisco, CA: Jossey-Bass, Inc., Publishers.

Csikszentmihalyi, M. (1990). *Flow: The psychology of optimal experience.* New York, NY: Harper & Row Publishers, Inc.

Csikszentmihalyi, M. and Kleiber, D. (1991). Leisure and self-actualization. In B. Driver, P. Brown, and G. Peterson (Eds.), *Benefits of leisure* (pp. 91-102). State College, PA: Venture Publishing, Inc.

Csikszentmihalyi, M. and Larson, R. (1984). *Being adolescent.* New York, NY: Basic Books.

Dawson, L. (1990). Self-affirmation, freedom, and rationality: Theoretically elaborating "active" conversions. *Journal for the Scientific Study of Religion, 29*, 141-163.

de Grazia, S. (1962). *Of time, work and leisure.* New York, NY: Twentieth Century Fund Press.

Driver, B. (1976). Quantification of outdoor recreationists' preferences. In B. Van Der Smissen (Comp.), *Research, camping and environmental education*, Series II (pp. 165-187). State College, PA: Health, Physical Education and Recreation, The Pennsylvania State University.

Driver, B., Brown, P., Stankey, G., and Gregoire, T. (1987). The ROS planning system: Evolution, basic concepts, and research needed. *Leisure Sciences, 9*, 201-212.

Driver, B., Tinsley, H., and Manfredo, M. (1991). The paragraphs about leisure and recreation experience preference scales: Results from two inventories designed to assess the breadth of the perceived psychological benefits of leisure. In B. Driver, P. Brown, and G. Peterson (Eds.), *Benefits of leisure* (pp. 263-286). State College, PA: Venture Publishing, Inc.

Driver, B. and Tocher, S. (1970). Toward a behavioral interpretation of recreational engagements, with implications for planning. In B. Driver (Ed.), *Elements of outdoor recreation planning* (pp. 9-31). Ann Arbor, MI: The University of Michigan Press.

Einstein, A. (1992). What I Believe. In J. Kaplan (Ed.), *Bartlett's familiar quotations* (16th ed.) (p. 635). Boston, MA: Little, Brown and Company.

Graef, R., Csikszentmihalyi, M., and Gianinno, S. (1983). Measuring intrinsic motivation in everyday life. *Leisure Studies, 2*, 155-168.

Greeley, A. (1974). *Ecstasy: A way of knowing.* Englewood Cliffs, NJ: Prentice-Hall Press.

Gunter, B. (1987). The leisure experience: Selected properties. *Journal of Leisure Research, 19*, 115-130.

Hardy, A. (1979). *The spiritual nature of man.* Oxford, UK: Clarendon Press.

Hartig, T. and Evans, G. (1993). Psychological foundations of nature experience. In T. Garling and R. Golledge (Eds.), *Behavior and environment: Psychological and geographical approaches* (pp. 427-457). New York, NY: Elsevier Science Publishers.

Henderson, K. (1990). An oral life history perspective on the containers in which American farm women experienced leisure. *Leisure Studies, 9*, 121-133.

Henderson, K. (1992). *Dimensions of choice.* State College, PA: Venture Publishing, Inc.

Hood, R. (1975). The construction and preliminary validation of a measure of reported mystical experience. *Journal for the Scientific Study of Religion, 14*, 29-41.

Hood, R. (1977). Eliciting mystical states of consciousness with semistructured nature experiences. *Journal for the Scientific Study of Religion, 16*, 155-163.

Hood, R. and Morris, R. (1981). Sensory isolation and the differential elicitation of religious imagery in intrinsic and extrinsic persons. *Journal for the Scientific Study of Religion, 20*, 261-273.

Hood, R., Morris, R., and Watson, P. (1990). Quasi-experimental elicitation of the differential report of religious experience among intrinsic and indiscriminately proreligious types. *Journal for the Scientific Study of Religion, 29*, 164-172.

Iso-Ahola, S. (1979). Basic dimensions of definitions of leisure. *Journal of Leisure Research, 11*, 28-39.

James, W. (1902). *Varieties of religious experience.* New York, NY: Longmans & Green.

Johnstone, R. (1988). *Religion in society: A sociology of religion.* Toronto, Canada: Prentice Hall Canada.

Kass, J., Friedman, R., Leserman, J., Zuttermeister, P., and Benson, H. (1991). Health outcomes and a new index of spiritual experience. *Journal for the Scientific Study of Religion, 30*, 203-211.

Kelly, J. (1983). *Leisure identities and interactions.* London, UK: Allen & Unwin.

Kleiber, D. and Dirkin, G. (1985). Intrapersonal constraints to leisure. In M. Wade (Ed.), *Constraints on leisure* (pp. 17-42). Springfield, IL: Charles C. Thomas, Publisher.

Kleiber, D., Larson, R., and Csikszentmihalyi, M. (1986). The experience of leisure in adolescence. *Journal of Leisure Research, 18,* 169-176.

Larson, R. and Csikszentmihalyi, M. (1983). The experience sampling method. In H. Reis (Ed.), *Naturalistic approaches to studying social interaction* (pp. 41-56). San Francisco, CA: Jossey-Bass, Inc., Publishers.

Larson, R., Mannell, R., and Zuzanek, J. (1986). Daily well-being of older adults with friends and family. *Journal of Psychology and Aging, 1,* 117-126.

Lee, P., Ornstein, R., Galin, D., Deikman, A., and Tart, C. (1976). *Symposium on consciousness.* New York, NY: Penguin Books.

Lofland, J. and Skonovd, N. (1981). Conversion motifs. *Journal for the Scientific Study of Religion, 20,* 373-385.

MacCannell, D. (1976). *The tourist: A new theory of the leisure classes.* New York, NY: Pantheon Books/Schocken Books.

Mannell, R. (1979). A conceptual and experimental basis for research in the psychology of leisure. *Society and Leisure, 2,* 179-194.

Mannell, R. (1980). Social psychological techniques and strategies for studying leisure experiences. In S. Iso-Ahola (Ed.), *Social psychological perspectives on leisure and recreation* (pp. 62-88). Springfield, IL: Charles C. Thomas, Publishers.

Mannell, R. (1993). High investment activity and life satisfaction among older adults: Committed, serious leisure and flow activities. In J. Kelly (Ed.), *Activity and aging* (pp. 125-145). Newbury Park, CA: Sage Publications, Inc.

Mannell, R. and Bradley, W. (1986). Does greater freedom always lead to greater leisure? Testing a person X environment model of freedom and leisure. *Journal of Leisure Research, 18,* 215-230.

Mannell, R. and Zuzanek, J. (1991). The nature and variability of leisure constraints in daily life: The case of the physically active leisure of older adults. *Leisure Sciences, 13,* 337-351.

Mannell, R., Zuzanek, J., and Larson, R. (1988). Leisure states and "flow" experiences: Testing perceived freedom and intrinsic motivation hypotheses. *Journal of Leisure Research, 20,* 289-304.

Maslow, A. (1968). *Toward a psychology of being.* New York, NY: Van Nostrand Reinhold.

McDonald, B. and Schreyer, R. (1991). Spiritual benefits of leisure participation and leisure settings. In B. Driver, P. Brown, and G. Peterson (Eds.), *Benefits of leisure* (pp. 179-194). State College, PA: Venture Publishing, Inc.

Meyersohn, R. (1981). *Tourism as a sociocultural phenomenon: Research perspectives.* Waterloo, Ontario, Canada: OTIUM Publications, Research Group on Leisure and Cultural Development, University of Waterloo.

More, T. and Payne, B. (1978). Affective responses to natural areas near cities. *Journal of Leisure Research, 10,* 7-12.

Neulinger, J. (1974). *Psychology of leisure.* Springfield, IL: Charles C. Thomas, Publisher.

Pieper, J. (1952). *Leisure: The basis of culture.* New York, NY: Pantheon Books/Schocken Books.

Pigram, J. (1993). Human-nature relationships: Leisure environments and natural settings. In T. Garling and R. Golledge (Eds.), *Behavior and environment: Psychological and geographical approaches* (pp. 400-426). New York, NY: Elsevier Science, Inc.

Przeclawski, K. (1985). The role of tourism in contemporary culture. *The Tourist Review, 40,* 2-6.

Rosegrant, J. (1976). The impact of set and setting on religious experience in nature. *Journal for the Scientific Study of Religion, 15,* 301-310.

Samdahl, D. (1988). A symbolic interactionist model of leisure: Theory and empirical support. *Leisure Sciences, 10,* 27-39.

Samdahl, D. and Kleiber, D. (1989). Self-awareness and leisure experience. *Leisure Sciences, 11,* 1-10.

Schreyer, R. and Driver, B. (1989). The benefits of leisure. In E. Jackson and T. Burton (Eds.), *Understanding leisure and recreation in an era of change: Mapping the past, charting the future* (pp. 385-419). State College, PA: Venture Publishing, Inc.

Shaw, S. (1985). Gender and leisure: Inequality in the distribution of leisure time. *Journal of Leisure Research, 17,* 266-282.

Spilka, B., Hood, R., and Gorsuch, R. (1985). *The psychology of religion: An empirical approach.* Englewood Cliffs, NJ: Prentice Hall.

Stace, W. (1960). *Mysticism and philosophy.* New York, NY: Macmillan/McGraw-Hill School Publishing.

Stringer, A. and McAvoy, L. (1992). The need for something different: Spirituality and wilderness adventure. *The Journal of Experiential Education, 15,* 13-20.

Tellegen, A. and Atkinson, G. (1974). Openness to absorbing and self-altering experiences ('absorption'), a trait related to hypnotic susceptibility. *Journal of Abnormal Psychology, 83,* 268-277.

Tinsley, H. and Tinsley, D. (1986). A theory of the attributes, benefits, and causes of leisure experience. *Leisure Sciences, 8,* 1-45.

Wells, A. (1988). Self-esteem and optimal experience. In M. Csikszentmihalyi and I. Csikszentmihalyi (Eds.), *Optimal experience* (pp. 327-341). New York, NY: Cambridge University Press.

Williams, D., Patterson, M., Roggenbuck, J., and Watson, A. (1992). Beyond the commodity metaphor: Examining emotional and symbolic attachment to place. *Leisure Sciences, 14,* 29-46.

Wuthnow, R. (1978). *Experimentation in American religion*. Berkeley, CA: University of California Press.

An Integrated Approach to the Scientific Study of the Human Spirit

John Davis
Department of Psychology
The Naropa Institute
Boulder, Colorado

CHAPTER 35

Good scientific research on spiritual and other hard-to-define values and experiences can be done. The purpose of this chapter is to review several aspects of a scientific approach which is appropriate to the study of the human spirit and its relation to nature. Along with several calls for a more expansive approach to science the value and characteristics of science are reviewed. The two approaches of natural and human science described will show that while these two approaches differ in some important assumptions about the study of human behavior and experience, they share common goals and values. The discussion of human science leads to an overview of arguments for a methodological pluralism. The question of scientific adequacy is considered because it is central to evaluating any approach to science. Finally, three examples of research are given to illustrate the value of an integration of methods in studying nature and the human spirit. The conclusion of this chapter is that a methodological pluralism offers behavioral and social scientists, policymakers, and land managers the means to a more thorough accounting of the full range of human experience and behavior.

The view that spirituality can be scientifically researched may present challenges to both scientists and those in the humanities. Conventional science has ruled most aspects of the human spirit out of bounds. Good science, in this view, requires that the phenomena we study be quantified, controlled, and repeated. Since spiritual experience, or for that matter, experience of any kind cannot easily be studied in this way, it cannot be approached scientifically. In most cases, conventional scientists have dismissed the human spirit as fantasy or superstition. Others have argued that such matters are the province of philosophy or religion but not science. Thus, conventional science is skeptical, at best, about the existence—or at least, the scientific study—of the human spirit. At the same time, many of those most committed to the study of consciousness, spirituality, and related aspects of human existence object to attempts by conventional science to manipulate and control these phenomena. They argue that the essential character of deep emotional experience, self-transcendence, and the miraculous is lost by subjecting it to the materialistic demands of modern science.

Most conventional scientists discount the value of spiritual experience, and many spiritual seekers discount the value of science. However, there is an approach to science that is adequate to the task of studying the human spirit. The essence of this approach is an integration of complementary scientific approaches, a "methodological pluralism." This approach challenges the limiting assumptions and practices of conventional science without rejecting its deepest values—valuing truth over dogma and careful, critical analysis over bias. Similarly, it challenges the notion that spiritual experience is completely beyond empirical analysis. Scientists and spiritual seekers can come together, and the outcome will be better information on which behavioral scientists, policymakers, and public land managers can base decisions.

The Human Spirit

In this discussion the human spirit refers to a wide range of experiences and values including both quantitative and qualitative psychological dimensions of self-transcendence, meaning, spirituality, and one's relationship to the sacred. Spiritual values and experiences, in this broad definition, range from a felt sense of appreciation, coherence, and value to experiences of rapture, awe, and mystical oneness which seem beyond description. They might also be said to include difficulties and crises of the human spirit such as apathy, alienation, existential anxiety, and despair.

It should also be made clear at the outset that there are vital realms of human experience and activity that cannot be described adequately in ordinary, discursive language. These dimensions are either inaccessible to or beyond rational analysis (Wilber, 1980). As much as good science can contribute to understanding, supporting, and expanding the human spirit, it is no substitute for poetry, art, song, love, and awe. Contemplation, along with careful philosophical analysis and empirical data gathering, is a necessary component of greater understanding. Science can expand one's understanding of the spiritual, but it can never substitute for direct experience of it.

Two Metaphors

A fitting metaphor for the approach in this chapter is the relationship of the brain's left and right hemispheres. In most people, the left hemisphere is specialized for linear, atomistic, and quantitative information processing; the right hemisphere is specialized for spatial, holistic, and qualitative information

processing. Logic and analysis are associated with the left brain while imagery, song, rhythm, and synthesis are associated with the right brain (Ornstein, 1977). By analogy, science has been considered a left brain activity while the right brain is the realm of artists and poets. This chapter presents a scientific method that can encompass both a right and left brain approach. Just as two brain hemispheres, with different styles, strengths, and functions are integrated in a fully functioning person, these two ways of knowing can be integrated. A fully functioning science must be whole brained.

A second metaphor comes from Abraham Maslow, the founder of both humanistic and transpersonal psychology (see Schroeder, Chapter Five, in this volume). Maslow criticized the reductionistic and mechanistic views of psychology promoted by the behaviorists and psychoanalysts and called for a psychological science which could study optimal psychological health including the human spirit. Pointing to the limits of conventional psychological research methods, he wrote, "I suppose it is tempting, if the only tool you have is a hammer, to treat everything as if it were a nail" (Maslow, 1966, p. 15-16). There are some scientific tasks which require a hammer, as it were, but other tasks call for different tools. This chapter suggests a more inclusionary approach to methodology, arguing for a well-rounded tool box.

Values and Limits of Science

At its best, science is an alternative to dogma. Scientific research is a means of confirming the credibility and accuracy of differing accounts of human behavior. It enables us to choose among different accounts of a phenomenon, examine conclusions, audit decisions, and evaluate programs. Without some reliable means of evaluating claims of truth and efficacy, decisions will be limited. A program may be effective, but without documentation and hypothesis testing there is no way to demonstrate its effectiveness to detractors or show its failures to supporters. The process of scientific research requires honesty and willingness to be proved wrong, regardless of one's original position. As the physicist David Bohm (1993) pointed out, "Science, when done properly, acknowledges a fact whether we like it or not—that is, whether it agrees with our deeply held beliefs or not" (p. 147).

A second value of good scientific research is communication. Science provides a neutral language for communicating across disciplines and value systems. Once a community has agreed on the rules of research methods, science provides a means of evaluating claims that can be shared by all. It is no surprise, for instance, that the most open discussions between Americans and Soviets during the Cold War were held not by politicians but by scientists interested in nuclear winter research. Similarly, meditation techniques became widely available to the public after they were described in the scientific literature by the Harvard physiologist Herbert Benson and his colleagues. This research did not show anything new to those who had been practicing these techniques that were thousands of years old. However, it was a kind of translation of that knowledge into a modern cultural context. Redefined as the relaxation response, his research made meditation more acceptable and accessible.

What is the character of "good science"? Good science is open to new information, and it is open to all aspects of information. It urges constant examination of personal and cultural biases, while at the same time offering reminders that research is never entirely free of such biases. It facilitates discrimination of component parts from a whole identification of relationships and larger wholes. It allows creativity and a means to constantly seek new understandings that take us beyond what we know. There is a quality of patience and tolerance for ambiguity in good science because the depth and richness of a phenomenon often takes time to emerge. There is also a quality of humility in good science. A hypothesis or explanation might be wrong. Good science is willing to say so and move on, not holding dogmatically to unsupported beliefs or positions.

Good science is rooted in curiosity, joy in the process of inquiry, and what has been described in the two-year-old child as a "love affair with the world" (Kaplan, 1978). A typical two-year-old child seems to be constantly exploring, testing, tasting, never getting enough of the world. It could be said that this "love" and curiosity matures into the driving force behind good science. In the final analysis, good science is a means to compassion. It is a tool for relieving suffering, finding new ways of solving and preventing problems, and facilitating the full realization of each part of the greater whole. In short, good science is of service to the world.

Calls for an expanded approach to science which can include study of the human spirit are not new. In the early 1900s, William James, the first American psychologist, included the study of consciousness and religious experience in the subject matter of psychology while advocating and practicing a thoroughly empirical approach. Abraham Maslow was one of the strongest champions of science in the service of what he called "the farther reaches of human nature." He was trained first as a behaviorist under Harry Harlow, known best for his research on attachment and love in infant monkeys, and later worked with such influential psychoanalysts as Karen Horney. While Maslow criticized the limits of behaviorism and psychoanalysis, he never sought to replace them but to extend them. He advocated a blend of good science and what he called *resacralization*, rediscovering a sense of the sacred in everyday life. He suggested that a science which disallows the human spirit is rooted in a psychological defense mechanism. In *The Psychology of Science*, Maslow (1966) wrote:

> *Briefly put, it appears to me that science and everything scientific can be and often is used as a tool in the service of a distorted, narrowed, humorless, de-eroticized, de-emotionalized, desacralized, and desanctified Weltanschauung. This desacralization can be used as a defense against being flooded by emotion, especially the emotions of humility, reverence, mystery, wonder, and awe.* (p. 139)

However, he maintained that this desacralization was not necessary in a scientific approach to psychology. Maslow (1966) explained the integration of science and the spirit this way:

> *Many people still think that scientific study or detailed knowing is the opposite and the contradiction of the sense of mystery. But this need not be the case. Studying the mystery does not necessarily profane it. Indeed, this is the best way toward greater respect, richer understanding, and greater sacralization and sanctification at a much higher level of richness. . . . Science at its highest level is ultimately the organization of, the systematic pursuit of, and the enjoyment of wonder, awe, and mystery.* (p. 151)

Unfortunately, this analysis of science as desacralized is almost as true today as it was in 1966 when Maslow wrote it. If good science blends curiosity, compassion, and a sense of mystery, there is a lot of bad science around. While science can be a powerful tool for evaluating differing claims of truth and accuracy, a misconceived science can be limiting. Conventional science has operated under assumptions that have made research on many aspects of human behavior and experience impossible, and rigid adherence to these assumptions have limited the value of science. The style of science characterized by dogmatic belief in mechanism, materialism, and reductionism has been called *scientism*. Scientism is a conviction that there is only one correct and valid way to "do" science (i.e., by the rules of natural science). It is the application of conventional science to all phenomena without questioning the appropriateness of the assumptions or methods of that paradigm. Along with this conviction is a corollary belief that anything other than natural science is not "real" science and is, therefore, not valid for finding truth or making decisions. However, scientism violates some of the basic tenets of science. Its presuppositions are never questioned, the humility and curiosity that characterize good science are dropped, and much that we know to be important is ignored or dismissed. Clearly, scientism is inadequate for careful, systematic, and adequate study of hard-to-define human values and experiences.

In the scientistic approach the questions relevant to most aspects of the human spirit are not even asked, the methods capable of systematically studying the spirit are ruled inadequate, and the set of possible explanations is severely limited. Essential aspects of human existence are considered to be beside the point and, since they are excluded from scientific research, they are omitted from planning, policymaking, and evaluation.

Postmodern Science

Many of the challenges to the conventional view of science are connected with calls for a postmodern science. Postmodernism is a complex issue with a variety of definitions and approaches. (For reviews of modernism and postmodernism, see Rothberg, 1993; Spretnak, 1991; and two collections edited by Griffin, 1988a, 1988b.) A postmodern philosophy view of science can be contrasted to a modern view and described by some general insights.

A modern view of science asks of the phenomenon under study, "Is it real?" and assumes there is a single correct answer to the question. This view is based on the tenet that reality can be described by mechanical laws that are constant, universal, and unchanging. Griffin (1988b) argues that the key to the "modern" approach to science is a mechanistic philosophy and disenchantment of nature. If nature is purely mechanical, it has no subjectivity, experience, or feeling, no aims, purpose, ideals, or direction, and no intrinsic value. Its relations are limited to simple cause-and-effect relations where all causes are elementary, impersonal processes. There can be nothing sacred or spiritual, nothing of ultimate value or connection. Since humans must be considered part of nature and, to a degree at least, subject to natural processes, the modern view also denies meaning, purpose, and intrinsic value to humans as well. According to the modern view of science, there is no human spirit.

Griffin (1988b) in reviewing the challenges to this view points out that historians and sociologists of science have called attention to the nonrational factors (such as paradigms, culture, power dynamics, personal motivations, gender, race, and class) which influence science. He demonstrates that the roots of modern science lie outside science in political and theological developments during the seventeenth century. Similarly, recent developments within science such as quantum physics (Zukav, 1979), the Gaia hypothesis (Lovelock, 1988), and cognitive biology (Maturana and Varela, 1988) point to an irreducible role for consciousness and holism. Griffin (1988b) shows that the modern view of science leads to the necessary conclusion that:

> There are no norms, not even truth, and everything is ultimately meaningless. The ironic conclusion is that modern science, in disenchanting nature, began a trajectory that ended by disenchanting science itself. If all human life is meaningless, then science, as one of its activities, must share in this meaninglessness. (p. 3)

A postmodern approach to science holds that reality is, to a degree, soft (cf., Hayward, 1987). While it is not infinitely malleable, what we consider real is partly a function of paradigms, language, conceptual frameworks, culture, class, and gender. The answer to the question "Is it real?" becomes "It depends." In some postmodern versions of science, reality is seen to have multiple levels. Mechanistic principles are appropriate to describe some of these levels, but other levels of reality are better described by the workings of consciousness.

In a postmodern view of science, narrative, story, and myth may be the primary tools for describing reality. In a modern view, myths are those descriptions of reality that have been proven to be false. In a postmodern view, however, myths describe that which is most real (i.e., the meaning and deep structure of experience). Myths contain multiple layers of interpretation and meaning, myths carry us beyond the surface to the depth of experience, and myths evolve. Thus, postmodern science reintroduces a sense of enchantment, mystery, aliveness, and meaning to the world that modern science has sought to eliminate.

The insights of systems theory are generally consistent with postmodern science (e.g., Macy, 1991). What appear to be independent entities are themselves systems and exist only insofar as they are parts of larger systems. These elements may be biological entities such as cells, organisms, and ecosystems or psychological elements such as behaviors, thoughts, and values. Experiences and actions are always part of a larger whole and only make sense taken in the larger context. Thus, transcendent experiences, one expression of the human spirit, can be seen as a psychological movement from one level to a higher, more inclusive level. One definition of mystical experience, then, is that which approaches the highest, all-inclusive level. At this level of the system, duality disappears—all is one (i.e., the whole and each part of the whole has intrinsic value and meaning). The higher levels in a system give meaning to lower levels, and the highest level sets the boundary conditions for all phenomena at lower levels of the system. Thus, examining the human spirit is not just possible in this view, it is necessary.

Behavioral and social scientists operating under the modern view of science have a goal of discovering facts and universal laws of behavior. Such knowledge is aimed at supporting progress toward the control and manipulation of nature (including human nature) for greater human good. In contrast, scientists using a postmodern view have as a goal constructing and vindicating descriptions of the world that are better than what was previously available. Science becomes a way of telling a story that is internally consistent, rich, deep, and useful, as well as subjecting that story to careful, system-atic evaluation. Postmodern science shifts the focus from control and progress to realization of the full potential of the whole and its parts. Postmodern science fosters liberation, not manipulation.

Natural Science and Human Science

A closer examination of two approaches to science may reveal ways to foster an integrated approach to a more adequate science. Natural science, the basis of conventional scientific methods, is rooted in the modern view of science described previously, while an alternative, human science, exemplifies a postmodern view of science. Natural science is based on an interwoven set of assumptions including positivism, operationism, reductionism, and mechanism. Positivism suggests that science should study only those aspects of the world about which we can be positive (i.e., only those phenomena which can be measured, quantified, and verified by independent observation). Height, weight, miles, and hours are legitimate to scientific exploration, but intangibles such as values, feelings, and states of consciousness are not except as they can be treated as quantifiable phenomena. Closely related to positivism is the doctrine of operationism which requires that all phenomena being studied be defined a priori in terms of the operations used to observe them. This restricts scientific discovery by limiting observations to those aspects of phenomena which are already known or predicted. Reductionism suggests that complex phenomena should be explained at lower levels of analysis. For instance, emotions should be explained at the level of physics and chemistry as exclusively biochemical and neurophysiological happenings. Mechanism suggests that the world is made up of discrete objects which interact through cause-and-effect laws. A related assumption is that researchers should be distant from the phenomenon being observed so as to not interfere with it. Similarly, manipulation of independent variables and control of extraneous variables is said to allow certainty about the causes of behavior.

This view of science has been responsible for substantial contributions in dealing with mechanical phenomena in the natural world, but it has been found to be wanting in dealing with human experience and values. Having excluded deeper psychological values and experiences from scientific study, the only two alternatives left are to study only the surface of these phenomena, reducing them to manageable, quantifiable data or to ignore them altogether. When taken as the sole means of arriving at knowledge, natural science becomes scientism.

Human science, on the other hand, focuses on those phenomena which are most human, including experience, values, meaning, feelings, and a sense of the spiritual (Giorgi, 1970; Polkinghorne, 1983). Seamon (1982) discusses a similar contrast in environmental psychology in terms of positivist and phenomenological approaches and shows that central questions in environmental psychology can only be studied through a phenomenological approach. Human science is a strong example of a postmodern approach to scientific research. Within psychology, human science approaches include humanistic, phenomenological, and transpersonal psychology.

The philosophical roots of human science include phenomenology, hermeneutics, and holism. Phenomenology refers to the study of experience as such. The focus is on immediate experience and the meaning associated with it rather than simply on overt behavior or physical phenomena (Seamon, 1982). Here, the focus is shifted from behaviors to the meaning of behaviors and experience. Hermeneutics (Messer, Sass, and Woolfolk, 1988) refers to, among other things, the interpretation of phenomena in their larger contexts. The term originally referred to the interpretation of Biblical texts by scripture scholars. The meaning of a word, story, verse, or parable depended on its context, both in the larger text and in its sociohistorical context. Behavioral scientists have used this same notion to understand how the meaning of a given behavior is, to a degree, context-specific. A day hike in a natural area can be survival, work, health promotion, recreation, or worship. Hermeneutics points to the centrality of context, including the person's motivations, value system, beliefs, needs, and state of consciousness in understanding experience. Holism recognizes that the whole is greater than the sum of its parts. Wholes are not merely collections of parts; the properties of these wholes cannot be understood or even predicted from the parts. By the same token, an experience cannot be reduced to a collection of behaviors and cognitions but must be viewed as a *gestalt*.

The goal of human science is to construct and support descriptions of experiences which are deeper, richer, and more useful. Depth refers to the match between a description and the experience or action being described. A deeper description is one that describes more aspects of a phenomenon. It can also be said that a deeper description is one which comes closer to a person's experience of a phenomenon. A profound description has extraordinary depth. However, the notion of depth does not assume that there is a "final," complete description. Particularly in describing the human spirit, any description, no matter how deep, will include a recognition of mystery and depth that cannot be fully captured in descriptive language. Richness refers to the connections with other phenomena. A richer description provides more links to other phenomena. Usefulness refers to practical applications. A more useful description provides more ways to alleviate suffering and promote well-being. Well-being, in this sense, is taken in the broadest terms. Well-being is not just material, but it includes dimensions of wellness such as the sense of community, understanding, aesthetics, and meaning. The object of well-being is not just humans but the larger whole including the environment. For advocates of human science, greater understanding and better descriptions are inseparable from service to the world.

Methodological Pluralism and Complementarity

In the view of natural science, the goal of research is to determine cause-and-effect by eliminating extraneous variables and identifying the independent variable which caused the changes in the dependent variable. A true experiment with the experimenter controlling or manipulating all conditions does this best. In circumstances where the researcher cannot control all aspects of the experiment, especially in social and behavioral research, one may be willing to accept a quasi-experimental design. Quasi-experimental designs are those in which some degree of control is lost or sacrificed as, for example, in a control group design where it is impossible to assign subjects to groups randomly. This limits the researcher's ability to eliminate all extraneous variables such as subject selection effects. When still less control is possible, one may even have to settle for a correlational design. In the natural science view, an experiment is best, and all other designs and research strategies are more or less deficient approximations of an experiment. This approach tends to be exclusionary in terms of methods, specifying a very limited number of valid scientific research methods and resulting in what Taylor calls "the great fault of modern psychology . . . that it is entirely too quantitative" (Taylor, 1992, p. 293).

In the view of human science, the questions asked in scientific research guide the choice of methods. Quantitative methods are appropriate for some questions while other questions call for qualitative methods. Since many of the central questions for the human sciences are qualitative, important research methods include ethnography, naturalistic inquiry, and interpretive research (see Stynes and Stokowski, Chapter Twenty-Seven, in this volume). These qualitative methods rely primarily on careful observation and in-depth interviews to reveal the deep structure of informants' experiences. There is no single "recipe" that guarantees truth and understanding. Each method has value depending on the situation, and often a combination of methods is best.

Rather than seeing research methods arranged in a vertical hierarchy with an experiment at the top and other methods arranged below, human science encourages a methodological pluralism in which the variety of research methods are arranged in a sort of horizontal menu. Therefore, true experiments are the best way to approach questions in which the goal is to establish cause and effect within a specific and carefully controlled set of circumstances. However, other methods are called for by other kinds of questions. For example, correlational methods are the best way to approach questions in which the goal is to describe the relationship between naturally occurring phenomena. Other research questions, in which the focus is on experience and meaning, call for qualitative methods. Each research method has equal intrinsic value. Which one is the "best" depends on the question and the context. To use Maslow's metaphor, nails still call for hammers but a board that is too long calls for a saw.

An example of such a combination of methods in the context of environmental perception is a study of arboretum landscapes. Schroeder (1991) asked people to complete a quantitative evaluation of a number of scenes from the Morton Arboretum near Chicago and to write qualitative descriptions of their experiences there. He then compared the two measures. Schroeder concluded, "Thus the two approaches provide different kinds of information, but when taken together they give a consistent picture of people's landscape perceptions and experiences" (p. 245). Schroeder's general conclusion supports the integration of qualitative and quantitative methods:

> *Qualitative responses provide useful information about landscape perception that is not obtained through quantitative preference ratings. . . . Combining the precision and analytic power of quantitative ratings with the richness and depth of qualitative responses provides a much fuller understanding of user responses to landscapes than could be gained from either method alone.*
>
> Bevan, 1991, p. 247

One of the strongest calls for methodological pluralism has come from William Bevan (1991). His critique of a narrow, overly quantified approach to psychological science is particularly credible because of his exceptional scientific credentials. Bevan is a former president of the American Psychological Association (APA) and its Divisions of Experimental and General Psychology. He is also a former president of the American Association for the Advancement of Science and former editor of *Science*. On the occasion of his acceptance of APA's Scientific Contribution Award, he wrote about the need to question the social and behavioral sciences' insistence on natural science methods and the need to reach beyond the natural sciences to the humanities for methods appropriate to the human sciences:

> *Increasingly, people are coming to believe that the subject matter of the human and social sciences is fundamentally different from that of the natural sciences. . . . When one recognizes that science is influenced by its ideological context, one must raise serious questions of an epistemological nature. For psychology and the other social sciences, these chiefly concern the appropriateness of the epistemology identified with the intellectual tradition that we have borrowed without question from classical physical science. Some among us who care about these matters now see our 100-year-old intellectual commitment to be wanting. To set aside this orthodox epistemology is either*

to cut ourselves adrift without a methodological anchor or to recognize that there are multiple epistemological alternatives, some presumably more appropriate than others for the human sciences. (p. 477)

Bevan (1991) advocates a broader range of research methods and reinforces the need to expand our vision beyond the limitations of methodological orthodoxy or a "science by the numbers."

It is better to speak of methodologies in the plural, for it is important to assume a far less rigid, more pragmatic view towards what scientists may or may not do. The great disservice that results from the generic methodology associated with modernism lies in its stamping some procedures as scientific and the others as unscientific, some as legitimate and others not. (The narrowly conceived quarantine against introspection, in effect for so many years, is a useful example of what I have in mind here.) . . . Be wary of rule-bound methodology. Use any method with a full understanding of what it does for you but also what constraints it may place on you, and whether it violates assumptions about the phenomena that you are studying. Free yourself of the worry that you are behaving badly if you don't use officially certified scientific methodology. Rule-bound methodology frequently degenerates into methodology by formula. (p. 480)

A related argument takes the notion of pluralism one step further, suggesting that psychology, and indeed all scientific research, should use a principle of complementarity (Rychlak, 1993). Complementarity is a familiar concept in physics where it refers, for example, to the finding that light can be both particle and wave. The psychological version of complementarity proposes that there are four different theoretical perspectives or grounds for studying psychological, behavioral, and social phenomena. One ground is taken from physical science and deals with psychological phenomena as physical phenomena, a second is grounded in biological systems, a third in social systems, and a fourth in values, meaning, and purpose. Spiritual values and phenomenological research have their place in Rychlak's (1993) scheme, as do physical, biological, and social processes.

In Rychlak's (1993) view, these four perspectives are independent and irreconcilable; that is, none can be reduced to any other. This view is similar to a systems view in which explanations at one level of complexity are inappropriate at another. Each perspective is appropriate for certain questions and not for others and each is necessary for a complete picture. The physics of light is an analogy; both views of light as particle and as wave are appropriate and necessary under different conditions of observation. Complementarity points to the role of each perspective in adding what is missing in any single perspective.

It is important to understand that Rychlak's (1993) four perspectives are preempirical and they, in turn, lead to different research strategies. First a perspective or theoretical ground is adopted followed by an appropriate set of research methods. For instance, a perspective derived from physical science and directed at physical phenomena would use methods drawn from physical science, while a perspective derived from human science and directed at values, experiences and meaning would use methods drawn from human science. Carefully controlled experiments cannot, therefore, answer all important psychological questions. Methodological pluralism is rooted deeply in a broad base of theoretical grounds and, therefore, is even more essential to the proper study of a full range of human behavior and experience.

The Question of Adequacy

The question of adequacy of scientific research has been a key issue for human scientists. Natural scientists argue that research methods must be rigorous and that the way to achieve rigor is to quantify, operationalize, manipulate, and control the phenomenon under study. Since much human science research does not quantify, manipulate, or control, it has been deemed inadequate. However, both natural science using a positivist model, and human science with a phenomenological orientation share a concern for adequacy:

It can be seen that positivism's broad evaluative criteria are reasonable standards for existential-phenomenological [i.e., human science] research. That is, research conclusions should be empirically based; research should strive to be free of personal biases, prejudices, and dogma; other individuals should be able to agree that conclusions are justified by the data; and criteria should be provided for evaluating competing knowledge claims. . . . Although the ontological and methodological assumptions of existential phenomenology and logical positivism differ, both share a common commitment to conducting rigorous, empirical research that is open to careful scrutiny.

Thompson, Locander, and
Pollio, 1989, p. 142

While human science researchers often use the term "rigorous" to describe their research methods, "adequate" may be a better term. The notion of adequacy suggests research methods that are equal to the task of understanding, are responsive to the nature of the subject matter, and are open to critical evaluation. Although the underlying standards of good research are the same, the particular criteria for scientific adequacy differ in natural science and human science (Kirk and Miller, 1986). Lincoln and Guba (1985, see also Guba and Lincoln, 1994) identify the primary aspects of rigor or adequacy in scientific research and detail how these aspects are expressed differently in the two approaches. Three of these aspects of adequate scientific research (truthvalue, consistency, and neutrality), along with their parallel versions in natural science and human science, will be examined.

The foundation of the adequacy of scientific research is its truth-value. In this sense, truth-value can be understood as conducting research that is true to the phenomenon under study and drawing trustworthy conclusions that are faithful to empirical observations. In natural science, where the goal is to determine cause-and-effect relationships, truthvalue depends on internal validity. Internal validity is a means for establishing that the independent variable is the major cause of changes in the dependent variable. This is accomplished by controlling extraneous variables in order to eliminate alternative hypotheses such as subject selection, history, and demand characteristics. Control and systematic manipulation of conditions are central requirements for establishing internal validity. However, achieving such control and manipulation cannot be done with many kinds of psychological phenomena, including experiences of the human spirit. An alternative in human science aims for constructing credible accounts of a phenomenon in its context, rather than control. This is based on describing the deep structure or pattern of an experience or phenomenon in a way that is faithful to the experience. According to

this standard, credibility is achieved when someone who has had the experience can say, "This captures my experience better than I could have." By this standard, the truth/value of accounts of the human spirit can be evaluated and established.

Consistency is another critical aspect of scientific adequacy. A particular scientific method must be consistent from one study to another and from one setting to another. Inconsistent methods are akin to using a rubber ruler to measure. In natural science, reliability of both tests and experimental settings is one of the first requirements for rigorous research. However, in the view of human science, many phenomena, by their very nature, cannot be replicated. This makes it difficult or impossible to establish reliability for most experiences of the human spirit. An alternative to reliability is auditability. To achieve auditability, the research provides enough details of the research setting, the informants, the data collection methods, and the data analysis to allow other researchers to come to their own conclusions (i.e., to audit the original research process). In good human science, auditability allows other researchers to follow and evaluate a research study. These auditors may reach different conclusions which leads to dialogue and, ideally, a deeper understanding. In any case, other researchers can see how and why the original researchers arrived at their conclusions.

Neutrality is one element which distinguishes scientific research from dogma or propaganda and may be conceived as objectivity or confirmability. Mechanistic natural science seeks to establish objectivity by maintaining distance between researcher and subject. Their relationship is mediated by protocol, theory, and instrumentation. The more the interaction can be mechanized and the person-to-person intimacy reduced, the more objective the research will be. Human science, on the other hand, argues that this distance is not possible or even desirable. Attempts to achieve this kind of objectivity run the risk of removing the meaning of the experience which Mishler (1986) called "context-stripping." In the attempt to remove the researcher from the research and to quantify experiences, the experience is removed from its context and meaning is altered. Yet, the need to keep scientific conclusions neutral and free from bias remains. Human science suggests that this is possible in qualitative research by a combination of credibility, fittingness, and auditability. Confirmability allows researchers' conclusions to be evaluated in terms of their depth, richness, usefulness, and faithfulness to informants' experiences. It allows evaluations of the degree of fit in other situations. Finally, it allows for thorough examination of the research process. By virtue of allowing confirmation of human science research, researchers can be involved with informants and, at the same time, be neutral; they can be scientifically honest while retaining their focus on the subjective realities and meanings given to and derived from informants' life experiences.

Human science recognizes that a phenomenon is affected by being researched; the act of observing a phenomenon changes it. For example, asking informants to report their experiences (either on a quantifiable survey instrument or in an open-ended interview) may induce more careful self-examination which leads to a different, often fuller, experience. While natural scientists view such reactivity as an extraneous variable to be eliminated in the interest of objectivity, human scientists recognize it as a central feature of human experience and interactions. The concepts of credibility, auditability, and confirmability are reminders that attempts to be objective limit the vitality and meaning of the phenomenon being studied and offer alternatives for research that meets the requirements for adequate, rigorous research. These concepts can serve as guidelines for good scientific research methods in the realm of the human spirit.

Three Examples

Three brief examples can demonstrate the value of methodological pluralism in studying aspects of the human spirit. Two of these examples show that different methods lead to different conclusions, supporting a need for both methods. The other shows that different methods can lead to similar conclusions. Methodological pluralism does not always lead to conflicting conclusions but can lead to a kind of triangulation which may clarify and reinforce our understanding.

Research on Life Satisfaction

Thomas and Chambers (1989) studied life satisfaction in elderly men using two samples—men over seventy in England and in India. A quantitative component of the research used three standard measures of life satisfaction which had been used in previous research. There were no differences between the two groups on these measures; the elderly men in England and India who were surveyed were equally satisfied with their lives. However, a qualitative component of the research showed marked differences. In-depth, open-ended, nondirective interviews were conducted with men from both groups. Analysis of the interviews consisted of identifying meaning units (i.e., any words, phrases, or expressions which could be said to carry information or meaning). Researchers combined meaning units into themes and the overarching themes for each group were identified. Data analysis entailed examination of the interview texts and themes along with ongoing dialogue between researchers. These dialogues produced a high level of agreement but, as with any dialogue, there were differences which required negotiation to reach consensus.

In the qualitative data analysis, the differences between the two groups were strong, with the English men being more concerned about their physical well-being and loss of independence and the Indian men being more concerned with their spiritual and religious well-being and with their families. In the realm of the human spirit, including morale, meaning, and purpose, the qualitative research revealed a different understanding than did the quantitative research. Thomas and Chambers conclude, "Perhaps it is time to acknowledge that quantitative measures alone are not able to encompass the full breadth of these intensely subjective domains" (p. 66). This conclusion applies to nature-based experiences and values as well.

Research on Meditation

Relying primarily on experimental techniques in a reductionist framework, a natural science perspective has approached meditation in terms of quantifiable variables such as physiological arousal levels. A review of this research by Holmes (1984) showed meditation to be as effective as, but not better than, progressive relaxation or napping. However, using a human science approach, transpersonal psychologists have explored not only quantitative but also qualitative phenomenological data (e.g., Goleman, 1987; Shapiro and Walsh, 1984). The phenomenology of meditation explores meditators' goals and the meaning of meditative experiences. Based on this research, the effects of meditation include not only relaxation and self-regulation but also altered states of consciousness, self-transcendence, personal growth, and spiritual transformation. From a human science perspective, the effects of meditation are clearly distinguishable from those of napping and other self-regulation or behavior modification practices (Shapiro, 1985, 1992).

Here, the human science approach provides a description of meditation using both quantitative and qualitative research methods. Compared to a natural science approach, this description is deeper in that it comes closer to the experiences of the many people who, for thousands of years, have used meditation as part of a spiritual practice. It is richer in that it connects meditation to other spiritual and personal growth practices such as prayer and ritual as well as to relaxation. It is also more useful because it connects meditation to the concepts and theories of modern psychology. For instance, the human science approach reveals the similarities and differences between meditation and relaxation training and shows the potential dangers of meditation to those for whom such altered states of consciousness might be problematic, such as psychotics or those in psychological crisis.

Research on Nature-Based Peak Experiences

The third example integrates several studies on nature-based spiritual and peak experiences. Survey methods have been used to study experiences which the researchers defined as peak experiences (Maslow, 1962; Wuthnow, 1978) and spiritual or transcendent experiences (Greeley, 1974; Keutzer, 1978). Wuthnow used three specific operational definitions of peak experiences in his research. He asked a large representative sample the following questions: "Have you ever had the feeling that you were in close contact with something holy or sacred? Have you ever experienced the beauty of nature in a deeply moving way? Have you ever had the feeling that you were in harmony or at one with the universe?" The most frequent affirmative response was to the question about the beauty of nature. Eighty-two percent of those sampled said they had experienced the beauty of nature in a deeply moving way, and 49 percent of the total

sample reported that this experience had a lasting influence.

Greeley (1974) and Keutzer (1978) asked, "With what frequency have you felt as though you were very close to a powerful, spiritual force that seemed to lift you out of yourself?" Greeley found 35 percent of a large sample of the U.S. population reported such an experience, and Keutzer found 65 percent of a sample of college students giving similar reports. When asked what had triggered such experiences, some reference to nature or outdoor experience was the most common trigger in both surveys.

Kaplan and Talbot (1983), using both quantitative and qualitative methods, arrived at a similar conclusion; namely, encounters with nature can lead to spiritual experiences. The Outdoor Challenge Program which they were evaluating involved wilderness backpacking trips in Michigan's Upper Peninsula. A qualitative analysis of participants' journal entries showed what Kaplan and Talbot (1983) called a "surprising" depth of spiritual content. For instance, they report that during the backpacking trip:

> *For many participants there is eventually a surprising sense of revelation, as both the environment and the self are newly perceived and seem newly wondrous. The wilderness inspires feelings of awe and wonder, and one's intimate contact with this environment leads to thoughts about spiritual meanings and eternal processes.* (p. 178)

Kaplan and Talbot (1993) report that after the trip:

> *There is a growing sense of wonder and a complex awareness of spiritual meanings as individuals feel at one with nature, yet they are aware of the transience of individual concerns when seen against the background of enduring natural rhythms.* (pp. 179-180)

As this research demonstrates, an integration of quantitative and qualitative research methods is a powerful means of studying experiences of the human spirit which emerge in natural settings.

Conclusion

These examples demonstrate that a methodologically integrated human science approach works in understanding spiritual and other hard-to-define phenomena. If defining experiences requires reduction and quantification, such definitions will be impossible.

However, if defining means revealing their deep structure and characteristics, the task becomes possible and potentially rewarding. While some research questions about nature-based experiences do call for experiments, surveys, and other natural science methods, the deeper subjective domains of the human spirit call for an integration of qualitative and quantitative research.

The human science approach including aspects of the human spirit is an appropriate basis for the study of human behavior and experience. Being open to the full range of human experience, combining quantitative and qualitative research methods, valuing phenomenological reports as a key source of data, and providing systematic means to evaluate its adequacy, a human science approach provides scientific access to studying the deeper psychological essence of human/nature relationships. It avoids the limitations of a narrow scientism with its dependence on natural science methods while furthering the basic goals and values of science.

Such an integrated approach to scientific research is consistent with the development of a new land management ethic. Such an ethic must consider aspects of human action and experience that, though difficult to quantify, are central in the lives of individuals, communities, cultures, and the environment. A human science approach provides the basis for data-based decisions which incorporate these deeper aspects. This expanded view of science enables dialogue and policy decisions which recognize the essential place of the human spirit in public land management.

Literature Cited

Bevan, W. (1991). Contemporary psychology: A tour inside the onion. *American Psychologist, 46*(5), 475-483.

Bohm, D. (1993). Science, spirituality, and the present world crisis. *ReVision, 15*(4), 147-152.

Giorgi, A. (1970). *Psychology as a human science*. New York, NY: Harper & Row Publishers, Inc.

Goleman, D. (1987). *The meditative mind: The varieties of meditative experience*. New York, NY: St. Martins.

Greeley, A. (1974). *Ecstasy: A way of knowing*. Englewood Cliffs, NJ: Prentice-Hall.

Griffin, D. (1988a). *Spirituality and society: Postmodern visions*. Albany, NY: State University of New York Press.

Griffin, D. (1988b). *The reenchantment of science: Postmodern proposals*. Albany, NY: State University of New York Press.

Guba, E. and Lincoln, Y. (1994). Competing paradigms in qualitative research. In N. Denzin and Y. Lincoln (Eds.), *Handbook of qualitative research* (pp. 105-117). Thousand Oaks, CA: Sage Publications, Inc.

Hayward, J. (1987). *Shifting worlds changing minds: Where the sciences and Buddhism meet*. Boston, MA: Shambhala Publications, Inc.

Holmes, D. (1984). Meditation and Somatic Arousal Reduction. *American Psychologist, 39*(1): 1-10.

Kaplan, L. (1978). *Oneness and separateness*. New York, NY: Simon and Schuster, Inc.

Kaplan, S. and Talbot, J. (1983). Psychological benefits of a wilderness experience. In I. Altman and J. Wohlwill (Eds.), *Behavior and the natural environment* (pp. 163-203). New York, NY: Plenum Publishing Corp.

Keutzer, C. (1978). Whatever turns you on: Triggers to transcendent experiences. *Journal of Humanistic Psychology, 18*, 77-80.

Kirk, J. and Miller, M. (1986). *Reliability and validity in qualitative research*. Newbury Park, CA: Sage Publications, Inc.

Lincoln, Y. and Guba, E. (1985). *Naturalistic inquiry*. Beverly Hills, CA: Sage Publications, Inc.

Lovelock, J. (1988). *The ages of Gaia*. New York, NY: W. W. Norton and Company, Inc.

Macy, J. (1991). *World as lover, world as self*. Berkeley, CA: Parallax Press.

Maslow, A. (1962). Lessons from the peak-experiences. *Journal of Humanistic Psychology, 2*, 9-18.

Maslow, A. (1966). *The psychology of science*. New York, NY: Harper and Row Publishers, Inc.

Maslow, A. (1971). *The farther reaches of human nature.* New York, NY: Viking, Penguin, Inc.

Maturana, H. and Varela, F. (1988). *The tree of knowledge: The biological roots of human understanding.* Boston, MA: Shambhala Publications, Inc.

Messer, S., Sass, L., and Woolfolk, R. (Eds.). (1988). *Hermeneutics and psychological theory: Interpretive perspectives on personality, psychotherapy, and psychopathology.* New Brunswik, NJ: Rutgers University Press.

Mishler, E. (1986). *Research interviewing: Context and narrative.* Cambridge, MA: Harvard University Press.

Ornstein, R. (1977). *The psychology of consciousness* (2nd ed.). New York, NY: Harcourt Brace Jovanovich.

Polkinghorne, D. (1983). *Methodology for the human sciences.* Albany, NY: State University of New York Press.

Rothberg, D. (1993). The crisis of modernity and the emergence of socially engaged spirituality. *ReVision, 15*(3), 105-114.

Rychlak, J. (1993). A suggested principle of complimentarity for psychology. *American Psychologist, 48*(9), 933-942.

Schroeder, H. (1991). Preference and meaning of arboretum landscapes: Combining quantitative and qualitative data. *Journal of Environmental Psychology, 11*, 231-248.

Seamon, D. (1982). The phenomenological contribution to environmental psychology. *Journal of Environmental Psychology, 2*, 119-140.

Shapiro, D. (1985). Clinical use of meditation as a self-regulation strategy: Comments on Holmes' conclusions and implications. *American Psychologist, 40*, 719-722.

Shapiro, D. (1992). A preliminary study of long-term meditators: Goals, effects, religious orientation, and cognitions. *Journal of Transpersonal Psychology, 24*(1), 23-33.

Shapiro, D. and Walsh, R. (Eds.). (1984). *Meditation: Classic and contemporary perspectives.* New York, NY: Aldine de Gruyter, Inc.

Spretnak, C. (1991). *States of grace: The recovery of meaning in the postmodern age.* San Francisco, CA: HarperCollins San Francisco Group.

Taylor, E. (1992). Transpersonal psychology: Its several virtues. *The Humanistic Psychologist, 20*(2 and 3), 285-300.

Thomas, L. and Chambers, K. (1989). Phenomenology of life satisfaction among elderly men: Quantitative and qualitative views. *Psychology and Aging, 4*, 284-289.

Thompson, C., Locander, W., and Pollio, H. (1989). Putting consumer experience back into consumer research: The philosophy and method of existential-phenomenology. *Journal of Consumer Research, 16*, 133-146.

Wilber, K. (1980). Eye to eye: Science and transpersonal psychology. In R. Walsh and F. Vaughan (Eds.), *Beyond ego: Transpersonal dimensions in psychology.* Los Angeles, CA: Jeremy P. Tarcher, Inc.

Wuthnow, R. (1978). Peak experiences: Some empirical tests. *Journal of Humanistic Psychology, 18*, 59-75.

Zukav, G. (1979). *The dancing Wu Li masters: An overview of the new physics.* New York, NY: Bantam Books.

RESEARCH NEEDED ON HARD-TO-DEFINE NATURE-BASED HUMAN EXPERIENCES

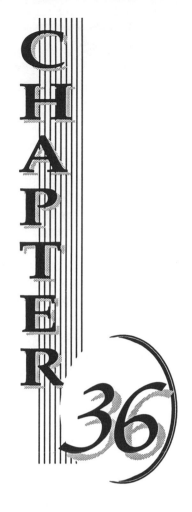

B. L. Driver
Rocky Mountain Forest and Range Experiment Station
USDA Forest Service
Fort Collins, Colorado

Icek Ajzen
Department of Psychology
The University of Massachusetts
Amherst, Massachusetts

Purposes and Orientation

The purpose of this chapter is to summarize and list the many types of information identified in the other chapters of this text that are needed to better understand:

1. the psychologically deep meanings of natural areas to humans;

2. how managers of the public lands can more effectively provide opportunities for the realization of these values; and

3. the relationships between psychologically deep nature-based human experiences and an expanded land management ethic that more explicitly incorporates these values and meanings of nature.

Hopefully, these listings will help stimulate additional research on this increasingly important dimension of public land management.

The various types of informational needs identified by the authors of this text cover philosophical questions, needs for improved managerial technologies, and better basic understanding of psychologically deep nature-based human experiences. While all of these informational needs might not fall within some readers' concept of research needs, we identify them as such. We use the word "research" quite broadly to include any type of study or analysis that advances knowledge, and we do not limit our use of the word simply to the creation of new knowledge. Thus, we include case studies, administrative studies, literature reviews, conceptual analyses, philosophical inquiry, and integrative interpretations as well as the more conventional quantitative and qualitative approaches.

Given our major purpose of identifying needed research, we do not discuss alternative research approaches. Chapter Thirty-Five by Davis and Chapter Thirty-Seven by Stynes and Stokowski cover that. The topic is also addressed in several of the other chapters, especially Chapter Five by Schroeder and Chapter Thirty by Lee and Tainter. Since Mannell addresses past research on hard-to-define values in Chapter Thirty-Four, we will not elaborate on the research that has been done.

This chapter has two parts. The first part lists research needs; the second part illustrates the approach we would use to identify and measure nature-based, spiritual experiences.

Needed Research

The first part of our chapter on needed research covers the five major sections of the text. It summarizes what we consider to be the most important research needs identified by the authors in each of those five sections. The major task of those authors was not to identify research needs, but we have interpreted their chapters from that perspective. These interpretations reflect our judgments. The authors might disagree with our assessments and believe that we have read in research needs they never thought of, omitted some needs they identified, emphasized some needs more than they would, or left out some they would have included. This is the nature of an effort such as this, and our concern is not that those authors might disagree with our assessments of the research needs they have identified but that we might have misrepresented what they wrote. We hope we have not. For the reader's reference, we show in parentheses at the end of each listed research need the last name of the author(s) of the chapter in which we identified that need. Given the exceptionally wide scope of the text and the different orientations of its several major sections, some of the chapters identify more research needs than others.

Sections I and II: Needs and Context

The purposes of the first two sections of the text were to establish the needs for the text, describe its scope and purposes, establish definitions, and develop the conceptual scaffolds around which the text is built. In no particular order of relative importance, the research questions and needs identified by the authors in these sections are given below (if other authors raised similar research needs in later chapters, we give their names too):

1. More study is needed of what people "feel" about nature to supplement the many studies of what people are "doing" in nature (Elsner, Lewis, Snell, and Spitzer, Introduction).

2. We need to understand how to integrate information about the psychologically deep nature-based human experiences and values into ecosystems management by public

agencies (Elsner, Lewis, Snell, and Spitzer, Introduction).

3. We need a better understanding of the trends in these hard-to-define values over time (Elsner, Lewis, Snell, and Spitzer, Introduction).

4. How can we better sensitize and educate both public land managers and the general public about these values (Elsner, Lewis, Snell, and Spitzer, Introduction; Hammond and Judy, Chapter Thirty-Two; and Roggenbuck and Driver, Chapter Thirty-Three)?

5. How can we better represent in land policy and managerial decisions the multicultural diversity that is reflected by these values (Elsner, Lewis, Snell, and Spitzer, Introduction)?

6. How can we better understand the attitudes held by some people that public land management agencies should not be considering these values, and how do we address that point of view (Elsner, Lewis, Snell, and Spitzer, Introduction)?

7. How can we "deepen" the perspectives of public land managers so they can better understand the fundamental spiritual aspects of nature (Rolston, Chapter One, and Hammond and Judy, Chapter Thirty-Two)?

8. What are the essential psychological dimensions of a nature-based, spiritual experience (Rolston, Chapter One)?

9. Does purposeful management of the public lands to provide opportunities to realize generic, noninstitutionalized, multicultural spiritual values violate the clauses of the First Amendment of the United States Constitution pertaining to religion since the word "religion" in that clause was used in a narrower institutionalized sense (Rolston, Chapter One, and Friesen, Chapter Twenty-Two)?

10. Which "value paradigm" is the most appropriate for guiding management of the public lands under an expanded land management ethic that clearly includes psychologically deep, nature-based values and experiences considered in this text (Peterson, Chapter Two)?

11. To what extent would the use of General Systems Theory help structure thinking about these values (Peterson, Chapter Two)?

12. Historiographically, what are the likely near-term trends in Western countries in relationships between established, institutionalized religions and hard-to-define, nature-based values and experiences (Kaza, Chapter Three)?

13. To what extent are the high levels of public concern about management of the public lands possibly related to the past relative inability of managers of those lands to appreciate and understand the spiritual values people associate with those lands (Kaza, Chapter Three)?

14. Could courses about nature in comparative perspectives of world religions help develop greater sensitivity in land managers regarding hard-to-define values (Kaza, Chapter Three)?

15. There is a need for an expanded treatise on the topic addressed by Kaza that isn't limited by the maximum page number constraint she faced in Chapter Three (Driver and Ajzen, Chapter Thirty-Six).

16. What are the relationships between understanding the experience of place and understanding how humans belong to the land (as described by Leopold in *A Sand County Almanac* when he says, "We abuse land because we regard it as a commodity belonging to us. When we see land as a community to which we belong, we may begin to use it with love and respect.") (Roberts, Chapter Four, and Greene, Chapter Twenty-Seven)?

17. What sense of connectedness do most urban residents have with nature and what are the likely trends (Roberts, Chapter Four, and Greene, Chapter Twenty-Seven)?

18. We need case studies of the consequences of managing public lands according to the criteria established at the end of Chapter Four by Roberts—for wildness, for regional identity, for authenticity, to educate, and to restore.

19. What are the essential dimensions of sense of, and attachment to, place? How are they developed? Can they be inculcated through modern techniques of attitude change (e.g., persuasive communication)? How do they differ by individuals and subcultures (Roberts, Chapter Four, and Greene, Chapter Twenty-Seven)?

20. What are the salient attributes of special places to which strong attachments exist (Roberts, Chapter Four, and Greene, Chapter Twenty-Seven)?

21. What are the most appropriate research methods to study the "implicit, prelogical, subliminal, deep, . . . unconscious" psychological experiences and responses to nature? What are the advantages and disadvantages of different approaches? How can scientists be best guided in deciding which approach(es) to use (Schroeder, Chapter Five)?

22. Are there environmental "dispositions" that cause individuals to differ in how they experience hard-to-define, nature-based experiences (Schroeder, Chapter Five)?

23. Can the Jungian, nature-based archetypes (deep inherited-instinctive motives and meanings that "are characteristic of humanity as a whole" or "a collective unconscious that is shared by all people") be identified, and if so, are there, in fact, cross-cultural patterns of similarity in these archetypes (Schroeder, Chapter Five)?

24. How can we modify the dominant rational/scientific paradigm that guides land management agencies to incorporate better the "felt experiences that move and motivate us" which are hard-to-define and hard-to-measure, when the tradition and biases have been toward things that can be measured and maximized (Schroeder, Chapter Five)?

25. What are the likely near-term trends in continued structuring and commodification of leisure contrasted with the Aristotelian notion of leisure being "to develop excellence of the soul" or of Joseph Pieper's notion of "contemplative attention to things in which man begins to see how worthy of veneration they really are" (Goodale and Godbey, Chapter Six)?

26. What is needed to help reorient leisure more toward those higher and deeper ends articulated by Aristotle and Pieper and by Goodale and Godbey (Chapter Six)?

27. What are the health and well-being related restorative, preventive, maintaining, and promotional aspects of nature (Montes, Chapter Seven)?

28. What are the health-restoring, maintaining, and promotional aspects of spiritual experiences and spirituality as an orientation to life, and how does nature-based spirituality fit in (Montes, Chapter Seven)?

29. What can Western societies learn from the practices of, and mind sets required for, traditional Chinese Medicine (Montes, Chapter Seven)?

30. What does it take to promote and achieve more widely the practice of preventive medicine (Montes, Chapter Seven)?

Section III: Describing Diverse Perspectives

The purpose of this third major section of the text is to show the diverse range of perspectives about psychologically deep, nature-based human experiences that are held by different subcultures and by people with different personal and professional orientations. The research questions we gleaned from the chapters in this section are listed below, again in no particular order of priority:

1. How do different styles of communication—especially languages and uses and meanings of particular words—affect understanding and lack of understanding and trust between subcultures and between public land managers and the people they serve (Kopper, Chapter Eight, and Redmond, Chapter Nine)?

2. How can public land managers more effectively understand, establish trust, and build and maintain collaborative partnerships with the stakeholders they serve at all administrative levels of an agency, especially regarding the hard-to-define experiences, values, and land uses on which this text focuses (Kopper, Chapter Eight; Wondolleck,

Chapter Twenty-Three; and Stynes and Peterson, Chapter Twenty-Five)?

3. We need to understand better the world-views or core values that direct much of the thoughts and behaviors of particular groups of users of the public lands (Redmond, Chapter Nine).

4. We need to understand better the considerable diversity of values, attitudes, opinions and world-views that exist within a particular subculture that has strong ties to the land, (i.e., a particular tribe or clan of Native Americans), especially as these differences relate to management of the public lands (Redmond, Chapter Nine).

5. What spiritual and other psychologically deep, nature-based values can be derived from small natural areas such as gardens (Bagby, Chapter Ten)?

6. What are the historical roots of nature-based values, especially as expressed in poems and hymns (Bagby, Chapter Ten)?

7. We need to understand better the approaches and models for understanding contemporary uses of and orientations to the land by specific subcultures (i.e, Hispanics) within a historiographic context. How can we encourage managers of the public lands to think more about the cultural history of the areas they manage (Garcia, Chapter Eleven)?

8. We need to understand better how different ethnic groups interpret and practice "community" or communal use of the land (Garcia, Chapter Eleven)?

9. How do ethnic groups differ in their natural resource-based amenity-related preferences and behaviors (Garcia, Chapter Eleven)?

10. To what degree are past violations of treaties affecting contemporary management of the public lands for hard-to-define values (Garcia, Chapter Eleven)?

11. We need to know more about female views of, and relationships with, nature to supplement male views as "the voices of women have not always been heard" (Henderson, Chapter Twelve).

12. Do women focus on different aspects of the environment than men, and do they relate and respond to the environment differently (Henderson, Chapter Twelve)?

13. To what extent have "... differences such as male/female, nature/culture, body/spirit, and intellect/emotion ... been placed in false dichotomies that tend to polarize relationships between people and the Earth" (Henderson, Chapter Twelve)?

14. What contributions can the female perspective bring to topics such as an expanded land management ethic, spirituality and earth religions, and approaches to management of the public lands (Henderson, Chapter Twelve)?

15. What have been the past traditions of outdoor writers regarding hard-to-define experiences and values, and what role can they play in promoting an expanded land management ethic that better incorporates these values (Madson, Chapter Thirteen)?

16. In the United States, what is the relationship between land and human freedom (Madson, Chapter Thirteen)?

17. More introspective writings about the psychologically deep, nature-based values and experiences are needed from the commercial users of natural areas (Madson, Chapter Thirteen; Budd, Chapter Fourteen; and Tims, Chapter Fifteen).

18. What have been the trends during the past 30-40 years in the stewardship values and actions of commercial users of both public and private lands (Budd, Chapter Fourteen; Tims, Chapter Fifteen; and Rey, Chapter Seventeen)?

19. How can we achieve greater common understanding about the differences and similarities in the land stewardship values and behavior of different groups that use public and private natural areas (Budd, Chapter Fourteen; Tims, Chapter Fifteen; and Rey, Chapter Seventeen)?

20. To what extent do guides and outfitters who use the public lands promote and advance the hard-to-define, nature-based experiences and values on which this text focuses (Tims, Chapter Fifteen)?

21. How can art be used to better sensitize public land managers to psychologically deep, nature-based experiences (Driver, Chapter Sixteen)?

22. What accounts for the "perception gaps" concerning stewardship values between commercial forest-using companies and other users, academicians, and the general public (Rey, Chapter Seventeen)?

23. How different are "commodity users" of the public lands in their hard-to-define experiences and values from other users (Rey, Chapter Seventeen)?

24. What can the nonindigenous cultures of a country learn from the indigenous cultures about the psychologically deep, nature-based values and their relationship to an expanded land management ethic (Birckhead, Chapter Eighteen)?

25. Cross-cultural comparisons are needed of how different countries (e.g., United States, Canada, New Zealand, Australia) are responding to standing treaties with indigenous populations (Birckhead, Chapter Eighteen).

26. We need cross-cultural studies of similarities and differences in the hard-to-define values, their relative importance, and their historical bases (Birckhead, Chapter Eighteen; Sidaway, Chapter Nineteen; and Reunala, Chapter Twenty).

27. Why have different cultures and countries adopted different attitudes about access to public and private lands (e.g., the Scandinavian "right of common access")? And how might policies in one country benefit other countries (Reunala, Chapter Twenty)?

28. What is the role of formal forestry education in nurturing professional land managers' attitudes toward hard-to-define values (Reunala, Chapter Twenty; Wondolleck, Chapter Twenty-Three; and Hammond and Judy, Chapter Thirty-Two)?

Sections IV and V: Public Land Management Concerns and Directions and Research Directions

These two sections of the text have a managerial and research focus and their chapters evaluate different paradigms of land management, consider specific managerial issues, recommend managerial practices that could better accommodate hard-to-define experiences and values on which the text focuses, and consider alternative research approaches. The needed research identified by the authors of the chapters in these sections follows:

1. How do different managerial paradigms affect land managing agencies' approaches to the provision of opportunities for psychologically deep, hard-to-define nature-based experiences, and a land management ethic (Grumbine, Chapter Twenty-One)?

2. How can we better define sustainable ecosystems management and establish managerial guidelines for such management that explicitly incorporate provision of opportunities for psychologically deep, hard-to-define values (Grumbine, Chapter Twenty-One)?

3. What legal reasons can be given to justify a deliberate policy to manage public lands in a way that facilitates their use for spiritual purposes (Friesen, Chapter Twenty-Two)?

4. Do broad based and differentially interpreted spiritual uses of the public lands constitute religious uses under the first amendment of the Constitution of the United States (Friesen, Chapter Twenty-Two)?

5. What would be the impact on management of the public lands if broadly defined and widely different spiritual uses of the public lands were not viewed strictly as religious uses (Friesen, Chapter Twenty-Two)?

6. How can formal training of professional resource managers be changed to prepare them to be more adept in building and maintaining collaborative partnerships with stakeholders (Wondolleck, Chapter Twenty-Three, and Hammond and Judy, Chapter Thirty-Two)?

7. How can professional resource managers most effectively adopt the perspective that there is not a single technically "right" decision but a range of feasible alternative decisions each of which is "right" from different perspectives (Wondolleck, Chapter Twenty-Three)?

8. How can public land managerial decision processes be changed so they are more open, trusted and respected with all parties being involved fairly and with civility (Wondolleck, Chapter Twenty-Three, and Stynes and Peterson, Chapter Twenty-Five)?

9. What combination of managerial frameworks can be used for public land managers to incorporate hard-to-define, nature-based values into their management practices (Stynes and Peterson, Chapter Twenty-Five)?

10. What interpretive, communicative, educational, and public involvement methods best serve managers in both articulating and responding to public demands for hard-to-define, nature-based values and experiences (Stynes and Peterson, Chapter Twenty-Five)?

11. If "... a land ethic cannot be prescribed ... but only evolve through a learning process embedded in human experiences and relationships in the natural world," how can this learning best be achieved (Baltic, Chapter Twenty-Four)?

12. How can our educational systems better teach people how to perceive and prevent "social traps" and "counterintuitive behavior" (Baltic, Chapter Twenty-Four)?

13. Is Magary correct that "government clearly cannot nurture, much less 'promote' spiritual values but only ... create space within which spiritual experience can occur" (Magary, Chapter Twenty-Six)?

14. What are the hazards of the attempts of public land managers to interpret nature-based, spiritual values for users (Magary, Chapter Twenty-Six)?

15. What can managers do to enhance opportunities for the realization of spiritual values on the public lands they manage (Magary, Chapter Twenty-Six)?

16. How can managers of the public lands better understand and manage the "special places" on those lands (Greene, Chapter Twenty-Seven)?

17. How idiosyncratic are place experiences (Greene, Chapter Twenty-Seven)?

18. "If place experiences are completely idiosyncratic . . . and cannot be aggregated statistically," how can they best be researched to provide managerially useful information (Greene, Chapter Twenty-Seven)?

19. How important are senses other than vision in landscape aesthetics (Bacon, Chapter Twenty-Eight)?

20. How can multisensory landscape aesthetics be better incorporated into land management practices (Bacon, Chapter Twenty-Eight)?

21. How important are early American landscapes (EALs) to people (Bruns and Stokowski, Chapter Twenty-Nine)?

22. What can be done to help preserve EALs in rural America and to ensure that their use does not destroy them (Bruns and Stokowski, Chapter Twenty-Nine)?

23. What are the relationships between psychologically deep, nature-based values and experiences and tourism, especially nature-based, heritage, and ecotourism (Bruns and Stokowski, Chapter Twenty-Nine)?

24. How can a "kinder and gentler" type of tourism be promoted (Bruns and Stokowski, Chapter Twenty-Nine)?

25. How can the formal education of public land managers escape the problems associated with the "empiricist/positivist" mode of thinking about nature-based, hard-to-define uses and values (Lee and Tainter, Chapter Thirty)?

26. What motivates people who reenact past historical events such as Civil War battles, and how do they benefit from these behaviors (Lee and Tainter, Chapter Thirty)?

27. What is the value of cultural/heritage resources in promoting understanding of, and pride in nation and community (Lee and Tainter, Chapter Thirty)?

28. How can cultural/heritage resources best be managed for their diverse uses and values (Lee and Tainter, Chapter Thirty)?

29. Are hard-to-define values objectively intrinsic to nature, or are they assigned subjectively (i.e., spiritually, inspirationally, emotionally) by humans, or are they both (Lee and Tainter, Chapter Thirty; Stynes and Peterson, Chapter Twenty-Five; and Rolston, Chapter One)?

30. How can public land managers better meet the needs of special populations, especially physically challenged people, to realize hard-to-define, nature-based values (McAvoy and Lais, Chapter Thirty-One)?

31. Are Hammond and Judy correct in saying ". . .there is no way to teach anyone how to analyze or quantify spiritual values" and that "spiritual values must be accepted; they cannot be defined" (Hammond and Judy, Chapter Thirty-Two)?

32. What are the characteristics of "traditional Western thought patterns" that impede understanding of nature-based spiritual values (Hammond and Judy, Chapter Thirty-Two)?

33. How can public land managers best realize "experiential and participatory modes of learning" about nature-based spiritual values (Hammond and Judy, Chapter Thirty-Two)?

34. What are the responsibilities of public land managers to promote environmental education oriented toward an expanded land management ethic that better incorporates psychologically deep, nature-based values (Roggenbuck and Driver, Chapter Thirty-Three)?

35. If public land managers should be more active in promoting environmental education, what are the best means for doing so (Roggenbuck and Driver, Chapter Thirty-Three)?

36. What can we learn from past research on religion relative to the theme of this text (Mannell, Chapter Thirty-Four; Davis, Chapter Thirty-Five; and Schroeder, Chapter Five)?

37. Assuming that both qualitative and quantitative approaches will be needed to better define, measure, and understand hard-to-define experiences and values, how can the required methods be developed or refined (Mannell, Chapter Thirty-Four; Davis, Chapter Thirty-Five; Stynes and Stokowski, Chapter Thirty-Seven; and Schroeder, Chapter Five)?

38. From a managerial perspective, what are the highest priority research questions regarding hard-to-define, nature-based values and uses (Stynes and Stokowski, Chapter Thirty-Seven)?

How We Would Try to Measure Nature-Based Spiritual Experiences

Our purpose in this second part of the chapter is to outline a program of research for measuring nature-based spiritual experiences (SEs). Not too surprising to readers familiar with our past research, the proposed approach is based in attitude theory. But in line with the recommendations of the authors of several chapters in this text, we call for considerable qualitative research in our proposed approach.

The program of research we propose is comprised of seven major tasks:

1. Identify and define specific dimensions of an SE.

2. Develop psychometric scales to measure these dimensions.

3. Measure the importance of the SE dimensions.

4. Determine how SEs are derived and how land management practices and other uses impact them.

5. Determine trends in SEs and their values.

6. Determine how these experiences impact other behaviors and are impacted by them.

7. Determine barriers to experiencing SEs and how to remove them.

Identify and Define Specific Dimensions of an SE

This first phase will consist of two complementary tasks that can be done concurrently. One will focus on behaviors or activities that people engage in to realize an SE. The other will focus directly on the dimensions of such an experience. The purpose is to identify and define specific dimensions of an SE. These tasks will include reviews of the literature, unstructured talks with experts and laypersons, and especially use of qualitative research methods which would use focus groups as well as in-depth, open-ended interviews with users who report nature-based spiritual activities and experiences. These descriptions will record what was happening and how the respondents felt (e.g., "After getting up at sunrise, I drove to the overlook and, among a myriad of colors, watched the sun rise over the canyon, casting and erasing its shadows. I was struck with awe, overwhelmed by the majesty, and felt humble."). The unstructured interviews will be analyzed for meaning units, higher-order themes and overarching themes and patterns. The results of the literature reviews and interviews will then be cross-checked to produce a complementary picture of common dimensions and differences of nature-based SEs.

These descriptions of the SEs will next be subjected to multidimensional scaling analysis. Naive subjects will be asked to judge the similarity or difference of pairs of descriptions of spiritual experience. The result will be a number of groups of related constructs which we will call dimensions of an SE (e.g., serenity). Some will be quite abstract, and each dimension will need to be interpreted, with the help of experts, to determine overlap and correspondence. At this time, each dimension will be interpreted as to what it means and will be given a name that best captures that meaning.

Develop SE Scales

The next step will be to make up scale items (e.g., relaxed, humbled, awestruck) to tap the theme of each dimension identified by the multidimensional scaling. A new sample of respondents will then rate the original SE descriptions on the scale items designed to tap each of the dimensions. Items that discriminate between experiences that differ on a given dimension will be retained for development of a general measuring instrument. They will be subjected to validity and reliability testing commonly used in psychometric scaling. Given the research process proposed, those scales should tap most, to all, of the dimensions of an SE that humans can meaningfully articulate.

Measure Importance of the SE Dimensions

Once a comprehensive set of reasonably valid and reliable SE scales has been developed, it should be applied to subjects within different contexts defined by different hypothetical or actual behaviors, some of which are known to create an SE, and some of the subjects must have past experience with those behaviors. The purpose here is to determine the relative desirability and/or perceived psychological importance of the SE dimensions for the specified context. The results will be knowledge about which types of behavior provide opportunities for specific dimensions of SE and the relative importance of those dimensions for those behaviors. One can also solicit sociodemographic and other descriptive information from the subjects to determine the types and dimensions of an SE that differentiate people with different characteristics.

Determine How an SE Is Derived and the Impacts of Management Actions and Other Uses

By definition, the SE scales will identify and define the essential dimensions of an SE. Given that information, targeted subjects (e.g., different types of users of natural areas) can be questioned about the degree to which different land management practices and different types of land use either facilitate or prohibit realization of the specific dimensions of an SE that are tapped by the SE scales. Again, these perceptions can be classified for subjects with different sociodemographic and other characteristics.

Determine Trends

The SE scales can be administered over time to determine trends in the importance of an SE (and its dimensions) and in the numbers of specified types of people who value them to different degrees.

Determine Impacts on Other Behaviors

This research would evaluate how differential valuing of the SE dimensions correlates with other behaviors. Included could be objective measures of mental and physical health, personal relations with other people inside and outside of the subject's immediate family, and environmental dispositions and behaviors (e.g., participation in conservation activities). Other studies could employ techniques of modern persuasive communication theory and methods to determine the subjects' awareness of their SE or specific dimensions of such and to enhance such awareness.

Determine Barriers to Experiencing SEs and How to Remove Them

It is highly likely that most, if not all, people have the potential for realizing nature-based SEs; it is not known how many really do. More relevant to the purposes of this text, little is known about the psychological, cultural, economic and physical barriers that constrain people from realizing nature-based SEs. While quite speculative, we conjecture that these barriers would include institutionalized religious and other cultural norms, personal prejudices and world-views that deter realization of the SEs, conditions in home environments that do not nurture orientations toward nature-based SEs, and physical and economic constraints. Much research is needed to identify and quantify the magnitudes of these constraints and how they might most efficiently and effectively be removed.

Alternative Research Approaches for Studying Hard-to-Define Nature-Based Human Values

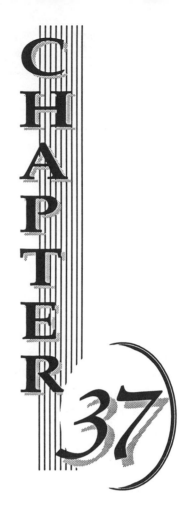

Daniel Stynes
Department of Park, Recreation, and Tourism Resources
Michigan State University
East Lansing, Michigan

Patricia Stokowski
Department of Recreation, Park and Tourism Sciences
Texas A & M University
College Station, Texas

Introduction

The purpose of our chapter is to review alternative research approaches for studying hard-to-define, nature-based human values. In Chapter Thirty-Six, Driver and Ajzen compile a broad list of questions and information needs that are identified by various authors throughout this text. Some of these questions raise philosophical and ethical issues, some pose alternatives for management to consider, and some suggest scientific research topics. Most of the problems associated with hard-to-define values and public land management involve all three kinds of questions. As we discuss research approaches in this chapter, we necessarily pay primary attention to scientific questions. Many of the general qualitative and quantitative research approaches discussed here are, however, widely applied to individual and organizational problem solving in somewhat less formal ways.

Research methods must fit the problems to which they will be applied. Identifying the critical research questions is both more important and more difficult than choosing suitable methods once the problems are understood. As the chapters in this text illustrate, the questions are numerous and, like

the values we seek to clarify, are equally hard to define. We therefore begin by outlining a broad set of research themes or areas, beginning with the applied problems faced by public land management agencies (PLMAs) and their constituencies. We then briefly discuss value concepts before presenting qualitative and quantitative approaches to the study of values. Given a wide range of relevant research questions, a variety of possible approaches to each, and numerous relevant theories and disciplinary perspectives, we necessarily limit our presentation of research approaches to some general comments and a few illustrative examples.

The Research Questions

The applied research questions flow from the management problems they are to address. PLMAs must make and implement decisions about how to manage public lands to serve a variety of people and uses. Individuals and various stakeholder groups must assess their interests in public lands and how to foster these interests through their own use of public lands or their involvement in public land management decision processes. Management questions arise in identifying problems, developing management alternatives, evaluating them, and reconciling competing and conflicting interests.

Decisions must take into account physical, biological, economic, social, environmental and political processes and constraints. Values help to guide public land management agencies and their publics. As the word implies, values provide a means of evaluating, whether it be a personal decision to litter or not, or an agency decision over which of several policy or management alternatives to choose.

Viewing public land management from a systems perspective helps to identify specific research themes. Public land management systems may be characterized via three subsystems:

1. a resource subsystem of natural and cultural resources;

2. a user subsystem consisting of various people, stakeholders, and users of public lands; and

3. a management subsystem consisting primarily of the PLMAs themselves but also including management activities of individuals and other organizations.

The resource, people, and management subsystems operate within a broader social, political, and natural environment that plays a major role in influencing values and establishing opportunities and constraints. The task for research is to better understand each of these subsystems and, more importantly, to understand how they interact within a complex and dynamic environment to make and implement decisions about the management and use of public lands.

A systems perspective directs attention to the interrelationships between subsystems. Systems models typically measure interrelationships as flows of people, energy, money, or information. Our interest in hard-to-define values suggests a focus on flows of value and value information in this system. Three subsystems yield ten categories of flows and corresponding potential research thrusts:

1. *Resource-resource interactions* is a place for studies of some of the intrinsic and functional values of natural environments proposed by Rolston (1982). Resource-resource interactions capture ecological relationships and the dynamics of natural systems

(change over time). Ecosystem relationships and natural processes involve both intrinsic and instrumental values. Our understandings of these processes influence how we value ecosystems and their components.

2. *Resource-people interactions* is perhaps the central area of resource value research as it addresses flows of value from resources to people. The need here is to extend research from commodity and easier to measure use values to investigations of the characteristics of public lands that foster particular values of individuals, social groups, and society as a whole (e.g., What characteristics of natural environments enhance the human spirit and through what mechanisms?).

3. *Resource-management interactions* acknowledge that public lands also provide values to management organizations themselves. Some of these are of the same type as those for people in general, while others arise from the special public service, management, and stewardship roles of PLMAs. How do the lands and resources being managed affect the spirit of the managers and land management organizations?

4. *People-people relationships* cover the communication and exchange of value information between individuals and population subgroups, including the passing on of values across generations. Value information is sometimes explicit, but more often is implicit in the communications and behaviors of people. A better understanding of the role and value of natural environments for both individuals and societies can be obtained by studying the communications and exchanges between people (e.g., verbal exchanges among members of a backpacking party, trading of natural objects—be they gemstones or rhino horns—or communications about nature-based values in the mass media, art, poetry, and literature).

5. *People-resource flows* are the other side of the resource-people interactions. If we adopt the usual social scientific perspective on values as human attributions, then values are assigned to objects, resources, and behaviors by people. A central theme of research on

hard-to-define values must be to understand how these attributions are made and the impacts of human value attributions on resource subsystems. What makes people value certain places, environments, species, and what is the nature of these values?

6. *People-management interactions* cover the communication of value information from various publics and public land users to management organizations. People communicate values through their behaviors and via various formal and informal public involvement vehicles.

7. *Management-resource interrelationships* are the primary stuff of traditional resource management, covering all of the ways that PLMAs manipulate public lands to protect resources or provide for various uses. Of interest here is how management practices may alter resources in ways that either change how people value public lands or alter the ability of public lands to provide various goods and services that people value. How can PLMAs manage for hard-to-define values?

8. *Management-people flows* encompass communications and exchanges between PLMAs and the public. PLMA educational, informational, and user management programs influence attitudes, behaviors, and values. How do these interactions affect the often hard-to-define varied groups? How are some of the values expressed in this text communicated by PLMAs, if at all?

9. *Management-management interactions* cover the interrelationships within PLMAs where management frameworks are established and the values and competing views among agency personnel are exchanged in the process of making and implementing decisions. This category also includes exchanges of value information between different PLMAs. How is information about hard-to-define values communicated within and between PLMAs?

10. *System-environment interactions.* Finally, the largest category of interactions of all is the set of complex interrelationships between these three subsystems and the broader environment. These relationships are two directional with the PLMA resource-people-management system both influencing and being influenced by the broader environment. To fully understand the role of PLMAs in serving hard-to-define, nature-based values, we suspect that significant attention will need to be directed toward the broader social, cultural, and political environment both to understand the sources and nature of these values and to understand what role PLMAs might play in fostering or serving them. Does the "public" in public land define or modify the nature of some of these values? What can we learn about some of these values from private lands where the user and manager are the same person?

Public land management research activity, especially research with a values component, has usually focused on one of the three subsystems. Focusing on the resource subsystem usually leads to an inventory and assessment of the values of resources, usually as commodities and generally using market prices or subjective assessments of importance or quality. Most forest plans implement this type of analysis. Hard-to-define values are sometimes identified in a qualitative fashion in such inventories. Focusing on users and other stakeholders produces studies of the benefits that people derive from public lands or the values they attribute to them. Quantitative studies typically measure user benefits or willingness to pay while qualitative studies attempt to understand the meaning of individuals' nature-based experiences. Finally, a few studies have focused on public land management organizations to understand their values and decision processes (e.g., Mohai, Stillman, Jakes, and Liggett, 1994).

A systems perspective recommends that more attention be directed at the interactions between these three subsystems (i.e., the relationships between users, management, and resources). Boulding (1969) notes that "value" was a verb before it became a noun. A value expresses a relationship between a thing that is valued and the individual or group that makes the value attribution in a particular situation. To understand nature-based values, one must understand people-environment relationships (i.e., the exchanges of information, energy, goods and services between people, land management organizations and the environment). One must also understand the particular historical, political and social context of these exchanges and relationships.

The systems perspective defines a broad potential research agenda with ample room for both reductionist and holistic approaches. The topic is clearly interdisciplinary. One can anticipate important contributions from several disciplines and suggest that the most important will come from approaches that cut across disciplinary boundaries. There are important basic, applied, and methodological research questions to address. The term *hard to define* indicates that a first priority is to better understand and define these values. There is little scientific agreement about the concept of "values," so the notion of "hard-to-define values" is doubly problematic.

Value Concepts

While various concepts of value can be found in the social and management science literature, there does not exist a commonly accepted definition of value or a universally accepted framework for studying values. While there are numerous philosophical treatments of ethics and values, empirical studies are rare. Empirical information about values comes from three principal sources:

1. economic efforts to measure nonmarket values (Sinden and Worrell, 1979),

2. social surveys which measure broad societal values (e.g., Rokeach, 1973), and

3. value information revealed in attitude, preference and choice research (e.g., Louviere, 1988).

Scientists have generally not studied values specifically for the purpose of describing, explaining, or predicting them. Social scientists have tended to treat values as orienting concepts (Homans, 1967) by directing attention to a general topic rather than defining notions of value in operational terms. What is actually studied under the term "values" may be benefits, preferences, ethics, willingness to pay, perceptions, importance, attitudes, beliefs, or feelings. Subtle differences between these different concepts of value have frequently been obscured, yielding little agreement about theories of value or how to study values.

The absence of a substantive body of empirical research or science of values may be because the subject is not sufficiently well-defined to permit serious study. An equally likely reason is that the topic falls between disciplinary cracks, with separate disciplines addressing values in different ways and usually as a side issue rather than a central concern. Within the public land management field, the topic of values has largely been left to economists yielding a somewhat one-sided perspective.

There are many different notions of value arising from distinct disciplinary and theoretical positions. Most scientists treat values as expressions of human preferences and, hence, the topic largely falls within the realm of the social and management sciences. There are, however, parallels to the idea of value in the physical and biological sciences. One could, for example, infer preferences and values from the behavior of planets, rocks, animals, plants, and even molecules (nature abhors a vacuum!), but it is unclear what this would add to these sciences. The rationale for a concept of value in the social sciences is that it aids in better understanding and explaining human behavior.

For most social scientists, values surface in studying human decision making or behavior. Definitions of value are generally embedded in a particular theory which also dictates the appropriate interpretations and uses of given value concepts. Confusion often arises when particular notions of value are applied outside of their defining theory (e.g., using prices as measures of value without some kind of market or assumed rules of exchange between people).

While values are almost universally recognized as a fundamental part of decision making, there is little consistency in how values are conceptualized and used in analyzing decisions. For some, values are desired goals or end states, while for others values are attributes of objects. When applied to behaviors, the words "norm" or "ethic" often replace the word "value." Values may also be classified as intrinsic or extrinsic, instrumental or terminal, and held or assigned (Brown, 1984). Andrews and Waits (1978) distinguish between values as individual preferences, social obligations, and functions. These distinctions are not typically made when considering values in the context of decisions or when people and organizations communicate value information.

Not surprisingly, uses of the term "value" by public land managers and the public in general suffer from the same fuzziness and diversity of meanings. The idea of "hard-to-define" values comes largely from a quantitative reading of the underlying problems. The fine and not so fine distinctions in conceptions of value pose problems primarily for quantitative research where concepts must be clearly defined and measured. The diversity and openness of meanings of the term "value" in general use mirror how qualitative studies would approach the topic. Qualitative researchers do not generally use the term "value" at all. They speak of "meanings" or "interpretations" of individual experiences.

The formats of a qualitative versus quantitative research agenda to address hard-to-define values and public land management are therefore quite different. Lists of specific research topics come more readily from a quantitative perspective on public land management research. This is currently the dominant paradigm among both researchers and public land managers. Qualitative methods are, however, widely used in an informal manner by public land managers and are increasingly being recognized for their value in more formal research.

Qualitative and Quantitative Approaches

We intentionally selected a systems model over several alternative ways to organize this topic, as it seems to be able to embrace both quantitative and qualitative perspectives. The model is not meant to imply any philosophical or scientific position about how to study values or their role in public land management. Empiricists and positivists, as well as interpretive scientists (phenomenologists, humanists, postmodernists, and others) all share a common goal of understanding the world in which we live. Their approaches differ because of distinct perspectives about the nature of reality. These perspectives lead to somewhat distinct purposes of research and significantly different procedures.

Most public land managers and scientists working on public land management problems lean toward quantitative approaches. Quantitative research approaches are based in logical positivism and encompass "traditional science" (Kaplan, 1964). A somewhat distinct set of methods, loosely termed "qualitative research," are based in phenomenology and other nonpositivist theories of knowledge (Glaser and Strauss, 1967). With roots in sociology and anthropology, qualitative methods are now used in almost all human sciences. In the past ten years, qualitative approaches have become increasingly popular in those areas of resource management with strong social science orientations, such as recreation and community development (Henderson, 1991). Qualitative methods include ethnography, focus groups, in-depth interviews, case studies, historical analysis, participant observation and related techniques (Denzin and Lincoln, 1994). Quantitative approaches, involving systematic observation, surveys, experiments, and analysis of quantitative data are more commonly used and understood in the public land management professions.

Perspectives

Positivist or quantitative science assumes that reality is "objective" and that researchers must systematically identify and measure elements of this reality in order to understand the world. Interpretive or qualitative science assumes that reality is subjectively constructed and that researchers must enter into the lived worlds of their subjects in order to understand meanings and experiences. The quantitative model examines the world from the researcher's perspective while qualitative methods attempt to understand the world from the subject's point of view. This "insider" perspective leads to relativist interpretations of the world rather than the assumed objective reality of traditional science.

We also acknowledge the relevance and usefulness of humanist, artistic, religious, and many other nonscientific perspectives on values and public land management. In this chapter, however, we do not approach these ways of knowing as means of accumulating scientific knowledge (Casti, 1989). There are, however, potential contributions to our topic from the scientific study of religion, art, literature, transcendental experience and the like, including the role that these ways of knowing play in forming human values and perceptions of nature.

Purposes

The purpose of quantitative approaches is to establish general knowledge through careful measurement, hypothesis testing and verification. Qualitative approaches are more likely to study the particular than the general, seeking to understand human experience rather than to predict it. While quantitative approaches seek to explain and predict behavior, qualitative researchers want to understand the meanings and interpretations that individuals attach to their experiences. All of these purposes are relevant to public land management. Managers must seek solutions to general problems while also responding to unique circumstances and situations.

Procedures

Quantitative procedures tend to be highly structured and standardized and require operational definitions of concepts, formal measurement procedures, probability sampling and statistical analysis of quantitative data. Qualitative approaches generally involve in-depth observation or interviews with small purposeful samples employing multiple sources of evidence and research strategies. Quantitative approaches tend to be reductionist, dividing complex problems into smaller parts that can be studied somewhat independently. Each subproblem is addressed by identifying a small set of the most important variables and either controlling for or assuming away the rest. Qualitative methods are more holistic.

There is a clear trade-off between depth and breadth in the two approaches. A single quantitative study tends to be quite narrow, permitting detailed analysis of a small set of variables. Quantitative science attempts to achieve broader explanations through the cumulative contributions of many narrowly defined studies, each taking a somewhat different focus. Qualitative investigations are able to consider a much wider range of variables, particularly historical and situational, by narrowing the study to a small number of cases, sometimes to a single individual or case study. Qualitative studies seek "deep" understanding by examining a large number of variables for a small number of subjects, while quantitative depth comes from focusing intensively on a small number of variables across many subjects.

Quantitative approaches strictly separate procedures for data gathering and analysis from interpretation, where these procedures tend to be inextricably linked in qualitative studies. This makes assessments of reliability and validity of qualitative research more difficult. While quantitative researchers infer conclusions about populations based on representative samples and repeatable measures, qualitative investigators "support claims by

citing prototypes or examples that illustrate the reasonableness of the conclusions . . . (or by showing) that no outstanding counter examples contradict conclusions" (Smith, 1988, p. 246).

While quantitative and qualitative perspectives are often presented as competing scientific paradigms, in terms of advancing knowledge they are more complementary than competitive. Both qualitative and quantitative approaches are useful, although usually for quite different purposes. The key is matching the methods with the study purpose. Although this is not their only use, qualitative methods tend to be used more for exploratory research. Ideally, qualitative and quantitative methods should be integrated to study a particular problem. One may start with a qualitative approach talking with key informants, observing as a participant, and so forth. From these investigations, concepts and hypotheses are generated which then may be measured and tested within a quantitative approach, perhaps as a survey or experiment. Results of a quantitative study may help assess the generalizability of the qualitative findings and suggest additional questions. These may be addressed in a further qualitative study, perhaps followed again by a quantitative approach.

There are too many different research questions and alternative research approaches to attempt to propose very specific recommendations for applying qualitative and quantitative methods to the topic of hard-to-define values. We therefore outline the general types of questions that qualitative and quantitative approaches seem best suited for and present a few examples illustrative of applications that seem worthwhile.

Applications of Qualitative Methods

The stage of research on the values topic along with interest in hard-to-define values suggests an important role for qualitative investigations. Virtually all of the qualitative approaches are tailored to understanding the unique perspectives and interpretations of individuals and special groups. The methods are readily adaptable to studying different perspectives on public land management issues within particular contexts.

Qualitative methods are well-suited in helping to understand the nature of the values that particular individuals or population subgroups associate with public lands. A particular strength of qualitative methods is that values may be examined within a particular historical, social, and cultural context. Qualitative approaches will not provide any quantitative measures of value, and the approaches are limited in providing predictions or explanations beyond the particular individuals and situations that are studied. Qualitative approaches can yield some insights into how and when individuals make trade-offs, but they will not provide clear-cut rules for deciding among conflicting uses or users. Indeed, the relativist perspective of qualitative approaches provides no guidance for reconciling competing points of view. Qualitative methods are, however, appropriate for understanding how different individuals and groups interpret public lands, public land management decisions and decision processes. Such understanding could likely suggest a number of possible improvements, including how to adapt management and decision processes to different perspectives and communication styles.

Examples of Qualitative Methods

1. *In-depth studies of user groups.* Participant observation, focus groups, or in-depth interviews may be conducted with various public land management user groups to better understand how they use public lands and the values they associate with them. The same qualitative approaches used to understand bridge players (Stebbins, 1992), auction goers (Glancy, 1988), and fantasy baseball camps (Brandmeyer and Alexander, 1986) can be applied to understand particular public land stakeholder and user groups.

2. *Ethnographic studies.* Studies may be conducted of public land resource-dependent communities, of public land management agencies, and of special interest and minority cultural groups. Examples include Kaufman's (1960) study of the forest ranger, Colfer and Colfer's (1978) study of a Pacific Northwest logging community, and Bellah, Madsen, Sullivan, Swidler, and Tipton's

(1985) influential *Habits of the Heart*, in which the authors apply social science to public philosophy by exploring American values and the ways that people make sense of their lives and their society. Sutherland and Nash (1994) use field trips, interviews, and reviews of films and brochures to examine the values and perspectives of animal rights groups.

3. *Case studies of particular public land management decisions and events.* Case studies may explore how a particular decision or event came about (e.g., Nash's [1967] examination of the Hetch Hechy reservoir); may document distinct interpretations of an event or decision as it occurred (e.g., Gephart's [1993] study of a gas pipeline disaster); or may examine perceptions of changes or impacts after the fact (e.g., Stynes and Stewart's [1991] study of the impacts of a major resort development on a community in northern Michigan). Yin (1984) formally defines case studies as using multiple sources of evidence to investigate real-life phenomena when "the boundaries between the phenomenon and context are not clearly evident."

4. *Historical studies.* A variety of historical analyses of individuals, communities, public lands, public land agencies, and various stakeholder and user groups would help us better understand the historical context of current PLMA problems and issues. Roderick Nash's (1967) historical analysis of wilderness values and concepts is one of the best and most well-known examples of this genre. Histories of public land management organizations (e.g., Albright and Cahn, 1985; Clawson and Held, 1957; Frome, 1971; Hummell, 1987) and stakeholder groups (e.g., Nash, 1989; Snow, 1992; Worster, 1973) also shed considerable light on values and perspectives from both internal and external points of view.

Applications of Quantitative Methods

Quantitative research is routinely carried out to support public land management decisions. Quantitative studies are particularly recommended when study results must yield quantitative measures that are representative of and projectable to some larger population. There are a number of contributions that quantitative research can make to our understanding of nature-based values and their role in public land management decisions. Quantitative studies that are easiest to anticipate are simply extensions of previous research on human attitudes, preferences, and values. Current economic, sociological, and psychological theories and approaches can potentially be extended to cover many of the values of interest here. We encourage such attempts, while also cautioning against overextending theories and approaches that may not apply.

The modifier "hard-to-define" suggests that the development of new research thrusts, theories, and measurement approaches receive as much attention as adaptations and extensions of old ones. Some values may only be hard to define because our theories, perspectives, or approaches are too narrow. Whether a value can be defined and measured is determined as much by our own creativity as any characteristics of the value itself. Measuring the biomass of an old growth forest does not seem inherently easier than measuring its spiritual value to an indigenous population. People simply have invested considerably more time and effort on a science of forest ecology than a science of human values. There was a time when concepts and measurements of mass were as fuzzy and crude as the current notions and measures of spiritual values. Definitions and measures of value rest heavily on having appropriate theories of how humans and natural systems behave. Qualitative studies could be especially useful in helping to ground some revised value concepts, theories, and decision frameworks.

As with any topic, quantitative research approaches should begin by defining concepts, linking these to existing research and theory, building new theory as required, and finally making measurements and conducting empirical tests. Research on hard-to-define values must proceed in the usual way from exploratory studies to descriptive studies, to explanatory research. The standard quantitative approach is to:

1. define the value,
2. measure it, and
3. incorporate it analytically into existing theoretical, management and decision-making frameworks (Driver, Brown, and Peterson, 1991).

Defining concepts primarily involves basic research, developing suitable measures entails a mix of basic and applied studies, and the final step largely involves applied research.

Quantitative approaches rest heavily on existing theory. In using quantitative tools to study values, it is important to recognize that the conceptions of value being used are intimately tied to a body of theory. The economic notion of value as a measure of exchange rests on assumptions about markets. The idea of value as a mental construct or human attribution is embedded in psychological theories of attitudes and behavior. Sociological and anthropological notions of value as expressions of group norms or acceptable modes of behavior stem from quite different theories about the behavior of social groups.

These distinct value concepts imply somewhat different measurement procedures and research approaches. The economic concept of willingness to pay, for example, is measured via market transactions when suitable markets exist. When they do not, measures of willingness to pay are generated using travel cost or contingent valuation methods (Mitchell and Carson, 1991). Values conceived as attitudes are measured using accepted attitude measurement techniques (Eagly and Chaiken, 1993), frequently including the development of standardized instruments and measurement scales (e.g., Rokeach, 1973).

Social science theories relevant to our topic are too numerous to discuss here. Suffice it to say that each theory of individual, group, and organizational behavior suggests a somewhat different research agenda and distinct value concepts, measures, and research approaches. These theories tend to follow disciplinary lines. Four research or data gathering approaches common to all disciplines are:

1. surveys,
2. observations (human or via physical instruments),
3. experiments, and
4. secondary data.

All of these approaches offer some potential for studying hard-to-define values and their role in land management decisions. Since measurement is the beginning of quantitative science, we comment briefly about uses of these approaches to measure values before giving some illustrative examples of typical quantitative studies.

Examples of Quantitative Approaches to Measure Values

1. *Direct measurement of preferences and values using survey methods.* The most direct approach to measure values is to simply ask people about their values through surveys. If one can articulate the values of interest in a manner that is understood consistently across subjects, standard attitudinal and behavioral measures of value or preference can be employed. In Chapter Thirty-Six, Driver and Ajzen summarize how standard attitude measurement techniques may be extended to develop measures and scales relevant to spiritual experiences. Attitudinal approaches are quantitative tools that are widely applicable to understanding human preferences and behavior and are, therefore, frequently used to inform public land management decisions.

   Psychologists and social psychologists tend to focus on individual attitudes and their relationship to behavior. The development and applications of recreation experience preference scales provide good examples of relevance to the topic of values and public lands (Driver, Tinsley, and Manfredo, 1991). Illustrative examples of surveys measuring values at a community or societal level include Rokeach (1973), Zwick (1990) and Dunlap and van Liere (1984). The research questions raised throughout this text suggest many new challenges for value and attitude surveys, including greater attention to potential value

and attitude measurement problems across distinct cultures and world-views.

Two other direct survey approaches to measuring preferences or values are policy referenda and contingent valuation surveys (Mitchell and Carson, 1991). When studying public policy questions that involve clear trade-offs among competing alternatives or interest groups, these methods are favored by political scientists and economists over attitude surveys. Both the contingent valuation and policy referendum formats have clear applications in studying hard-to-define values in the context of particular public policy questions.

Economists have extended traditional market valuation methods to a variety of so-called "nonmarket valuation" techniques suitable for application to environmental goods and services like recreation, endangered species, and water quality. These methods have considerably broadened the range of goods and services that can be valued, while raising many questions about both the nature of values and the validity and reliability of measures of value. Tackling hard-to-define values requires that this line of research and the available methods be extended. This will undoubtedly yield additional insights into both the limits and potentials of quantitative economic approaches to value.

2. *Inferring preferences and values from observed behavior and choices.* Quantitative researchers have developed deeper insights into preferences by inferring values from actual choices. Multinomial logit choice models (Stynes and Peterson, 1984) and conjoint measurement techniques (Louviere, 1988) are used to sort out part worth utilities of various attributes of the objects of choice. Preferences for some hard-to-define attributes of particular choice objects may be measured in the same ways that researchers have identified consumer preferences for transportation modes (Ben Akiva and Lerman, 1985), environmental features (Zube, Brush, and Fabos, 1975) and the presence and quality of various product and service attributes (Louviere, 1988).

The constraints and obstacles in extending these methods are largely in identifying and measuring the attributes that capture the hard-to-define values of interest. Hard-to-define values are often not conceptualized as separable attributes of choice objects, although this does not mean they cannot be. To apply discrete choice methods, we also must be able to observe a sufficient number of choice events under varying levels of the attributes to statistically identify their relative importance. These methods assume separability of attributes and a compensatory choice process which limits their application to understanding values that may be of a more holistic nature.

Inferences about human preferences are not limited to behavioral evidence. Psychophysiological measures have clear applications to measuring emotional and physical responses to natural environments and experiences (Ulrich, Dimberg, and Driver, 1991). By relating such responses to some of the values of interest, we may obtain additional insights into human preferences. Psychophysiological approaches seem particularly applicable to understanding values that may be subconscious or otherwise difficult to express through words or behavior.

3. *Inferring preferences and values from choice experiments.* A wider range of attributes and choices may be considered using real or hypothetical choice experiments. Experiments have considerable advantage over surveys in establishing causal linkages. In choice experiments, the researcher is not constrained by currently available alternatives but may construct hypothetical alternatives or alter existing ones to better reveal underlying preferences and values. There are hundreds of examples of the application of contingent valuation experiments (Mitchell and Carson, 1991) and conjoint experiments (Louviere and Timmermans, 1990) to measure values that were formerly seen as hard to define. These methods should therefore be carefully examined for potential extensions to even harder to define values.

For example, to measure the values that individuals or groups may assign to the protection of Native-American sacred lands, people could be asked to choose among land management alternatives that afford varying levels of protection. This approach forces subjects to make trade-offs between this value and other competing values, or perhaps to protest the choice itself. Similarly, to measure preferences for a spiritual dimension of a wilderness experience, one must be able to construct actual or hypothetical experiences with and without a given level of this attribute. The nature of the attributes and alternatives must also be communicable to the subjects. These conditions may not hold for many hard-to-define values, but for others the approach seems worth pursuing.

4. *Inferring preferences and values from secondary data.* Secondary data offers opportunities to study hard-to-define values, but will call for some creative approaches backed up by sound theories. Although there is no "Census of Values," there is surely value information in virtually all existing data. Just as with behavioral information, verbal reports, and physiological measures, the problem is developing theories and statistical techniques for extracting the value information in a valid manner. Sufficiently creative researchers can likely draw value inferences from as far ranging sources as garbage cans, mass media coverage, children's textbooks, voting patterns, organizational memberships, and consumer purchases. Human values are reflected as much in how people spend their time and energy as well as their money. Reexamination of survey data sets, historical records, documents, and trace evidence with a clearer focus on values and public lands will likely yield many new insights. For example, content analysis methods are one set of tools that could be applied to identify values in documentary evidence (Holsti, 1969).

Organizational and Institutional Issues

Choices of research approaches go beyond purely methodological issues, particularly for research with a clear applied orientation. A host of political, social, institutional, and economic factors are as important as scientific ones in setting both the research agenda and choosing among alternative methods. The natural conservatism of science, organizations, and cultures suggests that changes in research approaches, public land management decisions, and human values are more likely to be incremental than revolutionary.

Quantitative methods are clearly the established approach for injecting scientific information into public decisions, particularly for public land management decisions. Managers, researchers, and traditional stakeholder groups share a common set of "quantitative" values—a preference for objective facts, open and explicit analysis, analytical frameworks, and "hard" evaluation criteria. These values are reinforced by legislation, judicial rulings, administrative rules, and operating procedures which frequently require quantitative analysis and analytical decision frameworks. All of this has tended to relegate qualitative approaches to more of a supporting role in public land management research.

Qualitative methods do have some clear advantages in understanding hard-to-define values and solving public land management problems that involve more than simply a technical solution. Increasingly, PLMAs look for solutions that are acceptable to the public by seeking compromises among competing interests. In these situations an understanding of the perspectives of different stakeholders and the process itself may be much more useful than explicit quantitative measures of benefits and costs.

The contributions of systematic qualitative approaches in public land management will likely be seen first through their role as management, public involvement, and communication tools rather than as formal research tools. Focus groups, in-depth discussions, participant observation, textual analysis, and most other qualitative techniques can significantly improve communication and understanding between and among public land managers and their stakeholder groups. Many of these uses of qualitative approaches need not be seen as "research" but simply as good management and communication practices.

It will take longer for many qualitative methods to be readily accepted as research tools by PLMAs. Management personnel and researchers with primarily biological, engineering, and technical training are unlikely to readily understand or accept many qualitative approaches. Physical scientists and engineers receive little exposure to these methods and are firmly steeped in quantitative approaches and philosophies. The general public is also accustomed to seeing science in its quantitative, positivist form. Qualitative methods will also suffer because of weak links to budgeting and financial matters which drive many public decisions. The difficulty of concisely communicating the results of qualitative research, plus the interpretive and relativist position of qualitative science will also pose problems in the public policy arena.

The intent in noting these problems and weaknesses is not to discourage the use of qualitative approaches, but to be realistic about where qualitative methods may initially prove most useful and what obstacles will need to be overcome to more fully utilize these techniques.

Conclusion

While we have presented qualitative and quantitative methods as distinct approaches to research, we see these techniques as more complementary than competitive. Both sets of methods have important contributions to make to our understanding of values, nature, public land management, and the human spirit. Multiple perspectives are as valuable in the research arena as in matters of public policy. Managers and researchers should develop an appreciation of both qualitative and quantitative approaches including the advantages and disadvantages of each. This is not to say that both qualitative and quantitative approaches must be embraced in a single study although some studies certainly do. Since qualitative and quantitative approaches begin from quite distinct assumptions about reality, it will be more common for quantitative and qualitative studies to be carried out somewhat independently.

Debates about quantitative versus qualitative approaches make the mistake of assuming that a single study, perspective, or research approach can somehow yield complete understanding of any given phenomenon. Science and knowledge are cumulative processes that benefit from a variety of perspectives and approaches. We therefore urge greater tolerance and understanding among various research subcultures and recommend that public land management decisions be based on inputs from both qualitative and quantitative perspectives.

Hard-to-define value problems are inherently multidisciplinary and cut across the traditional boundaries between the sciences and humanities. Quantitative approaches should strive to extend existing theory and applications to values and behaviors that have historically been neglected. Some of this work can take place within existing disciplinary paradigms, although we feel some of the most productive approaches will come from integration and bridging of disciplinary perspectives. Improved taxonomies of values, new theories, and a clearer science of values is needed. Attempting to cover hard-to-define values within existing theoretical frameworks will help to identify both the limits and limitations of these theories.

Qualitative methods offer many opportunities to inform both research and management. As research extends into even harder to define areas, it is imperative that concepts and theories be adequately grounded in human experience. Qualitative methods should play a much stronger role in defining the research questions as well as the management issues and alternatives. Qualitative paradigms also provide a potential bridge between the scientific and humanistic spheres of activity.

Quantitative methods will remain the primary approach for generating "hard," "objective," quantitative information necessary for wise public policy and management decisions. Qualitative approaches will help us better understand the meanings of public lands and nature-based experiences to various individuals and stakeholder groups. By drawing on both epistemologies and sets of methods, researchers and managers can perhaps achieve a clearer balance between the positivist notion of a shared and communicable sense of reality and the postmodern, interpretive, and relativist perspectives on human experience. Both types of information are important and relevant to public land management decisions.

Two related but somewhat distinct research areas identified by Andrews and Waits (1978) almost twenty years ago still form the primary research agenda today:

1. characterizing values associated with nature and public lands, and

2. understanding the roles that values play in public and private decision processes.

Quantitative and qualitative approaches each have significant contributions to make in both research areas.

Literature Cited

Albright, H. and Cahn, R. (1985). *The birth of the National Park Service: The founding years 1913-1933.* Salt Lake City, UT: Howe Brothers.

Andrews, R. and Waits, M. (1978). *Environmental values in public decisions: A research agenda.* Ann Arbor, MI: University of Michigan School of Natural Resources.

Bellah, R., Madsen, R., Sullivan, W., Swidler, A., and Tipton, S. (1985). *Habits of the heart: Individualism and commitment in American life.* Berkeley, CA: University of California Press.

Ben Akiva, M. and Lerman, S. (1985). *Discrete choice analysis theory and application to travel demand.* Cambridge, MA: The MIT Press.

Boulding, K. (1969). The formation of values as a process in human learning. In *Transportation and community values, Highway Research Board Special Report 105* (pp. 31-38). National Research Council.

Brandmeyer, G. and Alexander, L. (1986). "I caught the dream": The adult baseball camp as fantasy leisure. *Journal of Leisure Research, 18*(1), 26-39.

Brown, T. (1984). The concept of value in resource allocation. *Land Economics, 60*(3), 231-246.

Casti, J. (1989). *Paradigms lost: Images of man in the mirror of science.* New York, NY: William Morrow & Company, Inc.

Clawson, M. and Held, B. (1957). *The federal lands.* Baltimore, MD: The Johns Hopkins University Press.

Colfer, C. and Colfer, A. (1978). Inside Bushler Bay: Lifeways in counterpoint. *Rural Sociology, 43*(2), 204-220.

Denzin, N. and Lincoln, Y. (1994). *Handbook of qualitative research.* Thousand Oaks, CA: Sage Publications, Inc.

Driver, B., Brown, P. and Peterson, G. (Eds.). (1991). *Benefits of leisure.* State College, PA: Venture Publishing, Inc.

Driver, B., Tinsley, H. and Manfredo, M. (1991). The paragraphs about leisure and recreation experience preference scales: Results from two inventories designed to assess the breadth of the perceived psychological benefits of leisure. In B. Driver, P. Brown, and G. Peterson (Eds.), *Benefits of leisure* (pp. 263-286). State College, PA: Venture Publishing, Inc.

Dunlap, R. and van Liere, K. (1984). Commitment to the dominant social paradigm and concern for environmental quality. *Social Science Quarterly, 65,* 1013-1028.

Eagly, A. and Chaiken, S. (1993). *The psychology of attitudes.* Fort Worth, TX: Harcourt Brace Jovanovich College Publishers.

Frome, M. (1971). *The Forest Service.* New York, NY: Praeger.

Gephart, R., Jr. (1993). The textual approach: Risk and blame in disaster sensemaking. *Academy of Management Journal, 36*(6), 1465-1514.

Glancy, M. (1988). The play world setting of the auction. *Journal of Leisure Research, 20,* 135-153.

Glaser, B. and Strauss, A. (1967). *The discovery of grounded theory: Strategies for qualitative research.* New York, NY: Aldine de Gruyter, Inc.

Henderson, K. (1991). *Dimensions of Choice: A qualitative approach to recreation, parks and leisure research.* State College, PA: Venture Publishing, Inc.

Holsti, O. (1969). *Content analysis for the social sciences and humanities.* Reading, MA: Addison-Wesley Longman Publishing, Inc.

Homans, G. (1967). *The nature of social science.* New York, NY: Harcourt, Brace and World.

Hummell, D. (1987). *Stealing the National Parks.* Bellevue, WA: The Free Enterprise Press.

Kaplan, A. (1964). *The conduct of inquiry: Methodology for behavioral science.* San Francisco, CA: Chandler Publishing.

Kaufman, H. (1960). *The forest ranger: A study in administrative behavior.* Baltimore, MD: Johns Hopkins University Press.

Louviere, J. (1988). *Analyzing decision making: Metric conjoint analysis.* Beverly Hills, CA: Sage Publications, Inc.

Louviere, J. and Timmermans, H. (1990). Stated preference and choice models applied to recreation: A review. *Leisure Sciences, 12,* 9-32.

Mitchell, R. and Carson, R. (1991). *Using surveys to value public goods: The contingent valuation method.* Washington, DC: Resources for the Future.

Mohai, P., Stillman, P., Jakes, P., and Liggett, C. (1994). *Change in the USDA Forest Service: Are we heading in the right direction?* (General Technical Report NC-172). St. Paul, MN: USDA Forest Service, North Central Forest Experiment Station.

Nash, R. (1967). *Wilderness and the American mind.* New Haven, CT: Yale University Press.

Nash, R. (1989). *The rights of nature: A history of environmental ethics.* Madison, WI: University of Wisconsin Press.

Rokeach, M. (1973). *The nature of human values.* New York, NY: The Free Press.

Rolston, H. (1982). Are values in nature subjective or objective? *Environmental Ethics, 4*(2), 131.

Sinden, J. and Worrell, A. (1979). *Unpriced values: Decisions without market prices.* New York, NY: John Wiley & Sons, Inc.

Smith, M. (1988). *Contemporary communication research methods*. Belmont, CA: Wadsworth Publishing, Co.

Snow, D. (Ed). (1992). *Voices from the environmental movement*. Washington, DC: Island Press.

Stebbins, R. (1992). Costs and rewards in barbershop singing. *Leisure Studies*, *11*, 123-133.

Stynes, D. and Peterson, G. (1984). A review of logit models with implications for modeling recreation choices. *Journal of Leisure Research*, *16*(4), 295-310.

Stynes, D. and Stewart, S. (1991). *The impacts of the Grand Traverse Resort on a local community*. East Lansing, MI: Department of Park and Recreation Resources, Michigan State University.

Sutherland, A. and Nash, J. (1994). Animal rights as a new environmental cosmology. *Qualitative Sociology*, *17*(2), 171-186.

Ulrich, R., Dimberg, U., and Driver, B. (1991). Psychophysiological indicators of leisure benefits. In B. Driver, P. Brown, and G. Peterson (Eds.), *Benefits of Leisure* (pp. 73-89). State College, PA: Venture Publishing, Inc.

Worster, D. (Ed). (1973). *American environmentalism: The formative period 1860-1915*. New York, NY: John Wiley & Sons, Inc.

Yin, R. (1984). *Case study research: Design and methods*. Beverly Hills, CA: Sage Publications, Inc.

Zube, E., Brush, R., and Fabos, J. (Eds.). (1975). *Landscape assessment: Values, perceptions, and resources*. Stroudsburg, PA: Dowden, Hutchison and Ross.

Zwick, R. (1990). *Rural resident values and attitudes towards tourism*. Proceedings of the 1990 Northeastern Recreation Research Symposium (General Technical Report NE-145). Burlington, VT: USDA Forest Service, Northeastern Forest Experiment Station.

Section VI

Summary

Where Do We Go from Here?

[This text] is only a beginning. . . . Although wolf dogs may unravel some of what we have done, we, and others, will keep returning to weave again. Ours has been but a first step in what promises to be a most rewarding intellectual, emotional, and spiritual journey toward a deeper understanding of our relationship with the Earth that sustains us.

from the Preface

Moving Toward an Expanded Land Management Ethic

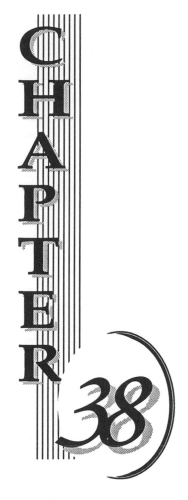

CHAPTER 38

Peter List
Department of Philosophy
Oregon State University
Corvallis, Oregon

Perry Brown
School of Forestry
University of Montana
Missoula, Montana

The cultural diversity and urban character of American society have grown immensely since the nineteenth century, and American attitudes toward nature have evolved in parallel with these social developments. During most of this period, the predominant world-view has seen the land as having primarily utilitarian and commercial value, as a resource for some rather limited human purposes. At the turn of this century, the conservation philosophy of Gifford Pinchot expressed this view when it defined conservation as the use and development of natural resources for the greatest good for the greatest number for the longest time (Pinchot, 1947). Under this philosophy, the first obligation of public land managers is to promote the wise human development of public lands for economic and commercial goals.

Clearly, public lands have long been a significant source of national wealth, and have provided many of the raw materials needed to support the American economy and personal livelihood. The main value of the land has been seen in its economic worth rather than in its aesthetic, religious, spiritual, ecologic, historic, or intrinsic qualities. More recently, however, one can see a philosophical shift toward a more expansive land ethic, a more holistic view that emphasizes multiple values in the landscape.

The idea that nature has deeper, nonmaterialistic meanings is also to be found in American culture. Many of our poets, scientists, farmers, philosophers, ministers, explorers, writers, and pioneers have given voice to this deep-seated dimension of the land's meaning, and Native American cultures have expressed this point of view in their traditions and behavior (Nash, 1982; Hughes, 1983). Until recently, however, this viewpoint has been submerged in individual and corporate efforts to carve a way of life out of wild nature. The development of the environmental movement and the greening of public attitudes in the past thirty years have reinstalled this perspective in American public life, and now the emergence of more diverse and less materialistic attitudes toward the land is being seen (Dunlap, 1992).

Two of the philosophical prophets who led this evolution in thinking were John Muir and Aldo Leopold. Muir was famous as a nature writer, publicist, environmental activist, and thinker who in the 1800s and early 1900s was fond of roaming the forests and wild lands of the United States, especially western North America and Alaska. His love for wild nature had a profound impact on his world-view (Cohen, 1984). Muir recognized the commercial value that existed in forests. For example, trees obviously had to be used for ship building, home construction, and the like, but he was particularly attentive to the beauty in wild nature. He argued that nature was not ugly as long as it was wild, and he applied this idea not only to forests and their component animals and plants but also to the sea and sky, the light from the stars and sun, and the glaciers and canyons as well (Muir, 1898). Nature had a grandeur and sublimity in whatever wild shape it took, no matter how magnificent or low. Muir compared nature to a large painting by a supremely talented artist. The mountains and tundras, the plains and rivers were all good the way they were painted, in an unspoiled and pristine condition exhibiting an incredible variety of shapes, colors, hues, and structures.

To argue that wild lands have a natural beauty is to locate their value in the pleasures or satisfactions they bring to one's consciousness. But Muir's reasoning also reflects the nonutilitarian values in nature. Wild creatures have their own purposes and lives to live and to enjoy, independent of humans. In fact, Muir thought that the purpose for which wild animals and plants exist is first and foremost their own happiness. Humans, after all, are only one small part of the creation, and while the cosmos might be incomplete without them, it would also be incomplete without "the smallest transmicroscopic creature that dwells beyond our conceitful eyes and knowledge" (Teale, 1954). Thus, while wild nature and its inhabitants provide aesthetic pleasures to humans who gain value as a result, they also have a value that has nothing to do with humanity, a deeper value independent of human life, a value just because of what they are in nature's scheme.

Leopold, author of *A Sand County Almanac* and many essays on land ethics, also argued for deeper, hard-to-define nature-based values (Leopold, 1949). Leopold's influence on the thinking of land managers and resource scientists has been steadily growing for some 45 years and is evident throughout the chapters in this text. Leopold was trained as a forester at Yale in the first decade of this century, and for some 20 years, while working for the Forest Service and other groups in the Southwest, he embraced a land philosophy that was production-oriented and that focused on timber, rangeland, and wildlife issues (Meine, 1988). One of his main aims as a public servant was to enhance the interests of the dominant land users in the national forests and to encourage more efficient commercial exploitation of forest and range resources. But his vision began to change in the 1920s as he came to study the newly emerging science of ecology and as he learned more about the ecological consequences of existing land uses. Land management, he came to believe, could be freed from its more limited resource conservation and commercial roots to become a means of promoting land health and of discovering the many noneconomic values in nature.

Leopold led the way to a more inclusive land philosophy that conceived of humans not as conquerors of nature but as "plain members" and "biotic citizens." This meant that land users had to move beyond the narrower model of the land as a material resource for human use to a broader model that includes the aesthetic, historic, cultural, philosophical, scientific, and ecologic values in the land. In fact, in his scheme, economic thinking about the land is the tail wagging the aesthetic and ecological dog, and he recommended a new ethical principle that extends value and ethical status to all components, organisms, and systems in the land community, not only to those that are of human commercial significance.

In his efforts to identify the "cultural harvest" that the public lands can yield, Leopold clearly articulated some of the hard-to-define values that are mentioned in earlier chapters of this work. For example, his essay "Wildlife in American Culture" isolates several kinds of cultural value in the customs and experiences one may have with wild creatures and wilderness (Leopold, 1966). These include the "split-rail" value that can come from imitating historic methods of hunting, fishing, or woodcraft in one's excursions into the wilds and also the "man-earth" value that results from having experiences that remind one of one's dependency on other animals and organisms in the food chain. Leopold implied that these are instrumental values for humans since they express the significance of wild things in terms of our own social and individual welfare; wildlife and wilderness are a human social asset. But he also believed that wild creatures, wild plants, and wild areas have value in a deeper, more philosophical sense that cannot be expressed in these "civilized" terms or in the more common monetary exchange terms of our economic system.

The question "what is a wild goose worth?" revealed to him this deeper value that is neither quantifiable nor instrumental. In his essay "Goose

Music" he wondered how the opportunity to hear goose music compares to a ticket to a symphony concert (Leopold, 1966). His answer was that, comparatively speaking, there is value in wild geese and goose honking just as there is in music and the other arts. On the one hand, both wild things and art are valuable because of the experience and appreciation one has of their qualities once one becomes familiar with them; they both have a "beauty" of their own. The music of wild geese is just as valuable in this sense as Homer's *Iliad* or Beethoven's *Fifth Symphony*. On the other hand, the value of wild organisms is more than this, he suggested, for wild geese are also part of the biotic community of life on Earth and have an ecological value that results from their being functional members of the land community. All parts of the community are important to the health of the whole and thus have biotic value, whether they are means to human ends, whether they can be priced in a market, or whether any human is willing to pay anything for them.

Muir and Leopold thus identified some important noneconomic values in nature as well as a deeper value in wild organisms and wild lands that goes beyond the direct utility they have in the human economy. There are aesthetic, historical, and ecological values in public wild lands, but there are also inherent or intrinsic values that defy ready definition. As suggested in the Introduction, these deeper values are manifold and complex. They may be entangled with emotions and feelings or with more refined thoughts and ideas. They may result from personal attachments to particular places or landscapes or from the experience of nature whenever and wherever encountered. They may be bound up with very specific historic, cultural, or ethnic traditions, or they may be more universally tied to human experience. They may include appreciation of particular life-forms or of all life in a more general way. They may be reflected in the awe, reverence, and mystery one experiences in nature, but they can also be tied to more mundane emotions and feelings. In any case, these are real values that real people experience, remember, and talk about in real places, and they are not to be dismissed because of their intangible character. At the same time, because of their elusive nature, they are values that are hard for managers to incorporate into land management. This is, then, yet another pur-

pose of this book—to bring home to managers some useful ideas about how they might incorporate these values in new land management strategies.

A Need to Hear and Understand Diverse Values

The personal history of Leopold shows how American values toward land and natural resources have evolved over time, and this evolution is evident in theories about land management. Early European immigrants brought with them the idea that wilderness needed to be tamed for human settlement. The land policies of the colonies, states, and federal government built on these ideas. In the 1800s the contrasting values of utilitarianism and romanticism emerged as prominent themes in the culture, and they influenced land management as well. At the beginning of the twentieth century, as Muir extolled the beauties of nature and Pinchot promoted its development, land and natural resource policies and practices expressed these sometimes conflicting perspectives. Congress created a more utilitarian Forest Service and a more aesthetic Park Service, it passed a mineral leasing act and an antiquities act, it developed a multiple use–sustained yield act and a wilderness act, and the nation continues to embrace these varying perspectives in natural resource stewardship today.

The reigning emphasis is on utilitarian values, however, and this has gone hand-in-hand with the idea that a small elite of leaders and professionals should make decisions about what the nation's natural resources are, what outcomes Americans should expect from them, what resource management institutions are appropriate, and what management tools and techniques should be used. However, this model was created for a different time and place than the present, and today it is recognized as inadequate (Brown, 1995). The current model is more broadly democratic in practice and requires much greater public involvement in how natural resources are to be managed and for what purposes.

With tremendous changes in information technology, a move toward a more participatory democracy, a recognition of complex technical problems, a deeper public concern for the environment, and increased scientific understanding of natural systems, guidance by a fairly narrow elite has been replaced by reliance on a plurality of interests, pulling, tugging, and coalescing in the development of public resource policies and practices. A wider array of people than ever before is interested in natural resource policy formation and desires to participate more actively in resource allocation decision making (Shindler, List and Steel, 1993). No longer can the ideas of a small number of individuals and the institutions they created exclusively control natural resource management on public lands.

This means that public land managers and administrators need to understand more clearly how different kinds of citizens define and relate to the public lands, and how diverse groups satisfy their needs on the public lands. Land management has thus become more challenging, but the broader perspectives about land and its uses that are discussed in this text are vital if the goal is to manage public lands so that some needs are not ignored. Resource management at the close of the twentieth century must become profoundly pluralistic and must reflect the many relevant voices in this country. Commodity (e.g., timber) and service (e.g., recreation opportunities) outputs on public lands remain important to people, but managers now recognize that there is much more to the land and to the human spirit, and issues of place, heritage, personal identity, spirituality, culture, and ethnicity ought to be reflected in decisions about the land. While these values may be harder to grasp than commodity and service values, they are no less essential or real; they are deeper and more open-ended and are significant in the lives of individuals. Public land managers also know that there are different perspectives on each of these values as they listen to people from different ethnic, religious, and cultural backgrounds. This book was put together in order to present a sample of the voices managers need to hear as they formulate strategies and techniques for managing our natural resource heritage. In what follows, we will isolate some of the common themes present in the previous chapters.

A Sampling of Themes

The Deeper Meaning of the Land

First and foremost is the theme that the land has deep meaning to individuals in this society. As several authors explain, relationships with the land consist of more than an appreciation of the material values in particular geographical places, wilderness landscapes, or natural resources. The land and its resources are not only the basis of material existence providing sustenance for life and livelihoods, but they are also a wellspring of spiritual insight and psychological well-being. Most important, the land is a basic organizing conception in human social life because it encompasses the traditions, institutions, and customs that have arisen out of the many connections to specific places and pieces of ground. In this broad sense, the land represents a vast cultural heritage that is shared nationally, distinguishing Americans from other nations and societies.

Within cultural history there are several different philosophical ideas about the deeper meaning of the land, and these coexist today in the consciousness and attitudes Americans have about private and public lands. First, throughout American history, the land has been defined as private property to which humans have natural rights of ownership. Land is something that can be possessed by individuals and corporate organizations and can be manipulated and disposed of as a commodity for private profit and personal economic use. A second philosophical idea views the land as a collection of natural resources, some of which are renewable and removable, some of which are exhaustible. Here, land is to be developed and conserved for various economic and noneconomic purposes. It can be either privately or publicly owned and exploited, but it must be used for some public good. A third notion considers the land to be the spiritual source of being, something much more powerful and important than any one individually or collectively. It surrounds social and personal lives, is imbued with spiritual values, and is the total basis of human existence. A fourth idea sees the land as a complex ecological system that is to be valued and preserved for its ecological and scientific values.

Though these basic ideas are not mutually exclusive, a different "land ethic" is typically connected with each of them and ranges from a more exploitative ethic that rests on individual self-interest and personal benefit to a conservation ethic that emphasizes the social and public utility of the land, and a spiritual ethic or a way of life that sees our land behavior to be sacred or profane, and an ecological ethic that develops its ethical standards from general features of the whole land system itself. At different times in American history and in different parts of

American culture, all of these conceptions can be discovered in the actions and beliefs of individuals and cultural groups, though the dominant ideas throughout American history define land to be either property, economic commodity, or natural resource.

In a pluralistic and diverse society, all of these meanings should be acknowledged and should have their place in our cultural schemes, though some of them should obviously be more appropriate for certain kinds of land than others. For example, the use of private lands has been motivated by the goal of economic profit, but it also has been seen to be the basis for individual happiness and well-being. This private property ethic owes a debt to people like John Locke, Adam Smith, and the other founders and defenders of capitalism. On the other hand, parts of our public lands were once "owned" collectively by various Native-American cultural groups and were either purchased, taken by force, or stolen for the collective convenience of European Americans and their descendants. These lands, too, have been a source of personal profit, but in time their mission has been broadened to embrace a conservation ethic and, more recently, a new layer of aesthetic and ecological standards. The ethic that is evolving for public lands owes its debt more to Pinchot, Muir, and Leopold. They set down some of the important ethical ideas that result from discovering hard-to-define values in the land.

Meanings and Connections

Several authors in this text raise a long-standing question about relationships to the land; namely, what does it mean to say that today people are not fundamentally connected to the land? The standard answer is that because urbanites in our society did not grow up in a rural area or community, or have not worked on a farm or ranch, they do not understand the deep feelings of stewardship attached to living on and caring for the land, and they do not appreciate the utilitarian values associated with working the land. In essence, urban people just do not understand what farmers and foresters do, why they do it, or how their utilitarian management perspective can include a sense of responsibility and stewardship.

While there may well be differing senses of relationship to the land, the contents of this book demonstrate that many people, including people in cities, feel intimately connected to the land. However, they are connected in very different ways and find different meanings in the process. Obviously many urban citizens do not understand farming, ranching, or forestry, or how commercial lands are managed for production of goods and services. Nevertheless, they do express deep values about the land and have meaningful connections to it. There are several signs of this attachment in their beliefs and behavior: their acceptance of aesthetically and environmentally oriented attitudes about nature; their appreciation of special and sacred places on public land; their support for and use of urban parks and programs that naturalize cities; and their enthusiastic use of national parks and recreation lands. People from urban backgrounds often have substantial appreciation for the artistic and aesthetic values in the land and the many recreational functions it offers, even if they have not lived on or made their living from it. As American attitudes about the land have evolved, these elements of urban consciousness express no less legitimate connections to land than do those so often assigned to farmers and foresters.

Do all Americans have deep connections to the land? Surely not, and because there is a large population, the number who do not is surely large also. But many expressions of deep attachment and appreciation are woven into the contributions in this text. The land values of ranchers, artists, outfitters and guides, recreationists, and managers are represented here in a rich and diverse way, as are the values of different ethnic and cultural groups not normally associated with rural areas. These authors believe that there exists a great plurality of land connections in America, and these give land managers many opportunities for listening and learning about the land. As land resources are defined, benefits are derived both directly and in terms of decision-making capabilities.

Sense of Place

Several authors in this book make it clear that specific landscapes are often the location of cultural meaning and that a sense of place is part and parcel of the effort to find meaning in the land and to create personal and cultural identities. Places in the landscape are infused with meaning and are more than the sum of their biophysical attributes or their associated plants, animals and landforms. The meanings associated with places obviously are derived from experiences in them, and these experiences are quite variable. They can come from growing up in a particular region, such as the flat openness of the Midwest, from listening to grandparents and relatives describe their lives on the family farm, or from adventure experiences traveling the wild rivers of the West. These personal experiences are tied to other people and their lives, to ways of life and play, and to a culture that has been greatly shaped by the natural environment.

As Wallace Stegner has remarked, the American land and its resources are the main elements that define who and what Americans have become, and it is the special places that most often provide particular meaning, no matter what culture or nationality is involved (Stegner, 1961). In their use, destruction, reestablishment, and influence on culture and personality, places are major threads in the social fabric. As one reads of the people, forests and lake mosaics of Lapland, the arid bush of Australia, the forests and farms of the Shenandoah Valley, the Rocky Mountain Front of Montana, the prairies of Manitoba, the rain forests of the Pacific Northwest, and the cypress swamps of Louisiana, one realizes that these are environments that shape regional cultures and identities, sometimes on a large scale. When one experiences them, one understands how they are so significant in the lives of their past and present inhabitants. But the same is true of the less grandiose and more intimate places people have come to love in their backyards and local environments. They, too, have subtle effects on one's consciousness.

The ideas of place and a sense of place are an important theme in this book, yet they are elusive because they represent a personal dimension of experience and operate at many scales and meanings of landscape. They are elusive to the land manager because personal meanings define specific places and somewhat different meanings are attached to particular geographic spaces. At the same time, when moving from smaller to larger spatial scales, one finds shared regional meanings about the land that are expressed in literature, painting, photography, music, folk tales, religion, and other cultural media. To ignore the power of places in land management is to ignore the people, ideas, and mean-

ings that are attached to those places. These meanings and ideas are as important as the biophysical attributes of specific landscapes and ecosystems. Land managers know from experience that few acts engender more hostility between them and their constituents than do management-caused changes in personal and sacred places. It is imperative, then, that managers consider the psychological and spiritual consequences of land management decisions in addition to the economic, scientific, and environmental consequences. Land managers have a responsibility to ensure that their land policies and procedures do not obstruct or degrade the public's need for psychological and spiritual connections to the land, connections that will always be inherent in the specific places and landscapes they manage.

Cultural Diversity

Cultures and places so intertwine that it can be difficult to separate one from the other. The chapters in this text touch on only a small sample of the possibilities for exploring this theme, but they include contributions from a Native American, an Hispanic American, and an African American, in addition to writers from Europe and Australia. From this sample, it is clear that there is considerable pluralism among individuals and groups in their relationships to the land. There are different world-views and resource management practices that characterize different cultures, and these are tied to the qualities of the land and landscapes in different places.

What this means for land managers, especially if they are products of different traditions and world-views from the constituents with whom they interact, is that they must first develop respect for cultural perspectives that already exist in their areas and then pursue land management on a case-by-case or situational basis. There is no single management template that can be placed over all land or even all land within a management region. Cultural diversity affects both the definition of land resources and the proper uses of these resources and must become a component of an integrated, collaborative land management approach. This demands that managers consider carefully the cultural and social meanings associated with places and landscapes as they are embodied in local cultural traditions and land attitudes. Moreover, as land managers formulate management prescriptions for given areas, they will have to learn how to cope with a diversity of land cultures just as they have to consider the physical and biological diversity of an area. They should listen to, and read the land meanings of, different peoples recognizing the legitimacy of different land perspectives and the importance of the deep values that go with them.

Toward an Expanded Land Management Ethic

Given the diversity of meanings and values the land holds, what kind of land management ethic is needed to guide land managers into the future? The authors of this text begin to lay the necessary foundation when they remind public land managers of the Leopoldian tenet that a land ethic should take into account the deeper spiritual and psychological meanings of the land in addition to its economic meanings. The authors persuasively argue that public lands are locations for spiritual renewal and rejuvenation, for reconnecting oneself to nature and the Earth, and for discovering specific natural and human values in specific places. Public lands provide a refreshing vitality and spiritedness, a "spiritual resource" for the psyche. They provoke wonder, awe, a sense of the sublime and the sacred, a feeling of respect and reverence for all life on Earth. They permit affiliation with natural settings in a time of "spiritual famine." They satisfy the need for natural places that contrast with more urban existence. They contribute to one's mental and physical health because deep natural experiences result in stress reduction, relaxed and improved mental moods and to other psychological benefits. Moreover, they provide opportunity to utilize all of one's sensory connections to nature, not just sight or hearing, and to experience natural ecosystems as wholes.

An expanded land management ethic will also have to be based on the recognition that values in the land arise from many cultural and individual sources, insights, and experiences, and that there are many voices from many sectors of society that are relevant in defining these deeper meanings in the land. As emphasized so strongly in the Describing Diverse Perspectives section of this text, public land managers can learn from the manner in which

prehistoric cultures accommodated different interests in different natural places. Moreover, there is considerable diversity in world-views and traditions in Native American cultures, and this diversity is a positive value today in thinking about land management. The experiential foundation for an expanded land management ethic must therefore be broadened. It must recognize the manifold ways in which traditional and contemporary cultures have related to and used the land.

This means that public land management will have to become genuinely pluralistic and participatory. It will have to develop collaborative approaches that recognize cultural diversity and consensually integrate a variety of land perspectives. A diverse public, including such cultural groups as Hispanics, African Americans, and others who have traditionally been excluded from or ignored in land management—women, Native Americans, persons with disabilities, and those who represent spiritual orientations to the land—should be welcomed by public land managers not just for their "input" but to share genuine responsibility for determining how public lands and spaces ought to be managed. Groups that have typically been given special access to public land management, such as private land owners, ranchers, miners, and loggers, and more recently, recreationists and environmentalists, should no longer occupy privileged positions in the management decision process but should make room for others to join them. A small group of agency "leaders" and their traditional advisors should not determine alone how the public lands will be allocated to various uses. Moreover, land managers should recognize that the effort to incorporate and balance the diverse values of different groups cannot aim to produce one "right" answer about land management, especially in a public atmosphere of distrust of public officials, polarization of interest groups, adversarial behavior, and the promotion of extreme positions on land allocation issues. Managers must carefully figure out how to build bridges between groups, find common understanding, and facilitate useful dialogue.

An expanded land management ethic will also have to be based on the realization that land managers have much to learn about the public lands from people who already have deep connections to them. Land managers themselves must learn to care for the land, and this can be done, in part, by listening to those who are already good at doing so. The land management bureaucracy is not the only repository of land wisdom, especially when there are so many valid perspectives about land uses and so many land values. Land managers must understand how to learn from others and communicate with them whether they are "experts" or not. In fact, one mark of an expert manager will undoubtedly lie in the ability to communicate and work collectively and skillfully with many constituents and interest groups, to identify common and specific goals, to learn together what the land is and can do, and to implement jointly shared ideas about appropriate land uses. In sum, a land management ethic is needed that is based on a renewed sense of community.

Land managers are not infallible; they can only do so much to connect people with specific places and landscapes. As Leopold once said about wild lands, "no one who does not sense the value of wilderness 'in his bones' can learn that value through any process of logic or education" (Leopold, 1936). Land managers should not expect that they can create plans that will inevitably lead the public and land users to appreciate deep values in the land. Indeed, discovering hard-to-define values may be successful only when people are not purposely seeking them. Land managers may only be able to optimize public opportunities to experience deeper natural values for learners who will then create their own benefits from their land associations and experiences.

In addition, an expanded land management ethic will have to be based on the recognition that there are many public landscapes, both urban and rural, that generate deeper meanings and hard-to-define values. As Edward Abbey observed, there is wilderness in the deserted factory district of Hoboken as well as in the public wilderness areas of the West (Abbey, 1977). These diverse locations will have to be managed to accommodate the changeable and diverse experiences and values of the public, and it may be necessary, as argued in this text, to set aside some "spiritual landscapes" or "reserves" on the public lands to accomplish this. These would be landscapes where individuals could go and discover for themselves the deeper values in the land.

Finally, an expanded land management ethic will have to be founded on the latest baseline knowledge about ecosystems that ecology and the environmental sciences can produce, elevating the Leopoldian insight that what managers can do to the land is limited by what the land is *ecologically*. Ecologically, the land is a complicated natural system, a whole that is greater than the sum of its parts. It is a system that can lose its integrity and become so fragmented and degraded that its original ecological and aesthetic values are impoverished. Land managers must realize that the land cannot minister to all of the users' physical wants if it is to remain a healthy reservoir of natural values and natural processes for future generations. There are ecological limits to the demands that can be placed on the environment, and the ongoing challenge is to learn how to conduct oneself responsibly and respectfully within those limits.

Literature Cited

Abbey, E. (1977). *The journey home*. New York, NY: Dutton/Signet.

Brown, P. (1995). Forestry yesterday and tomorrow: Institutional assumptions and responses. XIX William P. Thompson Memorial Lecture. Flagstaff, AZ: Northern Arizona University.

Cohen, M. (1984). *The pathless way, John Muir and American wilderness*. Madison, WI: University of Wisconsin Press.

Dunlap, R. (1992). Trends in public opinion toward the environment: 1965-1990. In R. Dunlap and A. Mertig (Eds.), *American environmentalism: The U.S. environmental movement, 1970-1990*. Philadelphia, PA: Taylor and Francis Publishing, Inc.

Hughes, J. (1983). *American Indian ecology*. El Paso, TX: Texas Western Press.

Leopold, A. (1936). The cult of wilderness. *Journal of Forestry, 34*(4).

Leopold, A. (1949). *A sand county almanac and sketches here and there*. New York, NY: Oxford University Press.

Leopold, A. (1966). *A sand county almanac with other essays on conservation from Round River*. New York, NY: Oxford University Press.

Meine, K. (1988). *Aldo Leopold, his life and work*. Madison, WI: University of Wisconsin Press.

Muir, J. (1898). Wild parks and forest reservations of the west. *Atlantic Monthly, 81*:15-28.

Nash, R. (1982). *Wilderness and the American mind* (3rd. ed.). New Haven, CT: Yale University Press.

Pinchot, G. (1947). *Breaking new ground*. New York, NY: Harcourt, Brace & World, Inc.

Shindler, B., List, P., and Steel, B. (1993). Managing federal forests: Public attitudes in Oregon and nationwide. *Journal of Forestry, 91*(7):36-42.

Stegner, W. (1961). The wilderness idea. In D. Brower (Ed.), *Wilderness*: *America's living heritage*. San Francisco, CA: Sierra Club Books.

Teale, E. (Ed.). (1954). The philosophy of John Muir. In *The wilderness world of John Muir*. Boston, MA: Houghton Mifflin Company.

Models of Change in Municipal Parks and Recreation: A Book of Innovative Case Studies
edited by Mark E. Havitz

Outdoor Recreation Management: Theory and Application, Third Edition
by Alan Jubenville and Ben Twight

Planning Parks for People
by John Hultsman, Richard L. Cottrell and Wendy Zales Hultsman

Private and Commercial Recreation
edited by Arlin Epperson

The Process of Recreation Programming Theory and Technique, Third Edition
by Patricia Farrell and Herberta M. Lundegren

Protocols for Recreation Therapy Programs
edited by Jill Kelland, along with the Recreation Therapy Staff at Alberta Hospital Edmonton

Quality Management: Applications for Therapeutic Recreation
edited by Bob Riley

Recreation and Leisure: Issues in an Era of Change, Third Edition
edited by Thomas Goodale and Peter A. Witt

Recreation Programming and Activities for Older Adults
by Jerold E. Elliott and Judith A. Sorg-Elliott

Recreation Programs that Work for At-Risk Youth: The Challenge of Shaping the Future
by Peter A. Witt and John L. Crompton

Reference Manual for Writing Rehabilitation Therapy Treatment Plans
by Penny Hogberg and Mary Johnson

Research in Therapeutic Recreation: Concepts and Methods
edited by Marjorie J. Malkin and Christine Z. Howe

Risk Management in Therapeutic Recreation: A Component of Quality Assurance
by Judith Voelkl

A Social History of Leisure Since 1600
by Gary Cross

The Sociology of Leisure
by John R. Kelly and Geoffrey Godbey

A Study Guide for National Certification in Therapeutic Recreation
by Gerald O'Morrow and Ron Reynolds

Therapeutic Activity Intervention with the Elderly: Foundations & Practices
by Barbara A. Hawkins, Marti E. May and Nancy Brattain Rogers

Therapeutic Recreation: Cases and Exercises
by Barbara C. Wilhite and M. Jean Keller

Therapeutic Recreation in the Nursing Home
by Linda Buettner and Shelley L. Martin

Therapeutic Recreation Protocol for Treatment of Substance Addictions
by Rozanne W. Faulkner

A Training Manual for Americans With Disabilities Act Compliance in Parks and Recreation Settings
by Carol Stensrud

Understanding Leisure and Recreation: Mapping the Past, Charting the Future
edited by Edgar L. Jackson and Thomas L. Burton

Venture Publishing, Inc.

 1999 Cato Avenue

State College, PA 16801

Phone: (814) 234-4561; FAX: (814) 234-1651